Egypt the Cradle of Ancient Masonry

(1902)

Comprising a history of Egypt, with a comprehensive and authentic account of the Antiquity of Masonry resulting from many years of personal investigation and exhaustive research in India, Persia, Syria and the valley of the Nile. Extremely rare book. Illustrations. Partial Contents: Alexandria; Origin of the name Freemason; Scottish Rite philosophy; Supreme Architect; Esoteric teaching of the Scottish Rite; Pyramids; Solomon; Sun Worship; Ineffable Degrees; Masonic Teachings, Hindu beggar, Roman Catholicism; Ceremonies, Initiation, Blue Lodge; Jewish Traditions, & Customs; The Lost Word.

Norman Frederick de Clifford

ISBN 1-56459-524-2

CONTENTS.

CONTENTS.

CONTENTS.

LIST OF ILLUSTRATIONS.

LIST OF ILLUSTRATIONS.

INTRODUCTION.

IN this age of countless books and wide-spread literature there is still remaining a vast field, both for the attainment of knowledge and its dissemination, by means of that ever useful, instructive and entertaining type of literature,—the historical narrative.

In this connection *Egypt, the Cradle of Ancient Masonry* is entitled to more than passing notice, not only from the general reader, but more particularly from the Masonic Fraternity, for whose peculiar and especial benefit this work was conceived, undertaken and completed.

In all the ages which have elapsed since the mighty Pharaohs swayed the destinies of the surging masses, composing the ancient empires, whose silent and impressive memorials stand as mute witnesses to the exceeding grandeur and glory of Egyptian civilizations, the savant and the scholar have been delving and exploring for the secrets which have been hidden within the concealed recesses of her tombs and temples.

Years of untiring energy and zeal have been devoted by the author, Bro. N. F. de Clifford, to the accumulation of data, the very best part of whose life has been spent in personal investigation and actual research among the archives of India, Persia, Syria and the Valley of the Nile.

The work treats, primarily, as the title implies, of the infancy of Freemasonry, not only proving by natural deductions, and positive evidence its antiquity, but tracing its rise and progress, and the glorious fruition to which it has attained at the present day.

INTRODUCTION.

Beginning, in the opening Chapter, with the founding of the City of Alexandria B. C. 332, a vast store house of knowledge, beneficial instruction and pleasurable entertainment is unfolded in charming sequence, until the Lost Word is finally reached in the closing Chapter and the narrative ends.

To every Masonic student, in fact to every Mason, knowledge is an absolute essential in the attainment of that perfection on which depend the Higher Degrees, and toward which we should ever strive with unceasing effort.

An actual personal examination of the evidences inscribed upon the tombs, temples and monuments in the Valley of the Nile, in India, Persia and Syria would doubtless be of intense interest to every sincere and earnest Mason. but should environment prevent, the graphic description herein contained will constitute a most acceptable and authentic substitute.

With sincere gratification upon the completion of this valuable addition to Masonic literature; with due appreciation of the unselfish labor of love bestowed by the author for the advancement of Masonic knowledge; and with the earnest hope that " More Light " may result to every inquiring Mason, from the study and perusal of these pages, I have the honor to present *Egypt, the Cradle of Ancient Masonry*.

JOHN ARTHUR,

PAST MASTER ST. JOHN'S LODGE No. 9, F. & A. M.,
DEPUTY GRAND MASTER OF GRAND LODGE OF WASHINGTON,
PAST POTENTATE AFIFI TEMPLE, A. A. O. N. M. S.,
AND MEMBER OF ALL OTHER MASONIC BODIES.

SEATTLE, WASH., May, 1902.

John Arthur

Alexandria—Antiquity of Masonry.

The Nile! the Nile! I hear its gathering roar,
No vision now, no dream of ancient years —
Throned on the rocks, amid the watery war,
The King of floods, old Homer's Nile, appears
With gentle smile, majestically sweet,
Curling the billowy steeds that vex them at his feet.

—LORD LINDSAY.

EGYPT, THE CRADLE OF ANCIENT MASONRY.

CHAPTER I.

ALEXANDRIA—THE ANTIQUITY OF MASONRY.

THE city of Alexandria was founded by Alexander the Great, B. C. 332, and here at the age of thirty-two, in the thirteenth year of his reign, he was buried with all the pomp and splendor of that age, and to-day there is not a single stone to mark the spot where this great warrior was laid to rest. This city was bequeathed to the Roman Empire by Ptolemy Alexander, B. C. 80, but it was not until fifty years later that it became an Imperial city, with a Roman Governor who was appointed by the Emperor Augustus.

In A. D. 640 Alexandria was captured by the Arab Caliph under Amru, a Saracen, who wrote to his master the Caliph Omar " that he had taken a city containing four thousand palaces, four thousand baths, twelve thousand dealers in fresh oil, twelve thousand gardeners, forty thousand Jews who pay tribute, and four hundred theatres or places of amusement." From this account of Amru we are enabled to form some idea of what a magnificent city it must have been.

History informs us that this city was second only to Rome, with an immense population, very highly civilized, and possessed of a most wonderful knowledge in mechanical arts and sciences, greatly beyond the comprehension of our architects and men of letters. This city had two libraries, the Soter and the Serapeum, and it was in this celebrated city that Mark suffered martyrdom and Peter preached Christianity. The modern city stands partly on what in ancient days was known as the Island of Pharos, but which is now a peninsula. The old city was built on the main land close to and nearly adjoining the modern town. The ruined walls of this ancient city are to be plainly traced, and the

3

old reservoirs which were constructed over two thousand years ago are still in a good state of preservation. Few remains of the ancient city are to be found at the present time, and it is only when workmen make excavations that fragments of pilasters, statues, etc., may be seen, which belonged to the Alexandrian and Ptolemaic age.

How well I remember my first visit to Alexandria as we came steaming along up to the harbor of this remarkable city, on board the Peninsular & Oriental Company's side-wheel steamer Ripon from the Island of Malta, one never to be forgotten, lovely Sabbath morning. Shortly after sunrise we saw the sandy shores of this most wonderful country, and rising up into the clear azure sky, seemingly, from out the very ocean itself, was that far famed and justly celebrated column known as Pompey's Pillar. Next to view came the light house, and the boats with their lateen sails; the harbor and the shipping, from whose masts float the flags of many nations, then the very unpretentious looking palace of the Khedive with its whitewashed walls on the Ras-et-tyn, and last, but not least, the numberless wind-mills. All these various things seemed to impress themselves upon my brain, and these scenes remain with me and come back at memory's call whenever the name Egypt or Alexandria is mentioned.

I was quite a boy when first I saw that celebrated city and visited it with my father during a vacation from school, and since then I have travelled through nearly every country upon the face of the earth and sailed on every sea and ocean. I have visited Alexandria many times in later years, but the memories of my first visit seem to recall the scenes and incidents which charmed and fascinated me in my boyhood's happy days in the long ago.

The "donkey boys" of Alexandria are a feature in themselves, the hackmen of our own country, in their most palmy days, could not begin to compare with the cool, rascally impudence of these celebrated "boys." Just as soon as you land from your boat they will crowd around you, and *Nolens Volens* forcibly drag you along, actually lifting you into the saddle and compelling you to ride their patient, enduring little animals. These boys prevent their donkeys from running away, when not working, by simply tying up one of the forelegs, instead of hitching them as we do our animals to a post or fence. They give their donkeys very peculiar

POMPEY'S PILLAR FROM THE CEMETERY

names, such as: Napoleon, John Bull, Yankee Doodle, Mark Twain, Moses, Jesus Christ, etc.

The Grand Square or *Place Mohammed Ali*, formerly called the *Place des Consuls*, is the most noticeable place in Alexandria to-day, and reminds one of a European city. It is embellished with beautiful trees and fountains, with a very fine equestrian statue of Mohammed Ali erected in the centre. The statue is sixteen feet high and stands upon a pedestal of Tuscan marble, twenty feet in height, making the monument in all thirty-six feet. The whole square is surrounded with magnificent edifices, and among them are some very fine hotels with all our modern improvements. They have some very fine stores here that will compare favorably with any of those in our own cities. In this square are located some of the prominent public buildings, and it is the regular promenade for the Europeans and Americans who live there. In fact, all classes of people go there to enjoy themselves after the business hours of the day.

We visited Pompey's Pillar, located a short distance from the city, which stands upon a mound forty feet high, as near as I can remember. According to some historians, this was the site of the Serapeum, situated in the Egyptian quarter of Rhacotis near the catacombs. This celebrated pillar is constructed of red granite, no doubt brought from the quarries of Syene, near the first cataract of the Nile, on the borders of Nubia, to which we shall refer later on.

Pompey's Pillar stands upon a square base or plinth, and bears a Greek inscription which most certainly proves that it was erected to honor the Emperor Diocletian. The shaft is composed of a single piece of granite, seventy-three feet long and twenty-nine feet eight inches in circumference, crowned with a Corinthian capital nine feet high. The base is about fifteen feet square, making the column nearly one hundred feet in height. It is one of the first objects to be seen on approaching the harbor of Alexandria and it is well worth a visit.

A party of English sailors, while ashore on liberty one day, flew a kite over this monument, and in this way they placed a string over it, then they drew over a stouter and stronger one, until, eventually they succeeded in drawing up a rope ladder, by the means of which they ascended to the top and displayed the British flag upon its summit.

They discovered a cavity on the top, in the capital, showing that at some time or other something must have occupied the hollow, and it has been claimed by some writers that a statue once stood there. This pillar does not in any way owe its name to the great Pompey, who was murdered off the Egyptian coast by his ward Ptolemy, but to a Roman Prefect of the same name, who, as is proven by the inscription it bears, erected it in honor of the Emperor Diocletian " the guardian genius of the city," in return for a gift of grain he had sent to the Alexandrians (*during a year of famine, no doubt*).

The two obelisks that are called Cleopatra's Needles were erected at Heliopolis in B. C. 1,500 by Thothmes III, one of the greatest Egyptian Pharoahs, in order to commemorate victories over his enemies in the " Golden Age of Egypt." They were brought from that great City of the Sun for the express purpose of decorating the temple of Cæser (The Cæsereum), in Alexandria, during the reign of Tiberius. One of these stupendous monoliths was given to the English Government by Mohammed Ali, and after considerable delay it was finally shipped to England in the year 1877, where it eventually arrived, having passed through great danger of loss by shipwreck, and stands to-day upon the Thames embankment, a relic of one of Egypt's grandest monarchs. The dimensions of this stone are sixty-eight feet long and seven feet seven inches across the base. The other one was brought to New York, by Commander Goringe, in the year 1880. This obelisk is seventy-one feet long, and seven feet seven inches at the base, measured across the face of the stone. I have often sat upon the companion stone, as it laid lengthwise beside this monolith, deciphering the hieroglyphics and pondering upon the glory that belonged to a people who built such magnificent monuments to adorn the banks of their grand old river Nile. Both of these obelisks were quarried in Syene, and are composed of the same kind and quality of granite as that in Pompey's Pillar.

These monoliths were erected to honor one of Egypt's mighty warriors nearly thirty-five centuries ago, and yet, now, they are the admiration of people not in existence when this great and powerful king conquered the Maharania of Mesopotamia, and blazoned upon their stony sides the deeds that he had done to thoroughly establish his kingdom, upon the banks of the river Nile, in the hoary civilization of a far away past. When Commander Goringe lowered this magnificent monolith from its pedestal in Alexandria, in order to ship it to America, they found beneath the stone a number of Masonic emblems as,—an apron, a trowel, a trestle board, the two ashlars, etc. The discovery of these emblems, placed beneath this mighty monolith by our ancient Brethren, must most assuredly demonstrate to the present generation that the peculiar rites and ceremonies practiced by the speculative (?) masons of the twentieth century, in erecting and dedicating their monuments and temples, were not only performed by the practical, operative masons at the beginning of our present era, but in every epoch of the world's history. This proves the verity of our rituals, in the statement that Masonry has existed from time immemorial, and that the most intelligent men in every age have been members of our most Illustrious Fraternity.

There were two Libraries in Alexandria during the reign of the Ptolemies that were the envy and admiration of the nations of antiquity. Ptolemy Soter was the founder of the one that bore his name, and he collected a very large number of books for the especial purpose of drawing together the most eminent scholars and learned men of the world for the improvement of the Sciences, Arts, Philosophies, etc., and founding in Alexandria a Museum or College like that of the Royal Society of London, England, or the Royal Academy of Paris, France. There is no doubt but Ptolemy Soter communicated his love of learning, the development of the intellectual qualifications, as well as the collecting of valuable books, to his son Ptolemy Philadelphus, for we positively know, from the historical records of that age, that this young king, previous to his father's death, sent learned men to all parts of Greece and Asia, to collect the most valuable books to be found in those countries, and bring them to Egypt, in order to grace and adorn the shelves of the Library in Alexandria, and to enrich the collection that had already been made by his father. Ptolemy Philadelphus followed up the work, so ably begun by his predecessor, in enlarging the Soter Library, already established in the *Regio Brucheum*, then the most magnificent quarter of the city, the abode of royalty, and the location of the splendid palaces of the Ptolemies. He also organized and established a Library in the Serapeum, the celebrated temple of Serapis, the principal building of the *Regio Rhacotis*, or regular Egyptian quarter of the city. This celebrated building was of such remarkable magnificence and beauty that it rivalled those glorious buildings of the Roman Capitol.

According to the best authorities the Serapeum occupied the site of the mound whereon stands Pompey's Pillar, and that column is said, by some writers, to have formed a part of this remarkable edifice. The structure was supported by firmly built arches, distributed through various subterranean passages. The building itself was surrounded by a quadrangular portico, leading from which were most magnificent halls and corridors, wherein was placed exquisite statuary that demonstrated their knowledge in the arts, while the books upon the shelves showed the source from whence they derived their wondrous knowledge of science and philosophy; but the triumph of the Soter and Serapeum Libraries was in the presence of the most learned men and scholars, who came from all quarters of the earth, men who had passed through the various stages of culture and refinement, in their own countries, and had been attracted to this wondrous city of Alexandria by the stupendous development belonging to the Egyptian civilization during the dynasty of the Ptolemies.

Ptolemy Euergetus appropriated all the books that were brought into Egypt by foreigners, no matter from whence they came, or who they were. He placed them in the Libraries, and when the owners made complaint about the seizure of their books, they were given a copy, but the original would remain in the Library, and in this manner he was enabled to gather an enormous number of the most valuable works, all of which were added to either the Soter or Serapeum Libraries, until according to Calimachus, who was the librarian under Ptolemy Euergetus, a catalogue of the books was formed and the two Libraries classified. By arranging them into one hundred and twenty classes, he found that there were seven hundred thousand in the Soter and four hundred thousand in the Serapeum.

I do not wish to enter into a description of the Alexandrian School of Literature and Philosophy, but simply to state that all peoples were benefited by Egyptian civilization and her marvellous intellectual advancement. It is a well known fact that the Alexandrian philosophers and scholars devoted a vast amount of their time and attention to the translation, into Greek and other languages, of the priceless treasures that had been placed upon the shelves of these most magnificent Libraries. In disseminating their knowledge throughout the world, by translations into a language common among the learned men of that age, they benefited all mankind, some of whom made antiquity illustrious with the knowledge gained through drinking from this most glorious fount of ancient Egyptian wisdom.   There are various conflicting accounts of the destruction of the magnificent Soter Library, and it has been very difficult for me to decide as to which is the true or the false, because there has been a vast amount of evidence brought forward by various writers, for and against, which, as I say, makes it difficult to arrive at a decision; but after careful investigation I have come to the conclusion that all the priceless volumes upon the shelves of this stupendous library were destroyed by the order of the Caliph Omar, in A.D. 641, after Amru took possession of Alexandria and its libraries.

History informs us that a celebrated peripatetic philosopher and a friend of Amru, called John the Grammarian lived in Alexandria at the time it was forcibly wrested from the Persians by the Arabian General Amru, B.C. 640. John went to him immediately and requested that he give him the books contained in the Soter Library. Amru told him it would be impossible to grant such a request himself, but that he would write to the Caliph Omar for his consent. The Caliph on receiving the request from Amru made answer thereto that " If those books contain the same doctrine with the Koran, they could be of no use, since the Koran contained all necessary truths; but if they contained any thing contrary to that book, they ought to be destroyed; and therefore, whatever their contents, he ordered them to be burned," in consequence of which they were given to the public baths of the city to be used as fuel, and we are informed, by the best authorities, that these priceless treasures of knowledge and information supplied those furnaces with fire for a period of six months.

It is also positively asserted, by some historians, that by an order of the Christian, Theodosius, the Serapeum was sacked, the books destroyed, the magnificent building pillaged, and the exquisite statuary broken. What had been the admiration of the civilized world, the very centre and source of intellectual development, was completely destroyed by fanatical and bigoted Christians. There are many other accounts of the destruction of these libraries and their contents. One relates that a fire destroyed the valuable treasures, both books and building. Some writers give one account and some another; but one thing is certain, and that is they were destroyed. By whom, when, or how, it is difficult to decide, but we are positively certain that the destruction of these libraries was assuredly one of the most barbarous and unpardonable acts ever committed by the hand of man. This vandalism resulted in the suppression of the Greek School of Philosophy, and turned the European world into the dark night of Christian barbarism that hung over the people like a deadly nightmare for twelve hundred years. The Christians have branded this era of Christian domination "The Dark Ages."

Alexandria has two harbors, the *Old* or Western, and the *New* or Eastern. The former is most decidedly the better of the two. It has a good anchorage close to the town, with from twenty to forty feet of water. A very fine breakwater protects the Old harbor, allowing shipping to lie safely at anchor at all times of the year without fear of wind or storm. There are three entrances leading into this celebrated harbor, but the middle is the principal one, considered to be the best, and the one most generally used; it is fully a quarter of a mile wide, is well marked and buoyed, so that pilots have no difficulty in taking vessels through this channel into the deep water of the harbor and pointing out the anchorage.

The Eastern or New harbor is very seldom used on account of its exposure to the heavy winds from the North. At one time this harbor was the only place in which "Christian" vessels were allowed to anchor. It was never considered safe, in fact it was more like an open roadstead; but now we very seldom find vessels in the New harbor, because the Old harbor is now in common use. Shipping from all parts of the world may be seen lying safely at anchor, side by side, in one of the best ports in the Mediterranean Sea—the Old harbor of Alexandria.

Ah! what glorious days I have spent in sailing from one harbor to another, examining the various points of interest and listening to the

HARBOR OF ALEXANDRIA.

legends and stories told by my friend and companion, Abd-el-Belek. I have much enjoyed a visit to the breakwater, to the queer Turkish fleet of old-fashioned men of war, with their three and four tiers of guns, the palace on the Ras-et-tyn, and the ancient site of "Pharos," the celebrated lighthouse, as well as sailing around "pirates' bay," the stronghold of the ancient Greek and Phœnician sea rovers, who made this bay their headquarters long centuries before the great Alexander was born. I have often sat upon the thwart of our boat, when becalmed of a lovely moonlight night, and watched the twinkling lights of the shipping in the distance, and the swarthy faces of our boatmen, pondering upon the glory of ancient Egypt and the hoary civilization on the banks of the Nile, when our great ancestors were digging clams with stone hatchets in the lagoons of Europe, and the altars of the Druids ran red with the blood of human sacrifice.

The catacombs of Alexandria are not very extensive, and are of Egypto-Greek origin. Strabo states in book 17, page 795, that "the quarter where it is placed had the name of the Necropolis." I did not find anything of especial interest in these receptacles of the dead, but I simply call the attention of my readers to the place and the fact that they can be very easily found by simply calling a donkey boy, jumping on to his little animal and telling the boy where you want to go. It is not far and the trip will only cost you about a quarter of a dollar. It is close to Pompey's Pillar and you can visit both places on the same trip.

There are quite a number of places one may visit on donkey back, and very enjoyable ones, more especially if you have friends to accompany you.

The Pharos, or lighthouse, was situated on the extreme point of the Island of Pharos. Its foundation was commenced by Ptolemy Soter, but was not completed until the reign of his son and successor, Ptolemy Philadelphus, about the year B. C. 283, at a cost of eight hundred talents. It was constructed of beautiful white marble and built in the shape of a tower that was five hundred and fifty-two feet high, on the top of which a fire was kept continually burning, said to have been distinctly visible forty-two miles at sea. It was erected for the purpose of directing sailors into the bay and harbor of Alexandria. History informs us that the following inscription was carved upon it: " King

Ptolemy to the gods, the saviours, for the benefit of sailors," but Sostratus, the architect, who was desirous of having the honor of erecting this magnificent edifice, cut his own name upon the stones of the tower and covered it with cement, upon which he lightly chiselled this inscription. In the course of time the cement decayed, disappeared and dropped from the face of the stone or tower, taking with it the name of Ptolemy, and in its place was to be seen: "Sostratus the Cnidian, son of Dexphanes, to the gods, the saviours, for the benefit of sailors." This justly celebrated lighthouse, or tower, was considered to be one of the wonders of the world.

The population of Alexandria during the reign of the Ptolemies was estimated at nearly half a million, but it dwindled down to a few thousand at the end of the eighteenth century. To-day it has a population of two hundred and forty thousand, sixty thousand of whom are Europeans, principally Greeks, Italians, French and English. According to Josephus 1: 31, he estimated the population of this city at three hundred thousand, and the whole of Egypt at seven million.

It was in this city, on the steps of the Cæsereum, that Hypatia, the maiden philosopher of Greece, was brutally murdered by order of Archbishop Cyril in the year A. D. 415. She had been lecturing to the assembled thousands in the immense auditorium of this magnificent structure upon her favorite questions: "Where are we? What am I? What can I know? and Where am I loved?" By her eloquence and the subjects chosen for her lectures she drew immense numbers to hear her, at the same time evoked the envy and wrath of the Christians, which eventually led to her destruction and the suppression of the Greek School of Philosophy, to which I have previously referred. At her death, when the glorious Theosophical and Philosophical truths were stamped out, it gave great power into the hands of the early Church Fathers, revolutionizing the whole world and bringing on the "Dark Ages" of Christian barbarism, or the rule of the Catholic Church over the people, for long, weary centuries. At this time it was considered proper to kill any one, even a bosom friend or nearest relative, if they dared to advocate a religion that was inimical to the Catholic faith, and we should ever remember that from the fourth to the end of the seventeenth century, the Catholic Church dominated the whole of the European nations, their governments, laws, literature, religion, sciences, and philosophies. Human rights were unknown, while ignorance, outrage, oppression, and injustice ruled supreme. The tentacles of the Roman Catholic Octopus enwrapped the most intelligent men of the age in its deadly fold and drank the life-blood of countless thousands.

All literature not officially sanctioned or approved by the Romish Church was proscribed under the penalty of death, and Dr. Draper informs us that "men in terror burned their libraries in order to save themselves and families from destruction." From the commencement of the Christian era until the end of the eighteenth century, the Romish Church, in its cruelty and bigotry, gave to human rights and individual liberty not the shadow of a chance to believe according to the dictates of its own conscience, in fact the Romish Church in those days was kept busy hunting out, condemning, and burning at the stake "witches" and heretics. During this age the *rack* and *stake* were the "*mild*" persuaders to bring both men and women into the bosom of "Holy Mother Church." Dr. Dick, an ecclesiastic writer, says that one hundred thousand of Germany's most intelligent men and women were burned alive at the stake during the fourteenth century for the crime of witch-craft alone.

John Wesley, the celebrated divine, informs us in his sermons that the religious contentions and persecutions were so fierce and unsparing during this age of Christian "Brotherly Love" that forty millions were slaughtered within the short space of *forty* years. Was ever record of death so awful and appalling as this? But, thank God, we have passed beyond the damnable power of this Roman Catholic Octopus. They know their hold upon the people is gradually but surely slipping away, and it is only a question of time when the Romish Church will be, like her most firm adherent and supporter—Spain—a thing of the past, for with her downfall on this American continent, the dawn of a New Light and a New Era will beam forth. As man stands erect within the rays of effulgent glory, with arms outstretched to welcome the coming of this New Light that will give him Free Thought, Free Conscience and Free Government, the cross of bondage falls behind him into the shadows of the dark past, among the falling ruins of the

Romish institutions that have in every age been the most bitter and relentless foe of education, in free secular schools, because, so long as they can keep the world and people in ignorance, just so long will they be enabled to rule it with their mummeries.

My dear Brothers, let me quote you parts of two speeches that were made by two Methodist ministers at the Methodist Convention held in St. Paul's Methodist Episcopal Church, New York, November 19th, 1900. Bishop Goodsell, of Tennessee, while speaking of the work that was being done by their Missionaries in Southern Europe, said: "There are many who doubt whether we have done any work in Italy, the land of superstition and priestcraft; whether we could ever hope to accomplish anything there, in the face of the tremendous press of adverse thought with which we are confronted. The fact is, we sent one of our workers into Italy. He soon made up his mind that in Rome we had to do as do the Romans. He began by training the young, by taking them into our schools and seminaries. The work is slow, but its value has been recently testified to by the pontiff himself, who has honored us by excommunicating every one, teachers and pupils alike, connected with our institutions of learning. In his effort to preserve for himself the triple crown of papacy, he has issued a sweeping interdiction against the schools, and every one passing through their gates. This, however, has only made us more determined to wipe out a system which has created, out of a former man of empire, a cringing beggar with a monkey and a grind-organ."

At the same place and during the same Convention the Rev. Dr. C. W. Drees said: "Christendom is divided into two camps, with Protestantism on one hand and Greek and Roman Catholicism on the other. The time is upon us when, anew, the questions which appeared in the Protestant reformation will begin to agitate the world, and demand to be pushed to their final issue. After slumbering through four centuries, these self-same questions were awakened, by the last act of infamy, of the pontiff in declaring himself infallible. Within twenty-four hours after that blasphemous declaration had been written, on the triple crown of Rome, the Prussian armies invaded Catholic France. Forty-five days later the battle of Sedan was fought, with Protestant Prussia the victor, and twenty days only had elapsed when the united armies entered the 'holy city' where the pope held sway, bringing with them carloads of Bibles. The pope lost his temporal power, and since that day the creed has been weakening.

"The Roman Church at one time held sway everywhere, but now both that church and Spanish domination have fallen off their high pedestals. When Spain is arraigned the Catholic church should be arraigned with that power as co-respondent. Ever since Isabella signed away the liberty of Spain to the pope there has been illegitimate alliance between statecraft and priestcraft against human liberty and human progress."

The Cæsareum was commenced by Cleopatra, but, it was not finished until long after her death, then it received the name Cæsareum, to honor the Emperor Augustus, in whose reign it was finished, and it was dedicated to his worship. Philo, of Alexandria, who lived in A. D. 60, gives us a description of this magnificent temple, stating that it was "facing a secure harbor, filled with votive offerings consisting of pictures and statues of gold and silver, and surrounded with a vast enclosure containing priestly residences, a library, sacred grove, propylæ, and large apartments, all open to the air, and all richly ornamented." It became a Christian Cathedral during the reign of Constantine. It was burned by the soldiers of Constantius, restored in A. D. 365 and completely destroyed by the Pagans during the reign of Valentinian and Valens. It was then rebuilt once more in the year A. D. 368 by Athanasius and remained the Cathedral church of the Patriarch of Alexandria until it fell into the hands of the Arabs in the year A. D. 640, when Amru captured the city. It once more became a Christian church in the year A. D. 727, and remained so until it was completely destroyed by fire in the year A. D. 912. There are a great many places of interest in the city and immediate vicinity that will well repay one for the time expended in visiting them; for instance: The Mahmudiya Canal, Lake Mareotis, the Saltworks, the Palace on the Ras-et-tyn, Pompey's Pillar, Catacombs, etc.

One of the most delightful trips for me was a visit to the site of the celebrated Pharos, whose tower is said to have been destroyed by an earthquake in the year A. D. 1203, the ruins of which are still visible beneath the waters of the sea on any calm day when the water is smooth and unruffled. One can spend a very pleasant day in visiting the town of Ramleh. The botanist will here find a fertile field in which to ramble for collections; as here, around Alexandria, he or she will be enabled to obtain specimens of over one-half the entire Flora of Egypt. The flowering season is said to begin about Christmas in the vicinity of Alexandria, after the winter rains are over, but, of course the abundance of flowers depend in a great measure upon the Autumn rainfall. If these rains start about the latter part of October and continue through November, flowers of every variety will be found in plenty in the following season, which is said to begin about the first of January. At this time dame nature comes forth in her most charming colors, although many beautiful plants and flowers are to be found at all seasons of the year. The only fern that is to be found in Egypt is the common maiden-hair (*Adiantum capillus—Veneris L.*). There are many Southern European and British plants to be found in the marsh-lands at Gabari, near the shore of Lake Mareotis. The most characteristic part of the botany of Egypt are the aquatic plants that are generally found in various canals and many of the ancient water courses of the old river, as well as the lakes and marshes near the shore, where the water is quiet and placid. The average rainfall at Alexandria is twelve inches.

Alexandria! Egypt! what a host of recollections these names recall! They carry me back to the land of stupendous temples and the ruins of a prehistoric civilization. After carefully examining the ruined temples in the wondrous valley of the Nile, searching among the tombs and ruins that lie scattered broadcast from one end of it to the other, I find that Masonry has existed through all ages, and has been the admiration of the most intelligent men of every epoch of the world's history, verifying the statements made by our rituals that "Masonry has been in existence from time immemorial," and I most firmly believe that our glorious Fraternity can date its origin back more than two thousand years before the building of the temple by our three Grand Masters. This event took place, according to Josephus, in the second month, which the Hebrews call Jur, and in the eleventh year of the reign of our Grand Master, Hiram, King of Tyre. I also firmly believe that it would have been simply impossible, for such a grand and glorious Fraternity as ours, to have sprung into an immediate existence simply in building the temple

CLEOPATRA'S NEEDLE, ALEXANDRIA,

NOW STANDING IN NEW YORK CITY.

upon the threshing-floor of Ornan, the Jebusite. Practical, Operative Masonry was thoroughly comprehended long centuries before that event, as is evidenced by those stupendous and magnificent temples that existed in the Land of old Khemi, upon the banks of the Nile, ages before David, King of Israel, bought the land from Ornan, whereon to erect a temple to the most High God, in which to practice the esoteric teachings handed down to us from one generation to another.

There is, at the present day, scattered all over Egypt, India, Syria, the valley of the Euphrates and the plains of Shinar, monuments and ruins of temples covered with hieroglyphic inscriptions, showing beyond the shadow of a doubt, that Ancient Masonry had its origin long centuries before the dawn of authentic history; aye, back beyond the dim realms of the ancient myths. These wonderful fabrics were erected by our ancient Brethren, who most assuredly possessed a far greater knowledge of the mechanical arts and sciences than is known to the architects of the present day. Otherwise they could not have built such stupendous buildings, or carried across the desert sands such enormous blocks of stone, with which to build the temples in which to perpetuate the peculiar rites and ceremonies of our most illustrous fraternity, as well as to celebrate the most High God of Israel; and I firmly believe that those ancient teachings have been handed down to us, until we find them, at the present day, across the threshold of this wonderful twentieth century, a monument of glory to the most eminent men of all ages and through all time.

Herodotus informs us that the high priests of Thebes were in direct line for three hundred and forty-five generations, and instances are recorded wherein the occupation of architect has descended from father to son for twenty-two generations. It is a well-known fact that the knowledge of the Egyptians was concealed from the lower classes, and if they wished to communicate any of their esoteric teachings to the learned men of other countries, it was given to them, accompanied with peculiar signs and symbols. Certain rites and ceremonies had to be performed by the priests at the initiation of the neophyte into the fraternity, and every Brother, Elu, Knight, or Prince had proof positive that each and all of these sublime Theosophical and Philosophical teachings and ceremonies originated in the far away East, the "Land of the

2

Vedas," under the very shadow of the Hindu Kush and Himalaya Mountains.

The student in Masonic lore will find the signs and symbols used in our illustrious fraternity to-day identical with those used by our ancient Brethren long centuries before Christ, and many of these signs and symbols are to be found engraved upon the walls of the tombs and temples of the ruined cities throughout Egypt, Assyria and India, from the cave temples of Nubia, across the dark waters, and beyond the cave temples of Elephanta and into the far interior of the "Land of the Vedas." He will realize that there is no portion of these countries in which traces of Masonry cannot be found, from the symbolic serpent of the Garden of Eden to the symbol of Christianity, the cross, or ancient Nilometer, that was in use long centuries before Moses was born, even to the emblems placed thereon. To the student of symbolism the field is inexhaustible, and the true meaning of each and every one of them ought to be especially interesting to the members of our ancient fraternity, because we practice the rites and perform the ceremonies just as they have been handed down to us, ever remembering as Brother Albert Pike says in his "Morals and Dogmas," page 106:

"The ceremonies and lessons of these degrees (Blue Lodge) have been for ages more and more accommodating themselves by curtailment and sinking into commonplace, to the often limited memory and capacity of the master and instructor, and to the intellect and needs of the pupil and initiate; that they have come to us from an age when symbols were used, not to *reveal*, but to *conceal*, when the commonest learning was confined to a select few, and the simplest principles of morality seemed newly discovered truths; and that these antique and simple degrees now stand like the broken columns of a roofless Druidical temple, in their rude and mutilated greatness; in many parts also corrupted by time, and disfigured by modern additions and absurd interpretations. They are but the entrance to the great Masonic temple, the triple columns of the portico."

Yet, notwithstanding all these things, we must certainly admit that Masonry and its precepts have been miraculously preserved, through the long drifting centuries, by our ancient brethren, who endeavored to re-veil the symbology that had come down through various epochs from time immemorial. Every initiate must assuredly admit that it is a wonderful organization, because through the rise and fall of empires, through the changing forms of civilization, in every country throughout the world, it has ever and always preserved its onward march, and time's devastating hand itself has, through every age, seemingly nurtured and fostered our most illustrious fraternity, through the wreck of mighty Empires.

It has withstood the shock and force that destroyed Babylon, the Queen city of the world, with her wonderful "Hanging Gardens" and stupendous palaces; Egypt and her golden age has passed away with her wondrous knowledge of the mechanical arts and sciences; cultured Greece with her marble miracles, and imperial Rome has bowed their mighty heads beneath the dust of centuries; aye, fallen never to rise again; while Masonry, our glorious fraternity, without any territorial possessions, without any particular race or power to sustain it, comes forth from the misty veil of the past, sublimely grand and beautiful. It stands to-day across the threshold of the twentieth century a monument of glory to those Elu's whose watchwords were MORALITY AND TRUTH, and who were ever and always opposed to *Tyranny and Fanaticism*, devoting their lives from one generation to another *to the destruction of ignorance*, whose hearts were filled with *Benevolence, Charity and Brotherly Sympathy to all Men*. They were ever directed, by *Honor and Duty*, to study the profound symbology of Ancient Masonry, to give it their most earnest and profound attention. By so doing they might thus be enabled to attain a far greater knowledge of its sublime meaning, and be better prepared to help their aspiring brother starting up the ladder, to a knowledge of those beautiful teachings that contain the same altruistic ideas which have ever led men on to LIGHT AND TRUTH, through every age of the world's history. These teachings enable them to practice the esoteric truths of high morality that bind us all in fraternal bonds of Masonic love, fitting us to lead higher and purer lives. In mingling with the outer world they might demonstrate to every man that Masonic precepts engender a love of morality, virtue and truth that will never die, but will live forever to the honor and glory of our most illustrious fraternity and to the Supreme Architect of the Universe.

The ladder to which I referred above, with its seven steps or rungs, are to be found in all the ancient mysteries, as a very important symbol, that will demonstrate to our aspiring candidate his passage from *Rock to Man*, or unfold to his wondering gaze nature's evolutionary processes. This symbol was used in the Indian Mysteries for the express purpose of reminding our aspirant that the "*Eternal Pilgrim*" or soul had to pass through seven different stages or planes in order to reach perfection.

The rites, as performed in India by those Hierophants of old, taught men that perfection is reached by gradual stages, and that knowledge could very easily be gained by simply reading the thoughts of others. If we desire to become *Wise* and attain *Wisdom* we must climb the ladder ourselves, or in other words, *We must think for ourselves.* In the Mazedean mysteries, in place of the ladder, they used the seven ascending caverns that led the aspirant on to the same conclusions—a knowledge of Self and its Divine possibilities. In fact, all the rites of the ancient Mysteries embodied the same idea of the *Septenary*, for in each and every one the candidate was conducted through variant states or stages, each representing different planes of being, until he stands upon the topmost rung of the ladder in the dazzling Light of WISDOM. Having thus attained the culminating point, he now understands himself, and consequently knows that he stands in the presence of his God, and realizes that *He and his Father are One*, and that "*He shall go no more out.*"

I do not wish to dilate upon the profound philosophy that underlies our symbology at the very start, but shall endeavor to lead you, by gradual stages, to the understanding of many of our beautiful symbols, and show you the road that will enable you to come to an understanding of the *Holy Doctrine*, a knowledge of which will unfold to you THE ROYAL SECRET. There are *Secrets or Hidden Truths*, and most profound ones, embodied in every emblem belonging to our glorious Fraternity, and we possess the Key to the *true* meaning of their sublime esoteric Truths, and will unfold them as we proceed with our work.

The temperature in the city of Alexandria is never so high as in Cairo or Upper Egypt, which is due to the blowing of the North West winds. The mean temperature here ranges from 60° F. in winter, to 75° in summer. There is considerable humidity in the atmosphere in

THE GRAND SQUARE,
ALEXANDRIA

all of the coast towns; hence the heat is much more oppressive than in the interior, although the days are much cooler and the nights much warmer than in those cities farther inland.

There are quite a number of Masonic Lodges in the city of Alexandria, working under the English, Scotch and other jurisdictions. The meetings are held in different buildings in various parts of the city. Those of the English meet in the Boulevard Ishmailiya. while those of the Scottish Jurisdiction meet in the Place Mohammed Ali. The Royal Arch Masons are well represented here, so is the Ancient and Accepted Scottish Rite, wherein are taught the glorious symbology of Ancient Masonry in all its sublimity and grandeur, from the time that our aspiring candidate passes between the two columns that *established in strength* the *Wisdom* that permeated her Sanctuaries. until he fully comprehends the true meaning of " THE MYSTERY OF THE BALANCE." Then. like the initiates of old, he *must* do his duty, stretch forth his hand, and lift his Brother by the way-side to a knowledge of Truth. In lifting the infant Moses from the throbbing bosom of the river Nile, Pharaoh's daughter gave to humanity one of the brightest men of the world's history. We also, who have ascended the ineffable heights, and have learned the esoteric meaning of the various symbols and allegories permeating the ceremonies of our glorious Rite should not hide its sublime teachings from the Brother who is searching for Light and Truth, and who is following the path that we ourselves have trod. We should share with him the knowledge that we have gained in our arduous climb, for by sharing with him the Light which illuminates our path, we may be enabled to help him on to higher planes of Spiritual unfoldment and to a knowledge of his *Higher Self.*

Masonry has its decalogue, which is a law to its Initiates. These are its Ten Commandments:

FIRST.

God is the Eternal, Omnipotent, Immutable WISDOM and Supreme INTELLIGENCE and Exhaustless Love.

Thou shalt adore, revere, and love Him!

Thou shalt honor Him by practising the virtues!

SECOND.

Thy religion shall be, to do good because it is a pleasure to thee, and not merely because it is a duty.

That thou mayest become the friend of the wise man, thou shalt obey his precepts!

Thy soul is immortal! Thou shalt do nothing to degrade it!

THIRD.

Thou shalt unceasingly war against vice!

Thou shalt not do unto others that which thou wouldst not wish them to do unto thee!

Thou shalt be submissive to thy fortunes, and keep burning the light of wisdom!

FOURTH.

Thou shalt honor thy parents!

Thou shalt pay respect and homage to the aged!

Thou shalt instruct the young!

Thou shalt protect and defend infancy and innocence!

FIFTH.

Thou shalt cherish thy wife and thy children!

Thou shalt love thy country, and obey its laws!

SIXTH.

Thy friend shall be to thee a second self!

Misfortune shall not estrange thee from him!

Thou shalt do for his memory whatever thou wouldst do for him, if he were living!

SEVENTH.

Thou shalt avoid and flee from insincere friendships!

Thou shalt in everything refrain from excess!

Thou shalt fear to be the cause of a stain on thy memory!

EIGHTH.

Thou shalt allow no passion to become thy master!

Thou shalt make the passions of others profitable lessons to thyself!

Thou shalt be indulgent to error!

NINTH.

Thou shalt hear much: Thou shalt speak little: Thou shalt act well!

Thou shalt forget injuries!

Thou shalt render good for evil!

Thou shalt not misuse either thy strength or thy superiority!

TENTH.

Thou shalt study to know men; that thereby thou mayest learn to know thyself!

Thou shalt ever seek after virtue!

Thou shalt be just!

Thou shalt avoid idleness!

But the great commandment of Masonry is this: "A new commandment give I unto you: that ye love one another! He that saith he is in the light, and hateth his brother, remaineth still in the darkness."

Brother Pike says: "Such are the moral duties of a Mason. But it is also the duty of Masonry to assist in elevating the moral and intellectual level of society; in coining knowledge, bringing ideas into circulation, and causing the mind of youth to grow; and in putting, gradually, by the teachings of axioms and the promulgation of positive laws, the human race, in harmony with its destinies."

Ruined Temples—Masonry and Its Symbols.

The ruins of Egypt are the tattered pages,
The archives of the nation passed away,
Whose Hierophants and ancient sages
Lived 'mid the scenes that we tread to-day;
We wander midst the stupendous glory
Of ancient Egypt, in her golden age,
And as we ramble read the story,
Then, passing on, we turn the page.

CHAPTER II.

RUINED TEMPLES—MASONRY AND MASONIC SYMBOLS.

SAIS was the most important city during the Saitic Empire, and the one which gave its name to the period when the Theban Empire yielded her exalted position to the growing power of the cities of the Delta, extending from the twentieth dynasty to the conquest of the valley of the Nile by Alexander the Great in the year B. C. 332. During this period many magnificent temples and tombs were erected that were the admiration of the learned men of Greece and other countries, many of whom went to Egypt for the express purpose of acquiring knowledge and information not obtainable in their own countries, and where they perfected their studies in science, art, and philosophy peculiar to the Golden Age of Egypt. The tutelar deity of this ancient city of Sais, was the goddess Neith, whom the Greeks identified with their Athene. She is very often represented with a weaver's shuttle, and is also frequently seen armed with bow and arrows, corresponding to the warlike goddess of the Greek *Minerva*, worshipped both by the Egyptians and the Libyans. There is no question in my mind, but, that this identification of Neith with Athene caused Pausanias to believe that Pallas-Athene originally came from Libia, to which Sais was frequently considered to belong. If the Egyptians did really conceive of the goddess Neith as weaving, it was only in a figurative sense, as *creating*. Upon her temple was inscribed: "*I am the things that have been, and that are, and that will be; no one hath ever me unveiled.*"

Herodotus gained a vast amount of knowledge and information from the priests of this city, as well as from his personal observations, and so did hundreds of other prominent men who came from all parts of Greece and distant countries to acquire a knowledge of the profound philosophies, sciences and architecture, which belonged to these ancient people, who not only erected the Pyramids and Sphinx, but adorned their wondrous valley and Delta of the Nile with such stupendous monuments, that they have been the admiration of the world down to the present day.

It was here in Sais that Solon associated with the Hierophants of Egypt, and Cambyses also visited this celebrated city after he had conquered the "Land of Egypt." He not only admitted his being an initiate, but he showed himself favorable to the rites and ceremonies of the mysteries, as practiced in the temple of Neith, by permitting it to stand as a monument to the fraternity in all its magnificence, just as he found it, and the very fact of his doing so proves that he was not only an initiate, but an Hierophant, who, like others before him had seen the "Light." His name was "Ameth." He had passed through the purifying elements, and had most assuredly witnessed the glory which filled the sanctuary beyond the veil shrouding the ivory portal. In seeing this ineffable mystic glory and having been thoroughly instructed in the esoteric teachings, like other Initiates, he recognized the presence of the Supreme Architect. as manifested in the beauty and grandeur of the outer world. His mind must have been enlightened by the "Holy Doctrine," a knowledge of which not only purifies the heart from sin, but drives ignorance from the mind, and insures the favor of the gods, thus opening the gates of immortal felicity to all who have passed beyond the veil.

The barriers have now been rent asunder and the initiate begins to understand himself and realizes that although he is blind to his surroundings and the knowledge which permeates the Kosmos, yet he carries the light of all knowledge within his heart, aye, within his own hand, that will light him on to the highest planes of intellectual and spiritual development. He will appreciate the fact that by the exercise of the inner vision all Wisdom is at his command. Every man who stepped across the mystic portals of the ancient Mysteries followed in the same paths trodden by those who had gone before. They learned the same lessons, received the same Light and vowed the same vows. In this way they were bound by a tie stronger than "chains of brass," and consequently they would always endeavor to build up rather than tear down. Thus it was that Cambyses permitted this celebrated structure to stand. He himself had fed the sacred fire upon the altar and had identified himself with the Hierophants who presided over the Ancient Mysteries within this celebrated temple.

To-day there is no trace of this wondrous temple, or the royal palace and mausoleum of the Pharoah's connected with it. Nothing now remains of the glory pertaining to this once celebrated city, but a few fellaheen dwellings, claiming the name of Sais, whose glory reached the four corners of the earth. But, to-day, the villagers only assume the first two letters of the old name and call it *Sa.* In the ancient city of Sais there was a chapel that had been hewn out of a single block of granite, brought from the quarries of Syene, the weight of which must have been fully three hundred tons.

Herodotus tells us of the magnificence of this wondrous city and the grandeur of the tomb of Osiris, whose columns were adorned with palm-capitals; the statues and the rows of andro-sphinxes which led up to the entrance of the temple were most magnificent specimens of the best Egyptian sculpture. He also tells us of the sacred lake, etc., but at the present time there is very little of it to be seen to give us an idea of its size and beauty, excepting an irregular sheet of water and portions of an immense wall that is sixty-five feet wide and about one thousand five hundred feet long. This wall, however, verifies the statement of Herodotus respecting the lake, and to satisfy one that it must have been a magnificent city, in its palmy days, as they never built such stupendous walls around ordinary cities. Few relics of this once famous city have been brought to light, and all that greets the eye of the traveller or tourist now visiting this place, is ruin, utter ruin.

San-Tanis, or ZOAN, was a city of very great prominence during the time of Moses, and it was in this place that both he and Aaron compelled Pharaoh to let the Israelites go "out of the land of Egypt and out of the house of bondage;" through the wonders they performed in the field of Zoan (*Exodus 7: 10, and Psalms 78: 12-43*). The site of this celebrated city is occupied to-day by Arab fishermen, who call their village *San*, which is the Arab form of the ancient Zan or Zoan. The inhabitants of this place are the lineal descendants of the Blamites and Bashmusites. They were also known as Malekites, who were, during the Christian domination, firm adherents of the orthodox church, but who were quite willing to embrace *El-Islam* when the opportunity offered.

These people are, in many respects, like their great ancestors, rude and uncultured, and extremely uncivil, treating all tourists and travellers with scant respect, but especially is this so if they be Christians. If it were not for the expectation of obtaining a goodly "baksheesh" from those who go to this place in order to examine the ruins and site of the "Field of Zoan," they would be far more uncourteous. The Greeks call this village Tanis, but the Egyptian name agrees with that in the Scriptures, which corresponds to the monumental name of this celebrated city. The truth of this assertion has verification from the statue found here, which is to be seen in the Museum of Antiquities, bearing an inscription stating that the individual it represents was "a governor in his town, a magnate in his province and a prefect in the towns and fields of Tan, 'meaning Zan or Zoan.'"

It was here the celebrated stone was found that was called by the French "La Pierre de San." It was that famous trilingual stone, containing Greek, hieroglyphic and Demotic characters, known to the Egyptologists as the "Decree of Kanopus," that constituted an edict promulgated by Ptolemy Euergetus in the year B. C. 237 at Kanopus, then the religious capital of the country. The original stone is now to be found in the Museum of Antiquities, Gizeh, near Cairo. There are two plaster casts of this stone, one of which has been placed in the British Museum, the other in the Aberdeen University, Scotland. This limestone tablet or "stele" was discovered by Dr. Lepsius in the year 1866. It was the writing on this stone which established the correctness of the method of deciphering the inscriptions on the celebrated "Rosette Stone," or stele, by Champolin and others.

Stele is the name that is given to tablets of granite, limestone, wood, or faience, so often found amid the ruins of tombs and temples in the valley of the Nile. They were used for the purpose of inscribing upon them the various decrees, historical records, victories of the various Pharaohs or kings of Egypt and biographical notices of prominent men and officials—in fact any thing of importance would be inscribed upon these stelæ. The largest number of these stones have been found placed inside the tombs, generally in the passage-way leading into the mummy chamber. They have also frequently been found placed just inside the door or entrance to the sepulchre, as well as at the bier, and a great many are to be seen set into the walls of various tombs throughout Egypt. They vary in size and shape, according to the fashion of the dynasty in which the individual lived. Sometimes they were rectangular, at other times lozenge or oval-shaped, but each and every one of them were inscribed with the name of the deceased, generally setting forth the principal events of their lives, as well as their pedigree, titles, etc., etc.

It is very difficult to tell the exact date of the origin of this city or by whom founded, but from the Scriptural account we are enabled to learn that the city of Zoan was built seven years after *Hebron* was established (*see Numbers 13 : 22*). The branch of the Nile on which this famous city of Zoan was situated was called the Tanitic. It was the most easterly branch of this grand old river and nearest to Palestine and Arabia, if we except that of the Pelusiac. There is no question but that the city grew in importance and power during the New Empire and when the Hyksos, in their warlike expeditions overran and dominated this northern part of Egypt, they found established here a race kindred to their own; consequently they made this city their capital, and at once proceeded to adorn and beautify it with most magnificent buildings and sculptures of all kinds, employing none but Egyptian artists to do the work, specimens of which were discovered by Mariette Bey, who threw a vast amount of light upon this period of Egyptian history. The rather peculiar type of sphinxes that he found here he attributed to these shepherd kings. He also stated that the probabilities were, that at the time one of these kings was reigning in Memphis, Joseph was sold into Egypt and may have served under him, for, as he says, this Pharaoh was not a pure born Egyptian, but of foreign parentage, of shepherd descent, like himself, and the treatment Joseph received, based upon this supposition, is far more easily understood.

Under the thirteenth dynasty this city received a great impetus. Quite a large number of very fine monuments and colossi were erected by Amenemhat and the two Usertesens, remains of which are to be found in the Museum of Gizeh, all testifying to the importance of Zoan at that period. Although the city had reached such importance at that time, the sanctuary of the great temple dates back to the sixth dynasty, B. C. 3703, plainly showing the rise and fall of this wonderful city during various epochs of Egyptian history.

During the lives of the monarchs of the twenty-ninth dynasty it was decorated and adorned with magnificent statues, obelisks and most exquisite works of art, and the rulers of this dynasty, Sethi, Rameses II and Meneptha often came here to hold their court and join in the sacred rites and ceremonies of the ancient mysteries.

It was under the twenty-first dynasty, B. C. 1110, that Tanis or Zoan became the capital of Egypt once more, and gave its name to the dynasty, and also to that branch of the river Nile on which it was situated. Under this administration the public buildings and temples were restored; the needs of the city carefully attended to, and its avenues beautified, but it again fell to a city of secondary consideration, although Marietta claimed that it was a town of great importance from the twenty-second to the twenty-sixth dynasty. He gave the name Tanite to the twenty-third dynasty. The city again began to decline during the reign of Amasis, by whom the capital of Egypt was removed to Sais, making Naucratis the sole port of entry for Egypt, and compelling all vessels to go *there* to load or discharge their freight. In consequence of which Naucratis soon grew into prominence, becoming one of the best known cities in Egypt. It was located about fifteen miles west of the capital of Egypt (Sais.) This decree of Amasis making Naucratis the sole port of entry for Egypt was the cause of its rapid growth, for it gave to this place special privileges.

Herodotus tells us that this king (Amasis) " was partial to the Greeks," and induced them to come and settle in Egypt. Amasis had recognized their bravery and power during his war with Apries, consequently, when they immigrated to this land of Egypt and established themselves at Naucratis, this great king did all in his power to help them, because he knew he would be enabled to depend upon them in case of war. He afterwards verified his good opinion of them, for when the Persians invaded Egypt he mustered them into the Egyptian forces, and led them on to assist him in repelling the invaders.

They responded to his call and assisted him in establishing himself more firmly in the hearts of his countrymen and in the land of Egypt.

Amasis was born in the town of Niouph, of poor and humble parents, but, through his wonderful abilities, his high intellectual power and force of character, he rose to the high and exalted position of ruler, or Pharaoh over Egypt, and over this great and mighty people. In attaining this exalted position he was not looked upon as a legitimate king by the higher classes, because they considered it to be an infringement upon the ancient constitutions of the Egyptians. The kings of Egypt had always been chosen from among the priests or soldiers of the country, but as he belonged to neither one nor the other he was considered to be ineligible, and the prominent men endeavored to have him deposed. As he was supported by the people, who had placed him upon the throne, they were compelled to abandon their opposition and acknowledge him as King and Pharaoh of Egypt.

Herodotus tells us in the second book (*Euterpe*, chapter 172), " At first his subjects looked down upon him, and held him in but small esteem, because he had been a mere private person, and of a house of no great distinction ; but after a time Amasis succeeded in reconciling them to his rule, not by severity, but by cleverness. Among his other splendors he had a golden foot-pan, in which his guests and himself were wont, upon occasion, to wash their feet. This vessel he caused to be broken in pieces, and made of the gold an image of one of the gods, which he set up in the most public place in the whole city ; upon which the Egyptians flocked to the image, and worshipped it with the utmost reverence. Amasis finding this was so, called an assembly and opened the matter to them, explaining how the image had been made of the foot-pan, wherein they had been wont formerly to wash their feet, and to put all manner of filth within it, yet now it was reverenced. And truly, he went on to say, it had gone with him, as with the foot-pan. If he was a private person formerly, yet now he had come to be their king. And so he bade them honor and reverence him. Such was the mode in which he won over the Egyptians, and brought them to be content in his service."

Amasis was one of the first kings of whose personal character we know anything, and from the records that have been preserved we find

3

that he had a very strict sense of honor and justice. It is positively known that he devoted himself to the interests of his country and the intellectual advancement of his fellow men. He possessed those qualities which not only endeared him to his soldiers and countrymen, but commanded the respect of the prominent men of all other nations. He loved pleasure, but when business of the nation required his services, he gave the whole of his time and attention to those requirements. He was a wise king, ruler, and Hierophant of the Mysteries, and enforced the law, compelling every Egyptian to appear once a year and demonstrate to the Governor of the Nome, in which he lived, that he was earning an honest living, to enable him to support his wife and family; failing to prove this the penalty was *Death*. Draco made this same law in Athens, but afterward Solon repealed it on account of its severity. This Egyptian King and Hierophant thoroughly understood the "Pole Star of Truth," and endeavored by his own conduct to demonstrate to all men that the teachings received from the ancient mysteries were most sublimely grand and beautiful. He knew full well there was no royal road to the understanding of its profound symbology, science and philosophies, and in order to attain to a knowledge of the rites, ceremonies and esoteric teachings of the various degrees, he would have to devote his time to it by earnest study, profound attention and the soul's deep meditation, before he would be enabled to comprehend the ineffable beauty of the rites and ceremonies. Like others who have passed beyond the mystic portals, he realized that without it he would simply pass through the ceremonies of the ancient mysteries of Egypt, but the sublimity and grandeur of the teachings would be as incomprehensible as the veiled statue of Neith, (Isis) in the temple of Sais.

"Masonry is a peculiar system of morality, veiled in allegory, and illustrated by symbols." But we must distinctly understand that ritualism is not Masonry. The glorious teachings embodied in the ethics of Masonry are, and ever will be, in existence, having been taught and promulgated through every age. And it did not require the building of the temple by Solomon to demonstrate the profound morality that belonged to our glorious Fraternity, for it has had a continuous existence through every epoch of the world's history.

EXTERIOR WALL OF THE TEMPLE OF DENDERAH

The profound wisdom contained in the veiled symbols is most beautiful and sublimely grand, and, as I have hereinbefore stated, the real meaning of the various symbols, belonging to Masonry, must be carefully searched out before the student can ever hope to understand the faintest glimmer of their true meaning. This cannot be told the aspiring candidate too often, that, in order to come to an understanding of the true meanings that are embodied in our symbology, he must learn the meaning contained in the very first degree, as herein lies the key or combination to those above.

Through all countries in the world, from the cave temples of India to those of Nubia, through the valley of the Nile and its Delta, as well as in Chaldea, Assyria, Greece, Rome and even amid the tropical growth of long drifting centuries in Mexico and Yucatan, are to be found, at the present day, in all these places, monuments and ruins of temples covered with signs, symbols and hieroglyphic inscriptions going to prove, beyond the shadow of a doubt, that our glorious fraternity has existed in each and every one of them. If you will take time to search for yourselves, as I have done, you will find that Free Masonry must have originated in India, and that it was cradled upon the banks of the Nile, beyond the dawn of authenticated history. Here in this extremely interesting valley will be found ocular demonstrations that our ancient brethren were not only speculative, but practical, operative Masons, who beautified and adorned the world with magnificent specimens of their work, from the Gopuras and temples of India, the Pyramids and stupendous fabrics of Egypt to the marble miracles of Greece and the grandest ruin of Rome—the Coliseum.

In the valley of the Nile our ancient brethren have demonstrated their knowledge in gigantic temples and colossal monolithic statues. The "Arundel Marbles" in the British Museum speak louder than a thousand tongues to testify to the sublimity to which they had attained in sculpture. The Acropolis and Parthenon are in ruins, but even as they are, in their mutilated grandeur, they testify to the men of cultured Greece and to the names of those craftsmen who wrought them. All these things go to prove that our practical, operative brethren of a prehistoric age thoroughly comprehended the mechanical arts and sciences, otherwise they never could have quarried and carried across the desert sands, such stupendous blocks of granite with which to build their imposing temples, wherein they practiced the rites and performed the ceremonies in a manner similar to our ancient craftsmen long before Moses officiated in the temples of Egypt. These same sublimely beautiful ceremonies stand to-day, across the threshold of the twentieth century, as a monument of glory to our most ancient and illustrious Rite and the Supreme Architect of the Universe. Those who believe in the Supreme Architect of the Universe can unite with us, in the Masonic fold, upon the level and true points of fellowship which unite and bind us all in fraternal bonds of Masonic love, teaching to each and every one the glory of the Fatherhood of God and the brotherhood of man.

Albert Pike states, in "Morals and Dogmas," page 726, that "Religion is the crown of morality, not its base. The base of morality is itself. The moral code of Masonry is still more extensive than that developed by philosophy. To the requisitions of the law of nature and the law of God, it adds the imperative obligation of a contract. Upon entering the Fraternity, the initiate binds to himself every Mason in the world. Once enrolled among the *Children of Light*, every Mason on earth becomes his brother, and owes him the duties, the kindness, and sympathies of a brother. On every one he may call for assistance in need, protection against danger, sympathy in sorrow, attention in sickness, and decent burial after death. There is not a Mason in the world who is not bound to go to his relief when he is in danger, if there be a greater probability of saving his life than losing his own. No Mason can wrong him to the value of anything, knowingly, himself, nor suffer it to be done by others, if it be in his power to prevent it. No Mason can speak evil of him, to his face or behind his back. Every Mason must keep his lawful secrets, and aid him in his business, defend his character when unjustly assailed, and protect, counsel, and assist his widow and orphans. What so many thousands owe to him, he owes to each of them. He has solemnly bound himself to be ever ready to discharge this sacred debt. If he fails to do it, he is dishonest and forsworn ; and it is an unparalleled meanness in him to obtain good offices by false pretences, to receive kindness and service, rendered him under the confident expectation that he will in his turn render the same, and then to disappoint, without ample reason, and just expectation. Masonry holds him also by his solemn promise to a purer life, a nobler generosity, a more perfect charity of opinion and action; to be tolerant, catholic in his love for his race, ardent in his zeal for the interest of mankind, and the advancement and progress of humanity."

We are positively certain that the esoteric teachings of both the Lesser and the Greater Mysteries were never revealed to any one who was not considered to be worthy and well qualified to receive them, but we must distinctly understand that all those who had received the light from the Lesser were not always considered worthy to pass across the threshold of the Greater Mysteries. In order to be enabled to attain to these rites and ceremonies, they had to stand the test of being proven worthy to receive them, and if they were permitted to enter through the sacred portals, they had to pass through the most profound and sublime ceremonies before they were entrusted with the key to the symbology which would enlighten them, and lift the veil to their searching and bewildered gaze, thus revealing the ineffable glories that lay beyond the mystic portals.

It must be thoroughly understood that in joining a Masonic Lodge a man does not immediately become a truer, purer, or better man; it simply shows him the light of truth, and impresses upon him " *That there is no Religion higher than Truth.*" Neither will he at first see the beauties, nor understand the mystic ceremonies, for he will be blinded, as it were, by the effulgent light that permeates the sanctuaries of our glorious Fraternity, when he will at once realize that the keynote to a thorough knowledge and understanding of the sublimity and grandeur of the ceremonies of our beloved Scottish Rite is *meditation and earnest study.*

Any Mason, be he Elu, Knight, or Prince, who is interested in the origin of the symbols and teachings of our ancient and accepted Scottish Rite of Free Masonry, can in India, Egypt and other countries, have ocular demonstration, in signs, symbols, and Masonic emblems, which have been in existance thousands of years before the building of the temple by our three Grand Masters, wherein to practice the esoteric teachings of our most illustrious fraternity, teachings that have been the admiration of the most profound men of every epoch in the world's history.

Symbols appeal to the eye, and impress themselves upon our memory, as oral instructors to the ear. The level is symbolical of equality and teaches us the universal brotherhood of man. The square is an emblem of justice, for, as Brother Fellows states, "It was the means in Egypt of establishing the boundaries of lands that had been obscured or carried away by the inundations." It is a very ancient symbol and like many others we cannot trace it to any particular nation or people. It does not derive its chief importance from the operative Mason, but rather from the speculative. We know that it was held, as a most profound sacred symbol, among the ancient Egyptians, for it was always carried in all their grand and solemn processions, by certain officials who were called Stolists. In our symbolic degrees it teaches us honesty of purpose, and fair dealing to all men. The plumb teaches us to learn to subdue our lower animal passionate nature; it is the symbol of unerring rectitude. The mosaic pavement is most assuredly symbolical of the human life, checkered with good and evil, forcibly emblematic of man's career, as each day we stand upon the bright square of hope or the black square of misfortune or adversity. To-day we are crowned with joy and happiness, to-morrow we may be filled with sorrow and tribulation. It teaches us to walk upright before all men, in humbleness of heart, and to assist our weary brother by the way-side, for we do not know the day nor the hour when we, ourselves, may need the help of those we have assisted. The tesselated border symbolizes the manifold blessings and comforts continually surrounding us, but the blazing star in the centre comes down to us from those ancient adepts, who named not only the signs of the Zodiac, but every star that glitters in the infinitude of space.

Let us go back beyond the " Golden Age of Egypt," when the arts and sciences were flourishing, which, centuries later, furnished the embers from which leaped Grecian culture and Roman civilization. What a sweep backward must the imagination take in order to appreciate the almost bewildering stretch of time from the present day, of this twentieth century, to the earliest ages of Egyptian civilization, when the people of this wondrous valley watched for the sign which assured them of all that was necessary for the sustenance of themselves, and the preservation of their domestic animals! And this sign was a brilliant, luminous star, appearing upon the eastern horizon in the early evening, which they called Sothis, or Anubis the barker, the same as we call Sirius, the dog star). Its appearance warned the people who occupied the lowlands adjacent to the river Nile, of approaching danger, that they might be enabled to go to higher ground and escape the flooding waters. About this time these waters came rushing down from its interior sources, from unknown regions in Central Africa, bearing within its bosom immense quantities of decayed organic substance that deposited itself evenly over the whole of the flooded country. This acted upon the parched and thirsty soil as a rich and powerful fertilizing agent, fructifying and causing all things planted to grow in abundance. All the fellaheen had to do was to scatter their seed broadcast upon the soil, trample them in with their domestic animals, and when the waters subsided watch their crops grow luxuriantly and reap a thousand fold what they had sown. No wonder, then, they eagerly longed for the coming of this glorious symbol which was to them a harbinger of the fruits of the earth and the fulness thereof, for to them the glorious river Nile was an emblem of God the Father, who brought to their very doors the necessaries of life. So we find it upon the floors of our temples—an emblem of faith in the goodness of the Supreme Architect of the Universe.

The overflowing of the river Nile was considered by the ancient Egyptians a demonstration of the activity of the Osirian Triad, because they considered that Isis personified the earth of the Nile valley and Delta, but not the whole earth universal like *Seb*, who was the representative of the earth in all its wonderful manifestations and differentiations. But they believed that Isis personified the rich black land of the Delta and valley of the Nile, on both banks of the river, as far as Thebes, and beyond, to the first cataract, where all things grew in such luxuriant abundance, and that she would continue to give to the ever succeeding generations, from her inexhaustible productive forces, all that was necessary for the sustenance of Man and his domestic animals living in this wondrous valley of the Nile. How did she produce these wonderful manifestations? Simply by the union of Osiris with Isis. Osiris personified the river Nile, which overflows its banks and takes Isis in his loving embrace, thereby uniting, every year, the river Osiris to his beloved Isis, and from this union comes forth the virgin harvest which represented Horus the Son, and thus we have the Egyptian triad of Osiris, Isis and Horus.

Egypt! how well I remember thy fertile valley, thy glorious river, and the evidences of thy former grandeur, whose splendors not only filled the ancient world with admiration and wonder, but compel the learned men of to-day to stand with awe before thy mighty monolithic statues and gigantic structures, whose very ruins represent the tattered pages of the archives of one of the grandest nations the world has ever known, and the evidences of a remote and wonderful civilization! We can gather a vast amount of knowledge and information respecting her manners and customs, science, arts and philosophies in the study of her tombs, temples and monolithic sculptures, as these things represent the stony leaves that have been written with pens of steel. Although her temples have fallen into decay and her innumerable statues and obelisks destroyed, broken into fragments and carried off by vandals, there remains no doubt a very large number of priceless treasures, still lying shrouded beneath the drifting desert sands, whose covering is even now being removed. We may possibly be enabled to recover many of the treasured secrets of the "Golden Age of Egypt" that will throw "more light" on the knowledge and Wisdom pertaining to Ancient Egyptians and the Craftsmen who wrought in the quarries in those golden days of long ago, in order to erect the temples which to-day lie scattered broadcast throughout the length and breadth of this most extraordinary valley.

In viewing these magnificent ruins I was filled with marvellous admiration for the majesty of their proportions, their wonderful strength and beauty, and the extraordinary knowledge of the mechanical arts and sciences possessed by the ancient craftsmen in their construction. I recognized that they represented the thoughts of men who lived in the hoary ages of a far away past, whose very names, if known, would command our most profound respect and admiration—men who rocked the cradle of Ancient Masonry in the land of the mighty Pharaohs, long centuries ago. There is but little to interest the traveller of to-day in "The field of Zoan," and he will realize that what was once the splendid palaces and temples of Egypt's mighty warlike kings, are now dwelling places for the lowly fishermen of San, amid ruins of tombs, temples, monuments and fragmentary statues that lie scattered around in the wildest confusion imaginable.

The drifting sands are slowly and silently covering up the remains of what was once one of the grandest cities of Lower Egypt, whose fame reached the four corners of the earth. The principal divinities worshipped in "The field of Zoan" were Ptah, Amen, and an Asiatic divinity called Set, or Sutek, but which was afterwards worshipped under the form of Ra, Horus, etc. The country in the vicinity of Tanis is low and marshy land, with scarcely any vegetation excepting reeds and dwarfed tamarask bushes, among which wild boars are often to be found. A canal runs through it now, and still it does not fertilize the soil. "Fire passed through Zoan, and it is desolate." (Ezekiel 30: 14.)

There are immense numbers of all kinds of water fowl that will afford good sport to the traveller or tourist, and help to replenish their larder if they camp as they go along. Whoever comes to this place should not forget to bring a goodly supply of insect powder and oil of pennyroyal—the first for the fleas whose name are legion, and outnumber those of San Francisco ten to one; the oil of pennyroyal to ward off attacks of the blood-thirsty mosquito and the pertinacity of the miserable Egyptian fly.

Egypt was divided into Nomes or Cantons, for administrative purposes, and each Nome was presided over by a Governor or *Monarch*, appointed by the king himself. A Nome consisted of one of the principal cities, and the surrounding villages that were in a measure dependent upon it. The duty of each Monarch was to superintend his Canton, see to the collecting of revenues, etc., in fact, all the details of the Government were attended to either by him or his deputies, and he was held personally responsible for all their acts, as well as his own. In the Delta there were, according to Strabo, (Book 17: 787,) ten of these Nomes, and the same in the Thebiad, while the intermediate country was credited with seven, growing at a later date into sixteen. Each Nome had definitely established boundaries, originally laid out by order of the early rulers. These Nomes eventually grew to the number of fifty, three among them being included in the Greater and Lesser Oasis and the Oasis of Amon. All these were divided into *Toparchies*, but of what size we are unable to say. Each of these Nomes sent delegates, who were accompanied, by the chief priests and priestesses, of the principal temple in their Nome, to the general convention that met, at stated times, in the magnificent palace of the Labyrinth, near Lake Moeris (of which I shall speak later on). At these conventions, possibly, the king presided and administered justice in accordance with the Law, and it was, no doubt, used for the same purpose as our legislature.

Bubastis.—This ancient city is now called *Tel Basta*. The Pi-beseth of the Scriptures (Ezekiel 30 : 17), is situated on the west bank of the Pelusiac branch of the Nile, about fourteen miles north of Belbeys, in very low marsy land pregnant with malaria, fever, etc. This was the site of one of the most ancient cities of Lower Egypt, and the ruins to be seen there to-day attest to her former magnificence and grandeur. The lofty mounds of brick that protected the city from the annual inundations of the Nile are sufficient proof of its antiquity.

Herodotus (in Book II, chapter 137) claims that these mounds were formed by Egyptians who, having committed some offence, were compelled to raise the ground in the vicinity of the city to which they belonged. In consequence of this a great many cities in the Delta of the Nile rose far above the plain, safe from the flooding waters of old God Nilus. He especially mentions Bubastis as having been raised to a greater elevation than any other city in Egypt, which was a noticeable fact in his time as well as in our own. As early as the reign of *User-Maat-Ra*, Rameses II., (The Great), these mounds began to rise around the city when that great warrior king connected the waters of the Red Sea with the river Nile, b. c. 1340. This city was no doubt of considerable importance, at least thirty-four centuries ago, during the reign of the " wall builder," Thotmes III. It received its death blow when Amasis made Sais his capital and fixed the seat of his power in his favorite city (*see ante*), and Bubastis, like Tanis, and other cities of importance, began to sink into insignificance.

Bubastis attained its highest importance and power under the twenty-second dynasty, whose first king was Sesonchis, the conqueror of Thebes, who united in himself the two crowns of Upper and Lower Egypt, besides making his native city the capital, and source from which emanated all his mandates. The student of ancient Egyptian history and Masonic tradition will recognize the magnificence to which this city had risen under the various dynasties, ranging from the Second

Memphite of the Old Monarchy (see Manetho) until its decline and subsequent fall. It began to lose its power when Amasis issued his famous edict making Naucratis the only port of entry in Egypt. The annals of the celebrated red granite temple of this city, extending back beyond authenticated history, constituted the glory of each succeeding dynasty. Its ruins of to-day form one of the grandest pages of the archives of ancient Egyptian history.

This magnificant city and red temple won the admiration of Herodotus (see Book II., Chapters 137-8), whose description is very accurate. In relation to it he says: "Here is the goddess Bubastis, which well deserves to be described. Other temples may be grander, and may have cost more in the building, but there is none so pleasant to the eye as this of Bubastis." Then he goes on to describe it as follows: "Excepting the entrance, the whole forms an island. Two artificial channels from the Nile, one on either hand of the temple encompass the building, leaving only a narrow passage by which it is approached. These channels are each a hundred feet wide and they are thickly shaded with trees. The gateway is sixty feet in height, and ornamented with figures cut upon stone six cubits high and well worthy of notice. The temple stands in the middle of the city, and is visible on all sides, as one walks around it. The city has been raised by means of an embankment, while the temple has been left untouched in its original condition. You can look down upon it wherever you are. A low wall runs around the enclosure, having figures engraved upon it, and inside there is a grove of beautiful tall trees, surrounding the shrine containing the image of the goddess. This enclosure is a furlong in length, and the same in breadth. The entrance to it is by a road, paved with stone for a distance of about three furlongs, which passes straight through the market place in an easterly direction and is four hundred feet in width. Trees of an extraordinary height grow on each side the road leading from the temple of Bubastis to that of Mercury."

This temple was sacred to the goddess Bast, who personified the spring-time warmth of the sun. Pasht, the Bubastis of the Egyptians, is often represented with the head of a cat, or, in the older sculptures, with a lion's head crowned with a disk and uraes, like the sun god Ra. The disk and lion indicate her connection with the solar deity, while the uraes was a symbol of immortality, and was generally worn upon the forehead of a king or queen. It is also an emblem of royalty. This deadly asp rears itself on the brow ready to strike and defend the wearer from his or her enemies. Bubastis of the Egyptians, is the same as the Artemis (Diana) of the Greeks. (*Her. 2 : 187.*) Bast is often represented both sitting and standing, with the cat or lion's head, disk and uraes holding the amulet of life the *anx*. She is sometimes found holding in her right hand a sistrum, carrying on her left arm a basket, and holding in her left hand an aegis. She is always represented as a woman, and very often a prayer accompanies the figure, one of which is, "May she grant all life, and power, all health and joy of heart," or "I am Bast, the Lady of Life."

The *panegyries*, or festivals, that were held by the people at the various temples of Egypt, sank into comparative insignificance compared with the festivities which took place in Bubastis, whose magnificent temple was the favorite resort of men, women and children. These came from every Nome in Egypt, to participate in the sacrifices and licentious festivities indulged in by all who sought Bast. They would come down the river and canals, by boats, in immense numbers, the men beating drums and playing on pipes, and the women beating cymbals in time with the music, while those who had no instruments, would accompany the harmony, by beating time with their hands, shouting, and behaving in a very indecent manner, much after the style of the women who participate in the festival of Ceres at Eleusis. On arriving at Bubastis, they would offer sacrifices and form processions, being led by men who played the pipe, the rest would follow and perform most indecent acts while dancing, shouting and making all kinds of gestures in a very debauched condition and in drunken abandonment. The number annually assembling here to participate in the panegyries of Bast, has been estimated at seven hundred thousand men and women, not including children.

The first king of the twenty-second dynasty, Sesonchis, or Sheshonk, was contemporary with Solomon, King of Israel. The scripture name of this Egyptian king was Shishak. During the latter part of the reign of Solomon he tried to kill Jeroboam. who in order to save his life, fled into Egypt, and no doubt to the city of Bubastis, taking refuge with Shishak. On his return he introduced some of the Egyptian divinities to the people of Israel. Afterwards Shishak invaded and captured the fenced cities of Judah and Benjamin, and took possession of Jerusalem, after which he carried away with him into Egypt the vast treasures that Solomon had collected. [*See 2nd Kings, Chap. 12*].

The historic names found upon monuments and sculptures of Bubastis, range from Khufu of the fourth dynasty to Ptolemy Euergetus second. There are also to be found among the ruins the name of Rameses second, Osorkon first, Amyrtaeus and others. The ruins of this magnificent city lie scattered around in bewildering confusion. There is, no doubt, many beautiful statues, lotus, palm-leaf, and Hathor-head capitals, shrouded in the drifting sands, which may never be brought to the light of day to testify to their wondrous skill and knowledge in the art of carving. One very important discovery was made in the ruins of this once famous city, and that was a fallen pylon of the time of Osorkon second. The carving upon it furnishes a description of a very important festival, which is of great interest to scholars of the present day, as it explains everything pertaining to it in all its details.

The temples of Lower Egypt differ considerably from those of Upper Egypt. In those above Cairo, or the Delta of the Nile, the walls are built of sandstone and the columns are made of different pieces, while granite is confined to the pylons, monuments, statues, etc. In the Delta the temples were built principally of granite, the vestibules, etc., having columns of a single stone of the same material. From the Hypostyle hall of this celebrated, magnificent red granite temple of Bubastis, came three valuable specimens of ancient Egyptian workmanship, now in the Boston Museum of Fine Arts, consisting of a Hathor-headed capital, a Lotus-bud capital, and a tablet on which Amen-Ra is represented enthroned on a dais that is reached by a series of steps, towards which a procession is apparently going for the purpose of rendering homage to the Great God of Egypt, the son of Ptah. The Egyptians affirmed of him, that he was ONE, the ONLY ONE. He formed the *first* in the great Triad of Thebes—Amen, Mut and Chansu.

.The ruins of Bubastis are composed of large dark mounds of debris, plainly visible from the railroad. There is little to be seen here that will interest the traveler of to-day, except the mutilated remains of this once magnificent city, unless he is desirous of identifying the shattered remains with the descriptions by Herodotus, Rawlinson and others; if so, he will be enabled to verify the statements made by these authorities respecting its site, surroundings, and magnitude. One thing is certain, he will see the great height of the mounds and the enormous blocks of beautiful red granite that Herodotus admired so much in the temple itself, and will also be enabled to recognize the site of both the temple of Bast and Mercury. Herodotus states in Book 2, Chaps. 66 and 67, that "If a cat dies in a private house by a natural death, all the inmates of the house shave their eyebrows; and on the death of a dog they shave the head and the whole of the body." Cats dying in any part of Egypt, were taken to the ancient city of Bubastis in order to be embalmed, after which they were deposited in a special place made for the purpose, but all dogs were buried in the various towns to which they belonged, and in certain receptacles provided for the burial of their bodies.

Ancient Cities—Osirian Myth—Karma.

47

"To thine abode, to thine abode, Oh come,
    To thine abode, god An, I thee implore,
    Thine enemies exist not any more;
Return, oh glorious sovereign, to thine home.

"I am thy sister, whom thou hast embraced,
    Look on me, I, thy sister, loving thee;
    Oh, beauteous youth, stay thou not far from me,
But come to thine abode with haste, with haste.

"I see thee not, and to my heart doth throng
    Anguish for thee, and bitterness untold;
    Mine eyes seek to thee, wishing to behold
Ere I behold will it be long?

"How long, oh glorious sovereign, must I yearn,
    Before the sight of thee mine eyes shall bless?
    God An, beholding thee is happiness,
To her who loveth thee, return, return.

"Oh, Un-nefer, the justified in state,
    Come to thy sister, come unto thy wife,
    Oh, Urt-het! Lo, one mother gave us life,
Thyself from me no longer separate.

"The gods and men towards thee turn their faces,
    Weeping for thee when they behold my tears.
    I make lament, but there is none that hears,
Yea, though with plaint, unto the heavenly places,
I, who so loved thee here on earth, do cry,
Thy sister, none hath loved thee more than I."

                —*Quoted from the Hymns of Ancient Egypt* (Rawnsley).

CHAPTER III.

ANCIENT CITIES—OSIRIAN MYTH—KARMA.

AFTER viewing the remains of the most extraordinary and wonderful cities mentioned in the preceding chapter, we must certainly realize the absurdity of giving credit to the stories that claim for certain men the honor of being the inventors and promoters of the early sciences, for instance:—It has been claimed by many that Archimedes, who was born in Syracuse, on the island of Sicily, in the year B.C. 237, conceived the application of the lever and screw. Why, there is not one of these buildings that I have mentioned, in which the lever, screw, and wedge were not practically applied by our ancient brethren long centuries before the dawn of authenticated history, to move the immense blocks of granite and sandstone used in the construction of the stupendous tombs, temples and monuments which adorned the whole length and breadth of the land of Egypt.

Go back to the Pyramids of Egypt, standing to-day in the plains of Gizeh, and we can realize that every one of them must have been known at that time, and were most assuredly used by our ancient craftsmen, who wrought in the quarries of the Mokattum hills, Libyan mountains, and elsewhere, and practically applied them in their work, not only of quarrying, but in the building of those wonderful fabrics. We have ocular demonstrations that the science of mathematics was thoroughly comprehended by the practical operative Masons long centuries before Abraham saw the stars glitter in the plains of Shinar. If we go to-day into the quarries of Syene we shall be enabled to see, not only their methods of quarrying, but the holes that were drilled for the wedges, and actually see the wedges, as they were placed by the craftsmen before Christ.

It has also been claimed by many that Galileo, an Italian mathematician and philosopher, who was born at Pisa, A.D. 1504, invented the telescope with a lead pipe and two lenses. Why, the ancient inhabitants

4

of Central America understood the method of focusing lenses in tubes, for one of their most ancient carvings represents a man looking through a telescope, thus demonstrating their knowledge in the use of them. Jensen is credited with having invented the compound microscope in the year A. D. 1590. We can prove that it was only a re-discovery of what had existed long before Christ was born. Cicero, who was born at *Arpinum*, B. C. 106, declares that he saw the whole of *Homer's Iliad* written on a skin, which might be rolled up and placed inside a walnut shell! Mr. Layard in his explorations discovered a rough magnifying lens *in the palace of Nimrod* that was made of rock crystal, and he also says, in writing of his discoveries in Nineveh, the "engravings on some of the stones were so small that they could only be read by the aid of very powerful glasses." Does this not show that the microscope must have been known at that period, otherwise how could the poem have been written or the stones carved? Aristophanes states that "Burning Spheres" were sold in the stores at Athens in his day, B. C. 400.

In the latter part of the wonderful nineteenth century we had arrived at a knowledge of manufacturing colored glass, and to-day in this twentieth century we have improved considerably in this art of making beautiful glass, for the purpose of decorating the windows of our cathedrals, churches and palatial residences, as well as for the various utensils for household purposes, as well as in imitation of precious stones. This art is claimed as a modern invention! In unearthing the celebrated city of Pompeii, destroyed on the twenty-fourth day of August, in the year A. D. 79, the workmen discovered a glass factory in which there was an immense quantity of glass, including magnificent specimens of gem imitations, capable of deceiving a dealer himself, if he were not very careful in his examinations. In the eleventh century the Arabians knew the secret of manufacturing malleable glass, and so perfect was their knowledge that they could anneal and draw it out into threads for weaving. During the reign of Tiberius malleable glass was known and glass cups were manufactured and used that could be crushed, but not broken.

The glass blowers of Thebes and Memphis are known to have been as proficient in the art of making all kinds of glass as is the most expert workman of to-day. The manufacturing of the beautiful opalescent glass that they produced could never have been carried on without a knowledge of the metallic oxides by which they colored, not only their glass, but their pottery as well, and this knowledge most assuredly involves an acquaintance with the science of chemistry, which science no doubt received its name from the ancient name of the " Land of Egypt," *Chemi*.

Rosseleni gives us an illustration of a piece of colored glass that is known to be four thousand years old. The priests of the temples, in both Memphis and Thebes, were experts in the art of manufacturing all kinds of glass. They thoroughly understood the art of vitrifying all the different colors, and the imitation of precious stones they brought to the highest state of perfection. The imitation gems they manufactured for the temples of Ptah at Memphis were so natural that, after the lapse of forty centuries, those lost in the shrouding desert sands, when found, would take an expert to distinguish, the true from the false.

In the British Museum there is an exquisite piece of stained glass, with a very fine engraved emblazonment upon it, of King Thothmes III., one of Egypt's celebrated monarchs who lived and reigned thirty-four centuries ago. This piece of work itself would prove to us that the ancient Egyptians made use of the diamond in cutting and engraving. The Hebrew people were very expert in the art of engraving, which they no doubt learned from the Egyptians, in the field of Zoan (see Exodus 28: 11).

Electricity, the force and power that is revolutionizing the world to-day, and contributes so immeasurably to our comfort, in driving our cars and carriages, lighting our houses, even carrying our very thoughts to the four-corners of the earth, was most certainly known to these ancient people and was possibly used for the very same purposes that we do to-day. (See Job 38: 35). It would be simply impossible for any man to describe something he had never seen or heard of, therefore, Job must have known of the working of the telegraph, otherwise he never could have described it.

Many people call this the age of steel, and look upon it as a discovery belonging exclusively to the nineteenth century. My dear Brothers, did you ever examine the implements of war belonging to ancient India, or the celebrated swords of Damascus? I assure you, my dear Friends and Brothers, steel has been used in every dynasty of Pharoanic history. In fact, her temples, tombs, sculptures, obelisks and hieroglyphic inscriptions were carved and written with pens of steel by our ancient craftsmen, when the songs of Solomon were not, ere Moses was lifted from the flowing waters of the river Nile.

Colonel Howard Vyse, during his investigations of the Pyramids, in the plains of Gizeh, found a piece of iron or steel in one of the joints of the stones that formed the *Great Pyramid*, which must certainly have been placed there during its construction by one of the workmen. In the tomb of Rameses fourth, the implements of war that are painted upon the walls are colored blue, to represent steel weapons. It would have been impossible for the craftsmen to have quarried the stones with which to build their extraordinary monuments, without a knowledge of steel, and how to make it. Mr. Layard, during his explorations in Nineveh, discovered sixty camel-loads of pickaxes. In the time of Saul there were no persons capable of forging among the Israelites (1st Samuel 13 : 15), but during the reign of David they had an abundance of cunning mechanics *who were capable.*

Any person who visits the tombs and temples of Egypt will certainly realize that their builders had a thorough knowledge, not only of the lever and wedge, but the pick, stone-saw, chisel and the various tools needed in quarrying and building such extraordinary edifices. One glance at those gigantic Pyramids will thoroughly demonstrate this fact to even the most skeptical.

The art of weaving fine linen and rich cloth is so very old that we are unable to trace it to the source from which it emanated, but there is one thing certain, the ancient Egyptians used linen of remarkable gossamer-like tissue. Wilkinson tells us in his "Manners and Customs" (Vol. III., 19), of a specimen of linen which "excites admiration at the present day, being to the touch comparable to silk, and not inferior in texture to the finest cambric. This has five hundred and forty threads to the inch in the warp, and one hundred and ten in the woof; being considerably finer than the richest cambric ever seen in this or any other country."

Ignatius Donnelly in "Atlantis" (page 365), tells us of the ancient Egyptians, that "they had clocks and dials for measuring time. They possessed gold and silver money, and were the first agriculturists of the Old World, raising cereals, cattle, horses and sheep. They also manufactured linen of so fine a quality that in the days of King Amasis (600 years B. C.), a single thread of a garment was composed of three hundred and sixty-five minor threads; worked in gold and silver, copper, bronze, and iron, and tempered iron to the hardness of steel. They were the first chemists. The word 'chemistry' comes from *chemi*, and chemi means Egypt. They manufactured glass and all kinds of pottery; made boats out of earthenware; and precisely as we do now, made railroad car-wheels of paper; and also manufactured vessels of paper. Their dentists filled teeth with gold, and their farmers hatched poultry with artificial heat. They were the first musicians, possessing guitars, single and double pipes, cymbals, drums, lyres, harps, flutes, the sambric and ashur. They had even castanets, such as are now used in Spain.

"In medicine and surgery they had reached such a degree of perfection that several years B. C. the operation for cataract upon the eye was performed among them, one of the most delicate and difficult feats of surgery, only attempted by us in the most recent times.

"'The Papyrus of Berlin' was discovered, rolled up in a case, under the feet of Anubis, in the town of Sekhem, in the days of Tet (or Thoth), after whose death it was transmitted to King Sent, and was then restored to the feet of the statue. King Sent belonged to the second dynasty, which flourished B. C. 4751, and the papyrus was old in his day. This papyrus is a medical treatise, containing no incantations or charms, but dealing in reasonable remedies, draughts, ungents and injections. The later medical papyri contain a great deal of magic and incantations.

"Egypt was the magnificent, the golden bridge, ten thousand years long, glorious with temples and pyramids, illuminated and illustrated by the most complete and continuous records of human history, along which the civilization of 'Atlantis,' in a great procession of kings and priests, philosophers and astronomers, artists and artisans streamed forward to Greece, to Rome, to Europe, to America. As far back in the ages as the eye can penetrate, even where the perspective dwindles almost to a point, we can still see the swarming multitudes, possessed of the arts of the highest civilization, passing forward from out that other and greater empire of which even this wonder-working Nile-land is but a faint and imperfect copy."

SEMMENUD is the site of the Sebenyte Nome that gave its name to the thirtieth dynasty. It was founded by its first King, Nectanebo I, who successfully defended his country against the attacks of the Persians and Greek mercenaries, under Pharnabazus and Iphicrates. After Nectanebo defeated these invaders of his country he spent the rest of his life in tranquillity and peace. It was during the reign of this King that Plato visited Egypt, for the purpose of investigating the religions and philosophies of this country, and he, like Pythagoras, was initiated into the ancient rites and ceremonies, from which our own glorious Scottish Rite has descended, of whose esoteric teachings I shall speak later.

The ancient Egyptian name of Sebennytus was *Teb-en-nuter*, which the cuneiform inscription translates *Zabnuter*. In this city Manetho, the celebrated Egyptian historian, is said to have been born. He was a High Priest of the temple of Isis in *Sebennytus*, the modern Semmenud. Manetho, in ancient Egyptian, was written *Mai-en-thot*, which signified "beloved of Thoth." He lived in the reign of Ptolemy Lagi and he was noted for his scholarly attainments, a man of the highest reputation, who thoroughly understood the Greek language, in consequence of which he was requested by Ptolemy II, Philadelphus, to translate the historical records that had been preserved in the sacred repositories of the temples of Egypt. He was an Egyptian priest, and authorized by Ptolemy himself to give to the world a history of his own country, *Egypt*, with which he was so thoroughly acquainted. He had access to the archives of all the temples throughout the "Land of Egypt," and I claim that these facts alone should impress the student with the truth of each and every one of his statements, ever remembering that he was a man of the highest reputation and ability. This history was held in high estimation, but was subsequently lost, and all that remains to us of this most valuable and scholarly work to-day, is the chronological list of the Kings of the various dynasties, transmitted to us through the Jewish and Christian chronographers.

Mariette Bey states, in his "Monuments of Upper Egypt," that "the system of contemporaneous dynasties is as yet supported by no really trustworthy proof; on the contrary, it seems certain that

Manetho was well aware that, at various epochs, Egypt was governed simultaneously by several dynasties, and he availed himself of the means at his disposal to strike out of his work all such dynasties as did not belong to the general series of royal houses who succeeded each other on the throne, so that the latter were alone officially enrolled in due order on the register of Kings."

The reason Mariette makes this statement is because there are many authorities who claim that Manetho cites various dynasties as successive that were contemporaneous. If this were truth and the fact could be proven, we should have to deduct from the total amount the duration of these various dynasties, said to have been falsely placed upon the roll belonging to regular consecutive dynasties of Egyptian history. The dates taken from Manetho are not in accordance with extracts culled from Julius Africanus and Eusebius, yet the two versions of the *Chronicle* of Eusebius do not agree with each other. Therefore the authority of Manetho, as a chronologist, remains unshaken, but on condition that we only take the dates which he gives us as approximate. It is certain that those dates are not absolutely exact, yet it is difficult to believe that they have been so radically altered as not in any degree to come near the truth.

The nearer we approach the source of those alterations the more we shall feel compelled to admit that if the original lists could but have reached us intact, from the hand of Manetho himself, we would find them extending over a still wider range of time. There is no question but that Manetho's figures have suffered serious alterations. But if we consider the figures as coming down to us through Christian writers, who had an evident purpose in curtailing them, we shall find, as a matter of fact, that this is far from ascribing too wide a range to them, and are bound, as fair critics, to accept them as having been systematically reduced in their total amount. There is no nation which ever existed in the world's history whose manners, customs, arts, sciences and philosophies are more easily traced than those of the ancient Egyptians, because she has not only written her own history, and carved it upon her tombs and temples, but she has given us keys by which we are enabled to decipher the hieroglyphic inscriptions and phonetic characters in the various *stele*, such as the Rosetta

Stone, the famous trilingual stone that was discovered by Dr. Lepsius, the stele found by Mariette Bey in the temple of Seti, and the many papyrus rolls that have been discovered at various times and places, despite the tooth of time and war's bloody hand, passing unscathed through the ravages of long drifting ages. These evidences of her civilization and intellectual advancement, with the treasures found in her buried cities, as well as those found under the drifting sands of the desert, in the Nomes of a prehistoric age, confirm what Manetho has written of his country.

I need not mention every or any special place from which we have obtained fragmentary records, but simply state that every tomb, temple, monument, mummy-case and contents have given us historical and genealogical records which not only confirm, but supplement what was written by our ancient Brother Manetho, whose name had been indorsed by the tongue of *good report*, who had been proven worthy and well qualified, "a man of the highest reputation," an Archamagus of the ancient Egyptian mysteries, whose name, like that of our revered Brother, the late General Albert Pike, Hierophant of the nineteenth century, will never die, but, like his works, writings and integrity, will stand the most crucial test and come forth from the trial and investigation, an honor to the ancient mysteries and its lineal descendant, our beloved Ancient and Accepted Scottish Rite of Free Masonry.

Semmenund or *Semmenud*, is a typical Egyptian town of about eleven thousand inhabitants. It is noted for its celebrated pottery, which is manufactured there and sent to all the larger cities, where it finds a ready sale throughout the whole of Egypt. It has the usual bazaars and mud hovels and all the peculiar concomitants that go to make up the peculiarities of typical Egyptian towns. Nectanebo XI was the last of the Sebennyte sovereigns, and was also the last of those native Egyptian Kings who ruled Egypt from B. C. 5004 to B. C. 340.

To the north of Semmenud, and south of Mansura lies the ancient city of Iseum, in the Sebennyte Nome. It is now called *Behbit-el-Hagar*, while the ancient Egyptians knew it as *Hebt* or *Pa-Hebt*. It was called the "town of the Panegyries," from the Egyptian name of Pa-Hebt. It is also called the "city of the stone," which derives its Arab name, Behbit-el-Hagar, on account of the very large number of stones to be seen there, once going to form a part of the beautiful decorations of this magnificent city, now scattered around in promiscuous confusion. The ruins of this celebrated city are very much inferior to the city in "the field of Zoan," as well as that of Bubastis, but notwithstanding this fact, it will well repay the traveller, or student of ancient Egyptian history, for the time spent in visiting these celebrated ruins, and in viewing the fragmentary remains of those beautiful carvings, executed in the peculiar colored granite, used to adorn and beautify this once famous city of the Ptolemies.

The traveller will most assuredly have unmistakable proofs of the deity that was worshipped here, in the numerous sculptures and carvings of an animal sacred to the goddess Isis, *the cow*, and also the exceedingly large number of figures with cow-heads. From this alone we judge that Isis was the principal deity worshipped there, as doubtless both the Greeks and Romans called this city *Iseum* or *Ision*. The chief deities that were worshipped in this city were the OSIRIAN TRIAD—*Isis, Osiris and Horus*. *Osiris* was a form of the sun god, *Ra*, and the child of *Seb*, the earth, and *Nut*, the heavens, in Egyptian mythology, who was the presiding judge in *Amenti*. His wife *Isis* represented *the dawn*, and their son was *Horus*, the sun, in his full power and glory. On a figure of the goddess found here was carved the following: "Isis, Mistress of Hebt."

There is another very interesting piece of work carved on a slab of grey granite, streaked with red, on which there is a representation of the king offering a gift of land to Osiris and Isis—"The great divine mistress of Hebit." The name of Ptolemy II., Philadelphus I., occurs in various parts of this temple, who founded it B. C. 284-246. His name appears in the dedications, while he presents the various offerings to the various gods. The temple alone must have cost an immense sum, as it was built of a very fine peculiar grey and red granite, now lying scattered around, broken and mutilated. There are among them fragments of architraves, slabs, columns, and blocks of all shapes and kinds of stone, some square, others circular-shaped, and many with very fine carvings upon them, both in intaglio and in relief.

Some of these have very large hieroglyphic inscriptions carved upon them, while others are comparatively small, but excellently well executed.

There is one peculiar feature about the ruins of this temple, and that is, a different kind of granite has been used in its construction from that which composed the temples of Upper Egypt. It seems as if an especial effort had been made to exclude every kind of stone from this building that was used in the construction of the other temples outside the Delta. It is too bad that this building should have been so completely demolished, because we are unable to trace, with any degree of exactitude. the plan of the temple. Its destruction is no doubt due to the natives undermining the building in order to procure the limestone, to burn and sell.

Murray describes one of the walls of this temple as follows: " On one of the walls about the centre of the temple is represented the sacred boat, or ark, of Isis. and in the shrine it bears the 'Lady of Pa-Hebt,' seated between two figures of goddesses, like the Jewish cherubim, who seem to protect her with their wings. They occur in two compartments, one over the other, at the centre of the shrine. These figures were, doubtless, the holy and unseen contents of the sacred repository which no profane eye was permitted to behold, being generally covered with a veil. In the upper one Isis is seated on a lotus flower and the two figures standing, while in the other all three are seated and below are four kneeling figures. one with a man's the other three with jackal's heads, beating their breasts. At either end of the boat is the head of the goddess, and the legend above shows it to have belonged to her. The king stands before it, presenting an offering of incense to Isis.

" There appears to be a very great variety in the sculptures, which mostly represent offerings to Isis, and the contemplar dieties, as in other Ptolemaic buildings. In one place the hawk-headed Hor-Hat conducts the king into the presence of the goddess of the temple; but the battle scenes and grand religious processions of old times are wanting here, as in other temples of a Ptolemaic and Roman epoch, and though the sculptures are rich, being highly finished, they are deficient in the elegance of a Pharaonic age—the fault of all Greco-Egyptian sculptures, and one which strikes every eye accustomed to monuments erected before the decadence of art in Egypt."

This temple, to-day, is in a demolished condition, with debris of all kinds piled and scattered promiscuously around, and all kinds of stone lying one upon another, in the wildest confusion. Notwithstanding this fact it is possible for one to go down beneath the masses of rubbish and stones, ten or a dozen feet, through various openings between the larger stones. where could be seen shattered parts of architraves, cornices, and large granite columns, crowned with the head of Isis, very fine specimens of the Ptolemaic age, but more especially of the granite carvings in relief, which must have taken an immense amount of time, labor and patience. One thing that was plainly to be seen, was parts of the ceiling, with the usual five pointed star upon a blue ground, just such stars as are to be found upon the ceilings of our own beloved Scottish Rite cathedrals to-day.

Herodotus says *Busiris* was situated in the very middle of the Delta, which was the next city in importance to Bubastis, for the splendors of its ceremonies during the festival of Isis (Book II, Chapter 59.) Diodorus informs us that there were two places called *Busiris* in Egypt. *Busiris* signifies " *the burial place of Osiris.*"

Wilkinson says, in note 6, chapter 61, of Herodotus, " The city of *Isis* was lower down the river, and it is more probable that the fete of Isis was held there than at Busiris." It is now called *Bebayt* and its site is marked by the ruin of a granite temple, the only one, except that at *Bubastis*, entirely built of that beautiful and costly material. It was doubtless thought worthy to succeed the very large temple that was dedicated to Isis, of which Herodotus speaks, for it was built during the reign of the Ptolamies and it was formerly called *Iseum*, and by the ancient Egyptians *Hebai*, or *Hebait*, of which Isis is named in the sculptures " *The Mistress of Hebt.*" Hebai signifies a " *panegyry*," or assembly, and this was the real meaning of the name of the place. Osiris is also sometimes spoken of in the legends as " *Lord of the land of Hebai.*"

Now this shows that it was not the city of Busiris that was second in importance in Egypt for the magnificence of its ceremonies, during the festival in honor of the goddess Isis, according to Herodotus, but *Behbit-el-Hagar*, or *Pa-Hebt*—" *the city of the stone*," or the town of the panegyries, the city I have just described to you.

I stated previously that Osiris was one of the principal deities worshipped in this city, in fact he was worshipped throughout the whole of Egypt, Ethiopia, Greece and Rome. No doubt the worship of this God was also introduced among the tribes of the children of Israel by Jeroboam on his return to his own country. Osiris is always represented with a human head sitting on a throne, as a king or *judge in the Halls of Amenti*, or in the form of a mummy; but in either case he always carries the scourge and crook, wearing upon his head the crown of Upper Egypt, which is very often decorated with the plumes of Truth, while beside him stands the *Thyrsus*, the vine and ivy twined staff of the Bacchantes, enwrapped with a leopard's skin. He was the judge of the Amenti or Lord of the Underworld, the King of Eternity. Of all the gods of Egypt he is the only one who has a regular, detailed, mythical history, like the gods of Grecian mythology. Herodotus says that Osiris was considered to be the Bacchus of the Greeks, and Diodorus states that *Osiris* "has been considered the same as Serapis, Bacchus. Pluto, or Amon. Others have thought him Jupiter, many Pan."

The ancient Egyptian hieroglyphic inscriptions identify Apis, the sacred bull, worshipped at Memphis during the second dynasty with Osiris, claiming that he was the god Osiris reincarnated in the shape of a bull. The mythical legend of this celebrated god is related by Plutarch as follows: "Rhea, having secretly united herself with Saturn, the Sun, becoming indignant, laid upon her a curse, that she should not bring forth in any year or month. Mercury, however, who was also a lover of Rhea, playing at dice with the Moon, took away the seventeenth part of each period of daylight, and from these made five new days, which are the *epagomenai* or intercalary days (seventy here stands, as elsewhere, a round number instead of the precise one, for seventy-two; five being the seventy-second part of three hundred and sixty). On each of these five days Rhea bore a child. On the first day Osiris, the son of the Sun, was born, at whose birth a voice was heard proclaiming that the Lord of all was coming to Light; or, according to another version, Paamyles, drawing water in the temple of Jupiter, heard a voice, which enjoined upon him to proclaim that the great and beneficient King Osiris was born. This Paamyles received him to nurse, and hence the festival of the *Paamylia*, which was a *phallephoria*. On the second day was born *Aroeris*, son of the Sun, whom they call *Apollo*, and the Elder Horus. On the third was born *Typhon*, not in the usual course, but bursting out with a sudden stroke from the side of Rhea. On the fourth day was born Isis, the daughter of Hermes. On the fifth *Nephthys*, who was called Teleute (the end), and Aphrodite, and according to some, Nike. Typhon and Nephthys were the children of Saturn and married each other. In consequence of the birth of Typhon, the third day of the *epagomenai* was a *dies nefastus*, and the Kings of Egypt neither transacted public business nor took the usual care of their persons till night. Isis and Osiris united themselves even before their birth and their son was called, according to some, Aroeris, or the Elder Horus. The more common account, however, made the son of Osiris and Isis to be the younger Horus."

Osiris being king, instructed the Egyptians in the arts of civilization, taught them agriculture, enacted laws for them, and established the worship of the gods. He afterwards traversed the world, for the same purpose, subduing the nations, not by arms, but by persuasion, and especially by the charms of music and poetry, which gave the Greeks occasion to identify him with Dionusos. In his absence Isis administered the regency so wisely that Typhon was unable to create any disturbance; but on his return he conspired against Osiris with seventy-two men and the Ethiopian queen, Aso, who having secretly obtained the measure of Osiris, caused a coffin, splendidly adorned, to be brought into the banqueting hall, promising to give it to the guest whom it should fit. Osiris put himself into it to make trial, and Typhon and his associates immediately pegged and soldered down the case and set it afloat on the river. It floated to the Tanitic mouth, which, on that account, the Egyptians held accursed. These things were done on the seventeenth of the month Athyr, in which the Sun enters Scorpion, and in the twenty-eight year of the reign, or as some said, of the age of Osiris. The Pans and Satyrs, who lived about Chemmis, hearing of these events and being agitated by them into sudden terrors, obtained the name of Panics. Isis cut off her hair and put on mourning at the place where she first heard the news; whence it obtained the name Coptos, signifying "to mourn for the dead." Meeting some boys, she heard from them where the coffin had floated, and hence the Egyptians deemed the words of boys to carry with them a divine meaning. Osiris had, by mistake, united himself with Nephthys, and a son had been born to him, whom Nephthys hid immediately from his birth. Isis sought him out and found him by the guidance of a dog, who attended her thenceforth, and was called Anubis.

"Meanwhile the chest had been floated to *Byblos*, and cast ashore; the plant *erica (a narrow leafed evergreen shrub)*, had grown up about it and enclosed it, and in this state it had been made use of as a pillar to support the palace of the king. Isis arrived, divinely conducted, in search of it, and recommending herself to the queen's maidens, had the charge of the young prince committed to her. She then obtained possession of the chest, and opening it carried it to Buto, where Horus was being brought up. The event of her return was celebrated by sacrifices on the seventeenth day of the month *Tybi*, and the figure of a hippopotamus bound, was impressed upon the sacrificial cakes, as an emblem of the defeat of Typhon. Here she deposited the body in secrecy, but Typhon, hunting by moonlight, found it and cut it into fourteen pieces. Isis in a *baris* made of papyrus, traversed the marshes and when she found one of the members, buried it there, whence the number of reputed places of interment of Osiris. In the end she found all the members but one, which had been devoured by the fishes *phagrus* and *lepidotus*.

"Isis, therefore, made an emblem of it, whence the honors still paid to it by the Egyptians (probably though Plutarch does not expressly say so, Isis was conceived to have recomposed the body from the limbs thus recovered). Osiris returned from Hades and gave his aid to Horus, who was preparing to overthrow the power of Typhon. Typhon fell into the hands of Isis, but she released him, at which Horus was so enraged that he plucked his mother's diadem from her head and Mercury supplied its place by a helmet in the form of cow's head. Two other battles took place before Typhon was finally subdued. Harpocrates was born from the union of Isis and Osiris, after the death of Osiris, and was consequently imperfect with a weakness in his lower limbs." Such is the myth as related by Plutarch and by Kenrick in "Ancient Egypt."

Baedeker's Lower Egypt tells us that Osiris was not actually killed by Typhon. He simply went to the underworld and there continued his existence. It was he who trained and armed his son Horus to do battle against Typhon, in which he eventually became victorious by defeating Typhon, but not in totally destroying him. With the assistance of Osiris they banished him to the infernal regions. Osiris is also regarded as the moisture falling upon the earth, the most perfect representation of which is the inundation of the river Nile. While Typhon and his seventy-two companions (the intercalary days), which represented the days of drought that dominated the earth, during which time Isis becomes sorrowful, longing, hoping for the return of Osiris, she mourns his absence, until eventually he returns, when Typhon is defeated and the fertile earth (Isis) is again dominated by the flooding waters of the river Nile (Osiris) when an abundance is assured.

Osiris is regarded as the principal of Life. Isis, the Earth, is the scene of the operation of that principal, while Typon represents death, and Horus the resurrection. If we regard Osiris, as the monuments so frequently do, as a pure and perfect being, the principle of the good, and the beautiful, in which case he receives the surname of *Un-Nefer*, we recognize in Typhon the discords with which life is so replete, but which seem to be permitted only in order that the purity of the harmonies into which they are resolved, through the intervention of Horus, may be the more thoroughly appreciated.

Osiris, according to the exoteric doctrine, is also the sovereign of the lower regions and judge of souls, which, if found pure, are permitted to unite with his. The dead, therefore, do not merely go to Osiris, but actually become Osiris.

" *Osiris*," according to Wilkinson, " was ranked or belonged to the third order of gods, and had the honor of being the god whose mysteries contained the most important secrets; his rites comprised the chief part of the Egyptian wisdom; he was the chief of *Amenti* or Hades and was a *heavenly* as well as an *infernal* deity. There was also an important reason for his being of the last or newest order of gods, related particularly to man, the last and most perfect work of the creation, and as the Deity was at first the Monad, then the Creator, 'creation being God passing into activity,' he did not become Osiris until man was placed upon the earth. He there manifested himself also, like Buddha for the benefit of man, who looked upon him for happiness in a future state."

In all the representation of the judgment of the dead Osiris is *always* represented " seated upon a throne, surrounded by certain gods and goddesses, paraphernalia, etc., holding within his hands the scourge and crook, and generally with his arms crossed upon his breast, while close beside him stands the thyrsus entwined with a spotted leapord's skin. He is generally attended by Isis and Nephthys, and in some pictures we see the four gods of the underworld. The centre of the paintings is generally occupied by a representation of a very large pair of scales and beam, standing beside which we recognize Thoth with a book or papyrus roll in his hand, noting the result of the process of weighing. In one scale the heart of the deceased is placed against the feather of Truth. One side of the scale is attended by the goddess of Truth, who places the feather against the heart of the deceased which has been placed there, within the opposite one by Horus. Then when the weighing has been finished Horus takes the tablet from Thoth, wherein has been recorded the decision which he announces to Osiris, the record of the good and moral qualities of the deceased against the feather of Truth and Justice. Then if the virtues of the deceased preponderate in his favor, Thoth introduces him into the presence of Osiris, but if the virtuous qualities of the candidate has been weighed and found wanting, Osiris rejects him and he is condemned and punished according to the judgment that has been rendered to the Lord of Amenti—Osiris.

The pictorial representations of this judgment scene differs in different places, some of them represent the forty-two assessors, corresponding to the earthly judges, who determined whether the deceased should be allowed to cross the river and enter into the abode of eternal bliss, or dwell on the confines of Hades and die a second death. Every Egyptian thoroughly believed that after death he would have to pass into the halls of Amenti in order to be weighed in the balance and judged according to his *just dues*. No matter what his station in life might be, he would have to undergo the ordeal of being weighed, and abide by the judgment rendered. In the same way, directly after death, his earthly judges rendered judgment for or against him. If he was found guilty, or unworthy, he would be excluded from burial in his own tomb or sepulchre, and during his trial all who knew him were allowed to testify for or against him, and according to the evidence he was judged.

This earthly judgment was typical of the one in the halls of Amenti. It was from this peculiar ancient custom that it was introduced into the ancient Mysteries, and during the peculiar rites and ceremonies the candidate died symbolically before he was raised to *Light* and *Life*. In the halls of Amenti, Osiris may be said rather to have presided over the dead than to have judged them. He gave admission to those who were found worthy to enter into the abode of happiness in the halls of peace. He was not the avenging deity; he did not punish, nor could he show mercy or subvert the judgment pronounced. It was a simple question of whether the deceased was guilty or not. If wicked, they were destined to suffer punishment according to their deeds. A man's actions were balanced in the scales against Justice and Truth; then, if they were found wanting, he would be excluded from all future happiness. Thus, though the Egyptians are said to have believed that the gods were capable of influencing destiny (*Esubcis, Pr., Ev., 111-4*), it is evident Osiris (*like the Greek Zeus*) was bound by it, and the wicked were punished, not because he rejected them, "but because they *were* wicked."

I have given a very lengthy account of the mythical story of Osiris, for the reason that it formed not only the basis of the Ancient Egyptian Mysteries, but also represented the scenes enacted in the great drama of life, if properly understood; and the teachings that emanated from the Ancient Egyptian Mysteries are to be found in every religion and every philosophy throughout the world, in every age and every epoch of its history. They have always been, and are now, covered with such a mass of rubbish that it is difficult to discover the glorious Truths that underlie their philosophy.

Now let us examine the Osirian myth, and take Osiris as the Judge or presiding deity of Amenti, and we shall find that the teachings of our Ancient and Accepted Scottish Rite inform us that he was not a god of vengeance, but a god of Truth and Justice. He judged no man, but simply pronounced the sentence that had been adjudged by Thoth, the Divine Nature, or "The Lord of Karma," *after* they had been weighed in the balance and their sentence declared to Osiris, who then and there pronounced it. Each and every man's "higher self" recognized that perfect Justice had been meted out to him. He knew that the acts of his life, in thought, word or deed, were to be harvested in their effects. It

5

was simply impossible for Osiris in any way to interfere with the Law of Cause and Effect; or, in other words, any man's "*Karma.*" When a man's life actions are weighed in the balance, his dues are rendered to him with perfect justice. He has made his own record and he will reap the full effects of it, *be it good or evil*, and this fact alone shows that "*Man is the master of his own destiny.*" What he has sown that must he also reap, and there is no power in earth or in heaven that can alter his Karma. Sir Edwin Arnold beautifully illustrates this in "The Light of Asia."

> "KARMA—All that total of a soul
> Which is the things it did, thoughts it had,
> The 'self' it wove with woof of viewless time
> Crossed on the ways of invisible acts."

A sin committed, or an evil thought permitted to go forth from your mind, for evil, is just the same as if the act itself had been performed. They are then beyond recall. You have sown the seed, and YOU, *yourself*, must suffer the consequence, and not somebody else, as nothing *you or any one else can do can ever destroy the result of your act or thought.* Repentance may possibly have a tendency to prevent one from repeating errors, but it never will, nor ever can destroy the effect of those already done. My dear Brothers, I do most earnestly and sincerely believe this, and most earnestly ask you, my dear readers and Friends, to take this matter under your careful consideration, and along these lines of thought I will quote you from "Re-incarnation," by E. D. Walker, page 302:

"The relentless hand which metes out our fortunes with the stern justice most vividly portrayed by the Greek dramatists in their Nemesis, Fates and Furies, takes from our own savings the gifts bestowed on us. 'Alas, we sow what we reap; the hand that smites us is our own.' In the domain of eternal justice the offense and the punishment are inseperably connected as the same event, because there is no real distinction between the action and its outcome. He who injures another in fact only wrongs himself. To adopt Schopenhauer's figure, he is a wild beast who fastens his fangs in his own flesh. But linked with the awful fact of our own individual responsibility for what we now are, gives the inspiring assurance, that we have under our control the remedy of evil and the increase of good. We can, and we alone can, extricate ourselves from the existing limitations, by the all-curing powers of purity, love, and spirituality. In Eastern phraseology, the purpose of life is to work out our *bad* Karma (action) and to stow away *good* Karma. As surely as the harvest of to-day grows from the seed-time of yesterday, so shall every kernel of thought and feeling, speech and performance bring its crop of reward or rebuke. The inherent result of every quiver of the human WILL continually tolls the Day of Judgment and affords immeasurable opportunities for amelioration."

This is just exactly what the philosophical degrees of our own beloved Scottish Rite teach us, and Brother Albert Pike says in "Morals and Dogmas" (pages 216-17): "We shall be just as happy hereafter, as we are pure and upright, and no more, just as happy as our character prepares us to be, and no more. Our moral, like our mental character, is not formed in a moment, it is the habit of our minds, the result of many thoughts and feelings and efforts bound together by many natural and strong ties. The great law of retribution is, that all coming experience is to be affected by every present feeling, every future moment of being must answer for every present moment. One moment sacrificed to vice, or lost to improvement, is *forever* sacrificed and lost; an hour's delay to enter the right path, is to put us back so far in the everlasting pursuit of happiness, and every sin, even of the best men, is to be thus answered for, if not according to the full measure of its ill desert, yet according to a rule of unbending rectitude and impartiality.

"The law of retribution presses upon every man, whether he thinks it or not. It pursues him through all the courses of life, with a step that never falters nor tires, and with an eye that never sleeps nor slumbers. If it were not so, God's government would not be impartial; there would be no discrimination; no moral dominion, no light shed on the mysteries of Providence.

"Whatsoever a man soweth, that, and not something else, shall he reap. That which we are doing, good or evil, grave or gay, that which we do to-day, and shall do to-morrow, each thought, each feeling, each action, each event, every passing hour, every breathing moment, all are contributing to form the character, according to which we are to be judged. Every particle of influence that goes to form that aggregate,—our character,—will in that future scrutiny, be sifted out from the mass, and particle by particle, with ages perhaps intervening, fall a distinct contribution to the sum of our joys or woes. Thus every idle word and idle hour will give answer in the judgment.

"Let us take care, therefore, what we sow. An evil temptation comes upon us, the opportunity of unrighteous gain or of unhallowed indulgence, either in the sphere of business or pleasure, of society or solitude. We yield, and plant a seed of bitterness and sorrow. To-morrow it will threaten discovery. Agitated and alarmed, we cover the sin and bury it deep in falsehood and hypocrisy. In the bosom where it lies concealed, in the fertile soil of kindred vices, that sin dies not, but thrives and grows, and other and still other germs of evil gather around the accursed root, until, from that single seed of corruption there springs up in the soul all that is horrible in habitual lying, knavery or vice. Loathingly, often, we take each downward step; but a frightful power urges us onward, and the hell of debt, disease, ignominy, or remorse, gathers its shadows around our steps, even on earth, and are yet but the beginning of sorrows. The evil deed may be done in a single moment; but conscience never dies, memory never sleeps, guilt can never become innocence and remorse can never whisper peace.

"Beware, thou who art tempted to evil! Beware what thou layest up for the future! Beware what thou layest up in the archives of eternity! Wrong not thy neighbor! lest the thought of him thou injurest and who suffers by thy act be to thee a pang which years will not deprive of its bitterness! Break not into the house of innocence, to rifle it of its treasure, lest when many years have passed over thee, the moan of its distress may not have died away from thine ear! Build not the desolate throne of ambition in thy heart, nor be busy with devices and circumventings, and selfish schemings, lest desolation and loneliness be on thy path, as it stretches into the long futurity! Live not a useless, an impious, or an injurious life! for bound up with that life is the immutable principle of an endless retribution, and elements of God's creating, which will never spend their force, but continue ever to unfold with the ages of eternity. Be not deceived! God has formed thy nature, thus to answer to the future. *His law* can never be abrogated, nor his justice eluded; and for ever and ever it will be true, that '*Whatsoever a man soweth, that also he shall reap.*'"

Madam H. P. Blavatsky says in "The Key to Theosophy" (page 237), "If our present lives depend upon the development of certain principles which are a growth from the germs left by a previous existence, the law holds good as regards the future. Once grasp the idea that universal causation is not merely present, but past, present and future, and every action on our present plane falls naturally and easily into its true place, and is seen in its true relation to ourselves and to others. Every mean and selfish action sends us backward and not forward, while every noble thought and every unselfish deed are stepping-stones to the higher and more glorious planes of being. If this life were all, then in many respects it would indeed be poor and mean, but regarded as a preparation for the next sphere of existence, it may be used as the golden gate through which we may pass, not selfishly and alone, but in company with our fellows, to the palace which lies beyond."

Buto, of whom I have previously spoken in this chapter, was identified by the Greeks in their *Latona.* She was worshipped principally in the town of Buto, which received its name from festivals held there in her honor, and an oracle was established there which was held in high esteem by the ancient Egyptians. "The most veracious of all the oracles of all the Egyptians" (Herodotus, Book II, chapter 152.) It was to this goddess that Isis entrusted her children while she went in search of lost Osiris. Buto acted the part of nurse and guardian to Horus and Bubastis, and watched over them very carefully during the whole time that Isis was absent, and when Typhon sought to persecute and destroy them she carried them away, hiding them in a floating island called Chemmis. In this way she prevented Typhon from obtaining possession of them. This island was situated in a lake not very far from the town of Buto, upon which Horus and Bubastis, with Buto, were worshipped together. .

I have not gone into the profound depths of the esoteric meaning of the Osirian Triad in this chapter, but shall leave that subject to another. Neither do I wish to enter into a long and useless article in order to prove that Scottish Rite Masonry has been in existence from time immemorial, but I do most assuredly claim that our most Illustrious

Ancient and Accepted Scottish Rite teaches the same grand truths, the same sublime philosophies, and solves the same scientific problems as elucidated in the esoteric teachings of the ancient mysteries, and I do most firmly and sincerely believe that these esoteric teachings originated in the valley of Hindustan, and that it was cradled on the banks of the river Nile, in the hoary ages of the past, from whence it found its way to all parts of the earth.

Every degree of the Ancient and Accepted Scottish Rite, from the first to the thirty-second degree, teaches by its ceremonial as well as by its instruction, that the noblest purpose of life and the highest duty of a man are to strive incessantly and vigorously to win the mastery in everything, of that which in him is spiritual and divine, over that which is material and sensual; so that in him also, as in the universe which God governs, harmony and beauty may be the result of a just equilibrium.

To achieve it, the Mason must first attain a solid conviction, founded upon reason, that he hath within him a spiritual nature, a soul that is not to die when the body is dissolved, but is to continue to exist and to advance toward perfection through all the ages of eternity, and to see more and more clearly, as it draws nearer unto God, the Light of the Divine Presence. This the Philosophy of the Ancient and Accepted Scottish Rite teaches him; it encourages him to persevere by helping him to believe that his free will is entirely consistent with God's omnipotence and omniscience; that He is not only infinite in power, and of infinite wisdom, but of infinite mercy, and has an infinitely tender pity and love for the frail and imperfect creatures that He has made.

The Nile—Origin of the Name Free Mason —Scottish Rite Philosophy.

It flows through old hushed Egypt and its sands, ·
Like some grave, mighty thought, threading a dream;
And times, and things, as in that vision seem,
Keeping along it, their eternal stands,
Caves, pillars, pyramids, the shepherd bands,
That roamed through the young earth—the flag extreme
Of high Sesostris, and that southern beam,
The laughing Queen that caught the world's great hands.
Then comes a mightier silence, stern and strong,
As of a world left empty of its throng;
And the void weighs on us; and then to wake,
And hear the fruitful stream lapsing along,
'Twixt villages, and think how we shall take
Our own calm journey on, for human sake.

—LEIGH HUNT.

CHAPTER IV.

THE NILE—ORIGIN OF THE NAME FREE MASON— SCOTTISH RITE PHILOSOPHY.

THE interpretation of the Osirian myth, according to Wilkinson's " Ancient Egyptians," (chap. 13, page 79), is as follows: " Osiris, the inundation of the Nile; Isis, the irrigated portion of the land of Egypt; Horus. their offspring, the vapors and exhalations reproducing rain; Buto. Latona, the marsh lands of Lower Egypt, where those vapors were nourished; Nephthys, the edge of the desert, occasionally overflowed during the high inundations; Anubis, the son of Osiris and Nephthys, the production of that barren soil, in consequence of its being overflowed by the Nile; Typhon, the sea, which swallowed up the Nile waters; the conspirators, the drought overcoming the moisture from which the increase of the Nile proceeds; the chest in which Osiris' body was confined, the banks of the river, within which it retired after the inundation; the Tanaitic mouth, the lake and barren lands about it which were held in abhorrence from their being overflowed by the river, without producing any benefit to the country; the twenty-eight years of his life, the twenty-eight cubits to which the Nile rises at Elephantine, its greatest height (*Plutarch, de Iside, 843*); the seventeenth of Athor, the period when the river retires within its banks; the Queen of Ethiopia, the southern winds preventing the clouds being carried south-wards; the different members of Osiris' body, the main channels and canals by which the inundations passed into the interior of the country, where each was said to be afterwards buried; that one which could not be recovered was the generative power of the Nile, which still continued in the stream itself, or as Plutarch thinks, it was thrown into the river, because ' water or moisture was the first matter upon which the genera-tive power of the deity operated and that principle by means of which all things capable of being were produced;' the victory of Horus, the powers possessed by the clouds in causing the successive inundations of the Nile; Harpocrates, whom Isis brought forth about the winter solstice, those weak shootings of the corn after the inundations had subsided."

Kenrick states in his "Ancient Egypt," page 346, vol. 1: "The order in which the different events of the myth succeed to each other, accords very well with the supposition that they relate to the disappearance of the sun from the northern hemisphere and the train of consequences which it produces to the earth. His burial and disappearance took place in the autumn; the voyage of Isis to discover his remains in the month of December; the search for them in Egypt about midwinter; and in the end of February, Osiris, entering into the moon, fertilizes the world. The representations of Osiris, as god of the invisible world and his being figured as a mummy naturally produced an explanatory myth. It accounts for an immortal god being subjected to death and for the association of Thoth and Horus, Isis, and Nephthys with him in his capacity of ruler of Amenti. The erection of the coffin at Byblos alludes to the use of Osiride pillars in Egyptian architecture. The story of the discerption of his body explained the circumstance that the honor of his interment was claimed by so many different places in Egypt and the ceremony of the *phallephoria* in his honor. The co-operation of a queen of Ethiopia in the plot against his life is significant of the national hostility of that people against the Egyptians and the prevalence of female dominion. The plotting against him in his absence may have been borrowed from the history of Sesostris, as the account of his expeditions to distant countries for the purpose of civilizing them, betrays its origin in times when the Egyptians had become acquainted with foreign nations, and were disposed to glorify themselves as the original source of knowledge and the arts. The story of the dog, who assisted Isis to discover the son of Nephthys and attended her ever afterwards, explained the form of the god Anubis, who belongs to the Osirian circle; that the animal with whose head this god is represented is not a dog, but a jackal, shows that the myth was accommodated to the general conception, not to the fact. The respect paid by the Egyptians to the words of children, a feature of their excessive superstitions, is explained by the aid which children gave to her in her researches. Another object of the myth was to explain the affinity which existed, or was believed to exist, between the worship of Isis in Egypt and that of the same or a similar divinity in Phœnicia, and especially at Byblos. The identity of these goddesses was believed and was the foundation of the legend of Io's wanderings. There was, at all events, a close resemblance between the rites which related to the death and revival of Adonis at Byblos and of Osiris in Egypt."

The river Nile has in every age been a source of mystery to those people who dwelt upon its banks and watched its annual inundations through the ever-succeeding centuries. The people who built such wondrous and stupendous fabrics, to adorn and beautify their fertile valley, were the men who had made extraordinary intellectual advancement and who had arrived at a wonderful knowledge of the arts and sciences. We, to-day, stand in awe and admiration before the records of their prehistoric civilization, manifested in the ruined tombs, temples, and monolith sculptures that graced and adorned the banks of this grand old river *Nilus*, which throbbed and pulsated through the parched and thirsty soil of this remarkable valley a veritable river of Life. The conquering armies of Egypt's grandest monarchs have been marshalled upon her banks in all the magnificence of barbaric splendor, glittering in all the panoply of war, laden with the spoils, followed by long trains of captives, who with trembling steps shrank from the mighty shouting populace, pouring forth from the various cities to welcome them home. Ah! what mad revels they must have held! What grand rejoicings and glorious feastings they may have had, we of to-day will never know, for there, where the earth shook with the tread of Egypt's mighty men of war, naught but silence remains. Where once swarmed the vast population of Egypt, and where shone resplendent the glorious temples of ancient Egyptian splendor, all is ruin, utter ruin; and yet those ruins are the records of the grandeur of the Golden Age of ancient Egyptian glory, and the old god Nilus still flows along in silent majesty, just as it did thousands of years before Pharaoh's daughter found the infant Moses sleeping upon its throbbing bosom (Exodus 2 : 5).

The Nile is without exception, so far as its historical and ethnographical features are considered, the river of the world, the Amazon alone surpassing it in length. It is claimed, according to the latest discoveries, that its source is located in the Victoria Nyanza, but I differ with this statement, and believe. like many others, that the actual source of this grand old river is in the *Shimiju, which rises fully 5° south of the Equator.* The true source of the river is positively unknown and "it ranks with the Amazon and Congo as one of the longest rivers of the world in length but not in volume."

This wonderful and mysterious river was worshipped by the ancient Egyptians as a god, for without it the drifting desert sands would soon render this fertile valley as desolate as the Great Sahara itself, thus verifying the statement made by Herodotus, that—"Egypt is the gift of the Nile."

Kenrick states, in his "Ancient Egypt." vol. 1, page 3: "The geography and history of every country are closely connected with the origin and course of its rivers. In cold and humid climates, like our own, their neighborhood may have been avoided by the early inhabitants, who found more healthy abodes on the open side of the hills; but in the East where many months succeed each other without any supply of rain, the vicinity of a perennial stream is the first condition of a settled and civilized life.

"The history of the world begins on the banks of the great rivers of China, Indian, Assyria and Egypt. The Nile, however, holds a far more important relation to the country through which its flows than any other river of the world. The courses of the Rhine, the Danube or the Rhone are only lines on the surface of Germany or France. The valleys of the Euphrates and the Tigris were a very small part of the dominions of the Assyrian and Babylonian Kings; but the banks of the Nile *are* Egypt and Nubia. To live below the Cataracts and to drink of its waters was, according to the Oracle of Amon, to be an Egyptian (Herodotus, Book II, chapter 28). Upwards or downwards, it is through the valley of the Nile that civilization and conquest have taken their course. We should, therefore, naturally begin by tracing it from its source to the sea; but this is still impracticable. The Mesopotamian rivers have been followed to their sources amidst the mountains of Armenia and Kurdistan; the traveller has even penetrated to the place where the Ganges bursts forth from the everlasting snows of the Himalaya; but the sacred river of Egypt still conceals its true fountains."

The question that Herodotus (Book II, chapter 28), asked of the priests of Egypt, Alexander, of the oracle of Ammon, and which learned

FIRST CATARACT OF THE NILE.

curiosity has so often addressed to geographical science, has been only partially answered. The source of this river has ever been a problem, as well as the cause of its annual overflow. Scientific men for thousands of years have ever endeavored to solve the mysteries surrounding it. The Egyptians themselves knew but very little about it, and all that we know respecting it is, that it comes pouring forth from the Victoria Nyanza into the Somerset River, thence to the Albert Nyanza, flowing on over the various rapids that are known as *Bahr-el-Gabel.* It then goes rushing on through *Gondokoro*, until it is joined by the great tributaries of the *Bahr-el-Ghazel* (gazelle river), on the West and the *Sobat* on the East, in about 9° North latitude. From here it is known as the *Bahr-el-Abyad* or the *White Nile*. Its course is now through the *Soudan* until it reaches *Khartum* at which place it receives the waters of the *Bahr-el-Azrek*, or *Blue Nile*, which name it receives from the dark color of its waters.

The white Nile is so-called on account of its contrast with the blue, or possibly from the whitish clay that is held in solution by its waters. The character of the white Nile is entirely and completely changed in its union with the turbid waters of the blue Nile, which furnishes about one-third of the volume of water now flowing along under the name of *Bahr-el-Nil.* During the spring and summer months the blue Nile becomes very much swollen by rains falling in the mountains of Abyssinia, and it may be considered the *True* Nile that furnishes the mud and rich fertilizing substances that so enriches the soil and causes the crops to grow in such luxuriant abundance throughout the length and breadth of this most remarkable valley.

This river rises according to Bruce ("Travels," volume 5, page 308,) "in North latitude 10° 59' and East longitude 36° 55', in the Kingdom of Abyssinia, at a height of nearly six thousand feet above the sea." He visited its sources, which had not been seen by any European for seventeen years, and he professed to have discovered the true sources of the Bahr-el-Azrek or blue Nile. He says, " They are three springs, regarded by the natives with superstitious veneration, not large, but deep. To the sweetness and purity of this stream the Nile is said to owe its reputation, which its waters have in all ages maintained."

We have traced the white Nile from its so-called source to its junction with the blue Nile at Khartum, a distance of one thousand five hundred miles, from which place it flows along uninterruptedly through a miserable, desolate country, an absolutely barren waste of desert sands, receiving but one single tributary in its long journey to the sea, and farther on to its two principal mouths, Rosetta and Damietta, that are distant from its confluence with the blue Nile, one thousand eight hundred miles.

The Atbara becomes an affluent of the river Nile in about 18° North latitude and one hundred and eighty miles to the Northeast of the confluence of the blue and white Niles. After receiving the waters of the Atbara it flows in one continuous stream through Egypt, forcing its way over the hills and down steep rapids or cataracts, until it arrives at and passes Aswan, at the first cataract, five hundred and ninety miles from Cairo. It continues its onward flow until it reaches a point of separation at the apex of the Delta, which remains to-day unchanged.

Murray informs us that at the first cataract the Nile "enters Egypt proper and continues at an average rate of about three miles an hour, increased to four and one-half at the height of the inundation, a quiet, winding course, varying in breadth from three hundred and fifty yards at Silsilis to one thousand one hundred yards at Minia. So far its course is the same as in the days of old, but a considerable change now takes place, for whereas it formerly discharged itself into the sea, by seven mouths, these are at present reduced to two. Its ancient name appears to have been Cercasorus, the modern representation of which may be placed at a point opposite Shubra. Here the river, anciently divided into three branches, the Pelusiac running East, the Kanopic running West, and the Sebennytic which flowed between the two, continuing the general northward direction hitherto taken by the Nile, and piercing the Delta through the centre. From this Sebynnitic branch two others were derived. The Tanitic and Mendesian, both of which emptied themselves between it and the Pelusiac branch. The lower part of the remaining two branches, the Bolbitine and the Phatmitic, were artificial and were constructed probably when the other outlets began to dry up. It is by these two mouths that the river at the present day finds its outlet. At the point of bifurcation the general direction of the two streams is probably that of the old Pelusiac and Kanopic branches, where they gradually quit the extreme East and West course and continue more in the center of the Delta, the one to Damietta, the other to Rosetta, from which places they derive their modern appellation."

The Atbara and the blue Nile are most assuredly the fertilizers of the valley of the Nile, giving to Egypt those wonderful productive forces for which it is so noted. These turbulent rivers are fed by a great number of mountain torrents in Abyssinia, which cut deep channels and gorges into the hillsides and mountains, carrying away with them immense quantities of a dark reddish-brown soil to the Atbara and blue Nile, whose waters are already charged with a black alluvial soil, very rich in fertilizing properties, which gives to the turbid waters of these rivers their peculiar color.

On the entrance of these two affluent streams into the clear flowing waters of the Nile its characteristics become entirely changed, from the beautiful river flowing through the grassy plains of Soudan, bearing within its bosom the pellucid waters of the mountain lakes of interior Africa, to the mud and decayed organic matter which discolors the waters of the Nile. It is this alluvial soil and decayed organic substance that come down annually within the bosom of this grand old river which sustains and forms the land of the Nile, "The gift of the river."

From Khartum this great and glorious stream falls one thousand, two hundred and forty feet in its course to the sea, cutting a deep groove through the rocks and Nubian sandstone, in many places to the depth of one thousand feet, bursting forth from a transverse barrier of beautiful Syenite granite that forms the boundary between Nubia and Egypt proper. In its wonderful passage through this immense obstruction, it opens to our view the magnificent red felspar crystals so extremely beautiful. Not far from here are the quarries of Syene, about a mile from Aswan. The site of this ancient city Syene is in latitude 24° 5' 28", and is located on the East bank of the river. It has both post and telegraph offices, and a population of about eleven thousand inhabitants. An immense amount of trade is done here with the Soudanese and Abyssinians, carried on through the medium of the camel. There is a very short railroad running from here, up above the cataract, to the town of Shellal, which was of great service to the British during the trouble in the Soudan. I shall give you, my dear Brothers, a more detailed account in a future chapter of this work. From the quarries of Syene many of Egypt's basalt and beautiful red granite monoliths have been taken, and this place is well worth a visit from the Masonic student desirous of seeing for himself these celebrated quarries of the ancient Egyptians. He will find specimens of work done by the craft long centuries before authenticated history, such as a very large obelisk, gigantic columns and peculiar stones that have never been removed, but remain just as the craftsmen left them when " *called from labor.*"

In viewing this unfinished work of the ancient craftmen, one can scarcely believe that long drifting centuries have passed and gone since these stones were quarried by hands the most skilled of any which the world has ever heard. One would hardly credit his senses if told that thousands of years have elapsed since our ancient brethren wrought in these quarries and exhibited such satisfactory specimens of their skill, the very chips looking as bright to-day as in the early ages of Pharaonic history. The whole world, to-day, stands in awe and admiration before the ruined tombs, temples and monuments which demonstrate their wonderful knowledge of architecture and sculpture, evidences of which are to be seen in the many ruined cities of ancient Egypt. Somewhere about the beginning of the *summer solstice* the people of the Nile valley began to look anxiously at the old god Nilus, for signs of the annual inundation; but more especially was this so of the peasant, because all his hopes were centered upon the overflow, as he was dependent upon the fruits of the field for the sustenance of himself, family and domestic animals. He longed to be enabled to plow the soil, sow his seed and reap an abundance therefrom, which was assured whenever the waters reached the heighth that insured good crops. When the expectations were realized what grand feastings and rejoicings took place in honor of the "*Lelet-en-Nukta,* or the *Night of the Drop*," which event occurred on the night preceding the eleventh of the Coptic month of *Beuna,* corresponding to the seventeenth of June.

One who has never been able to witness this celebrated festival should assuredly visit the village of *Embaba* on the west bank of the river on the *Night of the Drop.* It was believed by the ancient Egyptians that a miraculous tear-drop fell from the eye of the goddess Isis, upon the bosom of the water of the Nile, which caused the river to swell and overflow its banks and fructify the whole of this fertile valley, therefore on this special night the people of Egypt have, from time immemorial, feasted and rejoiced in honor of the coming of their god Nilus. At his appearance the same things that are done in Egypt to-day were done, no doubt, on a grander scale by the ancient Egyptians, long before the foundations of the Pyramids were laid, or that wonderful monolith the Sphinx "looked to the East," and long centuries before Homer sang of "hundred-gated Thebes."

Through every dynasty of Pharaonic history we find that the Egyptians have worshipped their old god Nilus, not as God, but only emblematic of the Divine Essence Itself. Both before and at every inundation, these people would perform certain rites and ceremonies, in order to insure a plentiful overflow. We learn from some Arabian writers that these ancient people prayed earnestly and incessantly for a bountiful inundation, and during some of the ceremonies sacrificed a virgin to the god of their river—a custom continued until Egypt passed under the yoke of Moslem rule. The Copts continued to observe certain rites and preserve a relic of the virgin sacrifice in their peculiar ceremonies. Heliodorus gives us an account of the festivals given in honor of the annual inundations, as do many other writers, and to-day the Khedive and state officials at the festival of "*Mosim el-Khaleeg*" (which takes place somewhere about the middle of August), cuts the dam at Cairo, letting the water of the High Nile flow through its old bed, when an heifer is slain and distributed to the people for food, who go about rejoicing, assured of a year of plenty, while every one is filled with joy, and happiness reigns supreme.

These ceremonies carry us back to the ancient days of Meneptah, B. C. 1400, when the people chanted their grand "Hymn to the Nile," one verse of which I quote you:

> "Hail, all hail, O Nile, to thee!
> To this land thyself thou showest,
> Coming tranquilly to give
> Life, that Egypt so may live:
> Ammon, hidden is thy source,
> But it fills our hearts with glee!

6

> Thou the gardens overflowest,
> With their flowers beloved of Ra ;
> Thou, for all the beasts that are,
> Glorious river,
> Art life-giver ;
> To our fair fields ceaselessly,
> Thou thy waters dost supply,
> And dost come
> Thro' the middle plain descending,
> Like the sun thro' middle sky ;
> Loving good, and without ending,
> Bringing corn for granary ;
> Giving light to every home,
> O thou mighty Ptah."

This hymn was no doubt the principal one sung during the festivals of the *Niloa.* I would have been pleased to have quoted the entire hymn, but it is too long, and I simply give the first verse. " Rawnsley " tells us that this " poem is specially interesting, as identifying the Nile with *Ra, Amon* and *Ptah,* as well as other gods. This assures us of the complete identification of the reigning monarch with deity, as well as giving a realization of how entirely unknown the sources of the Nile were at that day, and how the mystery of its risings affected the Egyptians with the thought of a hand unseen, working the yearly miracle of inundation, and giving its yearly blessing."

Through the drifting centuries the Egyptian people have ever observed this festival, and Christian domination has thus far never been able to stamp it out. The peculiarities and ceremonies still continue, but not on such a grand scale as in the hoary civilization of Egyptian splendor.

From this time forward the voice of the *Munadi en-Nil* (Nile Crier) will announce to the people the progress of the rising river. One of the first things observed in the swelling waters is its reddish color. As soon as this color makes its appearance the people hasten down to the river and collect a plentiful supply, which they store away in jars for future use. It begins, soon afterward, to assume a greenish color, during which period the water is considered very unhealthy. After this decayed, organic matter is swept away, it once more assumes the reddish color and with it the delicious, sweet and healthy drinking water such as the kings

VIEW OF ASWAN OR SYENE.

of Persia always used at their tables. The river increases continually for a period of almost three months, sometimes having a final rise in the early part of October, after which it gradually falls to its natural flow. The prosperity of the country depends, in a very great measure, upon the height of the inundation. Too great an overflow would cause an immense loss of life and property, while an insufficent rise would occasion a great deal of distress, simply because large portions of land could not be flooded, in consequence of which no crops would grow in a great many places throughout the land of Egypt.

To-day there are wonderful improvements going on for the purpose of preserving the waters of the river from running to waste. To this end two very large dams are under construction, and nearing completion, in Upper Egypt. One is to be constructed at Asyut, and the other at Aswan, both of which are expected to be completed during the year 1903. The dam at the latter place will form a reservoir fully one hundred and twenty miles in length, having a storage capacity of about one billion three hundred and ninety-three million and twenty thousand cubic yards of water, which will form quite a lake in itself. At the point selected for the building of the dam at Aswan the river is fully two thousand two hundred yards wide at "High Nile." The reservoir, when completed, will be one of the most magnificent specimens of engineering, for the purpose of irrigation, known to the world. The cost of construction of this stupendous piece of wcrk has been estimated at $25,000,000.

The inhabitants of this valley were taxed in ancient times, as well as at the present day, according to the rise of the river. In all ages the government had to be supported, just the same as any other nation, " by taxation," and the duty of seeing that taxation was duly administered belonged to the *Mudir* of every province, who would, of course, have to be assisted by a number of inferior officers, such as Vice-Governors, or *Wekil*, a chief clerk, a regular tax-gatherer, an accountant, a *Kadi* or supreme judge, a superintendent of police, a supervisor of canals, and the physician of the province. These were the officers that composed the general council for each province in Egypt, while in small towns the *Nazir el-Kism*, or sub-governor, was under the general supervision of the *Mudir*, as well as the *Sheikh el-Beled's* of the villages, who had to render an account of all monies collected to the general council. Those officials composed all the general officers, as well as a part of the inferior officers, who were legally authorized to collect the taxes of the provinces throughout the whole length and breadth of Egypt. The principal ones were, the land tax, income tax, market tax, and palm tax. These are some of the taxes collected to-day, but C. Ritter says in Baedeker *note*, page 319, "Lower Egypt:"

"The rate of taxation was determined in ancient times in accordance with the height of the inundation. All the authorities from Herodotus down to Leo Africanus agree in stating that the Nile must rise sixteen cubits, or Egyptian ells, in order that the land may produce good crops. The famous statue of Father Nile, in the Vatican, is accordingly surrounded by sixteen figures of genii, representing these sixteen ells. To this day the height of the overflow influences taxation and the land which is artificially irrigated pays less than that reached by the river itself. The object of the government is always to induce belief that the inundation is favorable, and the sworn Sheikh of the Nilometer, is therefore, subject to the influence of the police at Cairo. The same political motives from which, in ancient times, the custody of the Nilometers was entrusted to the priests alone, still prevent the Egyptian public from obtaining access to the Mikyas (Nilometers) in the island of Roda. The real height of the water is always concealed and false statements made, as it is the object of the fiscal authorities to levy, if possible, the full rate of taxation every year, whatever the height of the Nile may have been. This traditional dishonesty in the use of the Nilometer was first discovered by the French engineers during the occupation of Egypt by Napoleon."

The waters which flood this fertile valley during every inundation contain such wonderful powers to stimulate vegetable life into remarkable growth, that no artificial fertilizing agent is needed, but only such as old god Nilus gives. This is sufficient for all purposes, as it contains, according to Kenrick, in every one hundred parts of water, "forty-eight clay, nine of carbon, eighteen parts of carbonate of lime, four of carbonate of magnesia, besides portions of silicia, and oxide of iron."

There is no question in my mind but that the river Nile was personified by the ancient Egyptians and received divine honors throughout the length and breadth of the Nile valley, as all the information I have gathered during my researches upon this subject among ancient authorities and modern historians only strengthens my belief in this matter. Heliodorus informs us that the river was personified, and from what Herodotus tells us in Book II, chap. 90, this fact is proven, consequently we have good ground for believing that *Old god Nilus* was worshipped throughout the whole of Egypt. We have no reason to doubt his statement, when he says that "none may touch the corpse, not even the friends or relatives, but only *the priests of the Nile*," showing that whenever a person was drowned in its waters it was the special duty of these priests to attend solely to the disposal of the body, hence, temples must have been erected in every Nome and every city throughout the "Land of Egypt." We have evidence of the fact that this god Nilus was worshipped in many cities.

The festival of the *Niloa*, of which I have already spoken, was for the express purpose of welcoming the rising river and the coming flood. Heliodorus states in *Eth* 9:9, that "it was one of the principal festivals of Egypt and was celebrated at the summer solstice, or at the first appearance of the rising of the waters." The ancient Egyptians believed that if all the peculiar rites and ceremonies were not properly observed and everything done in accordance with custom and usage, the river would not overflow its banks to the height required for an abundant crop, and an assured harvest, when a famine would result. In order to avert such a terrible catastrophe not one single ceremony should be neglected, and the priest would be required to give his offering in money, while the various officials of the different Nomes would have to cast their gifts of gold upon the throbbing bosom of the flowing river, in order to carry out the programme that had been established long centuries before the sons of Jacob went down into the "Land of Egypt" to buy corn from their brother Joseph; aye, long before the foundations of the Pyramids of Gizeh were laid or the Sphinx looked to the East and saw the glory of the Sun God Ra, when its glorious rays lit up this wonderous valley in the radiant beauty of Light.

Now this brings me to a very interesting subject, one that should interest every Masonic student and Free Mason throughout the world universal, and that is the meaning and origin of the word Free-Mason, because a thorough understanding of these two words *Free* and *Mason* will verify the statements that are made in our rituals, that "Free Masonry has been in existence from time immemorial, and that the best men of every epoch of the world's history have been members of our fraternity." It will also prove that our very name *Free Mason* originated in the Valley of the Nile, and that our glorious Fraternity existed thousands of years before Christ, as well as that the Craftsmen who wrought in the quarries and laid the foundation of the Pyramids were members of our beloved fraternity.

I have often asked Brethren of the "Royal Craft," when in conference assembled: Why are we called Free Masons? Not one of the many to whom this question has been propounded could give a definite or lucid account of its origin, or why we are called by this name. In the third chapter I make the claim that our glorious fraternity originated in the "Land of the Vedas" and was cradled on the banks of the Nile. Therefore in order to prove this fact I will state that the very name Free Mason proves its antiquity, as well as the country in which it was cradled, and consequently verifies my statement that "*it is a lineal descendant of the Ancient Egyptian Mysteries.*"

Now, my dear Brothers, the words Free Mason do not belong to the English language, neither do they originate in the Latin or Greek languages, all of which they antedate, by thousands of years, and come to us from the Egypto-Coptic language, the language that was used by the Ancient Egyptians in the Golden Age of Egypt The Copts are most certainly the lineal descendants of the people who migrated from India to the valley of the Nile and adorned its banks with stupendous specimens of Cyclopean architecture, whose written language was expressed in three distinct forms. The first of which was the *Hieroglyphs*, the second the *Hieratic* and the third the *Demotic*.

Champollin was one of the most indefatigable students of those ancient Egyptian writings and after very careful and painstaking investigation of the various hieroglyphic inscriptions throughout the tombs, temples and papyrus of Egypt, he gave to the world his celebrated *Grammaire Egyptienne*, wherein he proves that the Hieratic was derived from the hieroglyphs. There is no question but that the Hierophants and priests of Egypt preserved all their sacred writings, secrets, etc., in these early hieroglyphs, as the first two of these writings belonged especially to the priesthood, while the Demotic was used principally by the people for commercial purposes. This latter was a degenerate from the other two and it was the most difficult to understand. I do not desire to enter into a long description of the writings of this ancient people, but simply to state that the words Free Mason are derived from the ancient Egypto-Coptic. In that language the word " PHREE " meant —*Light, Knowledge, Wisdom,* or *Intelligence,* while " MASSEN " was the plural of " *Mes* " signifying children; hence we were and are known as *children of,* or *Sons of Light, Wisdom,* or *Intelligence,* because *Light* signified knowledge to the *Candidate or Initiate,* and it is that which every Brother is in search of, MORE LIGHT. *Thoth* signifies the intellect and *mes* a child, consequently Thothmes means child of Thoth, or a man of intelligence. *Ra* was the Sun God and *Mes* the child, therefore the Great Rames-es was considered to be a child of the sun god Ra, or *Son of the Sun.*

Surely the very name Free Mason ought to convince any person from whence it is derived, prove the antiquity of the Fraternity, and demonstrate beyond the shadow of a doubt that it is far older than the " Golden Fleece, or Roman Eagle," as the Coptic language was, in substance, the same as the spoken language of the Ancient Egyptians. Now, in proving the name Free Mason to have been of Ancient Egyptian origin, it follows, that it must have been connected with the Ancient Egyptian Mysteries, for the teachings of the one are identical with the other, if rightly understood, and I do not stand alone in this opinion. I may possibly claim for it more than some other authorities, who have not thoroughly investigated this subject. Yet I feel positively certain that I shall adduce sufficient evidence to prove and sustain my assertions, that the *esoteric teachings* of our beloved *Scottish Rite of Free Masonry is a lineal descendant of the Ancient Mysteries,* whose esoteric teachings have ever been a guide to higher planes of spiritual unfoldment, through an understanding of Nature and her wonderful manifestations; whose revelations from the known to the hitherto unknown, from the land of effect to the realm of cause, from man through a profound Pantheism to his God, binding us, the human family, together in stronger bonds than were ever imposed by any human law, because the *Perfect Mason* is taught to understand HIMSELF and in so doing he understands the true meaning of the UNIVERSAL BROTHERHOOD OF MAN, irrespective of race, creed, caste, or color.

I had the pleasure of sitting in the Grand Lodge F. & A. M. of the State of Washington, when the Committee on Jurisprudence (Brothers T. M. Reed, of Olympia, J. E. Edmiston, of Dayton, and Wm. H. Upton, of Seattle) laid before that body the question pertaining to Negro Masonry. Two of this committee, who submitted the report recognizing the negro as a man and Brother, were born and raised in the Southern States. In making their report they declared that honor, justice and right were insurmountable, and that prejudice was a secondary considera-tion with them, as all they wanted was to have justice done to those who, like ourselves, were searching for " More Light " on the esoteric teachings of Masonry, in order to come to a better understanding of themselves and the potential forces latent within them.

Our revered Brother Albert Pike, states in " Morals and Dogmas," page 220, that :—" The whole world is but one Republic, of which each Nation is a family, and every individual a child. Masonry, not in any wise derogating from the differing duties which the diversity of states requires, tends to create a new people, which, composed of Men of many nations and tongues, shall all be bound together by the bonds of Science, Morality and Virtue.

" Essentially philanthropic, philosophical and progressive, but it is neither a political party nor a religious sect. It embraces all parties and all sects, to form from among them all a vast fraternal association. It recognizes the dignity of human nature, and man's right to so much freedom as he is fitted for ; and *it knows nothing that should place one man below another*, except ignorance, debasement and crime, and the necessity of subordination to lawful will and authority."

Rebold, in his " History of Masonry," page 62, says : " The real object of Freemasonry may be summed up in these words: To efface from among men the prejudices of caste, the conventional distinctions of color, origin, opinion, nationality ; to annihilate fanaticism and supersti-tion ; to extirpate national discord, and with it extinguish the firebrand of war ; in a word—to arrive, by free and pacific progress, at one formula or model of eternal and universal right, according to which each individual human being shall be free to develop every faculty with which he may be endowed, and to concur heartily, and with the fulness of his strength, in the bestowment of happiness upon all, and thus to make of the whole human race one family of brothers, united by affection, wisdom and labor.

J. D. Buck, in his very valuable little work entitled, "Mystic Masonry," states that "The qualified Brotherhood of Man is the basis of all ethics, and the Great Republic is the ideal state. If these concepts were accepted and acted upon, there would result time and opportunity, and the power to apprehend the deeper problems of the origin, nature, and destiny of man. 'Man is not man as yet.' What he may be, and what he might do, under favorable conditions, is very seldom even dreamed. We never build beyond our ideals. We habitually fall below them."

I do not wish to dwell upon Man or Universal Brotherhood now, but shall speak of the subject in another chapter, when entering into a full interpretation of the building of man under the badge of a Mason. In order to do this, I shall bring forward the profound philosophy of the far East, and the design upon my trestle board will be: the white leather apron with the bib turned up, to demonstrate the Lower Quarternary and the Upper Triad. In my demonstrations I shall trace nature in all its gradations, through elements, crystals, plants and animals to quarternary man, up to the present.evolution, thence through body, soul and spirit into the eternal essence of all things.

Our Rite came down to us from the masters and adepts of India, and made its dwelling place upon the banks of that wonderful river Nile, where, as the ancient mysteries, it preserved those sublime and beautiful esoteric teachings of the ancient Wisdom which will eventually enlighten the world and point out the way leading to an understanding of the symbology. Then will the aspirant begin to realize that the ceremonies, at the initiatory services, are simply unwritten aids, more suggestive than words and far more pregnant with meaning than knowledge imparted by books. It appeals to his eye, impresses itself upon his brain, and stimulates his memory to action, so that long after the ceremonies have passed, he will be enabled to recall every incident by a simple effort of his will. Thus through memory he can interpret, study and develop for himself the true meaning of the symbols and ceremonies of our glorious Scottish Rite.

What the world of to-day, and generations unborn, owe to Free Masonry will never be fully realized. The fraternity has always been, and always will be an incentive to enlightenment, liberality and education. During the "Dark Ages" it was only in the lodge-room that our scientific and philosophical brethren dared make known any of the invaluable discoveries, or profound philosophical knowledge, for fear of the inquisition, which was supported by the bigotry, fanaticism and ignorance of tyrants, backed by a superstitious and uncultured populace. But to-day we find it working, as it has ever done, in the interest of humanity. *In fact it is the Advocate and Champion of the Rights of the People* by the best men of the world, who have an advantage over our ancient brethren, by being enabled to exemplify openly, the grand truths taught behind the closed doors of our Lodges, Chapters, Councils and Consistories; the glorious heritage of man, LIBERTY, EQUALITY AND FRATERNITY.

Brother Albert Pike says in "Morals and Dogmas," page 25, *et seq:* "The best gift we can bestow on man is Manhood. It is that which Masonry is ordained of God to bestow on its votaries; not sectarianism and religious dogma; not a rudimentary morality, that may be found in the writings of Confucius, Zoroaster, Seneca and the Rabbis in the Proverbs and Ecclesiastes; not a little and cheap common-school knowledge; but Manhood, Science and Philosophy.

"Not that Philosophy or Science is in opposition to Religion. For Philosophy is but the knowledge of God and the Soul, which is derived from observation of the manifold action of God and the Soul, and from a wise analogy. It is the intellectual guide which the religious sentiment needs. The true religious philosophy of an imperfect being is not a system of creed; but as SOCRATES thought, an infinite search or approximation. Philosophy is that intellectual and moral progress which the religious sentiment inspires and ennobles.

"As to Science, it could not walk alone while religion was stationary. It consists of those matured inferences, from experience, which all other experience confirms. It realizes and unites all that was truly valuable, in both the old schemes of mediation,—one *heroic*, or the system of action and effort; and the *mystical* theory of spiritual, contemplative communion.

"The first Scriptures for the human race were written by God on the Earth and the Heavens. The reading of these Scriptures is Science. Familiarity with the grass and the trees, the insects and the infusoria, teaches us deeper lessons of love and faith than we can glean from the writings of FENELON and AUGUSTINE. The great Bible of God is ever open before mankind."

Masonry is not a Religion, for Religion does not exist without a dogma, a creed and a priesthood; it is the basic philosophical idea which underlies all religions, and which appears distinctly as soon as the mass of theological allegories and interpretations are removed. This fact can be conclusively demonstrated by any thoughtful Mason, be he *Elu*, Knight or Prince, and he will be astonished at the identity of the claims that are made by the various sects into which mankind is divided. Their metaphysical conceptions of the Divine Principle of man's essence and future destiny are almost the same; their ethical conclusions and rules for daily conduct in life are absolutely identical. It is quite plain that the conflict between them is merely a war of words and petty details, showing Religion is but an effort to satisfy the innate religious feeling existing in every human being. Each and every one is a *partial* revelation of the *One* Truth, adapted to the special capacities of comprehending the epoch in which they appeared, more or less adored by the peculiar mental bias of the people among whom it was evolved. The Masonic student will find connecting links between the ancient teachings of long ago and those of to-day, tending to prove the existence of a very ancient system, or body of occult knowledge, which can be traced in its influence and esoteric forms, through the middle-ages; through and beyond the Greek and Roman civilizations, and their contemporary dynasties in the East; through Egypt, Persia and India, until it is lost in the hoary ages of the past, far back into those ages which saw the birth and childhood of the Aryan race in the valley of Hindustan.

This great fact will be forced upon every student and thinker that ALL Religions of the World have been derived from the one primal source—the GREAT WISDOM RELIGION—THE SECRET DOCTRINE of the Initiates of old. Many names have been given at different periods of the world's history, to this body of occult knowledge, the key to which was kept a profound secret by its custodians, those who, through Initiation had earned a right to its deepest mysteries. Sages, philosophers, Adepts, and Mystics in all ages have drawn upon this *Secret Doctrine* for their knowledge and inspiration; who have hinted as plainly as they dared, at its more recondite secrets, and transcendental knowledge. The nineteenth century has witnessed a very great revival of knowledge and science which has excited widespread and profound attention, and it is not to be wondered that such has been the case, when we take into consideration that Initiates have ever warred against *Ignorance*, and contended against *Tyranny* and *Fanaticism*.

These forces caused the Secret Doctrine to emerge from the obscurity into which it had fallen through the superstition, ignorance and fanaticism of the Middle Ages, as well as the influence of ecclesiastical religions, which dominated the world for so many long and weary centuries. The element of supernaturalism is fast disappearing under the exertions and influence of the teachings of our Rite and its scientific generalizations. Any doctrine or teaching, presenting itself for acceptance among the readers and thinkers of this twentieth century, must undergo this test first, as whether it can stand in line with the law of conservation, of energy, and the ordered sequence of *Cause and Effect*, discoverable in every domain of natural phenomena. This is the fundamental claim of our beloved Ancient and Accepted Scottish Rite of Masonry, which obtained its knowledge and Wisdom from the Secret Doctrine of the Ancient Mysteries, the fountain from which learned men of every age have drawn their high inspirational force and intellectual development. From this source it can be proven, fully and undisputably, that a transcendental knowledge of man's nature has always existed in the world— so far at all events as we have any historical records—and that all these great Religions and Philosophies are but the echoes or reflections of these occult doctrines, overlaid and perverted in most instances by ages of superstition and ignorance.

The revival of this knowledge will clear away entirely that element of supernaturalism in religion which is the great cause of the total rejection of all religious doctrines by the intelligent thinkers of the present day. It will do more than this. In freeing religion from its supernatural element, its work will be constuctive of a new and surer basis for the practice of religion, as a matter of conduct instead of belief. The present crisis in the religious world is produced, not so much by sheer disbelief, as by uncertainty. This is above all an age of inquiry, and woe betide any teaching, religious or scientific, which cannot make a decent pretense of fulfilling its undertakings, and giving its *raison d'etre* in no uncertain voice. That religion, to-day, is making little or no headway toward the regeneration of the world, is manifest to any one who has taken the trouble to make himself acquainted with the social life of the people.

Hideous misery, and open unblushing vice, have never been more rampant than to-day, and in the presence of this, official religion is dumb and helpless. It knows not the cause and still less the remedy. It is deaf to the voice of materialism, loudly scoffing at its claims and derides its fancied remedies.

It must not be supposed that Masonry is adverse to Christianity, or to any other religion in a pure form. It does, however, assert that the pure gem of Truth, upon which it is founded, is obscured by a mass of useless creed, under which it is lost to sight. Masonry desires to strengthen and not to weaken the hands of the Religionist. It does not proclaim nor teach any new revelation for a chosen people, but a complete philosophy, explaining every problem of human life to the entire satisfaction of the most severe logician. There is an array of Truths as old as mankind itself, scattered here and there in the fragments which are found in every religion, ancient or modern, tested to the utmost by strict philosophical and scientific processes, divested of all the fanciful additions of superstition, based not on authority, not on blind faith; but on reasonable demonstrations by comparisons, analysis and universal applicability; the crucial test of all hypothesis.

Masonic esoteric teachings do not crave acceptance from her initiates, but only asks loyal investigation. "Every one is entirely free to reject and dissent from whatsoever may seem to him untrue or unsound. It is only required of him that he shall weigh what is taught, and give it fair hearing and unprejudiced judgment." It does not demand belief, but knowledge. It is a science, not a Religion—the science of man's relation to the Universe. It is a well known fact, that in ancient times, religion and science were not the irreconcilable adversaries they are to-day, and that the sages of India and Egypt were, at the same time, the spiritual advisors of the people, and the zealous keepers of the scientific knowledge. Did not Plato and Pythagoras, the great Grecian philosophers, go to the Egyptian priests for instruction? Did not Jesus of Nazareth dispute with the doctors of his time, and astound them by his unaccountable knowledge? Were not the so-called miracles of all religious reformers or prophets, but a mere manifestation of superior knowledge of the laws of nature, which, to the ignorant, appeared as supernatural?

Unfortunately both science and religion have long forgotten their palmiest days, when they were twins, walking hand in hand together. But, at the present time, they have degenerated into gross materialism. Science purposely narrowing its field of observation to the domain of matter, leaving metaphysical investigations to people untrained in the accuracy of scientific methods. Religion dwarfs the conception of God into that of a personal being, whom each votary endows with more or less human attributes, while Masonry avoids both errors. It follows Science on its chosen ground, antagonizing it only when it becomes materialistic, negative and narrow minded. It respects the religious feelings of all, when sincere, regardless of the form in which they may be clothed; but refuses to any kind of religion the monopoly of Truth.

Ancient Mysteries—Scottish Rite Philosophy.

"A babe, new-born, lay on its mother's breast,
It was not new, but old! Aye, older than the stars!
For 'twas the self-same soul whose essence was
The gathered rays from Hierarchies, higher far
Than present man with his small brain can dream!
The Hierarchies who their essence draw
From the One Absolute.
Nay! nor was the body new, except in shape,
But formed of that which is imperishable,
Whose spirit of all matter essence is;
Whose atoms had built many forms, the abodes
Wherein this soul had dwelt—this pilgrim of old."

CHAPTER V.

ANCIENT MYSTERIES—SCOTTISH RITE PHILOSOPHY.

AFTER carefully searching through many countries and various sources, I find that the ancient mysteries originated in the hoary civilization of a prehistoric age. That all knowledge of Science, Arts and Philosophy are due to the ancient wisdom that permeated the Indian, Mazdean and Egyptian mysteries, whose Hierophants gave forth freely the sublime teachings of this ancient wisdom, to all those who, after due trial, were found worthy and well qualified to receive them, and then only, under deep and binding obligations., I also found, that in all those different countries, these mysteries had a common origin, with a purpose in view identical one with the other. That purpose was for the upbuilding of humanity by instructing it in the sublime and profound truths of the ancient wisdom, which truths to-day underlie all religions and all philosophies. The principle of these mysteries, and the "*fons et origo*" of all the rest, was the *Mysteries of India*, whose basic source of all knowledge and intellectual advancement was the SECRET DOCTRINE of the adepts and sages of that country, who taught that "*there is an Omnipresent, Eternal, Boundless and Immutable Principle back of all manifestations.*" It is that which we call the Supreme Architect of the Universe, THE ABSOLUTE AND INFINITE DEITY. This fact was impressed upon the initiate of old, that he might be enabled to know that this Eternal Absolute Reality, is the eternal cause of all the manifestations and differentiations in the Kosmos. It was also taught that the Universal Brotherhood of Man is the basis of all ethics, and that the grandest study for man, was man, as in coming to an understanding of himself and his own potential forces he would be enabled to come to a better comprehension of God and Nature.

The esoteric teachings of the ancient mysteries is what gave to Greece her civilization and culture, which resulted in her wonderful intel-

7

lectual advancement; force of character to her citizens, wisdom to her statesmen, and placed her at the head of all civilized nations. This fact is demonstrated in history as, after the "Golden Age" of Egypt, she was pre-eminently above all other nations and peoples, through the development of her knowledge of science, art, philosophy, literature, poetry, etc. All this was due to the profound and sublime teachings that permeated the ancient mysteries.

In order that you, my dear Brothers and readers, may be enabled to understand something about these ancient mysteries, I shall quote you from various authorities, and try to explain the sublimity and grandeur of the teachings which pertained, not only to the Ancient Mysteries, but to our own glorious Scottish Rite, a true and lineal descendent of those ancient institutions or fraternities. These gave to Greece her culture and refinement, and to Rome her civilization. I want you, my dear Brothers, to distinctly understand that all the knowledge and wisdom that belonged to the Indian, Mazdean, and the ancient Egyptian Mysteries, have been preserved, and are now taught, in all their sublimity and grandeur, in our own beloved Ancient and Accepted Scottish Rite.

Grote in his "History of Greece," Vol. I, Chapter xvi, page 388, says: "In the Elusinian and Samothracian Mysteries was treasured up the *Secret Doctrine* of the theological and philosophical myths, which had once constituted the primitive legendary stock of Greece, in the hands of the original priesthood, and in ages anterior to Homer. Persons who had gone through the preliminary ceremonies of initiation, were permitted at length to hear, though under strict obligations of secrecy, this ancient and cosmogonic doctrine, revealing the distinction of man, and the certainty of posthumous rewards and punishments, all disengaged from the corruptions of poets, as well as from the symbols and allegories under which they still remain buried in the eyes of the vulgar. The Mysteries of Greece were thus traced up to the earliest ages, and represented the only faithful depositories of that purer theology and physics, which had originally been communicated, though under unavoidable inconveniences of a symbolical expression, by an *enlightened priesthood, who were highly educated* in the sciences, philosophies, arts and ethics, and thoroughly instructed, having their origin either in Egypt, or in the East among the rude and barbarous Greeks, to whom their knowledge was communicated under the veil of symbols." These teachings embodied a profound theological philosophy and inculcated great and glorious moral truths upon those Initiates who desired a knowledge of the *Ancient Wisdom*, and these teachings eventually became lost, that is to the great majority; but they were preserved by the few and taught in the various Mysteries handed down from generation to generation, until to-day we find them in all their sublimity and grandeur in our own glorious Ancient and Accepted Scottish Rite.

Should any man or Mason doubt the verity of this statement, let either him or them read that scholarly production of our revered Brother General Albert Pike, "Morals and Dogmas," page 328 *et seq*, where he positively states that, "We use the old allegories, based on occurrences detailed in the Hebrew and Christian books, and drawn from the Ancient Mysteries of Egypt, Persia, India, Greece, the Druids and the Essenes, as vehicles to communicate the Great Masonic Truths; as it has used the legends of the Crusades, and the ceremonies of orders of Knighthood.

"The Ancient and Accepted Scottish Rite of Masonry has now become what Masonry was at first meant to be, a teacher of Great Truths, inspired by an upright and enlightened reason, a firm and constant wisdom, and an affectionate and liberal philanthrophy.

"We teach the truth of none of the legends we recite. They are to us but parables and allegories, involving and enveloping Masonic instruction ; and vehicles of useful and interesting information. They represent the phases of the human mind, its efforts and struggles to comprehend nature, God, the government of the universe, the permitted existence of sorrow and evil. To teach us wisdom, and the folly of endeavoring to explain to ourselves that which we are not capable of understanding, we reproduce the speculations of the Philosophers, the Kabalists, the Mystagogues and the Gnostics. Everyone being at liberty to apply our symbols and emblems as he thinks most consistent with truth and reason, and with his own faith. We give them such interpretation only as may be accepted by all. Our degrees may be conferred in France, or Turkey, at Pekin, Ispahan, Rome, or Geneva, in the city of Penn, or in Catholic Lousiana, upon the subjects of an absolute government or the citizens of a free State, upon sectarian or theist. To honor the Diety, to regard all men as our brethren, as children, equally dear to him, of the Supreme

Creator of the Universe, and to make himself useful to society and himself by his labors, are its teachings to its initiates in all of the degrees.

"Preacher of Liberty, Fraternity and Equality, it desires them to be attained by making men fit to receive them, and by the moral power of an intelligent and enlightened people. It lays no plots and conspiracies. It hatches no premature revolutions. It encourages no people to revolt against the constituted authorities; but recognizing the great truth that freedom follows fitness for freedom, as the corollary follows the axiom, it strives to *prepare* men to govern themselves.

"Except as mere symbols of the moral virtues and intellectual qualities, the tools and implements of Masonry belong exclusively to the first three degrees. They also, however, serve to remind the Mason who has advanced further, that his new rank is based upon the humble labors of the symbolic degrees, as they are improperly termed, inasmuch as all the degrees are symbolic.

"Thus the initiates are inspired with a just idea of Masonry, to wit, that it is essentially WORK; both teaching and practising LABOR; and that it is altogether emblematic. Three kinds of work are necessary to the preservation and protection of man and society; manual labor, specially belonging to the three blue degrees; labor in arms, symbolized by the knightly or chivalric degrees; and intellectual labor, belonging particularly to the philosopical degrees.

"There was a distinction between the lesser and greater mysteries. One must have been for some years admitted to the former before he could receive the latter, which was but a preparation for them, the Vestibule of the Temple, of which those of Eleusis was the sanctuary. There, in the lesser mysteries, they were prepared to receive the holy truths in the greater. The initiates in the lesser were called simply *Mystes*, or initiates; but those in the greater, *Epoptes*, or seers. An ancient poet says that the former was an imperfect shadow of the latter, as sleep is of death. After admission to the former, the initiate was taught lessons of morality, and the rudiments of the sacred science, the most sublime and secret part of which was reserved for the Epopt, who saw the truth in its nakedness, while the Mystes only viewed it through a veil and under emblems fitter to excite than to satisfy his curiosity.

THE RUINED TEMPLE OF RAMESES,
KARNAK.

"Before communicating the first secrets and primary dogmas of initiation the priests required the candidate to take a fearful oath never to divulge the secrets. Then he made his vows, prayers and sacrifices to the gods. The skins of the victims consecrated to Jupiter were spread on the ground, and he was made to set his feet upon them. He was then taught some enigmatic formulas, as answers to questions, by which to make himself known. He was then enthroned, invested with a purple cincture, and crowned with flowers, or branches of palms or olive."

Our very learned and ancient Brother Pythagoras divided his schools into two classes, to whom he gave instruction, both day and night. To those attending his day class, his lectures or teachings were to admonish his pupils as to the path they should follow, in order to acquire a knowledge of morality, virtue and truth, as well as continually warning them of their lower nature, and instructing them how to kill the animal within themselves, so as to allow the higher spiritual to dominate and guide him. Those who attended his night class were selected from the pupils who had proved themselves by earnest study and profound meditation, to be worthy and well qualified to live in union with a community who enjoyed a common property. These he instructed by allegories and symbols. The emblems used were taken from geometrical and numerical figures, believing that, "Number lies at the root of manifest universe. Numbers and harmonious proportion guide the first differentiation of homogeneous substance into heterogenous elements; and number and numbers set limits to the formative hand of nature. Know the corresponding numbers of the fundamental principle of every element, and its sub-elements; learn their interaction and behaviour on the occult side of manifesting nature, and the law of correspondences will lead you to the discovery of the greatest mysteries of macrocosmical life." (*Secret Doctrine.*)

After the pupil had thoroughly mastered and comprehended the primary instructions, he was then advanced to another plane of thought, and instructed in the profound, sublime teachings of the Secret Doctrine, that fountain of Ancient Wisdom, wherein he learned that man is not the highest being in Nature's evolutionary process; but that he has within him the potentiality of becoming so.

We learn from Clement of Alexandria that—"The Egyptians neither entrusted their mysteries to everyone, nor degraded the secrets of divine matters by disclosing them to the profane, reserving them for the heir apparent of the throne, and for such of the priests as excelled in virtue and wisdom."

Wilkinson, commenting on this, in "Ancient Egyptians," Vol. I, page 174, says: "From all we can learn of the subject, it appears that the Mysteries consisted of two degrees, demonstrated the greater and the less, and in order to become qualified for admission into the higher class, it was necessary to have passed through those of the inferior degree, as each of them were probably divided into ten different grades. It was necessary that the character of the candidate for initiation should be pure and unsullied, and novitiates were commanded to study those things which tended to purify the mind and encourage morality. The honor of ascending from the less to the greater mysteries, was as highly esteemed, as it was difficult to attain. No ordinary qualifications recommended the aspirant to this important privilege and independent of enjoying an acknowledged reputation for learning and morality, he was required to undergo the most severe ordeal and to show the greatest moral resignation; but the ceremony of passing under the knife of the Hierophant was merely emblematic of the regeneration of the Neophyte. That no one, except the priests, was privileged to initiation into the greater mysteries, is evident from the fact of a prince, and even the heir-apparent, if of the military order, neither being made partakers of those important secrets, nor instructed in them, until his accession to the throne, when in virtue of his kingly office he became a member of the priesthood and the head of the religion. It is not, however, less certain that at a later period many besides the priests and even some Greeks were admitted to the lesser mysteries; yet in these cases also their advancement through the different grades must have depended on a strict conformance to prescribed rules."

J. Septimius Florens Tertullianus, a pagan philosopher, who afterwards embraced Christianity, and flourished about A. D. 196, was an able writer and in his "*Apology for the Christians*," says: "None are admitted to the religious mysteries without an oath of secrecy. We appeal to your Thracian and Elusinian mysteries, and we are specially bound to this caution, because if we prove faithless we should not only provoke Heaven, but draw upon our heads the utmost rigor of human displeasure. And should strangers betray us? They know nothing but by report and hearsay. Far hence, ye Profane, is the prohibition from all holy mysteries."

Clemens of Alexandria tells us in his "*Stromata*," that "he cannot explain the mysteries, because he should thereby, according to the old proverb, put a sword into the hands of a child." He frequently compares the discipline of the Secret with the heathen Mysteries, as to their internal and recondite wisdom.

Origen, a celebrated Greek writer, surnamed *Adamantus*, a rigid Christian who made himself a eunuch, tells us that "Inasmuch as the essential and important doctrines and principles of Christianity are openly taught, it is foolish to object that there are other things that are recondite; for this is common to Christian discipline with that of those philosophers in whose teachings some things were exoteric, and some esoteric." It is enough to say that it was so with some of the disciples of Pythagoras, and he, like Tertullian, informs us that, just before the church opened in regular form, those present were warned in the following words: "Depart ye Profane! Let the Catechumens and those who have not been admitted or initiated go forth."

Cyrillus, Bishop of Jerusalem, informs us that "The Lord spake in parables to his hearers in general; but to his disciples he explained in private the parables and allegories which he spoke in public. The splendor of glory is for those who are early enlightened; obscurity and darkness are the portion of the unbelievers and ignorant. Just so the church discovers its mysteries to those who have advanced beyond the class of Catechumens; we employ obscure terms with others."

Ambrosius, Bishop of Milan, who compelled the Emperor Theodosius to do penance for the murder of the people of Thessalonica, tells us in his "*de Officis*" that "All the mystery should be kept concealed, guarded by faithful silence, lest it should be inconsiderately divulged to the ears of the profane. . . . . . It is not given to all to contemplate the depths of our mysteries . . . . . that they may not be seen by those who ought not to behold them; nor received by those who cannot preserve them . . . . . He sins against God who divulges to the unworthy the mysteries confided to him. The danger is not merely in violating *truth*, but in telling truth, if he allows himself to give hints of them to those from whom they ought to be concealed. . . . . . Beware of casting pearls before swine ! . . . . . Every mystery ought to be kept secret, and as it were, to be covered over by silence, lest it should be rashly divulged to the ear of the profane."

Brother Pike, in " Morals and Dogmas," page 624, says, " In the mysteries, wherever they were practiced, was taught that truth of the primitive revelation, the existence of One Great Being, infinite and prevading the universe, who was there worshipped without superstition ; and his marvellous nature, essence and attributes taught to the initiates, while the vulgar attributed his works to secondary gods, personified and isolated from Him in fabulous independence.

" These truths were covered from the common people as with a veil, and the mysteries were carried into every country, that, without disturbing the popular beliefs, truth, the arts and the sciences might be known to those who were capable of understanding them, and maintaining the true doctrine incorrupt ; which the people, prone to superstition and idolatry, have in no age been able to do ; nor, as many strange aberrations and superstitions of the present day prove, any more now than heretofore. For we need but point to the doctrines of so many sects that degrade the Creator to the rank, and assign to Him the passions of humanity, to prove that now, as always, the old truths must be committed to a few, or they will be overlaid with fiction and error and irretrievably lost.

" Though Masonry is identical with the ancient mysteries, it is so in this qualified sense : that it presents but an imperfect image of their brilliancy ; the ruins only of their grandeur, and a system that has experienced progressive alterations, the fruits of social events and political circumstances."

Augustinus,, Bishop of Hippo, in Africa, was a celebrated writer of his age. He died in the seventy-sixth year of his age, A. D. 430. He tells us that " Having dismissed the catechumens, we have retained you only to be our hearers, because, besides those things which belong to all Christians in common, we are now to discourse to you of sublime mysteries, which none are qualified to hear, but those who by the

Master's favor are made partakers of them. . . . . . To have taught them openly would have been to betray them."

Chrysostom, a Bishop of Constantinople, died in A. D. 407, in his fifty-third year. He was a very great disciplinarian and made himself many enemies by preaching against the vices of the people. He was banished by the empress for opposing the raising of a statue to her. He was a truly good man, and in his writings says, " I wish to speak openly; but I dare not, on account of those not initiated. I shall therefore avail myself of disguised terms, discoursing in a shadowy manner. . . . . . Where the holy mysteries are celebrated we drive away all unitiated persons and then close the doors." He also informs us, respecting the acclamations of the initiated, that he " will pass them over in silence; for it is forbidden to disclose such things to the profane."

Basilius, a celebrated Bishop of Africa, was a very eloquent orator, who died in his fifty-first year, A. D. 379. He informs us that, " We receive the dogmas transmitted to us by writing and those which have descended to us from the Apostles, beneath the mysteries of oral tradition; for several things have been handed to us without writing, lest the vulgar, too familiar with our dogmas, should lose a due respect for them. . . . . . This is what the uninitiated are not permitted to contemplate, and how should it ever be proper to write and circulate among the people an account of them?"

I have made various quotations to verify my own assertions as to the mysteries having a common origin and being the original source and depository of those pure Theosophical and Philosophical truths that are to be found in all religions, all philosophies, and all science. That in every epoch of the world's history these sublime and profound teachings have always existed. I want to show the intimate relation between the esoteric truths and teachings of our own beloved Scottish Rite of Freemasonry, with the mysteries of ancient India. From this source ramified all the other mysteries, through those of the Mazdean, Egyptian, Orphic, Cabirian, Samothracian, Elusinian, Sidonian, Dionysian, Pythagorean, Druids, Christian, Basilidean, etc. Every intelligent Masonic student will recognize the connecting links between the ancient wisdom of India and the Theosophical and Philosophical esoteric teaching of Scottish Masonry; but he must not expect to find a regular, unbroken chain of evidence running down from the hoary civilization of prehistoric ages to the present day. He will be enabled to trace the links in regular interrupted lines of transmission, and though interrupted the proof of their continued existence will be most assuredly unmistakable, as the thread which connects it will mark its descent from age to age, until we find it in all its sublimity and grandeur echoing through the temples of our own beloved Scottish Rite of Masonry, as it did in those of India, in the cave temples of Mazdean Hierophants, and the temples and pyramids of ancient Egypt, back to the dawn of time. These glorious truths and teachings which illuminated the path and mind of the aspirant in the hoary ages of the past, have descended to us from the "Land of the Vedas," and it demonstrates to the Neophyte of to-day the same grand system of philosophy. The self-same teachings that were concealed in the lesser and the greater mysteries are now taught and used in this glorious rite of ours, for the same purpose and in the same manner as in the civilization of the far away past.

Ah! how magnificent and impressive must have been the ceremonies of the ancient Egyptians in their stupendous temples! What transition from sorrow to joy! Light wandering in darkness, bereft of all save Hope, and the Light of Truth, carried deep down within the heart of every man; even passing through the very shadow of death, pondering upon the threshold of the tomb, battling for very life; wandering through weary wastes of desert, seeking for Light through cavernous depths; but ever rising above *Ignorance, Tyranny and Fanaticism* into the realm of the highest degree of intellectual knowledge and perfection.

This most profound Theosophical Philosophy and science is written in symbols and veiled in such a manner, that only those Elus, Masters and Adepts, who have seen the Light, are enabled to interpret or explain the true meaning of them, as they were and are used for the purpose of concealing the profound and sublime teachings of the Ancient Wisdom, instead of revealing. In fact, as I have heretofore stated in the early part of this work, that "*Masonry is a peculiar system of Morality, veiled in Allegory and illustrated by Symbols.*" In the ancient days these allegories and symbols were most carefully guarded from the Profane, and people who had not seen the Light, were never permitted to cross the threshold of the temples, wherein was practiced the secret teachings of the ancient mysteries. Chrysostom, in his letter to Pope Innocent, informing him that on account of his opposing the empress, he excited quite a number of the people against him, who forced "their way into the most secret parts of the temple, even into the inner sanctuary, and there saw what was not proper for them to behold." But they could not have understood the meaning of the things they had seen, no more than the uninitiated could, of the symbology of our own beloved Rite. In fact, some of our Initiates themselves do not understand the meaning of many of the symbols revealed to them, simply because they are looking beyond, instead of at, what lies before them. I am very sorry to say that just as soon as our aspiring candidate receives his Morals and Dogmas, he turns on toward the end, instead of the beginning, and is thus retarded in his comprehension of the glories pertaining to our philosophy.

No one was allowed to enter the portals of the ancient mysteries for initiation who was not Just, Upright and True, and possessed of a good moral character, who had been heard of "under the tongue of good report." They did not depend entirely upon the report or reputation; but rather upon the true character of the man who sought initiation. The wise and good of all nations and peoples were allowed to enter into and receive the "Light" of initiation, irrespective of creed, caste or color, because the Universal Brotherhood of Man was one of the first things taught the Neophyte. Neither rank nor power would open the gates for initiation, to any man, unless he was found worthy and well qualified. The pre-requisite was to be, JUST, UPRIGHT AND TRUE to all men. If he was found possessed of these requisites he was permitted to cross the threshold; but before he could advance, from one degree to another, he would have to be well versed in the esoteric teachings of the preceding degrees, as well as the symbolic meaning of the various emblems presented to him for inspection. Not until he had made suitable proficiency in the lesser, was he allowed to proceed to the higher and more sublime mysteries.

The Hierophants of ancient Egypt were very careful to thoroughly investigate the character of the Aspirant before permitting him to drink from the *Sacred Fount* of Ancient Egyptian Wisdom, and when Pythagoras presented himself for initiation, he underwent the most searching investigation, before being allowed to proceed with the initiatory ceremonies. Historical records inform us that he displayed the most remarkable fortitude and incredible patience, before obtaining the privilege of searching through the profound philosophies of the Sacred Science. After having done so, like all good men who had preceded him, he began to realize the sublimity and grandeur of its profound philosophies. One of the very first things taught was that all men were Brothers, and part of the Divine Whole.

When Plutarch endeavored to attain an entrance into the ancient mysteries by initiation, the Hierophants requested him to confess every wicked act committed during the whole course of his life. These Hierophants positively knew that initiation into their mysteries would never be allowed, nor the initiatory degree conferred upon any one who could not prove themselves to be good men and true, moral and virtuous. Unless they were able to do this they were not considered worthy of the high honor, and the consequence was, the sacred portals were closed against them.

Proclus said that initiation into the mysteries was so sublime that all those who had been selected to enter into the sacred precincts should prove themselves to be virtuous. He also said that, " It drew the souls of men from a material, sensual and merely human life, to join them in communion with the Gods."

In the " Book of the Dead," Chapter 125, called " The Hall of the Two Truths," the soul, in passing through Amenti, thus addresses the Lords of Truth : " I have not afflicted any. I have not told falsehoods. I have not made the laboring man do more than his task. I have not been idle. I have not murdered. I have not committed fraud. I have not injured the images of the Gods. I have not taken scraps of the bandages of the dead. I have not committed adultery. I have not cheated by false weights." Again he goes on to confess, saying : " That he has loved God, that he has given bread to the hungry and water to the thirsty, garments to the naked and a home to the homeless." This examination, herein related, was no doubt the key to the examination which the candidate had to pass through before being accepted and allowed to pass between the columns and enter the sacred portals of the Egyptian Mysteries. We can now thoroughly understand how difficult it was to obtain admission into the Mysteries, and why it was that the Hierophant was so searching in his questions, not permitting any one to take even the initiatory degrees who were not thoroughly virtuous, free from sin and vice. Minor offences were, no doubt, purged and purified during the initiatory services by passing through certain ceremonies *and in being baptized anew, and consecrated* to RIGHT, JUSTICE AND TRUTH. But to all such applicants as Constantine, Nero, and many others, the gates of the sublime Mysteries were forever closed, on account of their awful crimes, which could not be condoned.

The principal object of initiation was to instruct and assist the Neophyte in his search for "Light." As I have previously stated, "Light" meant Wisdom, Knowledge and Information. It is that knowledge which leads us all to a comprehension of the Divine Principle, the Supreme Essence, the source of all *Life, Light and Love.* It taught the Initiate to thoroughly understand himself, and the potential forces latent within him. It also teaches him that as his moral, intellectual and spiritual nature develops he will be far better enabled to consciously know the intents and purposes of human life. In consequence of this he becomes more earnest and eager to help accomplish that purpose in his own person, by practicing LOVE AND SELFLESSNESS. In loving his neighbor as himself and giving up the avaricious, grasping desire of self gratification.

The instructions received were not only on Nature and Man; but all the various phenomena emanating from the unseen world, as well as in comprehending the Occult science. He would understand that what is seen is not the reality, but only the manifestation of the unseen, which is the reality, *The noumenon.* He was taught that the director of the Mind, the *Higher Self,* was the *true Immortal Man,* the real *I* that continually clothes itself with various personalities which live, and die, and pass away with each and every one. But, the *true man,* the Immortal "*Thinker,*" lives through all and endures for ever. "We are all of us conscious that the individual, as we see him with our eyes and perceive with our bodily senses, is not the actual personality. If he should fall dead in our presence, there would still be a body to look upon as distinctly as before. But the something has gone forth which had imparted sensibility to the nerves and impulse to the muscles. That something was the real individual. It accompanied the body, but has departed, leaving it behind." The "*He*" or "*She*" has thus given place to "*It.*"

We witness *phenomena* and may now ask to learn the *noumena.* ("A Wilder.") The "voice of *the real man* comes to him by a process as direct and swift as bodily vision, or the sense of feeling, and this voice which never deceives him is *Intuition.*"

Masonic Knowledge is the highest and most sacred deposit that has come down to us from the ancient days of Egyptian splendor and beyond. It is the most sacred and profound Wisdom of human life and experience, because it helps man to understand the presence of a mysterious and inscrutable POWER, the knowledge of which thrills him to the very centre of his being, and calls into existence the susceptibilities and faculties which appropriates knowledge gained along these lines for the upbuilding of his *Higher Self,* so that he may eventually attain to perfect wisdom and become at one with the POWER that permeates the Kosmos. There is no question in my mind but that the problem of Life was a study for the candidate as well as Death and Reincarnation.

I quite agree with Brother J. D. Buck, 32°, in his "Mystic Masonry," page 51, wherein he says: "In the Ancient Mysteries, Life presented itself to the candidate as a problem to be solved, and not as certain propositions to be memorized, and as easily forgotten. The solution of this problem constituted all genuine initiation, and at every step or 'degree' the problem expanded. As the vision of the candidate enlarged in relation to the problems and meaning of life, his powers of apprehension and assimilation also increased proportionately. This was also an evolution. It may reasonably be supposed that the lower degrees of such initiation concerned the ordinary affairs of life, *viz ;* a knowledge of the laws and processes of external nature ; the candidate's relation to these, through his physical body, and his relations on the physical plane, through his animal senses, and social instincts, to his fellow-men. These matters being learned, adjusted, Mastered ; the candidate passed to the next degree. Here he learned, theoretically, at first, the nature of the soul ; the process of its evolution, and began to unfold those finer instincts. If he was found capable of apprehending these, and kept his 'vow' in the preceding degree, he presently discovered the evolution within him of senses and falculties pertaining to the 'soul-plane.'

His progress would be instantly arrested, and his teacher would refuse all further instruction, if he was found negligent of the ordinary duties of life; those to his family, his neighbors, or his country. All these must have been fully discharged before he could stand upon the threshold as a candidate for the Greater Mysteries; for in these he became an unselfish Servant of Humanity as a whole; and had no longer the right to bestow the gifts of knowledge or power that he possessed, upon his own kinsmen, or friends, in preference to strangers. In the higher degrees, he might be precluded from using these powers even to preserve his own life. Both the Master and his Powers belong to Humanity. If the reader will but reflect for a moment, how the tantalizing Jews called upon Jesus to 'save himself and come down from the cross,' if he were the Christ, it may be seen that this doctrine of Supreme Selflessness ought, long ago, to have been better apprehended by the Christian world; for while it is a Divine Attribute, the Synonym of the Christ, it is latent in all humanity and must be evolved as herein described.

"That which makes such an evolution seem to modern readers impossible, is, that it can not be conceived as being accomplished in a single life, nor can it be. It is the result of persistent effort, guided by high ideals, through many lives. Those who deny Pre-existence may logically deny all such evolution. There must, however, come a time when all the consummation is reached in one life, and this is the logical meaning of the saying of Jesus—IT IS FINISHED."

There is no question but the Mysteries, the Ancient Wisdom, and the Scottish Rite of Freemasonry exists for the express purpose of teaching man to understand himself; the attributes of Life and its Forces; the soul and its attributes, Thought, Will, and Cognition, and Death and its meaning. It teaches us that every object in the manifested universe, even the tiniest atom that floats in the sunshine, has a soul within itself. This soul with *Matter* and *Spirit*, forms the Trinity which comprises *Unity*. It is this Soul, Energy, Force or vibration that causes every atom to float in the sunlit ray and manifests that Force by its own individual energy or motion. In fact, it is this Force within itself, which produces motion, and is contained in all bodies animate or inanimate. It is known to the Masters and Adepts as the Incarnation of the Force. This is a Universal Law.

Look around you, in every direction, and you will perceive that Force, Type, Idea, is ever changing, manifesting itself again and again in varying phases. In this way it is continually evolving into higher forms of development. Energy or Force is never annihilated, but continues its protean appearance, clothed in various garbs; yet still moving onward in its upward march, ever finding variant forms with which to express or manifest itself. The self-same law applies to all Kingdoms; but more especially to the Human Kingdom. Man being a part and parcel of the Divine Whole, cannot be separated from it no more than the tiniest grain of sand upon the sea-shore, without disturbing the Equilibrium of the Balance, and the Kosmos with it. Therefore human Energy, Force, or Soul, continually reincarnates, in order to grow and attain spiritual perfection and Wisdom, such as was reached by the Master and Adept, Jesus of Nazareth—The Christ. The *Atharva Veda* says "Nothing is commenced or ended. Everything is changed or transformed. Life and Death are only modes of transformation which rule the vital molecules, from the plant up to Brahma himself." The Atharva-veda is one of the sacred books of the Hindus and of great antiquity.

In speaking of India and her sacred writings I am reminded of the many happy years spent in that extraordinary country, studying the manners and customs of the people. I travelled from Calcutta to Bombay, not by cars alone, but by regular "Dak gharreh," and after leaving Moultan, by the steamer, down the river Indus and cars to Khurrachee, from thence by steamer to Bombay. I stopped at all the principal cities *en route* and while writing of the Ancient Mysteries and their teachings, memory carried me back to the celebrated cave temples in the immediate vicinity of Bombay, and especially to the Cave Temple of Elephanta, with its wonderful Trimurti.

"I am all in all" says the Trinitariun inscription in this ancient Temple, which is situated on the island of Elephanta, about four or five miles from Mazagong, a suburb of Bombay, where boats can be secured to take you across to the island. From the landing place up on the beach you can make the ascent by stone steps, winding their way up to the entrance, which is located about midway on the hillside from the beach. Here we found a level space fronting the entrance of the cave. On entering we found ourselves in a large hall, about one hundred and

ENTRANCE TO THE CAVE TEMPLE OF ELEPHANTA,

BOMBAY, INDIA

fifty feet long, by eighty feet wide, with four rows of very strong massive columns at regular distances, forming three avenues leading to the extreme end of the hall. The cave has been cut right into the face of the solid rock. There are halls or rooms, of much smaller dimensions, opening into the larger hall from each side of it. Very fine carvings beautify and adorn the large and massive pillars of the rock, left to support the tremendous weight of the mountain above, forming the roof. These pillars or columns are eighteen feet high, and have a majestic appearance; in fact, everything here will have a tendency to surprise the traveller and fill him with awe and admiration. The ceiling or roof is flat, with very fine imitations of architraves running from column to column. These pillars differ entirely from the variant orders of Greece and Rome, in their peculiar shape, yet such columns seem to be quite in keeping with their surroundings, and very appropriate to their function, reminding one of the more massive pillars of ancient Egypt.

I saw here a large number of carvings relative to Hindu mythology, and one chamber with the Lingham and Yoni. Another small temple had a different style of columns, the walls adorned with sculptures, while the roof and cornice were ornamented with painted mosaic patterns, still bright with various colors. But the most striking, remarkable and artistically carved figures, are situated at the extreme end of the middle row of columns, in the large hall. It is the *Trimurti*, or triune god, representing *Brahma*, Vishnu and Siva united in one body. It is eighteen feet high. These figures represent the Creator, Preserver and Destroyer—*Evolution, Involution*, and *Brahma*, the container of both— the whole surrounded by minor figures cut deep into the solid rock. This trinity represents Brahma, the incomprehensible and infinite god, the substratum of all Being, just dawning into multiple existence— permitting himself to be seen in his first conceivable form. In this trinity *Vishnu* represents the idea of *Evolution*—the process by which the inner spirit unfolds and generates the universe of sensible forms. *Siva* represents the idea *Involution*, by which the thought and the sensible universe are indrawn again into the unmanifested; and *Brahma* represents that state which is *neither Evolution nor Involution*—and yet is both—existence itself, now first brought into the region of thought through relation to Vishnu and Siva. Each figure has its hand turned

8

upwards, resting upon the base of the neck, holding an emblem: Vishnu the Lotus flower of generation, Brahma the gourd of fruition, and Siva the "good snake," *the cobra de cappello*, whose bite is certain death. The faces of Vishnu and Brahma are mild and serene, while the features of Siva are peculiarly characteristic of her destroying propensities and attributes. Siva also has the third eye—the eye of the interior vision of the universe, a vision that comes to the man who adopts the method of involution. This eye is situated in the Pineal gland and lies surrounded by the Nates, Velum Interpositum, Optic Thalmus, and the Third and Fourth Ventricle.

The ancient Egyptian and Hindu Hierophants never admitted a creation out of nothing, but, as Herbert Spencer says, " an evolution by gradual stages of the heterogeneous and differentiated, from the homogeneous and undifferentiated." No mind can comprehend the Infinite and Absolute unknown, which has no beginning and shall have no end; which is both last and first, because, whether differentiated or withdrawn into itself, it ever is. All things emanate from a single Principle, a Primal source, which is the governing Force or Energy. The Moving Power which vibrates through all and controls all is *Life, Motion, Vibration, Harmony*. It is THAT which permeates all, governing and controlling everything in the Kosmos. Manifested or Unmanifested. It ever is, it ever will be.

Albert Pike, in " Morals and Dogmas," page 517, *et seq.* says, in speaking of the doctrine of the immortality of the soul, that " Egypt and Ethiopia in these matters learned from India, where, as everywhere else, the origin of the doctrine was as remote and untraceable as the origin of man himself. Its natural expression is found in the language of Krishna, in the *Bahgavad Gita*. I myself never was non-existent, nor thou, nor these princes of the Earth; nor shall we ever hereafter cease to be. . . . The soul is not a thing of which a man may say, it hath been, or is about to be, or is to be hereafter; for it is a thing without birth; it is pre-existent, changeless, eternal, and not to be destroyed with this mortal frame. According to the dogma of antiquity, the thronging forms of life are a series of purifying migrations, through which the Divine Principle reascends to the unity of its source. Inebriated in the bowl of Dionusos, and dazzled in the mirror of existence, the souls, those fragments or sparks of Universal Intelligence, forgot their native dignity and passed into terrestrial frames they coveted. The most usual type of the spirit's descent was suggested by the sinking of the Sun and Stars from the upper to the lower hemisphere. When it arrived within the portals of the proper empire of Dionusos, the God of this World, the scene of delusion and change, its individuality became clothed in a material form, and as individual bodies were compared to a garment, the World was the investiture of the Universal Spirit.

"In the course of Nature the Soul, to recover its lost estate, must pass through a series of trials and migrations. The scene of those trials is the Grand Sanctuary of Initiation, the world. Their primary agents are the elements and Dionusos, as Sovereign of Nature, or the sensous world personified, is official Arbiter of the Mysteries, and guide of the soul, which he introduces into the body and dismisses from it. He is the Sun, that liberator of the elements, and his spiritual mediation was suggested by the same imagery which made the zodiac the supposed path of the spirits in their descent and their return, and Cancer and Capricorn the gates through which they passed.

"Thus the scientific theories of the ancients expounded in the mysteries, as to the origin of the soul, its descent, its sojourn here below, and its return, were not a mere barren contemplation of the nature of the world, and about the soul, but a study of the means for arriving at the great object proposed—the perfecting of the soul; and as a necessary consequence, that of morals and society. This earth to them was not the soul's home, but its place of exile. Heaven was its home, and there was its birthplace. To it, it ought incessantly to turn its eyes. Man was not a terrestrial plant. His roots were in Heaven. The soul had lost its wings, clogged by the viscosity of matter. It would recover them when it extricated itself from matter and commenced its upward flight.

"Matter being in their view, as it was in that of St. Paul, the principle of all the passions that trouble reason, mislead the intelligence, and stain the purity of the soul, the Mysteries taught man how to enfeeble the action of the matter on the soul, and to restore to the latter its natural dominion, and that the stains so contracted should continue after death, lustrations were used, fastings, expiations, macerations, continence, and above all, initiations. Many of these practices were at first merely symbolical,—Material signs indicating the moral purity required of the initiates, but they afterwards came to be regarded as actual productive causes of that purity.

"The effect of initiation was meant to be the same as that of philosophy, to purify the soul of its passions, to weaken the empire of the body over the Divine portion of man, and to give him here below a happiness anticipatory of the felicity to be one day enjoyed by him, and of the future vision by him of the Divine Beings. And therefore Proclus and the other Platonists taught—'that the mysteries and initiations withdrew souls from this mortal and material life, to re-unite them to the gods, and dissipated for the adepts the shades of ignorance by the splendors of the Deity.' Such were the precious fruits of the last degree of the Mystic Science—to see Nature in her springs and sources, and to become familiar with the causes of things and with real existences.

"Cicero tells us that 'The soul must exercise itself in the practice of the virtues, if it would speedily return to its place of origin. It should, while imprisoned in the body, free itself therefrom by the contemplation of superior beings, and in some sort be divorced from the body and the senses. Those who remain enslaved, subjugated by their passions, and violating the sacred laws of religion and society will reascend to Heaven, only after they shall have been purified through a long succession of ages. The initiate was required to emancipate himself from his passions, and to free himself from the hindrances of the senses of matter, in order that he might rise to the contemplation of the Deity, or of that incorporeal and unchanging light in which live and subsist the causes of created natures.' Porphyry distinctly informs us that we must 'flee from everything sensual, that the soul may with ease reunite itself with God, and live happily with Him.'

"The object and aim of Initiation, Hierocles tells us, is 'To recall the soul to what is truly good and beautiful, and make it familiar therewith, and they its own. To deliver it from the pains and ills it endures here below, enchained in matter, as in a dark prison; to facilitate its return to the celestial splendors and to establish it in the fortunate isles by restoring it to its first estate. Thereby, when the hour of death arrives, the soul, freed from its mortal garmenting, which it leaves behind it, as a legacy to earth, will rise buoyantly to its home among the Stars, there to retake its ancient condition, and approach toward the Divine nature as far as man may do.' "

This evolution of the soul has ever been a source of study in all ages and through all time. It is one of the most profound and sublime problems handed down to us from the Ancient Mysteries of India. It requires deep and earnest meditation on the part of the Initiate, in order that he may be enabled to trace *it* through variant molecular forms, to states of consciousness in the mind of man. Of course there is a consciousness in all things, and this consciousness varies in all the varying forms in the Kosmos. In tracing it through the various kingdoms, so as to come to an understanding of consciousness, we must carefully note that before plant life could exist upon the face of the earth the very *Rocks and Stones* would have to disintegrate, surrendering their lives for the purpose of building up higher forms to a higher grade or plane of intelligence, for though we may not recognize it, there is a consciousness hid deep within their stony covering. Everything in the Kosmos, throughout all kingdoms, is conscious, *i. e.*, dowered with a consciousness peculiarly its own, and on its own plane of perception. We must not say that there is no consciousness in either mineral or vegetable, because we are unable to perceive any. "There is no such thing as *dead* or *blind* matter, as there is no blind or unconscious law." By the disintegration of the molecular form of the mineral, life leaps forth into a higher stage of development, awakening to a new birth, a new revelation, and a new vibration of harmony fitted to its new conditions, rejoicing in its freedom, thus demonstrating the first evolution and the first law of self-sacrifice. Before this disintegration of the *Rock* or *Stone* we may not cognize either sound or motion within its stony heart; because, it is, as it were, sleeping, lying dormant, awaiting the magic touch of Dionusos to transform it into a higher form, and possibly into a different kingdom; for out of the very dust of the earth comes man himself, the head of the animal kingdom, and from the very self same *stuff* comes plant-life in the vegetable kingdom, with consciousness and feeling more fully developed. No one can deny this fact!

Do you mean to tell me that in plucking a rose from its bush it suffers no pain? Do you not see the very life-blood of the plant ooze forth from the fracture? Because *you* do not see any signs of consciousness, does that prove that it has none? I tell you, my dear Brother and readers, all nature pulses with *Life* and *Consciousness*, and each form manifests as much of the *One Life* as it is capable of expressing. What is Man that he can despise the more limited manifestations, when he compares himself, as life expression, to that which soars above him in infinite heights of being, which he can estimate still less than the rose can estimate him.

Every flower that blooms, every plant or blade of grass that lifts itself into light and sunshine, has its degree of intelligence. Intelligence is as common as the atmosphere itself, and the only difference is, some forms have more life than others. Spirit precedes time and space, builds its own structure, and makes its own environment. The unity is so unbroken that the tiniest gnat carries on its back the key to the universe. Life, traced to its lowest forms, always discloses unity, whether in the stone. the clod of earth, the growing tree, a herd of animals, or a host of men, it is the same gift. The universe is a single expression of that unity.

Every star and planet that glitters in the starry vault above is a ball of dirt like the earth. The sun has no fuel that our earth cannot duplicate; neither can Saturn, Jupiter or Uranus impose upon us with any airs of superiority. A drop of water and a drop of human blood have their origin in the same corpuscle. The fungus and the oak on which it grows; the animalcule and the scientist who studies it are alike. From out the slime and filth of the cesspool comes forth the lily in all its purity and splendor. Out from the refuse of the stable comes the blush of the rose and its fragrance. Filth and fertility are the same word. So we climb the evolving ladder, from the rock, dust, plant, animal, to man. Out of the lowliest forms man has come to be something and he will come to be much more. He is at the end of a long series of forms, through whose natural gradations he has passed, each stage of which has been toward a higher transformation. Evolution has forced him up a long ascending way, and still pushes him on; for he is yet bound to the soil, from whence his body came, much earthly matter loading him down and binding him fast to earth-life through his animal nature. In this present stage of evolution we are but human animals, parading as men.

Much of the human structure is a legacy from inferior organisms, which, in our next advent, we shall make superfluous. Such are some of the esoteric teachings of the Ancient Mysteries. Such thoughts have existed from time immemorial, and such thoughts the human mind still speculates upon, for they have come down to us from the "Land of Gobi," the land of ancient wisdom whose Hierophants ever strived to place their Brothers upon the *path* that led on to a knowledge of BIRTH, LIFE, DEATH, and THE EVOLUTION OF THE SOUL.

BIRTH is the emerging or coming forth from the unmanifested into a higher plane of spiritual unfoldment where experience is gained through suffering and pain, where Man is refined like gold in the crucible. LIFE is a battle to be fought by Man, a battle of the spiritual against the Material and Sensual, or in other words it is a battle that is continually going on between his lower animal passional nature and his Higher Spiritual Self. DEATH is a transformation, a disintegration of molecular form, or a return to the unmanifested universe. The teachings of the Sacred Mysteries inform us that "The SOUL of Man is Immortal; and not the result of organization, nor an aggregate of modes of action of matter, nor a succession of phenomena and perceptions; but an *Existence*, one and identical, a living spirit, a spark of the Great Central Light, that hath entered into and dwells in the body; to be separated therefrom at death, and return to God who gave it; that doth not disperse or vanish at death, like breath or a smoke, nor can be annihilated; but still exists and possesses activity and intelligence, even as it existed in God before it was enveloped in the body.

Suez Canal—The Druses, their Manners and Customs.

Ships are now passing from sea to sea,

    Midst a waste, of the desert sand;

As in the days of the Great Seti,

    When this Pharaoh ruled the land.

122

CHAPTER VI.

SUEZ CANAL—THE DRUSES, THEIR MANNERS AND CUSTOMS.

IN the opening of the third chapter the attention of my readers was called to the absurdity of giving to certain men the credit of being the promoters and inventors of the early sciences, and demonstrated my reasons for so doing. The same may be said of the cutting of the canal across the Isthmus of Suez; it is the height of absurdity to give Napoleon credit for having been the first to conceive the idea of the project, or the French people, or any other modern source, for the simple reason that it had been under contemplation fully thirty-four centuries ago. In fact, we have proof positive that the two seas were connected by a canal or waterway long centuries before Christ; consequently the work commenced and completed by M. de Lesseps, in cutting a canal between the Mediterranean and Red Seas, was no new idea, but rather the completion of a scheme that had been in existence in the days of Rameses the Great. Still I do not wish to detract, in any way, from the great work as completed by this celebrated engineer in the year 1869. I simply wish to state that what he, and the workmen under him, accomplished in connecting the two seas was an old idea, and that the thought of constructing such a waterway or canal did not originate in the nineteenth century. It had already been accomplished in the hoary ages of the past, in the Golden Age of Egyptian splendor.

The principal and most important idea in the construction of the Suez Canal was, first to find the place where the waters of the Mediterranean were the deepest and nearest to the coast of Egypt. After this was done, to establish a starting point from that place and make it a point of operation. Then to build a town, as close to this point as possible, and establish there immense workshops and dwellings for the men engaged in the work of cutting a canal from sea to sea, through which ships might be enabled to pass with little or no difficulty or danger.

There is no question that M. de Lesseps carefully matured his plans as to the mode of procedure in constructing this maritime canal. It was a great responsibility to undertake such an immense piece of work, but M. de Lesseps was just the man needed. When Mahommed Said Pasha became Viceroy of Egypt, in 1854, he used his utmost endeavors to carry on the work so ably planned by his father, Mohammed Ali. He sent for M. de Lesseps in order to consult him upon the possibility of constructing a canal across the isthmus, and the best way to proceed about it. The result of this interview was that a commission was signed and given to M. de Lesseps, authorizing him to organize a company. The said company was to be known as "The Universal Suez Canal Company," for the express purpose of raising funds and pushing the preliminary work as rapidly as possible; but there were many things which deferred the commencement of the work.

In 1856 an International Commission had been organized, with representatives from England, France, Prussia, Austria, the Netherlands, and Spain. This Commission modified the previous arrangements made, by altering the line originally chosen to one a little farther north, so as to reach a place where the deep waters of the Mediterranean came closer to land. Locks were done away with, and the breakwaters, or jetties at each end of the canal, were slightly changed. A fresh water canal from Bulak, to convey water for the use of the workmen was agreed upon, and other minor details settled. The details dragged along slowly, and M. de Lesseps was anxious to commence operations; but various obstacles held him back and compelled him to "wait and hope." On the 25th day of April, in the year 1859, a small ditch was cut in the sandy spit that separates the waters of the Mediterranean from Lake Menzala. This work was performed in the presence of M. de Lesseps and four directors of the Company, and may be claimed as the first formal commencement of the great work. The surveying and selection of the site, as well as marking the place for the work to begin, as planned and laid out by M. de Lessep, was performed by M. Laroche.

Let me here quote from Murray, rather than depend upon my notes (page 287): "From the mouth of the Damietta branch of the Nile to the Gulf of Pelusium there stretches a low belt of sand, varying in width from two hundred to three hundred yards, serving to separate the Mediterranean from the waters of Lake Menzala; though often, when the lake is full and the waves of the Mediterranean are high, the two meet across the slight boundary line. In the beginning of the month of April, 1859, a small body of men, who might well be called the pioneers of the Suez Canal, headed by M. Laroche, landed at that spot of the narrow sandy slip, which had been chosen as the starting point of the canal from the Mediterranean, and the site of the city and port intended ultimately to rival Alexandria. It owed its selection, not to its being the spot from which the shortest line could be drawn—that would have been the Gulf of Pelusium—but to its being that point of the coast to which deep water appproached the nearest. There eight metres of water, equal to about twenty-six feet, the contemplated depth of the canal, were found at a distance of less than two miles. At the Gulf of Pelusium that depth only existed at more than five miles from the coast. The spot was called Port Said, in honor of the then Viceroy. On the 25th of April, M. de Lesseps, surrounded by ten or fifteen Europeans and some one hundred native workmen, gave the first stroke of the spade to the future Bosphorus between Asia and Africa. Hard, indeed, must have been the life of the first workers on this desolate strip of sand. The nearest place from which fresh water could be procured was Damietta, a distance of thirty-six miles. It was brought thence across Lake Menzala in Arab boats, but calms or storms often delayed the arrival of the looked for store; sometimes, indeed, it was altogether lost and the powers of endurance of the little band were sorely tried. After a time distilling machines were put up, and, in 1863, water was received through pipes from the Fresh Water Canal which had been completed to the centre of the Isthmus."

The town of Port Said unquestionably owes its origin to the construction of the Suez Canal. It is located at the entrance end of a small island, belonging to that narrow strip of sandy beach which separates Lake Menzala from the Mediterranean Sea. It has been laid out with fine broad streets and handsome brick buildings. There is nothing to interest the tourist or student in the town itself, excepting its remarkable growth from an insignificant sand spit, to a city of over forty thousand inhabitants, and the largest coaling station in the world. But the immense amount of laborious dredging necessary before laying the foundation is simply inexpressible. The town soon became a regular manufacturing and repairing workshop, as it were, with machinery running day and night. Mechanics of all kinds were continually employed, some in laying the foundation of the rising city, others making the enormous stones for the jetties, carpenters and builders putting up houses, while hundreds of men were engaged in the construction of the harbors and basins. All was bustle and work, resulting in a city of about forty thousand in less than forty years, with beautiful hotels, mosques, hospitals, churches, dwelling houses; in fact, all the adjuncts of a modern sea port. In the construction of this canal they used some of the most extraordinary dredges ever known. In order that you, my dear brothers and readers, may be enabled to understand something about them and their value in the construction, I will quote you from Murray, page 284: "First among them was the *long couloir* (long duct), an iron spout of semi-elliptical form, two hundred and thirty feet long, five and one-half wide, and two deep; by means of which a dredger, working in the centre of the channel, could discharge its contents beyond the bank. This enormous spout was supported on an iron framework, which rested partly on the dredge and partly on a floating lighter. The dredgings, when dropped into the upper end of this spout, were assisted in their progress down it, by water supplied by a rotary pump, and by an endless chain, to which were fixed scrapers—large pieces of wood that fitted the inside of the spout and forced on pieces of stone and clay. By these means the spouts could deliver their dredgings at almost a horizontal line, and the water had the further good effect of reducing the dredgings to a semi-liquid condition, thus causing them to spread themselves over a larger surface, and settle down better. The work done by these long spouted dredges was extraordinary; eighty thousand cubic yards of soil a month was the average, but as much as one hundred and twenty thousand was sometimes accomplished. When the banks were too high for the long spouts to be used, another ingenious machine called an *élévateur*, was introduced. This consisted of an inclined plane, running upwards from over the water line, and supported on an iron frame, the lower part of which rested over the water, on a steam float, and the upper part on a platform, moving on rails along the bank. The plane carried a tramway, along which ran an axle on wheels, worked by the engine of the steam float. From this axle hung four chains. As soon as a lighter containing seven huge boxes filled with dredgings was towed under the lower part of this *élévateur*, the chains hanging from the axle were hooked to one of the boxes, and the machine being set in motion the box was first raised, and then carried along swinging beneath the axle to the top of the plane; then by a self-acting contrivance, it tilted over and emptied its contents over the bank. It was then run down again, dropped into its place in the lighter, and the operation repeated with the next box. No such dredging operations had ever been undertaken before."

The harbor of Port Said has an area of about five hundred and seventy acres, with an average depth of twenty-seven feet, the entrance to which is protected by two very strong and substantial stone piers. The one on the East running out into the sea in a northerly direction for fully a mile, while the one on the West extends into the sea in a north-easterly direction for about one mile and a half. Where these piers start from the land, they are seven hundred and twenty fathoms apart, but they approach each other, at their extremities, to about three hundred and eighty-five fathoms. There is a channel or entrance ranging from fifty to eighty fathoms wide, that is well marked and buoyed. These buoys are lit up at night so as to direct the pilot in the course he should take in his passage with vessels going into or out of the harbor. The lighthouse stands on the low sandy spit, that I have already referred to, which separates the Mediterranean from Lake Menzala. It is built of concrete fully one hundred and seventy-six feet high. It is furnished with electric lights that are distinctly visible at a distance of twenty-four miles at sea. It is a flash light that flashes every twenty seconds.

I do not wish to dwell upon the town of Port Said, or to give a full account of the moles and harbor, or the towns that sprang into existence through the construction of this remarkable canal, one of the grandest, if not the greatest piece of work ever performed during the wonderful nineteenth century—connecting the Red with the Mediterranean Sea at the enormous outlay of about eight hundred and fifty million dollars, up to the opening of the canal, on the seventeenth day of November, 1869. The canal was not entirely completed at that date, as it only had about nineteen to twenty feet of water in it, allowing only light draft ships to pass through, those drawing not over eighteen feet of water. At the present writing, however, there is an average depth of twenty-seven feet nine inches, from Port Said to the Red Sea, thus enabling vessels of large draft to pass safely through its entire length of one hundred miles, without difficulty or danger. The average width of this canal is two hundred and fifty-nine feet. But in some of the deep cuttings the width is only about one hundred and ninety feet wide on the water line, while in other places, where the banks are low, the water line is fully three hundred and twenty-eight feet, thus making the average width of the canal two hundred and fifty-nine feet.

The passage through the canal saves, on the voyage from England to Bombay, nearly five thousand miles, and from New York to the same place, there is a saving of about three thousand six hundred miles in distance, and possibly three weeks in time. As I previously stated, the scheme of connecting the two seas was no new idea, originating in the nineteenth century. It had been under contemplation long centuries before Christ; for it is recorded by Aristotle, Strabo and many other historians that Rameses II. cut a canal between the sea and the river Nile, B. C. 1340.

Wilkinson in his "Ancient Egyptians," Volume I, page 74, *et seq.*, quoting Herodotus, says, " Sesostris (Rameses) fitted out a fleet of war ships that went beyond the Red Sea, invading India." He supposes that Rameses II. was the first of the Egyptian monarchs who built ships of war, although he admits that they may have been used at a much earlier period. He also says, "And we may reasonably conclude the fleet to have been connected with the Indian trade, as well as the canal he cut from the Nile, to what is now called the Gulf of Suez. This canal commenced about twelve miles to the north-east of the modern town of Belbys, called by the Romans *Bubastis Agria*, although Strabo claims that it started from the village of Thecansa, not far from Pithom. After flowing in a direction nearly East for about thirty-three miles, it

SHIPS PASSING THROUGH THE SUEZ CANAL.

turned to South-southeast, and continued about sixty-three more in that line to the extremity of the Arabian Gulf."

Again he says although the old channel is " filled with sand its direction is still easily traced, as well from the appearance of its channel as from the mounds and vestiges of ancient towns upon its banks, in one of which I found a monument bearing the sculpture and name of Rameses II.; the more satisfactory, as being a strong proof of its having existed at least as early as the reign of that monarch.

"After the time of the Ptolemies and Cæsars it was again neglected and suffered to go to decay; but on the revival of trade with India, this line of communication, from the Red Sea to the Nile, was once more proposed, the canal was re-opened by the Caliphs, and it continued to be used and kept in repair till the commerce of Alexandria was ruined by the discovery of the passage around the Cape."

Notwithstanding this account there are other historians who claim that the work was done a century earlier by Seti, the father of Rameses, and they bring forward as evidence the scene on the outside of the North wall of the temple of Karnak in which he is said to have made his triumphant return from Asia by way of *Ta-tenat.*

Seti, the father of Rameses II., was the Pharaoh under whom Joseph served as governor, and history positively informs us that Joseph introduced a system of irrigation into Egypt, by cutting canals from the river Nile to various parts of the desert, thus bringing under cultivation an enormous amount of land, which had long lain waste, barren, and desolate. Therefore, possibly, from the cutting of these canals for irrigating purposes, Seti, or his son Rameses, might have conceived the idea of connecting the two seas by constructing a canal from the Red Sea to the Nile, and thus operate their ships during war, to transport their warriors to all parts of Asia in time of need.

According to Herodotus, Book II, Chap. 158, Necho (who is spoken of in the second book of Kings), reconstructed this canal, but sacrificed one hundred and twenty thousand men during the performance of the work. He only desisted from his operations on account of a warning received from an Oracle, which stated " *that he was laboring for the barbarian.*" This prophecy has been fulfilled, or verified, in our day, the canal now being used solely by barbarians for the express purpose

9

of sending their ships from Port Said to the Red Sea, and *vice versa*. By this route they are enabled to save much time going to India, etc., over the journey around the " Cape of Good Hope." The Egyptians called all men barbarians who lived above the first cataract, or spoke a different language from their own.

This canal was commenced by Necho, B. C. 610, at a considerable distance north of Suez, and it wound its way along in a north-westerly direction, until it reached and tapped the river Nile at the city of Bubastis, through the Pelusiac branch, near Zaqaziq. The length of this canal, according to Pliny, was about sixty-two Roman miles, or fifty-seven of ours. When Herodotus gives the length of one hundred and fourteen miles to this canal he must have included the distance from sea to sea, as by carefully examining the line from its start, and following the sinuosities of its course through the valley to the site of Bubastis, we shall find that Pliny's account will agree with our own measurements.

Necho, no doubt, constructed this canal for the purpose of saving the immense labor and trouble of transporting men and munitions of war across the desert. Seeing parts of the old canal of Seti or Rameses, no doubt first gave him the idea of making a waterway across the isthmus. The fact of there having been one, naturally suggested the idea to Necho of reopening it, or of making another, which work he most assuredly accomplished, for history informs us that he sent a fleet of ships to circumnavigate Africa, a feat which was accomplished in three years. Those making the voyage sailed from Egypt into the Southern Ocean, but stopped whenever and wherever they desired. It is specially mentioned that they went on shore at one place and planted a crop of corn, camping there and waiting for it to grow and ripen, and they harvested it before continuing their voyage around Africa. In this way they lost an immense amount of time.

When the Persians conquered Egypt, under Cambyses, B. C. 525, the canal was found to be no longer navigable, and it remained so until Darius I., in B. C. 520, re-opened it and restored it to its natural channel. He had the interest of this country at heart, consequently everything in his power was done to promote the commercial welfare of the country and the interests of the people. As the centuries rolled along it again became obstructed, by sand drifting in from the desert and filling it up in many places along its entire length ; but was opened up once more by the Emperor Trajan, during the latter part of the first century A. D., or the beginning of our present era. He cleared out the old canal and made it navigable; but started his work from a different place, and cut a canal to join the old one, which was at a point above Cairo, called Amnis Trajanus.

From this period the canal seems to have remained open until the country was dominated by the Arab Caliphs, when it was closed again, in order to prevent supplies being sent to the rebels in Medina. It was filled up by order of El-Mansur, brother of Abbas, the second Caliph of the Abbaside Dynasty, and remained closed until it was once more cleaned out, by order of El-Hakem in the year A. D. 1,000.

This Caliph was the third of the Fatimide Dynasty, the founder of the sect called the Druses, and a persecutor of the Christians. He believed himself to be an incarnation of the Deity. He was assassinated at the instigation of his sister. From this time nothing was done to the canal to keep it in repair, and consequently through sheer neglect it soon became choked and unnavigable. When cutting the canal was first talked of, and M. de Lesseps was trying to raise funds for the work, the nations ridiculed and scoffed at the idea, and none more so than the British. On its completion England recognized the full value of the canal, and was the first to profit by it. Seeing the immense advantage to be derived in controlling the canal, she purchased from the Khedive his interest in that wonderful piece of work, and to-day is enabled to keep in rapid communication with her India and China colonies, also reaping an enormous profit from her investment in this most magnificent water-course—the Suez Canal.

I mentioned above that El-Hakem was the founder of the sect or society known as the Druses, and thinking that it would be of some interest to you, my dear Brothers and readers, I shall give you quite a lengthy account of these very remarkable people, quoting fully from various able authorities, the first of which will be from the work of C. W. Heckethorn's " Secret Societies," Book IV, volume 1, page 126, wherein he says, in his remarks concerning the Druses, that: " Their sect may be said to date its rise from the supposed incarnation of God in Hakem Bamr Allah, publicly announced at Cairo in A. D. 1020."

This Hakem was the sixth Caliph of Egypt, and Darazi, his confessor, took an active part in promoting the imposture, which, however, was at first so badly received that he was compelled to take refuge in the deserts of the Lebanon, where, receiving liberal pecuniary support from Hakem, he found hearers among the Arabs and soon made converts. According to other accounts, Darazi was killed for preaching his doctrine, and thus became the first martyr to the new religion. A footing thus gained, correspondence was opened with Egypt, and Hamze, a Persian Mystic, and Vizier of Hakem, who had from the first been a zealous supporter of Hakem's divinity, hastened to avail himself of the favorable opening. Ten years did not elapse before the two clever rogues, or fiery fanatics, had converted nearly all the Arab tribes inhabiting the Lebanon, while one portion of them were set apart and initiated into the mysteries of the doctrines of Hamze. But he did not give his name to the sect. By a natural etymology the disciples of *Darazi*, the first teacher, obtained the name Druses, though they reject it and call themselves Unitarians. We may thus look upon the Fatimide Caliph Hakem, the Persian Hamze, and the Turk Darazi as the founders of the Druse system, Hakem being its political founder, Hamze its intellectual framer, and Darazi its expositor and propagator.

"'*Religious books of the Druses.*'—Hamze associated with himself four assistants, to whom, as well as to himself, he gave high-sounding names. He called himself, for instance, Universal Reason, the Centre, Messiah of Nations, Jesus United, *i. e.*, he who is ever united with God. He had, moreover, one hundred and fifty-nine disciples, who went about preaching. The Druses call their religious books, 'The Sittings of the Rulers, and Their Learned Men,' comprised in six volumes. The first has the title, 'The Diploma;' the second, 'The Reputation;' the third, 'The Awakening;' the fourth, 'The First of the Seven Parts;' the fifth, 'The Staircase,' and the sixth, 'The Reproaches.' In 1817 the Druses obtained a seventh volume from a Christian, who alleged to have found it in an Egyptian school, and which they call 'The Book of the Greeks.'

"The '*Murder of Hakem.*'—Hakem was one of the most cruel monsters on record, a Saracen Nero. Amidst carnage, and the most revolting persecutions, he spread his doctrine. But in Egypt, where he resided, his heresy outraged the true believers and his savagery the whole people. Sitt-El-Mulk, his own sister, headed the malcontents and one evening, when, according to his custom, he took his ride on a white ass, she caused him to be assassinated by some trusty followers, who having despatched him with their daggers, undressed him, and securely concealed the naked body. They then carefully fastened up his clothes again, by order of his sister, who did not wish the belief in his divinity to be destroyed. At last when the Caliph did not return and those sent to look for him returned with the news that they had found his clothes, but not his body, it was said that Hakem had simply rendered himself invisible, to test the faith of his followers, and to punish apostates on his return. And the Druses, to explain the miracle, say that Hakem possessed a body of more subtle substance than the usual human body, and could go forth out of his clothes without opening or tearing them. The dagger cuts in them are explained away as mysterious indications of certain purposes of the Deity.

" '*Hakem's Successors.*'—Hakem left two sons, but the sect did not acknowledge them as such. Ali Ess Ssahir, who succeeded his father as Caliph, is reported to have said to Hamze, 'Worship me as you worshipped my father;' but Hamze replied, 'Our Lord, who be praised, neither begat nor was he begotten.' Ali replied, 'Then I and my brother are illegitimate?' Hamze answered, 'You have said it, and borne testimony against yourself.' Thereupon the enraged Ali ordered the wholesale murder of the Unitarians, unless they returned to the Moslem faith. Those who refused were either slain or fled to Syria to their co-religionists. Ali, to conciliate the people who had, by his father's despotism and oppression, been greatly embittered against his dynasty, gave up all title to divine honors and the rights it implied.

" '*Doctrines.*'—The Druses believe in the transmigration of souls; but probably it is merely a figure, as it was to the Pythagoreans. Hakem is their prophet, and they have seven commandments, religious and moral. The first of these is veracity, by which is understood faith in the Unitarian religion they profess and abhorrence of that lie which is called polytheism, incredulity, error. To a brother, perfect truth and confidence are due; but it is allowable, nay, a duty, to be false toward men of another creed. The Sect is divided into three degress : *Profane*, *Aspirants* and *Wise*. A Druse who has entered the second may return to the first degree, but incurs death if he reveals what he has learned. In their secret meetings they are supposed to worship a calf's head ; but as their religious books are full of denunciations against idolatry, and as they also compare Judaism, Christianity and Mohammedanism to a calf, it is more probable that this effigy represents the principle of falsehood and evil, Iblis, the rival of Hakem. The Druses have also been accused of licentious orgies, and are said by Baspier in his ' Remarks on Recant ' (an English diplomatist), to marry their own daughters ; but according to the evidence of resident Christians, a young Druse as soon as he is initiated, gives up all dissolute habits and becomes, at least in appearance, quite another man, meriting, as in other initiations, the title of ' new born.' The initiated are known by the appellation of Ockals, and form a kind of priesthood in the midst of the general population.

"According to their traditions, the world was at the appearance of God, in the form of Hakem, three thousand four hundred and thirty million years old, and they believe, like the Chiliast of England and America that the Millennium is almost at hand. The Wise often retire into hermitages, whereby they acquire great honor and influence. When discoursing with a Mohammedan, the Druses profess to be of the same creed ; when talking with a Christian, they are Christians. They defend this deception by alleging that it is not lawful to reveal any dogma of their creed to a ' Black ' or unbeliever; and their secrecy with regard to their religion has led them to adopt signs and passwords, such as are in use among Free Masons and other secret societies. When in doubt whether a stranger with whom they conversed belonged to their sect, they would ask, ' Do people in your part of the country sow balm seed ?' If the other replied, ' Yes, it is sown in the hearts of the faithful,' he probably was a co-religionist; but he might be an Aspirant only, and therefore would question him further, as to some of the secret dogmas ; if he did not understand the drift of their questions, they would know that he was not initiated into the higher grades. But their signs and test words and phrases had frequently to be changed. their import having been discovered by the Blacks, which happened especially when the extensive hermit village of Bajjado, near Chasbai, was destroyed in 1838 by the troops of Ibrahim Pasha, and the sacred books of the Druses made publicly known.

"'*Customs of the Druses.*'—Every village has its meeting-houses, where religious and political affairs are discussed every Thursday night, the Wise men and women attending. The resolutions passed at such meetings are communicated to the district meetings, held in the chief village of every district, which again report to the general assembly in the town of Baklin on Mount Lebanon. This was the fortified seat of government until, in the last century, Deir El-Kammar (the moon monastery) was built as the Lebanon metropolis. At the general assembly the questions raised at the district meetings are discussed, and the deputies from the different villages who have attended, on their return home, announce the decisions arrived at; so that the Druses, in fact, have a regular family council to which, however, the Wise are only admitted, the uninitiated never being consulted on political or social matters. The civil government of the Druses is in the hands of the Sheiks, who again are subject to the Emir or Prince of Lebanon.

"They are warlike and industrious, and two traits in their character deserve notice and commendation; they refuse to give up any man who has sought refuge among them, and detest the European tall hat which they compare to a 'cooking pot,' and laugh at it. In the days when Burkhardt visited them, one of their maledictions was, 'May God put a hat on you!' The number of Druses does not exceed fifty or sixty thousand, exclusively occupying, in the Lebanon, upwards of forty large towns and villages, and nearly two hundred and thirty villages with a mixed population of Druses and Christians, whilst in the anti-Lebanon, they are also possessed of nearly eighty exclusively Druse villages."

In giving this account of the Druses I felt that it would deeply interest all Masons and students, because, whenever they go forth into those Eastern countries, or come in contact with the wandering Arabs of the desert, the descendants of Hagar and Ishmael, who went forth into the desert with a "jug of water and a loaf of bread," will recognize the similarity between their teachings and our own. Many of their signs are an exoteric recognition, as all may see them, though all who see them may not understand them. But, it is a positive fact that many of these people recognize a brother without either sign or word.

The Druses, like all other secret societies of antiquity, were not formed for political purposes, but more expressly for the better understanding of Man and Nature. Their teachings embraced the most profound philosophies, all arts, science and religion, and in coming to an understanding of these sublime teachings every one began to realize that they were receiving their *true* wages, "LIGHT," POWER and WISDOM. Then they would be enabled to travel in foreign countries, and receive and appreciate a "Master's Wages."

Ragon says in his "*Cours Philosophique de Initiations Anciennes et Modern,*" page 171: "That our Blue Lodge degrees demonstrate the following subjects to the initiate and Mason: 1st. The history of the human race, classified by epochs. 2d. The history of Civilization and of the progress of the human Mind in the Arts and Sciences, as produced by the Ancient Mysteries. 3d. The knowledge of Nature or the knowledge of the Divinity, manifested in his works and of all religions."

Brother W. H. Kingsbury in the "Trestle Board," Vol. IX, page 244, *et seq.,* in speaking of Brother Rawson's late travels through Arabia, Palestine and Syria, where he had especially investigated Masonry as practiced by the Druses, says: "The Master represents the unknown, the unseen, the all-powerful, and sits in the place of honor, whence he delivers his orders to his assistants, who are appointed at the time of meeting. The candidate is prepared—partly clothed—and after a strict examination, under the direction of the Master, is led before him screened from the assembly by a veil or shawl, held up by two brothers. The usual requirements as to age, free birth and free will are made, and also touching his general knowledge of men and things, as in the case of a literary degree among us. Not a word is said about religious faith or creed, not even as to belief in Deity. It is presumed that all rational men have consciousness of a Supreme existence, whether or not it is defined in words or symbols. The very word Allah (God) is an exotic in Arabia. The Bedouin idealizes the race, and imagines it personified into what he calls the '*Abram,*' the Great Father, usually written among us '*Abraham,*' from whom are derived all living men, and to whom they all return at death. The only world of being they know is the present, and the only things worth notice are those relating to Man. Their

Masonry is, therefore, a means of securing a better life here, without any reference to any other, past or future.

"The idea of collective man (humanity) is very ancient and its teachings are simple; that man was derived from the great source; that he returns to the same and that it is his duty to make life as important as possible; first for himself, which means with the Arab a discharge of duty to others for the sake of its return to himself. The will of the Sheikh (Master) is the law of the Lodge, but the will of the Master must be guided by the ancient law, which is invariable and inevitable. The teachings of the Lodge enlightens the conscience and lifts the neophyte above himself into a prevision of motives, the only sure guarantee of morals.

"The notion, which has grown into a belief, that an injury done to any member of the race will reflect upon any doer of the deed, not as an accident, but as a necessity of law, is a law of nature. Learning chiefly through observation, the Arab sees in the frequent exercise of the will of the Sheikh an apparent check or interference with the law of nature; but experience teaches him, through more careful observation, that the law invariably re-asserts itself. The Abraham is the ideal of excellence in human life, the type that the initiate is instructed to imitate in the daily walk of life. The esoteric work of the Lodge would be out of place here and intelligible to only a few initiates. A general idea, therefore, of the objects or purpose of the Lodge will be more acceptable to the reader.

"There is no Masonic literature in Arabic beyond the walls of the coast cities, and there is no true Masonry in those cities. The ritual, the whole framework of the craft in the cities, has become Europeanized, more or less, according to the locality, as having been the abode of merchants and others from Europe. The true Arab Mason never records anything except in memory. There can be no paper brother among them, no book Mason, and to advance the neophyte must have obtained from authorized sources.

"Masonry in the desert is the privilege of the few. None but the choicest men are admitted to the charmed circle. To a stranger in such a country, Masonic knowledge is an unqualified passport and introduction. An interesting feature of the craft is this: When one proposes a journey through a disturbed and dangerous country or district, some trusty brother is selected to whom the traveller is delivered, and the Masonic tie is renewed between them, when the guardian becomes responsible for his ward, life for life. This custom never fails of commanding respect, even between hostile tribes, except the traveller be guilty of shedding blood not in self defence. The protection of women and children is an obligation that is never neglected. Any shortcoming in this matter would heap dishonor on the head of the erring one.

"Literature has changed the character of our craft in so many points that careful study is required to ascertain the ancient meaning and practice, and even the closest application sometimes fails in tracing an ancient origin, for some things in frequent use in the Lodge and elsewhere by the brethren. No such innovation (removal of an ancient landmark) is possible in the desert, where the traditions of all the Tribal Lodges correct the errors that may have crept in through some over-zealous worker. The language in use in the Lodge is not that of modern literature; but is that of the early ages, known as *Yoktan*, in the centre; of Ishmael, in the West; of Yemen, in the South. The earliest language that has been preserved is poetic. The ritual of the modern Lodge is rhymned, questioned and answered in the choicest terms, according to the grammar of the present idiom, which also is the oldest. *To the philologist these items are proof of the antiquity of our Fraternity* more convincing even than monuments of stone, which can be made in every age, while language must grow, and is not made. The Egyptians recorded in writing and in pictures their rites and ceremonies, which make visible the condition of the fraternity and those matters at that time, about four thousand years ago. We reap in those pictures the same lessons that are taught to us now, although they are distributed through the several degrees from the first to the thirty-second.

"The work in the Arab Lodge shows a close connection between the members of the ancient brotherhood of Egypt and Arabia, and also established the antiquity of the origin of the Bedouin Lodges. *There is not a word in use in the modern Lodge that has any reference to modern discoveries in science, or to the political or religious changes of the last twenty centuries. Neither Christ nor Mohammed are mentioned.* This fact opens a charming vista to the antiquarian and philologist. The cost of indulgence in this storehouse of antiquity is a local residence among the Bedouin Arabs, and a thorough knowledge of their language and customs.

" *With the Arab the instruction of the Lodge is a preparation for a better life; with the Egyptians it was a preparation for death.* The Arab still lives in the same social conditions in which history noticed him forty centuries ago, while the Egyptian ceased to exist as a Nation about twenty-five centuries since. How much these different results were due to their peculiar ideas, is yet an unsolved problem. Arab Masonry furnishes a beautiful emblem of eternity, whose cycles are marked by supreme efforts for the redemption of mankind *from the slavery of Ignorance and Superstition;* while the Craft in our day lends itself for the perpetuation of errors peculiar to priest-craft.

" That mysterious Asiatic Peninsula, called Arabia, ever seems to be a geographic, historic and political wonder; for, while Empires like Assyria, Persia, India, Greece, and Rome were changing and vanishing, Arabia and Ishmael's children remained immutable. The Assyrians, Persians, Egyptians, Greeks, and Romans tried in vain to subjugate Hagar's progeny; they stand to-day with their language, manners, customs and traditions where they stood three thousand years ago. Renan, and Maspero have lately given the world some valuable hints on that mysterious people and country. Perhaps Freemasonry with its gentle, peaceful and persuasive methods of approaching people will succeed in opening that sealed country to the world; if so Dr. Rawson will be considered as a pioneer in the grand enterprise."

There were some very interesting articles published in Blackwood's Magazine by a student and Brother Mason, who claims that these people are the true lineal descendants of Hiram, King of Tyre. He had lived among the Druses and had studied their peculiar manners and customs and was thoroughly competent, worthy, and well qualified to write upon this subject. He tells us that after having carefully investigated the esoteric teachings of their mystic rites and ceremonies he found many things in common between their Rites and Freemasonry. He also says that he was very much astonished in finding many of the words identically the same and that their work for the pre-requisite of initiation was identical with the A. F. and A. M. In fact he, upon one occasion, received satisfactory evidence from one of these people, when making a contract with him, of his knowledge of the "*d*" of a Master Mason, for, in ratifying the contract he was very much surprised to hear the man mention what is generally given on many points. He adduces and summarizes the following for his belief as to their origin :—1st. "That they had lived from time immemorial where Hamze found them, on the slopes of Lebanon, towards Tyre and Sidon. 2nd. Their one great hero of Old Testament history is Solomon. 3rd. They stoutly maintain that they built King Solomon's temple. 4th. Their religious rites and ceremonies are to the present day intimately associated with the mystic rites of Freemasonry, which, as it is well known, are supposed to have originated at the building of Solomon's temple."

"Sir Charles Warren, R. E., K. C., M. G., Worshipful Master Lodge Quatuor Coronati, London, England," says Professor Marks, D. D., (one of the most profound Hebrew scholars), "found in an Arabic manuscript, written in Hebrew characters of the fifteenth century, that the keyword to the MS. was Mach or Mock, and on further investigation he discovered that each letter of the keyword was the beginning of a sentence, which ultimately read thus :—We have found our Master Hiram. He made out the meaning readily, inasmuch as the passage referred to Masonry, which, by-the-by, is traced up to the patriarchs, if not to Adam himself. Both Hebrews and Arabs make up a sentence upon one word, using each letter of it as expressive of a separate word."

Brother W. H. Kingsbury gives to Masonry an antiquity like myself and many other writers. He claims, however, that " Modern Masonry is a combination of the mysteries of the Hebrews, the Phœnicians and the Egyptians ; mysteries which were in older days unknown to any but the High Priests of the several Orders and which were entirely apart and distinct from the popular rendering of them. I take it that the knowledge derived from these severally was as follows : From the Hebrews *W* or Knowledge—God ; from the Egyptians *S* the Sciences ; from the Phœnicians *B* the Fine Arts, and these are symbolized in the Lodges; the W. M., *W.* a Hebrew, or Grand Master Solomon ; the S. W., *S.*, an Egyptian, or Grand Master Hiram ; the J. W., *B.*, a Phœnician, or Grand Master Hiram Abiff. In a word, I think there is not a doubt that in our Order we are the direct descendants from Phœnicians, who first moulded Masonry into its present form, and who were unable to openly worship the true God, for fear of the people.

"Masonry has unquestionably come down to us through the Gentiles and not through the Hebrews. The Lodge of the Phœnicians was constructed with windows at the East, South, and West. The *W. M.*, was placed in the East their sanctum. sanctorum; *S. W.* was placed in the West, at the great entrance to represent the sun at evening, and the J. W., was placed in the South to represent the sun at High Twelve.

"The arms of the Grand Lodge are still Masonically of unknown origin. They are purely Hebraic, and seem connected with the idea of the Ark of the Covenant. They were found among the papers of the learned Rabbi, Leon Judah, who lectured by Royal Patent in 1680 on a model of the temple of Solomon. Leon Judah, who was proficient in the Jewish Cabala, may also have been a member of the Hermetic Society."

I have quoted very extensively from various writers upon the Druses in order that you, my dear Brothers and readers, may get a general idea of the opinions of the various authors, as well as my own, upon these people. If we carefully examine what has been written about them, we shall find many things which will prove of great interest to us. For instance, if you will notice what Brother Kingsbury says in relation to Brother Rawson's account of his travels, you will realize that the Arab Mason in the Bedouin Lodges could not have been obligated on either the Bible or the Koran, because in the Bedouin Lodges neither Christ nor Mohammed are mentioned. I shall speak of this subject later on in another chapter.

They also tell us that the esoteric teachings of the Arab Mason was the preparation for a better life, and that of the Egyptian Brother was a preparation for death. So we find the teachings of both were the same, if properly understood, for the man who prepares to lead a purer, truer life, prepares for his future death, which is inevitable, and they both must realize that if they desire to die the death of the righteous they must live the life of the righteous. The act of death or dying does not make a man good or bad. He is what he has made himself through his thoughts and acts during life. I shall also speak of this later on. I simply call your attention to these points in the teachings of our ancient

Brothers, and compare them with our own to find simply a distinction without a difference. Brother Kingsbury states that "Masonry comes down to us from the Gentiles, and not through the Hebrew."

Now every Masonic student will realize that Masonry has passed through every epoch of the world's history. At the same time he will find that many things have been preserved to the fraternity by the Hebrew, whose forefathers were princes in Israel, when ours were digging clams with stone hatchets out of the lagoons of Europe. I myself make the assertion that we owe a great deal to the Hebrew people for the preservation of some of our symbology, of which I shall speak later on.

In the quarterly statement of the Palestine Exploration Fund there is some very valuable information relating to the Druses and their religions, meetings, beliefs, etc., furnished by a Mr. Joseph Jebrail, wherein he states that " reliable information regarding the Druses is not to be found everywhere, but the extracts here given are confirmed by Major Condor. The Druse places of worship are called chapels. They believe that there are many Druses in China, and that the religion of the English people is the Druse religion, though its votaries are not known by that name in England."

During my stay in the city of Los Angeles, Southern California, in the year 1897, I had the pleasure of meeting the Reverend Hasket Smith, M. A., who at that time was delivering a series of lectures on Egypt, Syria and the Holy Land, illustrated by sterioptic views. I had quite a long and enjoyable chat with him upon these people and countries, which I have already mentioned. We also spoke of ancient Masonry, when I told him that I had met quite a large number of Arabs in different parts of those countries who had certainly proved to my entire satisfaction that they had obtained the right Light of Truth from some source.

During the time that this gentleman lived among the Druses he had the good fortune to save the life of one of the prominent young men who had been bitten by a venomous snake. Mr. Smith sucked the wound, and in this way drew the deadly poison from the body of the young man. In performing this act he made a host of friends, and was welcomed by the entire people. Their homes were thrown open to him and he became popular among them. He was also initiated into different rites or degrees among them that were unknown to the general traveller in that country, and he, like Brother Rawson, was very much astonished at their knowledge of the various signs, grips and tokens of Ancient Masonry. He thoroughly believed the Druses to be the true and lineal descendants of the Hittites, a branch of those ancient Phœnicians who wrought in the mountains of Lebanon, near Joppa, and supplied Solomon with the cedar for the building of the temple on Mount Moriah.

Let me close this chapter by quoting you some passages from the Druse books: "When men were created, they knew not the origin of their existence, nor did they seek God by their works. Wherefore He impressed upon their souls conviction of truths, and the knowledge of truth, so that they knew and acknowledged Him. He manifested Himself unto them, by His works; and by His revelations of Himself in Nature taught them His greatness, and made them to know His unity, so that they said, 'God is great, There is no God but God.' Thus He calls them unto Him, saying, 'Am I not your God,' and they believed in the unity of the Most High.

"It was the Most Wise Intellect which was standing with God in the place of a priesthood, inviting the people to know their Creator, the Most High, and His unity. And this Intellect taught the people the arts and sciences, aided by the Creator, who gave him wisdom and spiritual sovereignty and potencies, and made him Priest, Prophet, Aider, Director, and Advisor.

"And this Intellect gave to men the faculty to distinguish between what is right and good, and wise, and what is wrong and bad, and foolish, enabling them to avoid excesses and follies, and evil deeds. And the benediction of the Lord God Almighty was over all the earth. May God make us and all our Brethren disciples of the true Faith, and deliver us from doubts after having attained to the truths! Amen.

"There are seven laws which every Akel or Ockal (Druse) will observe while the ray of the Divine light within him is not withdrawn from him, leaving him only his animal nature. *The first* is that of the Truth of the Tongue. It is the belief in the presence of the Word in Humanity; the belief in all those in different ages have taught men the truth; the belief in that wisdom which is the Religion in which alone is safety; the belief in the goodness of God, and in another life after this, and the reward or punishment that will there be decreed. *The second* is that of the preservation of Friendship among Brethren; to remember them in their needs and sorrows, and to love them whether they be near unto or far from us; to respect with manly self respect our superiors; to be gracious and kind to all those who are below us, and sustain them both secretly and publicly, giving them their due rights, whether temporal or spiritual, and proving ourselves to be their true Friends. *The third* is that of the abandonment of the worship of idols, formed in the mind by false and distorted conceptions of God, and seen with slavish superstition in the symbols which have usurped the places of the things symbolized and become the objects of an ignorant reverence, and the fruitful source of false and impure religions. It is also that of the abandonment of the doctrine of those who believe in legends and fables, and of those who say that God is not present everywhere, in symphathy with His creatures, but somewhere remote from them, where He looks unconcernedly on and sees the action of the Universe, and its forces, both of matter and intellect, proceeding under the operation of 'laws' enacted by Him, which make his personal intervention and concern and interest unnecessary. It is also that of the abandonment of the doctrine of those who believe in traditions and babble nonsense, and say that God is not one. *The fourth* is that of the disbelief in Evil Spirits in rebellion and antagonism against the one God. *The Fifth* is that of implicit truth and confidence in God, as infinitely merciful and loving, and of that worship of Him which has rested in every age and generation on the belief that He has personality by Unity of Will and Wisdom, but without body, form or shape, or confinement within limits; by imagining which men make a God after their own image, conceiving of themselves as infinitely magnified, and fancying this conception to be God. *The sixth* is that of being satisfied with the acts of God, whatever they may be, not endeavoring to avoid the operation of His laws, or condemning as wrong or criminal anything whatsoever that is done in obedience to them, as they appear and act in Nature and Humanity. And *the seventh* is that of resignation, cheerful and implicit, to His will, even when He afflicts us with sorrows, and what seem to us cruel and unnecessary desolations and deprivations. For in adversity we cannot know what evils and miseries, prosperity might have brought upon us, what enmities and slanders, what moral and mental and physical diseases; nor from what extremities of shame and agony, and sufferings, and sorrow He may have rescued by death the loved ones whom He has taken from us. *The conclusion* is, that whosoever knows and believes as the Seven Laws require, and is sound of mind and body, and of full age, and free from servitude, may be of those who are destined to the ranks, and entitled to be present at the private assemblies, at which whosoever is present must revere God and be true, and generous to his Brother and whosoever is absent with right to be present will repent it."

We can learn from these laws of the ancient Druses some very beautiful and forcible truths, as sublimely grand as those taught by Jesus Himself when He associated with the lowly fishermen of Galilee and preached the beatitudes throughout the Holy Land. They embody many of those eternal verities that have descended to us from the Wisdom Religion of the " Land of the Vedas," taught to the aspirants in the Indian, Mazdean and ancient Egyptian mysteries during the ceremonies of Initiation. They are exemplified to-day in the profound symbology of our glorious Scottish Rite throughout the world universal. Brothers of our obedience should give especial attention to *The Conclusion*. They in themselves should remind us of our duties to our Lodges, Chapters, Councils and Consistories. Therefore adorn your Lodge with your presence.

Agriculture—Irrigation—Lotus—Papyrus.

The waters flow o'er the burning soil,
    Of old Egypt's harvest bearing land,
And the fellaheen's task and daily toil
Is to direct it from the flowing Nile
    To the parched and thirsty sand

Where cotton, corn and the bean flowers grow
    In luxuriant abundance around,
The dikes and ditches that continually flow,
Where the sturdy fellaheen plies his hoe,
    To direct it over the ground.

CHAPTER VII.

AGRICULTURE—IRRIGATION—LOTUS—PAPYRUS.

THE agricultural part of Egypt is divided into what is known as *Rai* and *Sharaki* lands. The former is that portion of the soil subject to the annual inundations of the waters of the Nile, without any other assistance than in directing the course of the flooding turbid waters to where it is needed for irrigating the land over which it flows. The *Rai* land produces only one natural crop, but it can be made to yield a second, or even a third, if properly irrigated and attended. The *Sharaki* land is that particular part of the soil which requires artificial irrigation, for without water nothing would grow thereon, as it lies above the flooding waters of the river; therefore to make it produce abundantly, it is necessary to irrigate these parts by various methods, such as the Shaduf, Sakiyeh, Tabut and pumps, comprising machines that lift the water to the desired height for irrigating the soil.

The seasons are divided into three parts, of four months each. The most important of all is the WINTER SEASON (*es Shitawi*) which commences at the end of the inundation, or somewhere about the first of November, in Middle Egypt, and ends in the last days of February. During the early part of this season the whole of the Delta presents a very peculiar appearance, for it looks exactly like an immense checkerboard of water, whose dividing lines are the banks of the canals through which the waters of the Nile flow to all parts of Lower Egypt. Here and there, above the flooded country, stand villages, surrounded by clusters of palms and occasionally sycamores, that relieve the monotony of the scene.

As soon as the waters begin to subside and the fields are still moist, the staple food of the Egyptians is sown, as well as what is necessary for the use of their domestic animals, such as wheat, barley, beans, chickpeas, clover, vetches, etc. This seed is scattered broadcast upon the soft wet soil, and pressed into it by various very simple methods, one of which is by driving their domestic animals across the seeded soil. Sometimes they do not go to that trouble; but just leave the seed lying upon the surface of the soft wet mud or ground, when, by its own weight, it sinks beneath the surface and under the conditions of heat, light and moisture, very soon germinates and begins to grow luxuriantly and in abundance.

All sowing is done in the same old primitive way as in the time when Moses lived, and that is " by hand." The sower fills his basket full of seed, then slings it upon his shoulder and scatters it broadcast upon the wet shimmering soil. About four months from the time of sowing the seed, they begin to harvest the beans, lupins, clover, etc.; but the wheat and barley will take fully three months longer to mature and ripen, ready for harvesting, which is done in a very primitive manner, according to the ancient methods of their great ancestors. They either pull up the stocks by the roots, or cut them off with a sickle or knife, close to the ground, and pile them in a heap in the middle of the field. They then hitch up a couple of oxen to a " norag " (a kind of sled that rests upon a heavy roller, with sharp pieces of iron fastened to it) which is then driven over the pile, backwards and forwards, bruising and crushing the stalks and freeing the grain from the husk. They then gather up the larger parts of the stalks and throw them aside. The grain is separated from the husks and rubbish by throwing the crushed pile up into the wind; when the light chaff is blown away and the grain falls to the ground, after which it is gathered up and stored for future use.

THE SUMMER SEASON—*es Seffi*, begins with the month of March and ends in June. Very little is raised in Upper Egypt during this season, as during the whole of the time the cultivable land is very narrow and the greater portion nearly always under water, though they do raise considerable produce in many places. There are large quantities of millet, cucumbers, melons, etc., raised during this time, and they sow a great deal of sugar-cane during the commencement of this season; but it is not harvested, for conversion into sugar, until the latter part of January or the middle of February, although they cut large quantities for eating during the month of October. In Lower Egypt, or the Delta, the summer season is a very important one, for then is the time they plant indigo, cotton, rice, etc., which is harvested generally between the months of October and December. They plant cotton in April and then harvest it in November, and frequently reap quite a large amount from a second crop of this plant. This season is when their tobacco crop is harvested, of which they grow large quantities. Now is the farmer's delight in the Delta, as the whole of this part of Egypt is clothed in luxuriant vegetation, the gardens and fields are all laden with fruits that gladden the hearts of men. As far as the eye can reach we may see luxuriant crops of all kinds growing and ripening.

THE AUTUMN SEASON, (*ed Demira,*) begins with the rising or inundation of the Nile during the month of July, and ends in October. In the middle of this season the Delta was formerly covered with the flooding, rushing waters of the Nile, bearing out the statement which Herodotus makes in Book II, Chapter 97: "When the Nile overflows, the country is converted into a sea, and nothing appears but the cities, which look like the islands in the Ægean. At this season boats no longer keep the course of the river, but sail right across the plain. On the voyage from Naucratis to Memphis, at this season, you pass close to the Pyramids, whereas the usual course is by the apex of the Delta and the city of Cercasorus. You can sail also from the maritime town of Kanopus across the flat to Naucratis, passing by the cities Anthylla and Archandropolis."

During this season of the year corn is planted with millet, etc. And although it is a very short season, of but a little over seventy days, yet, during that time the fertile soil of the Delta matures and ripens the immense fields of growing grain, which is harvested somewhere about the latter part of September or the beginning of October. This season is really a harvesting time, not only of corn, millet, etc., but of all that which had been planted during the summer. At this time of the year (September) the Delta presents to view smiling fields of waving grain, when every spot of arable land is teeming in fertility, from Alexandria to Cairo. It will be a scene never to be forgotten by all those who travel through the Delta of the Nile during the latter part of Autumn.

There is a vast difference to-day in the inundations of the river Nile from those of ancient times; for now they are able to control, in a great measure, the flooding waters of old "God Nilus;" thanks to the efforts of Mohammed Ali, Ishmail Pasha and the British, in constructing places for the purpose of storing the surplus waters of the river, so as to distribute it when and where it would be most needed.

Mohammed Ali endeavored to build a barrage in order to preserve the surplus waters of the river. The construction of the dam was in charge of Mogul Bey, a Frenchman, who worked upon it for years, in the hope of making it a success; but it ultimately proved a miserable failure. The British afterwards reconstructed it and made it thoroughly secure. During their early occupation of this country they devoted a great deal of time and attention to this matter and appropriated considerable sums of money toward improvements along these lines, and to-day they have very nearly completed two most magnificent dams, of which I make mention in another chapter, to regulate the river's flow and reclaim a vast amount of desert land destined to support an additional population of from one to two millions of people. The prosperity of Egypt depends upon the storage of the water and controlling the flow of the river which runs to waste during the winter, and for that reason the British are constructing these enormous dams to prevent loss and utilize every gallon of water needed for irrigation.

The river Nile has created the soil of Egypt through its annual inundations, by depositing layer after layer of alluvial deposits brought down from the mountains of Abyssinia.

Herodotus says, in Book II, Chapter 4: "That the priests told him that when *Men* (Menes) was King, all Egypt, except the Thebaic canton was a marsh, and that none of the land below lake Moeris then showed itself above the water. This is a distance of seven days' sail from the sea up the river."

In Chapter 5: "What they said of their country seemed to me very reasonable. For any one who sees Egypt without having heard a word about it before, must perceive, if he has only common powers of observation, that the Egypt to which the Greeks go, in their ships, is an acquired country, the gift of the river. The same is true of the land above the lake, to the distance of three days' voyage, concerning which the Egyptians say nothing, but which is exactly the same kind of country. The following is the general character of the region: In the first place, Ly sea, when you are still a days' sail from land, if you let down a sounding-line you will bring up mud and find yourself in eleven fathoms of water, which shows that the soil washed down by the stream extends to that distance."

In Chapter 7.—" From the coast inland, as far as Heliopolis, the breadth of Egypt is considerable, the country is flat, without springs and full of swamps. The length of the route, from the sea up to Heliopolis, is almost exactly the same as that of the road which runs from the altar of the twelve gods at Athens, to the temple of the Olympian Jove at Pisa. If a person made a calculation he would find but very little difference between the two routes, not more than about fifteen furlongs; for the road from Athens to Pisa falls short of fifteen hundred furlongs by exactly fifteen, whereas the distance of Heliopolis from the sea is just the round numbers."

Fraas, quoted by Baedeker, in his "Lower Egypt," says: "Throughout the whole of Egypt the Nile mud rests on a bed of sea sand. The whole country between the first cataract and the Mediterranean was formerly a narrow estuary, which was probably filled by degrees, during the Pleiocene period with lagoon deposits, washed down from the crystalline Habesh. At a later period, when Egypt had risen from the sea, and after the isthmus had been formed, the river forced itself through these deposits of mud, sweeping away many of these loose particles at one place and depositing them again farther down."

Now, from my own personal observations, I do most firmly believe that at one time all that country, known as the Delta, was an estuary, and the river itself has been for ages bringing down a sedimentary deposit to build up this most important part of Egypt, the " Delta of the Nile," and continually renews it, by fresh accumulations, at every inundation or overflow of this remarkable old river, thus maintaining it, in a perpetual state of fertility, through the rich alluvial soil that is continually deposited upon the land by the flooding waters of the Nile.

After the Delta of the Nile had been formed, in the ancient days of Egyptian history, it was watered by seven different branches of the river, while to-day only two make their exit into the Mediterranean Sea by their regular channels, these two being known as the *Bolbetine* and the Phatnitic. The first is called the Rosetta branch, the other one is known as the Damietta branch of the Nile while the other five, the Kanopic, Mendesian, Sebennytic, Pelusiac, and Tanitic, are of but very little use or importance, except for irrigation purposes, as they are nearly always dry ; but are kept open simply for carrying water for irrigation.

The Bolbetine branch took its name from the ancient town of *Bolbitinum.* The ancient site of this town lies about a couple of miles South of the modern town of Rosetta, in Arabic *Rashid*, founded by one of the Caliphs of the Tülünide Dynasty, probably Ahmed-ibn-Tulün. It was formerly a very important and flourishing town of great commercial interest, to that branch of the Nile on which it stood, as well as the country tributary to it. At the present time its harbors are filled with the Nile deposit and only vessels of the smallest draft are enabled to enter ; in fact, since the completion of the Mahmudiyeh canal, opened on the 20th day of January, 1820, its importance began to decline, and its traffic diverted to the city of Alexandria. This town of Rosetta, at the beginning of the present century, had a population of between twenty-five and thirty thousand inhabitants, while at the present writing it has dwindled down to a population of less than one half of those figures. It is a very pleasant Arab town, chiefly celebrated for its gardens, then the principal attraction to the better class of Europeans as well as native Egyptians from interior cities. It was formerly a favorite summer resort, on account of the salubrity of the atmosphere and its picturesque beauty. There are several large mosques and khans in this town, as well as the typical bazaar of Egypt, the whole being surrounded by a wall with loopholes that have been cut at regular places for the purpose of firing through, in case of an attack from invaders ; but these walls would be of very little use if opposed to artillery fire. This city is also celebrated for the discovery of the famous trilingual stone, which was found here by a French officer while digging the foundation of Fort St. Julian. It is now in the British Museum, and is known as the " Rosetta Stone."

Off to the west of Rosetta and in plain sight is the bay of Abu-kir whereon was fought the celebrated " Battle of the Nile," on the first day of August, in the year 1798. Admiral Lord Nelson, while cruising along the coast discovered the French ships at anchor, which he immediately engaged, totally destroying fourteen vessels out of the seventeen composing the fleet under command of Admiral Bruéys. The completion of the

MAHAMUDIYEH CANAL,

ALEXANDRIA

victory was in the destruction of the L'Orient, commanded by the French Admiral himself. The destruction of this ship and fleet destroyed the power of the French and caused Napoleon to hurriedly return to Europe. Shortly afterwards Sir Ralph Abercrombie effected a landing at the battle of Alexandria, which, with the capitulation of Cairo, compelled the French to evacuate Egypt and return to France, very much demoralized at their losses. Sir Ralph Abercrombie was killed during the battle of Alexandria. East of the town of Rosetta is Lake Barulos which I shall speak of later on.

The Phatnitic branch of the Nile flows into the Mediterranean just west of the most northerly part of Lake Menzala, and the town of *Damietta* is situated on the east bank of the river, where it was once noted as being the most important town on the east side of the river and originally contained a population of about forty-five thousand inhabitants. Like its companion town Rosetta, it has fallen in importance through the growth of Alexandria and later Port Said, and to-day it has a population of about twenty-five thousand. This town was known to the ancient Egyptians as *Tamiathis*, when it was considered to be the Key to the Delta, during the crusades especially. Its principal revenues are derived from the manufacturing of leather and cloth, while the fishing industry enables its inhabitants to keep up a lucrative trade with the interior cities. The town lies due west of Lake Menzala and the extreme shallowness of its waters prevent vessels from entering the harbor; but there is some talk of cutting a canal to connect the Mediterranean Sea with the river Nile. If this were done it would no doubt restore a great deal of the trade lost through the difficulties of keeping the port open, that shipping could enter, discharge, and take on their cargoes for other ports.

The Delta of the Nile still preserves the same fan-like tract of land, lying between Alexandria and Port Said on the North, and Cairo at the apex of the Delta, on the South. From this last mentioned city the Delta begins to widen out into a regular fan-like formation, beginning at Lake Mareotis on the East, in about 30° East longitude, and ending with parts of the land extending into and helping to form, with Port Said and the Suez Canal, Lake Menzala, in about 32° East longitude. This land, roughly estimated, consists of about one hundred and sixty-five miles, running from Alexandria along the coast line, while the apex of the Delta lies very near Cairo, in about 32° North latitude, being distant from Alexandria nearly two hundred miles by river and one hundred and twenty-three by rail. The Delta has an area of about six thousand three hundred and fifty square miles, comprising good agricultural land. Its lack of woods and forests is one of its noticeable features. There is quite a number of trees to be seen in Lower Egypt but the most common is the date palm, which is cultivated and especially cared for on account of its fruit.

Mr. Poole, in his very interesting work on Egypt, says, on pages 31 and 32: "The interior of the Delta is a wide level plain, intersected by a network of canals, fed by the divided stream of the Nile, often running in ancient channels and fenced in by high embankments. The whole plain is clothed with rich crops of all manner of vegetation and the whole lit up with the snow-white blossoms of the cotton plant. Near the banks of the canals and river-arms are some three hundred small villages and a few towns, generally erected high above the inundation, on the lofty mounds of dark earth, the sites of ancient cities and temples, which are a prominent feature of the plain. At a distance the villages look almost a part of the mounds, for the most part merely a cluster of mud-huts surrounded by dove-cotes and palm groves, with a white-washed minaret standing out from the confused mass; but many of these villages take a fair share in the trade which the fertilizing Nile affords to the plain, and have developed into small but populous towns. They can be seen in every stage of progress, from the huddled head of mud-huts, piled up by the fellaheen who work the neighboring water-wheel, and sow the fields around, through the open door-holes of which the wretched poverty of the Egyptian peasant is plainly visible, to the well-to-do town, which boasts something like a definite street, and several mosques, where minarets overtop the houses and necessary palms. Houses and hovels are built of the same material, the inevitable Nile mud, though for the better houses in damp regions the bricks are baked, a precaution unknown in the villages higher up.

"The principal towns of the interior are—Demen-hur ("City of Horus"), west of the Rosetta branch, with a population of twenty-five thousand, possessed of considerable factories for cleaning cotton and preparing it for export, as well as El Mansurah, on the Damietta branch, the scene of the defeat of Jean de Brienne by a nephew of Saladin in 1221, and the prison of Saint Louis in 1250, at the disastrous termination of the *sixth* crusade. Tanta, between the two, a fine town of thirty thousand inhabitants, famous for its Saint *Amad El-Bedawy* and his annual festivals, improperly but appositely called fairs, that are held for a week and a day in January, April and August. The last and greatest of these festivals bring together half a million people to honor the Saint and obtain benefits for themselves from his intercession, as well as to enjoy the tricks of the jugglers, the dancing of the Ghawazy, and the fun and revelry which are the main characteristics of this religious festival. Ez-Zaqaziq, with forty thousand inhabitants, is the centre of the cotton trade of the Delta, situated in the midst of a fertile and wooded region, watered by a fine system of canals, and supporting a prosperous farming population. Near Ez-Zaqaziq runs the Fresh Water Canal which conveys the Nile water to Suez. This canal is of ancient construction and was built by the Pharaohs, perhaps four thousand years ago, and reopened by M de Lesseps to give drinking water to the workmen engaged upon the Suez Canal. It is now connected with Cairo by the Ismailia Canal and runs through the Wady Tumilat, which it fertilizes by its water, and after reaching Ismailia turns down to Suez. Though principally an aqueduct it is also serviceable for local traffic."

There are quite a number of towns in the Delta I have already written about, such as Sais, Tanis or Zoan, Bubastis, Semmenud, and others that could be described; but one town in the Delta is, in a measure, typical of all the rest, and therefore a description of them would simply be a mere repetition of words.

In approaching the apex of the Delta we are enabled to see the Libyan range of mountains and the Mokattum hills drawing closer together. In the middle distance the dark foliage marks the site of "Grand Cairo," with its citadel, splendid mosques and minarets, whose gorgeous beauties have been so highly praised by all Arabian writers, as well as by many modern historians. To say anything regarding its varied charms and beauties not already described would, indeed, be a difficult task ; but as all people do not see alike, I will leave my description of this peculiar city and its environs for a future chapter, and tell you what impressed me while sojourning in that quaint old city, the capital of Egypt. From our present view we can see very plainly the pyramids in the plains of Gizeh and the solitary obelisk that marks the site of the celebrated city of Heliopolis, " The city of the Sun," of which I shall speak later on.

There are five lakes of brackish water situated in the northern part of the Delta, which are separated from the Mediterranean Sea by long and narrow ridges of sand, through many of which the salt water filters and mixes with the fresh water of the river Nile during the overflow. The first is Lake Mareotis, not far from the city of Alexandria. In fact, after leaving this city by the Gabäri Gate the lake is right beside us. In the winter the waters of this lake are high, owing to the inundation ; but later on are surrounded by a vast area of swampy, ill-smelling bog-land, pregnant with malaria, etc. At one time this lake was not near so large as at present, and during the summer months is a disagreeable marsh. It was originally a fertile plain, with a beautiful lake of fresh, clear, pure water in the centre ; from which the city of Alexandria drew her water supply. When the British laid siege to this city, in the year 1801, they cut off the water supply from Alexandria by· digging an immense ditch from the Mediterranean Sea into the low land adjoining the lake, which not only flooded the country but destroyed the lake and a very large number of villages dotting the plain around it, thus sacrificing a great number of lives, but they succeeded in capturing Alexandria.

Lake Abukir originally belonged to and formed part of Mareotis, but when Mohammed Ali constructed the Mahmudiyeh canal in 1819 he threw up very high embankments which cut off the northern portion, entirely separating it from Mareotis, as the canal ran right through it to Alexandria.

Murray, on page 196, says this canal " received its name in honor of the Sultan Mahmud second. The cost is said to have been three hundred thousand pounds; and two hundred and fifty thousand men were employed about one year in digging it, of whom twenty thousand perished by accident, hunger and plague. It commences at the village of Atfih, on the Rosetta branch of the Nile, and has a total length of fifty miles, with an average width of about one hundred feet. A part of its course is identical with that of the ancient Kanopic branch of the Nile, and the old canal of Füa, which was used in the time of the Venitians for carrying goods to Alexandria, and existed, though nearly dry, in Savary's time, A. D. 1777. The right bank of the Mahmúdiyeh Canal is bordered for some distance with the houses and gardens of the wealthy inhabitants of Alexandria."

This part of the lake, at certain seasons of the year, is a very unhealthy place, a fact evidenced by the great number of men who died from the baneful influence of this part of the Delta during the construction of the Mahmudiyeh Canal. This branch of the Nile is the most westerly, and flows into the Abukir Bay, close to where the British destroyed the French fleet at the battle of the Nile.

It was upon the west bank of this arm of the Nile (Kanopic) that the town of Kanopus was located, and it is said to have derived its name from the pilot of *Menelaus*, who sailed to that place on his return from the siege of Troy. Strabo describes this town as follows : " Kanopus is a city which lies one hundred and twenty stadia (about fourteen English miles) from Alexandria, if one goes by land, and is named after the helmsman of Menelaus who died there. It contains the highly revered temple of Serapis, which, moreover, works such miracles that even the most respectable men believe in them, and either sleep in it themselves, or get others to sleep there for them. Some persons also record the cures, and others the effects of the oracle dreams experienced there. A particularly remarkable thing is the great number of parties of pleasure descending the canal from Alexandria; for day and night the canal swarms with men and women, who perform music on the flute and licentious dances in the boats with unbridled merriment, or who, at Kanopus itself, frequent taverns situated on the canal and suited for such amusement and revelry."

This city was noted for several temples, the chief of which was that of Serapis. This deity was worshipped here with the most profound respect. The Kanopic jars, which I shall describe in the chapter devoted to embalming, owe their name to this place. It was here that the celebrated trilingual stone called by the French savants " La Pierre de San " especially refers to what was known as the " Decree of Kanopus."

Directly east of Abukir is a long stretch of sand, separating it from Lake Edku, another body of brakish water of no especial interest. The ford which connects this lake with the sea is supposed by many to be the ancient Kanopic mouth of the river Nile. It is separated from the Mediterranean by a long dreary waste of sand, along which runs the railroad to Rosetta, lying to the northeast of Edku, and beyond the Bolbitinic branch of the Nile is Lake Brulus, situated between the two towns of Rosetta and Damietta. The Sebennytic mouth of the Nile empties into the sea from this lake, in about 31° east longitude and very near the long sandy ridge which divides it from the Mediterranean Sea.

The last of this series of lakes is Menzala, the most extensive lake in Egypt, an immense swamp at certain seasons, having an area of about five hundred thousand acres. It is a shallow lake, drifting off into marshy creeks, dotted here and there with number-less islands, many of which are flooded and disappear entirely during the inundations of the river, a most desolate region, pregnant with fever, etc. There are two ancient mouths of the Nile that flow into the sea from this lake, known as the *Mendesian* and Tanitic. A few of the islands in this lake will prove of great interest to the student and tourist. The principal ones are *Tuna* and *Tennes*. The first contains a small village called *Shekh Abdallah*, where there are some very interesting ruins.

Tennes is the ancient site of *Tennesus*, and contains a great many remains of vaulted tombs, baths and foundations that were constructed by the ancient Romans, after Egypt became tributary to the imperial power of Rome.

All through northern Egypt, in the vicinity of these lakes, are the grazing lands of the Egyptians, each of which furnish a very good field for the hunter; but one desirous of this privilege must first secure a permit before he is allowed to look across the sights of either gun or rifle. On all these lakes wild-fowl of varous kinds are to be found in abundance, such as wild duck, geese, coot, pelican, silver heron, flamingo, cormorant, etc. In many of these streams certain parts are especially reserved, where no shooting is allowed, excepting to those paying for the privilege. I have spent many glorious days

—aye, and weeks,—hunting on the lakes Menzala, Brulus and others, where many birds of all kinds were secured, and nearly devoured alive, at night in our tent, by the bloodthirsty mosquitos. During our hunting expeditions over these lakes we had a couple of good English punts, belonging to a friend, who had purchased them from an English captain for the express purpose of hunting. They were of very light draught and far superior to the old-fashioned, unwieldy Arab boats generally used here by sportsmen.

One thing seemed very strange to me, I did not see a single specimen of the papyrus plant during my ramblings through the whole of Lower Egypt. It used to be carefully cultivated by the ancient Egyptians, and grew in great abundance all over the Delta, more especially in those branches of the Nile and the streams flowing from them through this part of the country. The raising and manufacturing of papyrus into rolls was, at one time, a distinguishing industry in Semmenud.

Ebbers, in his article on the " Writing Materials of Antiquity," says, quoting Professor Schenk, in reply to inquiries asking his opinion upon the preparation of the specimens submitted to him : " I believe I am correct in the opinion that in the preparation, thinner or thicker lamella were cut from the inner texture or pith, and these were laid upon each other in such wise that the fibers crossed, the finer sorts being prepared of two and the rougher kinds out of three lamella; the thickness thus differing with the variety. They were then united by an adhesive substance, of what nature I can give no definite information. Its solubility in potash seems to indicate the use of the white of an egg, and possibly this alone was employed.

" Rolls and pieces of the different sort of papyrus used for writing materials are preserved in large quantities. The last decade has witnessed the most surprising increase in their numbers. As the result of thorough study, not of the writings with which they are covered, but of the papyri themselves, Professor U. Wilcken, of Breslau, discovered on which side of the papyrus the true page of the writing lay. It is invariably the one which, pending the fabrication, has lain uppermost and whose fibers, being laid upon the table, occupy a horizontal position ; that page of the leaf on which the fibers run vertically is the reverse side. Thus

11

on the page with the horizontal fibers, generally the smoother and better finished, which is recognizable at the first glance, the text was begun. That which is written on the reverse side may be the end of the writing, for which there was insufficient space on the principal page, or it may be a later addition. Thousands of papyri have confirmed this observation.

"Also the horizontal side is the one originally destined to be written upon. This can scarcely be otherwise, as from all the manipulations of its fabrications—pressure, beating smooth, etc.,—the upper side derived a much better finish than the one upon the table. Reversing the half-finished page, with a view to a similar treatment of both sides is unknown. The importance of the discovery rests in the fact that, when a papyrus is written on both sides, the writing on the horizontal side may be declared the more ancient. For example if a dated letter or contract is found on the vertical side, and on the horizontal the epigramme of a poet, the period of which we do not know, we may venture to assert that the poet lived prior to the date on the vertical side.

"Among the various kinds of papyrus the most excellent were those on which, in time of the Pharaohs, hieratic texts were inscribed and Strabo mentions the hieratic papyri as the best of all. It may perhaps be the same sort which was called, after the Emperor Augustus, 'the Augustinian.' Connected with this is another, which was called 'Liviana' after the Empress Livia, the consort of Octavia. Others were named from the places of their origin as Saitic, Tanitic, etc., or according to their uses as theatre programmes, wrapping paper, etc."

Many important discoveries of papyri have been made in Upper Egypt during the nineteenth century. To-day a vast amount of manuscripts pertaining to science, etc., are being found, which are proving of great value and interest to the scientific world in their investigations throughout the whole of this most extraordinary country. The papyrus was one of the most useful plants cultivated by the Egyptians. The roots and young shoots, as well as parts of the stem, were used as food in lieu of grain, to supply its want among the poorer classes of the Delta. Other parts were used for making baskets, mats, etc., while the stems were bound together and used for rafting purposes on the river and streams. The name of this plant became famous in the history of civilization for the manner in which writing material was manufactured out of its pith.

The papyrus was, as I have previously stated, found in great abundance principally in the lakes and watercourses of the Delta. In consequence of this it became the hieroglyphic symbol of Lower Egypt, as well as adjacent countries, while the lotus was far more prolific in Upper Egypt and was used to symbolize that country as well as Nubia and the bordering nations. The lotus is found carved upon every temple throughout the length and breadth of the valley of the Nile. Isis is invariably represented holding a lotus flower in one hand, while in the other she carries the crux ansata.

In the "Secret Doctrine," Vol. I, section 8, page 406, we find that " There are no ancient symbols without a deep and philosophical meaning attached to them, their importance and significance increasing with their antiquity. Such is the lotus. It is the flower sacred to Nature and her God, and represents the abstract and concrete universe, standing as the emblem of the productive powers of both spiritual and physical nature. It was held as sacred from the remotest antiquity by the Aryan Hindus, the Egyptians, and by the Buddhists after them. It was revered in China and Japan and adopted as a Christian emblem by the Greek and Latin churches, who made of it a messenger, as do now the Christians who have replaced it with the water lily.

" In the Christian religion, in every picture of the annunciation, Gabriel, the Archangel, appears to the Virgin Mary holding in his hand a spray of water lilies. This spray typifying Fire and Water, or the idea of creation and generation, symbolizes *precisely the same idea* as the Lotus in the hand of Bodhisattva who announces to Maha Maya, Guatama's Mother, the birth of Buddha, the world's Saviour. Thus, also, were Osiris and Horus constantly represented by the Egyptians in association with the Lotus-flower, both being Sun Gods, or Gods of Fire; just as the Holy Ghost is still typified by ' tongues of fire ' in the *Acts.*"

> "Love came to Flora asking for a flower,
>   That would of flowers be undisputed queen ;
> The Lily and the rose long, long had been
>   Rivals for that high honor.
> And Flora gave the Lotus ' rose-red ' dyed,
>   And ' Lilly white ' the queenliest flower that blows."

> —*Century Magazine.*

The Lotus has been exalted and religiously venerated by the Hindus, in the ancient days, as well as by all nations of the world, down to the Christians of to-day. Throughout the East, in prehistoric times, as well as the present, this flower was the theme of the poet. Its praise has been spoken and sung in every age and every land of the far East, immortalized in song and story. In our day *Heine, Tennyson,* and Sir Edwin Arnold have rendered homage in raphsodies of song to this flower of the " Land of the Vedas " and the glorious East.

This magnificent flower, emblem of the human soul, at whose birth the spotless purity of its glorious petals repelled the impurities from which it sprung. The muddy waters, coming in contact with its virgin blossoms, leaves or buds, roll back from them, leaving no stain. In the same way the pure in heart are impervious to the stain of sin, though surrounded by evil thoughts and evil deeds which permeate this world, as never resting upon or entering into the heart of the pure and true. Flowers of many varieties are found in all parts of Egypt which *are called* by the name of the Lotus, though none of them are the *true* or sacred flower of the Hindu or Buddhist. They are simply different species of the water lily having attached to them no sacred traditions.

The Egyptian Lotus is not the sacred Lotus of India; but very nearly approaches that glorious flower in its general characteristics. There are many Lotus-like flowers in Egypt of various hues, which rise out of the water at sunrise and disappear again at the setting of the sun. Many of the so-called Lotuses have been mistaken for *N. Nelumbo* the sacred flower of India. But it is not to be found in any part of Egypt. The *Nymphaea* Lotus, and *Nymphaea cerulea* are found in great quantities in both Upper and Lower Egypt, but as previously stated are not the sacred flower, the great brilliant rose-pink, the matchless Lotus of the Hindu and Buddhist, the royal lily of Siam. The true sacred Lotus of India is the universal symbol of the Kosmos, as the absolute totality, and the jewel is spiritual Man or God, and " *Om Mani Padme Hum,*" (O the jewel in the Lotus) points to the indissoluble union between Man and the Universe.

The full-grown Lotus flower is larger and more brilliant by far than the smaller and more compact water lily. It has not the stainless purity of the white lily. nor the rich, deep, ruby color of the darker lily, but its own brilliant rose-pink is matchless, unapproachable. The English heart goes out to it, reminded by its color-tone of the delicate brier-roses at home, and like the brier-rose its days are short. The petals that were perfect yesterday, are to-day parting and falling into the pool. But as they fall they reveal the most curious and botanically the most interesting of all the Lotus charms. This is the unique "receptacle" or fruit case, whose peculiarities at once distinguish the Nelumbian from the water lily. This receptacle occupies the central position in the flower, and the golden threads which surround it when the flower is in full bloom, fade away when the petals fall, and the receptacle is left alone on the top of the flower stalk. It is shaped like a boy's peg-top, with the narrow point downwards, and the broad circular end uppermost. The little fruits commonly called "seed" are immersed separately from its neighbors in this spongy receptacle. Now this is wholly a different state of things from those found in the water lily. There the little fruits, although individually free their entire length, are inclosed in a hollow case, and can thus touch each other. The degree of freedom is of course greater in the Lotus, where each little fruit has its own circle, instead of living in one large dormitory, with many other families, as the water lily carpels have to do. But in one respect, at any rate, the fruits of the water lily and the Lotus are alike—"they are all very wholesome eating."

The bulb of the Egyptian Lotus is very sweet and wholesome, and the seeds, when taken from the *ciborium* or capsule, are ground into flour and mixed with either milk or water. Baked in the same way as bread, and eaten warm, fresh from the oven, it is considered very wholesome. It supplies the place of corn to the poorer classes throughout Egypt, who are unable to obtain that commodity.

Before leaving the Delta of the Nile, I would like to call the attention of my readers to the natural chain of lakes that run from the Mediterranean Sea to the Gulf of Suez. First comes Menzala, next Balah, then Timsha and finally the Great Bitter Lakes, and the Gulf of Suez reaching down the Red Sea, giving one the impression that the two seas were originally connected. I incline to the same opinion, in relation to this matter, as Mr. Stanley Lane Poole. He says in his work "Egypt," page 113: "The Isthmus of Suez was originally a strait, and the only eminence on its low level surface—the hilly district called *El-Gisr*, or the causeway near the middle—is the result of the accumulation of sand produced by the meeting of the two seas; aided by the silting up of the country about the Isthmus, which is the counterpart of the depression still taking place along the coast of the Delta, in spite of the Nile deposit. The silting, however, did not cause the drying-up of the entire strait; but left a series of lakes or salt marshes," such as I have spoken of above.

These salt marshes extending over Lower Egypt are not cultivated, but are still valuable for the pasturage of cattle, as luxuriant herbage grows here in abundance. The men who herded and attended to the raising of stock were a wild, lawless race, according to Strabo and other historians. They dwelt in the midst of the marshes, upon the margins of the lagunes, or brackish lakes, and lived in huts made from the reeds and grasses that grew there. They subsisted on the roots of the papyrus, lotus and various other esculent plants, together with the leguminuous class, such as the lentils, etc., which formed the principal portion of their diet. The raising of oxen for agricultural purposes unquestionably received careful attention, as both in plowing and in treading out the grain no other animal was ever used. This fact made the maintenance of cows and oxen, not alone a necessity for agricultural purposes, but as beasts of burden. In the representations upon the walls of many of the temples we see cows drawing the sled upon which the mummy was conveyed to the tomb, while the stones brought from the quarries of Mokattum for the purpose of repairing the Memphian temple are represented as being drawn by three pair of oxen. According to the ancient paintings and the hieroglyphic inscriptions, I should judge their domestic animals were the source of much care and solicitude.

The ancient Egyptians also raised great quantities of sheep in the Delta, specially for their wool. Their flesh was eaten for food in Lower Egypt, but was not used in the Theban Nome, because the ram was held sacred to their great god of Thebas. We learn from *Diodorus* that the ewes were very prolific, bearing lambs and yielding wool twice in the year.

Wool, when woven into cloth was prohibited for use as under-garments, to be worn next the body as is largely done at the present day. Outer garments might be made from this staple for the priests or even

PROPYLON OF THE TEMPLE OF RAMESES III,

KARNAK.

all classes of people, but under no circumstances was it allowed to be worn or even carried into their temples, nor used for the purpose of embalming or wrapping their mummied dead.

Goats were raised throughout the whole of Upper and Lower Egypt in great quantities, but the Delta was the special place for raising stock of all kinds. After the flooding waters of the Nile had subsided the land over which it had flowed would produce a most luxuriant and abundant crop of herbage, making this part of Egypt the best place for pasturage and the raising of domestic animals.

In many of the tombs throughout the valley of the Nile we find paintings representing either the deceased or his overseer taking an inventory of the stock upon the farm, or belonging to him, or engaged in a tour of inspection for the purpose of numbering the cattle and domestic animals.

I could refer you to many of the tombs in both Upper and Lower Egypt where those engaged in this kind of work are depicted. There is one especial tomb at EL-KAB, the ancient *Eileithyia,* located about five hundred and ten miles above Cairo. on the East bank of the river. The painting is in the tomb of *Paheri* at this place, where either the deceased or his head-man is engaged in counting the domestic animals, attended by servants and scribe, and the number recorded is as follows: cattle, one hundred and twenty-two; sheep or rams, three hundred; goats, one thousand two hundred; and swine, one thousand five hundred. I have described this tomb in another chapter.

The paintings in many of these tombs are extremely interesting and will amply repay those who visit them because they explain a great deal of the home life of these ancient people.

There are two very familiar objects to be seen throughout the valley of the Nile, and they are the *Shaduf* and *Sakiyeh,* two machines used by these people in raising water from the river, for irrigating the land, after the waters have subsided. *The first* is a very simple one, worked by a man, to raise the water from the stream below to irrigate the land above. The machine is composed of two posts sunk into the ground, standing about four or five feet high and about three or four feet apart. On top of these two posts is fastened a cross-bar, on which is suspended a sweep or pole, something like the well-sweep so common in many parts of this country for drawing water from a well. To one end of this sweep is fastened a lump of Nile mud, or clay, and to the other is hung a leathern bucket. The sweep hangs directly over an irrigating ditch whose edge is protected from the wash of the water and the rub of the bucket by a piece of matting. This machine is generally operated by a *half-nude* man. When I say half-nude I mean that he very often wears a calico cap or an old fez. He dips the bucket into the water beneath him by pulling down the sweep, and filling it, the weight at the other end of the pole assists him in raising the bucket to the desired height, so that he can pour its contents into the ditch or pool above. Sometimes when the river is low and the banks are high, as many as four of these machines are required to raise the water to the height of the irrigating ditch and direct it to where it is most needed.

The *Sakiyeh* is a more modern arrangement, generally operated by oxen, the controlling power of which is a boy, nearly always asleep. He is brought into this peculiar hypnotic condition by the continuous turning of the oxen and the shrill monotonous creak of the ever-revolving wheel. "The Sakiyeh" is a large wheel, to which is fastened a large number of native earthen jars, which fill with water as the wheel revolves and empty themselves into a wooden box placed to receive the water and carry it off for irrigating the fields beyond. The wheel, as I have said, is turned by oxen, who go tramping round and round, accompanied by the continual shrieking noise of the ungreased bearings of the machine, which can be heard for quite a distance, while the boy sits perched up in a kind of basket, behind the oxen, nearly always asleep. These are two of the very old methods adopted by the ancient Egyptians to raise the water for irrigating the land. They also use another kind of machine called a *Tabut*, which is a wheel with hollow fellies that lifts the water to the desired height. It is a very light machine and easily worked, but only used in certain places. There is another kind of a wheel in use in the Fayum. It is so arranged that the wheel is turned by the weight or force of the water itself.

All through Egypt old-time methods are passing away, more especially where the banks of the river are high, and larger quantities of water are desired. In such places steam pumps are used, which are run night and day at certain seasons of the year. In this way very large quantities of water are obtained, for which there will be ample need, if the crop be sugar cane, as it requires far more water than any other crop grown in the land of Egypt. The water when raised is distributed over the land by little ditches, or furrows, just as the ranchers do in the southern part of California.

The waters of the Nile contain a very rich compost of Nile mud which enables the farmers to raise successive crops of corn, beans, etc., without manuring the soil. But in the case of sugar cane and cotton a fertilizing agent is needed after every planting, on account of the exhaustive nature of these crops upon the soil, when the fellaheen spreads over the impoverished soil a dressing of pigeon's dung. This fertilizer is far more easily obtained than any other, because these people keep countless numbers of these birds for this express purpose. If the ruins of a city or temple should be in the vicinity they haul the nitrous soil to their fields and use it as a fertilizing agent, which also has been found of great benefit. The inundations not only prepare the fields for the crops but deposits at the same time, a rich fertilizer that causes them to grow in greater abundance than without it. The rising of the river also fills the streams and water courses with an abundance of fish of all kinds, which are very often caught by the fellaheen while engaged in directing the water over the land. When the children of Israel fled out of the land of bondage and were wandering in the desert, they not only sighed for the flesh-pots of Egypt, but for the fish as well.

Kenrick informs us in his "Ancient Egypt," page 71, *et seq.*, that "the mean quantity of water brought down by the Nile, in normal years, as it depends on cosmical causes, probably continues the same from age to age, and the extent of land which it is capable of fertilizing by its overflow tends to increase, till its diffusion is stopped by the Arabian and Libyan hills. Long before the inundation reaches its maximum the dikes which close the communication between the canals and the Nile are opened and the water diffuses itself, first of all, over the lands which lie toward the Desert; gradually as it rises it irrigates the nearer country, but the immediate banks of the river are seldom covered, and serve as a highway for the people while the inundation continues. In the Delta, where the slope is small, the whole country is laid under water during an extraordinary rise, and boats take the place of the ordinary modes of communication. European travellers commonly choose the winter and spring for a journey through Egypt, and therefore do not see the Nile at its height; but those who have resided there through all seasons assure us that the description of Herodotus is still realized, the villages on their elevated sites rising out of a lake, like the Cyclades from the Ægean Sea.

" The trees which grew in Egypt were not numerous; two species of palm, beside their fruit, furnished material from different parts of the tree for every kind of work for which solid timber or tough fibre can be employed. The sycamore and various species of acacia also abounded, but no other trees of a large size were indigenous to the country. The products of the fields of Egypt were almost all the results of cultivation. Grain, herbs, and leguminous vegetables were produced in an abundance which no other country could rival; but its native botany was scanty, the yearly renewal of the soil preventing the seeds which had fallen on the surface from vegetating, and culture exterminating all plants which cannot be made serviceable to man. The fragrance of flowers was wanting in its landscape, for those of Egypt have very little odor. The sandy desert which lies beyond the reach of the inundation has a scanty vegetation of its own—stunted shrubs and herbs, which have generally an aromatic smell."

The construction of the dams, referred to elsewhere, will regulate the flow of water. The banks of the river and various canals will, under these new conditions, always be the highways for the people who live either in Upper or Lower Egypt, and instead of flooding the Delta and destroying villages, etc., it will be a thing of the past.

The Supreme Architect of the Universe.

Blessed is the man who hath obtained
The riches of the wisdom of God;
Wretched is he who hath
A false opinion about things divine.
God may not be approached,
Nor can we reach Him with our eyes,
Or touch Him with our hands.
No human head is placed upon His limbs,
Nor branching arms;
He has no feet to carry Him apace,
Nor other parts of men;
But He is all pure mind, holy and infinite,
Darting with swift thought through the universe,
From end to end.

—EMPEDOCLES.

CHAPTER VIII.

THE SUPREME ARCHITECT OF THE UNIVERSE.

WHEN a man becomes a Mason and takes upon himself the solemn vow that binds us all in bonds of fraternal love, it does not in any way interfere with his belief in God, or his religion, no matter what his belief may be. He need not cease to be a Christian, Mohammedan, Buddhist, Hindu, Jew, or any other denomination. If he earnestly studies the esoteric teachings of ancient Masonry, as taught in the Ancient and Accepted Scottish Rite, he will gain a far deeper insight into his own faith, and a far clearer conception, of his own creed, which will enable him to understand its sublime teachings and spiritual Truths. He will recognize that all religions must have emanated from a common source, originated from the same grand fountain, the "*Ancient Wisdom Religion*" whose eternal verities are to be found in all other teachings, in all other Religions, and may be summarized as follows :—1st. A belief in "One eternal, infinite, incognizable, real Existence. 2nd. From that the manifesting God, unfolding from unity to dualty, from dualty to trinity. 3rd. From the manifested Trinity many spiritual Intelligences guiding the Kosmic order. 4th. Man a reflection of the manifested God and therefore a trinity fundamentally, his inner and real self being eternal, one with the Self of the universe. 5th. His evolution by repeated incarnations, into which he is drawn by desire, and from which he is set free by knowledge and sacrifice, becoming divine in potency as he had ever been in latency."

I have read many works on religion, science and philosophy, and among them all, outside of the "Secret Doctrine," I have found none which gave me so much genuine pleasure, and from which I derived so much profit, as I did in perusing that most valuable and extraordinary work "Morals and Dogmas," from the pen of that most scholarly gentleman and Brother Mason, General Albert Pike. I most earnestly urge every Mason to possess a copy of this magnificent work, because it will help him to come to an understanding of the profound Symbology of the Masonic Fraternity, and thoroughly comprehend the sublime philosophical Truths of the esoteric teachings of our own beloved Ancient and Accepted Scottish Rite. Therefore, in order that you, my dear Brothers and readers, may have some idea of the writings of this most worthy exponent, I quote you from the preface, page 4 :—

" The teachings of these Readings are not sacramental so far as they go beyond the realm of Morality into those of other domains of Thought and Truth. The Ancient and Accepted Scottish Rite uses the word ' Dogma ' in its true sense, of *doctrine or teaching ;* and is not *dogmatic* in the odious sense of that term. Every one is entirely free to reject and dissent from whatsoever herein may seem to him to be untrue or unsound. It is only required of him that he shall weigh what is taught and give it fair hearing and unpredjudiced judgment. Of course, the ancient theosophic and philosophic speculations are not embodied as a part of the *doctrines* of the Rites ; but because it is of interest and profit to know what the Ancient Intellect thought upon these subjects, and because nothing so conclusively proves the radical difference between our human and the animal nature, as the capacity of the human mind to entertain such speculations in regard to itself and the Deity."

I shall once more quote you from " Morals and Dogmas," page 524, *et seq.*: " To every Mason there is a God One Supreme, Infinite in Goodness, Wisdom, Foresight, Justice and Benevolence ; Creator, Disposer, and Preserver of all things. How or by what intermediate He creates, and acts, and in what way He unfolds, and manifests Himself, Masonry leaves to creeds, and Religions to inquire.

" To every Mason the soul of man is immortal. Whether it emanates from and will return to God and what its continued mode of existence hereafter, each judges for himself. Masonry was not made to settle that.

" To every Mason, WISDOM, or INTELLIGENCE, FORCE, or STRENGTH and HARMONY, or FITNESS, and BEAUTY are the Trinity of the attributes of God. With the subtleties of Philosophy concerning them, Masonry does not meddle, nor decide as to the reality of the supposed Existences which are their personifications : nor whether the Christian

Trinity be such a personification or a Reality of the gravest import and significance.

"To every Mason the Infinite Justice and Benevolence of God give ample assurance that Evil will ultimately be dethroned, and the Good, the True and the Beautiful reign triumphant and eternal. It teaches as it feels and knows, that Evil, and Pain, and Sorrow exists as a part of a wise and beneficient plan, all the parts of which work together under God's eye to a result which shall be perfection. Whether the existence of evil is rightly explained in this creed or that by Typhon, the Great Serpent, by Ahriman and his armies of Wicked Spirits, by the Giants and Titans that war against Heaven, by the two co-existing Principles of Good and Evil, by Satan's temptation and the fall of Man, by Lok and the serpent Fenris, it is beyond the domain of Masonry to decide, nor does it need to inquire. Nor is it within the province to determine how the ultimate triumph of Light and Truth and Good, over Darkness and Error and Evil is to be achieved; nor whether the Redeemer looked and longed for by all nations, hath appeared in Judea or is yet to come.

"It reverences all the great reformers. It sees in Moses, the Lawgiver of the Jews, in Confucius, and Zoroaster, in Jesus of Nazareth, and in the Arabian Iconoclast, Great Teachers of Morality and Eminent Reformers, if no more; and allows every brother of the Fraternity to assign to each, such higher and even Divine character, as his creed and truth require.

"Thus Masonry disbelieves no truth and teaches unbelief in no creed, except so far as such creed may lower its lofty estimate of the Deity and degrade Him to the level of the passions of humanity, deny the high destiny of man, impugn the goodness and benevolence of the Supreme God, strike at the great columns of Masonry, Faith, Hope and Charity, or inculcate immorality and disregard of the active duties of the Fraternity.

"Masonry is a workshop; but one in which all civilized men can unite; for it does not undertake to explain, or dogmatically to settle those great mysteries, that are above the feeble comprehension of our human intellect. It trusts in God, and Hopes; it Believes, like a child, and is humble. It draws no sword to compel others to adopt its belief, or to be happy with its hopes. And it Waits with patience to understand the mysteries of nature and nature's God hereafter.

"The greatest mysteries in the universe are those which are ever going on around us; so trite and common to us that we never note them or reflect upon them. Wise men tell us of the *laws* that regulate the motions of the spheres, which flashing in huge circles and spinning on their axis, are also ever darting with inconceivable rapidity through the infinities of space; while we atoms sit here and dream that all was made for *us*. They tell us learnedly of centripetal and centrifugal *forces*, gravity and attraction, and all the other sounding terms invented to hide a *want* of meaning. There are other forces in the universe than those that are mechanical.

"The mysteries of the Great Universe of God! How *can* we with our limited mental vision expect to grasp and comprehend them! Infinite SPACE stretching out from us every way, without limit; infinite TIME, without beginning or end; and *we* HERE and NOW, in the centre of each! An infinity of suns, the nearest of which only *diminish* in size, viewed with the most powerful telescope; each with its retinue of worlds, infinite numbers of such suns, so remote from us that their light would not reach us journeying during an infinity of time, while the light that *has* reached us from some that we *seem* to see, has been upon its journey for fifty centuries; our world spinning upon its axis, and rushing ever in its circuit around the sun, and all our systems revolving round some great central point; and that, and suns, and stars, and worlds evermore flashing onward with incredible rapidity through illimitable space; and then in every drop of water that we drink, in every morsel of much of our food, in the air in the earth, in the sea, incredible multitudes of living creatures, invisible to the naked eye, of a minuteness beyond belief, yet organized, living, feeding, *perhaps* with consciousness of identity, and memory and instinct.

"God, therefore, is a mystery, only as everything that surrounds us, and as we ourselves, are a mystery. We know that there is and must be a FIRST CAUSE. His attributes, severed from Himself, are unrealities. As color and extension, weight and hardness do not exist apart from matter as separate existences and substantives, spiritual or immaterial; so the Goodness, Wisdom, Justice, Mercy and Benevolence of God are not independent existences, personify them as men may, but *attributes* of the Deity, the *adjectives* of One Great Substantive. But we know that He must be Good, True, Wise, Just, Benevolent, Merciful; and in all these, and all His other attributes, Perfect and Infinite, because we are conscious that these are laws imposed on us by the very nature of things, necessary and without which the universe would be confusion, and the existence of a God incredible. They are His essence, and necessary, as His existence.

" He is the Living, Thinking, Intelligent Soul of the Universe, the PERMANENT, the STATIONARY, of Simon Magus, the ONE that *always is* of Plato, as contradistinguished from the perpetual flux and reflux, or *Genesis of things.* And as the thoughts of the soul, emanating from the soul, become audible and visible in WORDS, so did THE THOUGHT OF GOD, springing up within himself, immortal *as* Himself, when once conceived,—immortal *before*, because *in* Himself, utter itself in THE WORD, its manifestations and mode of communication, and thus create the material, mental, spiritual universe, which, like Him, never *began* to exist."

This is the *real* idea of the *ancient nations:* GOD, the Almighty, Father and Source of all; His THOUGHT conceiving the whole universe, and *willing* its creation: His WORD *uttering* that THOUGHT and thus becoming the Creator or Demiourgos in whom was Life and Light, and that Light the life of the universe. Nor did that Word *cease* at the single act of Creation; and having set going the great machine and enacted the laws of its motion and progression, of birth and life, and change and death, cease to exist, or remain thereafter in inert idleness.

FOR THE THOUGHT OF GOD LIVES AND IS IMMORTAL. Embodied in the *Word*, is not only *created*, but it *preserves.* It conducts and controls the Universe, all spheres, all worlds, all actions of mankind and every animate and inanimate creature. It speaks in the soul of every man that lives. The stars, the earth, the trees, the winds, the universal voice of nature, tempest and avalanche; the sea's roar and the grave voice of the waterfall, the hoarse thunder and the low whisper of the brook, the song of birds, the voice of love, the speech of men, all are the alphabet in which it communicates itself to men, and informs them of the will and law of God, the Soul of the Universe.

12

Any man gazing up into the cosmic space, of a glorious summer's night, will see myriads of starry worlds rotating upon their axis, shining with a glory incomprehensibly grand, each and every one moving in rythmic harmony along its allotted path, according to the law governing these glorious stellar worlds. He will not only be impressed by the grandeur of their movements, but he will recognize that this planet of ours, sinks into comparative insignificance, when compared to those glorious orbs refulgent in the starry vault above, and he will begin to realize that they are not moving by chance, that their motions are not at random, but that each and all are a part of the Divine whole, and that they all perform their various motions in space according to Divine Ideation, or that Divine Principle that demonstrates to man that there is a something—an incomprehensible CAUSE, which directs and controls the motions of these planets through the spatial depths around him. Then will he dimly sense the Divine in their motions, and, like me, bow with awe and reverence before this Divine and incomprehensible Principle, a knowledge of which passeth all understanding.

Every human being, no matter how low in the ethnological scale of humanity we find him, no matter how degraded and brutal he is, no matter how deluded by superstition and ignorance he may be, in the silence of the night, surrounded by the grandeur and harmony of nature, and impressed by the sublimity of the underlying *ideation* that permeates it, is most assuredly capable of forming for himself, some abstract conception of a Deity, whereby to account for the sublime grandeur and glory of nature in all her differentiations and wonderful manifestations, which an anthropomorphic God could not logically explain.

He will see around him a world that is vibrating with life and harmony. He will see in every fronded fern and flower an expression of the Divinity. He will see a world cycling along in harmony, performing its various motions in space with an exactitude seemingly incomprehensible. He will hear in the mountain stream, as it flows along o'er its rocky bed, the voice of his Maker, and he would hear it in the rustling corn, the swaying pines, the song of birds or the hum of bees, and in the whisperings of insect life, as they revel in a glory of life and sunshine, in the rippling waves as they beat upon the shore, or the gliding river that goes murmuring by to its home in the sea. And from out the mire of doubt and hesitation he never loses completely the consciousness of Divine possibilities, and he will dimly sense the hallowed touch of his heavenly Father in these sublime and glorious manifestations.

This potential sensing of the Divine is most assuredly the true difference between man and the superior animals. It is this distinctive power in man which lifts him far above the level of his retarded brethren in evolution, the animal, and justifies his claim to having latent within him the *potentiality of becoming the highest being in nature's evolutionary processes.*

The faculty of reasoning and using an articulate language, places man at the head of the animal kingdom which he dominates, through the potential forces he has developed during the many lives that he has lived, and by the various experiences he has gained, makes all below him subservient to his indomitable will and energy. If we consider the animal kingdom as a whole, and mankind separated from it, and forming a class of its own, we shall find that articulated language is the result of the *Manasic* element within us, and of long ages of accumulated training, and that it is an essential attribute of man, while the phonetic expression of the animal, compared to the articulate of the human, is only of secondary consideration. We find that some animals seem to reason far better than some men, and the true difference between the two is not so very great, after all. The animal is just a little way below us on the path of evolution, dowered with instinctual cognition, while man has a self-conscious knowledge of the potential forces within him. Man has been illuminated with mind, and by its divine touch he has been transformed into the TRUE MAN, THE THINKER. But we must thoroughly understand that this transformation *comes from above.* Man's spiritual soul *comes from the Divinity itself,* and not from below, evolving through the brute. It is a ray of the Divine Spirit that makes him and his Father one. This God in man is the guide and director that helps him to gain experience and knowledge during the many lives that lie before him, on the path his feet must tread. It is that glorious Light which illuminates his path and leads him on to far higher planes of spiritual unfoldment, until he will eventually stand upon the threshold of complete perfection, when he will fully realize that he and his Father are one.

We have much to learn from the insect world, and more especially the *Ant*. Of all the insects that we know, none seem to me to possess so much intelligence as does the ant. Again look at the *Bees*, with their extraordinary mechanical skill and ingenuity, their wonderful industry and forethought, with the methods they adopt in building their comb, the shape and arrangement of their cells, their knowledge of what will give the most strength and greatest storage capacity for the amount of space and material used. These things command our most profound attention for they are all deeply interesting and well worthy of earnest study and thought. Look at the Elephant, the Horse and the Dog, and their remarkable power of finding methods by which to accomplish their desires. These animals are quite equal to the average man, in the practical application of selfish reasoning, and for the purpose of supplying themselves with the needs of every day life. Yet, notwithstanding all these remarkable instinctual developments, no animal has ever shown the slightest capacity for abstract reasoning or conceptions independent of its temporary wants or desires, and not the slightest tendency to worship the Divine principle that is manifested in the wondrous beauties of Nature surrounding him.

J. D. Buck, 32°, in his "Mystic Masonry," page 125, *et seq.*, says: "How much one's idea of God colors all his thoughts and deeds is seldom realized. The ordinary crude and ignorant conception of a personal God more often results in slavish fear on the one hand and Atheism on the other. It is what Carlyle calls 'an absentee God, doing nothing since the six days of creation, but sitting on the outside and seeing it go!' This idea of God carries with it, of course, the idea of creation, as something already completed in time; when the fact is, creation is a process, without beginning or end. The world—all worlds—are being 'created' to-day as much as at any period in the past. Even the apparent destruction of worlds is a creative, or evolutionary process. Emanating from the bosom of the all, and running their cyclic course; day alternating with night, on the outer physical plane, they are again *indrawn* to the invisible plane, only to re-emerge after a longer night and start again on a higher cycle of evolution. Theologians have tried in vain to attach the idea of *immanence* to that of personality, and ended in a jargon of words, and utter confusion of ideas. A personal Absolute is not, except in potency. God does not *think*, but is the cause of Thought. God does not love, he is Love, in the perfect or absolute sense; and so with all the Divine attributes. God is thus the concealed Logos the 'Causeless Cause,' the 'Rootless Root,' God never manifests Himself, to be seen of men. Creation is His manifestation, and as creation is not complete, and never will be, and as it never had a beginning, there is a concealed or unrevealed potency back of and beyond all creation, which is still God. Now, Space is the most perfect symbol of this *idea* of Divinity; for it enters into all our concepts, and is the basis of all our experiences. We cannot fathom it, or define it, or exclude it from a single thought or experience. Space is boundless, infinite, unfathomable, unknowable; in all, over all, through all. We know that It Is, and that is all that we know about it.

"But are not these just the attributes that are assigned to the Absolute and Infinite Deity? And they are all *negations*. God, says the Kabalah, is *No Thing*. But the theologian will hasten to say that this is pure Pantheism. It is no more Pantheism than it is Atheism, for, as already shown, the *Ain Soph* is before and beyond Creation, or Cosmos. It is not God deduced or derived from Nature, but precisely the reverse; nature derived from God, and yet God remains 'the same, yesterday, to-day and forever'—the CHANGELESS. The stability of nature is derived from the unchangeableness of God. God never tires, is not exhausted at His work, needing rest. That were so human as to be childish, and the idea perhaps, originated from the cyclic law found in the Kabalah of the 'Days and Nights of Brahm,' the 'Manvantaras and Pralayas,' or periods of 'outbreathing,' and of 'inbreathing' in the cycles of evolution."

God, according to Pythagoras, was ONE, a single substance, whose continuous parts extend through all the Universe without separation, difference or inequality, like the soul in the human body. He denied the doctrine of the Spiritualists, who had severed the Divinity from the Universe, making Him exist apart from the Universe, which thus became no more than a material work, on which acted the Abstract Cause, a God isolated from it.   The Ancient Theology did not so separate God from the Universe.   This Eusebius attests, in saying that but a small number of wise men, like Moses, had sought for God or the cause of all, outside of that ALL; while the philosophers of Egypt and Phœnicia, real authors of all the old Cosmogonies had placed the supreme Cause *in* the Universe itself, and in its parts, so that, in their view, the world and all its parts are *in* God.

Every man conceives of a Deity according to the dictates of his own conscience and expresses it in accordance with that conception.   For instance, the Red man that roams, in a semi-civilized condition, the mountains and plains of this continent, defies the forces of Nature he does not understand, and yet in the depth of his heart, makes his devotions to the Great Spirit that is just as incomprehensible.

Go to the Chinaman, and he will teach you the Law of Love that was taught by Lao-tze long centuries before Christ was born, and yet the same Truths are to be found in your own creed.   Go to the denizen of Central Africa and you will find him enwrapped in a knowledge of this Divine Principle to which I have referred above.

The following beautiful and expressive poem gives such a full and comprehensive idea of the Supreme Ruler of the Universe that I am constrained to publish it in its entirety for the benefit of those who may not have had the opportunity of seeing it before:

GOD.

O, Thou Eternal One! whose presence bright
    All space doth occupy, all motion guide;
Unchanged through Time's all devastating flight;
    Thou, only God! There is no God beside!
Being above all beings! Mighty One!
    Whom none can comprehend and none explore,
Who fil'st existence with Thyself alone—
    Embracing all—supporting—ruling o'er—
    Being whom we call God—now and evermore.

In its sublime research, philosophy
    May measure out the ocean deep—may count
The sands or the sun's rays—but God! for thee
    There is no weight nor measure—none can mount

A MINARET.

Up to Thy mysteries: Reason's brightest spark,
  Though kindled by Thy light, in vain may try
To trace thy counsels, infinite and dark;
  And thought is lost e'er thought can soar so high,
  Even like past moments in eternity.

Thou from primeval nothingness didst call,
  First, chaos—then existence—Lord, on thee
Eternity had its foundation—all
  Sprang forth from Thee—light, joy, harmony,
Sole origin—all life, all beauty, Thine.
  Thy word created all, and doth create;
Thy splendor fills all space with rays divine.
  Thou art and wert and shall be! Glorious! Great!
  Life-giving, life-sustaining Potentate!

Thy chains the unmeasured universe surround—
  Upheld by Thee, by Thee inspired with breath!
Thou the beginning with the end has bound,
  And beautifully mingled life and death!
As sparks mount upwards from the fiery blaze,
  So suns are born, so worlds sprang forth from Thee;
And as the spangles in the sunny rays
  Shine round the silver snow, the pageantry
Of Heaven's bright army glitters in Thy praise.

A million torches lighted by Thy hand
  Wander unwearied through the blue abyss;
They own Thy power, accomplish Thy command;
  All gay with life, all eloquent with bliss.
What shall we call them? Piles of crystal light?
  A glorious company of golden streams?
Lamps of celestial ether burning bright?
  Sun's lighting systems with their joyous beams?
But Thou to these are as the moon to night!

Yet as a drop of water in the sea,
  All this magnificence in Thee is lost;
What are ten thousand worlds compared to Thee,
  . And what am I, then? Heaven's unnumbered host,

Though multiplied by myriads, and arrayed
    In all the glory of sublimest thought
Is but an atom in the balance weighed
    Against Thy greatness, is a cypher brought
    Against infinity. What am I, then? Nought!

Nought! But the effluence of Thy light divine.
    Pervading worlds hath reached my bosom, too;
Yes, in my spirit dost Thy spirit shine,
    As shines the sunbeam in a drop of dew,
Nought! But I live, and on Hope's pinion's fly
    Eager towards Thy presence; for in Thee
I live and breathe and dwell; aspiring high,
    Even to the throne of Thy divinity.
    I am, O God! and surely Thou must be!

Thou art! Directing, guiding all, thou art,
    Direct my understanding, then, to thee;
Control my spirit, guide my wandering heart;
    Though but an atom 'midst immensity,
Still I am something, fashioned by Thy hand!
    I hold a middle rank 'twixt heaven and earth,
On the last verge of mortal being stand
    Close to the realms where angels have their birth.
Just on the boundary of the spirit land.

The chain of being is complete in me;
    In me is matter's last gradation lost,
And the next step is spirit—Deity!
    I can command Thy lightning, and am dust!
A monarch and a slave - a worm—a God!
    Whence came I here? And how so marvelously
Constructed and conceived? Unknown! This clod
    Lives surely through some higher energy, .
For from itself alone it could not be.

Creator! Yes, Thy wisdom and Thy word
    Created me! Thou source of life and good!
Thou spirit of my spirit, and my Lord!
    Thy light, Thy love, in their bright plentitude

Filled me with an immortal soul, to spring
 Over the abyss of death, and bade it wear
The garments of eternal day, and wing
 Its heavenly flight beyond this little sphere,
Even to its source—to Thee—its author there.

O thought ineffable! O vision blest!
 Though worthless our conceptions all of Thee,
Yet, shall Thy shadowed image fill our breast,
 And with it homage to the Deity,
God! Thus above my lowly thoughts can soar;
 Thus seek Thy presence, Being wise and good
Midst Thy vast works, admire, obey, adore;
 And when the tongue is eloquent no more,
The soul shall speak in tears of gratitude.
         —DERZHAVEN.

Civilized men of all nations formulate special gods to suit their own particular spiritual needs and endow them with the peculiar attributes, which are simply personifications of the general characteristics of the worshippers themselves. They make gods in their own image, and worship them with an extraordinary devotion. But as soon as the *Mind* rises above these social traits and personal characteristics; as soon as he or they become capable of seeing something more grand, more sublime, more ennobling, more spiritualizing beneath the frivolities of these personal gods, then will they be enabled to form some pure abstract conception, devoid of concrete symbolism, that senses the necessary existence of an underlying Divine Principle, manifesting Itself in, through, and by Nature. In its widest sense, feeling the mighty Presence of the Infinite. Then will the mind of Man bow down in reverence, making no rash attempt to comprehend the Absolute, yet fully conscious of the fact that being but an infinitisimal part of the SUPREME ALL it is simply impossible for the finite to understand the Infinite. The voice of the Divine is one and the same, whether coming from Indian, Chinese, African or civilized white man. The New teachings are like the Old, if we only understand them, for the underlying Truths of all Religions, all philosophies, and all sciences are identically the same. No common sense reasoning Man, who is capable of thinking for himself, will ever deny this fact.

The so-called Atheists and Agnostics are in open revolt only against the attributes, more or less fanciful and erroneous, with which sects and creeds describe their respective and exclusive gods. Not so much against the conception of a Divine Principle, *per se*, but only as to the absurd way in which the various gods are represented.

Voltaire derided and scoffed at the churches, creeds, dogmas and priest-craft, and those who believed in them, as well as what he called their mummeries and sophistry, ridiculing the Bishops and the Clergy. Yet, notwithstanding, he wrote—"If God did not exist it would be necessary to invent one."

Robert Ingersoll, the foremost and most aggressive agnostic in the closing years of the nineteenth century, brought forth the power of his wit and eloquence against abuses and errors born of ignorance and fanaticism. He assailed all religious forms of faith and practice with the keen, unphilosophical weapons of satire, obloquy and witticism, yet any thoughtful reader of his best efforts can feel vibrating between the lines a deep, true reverence for the unknowable, unconceivable, self-evident Divine Principle.

No matter where we force our investigations, even if we carry them into the very strongholds of the most terrible exponents of religious faith and practice, enemies of all creeds and dogmas; I refer to the materialistic scientists, or rather naturalists, or Darwinians, at whose head stood the author of the "History of Natural Creation," Professor Heackell, late of the University of Jena, whose history is diametrically opposed to the cosmogony of the Pentateuch, or the orthodox, super-natural or miraculous creation; yet, we shall find expressed in clear technical scientific terms, in that work, a positive recognition of the Divine Principle as the Eternal source of all that is, or ever will be. He refutes entirely the dualistic theory of Agassiz, because it supposes two distinct factors:—an extra cosmic God and Nature as a separate thing, and he closes his remarks by this unmistakable declaration: " But they overlook the fact that this personal creation is only an idealized organism endowed with human attributes. The more developed men of the present day are capable of conceiving that infinitely nobler and sub-limer idea of God which alone is compatible with the monistic conception of the universe, and which recognizes God's Spirit and power in all phenomena, without exception. It is of this noble idea of God that Gœthe says 'certainly there does not exist a more beautiful worship of God than that which needs no image, but which arises in our hearts from converse with Nature.' By it alone we arrive at the sublime 'Pantheistic' idea of the unity of God and Nature. Be it understood that Pantheistic here does not mean, as usually translated, many gods, but All God; from *pan* (all) and *theos* (God). It is synonomous with Monism and Deism." Can Heackell be charged with Atheism?

If we carefully examine the writings of the most eminent men of every age in the world's history, especially those who are and were sincere and truthful; no matter whether they be philosophers, scientists, materialists, spiritualists, freethinkers, poets or religious writers, we shall find that each one of them recognizes a Deity according to his own conception, differing in form and attributes from the individual conceptions by others. For instance, in examining "*The Zend-Avesta*," the sacred book of the Parsees or Sun worshippers of Persia and India; the followers of Zoroaster, the ancient teacher of the Religion of Magi, we shall find they believed in two spirits,—Good and Evil—typified by *Light* and *Darkness*, and that these two spirits, now and always have been engaged in antagonistic strife, making war one upon the other, until Light prevails, that is, until Man has conquered himself. We shall also find they believed that God has neither face nor form, color nor shape, nor fixed place and that there is no other like Him. He is Himself singly, such a glory that we cannot praise nor describe Him, nor can our mind comprehend Him.

Rollin says: "As the Magi held images in utter abhorrence, they worshipped God only under the form of *Fire*, on account of its purity, brightness, activity, subtlety, fecundity and incorruptibility as the most perfect symbol of the Deity."

"The Dabistan," compiled from the works of the ancient "*Guebers*," or "Fire Worshippers," states that the Persians long before the mission of Zoroaster, venerated a prophet called *Mahabad*, whom they considered the Father of Mankind. He taught "eternity," or boundless time, has neither beginning nor end, and is the only thing that can neither be created nor destroyed, but is that which creates and destroys everything else. Therefore time is considered the great first CAUSE or Creator.

The ancient Egyptians worshipped the Sun, as God, whom they considered to be *the cause* from which, and by which, all things were created. They believed that when the sun sank beneath the under-world and darkness covered the face of the earth he was engaged in fighting *Appepi*, the great serpent, who was at the head of a very large army of personifications of darkness, mist and cloud, trying to over-throw him, but, as he appeared again in the morning, day after day, in all his resplendent glory, they hailed him with joy and gladness as the victor, and worshipped him throughout the whole of Egypt. At Memphis he was worshipped as the creator god Ptah, the greatest of all gods. He was the ancient god of this city whom the Greeks called *Hephæstus*. The black bull was the symbol of this god; at Thebes Ammon-Ra or Amun-Ra "the veiled or unseen," the mystery of exist-ence. Osiris, the "Good," the beneficient principle pervading the universe, was one of those worshipped generally. Ra, or On, was origi-nally the sun-god, apparently a common object of worship to all prehistoric races. Heliopolis, or City of the Sun, being afterwards the Greek name of On, the town. Horus, the Light-bringer, weighed the heart of each man after his death; and as the welfare of the departed spirit or "double" was connected with that of the deserted body, the latter ought to be carefully preserved. Hence the great motive for embalming their dead and building massive tombs for the wealthy.

The sun was worshipped all through Egypt, under various names, as the creator and preserver of all things, because its motions demonstrated to them life, death and re-incarnation. When it appeared in the East it was emblematic of life coming forth into light and definition; in reaching its meridian height and glory, God the Creator giving forth to the world its fructifying, vivifying principles and demonstrating the fountain from which all things come. When it sank beneath the western horizon, leaving the earth enshrouded in darkness, it was emble-matic of death; but when it again re-appeared in the early morning, lighting up the eastern sky with a perfect halo of light and glory, tinting the magnificent tombs and temples in rainbow hues, when the feathered songsters burst into voluminous praise and harmony, men prostrated themselves in adoration before the emblem of that incomprehensible principle which holds Kosmos and solar systems within the hollow of his hand. This continual diurnal rising of the sun-god Ra was symbolical of the re-incarnation of the spirit of life; therefore to them life was emblematic of death, and death symbolical of life. Death is but an aspect of life, for the destruction of one material form is simply the prelude to the building up of others, a fact evidenced in all nature. " Death consists, indeed, in a repeated process of unrobing, or unsheathing. The immortal part of man shakes off from itself, one after the other, its outer casings, and, as the snake from its skin, the butterfly from its chrysalis, emerged from one after another, passing into a higher state of consciousness.

"The cardinal doctrines of the Kabalah embrace the nature of the Deity. the divine emanations or Sephiroth, the cosmogony, the creation of angels and man, their destiny, and the import of the revealed law. According to this esoteric doctrine. God who is boundless and above everything, even being and thinking. is called AIN-SOPH. He is the space of the universe. In this boundlessness He could not be comprehended by the intellect or described in words, and as such the Ain-Soph was in a certain sense—non-existent. To make this existence known and comprehended, the Ain-Soph had to become active and creative. As creation involves intention, desire, thought and work, and as these are properties which imply limit and belong to a finite being, and moreover as the imperfect and circumscribed nature of this creation precludes the idea of its being the direct work of the infinite and perfect, the *Ain-Soph* had to become creative through the medium of ten *Sephiroth*, or intelligences which emanated from him like rays proceeding from a luminary. Now the wish to become manifest and known, and hence the idea of creation is co-eternal, with the inscrutable Deity. The first manifestation of this primordial WILL is called *Sephira* or emanation. This first Sephira, this spiritual substance which existed in the Ain-Soph from all eternity contained nine other intelligences or Sephiroth. These again emanated one from another, the second from the first, the third from the second, and so on up to ten. The ten Sephiroth, forming among themselves, and with the Ain-Soph, a strict unity, and simply representing different aspects of one and the same being—' The Creator and Preserver of all things.'"

Albert Pike, in "Morals and Dogmas," says on page 221, *et seq:* "Man's views in regard to God will contain only as much positive truth as the human mind is capable of receiving, whether that truth is attained by the exercise of reason, or communicated by revelation. It must necessarily be both limited and alloyed, to bring it within the competence of finite human intelligence. Being finite we can form no correct or adequate idea of the Infinite; being material we can form no clear conception of the Spiritual. We do believe in and know the infinity of space and time and the spirituality of the soul; but the *idea* of that infinity and spirituality eludes us. Even Omnipotence cannot infuse infinite conceptions into finite minds; nor can God, without first entirely changing the conditions of our being, pour a complete and full knowledge of His own nature and attributes into the narrow capacity of the human soul. . . .

"The consciousness of the individual reveals *itself* alone. His knowledge cannot pass beyond the limits of his own being. His conceptions of other things and other beings *are only his conceptions.* They are not those things or beings *themselves.* The living principle of a living universe must be INFINITE; while all *our* ideas and conceptions are finite and applicable only to finite beings. The Deity is thus not an object of *knowledge*, but of *faith;* not to be approached by the *understanding*, but by the *moral sense;* not to be conceived, but to be *felt.* All attempts to embrace the infinite in the conception of the finite are, and must be, only accommodations to the frailty of man. Shrouded from comprehension in an obscurity from which a chastened imagination is awed back, and thought retreats in conscious weakness, the Divine Nature is a theme on which man is little entitled to dogmatize. Here the philosophic intellect becomes most painfully aware of its own insufficiency.

"Every man's conception of God must vary with his mental cultivation and mental powers. If any one contents himself with any *lower* image than his intellect is capable of grasping, then he contents himself with that which is false to *him*, as well as false *in fact.* If lower than he can reach, he must needs *feel* it to be false. . . . .

"God and Truth are inseparable; a knowledge of God is possession of the saving oracles of Truth. In proportion as the thought and purpose of the individual are trained to conformity with the rule of right prescribed by Supreme Intelligence, so far is his happiness promoted, and the purpose of his existence fulfilled. In this way a new life arises in him; he is no longer isolated, but part of the eternal harmonies around him. His erring will is directed by the influence of a higher will, informing and moulding it in the path of true happiness.

"The grand objects of nature perpetually constrain men to think of their author. The Alps are the great altar of Europe; the nocturnal sky has been to mankind the dome of a temple starred all over with admonitions to reverence, trust and love. The Scriptures for the human race are writ in earth and heaven. No organ or miserere touches the heart like the sonorous swell of the ocean wave's immeasureable laugh. Every year the old world puts on new bridal beauty, and celebrates its Whit Sunday, when in the sweet spring each bush and tree dons reverently its new glories. Autumn is a long All Saints' day; and the harvest is Hallowmass to mankind. Before the human race marched down from the slopes of the Himalayas to take possession of Asia, Chaldea and Egypt, men marked each annual crisis, the solstices, and the equinoxes, and celebrated religious festivals therein; and even then and ever since, the material was and has been the element of communion between man and God.

"Nature is full of religious lessons to a thoughtful man. He dissolves the matter of the universe, leaving only its forces; he dissolves away the phenomena of human history, leaving only immortal spirit; he studies the law, the mode of action of these forces, and this spirit; which makes up the material and the human world, and cannot fail to be filled with reverence, with trust, with boundless love of the Infinite God, who devised these laws of matter and mind, and thereby bears up this marvellous universe of things and men. Science has its New Testament; and the beatitudes of philosophy are profoundly touching. An undevout astronomer is mad. Familiarity with the grass, and the trees teaches us deeper lessons of love and trust than we can glean from the writings of Fenelon and Augustine. The great Bible of God is ever open before mankind. The eternal flowers of heaven seem to shed sweet influence on the perishable blossoms of the earth. The great sermon of Jesus was preached on a mountain, which preached to him as he did to the people, and his figures of speech were first natural figures of fact.

" Beautifully, above the great wide chaos of human errors, shines the calm, clear light of natural human religion, revealing to us God as the Infinite Parent of all, perfectly powerful, wise, just, loving, and perfectly holy too. Beautifully around, stretches off every way the Universe, the Great Bible of God. Material nature is its Old Testament, millions of years old, thick with eternal truths under our feet, glittering with ever-lasting glories over our heads, and human Nature is the New Testament from the Infinite God, every day revealing a new page as Time turns over the leaves. Immortality stands waiting to give a recompense for every virtue not rewarded, for every tear not wiped away, for every sorrow undeserved, for every prayer, for every pure intention, and emotion of the heart. And over the whole, over Nature, Material and Human, over this Mortal Life, and over the Eternal Past and Future, the infinite Loving-kindness of God the Father comes enfolding all, and blessing everything that ever was, that is, that ever shall be.

" In the Divine Pymander, and 5th book, we find Hermes Trismeg-istus saying of God ' It is His essence to be pregnant, or great, in all things, and to make them. As without a maker it is impossible that any-thing should be made, so it is that he should not always be, and always be making all things in heaven, in the air, in the earth, in the deep, in the whole world, and in every part of the whole that is or that is not. For there is nothing in the whole world, that is not Himself, both the things that are, and the things that are not. This is God that is better than any name ; this is He that is secret ; this is He that is most mani-fest ; this is He that is to be seen by the mind ; this is He that is visible to the eye ; this is He that hath no body ; and this is He that hath many bodies ; rather there is nothing of any body which is not He. For He alone is all things. And for this cause He hath all names, because He is the One Father and therefore He hath no name because He is the Father of All.' "

The ancient Greeks deified every force in Nature, weaving around each and all a poetical character which gives to them special character-istics and a personal history that is plainly traceable to two distinct causes. Every God in their mythology evidently sprang from their conception of Kronos—Time and Uranus—space, both emanating from chaos, and like the Persians and Chinese they believed that out from the darkness came forth Light with all its objective harmonious differentiations and wonderful manifestations. Plato reviewed the various systems of philosophies that preceded him, rejecting what he deemed to be false and adopting what he thought to be true. He claimed that as the world was sensible it must have been produced from an effectual *cause*. Pythagoras believed and taught that Number was the root basis of all forms, the world being regulated by numerical harmony. "Number lies at the root of the manifested Universe; numbers and harmonious proportions guide the first differentiations of homogeneous substance, into heterogeneous elements, and number and numbers set limits to the formative hand of Nature."

We find in the "*Sepher Jetsirah*" (which is considered the groundwork for students in the Kabala and Jewish writings) that "The number Ten (10) is a repetition of the One (1) being its multiple only; remove the one and there is no ten symbolizing God, the One, from whom all proceed. Thus the *Ten* brings all the digits back to *Unity* and ends the Pythagorean table. Such is the secret meaning of the 'strong grip of the Lion's paw, of the tribe Judah,' between two hands —the Master-Mason's grip—the joint number of whose fingers is *Ten*. This number also gives rise to the grand origin of the Cross, as also to the Covenant, which stands as an undivided one (Exod. xxiv, 27, 28). The sum of the nine digits added together equals 45, and 4 + 5 = 9; the sum of the ten numbers is 55, and 5 + 5 = 10. Ten is also the root of Four, for if you add the first four numbers you have ten; it is also the essential root of *Seven*, since the seven numbers added equal twenty-eight, and twenty-eight resolves itself into 10, thus 2 + 8 = 10."

Anaxagorus recognized a supreme Intelligence as the principle of Life and arranged the primitive chaotic atoms into perfect molecular forms.

Xenophanes maintained Unity—The Universe to be God. The Scandinavians have also their mythological ideas, adequate to their social characteristics, wherein the basic conception of an Eternal Divine Principle in its triple aspect of Creator, Preserver, and Regenerator, can be perceived amidst complicated myths and hidden allegories, which appear

13

as absurd superstitions only when we have not the Key of the mysteries they conceal.

Paracelsus says that, " The unmanifested Absolute cannot be conceived otherwise than as a mathematical point without any magnitude, and such a point in becoming manifest in all directions would necessarily become a sphere. If we imagine such a mathematical point as being self-conscious, thinking and capable to act, and desirous to manifest itself, the only thinkable mode in which it could possibly accomplish this would be to eradicate its own substance and consciousness from the centre towards the periphery. The centre is the *Father*, the eternal source of all (John 1:4); the radius is the Son (the *Logos*), who was contained in the Father from eternity (John 1:1), the substance of father and son from the incomprehensible centre to the unlimited periphery is the Holy Ghost, the spirit of truth manifested externally and revealed invisible Nature (John 15:26). We cannot conceive of a body without length, breadth and thickness; a circle or a sphere always consists of a centre, radius and periphery. They are three, yet they are one, and neither of them can exist without the other two.* God sends out His thought by the power of His will. He holds fast to the thought and expresses it in the *Word*, which is contained in the creative and conservative power, and his thought becomes corporified, bringing into existence worlds and beings, which form, so to say, the visible body of the invisible God. Thus were the worlds formed in the beginning by the thought of God acting in the Macrocosm (the Universal Mind), and in the same manner are forms created in the individual sphere of the mind of man. If we hold on to a thought we create a form in our inner world. A good thought produces a good, and an evil thought an evil form, each growing as they are nourished by thought or 'imagination.'"

There was appended a note to the above, where the asterisk is placed: " The doctrine of the Trinity is found in all the principal religious systems. In the Christian Religion as Father, Son and Spirit; among the Hindus as Brahma, Vishnu and Siva; the Buddhists call it Muleprakriti, Prakriti and Purush; the Persians teach that Ormuzd produced Light out of himself by the power of his word. The Egyptians called the first cause Ammon, out of which all things were created by the power of its own will. In China Kwan-shai-gin is the Universally manifested Word, coming from the unmanifested Absolute by the power of its own Will and being identical with the former. The Greeks called it Zeus (Power), Minerva (Wisdom), and Apollo (Beauty). The Germans, Wodan (the Supreme Cause), Thor (Power), and Feia (Beauty). Jehovah and Allah are trinities of Will, Knowledge and Power; and even the Materialist believes in Causation, Matter and Energy."

Albert Pike, in "Morals and Dogmas," page 576 *et seq*, speaking of the various religions and their belief in God, says: "While all these faiths assert their claims to the exclusive possession of the Truth, Masonry inculcates its old doctrine and no more. That God is One. That His Thought, uttered in His Word, created the Universe and preserved it by those Eternal Laws which are the expression of that Thought. That the Soul of Man, breathed into him by God is as Immortal as His Thoughts are. That he is free to do evil, or to choose good, responsible for his acts and punishable for his sins. That all evil and wrong, and suffering are but temporary, the discords of one great Harmony; to the great, harmonic final chord and cadence of Truth, Love, Peace, and Happiness, that will ring forever and ever under the Arches of Heaven, among all the Stars and Worlds, and in all souls of Man and Angels."

In the Secret Doctrine, Stanza II, Section 6, page 6, it states that: "The Divine Thought does not imply the idea of a Divine Thinker. The Universe, not only past, present and future—a human, and finite idea expressed by finite thought—but in its totality, the Sat (an untranslatable term), Absolute Being, with the Past and Future crystalized in an Eternal Present, is that Thought itself reflected in a secondary or manifested cause Brahman (neuter), as the Mysterious Magnum of Paracelsus, is an absolute mystery to the human mind. Brahma, the male-female, the aspect and anthropomorphic reflection of Brahman, is conceivable to the perceptions of blind faith, though neglected by human intellect, when it attains its majority. Hence the statement that during the prologue, so to say, of the drama of creation, or the beginning of cosmic evolution, the Universe, or the Son, lies still concealed 'in the Divine Thought' which had not yet penetrated into the 'Divine Bosom.' This idea, *note well*, is at the root and forms the origin of all the allegories about the 'Sons of God' born of immaculate Virgins."

This "Divine Thought," this Absolute, Eternal, Omnipresent Principal is the "Causeless Cause" of all the manifestations in the Kosmos, and it is beyond human speculation, exploration or similitude, being beyond the range and reach of human thought.

Therefore, "This Infinite and Eternal Cause is the rootless root of all that was, is, or ever shall be. This cause is, of course, devoid of all attributes and is essentially without any relation to manifested being, as it is Be-ness—the essence of Being—rather than Being. All manifested is the vehicle of this Be-ness rather than what might be strictly called its manifestations. This Be-ness is symbolized in the '*Secret Doctrine*' under two aspects: *First*—Absolute, abstract space, the only thing the human mind can exclude from any conception, or conceive of by itself. *Second*—Absolute, abstract motion (under law and therefore intelligent), representing unconditional Consciousness. Consciousness being inconceivable without change, abstract motion thus symbolizes change which is its essential characteristic. Thus, then, the first fundamental axiom of the '*Secret Doctrine*' is this metaphysical One Absolute Be-ness. This it might be said is the Theosophical definition of God and will not differ greatly from that given by the Churches, if the idea of personality be eliminated. The God postulated in the *Secret Doctrine* requires infinite space, eternity of time universal, and therefore Infinite consciousness, and matter for a manifestation, which of course includes man, with all forms of Life on and off the earth, in addition to all the planets, whether in this Solar system or any other throughout the infinity of Space."

The Theosophical and Masonic Student is often told that this is Pantheism. If so it is a Spiritual Pantheism, and all who recognize the Infinity, Omnipresence, Eternity and Immutability of God are Pantheists.

The Christian tells us that God is primarily, fundamentally and essentially—THOUGHT. St. John informs us in the first chapter and first verse that: "In the beginning was the Word, and the Word was with God, and the Word was God." Now what is the meaning of such an assertion? Does it explain to us what God is? In order to come to a better understanding of this statement of St. John let us first see what relation Thought bears to the "Word." The brain is (in a very limited sense) the organ of the mind, and thought functions through it; consequently when the brain receives a thought, in order to give it expression it needs a word. Now we can understand what the Christian conception of God is from the following: " In the beginning was the Word "—word is the expression of a thought. " The Word was with God "—then the expressed thought was with God. "And the Word was God "—therefore the Word or God was—*Thought or Mind*—Divine Ideation, from which the Thought and Word emanated   This is exactly the abstract Masonic conception of the Supreme Architect of the Universe—GOD.

The doctrine of the Trinity is to be found in all the principal religious systems as well as belief in the Absolute, the Unknowable, the Supreme Architect. Christianity offers in their Trinity: *The Son*, the manifested Logos. " The Word "—the falling of spirit into matter, or the manifestation on the objective plane. *The Holy Ghost*, the unmanifested " Word," that which is with the Absolute, Divine Ideation, seen only by its effects. *The Father*—" The Word," the highest conception of the Divinity, The Absolute, The Unknowable.

Therefore the God of the Free Mason is that which every man who is capable of thinking for himself is forced to admit, let him call *It* what he may. It makes no difference whether he calls it Almighty Matter, or Eternal Spirit, Brahm, Parabrahm, Abraham, Osiris, Ormuzd, Ain-Soph, Zeus, Allah, Jehovah, Adonai, Thor, God, or the Supreme Architect of the Universe. " What is there in a name? " We search for *Truth* in all religions, all sciences, and all philosophies, claiming that " There is no religion higher than truth," and I do most certainly believe that the Divine Principle is essential Truth manifested in the harmony of the spheres, manifested in all the variant phases of life.

Mosques—Tombs—Massacre of Mamelukes—Heliopolis.

While far as sight can reach, beneath as clear
And blue a heaven as ever blessed this sphere,
Gardens, and minarets, and glittering domes,
And high-built temples, fit to be the homes
Of mighty gods, and pyramid whose hour
Outlasts all time, above the waters tower.

—Moore.

CHAPTER IX.

MOSQUES—TOMBS—MASSACRE OF MAMELUKES—HELIOPOLIS.

ON the east bank and a little over a mile from the Nile, stands Cairo, the capital of Egypt, latitude 30° 6' North and longitude 31° 20' East of the meridian of Greenwich. This celebrated city includes four original sites. The first of which was founded by Amru after conquering Egypt. When the ancient fortress of Babylon surrendered in A. D. 641 to this celebrated general of the Caliph Omar he " pitched his tent " (Fostat) and the place where he camped was called " El Fostat," which eventually became the capital of Egypt. It remained such until, in the year A. D. 751, when Marwan II. was defeated by Abu-l'Abbas, who lost his life at Abusir in the Fayoum, then the Omayyade Dynasty ended in Egypt and the Abbaside Dynasty began under the reign of Abu-l'Abbas (a descendent of Abbas who defeated Marwan II). In A. D. 744 this ruler removed his residence a little farther to the northeast of the site that had been selected by Amru. It was again changed when Ahmed ibn-Tulun, Governor of Egypt, wrested the power from the ruling dynasty and founded a new line which bears his name.

This Caliph removed the site of the growing capitol still farther to the northeast and founded a suburb known as " El-Katiya," where he built the celebrated mosque bearing his name. At the restoration of the Abbaside Governor and during the rule of the Ikshidide dynasty they held their court at the palace of Ahmed ibn-Tulun, where it remained until El Muizz sent an army under Gohar to invade Egypt which he captured. He founded the new city of El-Kahira, or " The Victorious," which has been corrupted into " Cairo."

This city is the headquarters of nearly all the tourists that intend " doing Egypt." Here is the starting-place to many delightful jaunts, to various points of interest in the immediate vicinity of Cairo, as well as to those lying farther to the south and beyond the cataracts, up to the confluence of the Blue and White Nile and the city of Khartoum. Cairo is the principal starting-point for the pilgrimage to Mecca and for the examination of the Pyramids.

When I first visited the Capital of Egypt the railroad from Alexandria was not completed to the city of Cairo and the Suez Canal had not been started; but a very large force of Europeans were constructing a fine bridge across the river Nile, the first of a series of improvements destined to transform Egypt into a modern nineteenth century progressive country, with all the stir and bustle pertaining to many a European and American city. Civilization seemed to have touched Egypt with her magic wand and changed all things, connecting the two seas, building bridges, making railroads, introducing electric lights and power, giving them phonographs and all the wonderful inventions of the commencement of the twentieth century. Egypt was transformed from a semi-civilized barbarous condition into a new order and a new era.

I again visited this country and Cairo, on my return from India, and the memory of it will remain with me while life shall last. I came this time for the express purpose of carefully examining the various points and places of interest, to study the many tombs, temples, monuments, and mummies, as well as the symbology of Ancient Free Masonry and the evidence of its prehistoric existence.

I first saw the Light in India, the birthplace of our most Illustrious Fraternity, and discovered evidences that it was cradled upon the banks of the Nile, in the hoary ages of antiquity, long centuries before the Babylonian Magi had come into an existence, or the Hebrews were a people. I had often rambled with my father, when a boy, from one city to another, in order to see for myself the demonstrated thoughts of our ancient craftsmen, who had wrought in quarries, for the purpose of adorning the banks of the grand old river Nile with magnificient tombs and temples, whose very ruins are the wonder and admiration of the learned men of this twentieth century. I have stood in awe before many of these tombs and temples, and have spent years in careful examinations, for the express purpose of telling you, my dear brothers and readers, the result of my investigations. In this chapter I will describe some of the scenes and incidents which charmed and delighted me in

MOSQUE OF AKBAR,
CAIRO

this grand old city of the Caliphs, "Masr," the Mother of the World, "The Precious Diamond in the handle of the green Fan of the Delta."

One of the first places the student or tourist should visit in this wonderful old city of Cairo is the citadel, built by Saladin in 1166 with stones that were brought from the small pyramids in the plains of Gizeh. It was erected by the ruling power for the express purpose of protecting and defending the town from the assault of enemies. This fortress most certainly commands the whole city; but *it* is commanded by the Mokattum hills, which rise immediately above it. Mohammed Ali took advantage of this site, *Gebel Giyusha*, in 1805, when he was elected by the people to become their ruler.

At this time Khursid, who had been appointed the Turkish Pasha by the Sublime Porte, held the citadel until Mohammed Ali, at the head of a large body of Albanians, and assisted by the people, planted a battery upon the above-named site on the Mokattum hills, whence a continuous fire was kept up from the minaret of the mosque of Sultan Hassan, as well as from the battery at Gebel Giyusha, until he finally compelled Khursid to surrender the citadel into the hands of the people and gave the dominant power to their leader, Mohammed Ali.

On entering this celebrated fortress and inner court by the New Gate and following along a walled passage we come to the Alabaster Mosque, erected by Mohammed Ali, which occupies the site of Saladin's old palace, blown up in the year 1824. No one is allowed (European or American) to enter into this building without putting on straw or cloth shoes, and paying a fee of one piastre. The citadel stands overlooking the city, just where the Mokattum hills begin to descend to the plain beneath. Here rises the towering walls of this celebrated fortress that contain within them a veritable town itself, whose many very interesting objects and edifices are really worth seeing.

It was within the walls of this fortress that the massacre of the Mamelukes occurred and to me it was one of the most interesting places within its blood-stained walls. After Mohammed Ali had compelled the Turkish Pasha Khursid to surrender the citadel to him and had received the *firman* appointing him Governor of Egypt, his title was disputed by nearly every one outside the city of Cairo, but more especially by the Mameluke Beys, whose forces had been strengthened by the great majority of the army of Khursid Pasha, who had been deposed by Mohammed Ali. This fact caused the Governor to use all means in his power to destroy every one opposed to his rule. Therefore, in order that you may be enabled to read one of the best accounts of what led up to the actual massacre itself, I will quote you from that valuable little work of Stanley Lane Poole on "Egypt," page 168:

"An attempt was made to ensnare certain of the Beys, who were encamped north of the metropolis. On the seventeenth of August, 1805, the dam of the Canal of Cairo was to be cut and some chief of Mohammed Ali wrote informing them that he would go forth early in the morning, with most of his troops, to witness the ceremony, inviting them to enter and seize the city, and to deceive them, stipulated for a certain sum of money as a reward. The dam, however, was cut early in the preceding night, without any ceremony.

" On the following morning these Beys, with their Mamelukes, a very numerous body, broke open the gate of the suburb El-Hoseyniyeh and gained admittance into the city from the north through the gate called *Bab-el-Futuh.* They marched along the principal street for some distance, with kettle-drums behind each company and were received with apparent joy by the citizens. At the mosque called the *Ashrafiyeh* they separated, one party proceeding to the *Azhar* and the house of certain Sheiks, and the other party continuing along the main street and through the gate called *Bab-Zuweyleh,* where they turned up towards the Citadel. Here they were fired on by some soldiers from the houses and with this signal a terrible massacre commenced.

" Falling back towards their companions, they found the by-streets closed, and in that part of the main thoroughfare called *Beyn-el Kasreyn,* they were suddenly placed between two fires. Thus shut up in a narrow street, some sought refuge in the *collegiate mosque of the Barkûkiyeh,* while the remainder fought their way through their enemies and escaped over the city wall with the loss of their horses. Two Mamelukes had in the meantime, succeeded by great exertions, in giving the alarm to their comrades in the quarter of the *Azhar,* who escaped by the eastern gate called *Bab-el-Ghureyib.*

"A horrible fate awaited those who had shut themselves up in the *Barkûkiyeh.* Having begged for quarter and surrendered, they were immediately stripped nearly naked, and about fifty were slaughtered on the spot, while about the same number were dragged away, with the most brutal aggravation of their painful condition, to Mohammed Ali. Among these were four Beys, one of whom, driven to madness by Mohammed Ali's mockery, asked for a drink of water. His hands were untied that he might take the bottle, but he snatched a dagger from one of the soldiers, rushed at the Pasha and fell covered with wounds.

"The wretched captives were then chained and left in the court of the Pasha's house. On the following morning the heads of their comrades, who had perished the day before, were skinned and stuffed with straw before their eyes. One Bey and two other men paid their ransom and were released; the rest, without exception, were tortured and put to death in the course of the ensuing night. Eighty-three heads (many of them belonging to Frenchmen and Albanians) were stuffed and sent to Constantinople, with a boast that the Mameluke chiefs were utterly destroyed. This ended Mohammed Ali's 'first massacre of his two confiding victims,' which displays the ferocious and vindictive nature of this inhuman brute.

"The Beys were disheartened by this revolting butchery and most of them retired to the upper country. Urged by England, or more probably by the promise of a bribe from El-Elfy's, the Porte began a leisurely interference in favor of the Mamelukes; but the failure of El-Elfy's treasury, with a handsome bribe from Mohammed Ali, soon changed the Sultan's views and the Turkish fleet sailed away. The cause of the Beys then suffered an irreparable loss in the death of their rival leaders, El-Elfy and El-Bardisy, whose suicidal jealousy lasted to the end; and Mohammed Ali discomfited the chief surviving Bey, Shamin, in a decisive battle. An attempt of the English Government to restore the Mamelukes by the action of a force of five thousand men under General Fraser ended in disaster and humiliation, and the citizens of Cairo had the satisfaction of seeing the heads of Englishmen exposed on stakes in the Ezbekiyeh.

"Mohammed Ali now adopted a more conciliatory policy towards the Mamelukes, granting them land and encouraging them to return to Cairo. This clemency was only assumed, in order to prepare the way for the act of consummate treachery which finally uprooted the Mameluke power, and seated the author of the crime firmly on the throne, where his great grandson now sits. Early in the year 1811, the preparation for an expedition against the Wahhābis, in Arabia, being complete, all the Mameluke Beys then in Cairo were invited to the ceremony of investing Mohammed Ali's favorite son, Tūsūn, with a pelisse and the command of the army. As on the former occasion the unfortunate Mamelukes fell into the snare. .

"On the 1st of March, Shahin Bey and the other chiefs (one only excepted) repaired with their retinues to the Citadel and were courteously received by the Pasha. Having taken coffee they formed in procession and preceded and followed by the Pasha's troops, slowly descended the steep and narrow road leading to the great gate of the Citadel; but as soon as the Mamelukes arrived at the gate it was suddenly closed before them. The last of those who made their exit before the gate was shut were Albanians, under Sali Kush. To those troops their chief now made known the Pasha's orders to massacre all the Mamelukes within the Citadel. Returning by another way, they gained the summit of the walls and houses hemming in the road in which the Mamelukes were, and some stationed themselves upon the eminences of the rock through which the road is partly cut.

"Thus securely placed, they commenced a heavy fire on their defenceless victims, and immediately the troops who closed the procession and who had the advantage of higher ground, followed their example. Of the betrayed chiefs many were laid low in a few moments; some dismounting and throwing off outer robes, vainly sought, sword in hand, to return and escape by some other gate. The few who regained the summit of the Citadel experienced the same cruel fate as the rest (for those whom the Albanian soldiers made prisoners met with no mercy from their chiefs or from Mohammed Ali); but it soon became impossible for any to retrace their steps, even so far; the road was obstructed by the bleeding bodies of the slain Mamelukes, and their richly-caparisoned horses and their grooms. Four hundred and seventy Mamelukes entered the Citadel, and of these very few, if any, escaped. One of these is said to have been a Bey. According to some, he leaped his horse from the ramparts and alighted uninjured, though the horse was killed by the fall. Others say that he was prevented from joining his comrades and discovered the treachery while waiting without the gate. He fled and made his way to Syria.

"This massacre was the signal for an indiscriminate slaughter of the Mamelukes throughout Egypt, orders to this effect being given and transmitted to every governor. In Cairo itself the houses of the Beys were given over to the soldiery, who slaughtered all their adherents, treated their women in the most shameless manner, and sacked their dwellings. During the two following days, the Pasha and his son Tusun rode about the streets and endeavored to stop those atrocious proceedings; but order was not restored until five hundred houses had been completely pillaged."

Such is the account of this terrible massacre, so carefully planned and studied out by this ferocious Governor Mohammed Ali, which showed very plainly that he would not allow anything to stand in the way of his plans of progress. He was devoting the whole of his life and energy to the improvement of Egypt and her peoples, building canals, introducing printing presses, adopting more advanced ideas of agricultural processes, founding schools, etc. He realized that the Mamelukes were bitterly opposed to his rule and ideas of progress, hence they had to fall, so that Egypt might rise, and take her stand beside the other nations of the world to become a factor in the affairs of Europe.

Joseph's well as it is called, was discovered by the great Saladin when he laid out the site of this celebrated fortress. It was at that time filled up with sand; but after ordering it to be cleaned out he discovered that it was a most remarkable excavation of Ancient Egyptian origin, composed of two different parts, cut down through the solid rock to the depth of two hundred and ninety feet, which depth was supposed to correspond with the level of the river Nile.

It is a remarkable specimen of ancient Egyptian industry, perseverance and labor, and dates back beyond authentic history. The first part of this most extraordinary well is about one hundred and sixty feet in depth and the second or lower part is one hundred and thirty feet deeper. A landing marks the division between the upper and lower shafts. The bottom of the well is reached by a circular stairway, as near as I can remember, about ten feet wide.

When I first visited this celebrated well the water was raised by means of the Sakiyeh, two of which were used for the purpose, one right above the other, both worked by oxen, the water being far different from that of the Nile, that which I tasted being quite brackish and unpalatable. To-day they do not use the water of this well for drinking or household purposes, as the Citadel and city are both supplied with water by the Cairo Water Company.

Before closing my remarks on the Citadel, I desire to call your attention, once again, to the celebrated Mosque of Mohammed Ali, whose towering minarets are conspicuous from all parts of the city of Cairo and its surroundings; in fact, we may say that these graceful towers form one of its landmarks. From the southern side of this Mosque we are enabled to obtain one of the most magnificent views, not only of the city, but of the surrounding country. Rising directly in front of us is the magnificent Mosque of Sultan Hassan, situated just outside the gates of the Citadel, and the flat roofs of myriads of houses, nearly all of which are adorned with the "*nalkaf*" or ventilators which, catching the cooling breezes of the North Wind, circulates it through the different rooms below, making it far more pleasant for the people who live within them. We can see the Nile boats down upon the river, loading and unloading their cargoes, while some go skimming across the turbid waters like birds with their immense lateen sails swelling out before the breeze. We can plainly trace the green vegetation that fringes the river until it is lost in a misty haze, away off to the South. Rising in silent majesty from the plains of Gizeh, to the West, are to be seen the celebrated pyramids of Egypt, with the Sphinx crouching in the sand a short distance away from the Great Pyramid, still looking to the East, as in the golden days of long ago.

In this queer, quaint old city of Cairo everything seems new, strange and full of interest to the traveller. Here the antiquary, student, artist, or savant will find a rich field for his especial edification. Every street has a history of its own, and every mosque, tower and dome has an especial attraction for every one which sees them. There is not a building or ruined mosque in Cairo but has its own peculiar charms, and around each and every one there is woven a hundred associations of early Saracenic history. Every Mosque, dome and slender minaret, pointing into the starry vault above are exquisite specimens of ancient Saracenic Architecture, that will carry us back to the days of the

FELLAHEEN PLOWING WITH CAMELS.

Crusades. It was from this city that Saladin went forth in all the panoply of war, marshalling his Saracenic followers with blare of trumpet and rattle of drums, to do battle with Richard the "Lion-hearted" and the Crusaders, upon the field of Acre.

The very stones of which the city is built were priceless treasures (in a great many instances) of ancient Pharaonic days, that were torn from some of the most ancient cities of the world's history, such as Memphis, Heliopolis and others, in order to build up the remarkable city of El-Kahira. Standing to-day upon the Mokattum hills, overlooking the Citadel and city, we can see the ruins of cities, monuments, tombs, and temples which have been the wonder, not only of the ancient, but of the modern world. No matter where we turn our gaze something will present itself, full of the deepest interest.

The manners and customs of the people of Egypt, to-day, are in many instances like those of the ancient Egyptians in its Golden Age, and present the same scenes now as in the days so long gone by. Just as the physical make up of the inhabitants of this wondrous valley were in ancient times, so we find them now, across the threshold of the twentieth century. The very style of clothing worn by the lower classes to-day, in many parts of this remarkable valley, are identical with that of a prehistoric age. The toiler at the Shaduf, for instance, stands as nude as when Pharaoh's daughter saw the infant Moses sleeping on the throbbing bosom of old "god Nilus."

The men who work in the fields and till the soil scratch up the earth with the same kind of a machine their great ancestors used in the days of Rameses, although there are to be seen now, some of our modern gang plows. The poorer class of people may very often be seen plowing with a cow and camel hitched together before their primitive machines, toiling along in the same way their forefathers did when Joseph was sold into the land of bondage. They use the same old method of threshing their grain as in the Golden Age of Egypt, a method that I have described in a previous chapter.

The food of these people who wearily toil in the fields of Egypt, consists principally of beans and bread with a sauce composed of onions and butter. It is of very rare occurrence for them to partake of meat at their tables; but, upon special occasions they enjoy a sort of cake,

14

something like our cookies, with a fig stuck in the center of it. They make their coffee by grinding the bean as fine as flour, boiling it as we do chocolate and drinking it in the same way, grounds and all. It is a very palatable beverage, and I rather liked it. These people are very hospitable, without hypocrisy, and when once you have eaten at their table you are especially welcome among them.

The Bedouins are noted for their hospitality and if you have eaten salt with them your person is held sacred while among these sons of the desert, who make their homes in the wild wastes of the South and West, continually wandering from place to place, restless as the waves of the ocean, ever moving. The water-carriers in the larger cities of Egypt carry around the waters of the river Nile in skins, just as the ancients did in the days of Abraham, and the women, who go down to the river to obtain water for household purposes carry the jars upon their heads, after the same old style and in the self-same manner as did the women who lived in the days of Thothmes and his dynasty.

In walking through the streets in the evening one can very frequently see people performing their devotions, as mentioned in the scriptures. Just as mothers carried their children in the days of the builders of the Pyramids, straddled upon their shoulders, the infant holding its mother's head with its tiny hands, so is the child carried to-day by the mother in this celebrated valley of the Nile. When the Mummy of Rameses was seen by M. Maspero in the Boulak Museum, Cairo, June 1, 1886, his hands were henna-stained lying across his "ample breast." Upon many of the walls of the ancient tombs of Egypt are to be seen pictures of people whose hands are stained red henna colored, and to-day in the streets of Cairo and all through the land of Egypt are to be seen hands henna-stained, stretched out to us for baksheesh. The houses of those living in ancient times were built, as they are occasionally now, of sun-dried bricks, wood and sometimes cane and corn stalks, to last but for a day as it were, while their tombs and temples were built of the hardest kind of stone, to endure for ever, *comparatively speaking*.

As I have stated previously "The peculiar physical make-up of the ancient Egyptians are like the inhabitants of to-day." To verify this statement I will quote from Maspero's "Dawn of History." A statue called Kaápiru was discovered by Mariette Bey, at Sakkara, near

Memphis, "The head, torso, arms and even the staff were intact, but the pedestal was hopelessly decayed and the statute only kept upright by the sand surrounding it. Mariette repaired the statue and placed it in the Boulak Museum. Kaàpiru when found was the exact likeness of one of the 'Sheiks-el-Beled' or Mayors of the village of Sakkara. The Arab workmen noticed the likeness and called it the 'Sheik-el-Beled,' which name it has retained ever since. He seems to be coming forward to meet the beholder with an acacia staff in his hand, heavy, thick-set, broad shoulders of a bull and a common cast of countenance, whose vulgarity is not wanting in energy. The largely opened eye has, by a trick of the sculptor, an almost uncanny reality about it. The socket which holds it has been hollowed out and filled with an arrangement of black and white enamel; a rim of bronze marks the outline of the lids, while a little silver peg, inserted at the back of the pupil, reflects the light and gives the effect of a living glance. The statue is short in height and was carved from pieces of wood that had been fastened together. The statue is called by some authors Ra-em-ka. According to the chronological table of Mariette, this statue is over six thousand years old," and yet he has the same peculiar physical make-up of the men of our own day.

The donkey boys are quite a feature in Cairo. They are smart, quick-witted, well up-to-date, fond of a joke, full of quaint humor and love to take trips to the various points of interest in the immediate vicinity of Cairo. It is rather funny to see them running along behind their enduring little animals, carrying a bunch or wisp of clover for the dinner of the little animal that you bestride, and very often eating nothing themselves until their day's work is done. These boys and their donkeys are to be found at many places in the city, and should you desire one at any time during the night, all you would have to do, would be to stand out in the street and shout out the Arabic word "*hammar*" (donkey), when you would very soon find yourself surrounded by quite a number of them.

I was never bothered much myself about donkeys, as many of my acquaintances were, because I hunted for one that suited me directly I arrived in the city and immediately hired it by the week, giving the boy extra baksheesh for his care of me during my rambles. I have ridden a donkey all over this quaint old city of Cairo and have taken many delightful excursions to various points of interest within a radius of ten or twelve miles. One can go around and through the narrow streets of this city on donkey-back, and visit the numberless mosques and places of interest far better than with any other conveyance.

In this way I visited a number of celebrated mosques, among them *The Mosque of Akbar*, the place where the howling and whirling dervishes perform their peculiar *Zikr*. This mosque is a square building with a pointed dome, very finely ornamented with arabesque figures. The minaret is square and rises over one corner of the building in recessed stages. The entrance to the interior of the building is through a very fine trifoliate arch, the floor of which is of wood, worn smooth by the continual performance of their *Zikrs*, each one lasting about an hour. The center of the building is circular, fenced with a railing to keep the spectators from crowding in too close to the dancers, and the whole interior is painted in dark and horizontal bands.

The celebrated *Mosque El-Azhar* was founded about A. D. 973 and converted into a university by El-Aziz, of the Fatimide dynasty, during his rule. Very little of the exterior of this building is to be seen, from the fact that it is so enclosed by the houses surrounding it. There is nothing of especial architectural interest about this mosque and only a small portion of the eastern wall can be seen, which is of but little interest to the tourist or student. It has six minarets, erected by different people at various periods, some of which are painted in brilliant colors. The entrances to this mosque are by six gates, the principal one being known as the " Gate of the Barbers " (Bab-el-Muzeyinin). It has a very fine portal that is extremely interesting, and right here in this entrance many students are to be seen under the hands of the tonsorial artists, who congregate here to make a living by wielding their razors upon the heads of those who come here to study.

This mosque is celebrated as the principal existing Mohammedan University. It is the oldest in the history of the world, and is one of the richest institutions of its kind known to-day. It is still growing richer, as not a wealthy Mohammedan who dies but bequeaths some of his wealth to El-Azhar. There is one good thing about this university, no pupil is compelled to pay for his tuition; but he may, if so disposed, contribute toward the expenses of his education. This mosque contains within its archives unbroken records of about nine hundred and twenty years and there are to-day in attendance within its courts about nine thousand eight hundred students, who are taught by at least two hundred and thirty-one sheiks or professors.

The scholars who attend come from all parts, and wherever the Koran is accepted. The education given here includes grammar, arithmetic, logic and philosophy, after which they may enter into theology, with the Koran as a text book, enabling them to thoroughly comprehend the Mohammedan religion, according to the four great sects of Islam— the Shafeite, the Malakite, the Hanafeite and the Hambalite. Every student, before he can receive his diploma, must be thorough in all the various branches. Here, in this most extraordinary establishment, you may see the son of the rich man clad in silk and fine linen, sitting close beside those who are very scantily clad, in the coarse cotton garments of the peasant, with no evidence of any superiority among them, excepting their clothing, each one squatted upon the ground in a semicircle before the sheik, who occupies a seat upon a sheepskin rug at the base of one of the stone pillars, lecturing his especial class. While others, occupying similar positions, with their pupils are reciting passages from the Koran in concert, and all the time swaying their heads from side to side, in rythmic motion.

At another column you will hear the professor of another group addressing his class in low gutteral Arabic tones upon some especial subject in the curriculum of this wonderful old university in Cairo. Each sect and nationality has its own particular compartment wherein to study, for instance, the Turk is in one, the student from Morocco in another, while those that come from Algeria and other places are to be found in a separate compartment by themselves. A visit to this celebrated university of El-Azhar will well repay any one for the time and trouble.

The Mosque of Sultan Hassan stands immediately below the Citadel, and is considered to be one of the most beautiful specimens of Arabian architecture known to-day, ranking as one of the most superb and famous buildings in the City of Cairo. The foundation of this magnificent edifice was laid in the year A. D. 1356, and was completed in the year A. D. 1360. The high and lofty porch is a marvel of beauty, commanding the attention of all who visit it. The towering walls inclose a spacious court, and rise to the height of one hundred and thirteen feet, corbelled out fully six feet in successive lines of dentils that form a most magnificent cornice, beneath which are to be seen panels, arches and windows. This mosque is surmounted by two minarets and a painted brick dome, which rises over the mausoleum of the Sultan.

The minaret on the South is the highest in the world, being fully two hundred and eighty feet high. The other one was overthrown by an earthquake, killing an immense number of people in its fall. It was again rebuilt, but not according to its original dimensions. The stones that were used in the construction of this magnificent building were taken from the Pyramids. It is a well-known fact that the monuments, tombs and temples of ancient Egypt were used by the Arabs simply as a quarry, wherewith to build up their own quaint city of Cairo, and it is very much to be regretted that the priceless monuments of the golden age of Egypt should ever have been destroyed to supply materials for the upbuilding of that city. This mosque has been the chief center or rallying point for all who rebel against the government or ruling power. Mohammed Ali took possession of it, and used it as a fortress in order to drive Khursid Pasha from the Citadel. It bears the scars of many a hard fought battle, and to-day there are to be seen upon its walls the effects of the cannonading by the French when the inhabitants of this grand old city revolted against their rule. There are many other mosques and tombs that are well worth a visit, more especially the following :

The Tombs of the Circassian Mamelukes generally known as *The Tombs of the Khalifs.* The Tomb of Kait Bey is a beautiful specimen of Arabian architecture. It is not a large mosque, but its small dimensions are full of most exquisite grace and beauty. Fergusson, in his " Handbook of Architecture," says : " This mosque, looked at externally or internally, nothing can exceed the grace of every part of this building. Its small dimensions exclude it from any claim of grandeur, nor does it pretend to the purity of the Greek and some other styles ; but as a perfect model of the elegance we generally associate with the architecture of this people, it is perhaps unrivalled by anything in Egypt, and far surpasses the Alhambra or the Western buildings of its age."

MOSQUE OF SULTAN HASSAN,
CAIRO.

There is upon the slopes of the Mokattum hills the celebrated *Tombs of the Mamelukes*, well worth a visit, for amid the ruins are to be found some very fine specimens of Arabian architecture, with here and there some very beautiful minarets which will deeply interest any one willing to take the trouble of visiting this place and to hunt them up.

One of the best known places in Cairo is the *Esbekiyeh*, a public garden, which was named in honor of the Emir Ezbek, a celebrated general of the Sultan Kait Bey, one of the independent Mameluke Sultans who reigned in the year A. D. 1468. Originally there was a mosque erected here; but during the rule of Mohammed Ali it was simply a pond of water, formed by the inundations of the Nile, until he altered the site and laid out a garden, by filling in the pond and cutting a canal around it. Said Pasha improved upon what Mohammed had done; but it was not until Ishmael Pasha improved it by tearing down the old and building up anew that it reached its present state of perfection.

The gardens of to-day have beautiful walks and contain a very rare and choice collection of trees, shrubs and flowers. During the afternoon it is simply delightful to promenade the many charming pathways that wind around these beautiful grounds, with an area of over twenty acres. It contains a variety of places of amusement, such as cafés, a theatre and surrounding it are quite a number of the principal hotels. During the evening, from five to eight, either an Egyptian or an English band performs there. It used to be the special rendezvous for Americans and Europeans, but now it is used by all classes of people, and we may often see the veiled wives with their children, of both the rich and poor Arabs, promenading among the trees, shaded from the noonday sun, rubbing up against travellers and tourists from all parts of the world. What a contrast exists among them! Such a motley assemblage of people, and what a confusion of tongues. In these gardens one may hear nearly every language spoken upon the face of the earth. I have spent many a very pleasant evening in this delightful spot in listening to the band, watching the people, catching a few sentences from those who pass along, and pondering upon the rise and fall of nations and the mutations in Egypt.

The site of the celebrated old city of Heliopolis is situated about six miles to the northeast of Cairo, and the route to it lies along a very nice carriage road which passes through many places of historical interest to a person visiting the ruins of this celebrated city, one of the oldest in the history of the world.

How well I remember my trip to the various places I am about to describe. It seems to me but as yesterday that I came down the steps of Shepherd's Hotel and found my donkey and boy awaiting me, as well as a very large party of acquaintances and friends, who were going to make the trip with me. What a jolly, happy, rollicking, joyous lot we were, as we mounted our little animals, and skurried along the road, shouting and laughing, like so many school boys, as we started out to visit the various points of interest that lie along our pathway, which led us on to where Joseph found his wife, in the grand old city of *Beth-Shemesh, On,* or the *city of the Sun, Heliopolis.*

We rode out of the city at a rapid rate and kept it up until we reached a place where we stopped to arrange our refreshments, carried with us for luncheon; after which we started on our way again, passing quite a number of modern European residences and at length arrived at a rather peculiar looking building that is used as a Commissariat Depot of the English Army. During the French occupation it was used as a stronghold and was called Fort Zulkowski. The places where the loopholes used to be are in sight to-day.

Close to this place we passed through a gateway called *Bab-el-Hasaniya* and found ourselves upon the road leading to Abbasiya. We passed an Arabian tomb with a very fine sculptured dome, and still pushing along we see a public drinking fountain on our right, at which we refreshed ourselves and animals, after which we kept riding along until we arrived at and passed the barracks which were occupied by the English and Egyptian troops. We noticed the Astronomical Observatory and the Zaffaren Palace which Ishmael Pasha is said to have built in forty days, and then presented it to his mother. We now begin to realize that our way leads us on through pleasant paths, for our route is lined with orange and lemon groves, and vineyards that fringe the desert sands, showing what irrigation can do in reclaiming the arid sands of the desert. We now enter upon a beautiful shaded avenue and pass through some very finely cultivated grounds, until we arrive at the Palace of Qubba, which Ishmael built for his son Tewfik. We do not stop here, but continue along through groves and vineyards and through a beautiful olive orchard, coming out into a very richly cultivated plain, the scene of two decisive battles, long destined to live in the annals of Egyptian History. *The first* was when the Sultan Selim, on the twenty-sixth day of January, 1517, destroyed the power of the Mamelukes and made it a Turkish province. *The second* was on the twenty-first day of March, 1800, when the French, under General Kleber, conquered the Turks and regained Cairo.

We arrived at Matariyeh, the village near where these two battles were fought, and visited a living spring of water noted for being the only one in the valley of the Nile. Tradition informs us that originally the water flowing from it was salty; but that when the Holy Family visited this village "Our Lady, the Virgin Mother" bathed in it, when immediately it became soft and sweet. It was here in this place that were located the famous gardens belonging to Cleopatra, wherein grew the precious balsam, the true "Balm of Gilead," spoken of in the Scriptures; but, to-day, cotton has taken its place, and the balsam plants have been removed to Arabia where they flourish under the fostering care of the people who have charge of them. A short distance beyond the village we came to an old sycamore, called "The Virgin's Tree," from the fact, as tradition informs us again, the Holy Family rested beneath its spreading branches after their flight into "The Land of Egypt." About half a mile farther on we come to the site of Heliopolis and immediately recognize one peculiarity about it, that there were no heaps and mounds of rubbish representing the remains of the walls, tombs, temples, etc., for like Memphis, it too has been a quarry for the upbuilding of Cairo.

In the ancient days of Egypt this city was in the height of its glory, the very fact of Usertesen's obelisk standing there to-day proves its antiquity and links it with the beginning of the Middle Empire, in the year B. C. 3604. During the time that Mariette Bey was excavating here in 1858 he unearthed a great many stones bearing the names of Rameses Second and Thothmes Third, both of whom, no doubt, beautified and adorned some of the temples in this ancient city of On. It was celebrated for its temple of the Sun, which was a most magnificent edifice, standing at one end of an inclosure fully three miles in circumference, and leading up to it, from the entrance, were rows of beautiful sphinxes and obelisks.

The priests of Heliopolis were famous for their learning, and enjoyed the reputation of being the most learned men of their age. There Solon, Eudoxus and many others came to study and acquire some of the wisdom that flowed forth from their celebrated fountain, the college of priests, and yet, to-day, there is no remains of this most magnificent city standing to mark the spot where Moses drew his inspiration, nothing to tell of its vanished glory and the splendor of its tombs, temples and monuments, excepting one solitary obelisk to testify to the ancient grandeur and departed glory which existed B. C. 3000.

This obelisk is made of rose granite, and the length of the stone measures sixty-six feet, with an average face at the ground of six feet and one inch. The pyramidium or apex shows that it was encased at one time with a metal covering, and the inscriptions which are blazoned upon its stony sides inform us that Usertesen First (Ra-Kheper-Ka), King of Upper and Lower Egypt, dedicated and erected this monument at the beginning of a thirty years' cycle. There is only one other obelisk older than this, which is a very much smaller stone, and was found by Lepsius at Memphis.

Close to this ancient monolith we spread our luncheon, and amidst the popping of corks, the clatter of knives and forks, we feasted and talked of the wonderful civilization that belonged to these people, in the hoary ages of the past, whose architecture has been admired by people of every age, and continues to be the wonder and admiration of the people of the twentieth century, as in every other. We discussed the decadence of her Arts, Sciences and Philosophies, since the "Golden Age of Egypt," and the wonderful changes in the valley of the Nile and Delta since this grand old monument was quarried and erected on the borders of the desert in the city of *Beth-shemesh* (Heliopolis) close upon thirty centuries B. C.

It was to this city the Phœnix used to come, once in every five hundred years to reincarnate. This most extraordinary Arabian bird is said to have been the size of a full grown turkey, with the most beautiful plumage imaginable. Tradition informs us that about the time that this Arabian wonder was to arrive to reincarnate, a priest of the temple would prepare a fire upon an altar within its sacred precincts, into which the bird would fly and be consumed. The fire would then be allowed to die out and the embers to remain undisturbed for a certain number of days after, when the reincarnated bird would be seen to arise from the ashes, spread out its golden wings and with a plumage most exquisite soar away into the infinitude of space. There is no question but that this is an allegory which every one must interpret for himself.

There is one peculiar thing to be noticed in this wonderful valley of the Nile and that is there are three Sabbaths observed here. The first *Friday*—that of the Mohammedan. *Saturday*—that of the Hebrew and *Sunday* the Christian Sabbath. In fact, every day of the week is a Sabbath day to some nationality; for *Monday* is the Greek, *Tuesday* is the day of rest for the Persians, and *Wednesday* is the Sunday for the Assyrians. So you see every day is the Lord's day and is observed as such by different people in different places.

"The mean annual temperature at Cairo is about 71° F. The thermometer seldom falls to 40° F. at Cairo, but it is frequently lower on the Nile. The coldest months in the year are December and January and the hottest are June, July and August, but even then it is cool in the shade and at nights. The humidity in the atmosphere is principally controlled by the rise and fall of the Nile. Fogs prevail during the first two months of the receding of the waters. Evening fogs descend very quickly as the sun goes down and are as quickly deposited after the sun has set, leaving the sky clear and the air as fresh as after a good shower. Morning fogs are soon dispelled by the heat of the sun, and then follows the clear beautiful sky. On the desert the air is always dry and bracing and much cooler than that over cultivated land. Dews at night are common in the early and latter parts of the year. During the winter the nights are piercingly cold on the desert. The moonlight nights are singularly brilliant and when there is no moon the starlit sky is as wonderful as any moonlight night in Europe." (Murray.)

Esoteric Teaching of the Scottish Rite— Brain and Thought.

"Man is made free!—Man, by birthright is free,

    Though the tyrant may deem him but born for his tool.

Whatever the shout of the rabble may be—

    Whatever ranting misuse of the fool—

Still fear not the Slave, when he breaks from his chain,

For the Man made a freeman grows safe in his gain."

CHAPTER X.

ESOTERIC TEACHING OF THE SCOTTISH RITE—BRAIN AND THOUGHT.

IN speaking of this wonderful city of Heliopolis, " Fountain of the Sun," one of the most sacred cities of Egyptian history, I desire to call your attention to the knowledge pertaining to our Ancient Brethren, who officiated here, in the " College of Priests," " *The Grand East of Ancient Egypt.*" Here was the seat of the wisdom which belonged to the " Phree-Massen " whose teachings have been handed down to us, from generation to generation. Here Moses was initiated into the Sublime Mysteries of Ancient Egypt, of which our own beloved Ancient and Accepted Scottish Rite is a lineal descendant. Those Elus, Knights and Princes of every age who have ever followed the Pole Star of Truth through the drifting ages of time have handed down to us, from epoch to epoch, the wonderous knowledge taught in the Indian, Mazdean and Egyptian Mysteries, for the especial benefit of our Illustrious Fraternity. By this future generations are eventually enabled to stand upon the topmost rung of the ladder, the very pinnacle of Civil and Religious Liberty, when every Man and Mason shall be free from all usurpations of royalty and sacerdotal power, and be thoroughly competent to recognize the whole Truth in the Fatherhood of God and the Brotherhood of Man.

Masonry, successor of the mysteries, still follows the ancient manner of teaching. Her ceremonies are like the ancient mystic shows—not the reading of an essay, but the opening of a problem, requiring research and constituting philosophy the arch expounder. The symbols are the instruction she gives. The lectures are endeavors, often partial and one-sided, to interpret these symbols. He who would become an accomplished Mason must not be content merely to hear, or even to understand, the lectures; he must, aided by them, and they having, as it were, marked out the way for him; study, interpret, and develop these symbols for himself.

The Ancient and Accepted Scottish Rite of Masonry is like an immense tree, towering up into the glorious heights of Scientific Philosophy, whose ramifying branches spread o'er a vast area, enfolding in its arms the Light, Knowledge and Truth of all the Arts, Sciences, Religions and Philosophies of every age in the world's history; whose roots are watered by that great and glorious fount from which Moses drew his inspiration and knowledge. Iu fact this tree is the "*fons et origo*" of the "Wisdom" itself, which can be clearly demonstrated to all those who climb up into its glorious height. When the Neophyte first stands beneath its over-shadowing branches, in darkness visible, with ambition to know and understand the unknowable, his higher self will then prompt him to greater exertions. Clinging and climbing, he struggles upward and onward, grasping blindly for Light, until he stands upon the first of its multifarious branches. With awe and admiration he then begins to realize the Sublimity and Grandeur to be found in the very shadows of its magnificent foliage. He sees far above him scintillations of great and glorious Truths, descending through the drifting ages, to and across the threshold of the twentieth century, and will begin to understand what the poet meant when he said:

"Heaven is not reached at a single bound ;
    But we build the ladder by which we rise
    From the lowly earth to the vaulted skies,
And we mount to the summit round by round."

It is so with the Neophyte. He will begin to realize that Heaven (Wisdom) is not gained by a single bound; but is only to be obtained by mounting step by step, or degree by degree. Beset with many difficulties, and dangers, as he advances his view widens out, his horizon expands, for the Pole Star of Truth and Right has been his guide. Although he stands in the very shadow of Death, yet will he learn that within his own heart he carries the light which shall lead him through the valley of the shadow, to more sublime heights of the Ineffable degrees of our beloved fraternity. He will realize that there is no Death, for what we call Death is simply the disintegration of molecular forms, to be made manifest eventually in many others.

This disintegration of the physical body of man, animals, plants, etc., occurs as soon as the life forces or controlling soul departs. The mass of living elemental units, composing the physical body of man, being no longer controlled or co-ordinated, separate one from the other, putrefaction or decay ensues, and the body becomes a mass of unrestrained, unregulated lives, destroying the form or body by their own especial forces. The physical body of either man or animal once more becomes the dust of the earth, and he will now realize the Truth of the statement, " Though I die yet shall I live," for we must distinctly understand that Death is merely the Inn by the wayside, simply the bier upon which the body is laid. He will eventually realize that all men must pass through the gates of Death before they can enter on the road that leads to immortality. Death does not annihilate *the true spiritual man*, but just simply destroys the form or personality, the old shard or shell, the tegument of clay that has been the house in which the individuality, or higher self, has been enabled to manifest itself on the physical plane. And in reaching Death he must thoroughly understand that he has suffered, and will become purified, so that the works of the Divine Essence might be exemplified in him. Through the glory of Life, Man must mourn, sorrow, suffer pain and humiliation to the personality, while He, the *true man*, will know full well it is simply a refining process to bring him out purified. When man stands erect in his God-hood, before the Divine Glory of Light and Truth, with arms outstretched, and head uplifted, in conscious knowledge of Divine Love, willing to accept his Karma, then the cross will fall behind him and he will realize that he stands before his Higher Self, the Divine Presence of the Supreme Architect, and positively know that *he* and his Father are One. He will thoroughly understand that *Resignation* is what brings him perfect peace and happiness, and unlocks the door leading to Immortal bliss.

This faint glimmer of the Truth and proof of the immortality of the soul, proves to the initiate that he has passed from the square to the compasses, whose swinging leg circumscribes every moral virtue; in fact, he realizes that he has gone beyond the operative tools and now uses those of the speculative Mason. The instruments used by the Sages of the ancient world will now become familiar to him, and in their use he will discover that he has now risen to a higher plane of intellectual development, to a knowledge of Truth and the key to the Lost Word. Many things will now become clearer to his vision and

15

understanding, from these ineffable heights of Scottish Rite Masonry. He will see in the Pole Star a fit emblem of the Deity, a point within the circle of Eternity. Now is the opportunity for him to devote his time and attention to solving the great problems of life, to enable him to understand those sublime philosophical Truths permeating our beloved Fraternity. In attaining to a knowledge of these lofty Truths he should strive earnestly and faithfully to give them, just as freely as he received them, to his aspiring Brother by the wayside. Such a perfect Mason will be ever true to himself and the glorious fraternity to which he belongs. Like the ancient initiates of the Egyptian Mysteries he will faithfully obey the law and be true to the principles of Scottish Rite Masonry. Always ready to draw his sword in defense of his country for the preservation of free government, never consenting to despotism or civil or military usurpation, he will be guided and directed solely by honor and duty.

What the world of to-day, and even generations yet unborn, owe to Masonry and our glorious Scottish Rite will never be fully realized. Our fraternity has always been and always will be an incentive to enlightenment, liberality and education. During the " Dark Ages," in the Lodge room only did scientists and philosophers dare make known any of their important scientific discoveries, for fear of the Inquisition, that dread tool of tyrants and benighted superstition. To-day we find our beloved Rite working earnestly and faithfully in the interest of suffering humanity, to secure for all freedom of thought and free government, for the people and by the people. Our Elus, Knights and Princes of the twentieth century have an advantage over ancient Brethren in being able to exemplify openly the grand Truths taught behind the closed doors of our most illustrious bodies of the Scottish Rite, throughout the world universal. The faithful manner in which these duties are being performed are only known to the co-workers in the great and glorious undertaking *of that* which is *just, right and true.* We realize that we should not live for ourselves ; but devote our time to the welfare of our country, our neighbors, and practice charity toward all men in the fullest sense of the word, recognizing in every man a brother, and above all *practice self-less-ness* in all our dealings with our fellow man, without hope of honor or reward.

Once more I quote from "Morals and Dogmas," page 312: "The true Mason labors for the benefit of those to come after him, and for the advancement and improvement of his race. It is a poor ambition which contents itself within the limits of a single life. All men who desire to live, desire to survive their funerals, and to live afterward in the good which they have done mankind rather than in the fading characters written in men's memories. Most men desire to leave some work behind them which may outlast their own day and brief generation. This is an instinctive impulse, given by God, and often found in the rudest human heart; the surest proof of the soul's immortality and of the fundamental difference between men and the wisest brutes. To plant trees that, after we are dead, will shelter our children, is as natural as to love the shade of those our fathers planted. The rudest, unlettered husbandman, painfully conscious of his own inferiority, the poorest widowed mother, giving her life-blood to those who pay only for the work of her needle, will toil and stint themselves to educate their child that he may take a higher station in the world than they; and of such children are the world's greatest benefactors."

The first inhabitants of Egypt brought with them the eternal verities of the ancient wisdom from India, the birth place of the Aryan Hindu, the last offshoot of the first sub-race of the fifth Root race, who most assuredly preserved the secrets of the glorious teachings we so dearly love and practice to-day, in Scottish Rite Masonry. They are the self-same esoteric Truths taught by the Hierophants and Sages in the hoary ages of antiquity, during the initiatory services of the mysteries of India, by the Brotherhood of the *White Lodge*, the Hierarchy of Adepts, whose every thought and act has been for the upbuilding of humanity. These are the Brothers who have preserved the sublime Truths and teachings we are endeavoring to promulgate in our Lodges, Chapters, Councils and Consistories, of both the Southern and the Northern Jurisdictions of the Ancient and Accepted Scottish Rite, throughout the world Universal.

There has never existed a time, in the history of the world, when the teachings of those Great Adepts were not being given forth, in order to help poor struggling humanity on to a higher plane of intelligence and spiritual unfoldment. We must distinctly understand that a vast number of these great and glorious Truths are embodied in all Religions and Philosophies and are not new, but as old as the stars above. The scriptures tell us: "*Ein Chodosh tacash ha shemesh*" (There is no new thing under the sun) *See Eccles. 1st Chap. and 9th verse.* That man would be more than a God who could invent or discover anything which has never been in existence before. Ragon, in "Maconnerie Occulte," states that "Humanity only *seems* to progress in achieving one discovery after the other, as in truth it only finds that which it had lost. Most of our modern inventions, for which we claim such glory, are after all, things people were acquainted with three or four thousand years back. Lost to us through wars, floods, and fire their very existence became obliterated from the memory of man. And now modern thinkers begin to *rediscover* them once more" (see Chapters III and XIV of this work).

When the Ancient Craftsmen erected the Pyramids and carved the Sphinx upon the banks of the Nile, they must assuredly have been able to manufacture their tools in order to perform the work necessary in constructing such remarkable monuments. We have ocular demonstrations that they thoroughly comprehended the quarrying and carrying across the desert sands of Egypt, enormous blocks of stone, and raising them to the required position by methods peculiarly their own, to erect Tombs, Temples and colossal statuary to beautify and adorn the wonderous cities in the valley of the Nile. These ruins are scattered throughout its length and breadth and constitute fragmentary records of those ancient craftsmen, which to-day give evidence of their marvelous knowledge and skill, not only in Architecture, but in the Arts and Sciences.

Let us look back at the stupenduous buildings which adorned the banks of the Tigris and Euphrates, long centuries before Rhea Silvia officiated in the temples of Alba Longa and gave birth to Romulus and Remus. Let us follow in the footsteps of the men who delved into and unearthed the secrets of that Babylonian Empire, and we shall be astonished at the profound knowledge that pertained to this ancient people, who erected the "Hanging Gardens of Babylon" simply to gratify the whim of a daughter of Ebactana. Let us cross the dark waters of the Indian Ocean, and visit the "Land of the Vedas," where we may examine the most magnificent Gopuras and Cave Temples. We may here receive ocular demonstrations of the sublimity and grandeur

THE PERISTYLE,

of these extremely beautiful fabrics, which are the wonder and admiration of our learned men of the twentieth century. My dear Brothers and readers, the farther back we go into the realms of distant ages, searching for the wisdom and knowledge belonging to Brothers of a prehistoric age, the more will we be confronted with unmistakable evidences of their great learning and most extraordinary intellectual and spiritual development. We will recognize in the magnificent monuments of India, Assyria and the Valley of the Nile, tokens of their knowledge in Astronomy, as well as the state of perfection to which they had arrived in Mechanics, Mathematics, Architecture, etc. Besides these we have proof of the existence of a Science, which men of the present day cannot properly understand or interpret, or at best only dimly sense. Right here I will positively assert that all Religions, all Philosophies, and all Sciences for this Race had their origin in the "Land of the Vedas," whose links can be traced back to its original source, broken and disfigured as they are, yet still with fragments here and there to connect us with the glory belonging to the Ancient Wisdom of the "Great White Lodge," which was at its zenith when Science, Philosophy and Religion walked hand in hand together.

These great and glorious Adepts inherited all the wisdom belonging to the Atlanteans and Lemureans, whose mighty traditions they thoroughly comprehended, but which cannot be told to us, as we would be unable to understand them. These Great Teachers were the originators of a system of Philosophy that we of the present day are just beginning to comprehend. There is no man of this era who can truthfully say that the Sciences known to us of the twentieth century were unknown to our Ancient Brethren of India. The teachings of Anaxagoras, Empedocles, Democritus and others are being taught to-day in our schools and colleges. Gallileo was not the first man to discover the motions of the earth. The rotation of this planet upon its axis, as well as the heliocentric system, were taught by Pythagoras and others B. C. 700. As above stated, the motions of the earth were understood at this early date, and yet during the reign of the Emperor Constantine, in the year A. D. 217, his son Crispus Cæser was taught by his preceptor, Lactantius, that the earth was a plane surrounded by the sky, the earth itself being composed of fire and water; and his venerable preceptor, the Holy

Father, warned him against believing in the *heretical doctrine of the earth's globular form.*

Who can add or take away from Euclid and improve upon him? Many of the old Philosophers and Scientists of the ancient days had probably forgotten, during their lives, more than all our modern Scientists ever knew. What should we have known of the application of the theory of mathematics, for practical purposes, if it had not been for Archytus, the pupil of Pythagoras?

The Priests of Etruria, as well as the ancient Rishis of India, thoroughly understood the method whereby they could attract lightning, long centuries before Christ. What will better illustrate the peculiar methods of the teachings of the various ages, my readers will more fully understand, when they begin to search for themselves and find the truth of these statements, verified by the best writers of every epoch of the world's history. I know that it is very difficult to convince people of the truth of many things, more especially when these things clash with their preconceived ideas and notions of what is true or what is false. It is also very difficult to get men to believe and agree upon matters beyond their comprehension.

Suppose a man requested me to teach him square root without his having any knowledge of the first four rules of arithmetic; no matter how hard I tried to explain to him that the squares of the base and perpendicular equal the square of the hypothenuse, and that by adding the results of the squares of the two sides and extracting the square root from the sum of the sides would give him the required side of the hypothenuse. Why, it would be like talking Greek to him, he could not understand me, and it would be impossible for him so to do, until he had first mastered the basic principles: Addition, Subtraction, Multiplication and Division, as then, and then only, could he understand me and acquire a knowledge of Square Root.

Pythagoras was one of the greatest Philosophers of ancient Europe. He was the son of Mesarchus, an engraver, and was born about the year B. C. 580, either at Samos, an island in the Ægean Sea, or as some say, at Sidon in Phœnicia. Very little is known of his early life, beyond the fact that he won prizes for feats of agility at the Olympic Games. Having attained manhood and feeling dissatisfied with the amount of knowledge to be gained at home, he left his native land and spent many years in travel, visiting in turn most of the great centres of learning. History narrates that his pilgrimage in search of Wisdom extended to Egypt, India, Persia, Crete and Palestine, and from each country he gathered fresh stores of information and succeeded in becoming well acquainted with the esoteric Wisdom, as well as with the popular esoteric knowledge of each. He returned to his home, with his mind well stored and his judgment matured, intending to open there a college of learning; but this he found to be impracticable, owing to the opposition of its turbulent ruler, Polycrates. Failing in this design he migrated to Crotona, a noted city in Magna Græcia, and a colony founded by the Dorians, on the South coast of Italy. It was here this ever famous Philosopher founded his College or Society of students, which became known over the civilized world as the "Grand East," or central assembly of the learned men of Europe. It was here, too, that Pythagoras taught the Occult Wisdom gathered from the Gymnosophists and Brahmins of India, from the Hierophants of Egypt, the Oracles of Delphi, the Idean Cave and from the Kabbalah of the Hebrew Rabbis and Chaldean Magi.

For nearly forty years he taught his pupils and exhibited his wonderful powers; but an end was put to his institution and he was forced to flee from the city, owing to a conspiracy and rebellion which arose on account of a quarrel between the people of Crotona and the inhabitants of Sybaris. He succeeded in reaching Metapontum, where he is said to have died about the year B. C. 500. Pythagoras was intensely in earnest in his search for learning and a comprehensive knowledge of the profound and lofty Sciences possessed by the ancient Egyptian Hierophants. He was so very anxious to obtain all the esoteric secrets pertaining to the Ancient Egyptian Mysteries, that he consented to be circumcised that he might be eligible to become an Initiate, after which he was made familiar with the occult teachings of the Egyptian Hierophants.

Pythagoras founded the Grecian Mysteries and taught to his pupils all that he had learned from the Gymnosophists, Brahmins and Hierophants. It was within the Temples of these people that he studied the Hermetic Sciences and came to an understanding of the revelations of the Sybils; but he learned the geometrical theories in the Temples of Egypt. He was an apt scholar himself and grasped very readily all those high and lofty Sciences in which he had been instructed, until he stood preeminently above all the Philosophers of Ancient Europe, demonstrating this fact to all who studied under him.

Our revered Brother, Albert Pike, in "Morals and Dogmas," page 366, states that: "He taught the true method of obtaining a knowledge of the Divine Law; to purify the soul from its imperfections, to search for Truth, and to practice virtue; thus imitating the perfections of God. He thought his system vain, if it did not contribute to expel vice and introduce virtue into the mind. He taught that the two most excellent things were to speak the truth and to render benefits to one another. Particularly he inculcated Silence, Temperance, Fortitude, Prudence and Justice. He taught the immortality of the Soul, the Omnipotence of God, and the necessity of personal holiness to qualify a man for admission into the Society of the Gods. Thus we owe the particular mode of instruction in the Degree of Fellow-Craft to Pythagoras; and that degree is but an imperfect reproduction of his lectures. From him, too, we have many of our explanations of the symbols. He arranged his assemblies due East and West, because the Master represents the rising Sun, and of course must be in the East. The pyramids, too, were built precisely by the four cardinal points. And our expression that our Lodges extend upward to the Heavens, come to us from the Persian and Druidic custom of having to their Temples no roof but the sky."

" Thales, Orpheus, Pherecydes, Anaxagoras, Solon, Plato, in fact, all the ancient Philosophers visited Egypt for the express purpose of acquiring 'more light' in those wondrous realms of Mysticism, Metaphysics, and transcendental Anthropology, because they could not in their own countries get that higher and more intimate knowledge of Divine or Spiritual ideas which they so earnestly desired. They thoroughly realized that the sublime teachings of the ancient Egyptians were not cognized by the uninitiated, and, in fact, thoroughly comprehended they were not enabled, from the teachings received, to delve deeply into the ethereal realm of Thought or Being, and all they were enabled to comprehend was merely the phenomenal, cognizable by their senses alone ('*we must ever remember that with our physical senses alone at our command none of us can hope to reach beyond gross matter*') they distinctly understood that their investigations could go so far and no farther, but they positively knew

THE OSIRIDE COLUMNS—TEMPLE OF THE MYSTERIES.

that here, in Egypt, all those sublime teachings and glorious Truths, for which they had been searching, and so earnestly desired to comprehend, were to be found in the Ancient Egyptian Mysteries."

Every one of those ancient Philosophic Craftsmen, who lifted the veil of the Greater Mysteries and received the " Light " of those sublime teachings, which were the wonder of the ancient world, began to understand that before he or they could receive the Divine Wisdom so earnestly desired he would have to go from below upwards, and in order to attain to higher planes, he would have to build the ladder within himself, so as to rise above his lower, and free his higher self, that he might consciously know and understand all the causes " that have made him what he is, and that shall make him what he will be."

An oracle of Apollo, quoted by Eusebius, states that the " Egyptians were the first who disclosed by infinite actions the path that leads to the gods. The oracle is as follows :

> "The path by which to Deity we climb,
>   Is arduous, rough, ineffable, sublime :
>   And the strong massive gates, through which we pass,
>   In our first course, are bound with chains of brass.
>   Those men the first, who of Egyptian birth,
>   Drank the fair waters of Nilotic earth,
>   Disclosed by actions infinite this road,
>   And many paths to God Phœnicians showed,
>   This road the Assyrians pointed out to view,
>   And this the Lydians and Chaldeans knew."

Showing that the religions of the Egyptians comprised the essentials of all others, and that their moral code was both pure and exalted. But the real *nature* and attributes of God could only be communicated to such as were initiated into the Mysteries, and gave unquestionable proofs of their fidelity and zeal. And to the initiate it was a startling and solemn revelation. It was difficult, says Plato, to attain, and dangerous to publish the knowledge of the true God. Every Initiate in the Egyptian and Babylonian Mysteries were students deeply interested in the things seen, and the lessons learned, during their initiation, and they not only asked questions, but verified the statements made by the Hierophants, through their own personal investigations. In fact, they were endeavoring to acquire "Light" and Wisdom, consequently they looked up to those who initiated them for guidance, when they discovered that they must search and think for themselves, and in this way developed the power of Thought which could not otherwise have been done. "Knowledge is Power" but first let us understand what is meant by "Knowledge."

Many people are under the impression that "Knowledge" is comprised in simply knowing a thing to be hard or soft, hot or cold; that the object is a stone, a horse, dog or boy, is to know all about it; but that kind of knowledge is very superficial. There are many others who fancy that the result of experience places them in possession of certain facts, truths, etc., which is perfect knowledge. Now, I claim that true knowledge is a conscious realization of the law of phenomenal life, etc., a thorough understanding, of the underlying causes of the manifestations and differentiations of all things, and to be enabled to trace Nature from cause to Effect. For instance :—to have a Knowledge of Man we must trace the Monadic essence through elements to minerals, from minerals to plants, from plants to animals, from animals to quarternary Man, up to the present evolution, then on through body, soul and spirit, into the Eternal Essence of all things; this is knowledge, and such knowledge is only to be acquired by earnest study and the soul's deep meditation. Therefore, in our endeavor to solve any scientific problem, no matter how abstruse it may be, we should concentrate our mind firmly and persistently upon the subject, and then study it according to the law of analogy, or correspondence, which is the fundamental idea in all esoteric philosophies, whose right application is the key note to esoteric study.

Annie Besant, in the "Seven Principles of Man," page 14, states that, "The material centres of sensation are located in the Linga Sharira (*Ethereal Body*), which may be said to form the bridge between the physical organs and the mental perceptions; impressions from the physical universe impinge on the material molecules of the physical body, setting in vibration the constituent cells of the organs of sensation, or our 'senses.' These vibrations in their turn, set in motion the finer material molecules of the corresponding organs in the Linga Sharira (the 'Ka' of the ancient Egyptians), or the centers of sensation, the inner senses. From these, vibrations are again propagated into the yet rarer matter of the lower mental plane, whence they are reflected back until, reaching the material molecules of the cerebral hemispheres, they become our ' brain consciousness.'

" This correlated and unconscious succession is necessary for the normal action of ' consciousness,' as we know it. In sleep and in trance, natural or induced, the first and last stages are generally omitted, and the impressions start from and return to the astral plane, and thus make no trace on the brain memory; but the natural psychic, the clairvoyant who does not need trance for the exercise of his power, is able to transfer his consciousness from the physical to the astral plane without losing his grip thereof and can' impress the brain-memory with knowledge gained on the astral plane, so retaining it for use."

I consider consciousness to be the *Sixth* sense. It deals with the occult, the psychic, the purely mental, and is but little understood by the people of the Western world, simply because there is no money in it. Yet, by the use of this sense, we can work apparent miracles by the thoughts of others, like an open book. Consciousness develops intuition to such an extent, or degree, that to one who has cultivated this sense, by simply holding the hand of a person he can *feel* him talk, just as plainly and as intelligently as if you saw his lips move in speech and heard his voice. Now if we understand that Thoughts are things, that Thoughts are personal entities, just as much as a book or pen, a man or a tree we can thoroughly comprehend this fact. A word lightly spoken may not live, but the thought that embodied it does. Consequently to the psychic, the clairvoyant, there is no difficulty in reading one's mind, for the simple reason that the Thought forms are seen and easily understood, because he not only sees the Thought, but as I have already stated, he can *feel* him express himself.

Albert Pike says, in " Morals and Dogmas," page 573 : " The words I speak are but a succession of particular sounds, that by conventional arrangement communicate to others the Immaterial, Intangible, Eternal Thought. The fact that Thought continues to exist an instant, after it makes its appearance in the soul, proves it immortal: for there is nothing conceivable that can destroy it. The spoken words, being mere sounds, may vanish into thin air, and the written ones mere marks, be burned, erased, destroyed: but the Thought itself lives still, and must live on forever. A human Thought, then, is an actual existence, and a Force and Power, capable of acting upon and controlling matter as well as mind. Is not the existence of a God, who is the immaterial soul of the Universe, and whose Thought, embodied or not embodied in his Word, an Infinite Power of creation and production, destruction and preservation, quite as comprehensible as the existence of a Soul, of a Thought separated from the Soul, of the power of that Thought to mould the fate and influence the Destinies of Humanity?"

How sublimely grand is nature in her wondrous majesty and beauty, and how few there are who try to solve her mysteries. Science informs us of the harmony of nature's laws, which guide the glorious spheres in their orbits, and tries to explain the peculiar differentiation of molecular forms continually manifesting themselves from the unseen world around us; yet who is there among us that understands the mystery of either motion, sound or color? We tramp the stones, dust and grasses beneath our feet, seldom giving a thought about their peculiar differentiation and wonderful manifestations into higher forms of spiritual unfoldment, demonstrating what the poet says:

> " Every clod feels a stir of night,
>   An instinct within it that reaches and towers,
> Grasping blindly above it for light,
>   It climbs to a soul in the grasses and flowers.

Every object of which we know, every phenomenon we come across, has a soul in it. It is the moving power that produced the motion, the effect of which on us, we call an object. For all objects of which we have knowledge are objects of vibratory movement on us. This moving power may be, and is, in materialistic language called force. Now this force, or soul, is evolved and differentiated as it clothes itself in forms, a process which may be called the incarnation of force. This is a universal law. Everywhere we notice that force, type or idea is incarnated, or manifests itself in forms, again and again, and thus it grows. Force is never destroyed, but when the form, in which it clothes itself for the time being, is broken up, it finds some other form in which to express itself. The same law applies to the human kingdom; for human beings are just as much a part of nature as anything else. Human force, or type, or soul also reincarnates in order to grow. The only difference between the process, as working in the lower kingdom and that noticed in humanity, is that while in the lower kingdoms the force is a special one, human forces or souls are individuals. Each soul is an individual, and capable of no further subdivision and differentiation, but only of progress. Thus the soul in man, as an individual force, appears first in the crudest form. Then as it repeats its incarnation, or manifestation in form, it goes on progressing till it has completed the human evolution, and has reached the same perfection, as, for instance, was reached by Christ. Thus re-incarnation is the method of the evolution of the soul, and we must distinctly understand, that it does not mean transmigration, or reappearance of individuals of one incarnation, as the very same individual in the next.

The stone disentegrates and forms the dust of the earth, so that plant life might come into existence, and produce higher forms of unfoldment, leading on to higher spiritual development and divine consciousness, as manifested in her higher forms, for as the Reverend J. W. Lee, D.D., says, in the "Making of Man:"

"Not till the dust stands erect in the living man; not till the atoms throb in a human brain, and beat in a human heart was the intention under the drift of ages, spelled out in the unity of thought. Man is the head and heart of nature. Evolution and Involution is the coming and becoming of man. The world is because he is."

What mind can comprehend the Infinite and absolutely unknown, having no beginning and shall have no end; which is both last and first, because whether differentiated or withdrawn into itself it ever is? What mind can explain the mystery and power of "magnetism," the virtue or force which compels one pole of a magnetic needle to point direct to the north? And what is Light? What is electricity? Who can explain the process by which the rose received its delicious perfume? Whence comes the blush of its petals? And how does the lily come forth from the slime and filth of the cesspool, in all its dazzling brightness and purity? Is it any more a problem, whence comes Thought, Will, Perception and all the phenomena of the mind? Has the phonograph vocal organs? Has it a memory? Has this rotating cylinder which speaks to us a brain and tongue, that will articulate with an exactitude seemingly imcomprehensible—your vocal Thought?

How often we hear people say that "the brain is the organ of the mind and its secretion is Thought!" Are we to understand from this that *Thought* or *Mind* cannot exist without the *Brain?* If that is the idea they desire to convey, I for my part most emphatically object to such conception, and do most earnestly ask the reader to follow me in an argument along these lines, so that I may be enabled to show them that these assertions are not true.   Does it require a brain to direct?

> " Aldebaran, fairest in Germini's train,
>   That beams forth with Capella on high ;
> Where Orion's bright clusters splendidly reign,
>   And illumines the beautiful sky."

When Professor Tyndall delivered his celebrated address in Belfast, Ireland, upon the subject of " Matter and Mind," he stated " that Science would probably have entirely to recast its conception of matter," and this is just exactly what Science has been compelled to do ; and to-day, in this wonderful twentieth century, it does not give the same definition to matter it did when I was a boy, for now, we recognize matter existing under conditions that would have been regarded as an absurdity by the Scientific world, when Tyndall intimated the necessity for the reconsideration of preconceived ideas regarding matter.

Now this brings me to my first remark about " the brain being the organ of the Mind," etc. Nearly every person is under the impression that Thought is produced by the action of the " gray matter of the brain," and when the gray matter was not to be found working, in its peculiar convolutions, thought was not able to produce itself, and that with the presence of the brain thought is manifested. According to the old theory the development of thought in a child was entirely different in its character from that in man, or even in the child at a more advanced age. It was claimed that the thought in the child was infantile in its character, and as the child grew from boyhood to manhood, thought grew *pari passu* and became far more subtle and powerful, and that it was a more mature Thought, having developed through an advanced age, being produced simply by the physical development of the convolutions of the cerebral hemispheres.

Further, if at any period of man's life his brain was injured, or over-powered by use of strong liquors or narcotics, or under high feverish conditions, the blood supply would be impure and bad blood would function through the brain, in consequence of which he would have delirium, and his thoughts become confused through the peculiar condition of the brain.

Again, it is asserted that if a man's brain is injured by a heavy blow upon the head, crushing the bone in upon the gray matter, thought is immediately arrested, and in lifting the pressure of the bone from the brain thought will begin to function again. It is claimed that if a portion of the brain were destroyed or eaten away through disease, the faculty of thought expressed by that particular portion of the brain would disappear.

The conclusion arrived at would be, from the above, that thought grows, ripens and matures with the growth and development of the brain, and varies according to the condition of the brain, being destroyed if the brain is seriously injured, finally disappearing as the brain decays and the mind of man is destroyed—is lost. Now there is no question about the strength of these arguments, for they are most assuredly very strong, more especially to one who reasons, step by step, along the lines where this process of reasoning would lead him.

But I intend to show that this inductive method of reasoning is not at all times true, for many facts have been overlooked, and in consequence the entire argument falls to the ground, like a house built with a pack of cards. Annie Besant has said: " Unless you are sure that you know everything in the universe of discourse, inductive logic does not lead you to a certain and final conclusion," which most assuredly has not been done in this argument; therefore the whole superstructure falls to pieces.

In an argument based on the constant relation between two things, a relationship must positively be shown to exist. If you get the same two things moving in an opposite direction, varying inversely, then what becomes of the argument? Now that is exactly what has happened in connection with the argument based on brain and thought, and their constantly varying together. It has been found they do not so vary, and still more than that, sometimes vary inversely; that is, a condition may sometimes arise where the brain is partially paralyzed, but where the thought is much more active than when it is working in the brain.

Now I am going to prove to you by hypnotic and mesmeric experiment that intelligence can function when the brain is paralyzed. Charcot and his school have demonstrated this fact, and they have proved it over and over again. The learned doctors have not advanced a theory, but have just stated facts in their research and scientific observation. But first let me quote you from the "Medical Record" of New York, page 104, July 16th, 1898: "A man is reported by Porta to have lost the whole of his right cerebral hemisphere by an accident. He was unconscious for a few hours only, and *when he recovered he proved that immediately after the accident he had not been unconscious,* because he recollected being picked up and taken to a hospital. Eighteen months later the wound was closed. He had, of course, side paralysis; but his left cerebral hemisphere being intact his intellectual functions are said to be unimpaired."

We have an instrument called the *spymograph,* which distinctly shows, not only the throbbing of the heart, but it will record and show the movement of the lungs, as well as the contraction and expansion of the muscles. It is an instrument with a revolving cylinder and various attachments, such as levers, pencil, paper, etc., and when connected with various parts of the human body in a certain way we are enabled to register the peculiar motions of the various organs, such as the beating of the heart, the rise and fall of the lungs, etc., etc. Now, by applying certain parts of one of these machines to your heart, you would get a record of its motion, showing the slightest differentiation of its action, and this record would be traced by the recorder in all its variations upon the cylinder of the instrument itself. It will also record with exactness the motions of the lungs and muscles, however slight. If no perceptible motion is cognized by our physical senses, this instrument will mark it out in curved lines, easily recognizable by any physician, and these very lines prove the truth and fact of the motion, thus doing away with human testimony and the possibility of fraud by any human intervention.

Now we will hypnotize a man, and with this instrument find that the motions of his various organs, while in the hypnotic state, are so slight that without its use we should declare they were not functioning at all. This delicate instrument, with its wonderful mechanism, records the slightest movement in the lungs and heart, etc., thereby proving to us that the blood does not function through all parts of the brain, neither does it go to the lungs to be oxygenized and electrified and forced through the arterial system in all its wonderful ramifications on its life-giving mission to all parts of the body. Consequently the blood becomes over-charged with carbonic acid, which is produced through improper respira-tion, and its presence brings on a state of coma, a condition of the brain in which thought is unable to function. So far as the physical body of this man is concerned, as he is to all appearances dead, lying there so still and quiet, with all the attributes of death, yet, although in this con-dition, we shall find all his mental faculties in a remarkable state of activity.

We can obtain from him, in his present condition, a demonstration of memory and consciousness far more powerful than in his regular nor-mal or waking state. His memory has been immensely stimulated, in fact to such an extent that he can tell us of every incident in his life, from childhood up to the present day. He will be enabled to describe scenes of his schoolboy days, the school and schoolmates, the master, the interior and exterior of the building, and he will remember the houses and the people who lived in the immediate vicinity, indeed many things which in his waking state had long been forgotten, will now be described by him, as if they had occurred but yesterday. We shall also find that in his present state or condition his mental faculties have been so inten-sified, he can memorize to an extent truly remarkable, so much so that if we should read to him a half dozen stanzas from " Homer's Odyssey " in Greek, a language he does not understand, yet will he repeat it, word for word, from beginning to end without a mistake. If we restore him to his waking state we shall discover that he will not remember or be able to pronounce one word of it. Hypnotize him again and we shall find that he is able to repeat them, word for word, without blunder or mishap, thus demonstrating that when his brain is dormant, not functioning, and the man is in the hypnotic condition, we find a higher grade of intelli-gence and a grander memory, with no blank in his life, as he can describe accurately every incident, with an exactitude seemingly incomprehensible.

Many men which we meet in every-day life are dowered with an ordinary intelligence. Take one of these and throw him into a hyp-notic condition, when he will be far more brilliant in his reasoning, and

16

often argue from cause to effect with surprising ability, yet his brain is not working, and in this condition you can compel him to do nearly anything you may desire. You can destroy his senses or intensify them. You will realize that you can control his voluntary muscles, individuality, sympathies and antipathies, and perform many things with which, no doubt, you are perfectly familiar. We positively know that we can hypnotize an insane man and obtain from him intelligence and reasoning powers. Throw him back again to his waking state and once more he is a lunatic; but under hypnotic control he becomes an intelligent, reasoning, human being, who will talk and argue as well as one that is sane. I could continue my arguments along these lines, but think the above will prove that *though thought may always be expressed by the brain, it is also possible to express it without the brain.* Although many incidents in our normal lives have been forgotten, they are to be found impressed upon our consciousness and can be brought back, again and again, even when lost to our normal faculties.

We find, through these investigations, that instead of thought varying with the state of the brain, it varies against it; when the brain is in a state of coma, thought is far more active; when paralyzed the mental faculties are immensely stimulated and the man enabled to exercise a power far more keen and subtle than during his waking consciousness, by which fact we are *forced* to admit that *the brain is a limitation impressed on our consciousness, a partial instrument instead of the producer of Thought.* Therefore the Brain is not the organ of the Mind, and it does not secrete Thought in the same manner in which the Hepatic gland secretes bile for the digestive apparatus. For, as above stated, Thoughts are Things, and the Thoughts which come to Man have existed long ages before the physical body of the man was born.

We can readily prove the Power and Force of Thought; for instance: You are sitting at your window, or standing at some place where you can see another person—say—standing upon the sidewalk, waiting for some one, and, if you send out a thought to him, willing him to look around at you, the first thing you will observe will be a peculiar feeling of uneasiness about the individual, and he will turn his head, one way then the other, until finally he will direct his gaze to the spot where you are standing.

In the Appendix of Paracelsus, by Hartman, he states that : " By the magic power of the will a person on this side of the ocean may make a person on the other side hear what is said on this side, and a person in the East may thus converse with another in the West. The physical may hear and understand the voice of another man at a distance of a hundred steps, and the ethereal body of a man may hear what another man thinks at a distance of a hundred miles and more. What may be accomplished by ordinary means in a month (such as the sending of messages) may be done by this art in a day."

The thought goes forth with a force for good or evil, just as we think or send it out, and like a stone cast forth from our hand, falling into a pool of water, disturbs and displaces every molecule of that body. If we watch the falling stone we shall see, where it struck the water, an all embracing circular wave start out with a momentum which will eventually reach the surrounding banks, when, in order to preserve its equilibrium, it will return to the source from whence it emanated, thus proving that (Thoughts) " curses, like chickens, come home to roost." So we should ever be guarded in our Thoughts, for those we send out return to us, and we ourselves feel their influence, either for Good or Evil, as the case may be. Thoughts are perfect entities.

Thought has no language ! But in passing through the cerebral hemispheres of a Greek, Arab, Hindu, Chinese, or an American, it expresses itself in the language of the brain through which it passes. We can clearly demonstrate the locality of the brain, but who among us can locate the MIND ? " Mind (or Manas) belongs to the immortal man, the real *I* that continually clothes itself in various personalities, to live, die and pass away with each and every one of them. But the true man lives through all and endures forever," and the voice of the real man comes to us by a process as direct and swift as bodily vision, a voice which never deceives us *Intuition*.

Annie Besant says, in " Reincarnation," page 22 : " The brain no more produces the thought than the organ produces the melody, in both cases there is a player working through the instrument. But the power of the player to manifest himself, in thought or in melody, is limited by the capacities of the instrument."

Pyramids—Sphinx—Tombs.

My form stupendous here the gods have placed,
    Sparing each spot of harvest-bearing land;
And with this mighty work of art have graced
    A rocky isle, encompassed once with sand;
    And near the Pyramids have bid me stand:
Not that fierce sphynx that Thebes erewhile laid waste,
    But great Latona's servant, mild and bland;
Watching the prince beloved, who fills the throne
Of Egypt's plains, and calls the Nile his own.
    That heavenly monarch, who his foes defies
    Like Vulcan powerful, and like Pallas wise.

                               —ARRIAN.

CHAPTER XI.

PYRAMIDS—SPHINX—TOMBS.

WHEN first I visited the Pyramids of Egypt it was a far more difficult task than to-day, as then we had to cross the river Nile in row boats, and on arriving upon the west bank, hire donkeys and ride through the fields to the Pyramids and Sphinx, pestered at every step by the fellaheen, boys and girls, running along beside us, begging and shouting loudly for baksheesh; but now there is a very nice route that will take you direct to the Pyramids, lying along a very fine macadamized road, shaded with beautiful accacia or lebek trees leading directly to the foot of the Great Pyramid. You may take your choice of either a carriage or a donkey with which to make the trip from Cairo to the monuments and back. Should you choose the former, the charges will be about five dollars, and will take about one hour and a half to go and the same time to return. If you should start from the city with a carriage in the early morning, you would be enabled to devote the middle of the day to an examination of the Pyramids, Sphinx and other objects of interest in the immediate vicinity and return to Cairo in time for dinner in the evening; but, of course, your time would be very limited. Should you decide on a donkey for the trip, the expense would be about a dollar and a half a day and the difference in time will be fully half an hour longer going and coming, than it would be travelling with a carriage.

There are a great many people constantly visiting these stupendous specimens of ancient Egyptian Architecture and sculpture, who, after devoting a couple of hours to the examination of the celebrated Pyramids, come away with the impression that they know all about them. No greater mistake than this could be made, as it would be utterly impossible for any one, in so short a time, to realize the wonderful proportions and stupendous magnitude of the stones with which they are built, until they have thoroughly examined them in all their parts; both the exterior and interior of their geometrical proportions and astronomical position, then, and then only, can they say "*I know the Pyramids.*" In order to reach these celebrated fabrics, we cross the river from Cairo by the Kasr-el-Nil bridge, which will lead us on to the very fine road referred to above, constructed by his Highness, the Khedive, for the express purpose of accomodating the immense throngs continually visiting these celebrated Pyramids, Sphinx, etc., in the plains of Gizeh.

These wonderful monuments, which I am about to describe, occupy a site about eight or nine miles from the city of Cairo. After crossing the river Nile over the large iron bridge, we continue on and cross its western branch by a much smaller one, and then turning to the left enter the beautiful avenue shaded with accacias which leads us to the plains of Gizeh, and to these immense relics of ancient Egyptian Architecture. The view, as we ride along, is simply magnificent, the green fields of waving corn, clover, etc., presenting quite a contrast to the barren hills and desert sands which bound our horizon, while the pyramids themselves appear like huge mountains, rising into the clear blue sky above. It is not until we stand beneath their very shadow, looking upward along the gigantic steps leading to the apex, or summit, that we are enabled to fully realize their stupendous magnitude. Then their clear, sharply defined ontlines disappear and their immense proportions break in upon our senses, filling us with awe, admiration and amazement, for these wonderful monuments of a prehistoric age, now lying before us in all their rugged sublimity and grandeur. Even here the eye can hardly embrace them, nor the mind fully comprehend their gigantic proportions, and we stand bewildered, as it were, before one of the " Wonders of the World." An immense number of stones have been used in building the Great Pyramid weighing over thirty tons, each of which contain hundreds of cubic feet. In our ascent up its rough and rugged sides we could form no idea of the time, power, or force used, to quarry, carry across the desert sands, and place in position, such enormous blocks of stone, nor the machinery or number of men required in its construction.

The Pyramids of Gizeh occupy a rocky plateau considerably higher than the flooding waters of the river Nile, and they are built with their sides facing the four cardinal points of the universe. *The first* or Great Pyramid is known as Khufu or Cheops. *The second* Khafra and

THE KASR-EL-NIL BRIDGE,

CAIRO.

The third is called the Pyramid of Men-kau-Ra. Some Greek writers claimed that this pyramid was built for a tomb, wherein was placed the celebrated courtezan *Rhodopis*, being built for her, while others state that it was erected for *Nitokris*; but the discovery, by Col. H. Vyse, of a wooden mummy case bearing upon it the cartouce of King Men-kau-Ra, proves that he was the founder of this monument, and that it was erected for him. There is a story connected with this pyramid, which very much resembles our modern tale of Cinderella, for Strabo tells us that: " While Rhodopis was bathing, an eagle carried off one of her shoes, carried it to Memphis, and dropped it into the lap of the King, who was then sitting on the judgment seat. The king, admiring the neatness of the shoe, and surprised at the strangeness of the occurrence, sent out messengers to search for the owner of the shoe. She was found at Naucratis and brought to the king, who made her his wife and on her death erected the third pyramid to her memory." There are several smaller pyramids and a great many tombs and mummy pits of great interest, quite close to the greater pyramids and Sphinx and the *Granite Temple*, discovered by Mariette Bey in 1853. Campbell's Tomb was discovered by Col. H. Vyse, in 1837, during his exploring excavations, and he named it after the British Consul-General who filled that office at the time. Here we find numberless tombs and an immense quantity of buried tombs and mastabas of the early empire scattered promiscuously around, demonstrating that we are wandering through an ancient city of the dead. The great Pyramids stand about five miles from the river Nile, and they are just as much a problem to the human race to-day as they were in the days of Herodotus, who visited these celebrated monuments of the ancient Egyptians, and informs us that according to his judgment, the labor required to prepare for the construction of these wonderful fabrics was not less than that required to build the pyramids themselves.

The largest of the group (Cheops) is seven hundred and sixty-four feet at the base and covers thirteen acres of ground. It has a perpendicular height of four hundred and fifty feet, with about two hundred and six steps, varying from five feet to eighteen inches, which will bring you to its summit, a flat surface of about forty feet square, from which point a very fine view of the surrounding country may be obtained. Various writers give different dates for the founding of this wonder of the world, *Cheops,* and Wilkinson places its origin B. C. 2123. The best place to make the ascent is near the northeast angle, as there the stones are in a better condition for climbing, as on the other faces the stones have been broken and displaced, no doubt by the Caliphs, when they tried to destroy them. The steps are about two feet wide, and are all right for making the ascent; but coming down one does not seem to have sufficient foot room ; but there is really no danger, if you trust yourself to the attendants, who are quite strong and very careful of those under their care.

It was quite a long time before an entrance to the pyramid was discovered, and it was not until the Caliphs had finally established themselves at Cairo that the entrance was actually known. The Caliphs undertook to force a passage, by quarrying towards the centre, through the solid masonry, when, after reaching a distance of about one hundred feet, the workmen heard a noise like the sound of falling stones, which demonstrated an approach to some chamber or passage, and on continuing their work in the direction of the sounds, about fifteen feet to the left, they came across the original passage, made by the craftsmen, leading to the two interior chambers. They then returned by this discovered passage, clearing away the stones, etc., which had fallen into it during their tunneling. They traversed this passage until the original entrance was found, which formed a pointed arch or pediment on the North side of the pyramid, a little to one side of its centre, and about forty-five feet from the ground. This entrance is three feet eleven inches high, by three feet five inches wide, while the passage-way to the interior descends at an angle of 26° 41' for a distance of three hundred and forty feet, in a perfectly straight line, where it falls upon a horizontal passage of smaller dimensions, about thirty feet in length, terminating in a sepulchral chamber nearly a hundred feet below the base of the pyramid, which is forty feet long by twenty-seven wide and a little over eleven feet in height, though never completed, being left in the rough. From the southern side there is a very narrow passage extending fully fifty feet farther on, where it dies in the solid rock beyond. Col. H. Vyse, in his exploration of this chamber, sunk a shaft beneath it to a considerable depth, in the hopes of making some new discoveries, but was disappointed in his expectations.

At a distance of sixty-three feet from the entrance, down the incline already described, we find a very large block of granite, which closed the entrance leading to the chamber above. The exploring workmen were unable to remove this stone, so they quarried around it to the right (which road we took), and passing over some very rough steps we continued along the inclined passage that is blocked, until we arrived at what is known as the *Great Gallery*, a distance of about one hundred and thirty feet, at an angle of 26° 18' at this point, when a horizontal passage leads us to the " Queen's Chamber," but just before we enter it we have to descend one step.

This chamber is eighteen feet long, sixteen feet wide and twenty feet high in the centre, having a pediment roof, the stones of which are carried quite a distance into the solid masonry, in order to strengthen the roof. We noticed that the stones forming the sides of this chamber fitted so closely that it was difficult to discover their joints. This apartment is located directly under the centre of the apex of the pyramid and distant from it three hundred and seventy-three feet, or four hundred and seventy from the original summit, before it had been disturbed by the vandal hands of the Caliphs. On each side of this chamber are small holes, for ventilating purposes, and on the East side near the entrance is a recess formed by projecting stones, one above the other, the object of which has never been understood. Nothing was ever found in this apartment, and if anything had been concealed here, so far it has not been discovered.

Now let us return to the junction of the *Great Gallery* and the horizontal passage, where we shall find a well or inclined shaft two feet four inches square, and one hundred and ninety-one feet in depth, reaching down to the inclined passage, not far from the sepulchral chamber already described. It was, no doubt, used as a means of communication between the upper chambers and the sepulchral chamber after the passage had been closed by the block of granite previously described.

One can readily pass through it by means of the projections, which no doubt were made for this purpose. Right here where the horizontal passage leads to the *Queen's Chamber* is the *Great Gallery*, one hundred and fifty feet six inches long, twenty-eight feet high and seven feet wide above the vamp or seat, which extends along both sides of the gallery, being two feet high and projecting from the face of the sides nineteen inches, thus leaving a passage three feet ten inches in the clear. Overhead the projecting stones give this gallery the appearance of being arched, on account of the eight courses of stone laid in the side walls, approaching each other in every course. At the end of the *Great Gallery* we step or crawl upon a narrow horizontal passage way, twenty-two feet long, by three feet eight inches high at the beginning, but widening before reaching the end into a vestibule or ante-chamber to the principal apartment of this pyramid, the *King's Chamber*, the dimensions of which are thirty-four feet long from East to West, with sides from North to South seventeen feet wide, and its height is nineteen feet.

It is not situated exactly under the apex, but a little to the southeastward of it. The roof is flat and ceiled with immense granite slabs two feet wide and eighteen feet six inches long, whose ends are supported by the lateral walls. Within this chamber to-day, mutilated and unadorned, lies the lidless and empty sarcophagus, without name or carving. It is made of beautiful red granite, like the blocks which form the sides of the chamber itself, the joints demonstrating the knowledge and skill of the craftsmen, as they are fitted together so closely and with such perfect exactness that to insert the blade of a penknife between them would be impossible. What an immense amount of time and labor must the polishing of the stones which form the chamber and passages have entailed!

In the side walls of this chamber are tubular holes about three feet from the floor, which, when traced to their outlet, prove to be purely for ventilation. There are four or five rooms, or entresols, above the *King's Chamber;* but these are of very much smaller dimensions, being evidently made for the purpose of lessening the tremendous pressure from above upon its flat roof, thus testifying to the knowledge of architecture by the practical operative craftsmen of those days, and proving beyond the shadow of a doubt, as I have before stated, that they had a far greater knowledge of the mechanical arts and sciences than we possess to-day.

Before leaving the pyramids I desire to tell you of a rather amusing incident related in the autobiography of Sir W. Siemens. One day, with some companions, he was standing upon the summit of the Great Pyramid (*Cheops*) when " an Arab called his attention to the fact, that when he raised his hand, with fingers outspread, an acute singing note was heard, the sound ceasing as soon as he let his hand fall " " I found his assertion," he writes, " to be true. As soon as I raised one of my fingers above my head I felt a prickling in the fingers. That this could only be caused by an electrical phenomenon was proved by the slight electric shock, felt on trying to drink out of a wine bottle. So I wrapped a full bottle of wine that I had with me in damp paper, and thus converting it into a Leyden-bottle which was soon strongly charged with electricity by the simple device of holding it above my head. The Arabs had already become distrustful, on seeing small lightnings, as it were, issue from the wine bottles held up by myself and companions, and who now held a brief consultation. Suddenly at a given signal each of my companions were seized by the guide who had led him up, and now tried to force him to go down again. I myself was standing at the very top of the pyramid when the sheik of the Arabs came to me and told me, through my interpreter, that the Arabs had determined that we were at once to leave the pyramid, because we were practicing magic and it might damage their chance of making a living. On my refusing to obey this order, the sheik caught hold of my left hand. I had awaited this movement and held up my right hand with the bottle, in the attitude of a magician, afterwards lowering it slowly towards the point of the Sheik's nose. When quite close to that feature, I felt a violent shock run through the bottle to my own arm and was certain that the sheik must have received the equivalent. At any rate he fell senseless on the stones and a few anxious moments passed before he rose suddenly with a loud cry and sprang down the gigantic steps of the pyramid, with long strides. The Arabs, seeing this, and excited by the sheiks constant cries of magic! magic! released my companions and followed their leader, leaving us complete masters of the pyramids."

About six hundred yards to the southeast of the Great Pyramid, crouches the Sphinx, vainly endeavoring to arise from out the drifting sands of the desert, one of the most remarkable objects to be seen in the vicinity of the Pyramids. The age of this monolithic carving is unknown, as very little of the history of this fabulous monster has been handed down to us, for the simple reason that none of the ancient Greek authors furnish any account of it, and the Romans but very little and that unreliable. It is a positive fact that many people may now be found who actually believe that the Pyramids could not have been in existence when Moses led the Israelites from out the "Land of Egypt," and out of the "House of Bondage," simply because the Bible gives no account of them. It is the same with the history of the Sphinx, because no mention is made by ancient writers regarding this extraordinary monster it can have no claim to antiquity, and according to Roman historians, is simply of modern origin compared to the tombs and temples which surround it. In fact, Pliny tells us that, during his time, the Romans believed it to be the tomb of Amasis, one of the last kings of the XXVI Dynasty. Not many years ago, according to the investigations of some of our Egyptologists, it was believed to have been created by some one of the Kings of the Middle Empire. But it was not until the Stele was discovered by Mariette Bey, bearing upon its stony face a record of certain repairs made within the temple of the Sphinx by Thothmes IV, B. C. 1533, that its creation was positively known as due to one of the Kings of the Ancient Empire.

The record upon the Stele is as follows: "The living Horus, the King of Upper and Lower Egypt, Khufu, during his lifetime, had cleaned out the Temple of Isis, ruler of the Pyramid, which is situated at the spot where is the Sphinx, on the north-east side of the Temple of Osiris, Lord of Rostau. He had build his Pyramid where the Temple of this goddess is." There is a great deal more upon this stone that Mariette discovered, as well as other discoveries made by him, going to prove that the Sphinx must have existed during the reign of Khufu, or Cheops. Mariette says that: "Around this imposing relic of antiquity, whose origin is wrapped in mystery, a number of legends and superstitions have clustered in all ages; but Egyptology has shown, *first*, that it was a colossal image of Ra-Harmachis, and therefore of his human representative on earth, the King of Egypt, who had it hewn, and *second*, that it was in existence in the time of, and was probably repaired by, Cheops or Chephren, who had lived about B. C. 3700." Thothmes IV. placed a stone tablet fully fourteen feet high between the paws of this monolithic monster, whereon was inscribed an account of a vision he had seen during an after-dinner nap. There is also an account of the works and repairs done by him at the cities of Heliopolis and Memphis, etc. The Sphinx is carved out of solid rock, and where the rock was too small or hollow to follow the lines of the body, these places were filled with sandstone. The length of this monster is one hundred and forty feet; its extreme height, from the crown of the head to the pavement below, between its paws is nearly seventy feet; its extended paws are fifty feet; from the point of the chin to the top of the head is very nearly thirty feet; the width of the face is fourteen feet, and the mouth is seven feet long. It has been frightfully mutilated; but, notwithstanding this fact, one can, when standing in a proper position, still see a calm, peaceful expression upon its face, looking to the East, as it did when the rocky plateau above it reverberated with the sounds made by the craftsman who built the Pyramids in the ancient days of Pharaonic history.

Kenrick, in his "Ancient Egypt," says, Vol. I, page 115: "The design of carving a rock which broke the view of the Pyramids into a gigantic Sphinx was worthy of the grandeur of Egyptian conceptions in Architecture and Sculpture. It was probably the work of the same age as the Pyramids themselves. A Sphinx is the representative of the monarch whose name it bears; and as the name of *Chafre* (Chephren) is found upon the tablet before mentioned, it is natural to suppose that it was fashioned in his honor. (An opinion in which I do not concur.) The Greek mythology has accustomed us to speak of the Sphinx as a female, and the artists who carved, in the Roman times, those figures of Sphinxes from which antiquarians derived their first ideas of Egyptian antiquities, sometimes represented them as female. But in the genuine works of Pharaonic times, it is most rare to meet with a female Sphinx; and in these exceptional cases a female sovereign is represented, as in the Sphinx of the Museum at Turin, published by Champollion, in his letter to the Duke de Blacas. The junction of the human head, with the body of a lion, denotes the combination of sagacity with strength required in the administration of a King."

Before closing this article on the Sphinx I desire to quote you from Bacon's "Essays XXVIII," "SPHINX OR SCIENCE," to demonstrate the grandeur of Symbolism, but more especially in the relation to the Sphinx. It demonstrates the necessity of a depth of profound thought and study, in order to obtain a knowledge of such a beautiful solution to this ancient symbol. In our glorious Ancient and Accepted Scottish Rite of Masonry there are vast numbers of symbols, sublimely grand, which we shall be unable to realize or understand unless we devote time and most profound attention to a study of the beauties that lie imbedded within them. Not until we commence to study, in regular systematic order, the symbols in the various degrees of our most illustrious fraternity, from the 4° to the 32° inclusive, shall we begin to realize the sublimity and grandeur contained within them, and comprehend the "*Lost word*," understand the true meaning of *The Building of the Temple*, solve *The Mystery of the Balance* and find the *key* to the *Royal Secret*, by which the veil will be reft asunder and all the glories of our beloved Fraternity opened to our view and understanding.

Bacon says: "They relate that Sphinx was a monster, variously formed, having the face and voice of a virgin, the wings of a bird, and the talons of a griffin. She resided on the top of a mountain, near the city of Thebes, and also beset the highways. Her manner was to lie in ambush and seize the travellers, and having them in her power to propose to them certain dark and perplexing riddles, which it was thought she received from the Muses, and if the wretched captives could not solve and interpret these riddles she, with great cruelty, fell upon them in their hesitation and tore them to pieces. This plague, having reigned a long time, the Thebans at length offered their kingdom to the man who could interpret her riddles, there being no other way to subdue her. Ædipus, a penetrating and prudent man, though lame in his feet, excited by so great a reward, accepted the conditions, and with a good assurance of mind, cheerfully presented himself before the monster, who directly asked him: 'What creature that was, which being born four-footed, afterward became two-footed, then three-footed, and lastly four-footed again?' Ædipus, with presence of mind, replied: 'It was man, who, upon his first birth, and in infant state, crawled upon all fours in endeavoring to walk, but not long after went upright upon its two natural feet; again, in old age walked three-footed with a stick; and at last growing decrepit, lay four-footed confined to his bed;' and having by his exact solution obtained the victory, he slew the monster, and laying the carcass upon an Ass, led her away in triumph, and upon this he was, according to the agreement, made king of Thebes."

EXPLANATION.—This is an interesting, instructive fable, and seems invented to represent Science, especially as joined with practice. For science may, without absurdity, be called a monster, being strangely gazed at and admired by the ignorant and unskillful. Her figure and form is various, by reason of the vast variety of subjects that science considers; her voice and countenance are represented female, by reason of her gay appearance and volubility of speech; wings are added because the sciences and their inventions run and fly about in a moment, for knowledge, like light, communicated from one torch to another, is presently caught and copiously diffused; sharp and hooked talons are elegantly attributed to her because the axioms and arguments of science enter the mind, lay hold of it, fix it down, and keep it from moving or slipping away.

This the sacred philosopher observed when he said, " The words of the wise are like goads, or nails driven far in." Eccles. 12: 11. Again, all science seems placed on high, as it were on the tops of mountains that are hard to climb, for science is justly imagined a sublime and lofty thing, looking down upon ignorance from an eminence, and at the same time taking an extensive view on all sides, as is usual on tops of mountains.

Science is said to beset the highways, because through all the journey and peregrination of human life, there is matter and occasion offered for contemplation. Sphinx is said to propose various difficult questions and riddles to men which she received from the Muses, and these questions, as long as they originate with the Muses, may very well be unaccompanied with severity, for while there is no other end of contemplation and inquiry but that of knowledge alone, the understanding is not oppressed, or driven to straits or difficulties, but expatiates and ranges at large, and even receives a degree of pleasure, form and variety; but after the Muses have given over their riddles to Sphinx, that is to practice, which urges and impels to action, choice and determination, then it is that they become torturing, severe and trying, and unless solved and interpreted, strangely perplex and harass the human mind, rend it every way and perfectly tear it to pieces. All the riddles of Sphinx, therefore, have two conditions annexed, viz.: dilaceration to those who do not solve them, and empire to those who do.

17

For he who understands the things proposed, obtains his end, and every artificer rules over his work—(meaning that knowledge and power are reciprocal; so that to improve in knowledge is to improve in the power of commanding nature by introducing new arts and producing works and effects.) Sphinx has no more than two kinds of riddles, one relating to the nature of things, the other to the nature of man, and correspondent to these, the prizes of the solution are two kinds of empire: the empire over nature and the empire over man. For the true and ultimate end of natural philosophy is dominion over natural things, natural bodies, remedies, machines and numberless other particulars, though the schools, contented with what spontaneously offers, and swollen with their own discourses, neglect, and in a manner despise, both things and works. But the riddle proposed to Ædipus, the solution whereof acquired him the Theban kingdom, regarded the nature of man; for he who has thoroughly looked into and examined human nature, may in a manner command his own fortune, and seems born to acquire dominion and rule. It is with the utmost elegance added in the fable, that when Sphinx was conquered, her carcass was laid upon an ass; for there is nothing so subtle and abstruse, but after being once made plain, intelligible and common, may be received by the slowest capacity. We must not omit that the Sphinx was conquered by a lame man, and impotent in his feet; for men usually make too much haste to the solution of Sphinx's riddles; whence it happens that she, prevailing, their minds are rather racked and torn by disputes than invested with command, by work and effects.

The ancient city of Memphis was founded, according to Herodotus, by Menes, the first known king of Egypt. It has been called by different names at various times or periods. Originally it was known as the " City of the White Wall." Later it was called *Ha Ptah* (house of Ptah), which the Greeks eventually transformed into Hephaistopolis, and finally it received the name of *Men-nefer*, " the good place." In the course of time the letter *r* was dropped from *Men-nefer*, when the name of this celebrated city became known under the Coptic name of Menfi, or Memfi, which was soon changed to Memphis by the Greeks and Romans, from whom this name has been handed down to us of the twentieth century.

When Menes first formed the idea of establishing this city he realized that he would have to change the course of the river in order to obtain the amount of land necessary for the upbuilding of such an immense place as he had under contemplation. In order to accomplish his purpose he therefore built a large embankment across the river, compelling it to flow off in another direction, and by this means reclaiming a vast amount of land upon which to lay the foundation of one of the most celebrated and wonderful cities of the world's history—Memphis, the capital of ancient Egypt. At the point where he commenced to turn the course of the river he caused an enormous dyke to be constructed, to protect the city and prevent the river from ever returning into its old course, and to ultimately destroy the city established with so much labor. There is one thing respecting Herodotus and Diodorus, the two historians who wrote so much about this country, which is that Herodotus gives us a very full description of the city of Memphis, the capital of Lower Egypt, and a very poor account of Thebes, not even alluding to the monuments of that wonderful city; while Diodorus gives a full and complete account of the wonderful capital of Upper Egypt, Thebes, and tells but very little about Memphis, which does not even correspond with the account given by Herodotus.

It was within the walls of this city that Menes erected the wonderful " Temple of Ptah," a Temple so vast and so grand, that its fame was known throughout the ancient world. It was the first and probably the largest and most magnificent temple ever constructed by the hand of Man, in this extrordinary valley of the river Nile, and doubtless involved an enormous amount of time, material and labor in its completion. No accurate descriptions have been preserved of this stupendous fabric; but the best authorities agree that this wonderful Temple was begun by Menes, being enlarged and beautified by the various kings of succeeding dynasties, even up to the reign of Amasis, who dedicated therein a recumbent colossus, seventy-five feet long, the first of its kind known to have existed up to that time.

This famous temple of Hephaistos, or Ptah, was very much larger than the more modern temple of Karnak, which was, no doubt, modelled after this ancient temple of Ptah, in Memphis. There is a very curious story related in the " Library of Entertaining Knowledge," respecting a monolithic chamber which formed part of this wonderful temple, where Moses first studied the Wisdom peculiar to the priests of Memphis: "It was made of a single stone, nine cubits high, eight long, and seven broad, and was called the 'green chamber' and is described as being found among the ruins of Memphis. In the middle of the stone, a niche or hole is hollowed out, which leaves two cubits of thickness for the sides as well as for the top and bottom. All the rest forms the interior capacity of the chamber. It is completely covered, both outside and in, with intaglios in relief. On the outside is the figure of the Sun in the East and a great number of stars, spheres, men and animals. The men are represented in different attitudes, some stationary, others moving; some have their dresses tucked up to allow them to work, others carry materials, some are giving orders. It is evident that these representations refer to important things, remarkable actions and profound secrets. This niche was firmly fixed on supports of massive granite and placed in a magnificent temple (Hephaistos) constructed of enormous stones, put together with the most perfect art."

I do not wish to pass from this part of Egypt without speaking of the mastabas in this vast Necropolis of ancient Memphis, for they represent the tombs of private individuals who lived in the grand old days of Memphian splendor. These tombs of various sizes, range from ten to forty feet in height, differing one from another at about the same ratio. Approaching them from a distance they have the appearance of small truncated pyramids. These tombs have been thoroughly described by a great many writers, and I had intended giving an account of them myself, from personal observations, instead of which, however, I will substitute a quotation from Maspero's "Egyptian Archæology," page 110, *et seq*, because of special features in his account to which, later on in this work, I desire to call your attention. He states that "The ancient monumental tombs are found in the Necropolis of Memphis, between *Aboo Roash and Dashoor* (*or Dahshoor*) and belong to the Mastaba type, which is a quadrangular building, that from a distance might be taken for a truncated pyramid. They vary in size from thirty to forty feet in height, one hundred and fifty in length, and eighty feet in width; while others do not exceed ten feet in height. The faces are symmetrically inclined and generally smooth, though sometimes the courses retreat like steps. The materials employed in their construction are generally of stone or brick. At Gizeh, the Mastabas are distributed according to a symmetrical plan, and ranged in regular streets. At Sakkarah, at Abooseer and at Dashoor, they are scattered irregularly over the surface of the plateau, crowded in some places, and wide apart in others. The Mussulman cemetery at Siout perpetuates the like arrangement and enables us of this day to realize the aspect of the Memphite Necropolis towards the close of the ancient empire. The doors generally face to the East. They do occasionally face towards the North or South, but never towards the West. In theory there should be two doors, one for the dead, the other for the living. In tombs for single, or simply one person, a short passage led to an oblong chamber upon which it opened. In many instances just opposite the entrance, it was recessed and then formed a cross. This oblong chamber was the reception room of the Double. It was there that the relations and friends and priests celebrated the funerary sacrifices on the days prescribed by law; such as the feast of Thoth, the feast of Uage, the feast of Sothis, etc. The mummy was placed in a vault beneath, that was reached by a shaft, varying from ten to one hundred feet in depth and a low passage in which one could not walk upright. There sleeps the mummy in a massive sarcophagus. The corpse, left to itself, received no visits now save from the *Soul* which, from time to time, quitted the celestial regions wherein it voyaged with the Gods and came down to reunite itself with the body. The funerary vault was the abode of the Soul, as the funerary chapel was the abode of the Double."

It is to the latter part of this quotation, as well as another by the same author, whom I again quote in Chapter XIII of this work, that I wish to call the especial attention of my readers, to enable them to reach a better understanding of " Death and After," and why these ancient people embalmed their dead.

There are many things one could write about, and so many places of interest worthy a description in this most arable field of observation, " the Valley of the Nile," did time and space permit. These comprise specimens of highest Egyptian Art, fully demonstrating the knowledge of architecture, in addition to thorough understanding of the more abstruse Philosophical Sciences.

This ancient city of Memphis, like Heliopolis, furnished the stones for the upbuilding of Cairo. It constituted an immense quarry, from which those Arabian vandals drew the material with which to adorn and decorate their so-called "Mother of the World." The priceless treasures which have been lost and destroyed by these Arab Caliphs will never be fully known or realized. The whole of this vast Necropolis, from Gizeh to Sakkarah and farther, has been ransacked, torn up, excavated and delved into with the vain hope of recovering from the shrouding desert sands some of the inestimable treasures belonging to the hoary civilization which existed centuries before Abraham came to this country or Moses laid the foundation of his wisdom within those stupendous temples, among the Priests of Ptah, in Memphis. (Noph of the Scriptures.)

These Priests were noted for their wondrous learning and intellectual qualifications, ages before Greece produced her "Marble Miracles," or Rome led her mighty legions to conquer kingdoms. In those ancient days this grand old city flourished, and her Hierophants taught to those who were found worthy and well qualified, a knowledge of their Science, Arts, and Philosophies, also instructing them in the esoteric teachings of Ancient Egyptian Mysteries that at a far earlier period belonged to the Ancient Wisdom of India. At the time when Abd-el-Latyf, a very learned "Arabian Doctor" visited this country, in A. D. 1190, he found the city of Memphis in utter ruin, and remarked that the number and size of the various idols found among the ruins baffle description. He goes on to say that "I saw two lions facing each other within a short distance; their aspect inspired awe; for notwithstanding their colossal size, infinitely larger than that of life, the sculptor had succeeded in preserving the truthfulness of form and of proportion." Strabo also wrote a description of this old city of Memphis, wherein he says: "One finds also (at Memphis) a temple of Serapis in a spot so sandy that the wind causes the sand to accumulate in heaps, under which we could see many sphinxes, some of them almost entirely buried, others only partially covered, from which we may conjecture that the route leading to this temple might be attended with danger, if one were surprised by a sudden gust of wind."

This temple of Serapis had been the source of a long-continued search, but was never found until Mariette Bey, in 1851, having been sent out by his government to make an inventory of the various manuscripts in Oriental Languages, then to be found in the various Coptic convents in Egypt, wandered out one day to Sakkarah, when he chanced to pass by the place where the drifting sands had partly exposed to view the head of a sphinx, as he states, "obtruding itself from the sand. This one had never been touched and was certainly in its original position. Close by lay a libation table, on which was engraved, in hieroglyphics, an inscription to Osiris-Apis. The passage in Strabo suddenly occurred to my mind. The avenue which lay at my feet must be the one which led up to that Serapeum so long and so vainly sought for. But I had been sent to Egypt to make an inventory of manuscripts, not to seek for temples. My mind, however, was soon made up. Regardless of all risks, without saying a word, and almost furtively, I gathered together a few workmen and the excavation began. The first attempts were hard indeed, but before very long lions, peacocks and the Grecian statues of the dromos, together with the monumental tablets, or *stelæ* of the temple of Nectanebo, were drawn out of the sand, and I was able to announce my success to the French Government, informing them at the same time that the funds placed at my disposal for the researches after the manuscripts were entirely exhausted and that a further grant was indispensible. Thus began the discovery of the Serapeum."

This celebrated temple to-day is not in existence, but when it was, it no doubt resembled in appearance any other temple with its avenue of sphinxes that led up to the pylons which stood in front of it, and this especial avenue was fully six hundred feet long, within whose confines Mariette discovered and cleared from the drifting sands one hundred and forty-one sphinxes and a large number of pedestals whereon had stood many others which had been removed at some earlier period. But what most astonished him, on arriving at the end of this most extraordinary avenue, was to find a semicircle of statues, representing many of the most celebrated philosophers and writers of Greece. It was here, also, he found the mummy of *Kha-em-uas*, an ancient Governor of Memphis, and the favorite son of Rameses Second, and a discovery made in this way: While the workmen were exploring the ancient temple an enormous lot of stones and debris fell and blocked their further progress. Pending their removal, and an order being given to get through as quickly as possible, they resorted to blasting, and after the smoke had cleared away discovered this mummy, with its golden mask, scarabeus and other emblems of immortality, its breast covered with jewels and precious stones of all kinds, as well as golden chains and amulets of every description with hieroglyphic writings upon them, all identifying it as *Kha-em-uas*, the son of Rameses Second.

This celebrated mausoleum was erected for the especial purpose of receiving the dead bulls, which were called *Ausar-Hapi*, or Serapis, by the Greeks, hence the name of this mausoleum (*Serapeum*). But during the life of these so-called gods they were known as *Apis*, or *Hapi*, who were worshipped at Memphis as " The second life of Ptah, and the incarnation of Osiris." The marks of Apis, by which he was known, was a perfectly black hide, with a square or triangular white spot upon the forehead, while on his shoulders the resemblance of an Eagle, or Vulture, for some authors differ in their descriptions of this marking; under his tongue there should be a representation of a scarabeus, and the hairs upon his tail double. Now there is no doubt in my mind but some trickery was used in order to produce such a peculiar combination of markings, or else the populace were easily satisfied with general resemblances. Sometimes it was very difficult to obtain another *Apis*, after the death of the old one, but after it was found a house was built for this so-called god, which had to be built facing the East. The Apis was then placed on a milk diet for four months, after which he would be removed to Memphis on or about the full of the moon, in a boat most magnificently decorated. Amid great rejoicings he would be placed in the Apeum, where special apartments were provided for him and a very fine peristyle court in which he could walk about. Great care was taken in the selection of his food to prevent his getting too fat. He was not allowed to be seen by any one, excepting his attendants and the priest, for a period of forty days, and the women who attended to his wants were perfectly nude. Apis had free access to all the apartments in the Apeum, as well as to the court. If he passed into one apartment it was considered to be a very lucky omen; but if into the other it was deemed very unfortunate, in fact every act of Apis was oracular. It was considered a very lucky omen if he ate from the hand that offered him food; but if he refused to eat evil would result to those by whom it was proffered. If Apis did not die before his twenty-fifth year he would be drowned; but at his death, no matter how it occurred, he would be deeply mourned by the people throughout the whole of Egypt. He would be embalmed with great care and interred in the Serapeum with costly ceremonies. An Apis is to be found upon nearly every mummy case, as an emblem of immortality and a symbol of the reincarnation of the spirit.

One of the best specimens of a tomb of the Ancient Empire is the celebrated tomb of *Tih*, situated to the northeast of Mariette's house, and not far from the road to the pyramids of Abooseer. It is still in a remarkable state of preservation, no doubt due to its sandy covering, for the sculptures on the walls, as well as the paintings present a most magnificent series of pictures and carvings, even to-day. This man Tih was of humble birth, but attained to a very high position when he married a Nefer-hotep-s, a relative of one of the kingly rulers under whom he served. This tomb should be visited by all who go into this wonderful valley of the Nile, because the interior decorations illustrate the manners and customs of the dynasty in which he lived (*the Fifth*). Here upon the walls, you may see the man depicted in various scenes of everyday life. It would take too long to describe the whole of this remarkable tomb, but I will give you a general outline of things to be seen upon the walls of this most extraordinary building. Here we are enabled to see mechanics and laborers of all kinds working at their various trades, etc. Tih himself is depicted in various scenes, one of which seemed very remarkable to me. He is depicted as hunting in the marshes, and represented as standing in a boat holding in one hand some decoy birds, while with the other he is throwing a *boomerang* at another flock. The very fact of his having a boomerang in his hand proves that the ancient Egyptians had a knowledge of this most extraordinary instrument, one always considered an implement known and used solely by the natives of Australia.

It would be nearly impossible to describe all these pictures, in detail, such as hunting, fishing, farming and ship-building, as well as scenes in a court of justice, etc., etc., in a work of this kind; but I wanted to give you, my dear brothers, a general idea of what these pictures represent. They must be seen to be enjoyed and appreciated. To-day there are electric cars running to the Pyramids, so that one can go out there in a very little while, without being bothered with donkeys, or boys.

OFFICERS AND GRAND OFFICERS OF THE SOUTHERN JURISDICTION.

Solomon—Death of Hiram—Cross—Swastica.

And Pilate wrote a title, and put it on the cross.   And the writing was, JESUS OF NAZARETH THE KING OF THE JEWS.

—JOHN 19 : 19.

CHAPTER XII.

SOLOMON—DEATH OF HIRAM—CROSS—SWASTICA.

BEFORE proceeding with a treatment of the subjects embraced under the caption of this chapter, I desire to express astonishment at the apparent lack of interest taken in Masonic literature by many of the Brethren connected with our Fraternity. It is a lamentable fact that an immense number of brothers calling themselves Masons have no more idea of the esoteric teachings of our beloved Fraternity than the Neophyte who has not as yet received the light, being bewildered, as it were, by its refulgence. If you take the trouble to converse upon the teachings or symbology of the various degrees, you will find many sadly deficient upon the most simple subjects. Continue your investigations and you will find that seemingly they have no apparent interest in the actual knowledge needed to make them acquainted with the Ancient Landmarks of the Fraternity, or even to converse upon general topics of interest to the intellectual student, seeking more *Light*, more Truth; aye, more knowledge, not of Masonic interest only, but in the wonderful advance of Science, Philosophy, etc., as evidenced by researches in the realms of literature and the many remarkable discoveries made in the scientific world and utilized in this wonderful twentieth century.

The true Mason will never be satisfied with the simple ceremonies of the various degrees to which he has attained, but will search among the beautiful symbols permeating our beloved Fraternity to discover the sublimity and grandeur of the Truths underlying each and every one of them. Every word in these degrees is fraught with the deepest significance, and it is his bounden duty to endeavor to discover the hidden meaning of every symbol, as well as to understand the meaning of every word. If he is earnest in his endeavors, having passed through the profound and magnificent ceremonies pertaining to many of our Scottish Rite degrees, he will at length understand their seeming mysteries, and this translated knowledge will make him a Mason in Truth and in Spirit, plainly pointing out his Path and Duty. The great majority of Masons do not give enough study to the preceding degree before entering upon the threshold of another, and do not seem to consider or realize that the various degrees are like the links in a chain, connecting one with the other, forming among themselves a grand whole, and, as I have said before, the complete understanding of one degree is a keynote of comprehension to the one above. Possibly you may be able to get a better idea of my meaning when I say that the whole of the Ancient and Accepted Scottish Rite degrees are analogous to mathematics, because, in order to thoroughly understand the Science of Numbers and Arithmetic, we must begin at Addition, pass on to Subtraction, rise to Multiplication and then advance to Division, and so on, as without the knowledge of the one we could not possibly understand the true meaning of the other, and so it is with the beautiful Degrees of our Scottish Rite Bodies.

Hundreds of Masons do not care to study or learn the meaning of the beautiful symbols permeating our beloved Fraternity, but take the various degrees of our beloved Scottish Rite out of simple curiosity, while many others acquire them in the hope that it will aid them in their business affairs. Again, many are desirous of passing rapidly through the degrees and be received as a " Master of the Royal Secret," to be enabled to wear the jewel of that degree suspended from a watch chain, who yet know no more of the *Royal Secret* than a child unborn. Such Brothers are simply drones in the " Masonic Hive," and not *true* workers, otherwise they would endeavor to learn and acquire a knowledge of the profound Philosophies and Scientific problems which permeate our most illustrious Fraternity. But still there are a vast number of Brothers who are earnestly searching through the Symbology of the various degrees in our glorious Rite for the express purpose of understanding the grand Truths contained in its sublime Philosophies, and solving the problems of the Deity, Nature, the Immortality of the Soul and the development of the human intellect. Brothers who will ever be patient with the drones and sluggards and strive to help them along the path leading to greater exertions, and endeavor to implant within their hearts an earnest desire to know the Holy Doctrine and the Key to the Royal Secret. It is very difficult to solve some of the symbols of the ancient Mysteries and ancient

Masonry, and many of our modern writers give a wrong interpretation to them, often leading persons astray who are trying to understand them. The old secrets and symbols have been reveiled, or hidden, on purpose to conceal their real meaning from the Profane, and yet the earnest student who has obtained the key through profound study finds no difficulty in coming to an understanding of their sublime teachings. The word *reveal* is a very curious and misleading one, if taken in its general accepted sense, because the Latin word *revelare*, from which we derive the word reveal, or revealed, is just the opposite to the generally accepted meaning of it in English; for *re-velare* signifies to *reveil*, and not to reveal, *i.e.*, from *re* again, or back, and *velare* to hide, or cover; to veil from the eyes of those who were unworthy. One of the First to reveal (*reveil* or *hide*) the symbology of the ancient Mysteries of India, so as to preserve and practice them in the valley of the Nile, was Hermes, and long centuries after him the Jewish Lawgiver Moses, who reveiled or hid away in the Wisdom of the Ancient Egyptians all the Egypto-Chaldean theological legends and allegories.

To bear me out in the above statement I will quote you from " Morals and Dogmas," page 104: " Masonry, like all the Religions, all the Mysteries, Hermeticism and Alchemy, conceals its secrets from all except the Adepts and Sages, or the Elect, and uses false explanations and misinterpretations of its symbols to mislead those who deserve to be misled; to conceal the Truth, which it calls Light, from them, and to draw them away from it. Truth is not for those who are unworthy or unable to receive it, or would prevent it. So God Himself incapacitates many men, by color blindness, to distinguish colors, and leads the masses away from the highest Truth, giving them the power to attain only so much of it as is profitable to them to know. Every age has had a religion suited to its capacity. The teachers even of Christianity, are in general, the most ignorant of the true meaning of that which they teach. There is no book of which so little is known as the Bible. To most who read it, it is as incomprehensible as the Sohar. So Masonry zealously conceals its secrets, and intentionally leads conceited interpreters astray. There is no sight under the sun more pitiful and ludicrous at once, than the Prestons and the Webbs, not to mention the later incarnations of Dullness and commonplace, undertaking to 'explain' the old symbols of

Masonry, and added to and 'improving' them, or inventing new ones. To the circle, enclosing the central point, and itself traced between two parallel lines, a figure purely Kabalistic, these persons have added the superimposed Bible and even reared on that the ladder with three or nine rounds, and then given a vapid interpretation of the whole, so profoundly absurd as actually to excite admiration."

Brother J. D. Buck, in his very valuable little work, "Mystic Masonry" says, on page 253, that "The real secrets of Masonry lie concealed in its Symbols, and these, constituting as they do a Picture language, or Art Speech, are made to carry a complete philosophy of the existence and relations of Deity, Nature and Man. The average Mason, taking the symbols for the things symbolized and knowing nothing of the profound philosophy upon which they rest, is incredulous that it ever existed, and so he treads the 'burning sands' in search of a novel sensation, or a new joke. As mere pastimes these jovial entertainments are neither better nor worse than many others. They represent one extreme into which the Ancient Wisdom has degenerated. Let every intelligent Mason reflect on the sublimity and sanctity of the ceremonies in some of the Degrees, where the name of the Deity is invoked, where the highest moral precepts are inculcated, and where the purest and most exalted ethics are taught."

I have already spoken of Solomon's temple and alluded to the fact that a great many brethren actually believe Masonry to have originated with the building of that edifice by the Wise King of Israel, but, if they will only pause to consider this matter carefully, they will find that this, like many other things in Masonry, is purely Symbolical. For, as I have herein before stated, "Masonry is a peculiar system of Moralty, veiled in Allegory and Illustrated by Symbols," and this building of a temple by Sol-om-on is one of the most beautiful allegories in Masonry, full of profound symbology, as there is not a thing mentioned in relation to this temple that is not purely symbolical, which will probably account for the fact that to-day not a single vestige of it can be found among the squalid hovels in the ancient city of Jerusalem. The traditional history of this fabric, as well as many of the most magnificent temples of Egypt and Assyria have passed into the realm of fable.

We can, most certainly, find a grand account of the temple of Sol-om-on in all its dimensions in the Bible, and this very account demonstrates the Science of Numbers as taught by Pythagoras and his school, for Numbers were considered by him and his pupils to lie at the root of all manifestations, to understand every element of which was to thoroughly comprehend the upbuilding of molecular forms. In fact the Secret Doctrine tells us that " know the corresponding numbers of the fundamental principles of every element and its sub-elements ; learn their interaction and behavior on the occult side of manifesting nature, and the law of correspondences will lead you to the discovery of the greatest mysteries of macrocosmical life."

According to many of our Scientific Masonic writers, the building of Sol-om-on's temple is a beautiful allegory of the evolution or building of man.

Let me quote you once more from Brother J. D. Buck's " Mystic Masonry," pages 72, 102, 148 : " In the ritual of Masonry King Solomon's temple is taken as a symbol. The building and the restoration of the temple at Jerusalem are dramatically represented in the work of the Lodge, and in the ceremony of initiation, by a play upon words and parity of events, and applied to the candidate, with admonition, warning or encouragement, as the drama unfolds. The measurements and proportion of the temple are dwelt upon in order to bring in the science of numbers, form and proportion, so manifest in architecture, and to connect them with the 'spiritual temple' with which they all have the same, though less obvious, relations. The symbolism is fitted to ideal relations, rather than to actual existences or historical events. Sol-om-on represents the name of the Deity in three languages, and the biblical history is doubtless an allegory, or myth of the Sun-god. There is no reliable history of the construction of any such temple at Jerusalem, and recent explorations and measurements have greatly altered the dimensions as heretofore given. Hiram Abiff is dramatically represented to have lost his life when the temple was near completion, and yet it is recorded that after the completion of the temple he labored for years to construct and ornament a palace for the King. Add to these facts the statement that the temple was constructed without the sound of hammer or any tool of iron, and it is thus likened more nearly to that

18

other ' *Spiritual Temple*, not made with hands, eternal in the heavens,' and the literal and historic features disappear, and the symbolism stands out in bold relief. . . . . The real temple referred to from first to last in Masonry, as in all initiations, is the Tabernacle of the Human Soul.

"It is built, indeed, without the sound of hammer or any tool of iron. It is like (made in the likeness of) that other, spiritual temple, not made with hands; eternal in the heavens; for the old philosophy (Kabalah) teaches that the Immortal Spirit of man is the artificer of the body and its source of life; that it does not so much enter in, as overshadow man, while the Soul, the immediate vehicle of Spirit, inhabits the body, and is dissipated at death. The Spirit is Immortal, pure and forever undefiled. It is *Christos* or *Hiram*, the mediator between the Soul, or physical man, and the Universal Spirit. . . . . The ' designs on the trestleboard for the building of the temple' are the laws that determine the evolution of the Higher Self in Man ; while the execution of the plan or the construction of the temple in accordance with the plan, means a transformation of the earthly tabernacle—the lower nature—into a likeness with ' that other spiritual temple.'"

Brother Albert Pike, in "Morals and Dogmas," page 235, says, "How completely the Temple of Solomon was symbolic, is manifest, not only from the continual reproduction in it of the sacred numbers and of astrological symbols in the historical description of it ; but also, and yet more, from the details of the imaginary reconstructed edifice, seen by Ezechiel in his vision. The Apocalypse completes the demonstration, and shows the Kabalistic meanings of the whole. The Symbola Architectonica are found on the most ancient edifices, and these mathematical figures and instruments, adopted by the Templars, and identical with those on the gnostic seals and abraxæ, connect their dogma with the Chaldaic, Syriac and Egyptian Oriental philosophy. The secret Pythagorean doctrines of numbers were preserved by the monks of Thibet, by the Hierophants of Egypt and Eluesis, at Jerusalem, and in the circular chapters of the Druids ; and they are especially consecrated in that mysterious book the Apocalypse of Saint John."

There is no question to my mind but that the whole account of Sol-om-on and the temple is simply and purely allegorical, and I therefore consider it to be the greatest piece of absurdity imaginable, to claim Sol-om-on as one of our first Grand Masters, and that Masonry spang into immediate existence at the building of the temple, for this reason I quote various opinions from different Masonic writers, as well to substantiate my assertions as to demonstrate that I do not stand alone in this opinion, and desire to prove the Truth in relation to this matter through the assertion of other writers as well as my own.

I remember being in the city of San Francisco and in the office of the late Brother C. M. Plummer, manager and editor of the " Trestle Board," on California Street, when, during a lull in our conversation, I broached the subject of Sol-om-on's temple to my learned friend, when he said to me : " Doctor, you know my opinion respecting this subject; but, in addition to what I have told you, read this," and he handed me a copy of his book and pointed to an article, which reads as follows : " So far as regards the essential features of it (the temple) it was designed by the Almighty, and Sol-om-on had very little to do with it beyond the carrying out of specific directions. We may admire the proportions of it and magnify its glories to our heart's content, without in the least admitting that Sol-om-on was a Mason, for his connection with it by no means proves that he was such. If he was, then it follows that all the overseers, the workmen in the forests, and in the quarries, were Masons.

"This brings us to the position that at that time there were some one hundred and fifty thousand Masons in the little territory of Palestine, nearly twice as many as are now in the most populous State in this country, which is a palpable absurdity. We are told that there were eighty thousand fellows of the craft, seventy thousand entered apprentices, and three thousand overseers concerned in the building of the temple, not considering those who got away before they could be counted. If any one wishes to believe this he is free to do so, for there is no constitutional provision forbidding him to believe anything that may find lodgment in his mind. But to hold that a belief in these things is to condition one's standing as a Mason, is too ridiculous for serious consideration. If any one wants to believe that King Sol-om-on was a Free Mason, or that Prester John really had any existence, or that the man in the moon came down too soon, and burnt his mouth eating cold porridge, why, we have nothing to say except that it takes all kinds of people to make the world."—*Masonic Guide.*

I will make another quotation and this time from "The Secret Societies of All Ages," by C. W. Heckethorn, Vol. II, and pages as per articles quoted. I know that these articles will amuse my Masonic readers and friends and give them some very extraordinary ideas in relation to "The Legend of the Temple"—Solomon, Hiram, and the Queen of Sheba, and what led up to or caused the "death of Hiram"—every word of which will no doubt be of the deepest interest to many, as the greatest farce that was ever written upon Masonic history.

"The Legend of the Temple, Ancestry of Hiram Abiff," Vol. II, page 3-383: Solomon having determined on the erection of the temple, collected artificers, divided them into companies, and put them under the command of Adoniram, or Hiram Abiff, the architect sent to him by his friend and ally, Hiram, King of Tyre. According to mythical tradition, the ancestry of the builders of the mystical temple was as follows: One of the Elo-him, or Genii, married Eve and had a son called Cain (120), whilst Jehova or Adonai, another of the Elo-him, created Adam and united him with Eve to bring forth the family of Abel, to whom were subjected the sons of Cain, as a punishment for the transgression of Eve. Cain, though industriously cultivating the soil, yet derived little produce from it, whilst Abel leisurely tended his flocks. Adonai rejected the gifts and sacrifices of Cain, and stirred up strife between the sons of the Elo-him generated out of fire, and the sons of Abel the noble family that invented the arts and different sciences. Enoch, a son of Cain, taught men to hew stone, constructed edifices, and form civil societies. Ired and Mehujael, his son and grandson, set boundaries to the waters, and fashioned cedars into beams. Methusael, another of his descendents, invented the sacred characters, the books of Tau and the symbolic T, by which the workers, descended from the genii of fire, recognized each other. Lamach, whose prophecies are inexplicable to the profane, was the father of Jubal, who first taught men how to dress camel's skins; of Jubal, who discovered the harp; of Naamah, who discovered the arts of spinning and weaving; of Tubal Cain, who first constructed a furnace, worked in metal, and dug subterranean caves in the mountains to save his race during the deluge, but it perished nevertheless, and only Tubal Cain and his son, the sole survivors of the glorious and gigantic family came out alive. The wife of Ham, second son of Noah, thought the son of Tubal Cain handsomer than the sons of men, and he became the progenitor of Nimrod, who taught his brethren the art of hunting, and founded Babylon. Adoniram, the descendant of Tubal Cain, seemed called by God to lead the militia of the free men, connecting the sons of fire with the sons of thought, progress and truth.

384. "HIRAM, SOLOMON AND THE QUEEN OF SHEBA—By Hiram was erected a marvellous building, the Temple of Solomon. He raised the golden throne of Solomon, most beautifully wrought, and built many other glorious edifices. But melancholy amidst all his greatness, he lived alone, understood and loved by few, hated by many and among others by Solomon, envious of his genius and glory. Now, the fame of the Wisdom of Solomon spread to the remotest ends of the earth; and Balkis, the Queen of Sheba, came to Jerusalem to greet the great King and behold the marvel of his reign. She found Solomon seated on a throne of gilt cedar-wood, arrayed in cloth of gold, so that at first she seemed to behold a statue of gold, with hands of ivory.

"Solomon received her with every kind of festive preparation, and led her to behold his palace, and then the grand works of the temple, and the Queen was lost in admiration. The King was captivated by her beauty and in a short time offered her his hand, which the Queen, pleased at having conquered this proud heart, accepted. But on again visiting the temple, she repeatedly desired to see the architect, who had wrought such wondrous things.

"Solomon delayed as long as possible presenting Hiram Abiff to the Queen, but at last he was obliged to do so. The mystesious artificer was brought before her, and cast on the Queen a look that penetrated her very heart. Having recovered her composure, she questioned and defended him against the ill-will and rising jealousy of the King. When she wished to see the countless host of workmen that had wrought at the temple. Solomon protested the impossibility of assembling them all at once; but Hiram, leaping upon a stone, the better to be seen, with his right hand described in the air the symbolic Tau and immediately the men hastened from all parts of the works into the presence of their Master.

At this the Queen wondered greatly, and secretly repented of the promise she had given the King, for she felt herself in love with the mighty architect. Solomon set himself to destroy this affection, and to prepare his rival's humiliation and ruin. For this purpose he employed three fellow-crafts, envious of Hiram, because he had refused to raise them to the degree of Masters on account of their want of knowledge and their idleness. They were Fanon, a Syrian and a Mason; Amru a Phœnician and a carpenter, and Metusael, a Hebrew and a Miner. The black envy of these projected that the casting of the brazen sea, which was to raise the glory of Hiram to its utmost height, should turn out a failure. A young workman, Benoni, discovered the plot and revealed it to Solomon, thinking that sufficient.

" The day for the casting arrived, and Balkis was present, the doors that restrained the molten metal were opened, and torrents of liquid fire poured into the vast mould wherein the brazen sea was to assume its form. But the burning mass ran over the edges of the mould, and flowed like lava over the adjacent places. The terrified crowd fled from the advancing stream of fire. Hiram calm, like a god, endeavored to arrest its advance with ponderous columns of water, but without success. The waters and the fire mixed, and the struggle was terrible; the water rose in dense steam, and fell down in the shape of fiery rain, spreading terror and death. The dishonored needed the sympathy of a faithful heart; he called Benoni, but in vain; the proud youth perished in endeavoring to prevent the horrible catastrophe when he found Solomon had done nothing to hinder it. Hiram could not withdraw himself from the scene of his discomfiture. Oppressed with grief he heeded not the danger, he remembered not that this ocean of fire might speedily engulf him; he thought of the Queen of Sheba, who came to admire and congratulate him on a great triumph, and who saw nothing but a terrible disaster. Suddenly he heard a strange voice coming from above, and crying, ' Hiram, Hiram, Hiram.' He raised his eyes and beheld a gigantic human figure. The apparition continued, ' Come, my son, be without fear, I have rendered thee incombustible; cast thyself into the flames.' Hiram threw himself into the furnace, and where others would have found death, he tasted ineffable delights; nor could he be drawn by an irresistible force to leave it, and asked him who drew him into the abyss,

'Whither do you take me?' 'Into the centre of the earth, into the soul of the world, into the Kingdom of great Cain, where liberty reigns with him. There the tyrannous envy of Adonai ceases; there can we, despising his anger, taste the fruit of the tree of knowledge; there is the home of thy fathers.' 'Who then am I, and who art thou?' 'I am the father of thy fathers, I am the son of Lamach, I am Tubal Cain.'

"Tubal Cain introduced Hiram into the sanctuary of fire, where he expounded to him the weakness of Adonai, and the base passions of that god, the enemy of his own creatures whom he condemned to the inexorable law of death, to avenge the benefits the genii of fire had bestowed on him. Hiram was led into the presence of the author of his race, Cain. The angel of Light that begat Cain was reflected in the beauty of this son of Love, whose noble and generous mind roused the envy of Adonai. Cain related to Hiram his experiences, sufferings, and misfortunes, brought upon him by the implacable Adonai. Presently he heard the voice of him who was the offspring of Tubal Cain and his sister, Naamah: 'A son shall be born unto thee whom thou shalt indeed not see, but whose numerous descendants shall perpetuate thy race, which, superior to that of Adam, shall acquire the empire of the world; for many centuries they shall consecrate their courage and genius to the service of the ever-ungrateful race of Adam, but at last the best shall become the strongest and restore on earth the worship of fire. Thy sons, invincible in thy name, shall destroy the power of kings, the ministers of Adonai's tyranny. Go, my son, the genii of the fire are with thee!' Hiram was restored to the earth. Tubal Cain, before quitting him, gave him the hammer with which he himself had wrought great things and said to him: 'Thanks to this hammer, and the help of the genii of fire, thou shalt speedily accomplish the work left unfinished through man's stupidity and malignity!' Hiram did not hesitate to test the wonderful efficacy of the precious instrument, and the dawn saw the great mass of bronze cast. The artist felt the most lively joy, the queen exulted. The people came running up, astounded at this secret power which had in one night repaired everything."

385. "MURDER OF HIRAM.—One day the queen, accompanied by her maids, went beyond Jerusalem, and there encountered Hiram, alone, and thoughtful. The encounter was decisive; they mutually confessed their love. Had-Had, the bird who filled, with the Queen, the office of messenger of the genii of fire, seeing Hiram in the air make the sign of the mystic **T**, flew around his head and settled on his wrist. At this Sarahel, the nurse of the queen, exclaimed, 'The oracle is fulfilled, she recog· nized the husband which the genii of fire destined for Balkis whose love alone she dare!' They hesitated no longer, but mutually pledged their vows, and deliberated how Balkis could retract the promise given to the king.

"Hiram was the first to quit Jerusalem; the queen, impatient to join him in Arabia, was to elude the vigilance of the king, which she accomplished by withdrawing the ring from his finger, while he was overcome with wine, the ring wherewith she had plighted her troth to him. Solomon hinted to the Fellow-crafts that the removal of his rival, who refused to give them the Master's word, would be acceptable unto himself; so when the architect came to the temple he was assaulted and slain by them. Before his death, however, he had time to throw the golden triangle which he wore around his neck, and on which was engraven the Master's word, into a deep well. They wrapped up his body, carried it to a solitary hill, and buried it, planting over the grave a sprig of accacia. Hiram, not having made his appearance for seven days, Solomon, against his inclination, but to satisfy the clamour of the people, was forced to have him searched for. The body was found by three Masters, and they, suspecting that he had been slain by the three Fellow-crafts for refusing them the Master's word, determined, nevertheless, for greater security, to change the word, and that the first word accidentally uttered on raising the body should thenceforth be the word. In the act of raising it, the skin came off the body, so that one of the Masters exclaimed 'Machbenach!' (the flesh is off the bones, or the brother is smitten), and this word became the sacred word of the Master's degree.

" The three fellow-crafts were traced, but rather than fall into the hands of their pursuers, they committed suicide, and their heads were brought to Solomon. The triangle not having been found on the body of Hiram, it was sought for and at last discovered in the well in which the architect had cast it. The King caused it to be placed on a triangular altar erected in a secret vault, built under the most retired part of the temple. The triangle was further concealed by a cubical stone, on which had been inscribed the sacred law. The vault, the existence of which was only known to the twenty-seven elect, was then walled up.

402. "THE LEGEND EXPLAINED.—Taken literally, the story of Hiram would offer nothing so extraordinary as to deserve to be commemorated after three thousand years throughout the world by solemn rites and ceremonies. The death of an architect is not so important a matter as to have more honor paid to it than is shown to the memory of so many philosophers and learned men, who have lost their lives in the cause of human progress. But History knows nothing of him. His name is only mentioned in the Bible, and it is simply said of him that he was a man of understanding and cunning in working in brass. Tradition is equally silent concerning him. He is remembered nowhere except in Freemasonry; the legend in fact is purely allegorical, and may bear a two-fold meaning."

This account is most certainly correct in its claim of Hiram Abiff being unknown to history, outside the Bible and the Legends of Freemasonry, as with these exceptions his name is positively not mentioned. The Masonic student will, however, very readily recognize in Hiram the Osiris of the Egyptians, Mithras, the Sun God of the Persians, Bachus of the Greeks, etc., etc. He will recognize, in the celebrations of Christianity, in the Passion, death and resurrection of Jesus Christ, the same idea that permeated the ancient world thousands of years before he was born. History informs us that Christ, the Saviour, was crucified upon a cross, an emblem which has been in existence in every age of the world's history. In fact the Cross, Circle and Swastica are as old as Man himself, and represent symbols which express deep Scientific Truths that will unveil to the Masonic student profound Psychological and Physiological mysteries. These mysteries have been hidden from the "profane" in every country in which we find them. To all those who earnestly and diligently search for their origin, these symbols will take them back into the depth of the hoary Archaic ages of the long forgotten centuries, and they will realize that the farther they go back the more difficult will be their interpretation and the more abstruse their meaning.

These symbols can be plainly traced from the frozen Fjords of Norway throughout the whole of Europe. From Patagonia all through the South American continent up into the most Northern parts of British

Columbia and Alaska are to be found evidences of these universal symbols. All through India, China, Egypt, Persia, Chaldea and Babylon we find them, and even upon those extraordinary statues found on Easter Island, relics of the ancient Lemurians in the southern Pacific Ocean, these mystic emblems are blazoned. From out the shadowy depths of the cave temples of India these most extraordinary symbols greet our searching gaze. So we find in every "corner" of the earth, in every clime and country those emblems of antiquity, and realize that with all our efforts we are unable to trace them to any particular Nation or Race. We are compelled to stand before them with awe and reverence, full of profound thought, perplexed and bewildered before the endless shadows they cast backward into the hoary ages of Antiquity.

The Christian firmly believes the Cross to be the symbol of redemption, considering it to be purely and simply a Christian emblem, not knowing that it was used by the ancient Phœnicians long before Christ was crucified, or the Jews were a people, or a nation. The great majority claim that the Cross, with the Man upon it, is distinctly a Christian symbol, introduced into the Christian world and churches, after the Crucifixion of Christ on Calvary, which is a very strange assertion, for this emblem existed long centuries before Christ was born. And right here I wish to state that Christ was not the only Saviour crucified upon a Cross, as in the fourteenth chapter of this work I will give an account, as recorded in history, of Sixteen Saviours who died upon a Cross in the same manner that Christ did, and for the very same purpose, " for the sins and transgressions of the human race."

The Ancient Egyptians, or the people who colonized this country, settled upon the banks of the wondrous old river Nile, in the misty ages of the past, and no matter where they came from, they most certainly brought with them a knowledge of the Arts, Sciences and Philosophies, and very soon after their arrival overpowered the barbarous native population. They immediately began to adorn the banks of the grand old river with those stupendous architectural monuments whose very ruins are the admiration of the Scientific world of to-day, many of which have long since passed into the realm of fables. Notwithstanding the long drifting centuries which have rolled away since they established themselves upon that grand old river Nile, there still remain to us specimens

TEMPLE OF HATHOR,

DENDERAH.

of their handiwork, testifying to the knowledge that pertained to these Ancient Egyptians long ages before Babylon bowed her mighty head before the yoke of Cyrus.

After these ancient people had thoroughly established themselves in this wondrous valley they began to notice that although no rain ever fell in that country for agricultural purposes, yet the glorious old river would generally overflow its banks, when the crops would be assured and everything grow in abundance throughout the whole of the " Land of Egypt." After these ancient people had increased and multiplied in numbers, and the various parts of this fertile valley had been divided into Nomes, for administrative purposes, the people in all parts of Egypt, throughout the various Nomes, when crops were assured, and in order to determine the fact of a year of plenty, through an abundance of water, carefully observed the movements of the river and its annual inundations. The better to observe its rise and the height to which it attained, in order to tax the people, they drove down into the bosom of the river a perpendicular stake, or pole, whereon certain marks were made, that they could tell of its motions, as when it reached a certain point they would be enabled to tax the people, for the crops would be assured.

The men stationed to watch the rising river, "guardians of the Nile," were driven back by the flooding waters, and could not distinguish the markings upon the stake; in consequence they nailed a horizontal board at the required point and in this way the Nilometer became a Cross. Now, if the rising river reached the arms of the Cross they taxed the people accordingly. Every year of plenty when old God Nilus brought from the very heart of Africa to the very doors of the dwelling-places of these people the fruits of the field, in the plentiness thereof, they were exceedingly glad, and feasted and rejoiced in the fullness of heart, with grand processions and magnificent ceremonies, throughout the whole of the " Land of Egypt." They manifested their joy with sounding cymbals, tinkling sistrums, the double pipes, etc. Amid the revels were to be seen all classes, and at night the priests of the various temples illuminated them in honor of the goodness of their old god Nilus (hence the origin of the Christian feast of Candlemas).

But sometimes this grand old river would not overflow its banks, would fail to swell and increase in volume, when no water would flow upon the parched and thirsty soil and the corps could not grow. At such times the "guardians of the Nile," and the people themselves, with bated breath and anxious eyes, would gaze upon the Nilometer in fear and anxious expectancy, until, realizing with saddened hearts, that the river would not overflow its banks to fill their cisterns and furnish life to the seeds implanted in the soil. The consequence would be a drought and scarcity of food, as nothing would grow for that year for the sustenance of either themselves or their domestic animals.

Then throughout the "Land of Egypt" would go a wail of woe and mourning, in place of feasting and rejoicings; darkness instead of grand illuminations, while misery and gaunt Famine stalked throughout this wondrous valley. The "guardians of the Nile," when assured the river would not overflow its banks, would make small Nilometers (a cross), fasten upon them the emblem of a starving man, and send them out through the length and breadth of the valley of the Nile as symbols of Famine, warning the people to be careful of what store of food they had, for a drought was at hand, and that this year no crops would grow on account of the river not overflowing its banks. This emblem of famine has very often been mistaken by travellers for the emblem of Christianity, or Christ upon the Cross.

I will now quote you from the Introduction to "Mystic Masonry," page 15: "That superstructure known as Christianity has, it is true, many historical phases; of dogmas the most contradictory; of doctrines promulgated in one age and enforced with vice-regal authority and severe penalties for denial and disbelief, only to be denied and repudiated as 'damnable heresy' in another age. In the meantime, the origin of these doctrines, and the personality of the *Man of Sorrows*, around which these traditions cluster, receive no adequate support from authentic history. What, then, shall we conclude regarding the real genius of Christianity? Is it all a fable, put forth and kept alive by designing men, to support their pretensions to authority? Are historical facts and personal biography alone entitled to credit, while everlasting principles, Divine Beneficence, and the laying down of one's life for another are of no account? Is that which has inspired the hope and brightened the lives of the down-trodden and despairing for ages a mere fancy, a designing lie? Tear away every shred of history from the life of *Christ* to-day, and prove beyond all controversy that he never existed, and Humanity, from its heart of hearts, would create him again to-morrow, and justify the creation by every intuition of the human soul, and by every need of the daily life of man. The historical contention might be given up, ignored, and the whole character, genius and mission of *Jesus* the Christ, be none the less real, beneficent and eternal, with all of its human and dramatic episodes. Explain it as you will, it never can be explained away; the character remains; and whether Historical or Ideal, it is *real* and *eternal.* The real thread is to be sought for in the *theme* that runs through the symphony of creation; in the lofty *Ideals* that inspire the life of man, and lead him from the clod and the lowlands, where hover the ghosts of superstition and fear to the mountains of light, where dwell forever inspiration and peace. Such ideals are the *Christ Hiram*, and the *Perfect Master.*"

The teachings of Christ are as old as man himself, and embody the Fatherhood of God and the Brotherhood of Man, and the key-note to all is LOVE, and the practice of SELF-LESS-NESS. All men are brothers by the Laws of God and Nature, and as it is impossible to get away from this fact, the sooner it is understood the better it will be for the whole Human family. Everything in Nature goes to prove the Universal Brotherhood of Man, and that he is a part of the Divine Whole, subject to the laws and forces he himself has set in vibration. I have stood upon the shifting sands that border the gulfs, seas and oceans from India to Siberia, from the fjords of Norway to the Caspian sea, and have watched the surging waves as they came rolling in upon the beach in rythmic harmony, singing the same plaintive song in every country, in every clime; and while my wife and I were standing upon the beach at Santa Cruz, watching the long rolling waves, one lovely morning in November, when the wind was blowing fresh from the northwest, with the sun shining brightly from an unclouded sky, we looked around the ocean and saw the white caps come and go upon the crested waves, to the harmony of Nature's melody in F. As the wind increased, long combing waves came rolling in along the beach, in one continuous, ceaseless roar, up to our very feet, and the seething foam went drifting before the wind high up out of the waters upon the beach above. As we stood there, watching the hollow roaring waves, my attention was attracted to a tiny piece of shell or a very white grain of sand being driven hither and thither by the rushing, rolling waters. At one time it would be high up upon the beach, out of the drifting waters for awhile; but, behold, another wave, larger and stronger, drags it back again, into the surging, seething mass of foamy waters, and it is lost from our sight. Again it would be thrown up into view and as quickly dragged back again, by the ruthless under-tow, but once more it was thrown, with an irresistible force. upon the wet shimmering sands up to my feet. At last I stooped and picked it up from out the flecks of foam which surrounded it and held it within the hollow of my hand. As I gazed upon its tiny form I thought of "Karma," and said to my wife, How well this little speck of sand repre-sents man and the vicissitudes of Life, and how his previous acts, the seeds that he has sown, build up the powers that drag him this way, and the other, with overwhelming force, coming to him like the little grain of sand with irresistible strength and power, and smite him down; aye, when his hopes are at the very flood-tide of happiness and glorious realization.

Circumstances over which he has no control compel him to adapt himself to the Just and mighty Law of Cause and Effect, *Karma*, and verifies the teaching of Christ when he said "that which ye sow, that must ye also reap." And we recognized the insignificance of man in the tiny grain of sand, for it, like him, is part of the Divine whole, and began to realize that every grain of sand had at one time a different form; but like all molecular manifestations, it had changed its form for the purpose of the upbuilding of higher bodies, and recognized that the very rocks and stones were subservient to the great and mighty Law of self-sacrifice, and thought with the Hindu philosopher that "The dawn is in the sacrifice." The Masonic student and thinking man, of this twentieth century, knows this to be a positive fact. "The Eternal Pilgrim" in his passage from Rock to Man, demonstrates that every other kingdom is sacrificed for the upbuilding of humanity; but we must distinctly under-stand that the Lower kingdoms have to adapt themselves to this Eternal Law of sacrifice. There is no choice for them. With Man it is very different; he is dowered with a self-conscious knowledge, and he learns to choose and follow the Law under Divine guidance.

As I have previously spoken-of the antiquity of Swastica, or Svastica, I will now state that there is no symbol in existence to-day more pregnant with occult meaning than this emblem, if we except the white leather lamb-skin, the badge of a Mason. The Swastica is in the form of a Greek cross with the ends bent at right angles. It is found in every country upon the face of the earth and some of the best specimens found in America were discovered by a Mr. Morehead in an Indian mound in the State of Ohio. They were formed out of copper and are perfect specimens of their kind, demonstrating that they were known and used by the North American Indians. Le Plongeon mentions them as found in Yucatan, and I, myself, have seen these symbols in every country throughout the world, and we may see it in use to-day upon the seal of the Theosophical Society. Notwithstanding the universal identity of this symbol, I most firmly believe that it emanated from the "Land of the Vedas."

Let me quote you from the "Secret Doctrine," page 103, *et seq:* "The Svastica is the most philosophically scientific of all symbols, as also the most comprehensible. It is the summary in a few lines of the whole work of 'creation,' or evolution, as one should rather say, from Cosmotheogony down to Anthropogony, from the indivisible unknown, Parabraham, to the humble moneron of materialistic Science, whose *genesis is unknown* to that Science as it is that of the All-Deity itself. The Svastica is found heading the religious symbols of all nations. It is the 'Workers Hammer' in the Chaldean *Book of Numbers*, the 'Hammer' above, referred to the *Book of concealed Mystery*, 'which striketh sparks from the flint' (Space), those sparks becoming Worlds. It is Thor's Hammer, the magic weapon forged by the Dwarfs against the Giants, or the Pre-cosmic Titanic Forces of Nature, which rebel, and, while alive in the region of matter, will not be subdued by the gods—the agents of Universal Harmony—but have first to be destroyed. This is why the earth is formed out of the relics of the murdered Ymir. The Svastica is the Miölnir, the 'Storm-hammer,' and therefore it is said that when the Ases, the holy gods, after having been purified by fire—the fire of the passions and suffering in their life incarnations—become fit to dwell in Ida in eternal peace then Miölnir will become useless. This will be when the bonds of Hel—the goddess—queen of the region of the Dead—will bind them no longer, for the kingdom of evil will have passed away.

" Verily many are its meanings! In the Macrocosmic work 'Hammer of Creation,' with its four arms bent at right angles, refers to the continual *motion* and revolution of the invisible Kosmos of Forces. In that of the manifested Cosmos and our Earth it points to the rotation in the Cycles of Time of the world's axis and their equatorial belts ; the two lines forming the Svastica, meaning Spirit and Matter, the four hooks suggesting the motion in the revolving cycles. Applied to the Microcosm, Man, it shows him to be a link between Heaven and Earth, the right hand being raised of an horizontal arm the left pointing to the Earth. In the *Smaragdine Tablet* of Hermes, the uplifted right hand is inscribed with the word 'Solve,' the left with the word 'Coagula.' It is at one and the same time an Alchemical, Cosmogonical, Anthropological and Magical sign, with seven keys to its inner meaning. It is not too much to say that the compound. symbolism of this universal and most suggestive of signs, contains the key to the seven great mysteries of Kosmos. Born in mystical conception of the early Aryans, and by them placed at the very threshold of Eternity, on the head of the serpent Anenta, it found its spiritual death in the Scholastic interpretations of mediaeval Anthropomorphists. It is the Alpha and Omega of universal Creative Force, evolving from pure Spirit and ending in gross Matter. It is also the key to the Cycle of Science, divine and human ; and he who comprehends its full meaning is forever liberated from the toils of Mahâ-Mâyâ, the great Illusion and Deceiver. The Light that shines from under the Divine Hammer. Its more philosopical meaning will be better understood if the reader thinks carefully over the myth of Prometheus. It is examined farther on, in the light of the Hindu Pramantha. Degraded into a purely physiological great symbol by some Orientalists, and taken in connection with terrestrial fire only, their interpretation is an insult to every religion, including Christianity, whose greatest mystery is thus dragged down into Matter. The 'friction' of Divine Pramantha and Arani could suggest itself under the image only to the brutal conceptions of the German Materialists—than whom there are none worse. It is true that the Divine Babe, Agni with the Sanskrit speaking Race who became Ignis with the Latins, is born from the conjunction of Pramantha and Arani—the Svastica—during the sacrificial ceremony. But what of that? Tvashtri (Vishvakarman) is the 'divine artist' and *carpenter* ('The father of the fire'), and is also the Father of the Gods, and 'Creative Fire' in the Vedas. So ancient is the symbol and so sacred, that there is hardly an excavation made on the sites of old cities without its being found. A number of such terra cotta discs called *fusaioles*, were found by Dr. Schlieman *under* the ruins of ancient Troy. Some of these were excavated in great abundance; their presence being one more proof that the ancient Trojans and their ancestors were pure Aryans."

In every country throughout the world I have seen both the Cross and the Swastica carved upon the walls of the tombs, temples and gopuras and in many of the illustrations of this work you will have occular demonstration of this fact. Look particularly at the picture of Medinet Habu, where a group of native boys are standing before this temple, and just above the head of the third boy on the left, upon the wall, you will see very plainly the *Crux Ansata* cut into the hard stone. On the opposite side of the opening you will find another on a level with the first one. This cross is purely an Egyptian Symbol and is to be found upon nearly every tomb and temple throughout the whole of the valley of the Nile as well as those of Nubia. If you examine it carefully you will find that it is a cross with a circle on top, or rather a *tau cross* surmounted with an oval, which is known as the *Crux Ansata*. We find it nearly always borne in the hands of the ancient Egyptian Deities. This cross when entwined by a serpent is emblematic of Immortality and the cross singly was looked upon as the symbol of Life or the procreative forces, crowned with the oval it represented Life Eternal.

19

Mummification—Transmigration—Re=Incarnation.

Then came they forth, from that which now might seem
A gorgeous grave; through portals sculptured deep,
With imagery beautiful as dreams,
They went, and left the shades which tend on sleep
Over its unregarded dead to keep
Their silent watch. . . .
Then there came temples, such as mortal hand
Has never built; nor ecstacy, nor dream,
Reared in the cities of enchanted land.

—SHELLEY.

CHAPTER XIII.

MUMMIFICATION—TRANSMIGRATION—RE-INCARNATION.

THE natural tenderness felt by men for the bodies of those endeared to them, as well as the necessity of putting away from sight, or contact, objects which rapidly become offensive, in all ages has led to some disposition of the dead, by which these ends could be effected. Funeral rites have, in all ages, been interwoven with and consecrated by ceremonies. Portions of these rites have often survived the people and the religion to which they owed their origin. The Masonic student seeking for "*More Light*" is continually discovering the intimate relation between the manners and customs of the pagan philosophers of a prehistoric age and those practiced in the present day by the Christian Churches throughout the world universal.

The poet Virgil speaks of a peculiar mythological doctrine which declares that unless dust is sprinkled three times on a dead body, the soul, which had left its earthly temple, must wander for a thousand years on this side of the river Styx before Charon would admit him to his mysterious bark and ferry him to the gates of Hades. In the Christian Churches this peculiar ceremony is still performed at the burial of our dead, and the three-fold sprinkling upon the coffin, accompanied by the words, "Dust to dust, ashes to ashes," is most assuredly a custom that we have adopted from the pagan philosophers in a far-away past, long centuries before the Christian era had dawned, or Christ came upon the earth.

Four methods in times past have been employed in different countries for the disposition of the dead, which were as follows: Incineration, Mummification, Exposure, and Interment. I will describe these methods so that you may be enabled to have a general idea regarding the manner of disposing of the dead by various nations, and shall speak of them from my own personal observations throughout the world, obtained from the most reliable information and from various authorities.

The Hebrews generally buried their dead in cemeteries invariably situated outside the walls of their cities; yet, from a passage in Isaiah, chapter 30, and verse 33, it would seem that incineration was likewise practiced. Among the Greeks, in historical times, the bodies of the dead were indifferently interred or burned, a common word being used for either method. When the body was not burned it was placed in a coffin made of baked clay or earthenware and buried outside the town. Intramural interment was forbidden through the belief that the presence of the dead brought pollution to the living. If the ceremony was that of burning, the body was placed upon a pyre of wood, to which fire was communicated in the presence of those who had attended the funeral. When the flames were extinguished, the bones were collected and placed in urns made of various materials. These were preserved in tombs, built expressly for the purpose, on the road-side, just outside the city gates. After the funeral of the deceased, those who assisted at the disposal of the body partook of a feast, at the house of the nearest relative, whose duty it was to attend the funeral ceremonies, which, if neglected, subjected him to very grave accusations.

At Athens the period of mourning continued for thirty days, during which time feasts and sacrifices were celebrated. In the early part of the Republic, the Romans generally buried their dead, though burning was likewise practiced. Sylla appears to have been the first of his *gens* who was burned. Under the empire, burning became customary until subverted by the gradual spread of Christianity, and at the end of the fourth century it had again fallen into general disuse. The funeral rites varied, not only with the wealth of the deceased, but somewhat, too, in periods of the commonwealth. In the latter days of the Roman Republic, under the earlier emperors, the corpse of a man of wealth was washed, anointed with oil and perfumed by the slaves of the undertaker. The body was then dressed in the best clothes it had possessed when living, placed with the feet toward the door in the vestibule, upon a couch covered with flowers, a branch of cypress being placed before the door, and a coin put in the mouth of the corpse to pay the ferriage into Hades.

TOMBS OF THE CALIPHS,
CAIRO.

The funeral took place at night, the procession being headed by musicians, followed by hired mourners singing funeral songs; after these came the freedmen, wearing the cap of liberty. Immediately preceding the corpse were persons bearing masks made of wax, representing the ancestry of the deceased. The couch was borne by freedmen, or near relatives, the family following after; the men, contrary to custom, with heads covered; the women, with heads bare and hair disheveled, often beating their breasts and uttering piercing cries. Finally the corpse, with the couch upon which it was borne, was placed upon the funeral pyre, built in the form of an altar. The nearest relatives, with averted faces, kindled the fire, while perfumes, oils and articles of food were frequently thrown upon the body as it was being consumed. When the pyre was burned down, the embers were extinguished with wine, the bones and ashes sprinkled with perfume, and carefully collected by the nearest of kin, were then placed in an urn and buried in sepulchres common to those of the same family. After the funeral, mourning sacrifices were continued for nine days, though by the women. on the death of a husband, or father, mourning was sometimes worn for a year.

As the Christian religion gradually obtained the ascendancy a corresponding change took place in the mode of disposing of the dead. Bodies were no longer burned, but were interred and the offices of the Church were substituted for the rites of paganism. At a very early date it became customary to bury the dead in the immediate neighborhood of the churches, which, in large towns, led to scenes most shocking to the feelings of the community, while the disengagement of the gases, resulting from their decomposition, proved deleterious to the general health. In London some churchyards raised over four feet in a few years. Within thirty years there had been interred within a space not exceeding three hundred and eighteen acres, one million five hundred thousand. (Report of the General Board of Health, London, 1850).

The period taken by a body to decay, after inhumation, varies according to climate, soil and the covering in which it is enveloped. Orfila and Lesueur, in their experiments, found nothing but the skeletons of bodies that had been buried from eighteen months to two years; but this time is unusually short. Low, damp, moist grounds are best to hasten decomposition, especially if water percolates through.

The Parsees of Bombay, India, dispose of their dead by placing them upon iron gratings on the tops of high towers, called " Towers of Silence," built expressly for the purpose of exposing their dead to the approach of numberless vultures. These devour the body within an hour after it has been left alone, leaving nothing but the bones, which are thrown into a deep well in the centre of the tower, where they are left to decay. This receptacle for the remains is common to all, rich and poor, no distinctions being made. This method of disposing of the dead was adopted by these people because deemed by them as the most appropriate for this reason: They believe the Earth to be the Mother of Mankind, the producer of the fruits of the field. that source from whence comes plant life for the sustenance of not only man but his domestic animals.. They therefore considered it a defilement and a injury to the Earth to bury their dead within its sacred depths, in consequence of which they exposed them on the tops of these high towers and to the birds of the air. Fire was considered too pure and sacred to use for burning the body; like the Hindu, they considered exposure the best manner of disposing of their dead.

I do not wish to dwell too long upon the various methods adopted by different people of the world in the disposal of their dead, or to tire you, my dear Brothers, with a too lengthy article upon this subject, but shall confine my remarks especially to the Egyptian Mummy. It would have given me very great pleasure to have described the mummies and mummification of this American continent, but time and space will not permit my doing so. I will say, however, that I do firmly believe the religious ideas of the ancient Egyptians and the Incas of prehistoric times to have been identical.

Vestiges of an ancient Inca civilization are to be found to-day on the shores of Lake Titicaca. The tombs of the people who inhabited this country have been forcibly broken into and desecrated by miserable grave robbers, the ancient mummies taken from their sepulchres and broken into pieces, which they scattered over the ground in an endeavor to rob the dead of their eyes and the ornaments with which they were decorated.

Father Acosta says, in the sixth chapter " Royal Commentaries of the Inca," 1–92, that " these mummies were well preserved, with eyes that were made of pellets of gold, so well imitated that no one could have missed the real ones."

The following seems to have been the usual method adopted after death by the Ancient Egyptians: When a person of any consequence died the women of the family, as well as all the female relatives, smeared their faces and daubed their heads with mud, and going forth from their dead into the streets, with their bosoms bare and their clothing suspended from their waists, wandered through the city, all the time beating their bosoms with loud lamentations and loudly bewailing their loss. The male members of the family would gather together, their clothing arranged in a similar manner, and perform the same methods of flagellation, accompanied with loud cries and lamentations. These scenes are pictured in many of the tombs showing funeral processions with the mourners beating their breasts and throwing dust upon their heads.

The corpse of the male was at once committed to the care of the embalmers; but if it was a female it was retained at home until decomposition had begun. It was then, like the male, committed into the charge of the embalmers.

Herodotus says, in Chap-*Euterpe* 89, " The wives of men of rank are not given to be embalmed immediately after death, nor are indeed any of the more beautiful or valued women. It is not till they have been dead three or four days that they are carried to the embalmers. This is done to prevent indignities being offered them. It is said that once a case of this kind occurred, the man being detected by the information of his fellow-workmen."

After the body had been surrendered to the embalmers it was disrobed, when the principal embalmer, called a *Scribe*, drew a line with a reed pen down the left side, from the sternum across the ribs. Following this line a *paraschite* or flank incisor made a deep incision, and just as soon as it was made the operator would be driven away from the body by the people, who stoned, assaulted and cursed him, these *paraschites* being held in perfect abhorrence and dread. If any one should happen to come in contact with them they would be considered to be defiled, and one contaminated by their touch would immediately have to be purified, by certain ceremonies in their temples, performed by their priest, in order to purify them, that they might again mingle with friends and companions.

After the incision had been made another kind of embalmer called a *Taricheute* would then proceed to extract the entrails, which, according to Herodotus, were afterwards washed in palm wine and thoroughly cleansed, when they were put through different processes for their preservation, which, on being finished, were placed in canopic jars and dedicated to the gods of the underworld, representing the four cardinal points of the universe: 1st, *Mestha,* or *Amset;* 2d, *Hapi;* 3d, *Taumautef;* and 4th, *Quebhsennuf.* They received these names from the Ancient Egyptians who placed the viscera into jars because they thoroughly believed that it was necessary to have the whole of the body in the judgment of the dead, and if these jars did not contain the viscera of the deceased they were supposed to do so.

These four jars have each a different head, representing the separate gods, and are as follows: Mestha is human-headed, representing the South, and the jar of this god was supposed to contain the stomach and larger intestines. Hapi was dog-headed, and representing the North, and it was supposed to contain the small intestines. Taumautef was jackal-headed, representing the East, and was supposed to contain the lungs and the heart. Quebhsennuf is hawk-headed, representing the West, and is supposed to contain the liver and gall-bladder. These four jars were placed in canopic chests, or boxes, about two feet square, divided into four compartments of equal size, and in each space was placed one of the canopic jars that stood upright in the compartment to which it was allotted.

The earliest record of canopic jars occurs during the eighteenth dynasty, during which period these jars were made of alabaster, arragonite and a variety of beautiful stone. They were in many instances most magnificent and exquisite specimens of Egyptian Art. I have said above that these jars were *supposed* to contain the various interior organs of the human body, because both Porphyry and Plutarch claim that the viscera, when removed from the body, was cast into the Nile; but Mr. Pettigrew having received one chest for examination, which he opened, claims to have found the different jars used for the purpose as above described.

I myself firmly believe that the interior organs of the body were embalmed, preserved and kept for this reason: The ancient Egyptians most assuredly believed that the interior organs of the body exerted an influence upon every thought and act of a man's life, affecting not only his morality and virtue, but that they had a general tendency to lead into the downward path of vice and misery. In consequence they laid the blame for all the evil acts committed during the whole course of the man's life, as well as his evil thoughts, upon the viscera. Therefore, if the man was to be judged according to his every act and thought through life, all parts of the body should be there to undergo the examination, and whatever was adjudged to the body should also be adjudged to the various organs that made him either virtuous or immoral, and ought to be there with the body as testimony to the Truth of the Judgment. Budge states "that when the intestines were not buried in jars they were returned to the body, and figures of *Mestha, Hapi, Taumautef* and *Quebhsennuf* made of wax, sheet silver, gold, or porcelain were laid upon the parts these gods were supposed to protect," and yet Porphyry states that the viscera, after having been extracted, were laid in a box or chest and one of the embalmers would hold it up toward the sun, accompanied by the following invocation: "O sun, and all ye Gods, who give life to man, receive me, and give me to dwell along with the immortal Gods, for I have ever reverenced the Gods whom my parents taught me, and have honored the authors of my body; of other men I have neither killed any one nor deprived him of a deposit, nor have done any other grievous wrong. And if, throughout my life, I have committed any sin in eating or drinking, I have not done it on my own account, but on account of these, pointing to the chest containing the viscera, which was then thrown into the river and the body, as pure, submitted to embalmment." But this is clearly disproven by the fact that canopic jars have been found in immense quantities, containing the intestines of numberless bodies, as well as in finding the interior organs within the bodies of a vast majority of the mummies discovered throughout the Nile valley, demonstrating that the statement of Porphyry, only so far as the invocation is concerned, is not to be relied upon.

After the intestines had been removed, another *Tarischeute* extracted the brain, using a crooked instrument, made expressly for the purpose, with which to draw the brain down through the nasal cavities, after which the body was considered ready for the various salts and spices that were to be incorporated in all parts of it, necessary for its preservation. Further operations for the completion of the process of embalming depended in a great measure upon the amount paid for its decorations and preservation. Three methods prevailed for the purpose of embalming the bodies of the dead in Egypt.

The first was attainable only by the rich, the process being as follows: After the entrails, brains, etc., had been removed certain gums, spices and fluids were passed through the nostrils up into the hollow of the skull. The cavities of the chest and stomach were then thoroughly washed with palm wine, then filled with resins, gums and many now unknown substances, the incision made by the *Paraschite* being then closed up. The body was steeped in a bath, composed of carbonate of soda and other alkalies, for a period of seventy days; it was then taken from the bath and permitted to dry, after which they wrapped it in from eight hundred to one thousand yards of linen bandages, cemented together by gums and costly aromatics, which effectually preserved the body from decay. Its outer covering, or mask, was beautifully decorated with gold and silver leaf and artistically painted in many colors. It was then placed in a series of cases, the one fitting into the other. This completed the process adopted in the embalming of the bodies of the most wealthy and cost about three thousand five hundred dollars of our money, or one *silver talent* of theirs.

The second method consisted in removing the entrails, etc., injecting the cavities with cedar oil and soaking the body in natron for seventy days. It was then bandaged as above, inclosed in mask, and outer covering and coffin. This method cost about one thousand two hundred dollars in our money, or a mena in theirs.

The third process was for the poorer classes and consisted in removing the brains and viscera. It was then washed in the sap of a small tree growing in Arabia and Nubia, the juices of which were called myrrh. The body was then soaked in a saline bath for the usual seventy days, when it was dried and covered with linen bandages and mask. It was then decorated and put in a coffin or case. This mode of embalming cost about five hundred dollars.

When the bodies were prepared, or embalmed, they were often kept for a long time at home, being very frequently produced at festivals or banquets to recall to the guests the fact " that in life they were in the midst of death " and all the joys of life were but transient.

TOMBS OF THE MAMELUKES,
CAIRO.

Kenrick in his "Ancient Egyptians," Vol. II., page 48, says: " By a singular law passed, at a time when there was a great want of circulating medium (quoting from Herodotus), a man was allowed to pledge the mummies of his forefathers for debt, but was himself deprived of sepulture if he failed to redeem them before his death. The prohibition appears to have included his descendants as long as the debt remained unpaid."

Herodotus also related another peculiar custom, which was, whenever any Egyptian or foreigner lost his life through falling prey to a crocodile, or by drowning in the river, the law compelled the inhabitants of the city near which the body is cast up to have it embalmed and to bury it in one of the sacred repositories with all possible magnificence. No one may touch the corpse, not even any of the friends or relations, but only the priests of the Nile who prepare it for burial, with their own hands—regarding it as something more than the mere body of a man—and themselves lay it in the tomb.

The art of embalming reached its perfection during the eighteenth and nineteenth dynasties, or about the time of Thothmes III. to Rameses II. For a long time the dead were embalmed by compulsory law, so that rich and poor alike, whether at private or public expense, were submitted to the process, and it has been estimated by Rawlinson that "the annual expense of embalming in Egypt must have been not less than seventy-five million dollars."

The first mummy that was removed from this country and taken to England was in 1722, and quite a number were placed in the British Museum in 1803. These mummies are most interesting objects of study to all who desire knowledge of the remote and wonderful civilization of ancient Egypt. Mummification became one of the lost arts about A. D. 700, having continued for nearly four thousand years, and who can tell how long before that time?

The oldest mummy in the world, about whose antiquity there is no doubt, is that of Seker-em-sa-f, son of Pepi First, and elder brother of Pepi Second B. C. 3,200, was found at Sakkarah in 1881, and is now at Gizeh. The lower jaw is wanting and one of the legs have been dislocated in transporting, the features being well preserved and on the right side of the head is the lock of hair emblematic of youth. An examination of the body shows that Seker-em-sa-f died very young. A number of bandages found in the chamber of his pyramid at Sakkarah are similar to those in use at a later date, and the mummy proves that the art of embalming had already arrived at a very high state of perfection in the Ancient Empire.

The fragments of a body found by Col. Howard Vyse in the pyramid of Men-Kau-Ra (Mycerinus) at Gizeh, are thought by some to belong to a much later period than that of this king. There appears, however, to be no warrant for this belief, as they belong to a man and not to a woman, as Vyse thought, and may quite easily be the remains of the mummy of Mycerinus. The skeletons found in sarcophagi belonging to the first six dynasties fall to dust when air is admitted to them and emit a slight smell of bitumen.

ADDRESS TO A MUMMY OF THEBES.

And thou hast walk'd about (how strange a story!)
  In Thebes streets three thousand years ago,
When the Memnonium was in all its glory,
  And time had not begun to overthrow
Those temples, palaces, and piles stupendous
Of which the very ruins are tremendous!

Speak! for thou long enough has acted dummy;
  Thou hast a tongue—come - let us hear its tune;
Thou'rt standing on thy legs, above ground, mummy!
  Revisiting the glimpses of the moon—
Not like thin ghosts or disembodied creatures,
But with thy bones, and flesh, and limbs, and features.

Tell us—for doubtless thou canst recollect—
  To whom should we assign the sphinx's fame?
Was Cheops or Cephrenes architect
  Of either pyramid that bears his name?
Is Pompey's Pillar really a misnomer?
Had Thebes a hundred gates, as sung by Homer?

Perhaps thou wert a Mason, and forbidden
  By oath to tell the secrets of thy trade—
Then say what secret melody was hidden
  In Memnon's statue which at sunrise play'd?
Perhaps thou wert a priest—if so my struggles
Are vain, for priestcraft never owns its juggles.

Perhaps that very hand, now pinion'd flat,
    Has hob-a-nobbed with Pharaoh, glass to glass;
Or dropped a half-penny in Homer's hat,
    Or doff'd thine own to let Queen Dido pass;
Or held, by Solomon's own invitation,
A torch at the great temple's dedication.

I need not ask thee if that hand, when arm'd
    Has any Roman soldier maul'd and knuckled;
For thou wert dead, and buried, and embalmed
    Ere Romulus and Remus had been suckled:
Antiquity appears to have begun
Long after thy primeval race was run.

Thou could'st develop—if that withered tongue
    Might tell us what those sightless orbs have seen—
How the world looked when it was fresh and young:
    And the great deluge still had left it green.
Or was it then so old that history's pages
Contained no record of its early ages?

Still silent? Incommunicative elf,
    Art sworn to secrecy? then keep thy vows;
But prithee tell us something of thyself—
    Reveal the secrets of thy prison house;
Since in the world of spirits thou hast slumbered
What hast thou seen, what strange adventures numbered?

Since first thy form was in this box .extended
    We have above ground seen some strange mutations;
The Roman empire has begun and ended—
    New worlds have risen—we have lost old nations.
And countless kings have into dust been humbled,
While not a fragment of thy flesh has crumbled.

Didst thou not hear the pother o'er thy head
    When the great Persian conqueror Cambyses
Marched armies o'er thy tomb with thundering tread—
    O'erthrew Osiris, Orus, Apis, Isis,
And shook the pyramids with fear and wonder,
When the gigantic Memnon fell asunder?

If the tomb's secrets may not be confessed,
　The nature of thy private life unfold ;
A heart has throbbed beneath that leathern breast,
　And tears adown that dusky cheek have roll'd ;
Have children climb'd those knees and kissed that face ?
What was thy name and station, age and race ?

Statue of flesh ! Immortal of the dead !
　Imperishable type of evanescence !
Posthumous man—who quittest thy narrow bed
　And standest, undecayed, within our presence !
Thou wilt hear nothing till the judgment morning,
When the great trumpet shall thrill thee with its warning.

Why should this worthless tegument endure,
　If its undying quest be lost forever ?
Oh ! let us keep the soul embalmed and pure
　In living virtue—that when both must sever,
Although corruption may our frame consume,
The Immortal spirit in the skies may bloom.

HORACE SMITH.

　　Mummies of the eleventh dynasty are usually very poorly made ;
they are yellowish in color, brittle to the touch, and fall to pieces very
easily.　The limbs are rarely bandaged separately and the body, having
been wrapped carelessly in a number of folded cloths, is covered over
lengthwise by one large linen sheet.　On the little finger of the left hand
a scarab is usually found, but besides this there is neither amulet nor
ornament.　The coffins of the mummies of this period are often found
filled with baskets, tools, mirrors, bows and arrows, etc., etc.　From the
thirteenth to the seventeenth dynasties. also, mummies were made in such
a manner as to perish rapidly.　From the eighteenth to the twenty-first
dynasties the mummies of Memphis are black, and so dry that they fall
to pieces at the slightest touch ; the cavity of the breast is filled with
amulets of all kinds, and the green stone inscribed with the thirtieth
chapter of the Book of the Dead placed over the heart.

　　At Thebes, during this period, the mummies are yellow in color and
slightly polished, the nails of the hands and feet retain their places and
are stained with henna.　The limbs bend in all directions, without break-

ing, and the art of dainty bandaging attained its greatest perfection. The left hand wears rings and scarabs, and chapters of the Book of the Dead are found in the coffins, either by the side of the mummy or beneath it. After the twenty-first dynasty the custom arose of placing the mummy in a cartonnage, sewn or laced up the back, and painted in brilliant colors, with scenes of the deceased adorning the gods and the like. In the period between the twenty-sixth dynasty and the conquest of Egypt by Alexander the decoration of mummies reached its highest point, and the ornamentation of the cartonnage shows the influence of the art of Greece upon that of Egypt. The head of the mummy is put into a mask, gilded or painted in bright colors, the cartonnage fits the body very closely and the feet are protected by a sheath. A large number of figures of the gods and of amulets are found on the mummy itself, and many things which formed its private property when alive were buried with it. Towards the time of the Ptolemies mummies become black and heavy; bandages and body are made by bitumen into one solid mass, which can only be properly examined by the aid of a hatchet. About B. C. 100 mummies were very carefully bandaged, each limb being treated separately and retained its natural shape after treatment, and the features of the face, somewhat blunted, are to be distinguished beneath the bandages.

At the commencement of the Christian era mummification began to decline, as the process degenerated through neglect, and the art became lost in the seventh century. If we wish to understand the reason for embalming of the dead by ancient Egyptians, we must first come to a realization of what their conception was of man himself, while living. In order that my readers may be enabled to thoroughly understand this subject I shall quote from various authors, and give my own impressions, gleaned from personal investigation of the religions and philosophies of the far East.

Maspero tells us in " Egyptian Archaeology," page 108, that " The Egyptians regarded man as composed of various different entities, each having its separate life and functions. First there was the body, then the KA, or double, which was a less solid duplicate of the corporeal form —a colored but ethereal projection of the individual, reproducing feature for feature. The double of a child was a child; the double of a woman was a woman ; the double of a man was a man.

20

"After the double (*Ka*) came the soul (*Bi or Ba*) which was properly imagined and represented as a bird; after the soul came the ' *Khoo* ' or ' the Luminous,' a spark from the fire divine. None of these elements were in their nature imperishable. Left to themselves they would hasten to dissolution and the man would then die a second time; that is to say, annihilated. The piety of the survivors found means, however, to avert this catastrophe. By the process of embalmment they could for ages suspend the decomposition of the body; while by means of prayers and offerings they saved the Double, the soul, and the ' Luminous ' from the second death and secured to them all that was necessary for the prolongation of their existence.

" The Double never left the place where the mummy reposed; but the soul and the ' *Khoo* ' went forth to follow the gods. They, however, kept perpetually returning, like travellers who come home after an absence. The tomb was therefore a dwelling-house, the ' Eternal House ' of the dead, compared with which the houses of the living were but wayside inns. These ' Eternal Houses ' were built after a plan which exactly corresponded to the Egyptian idea of the after life. The ' Eternal Houses ' must always include the private rooms of the Soul, which were closed on the day of burial and which no living being could enter without being guilty of sacrilege. It must also contain the reception rooms of the Double, where priests and friends brought their wishes and offerings."

This same author also states, in his " Ancient Egypt and Assyria," that " The soul does not die at the same time that the breath expires upon the lips of man; it survives, but with a precarious life, of which the duration depends upon that of the corpse and is measured by it. Whilst it decays the soul perishes at the same time; it loses consciousness and gradually loses substance too, until nothing but an unconscious, empty form remains, which is finally effaced, when no traces of the skeleton are left. Such an existence is agony, uselessly prolonged, and to deliver the double from it the flesh must be rendered incorruptible. This is attained by embalming it as a mummy. Like every act that is useful to man, this one is of Divine origin."

The Ancient Egyptian belief in regard to a future life was that when death came the soul did not leave the body immediately, but con-

TOMB AND MOSQUE OF KA·T BEY,

CAIRO.

tinued with it until decay set in and if they could preserve the body by embalmment and prevent its decay the soul would then remain with it in a conscious state of existence. It was, therefore, with the greatest care they hastened to preserve the bodies of their dead in order to keep the soul within the dwelling-place prepared for it, the tomb. They gave a great deal more time and attention to building houses for the dead than to those for the living, because they believed houses occupied during life to be merely temporary dwelling places; but the tomb, wherein the mummied dead were laid, had apartments where friends could come on a visit and bring funeral offerings of all kinds to the deceased, seemingly at home, as it were, receiving his relations and friends. I have already described the custom in a previous chapter of this work.

A great many writers claim that the Ancient Egyptians believed in the Transmigration of souls, positively claiming they were the first people who declared that man possessed an immortal soul and taught that after the body decayed the soul would re-incarnate into a lower animal and thread itself through all terrestrial and marine animals, as well as birds; but after it had functioned through all these variant forms it would be re-born again as man, and that it would take no less than three thousand years in order to accomplish this cycle or round of Transmigration. Now in respect to Transmigration I do not think, for one moment, that the Initiates of the Ancient Egyptian Mysteries ever believed in the transmigration of souls, as generally understood by the profane in those days. In his wonderful allegory, Virgil shows a law of progression according to Nature's higher law, for he unfolds to us the doctrines as taught in the Mysteries, wherein he demonstrates that the most ancient philosophers believed in the existence of a primal source from which these souls emanated. That they were sparks from the Divine Fire, a part of that Divine Essence, which vivifies every star glittering in the infinitude of space and cycles along their allotted paths throughout the Kosmos, with the threefold purification of Fire, Water, and Air representing the Protean appearance employed by the *Eternal Pilgrim* in functioning through Nature's evolutionary processes, until it was made manifest in Man. In this way we are enabled to know that " Man is certainly *no* special creation, and that he is the product of Nature's gradual perfective work, like any other living unit of this earth.

But this is only so with regard to the human tabernacle. That which lives and thinks in man, and survives that frame, the masterpiece of evolution, *is* the 'Eternal Pilgrim,' the Protean differentiation in Space and Time of the One Absolute Unknowable" (" Secret Doctrine," Vol. II, page 728).

We have functioned all through the variant forms of Life and have wriggled and squirmed with the snake, and we have roamed, four-footed and fanged, through the forest and jungles and have left all that went with it behind us, yet we carry upon our tongue a venom far more deadly than the virus of the snake. Although the tiger's claws are gone and the fangs have been lost to us, yet we of to-day have claws far more treacherous and dangerous than the wolf or tiger, intensified for harm by having been humanized, more deadly than all the beasts of the jungle or forest.

The tiger and other wild beasts seek and kill their prey for food, as their very existence depends on killing weaker animals. But man is to be dreaded far more than other animals. I am under the opinion that those learned men, those Hierophants, esoterically who believe that according to the life a man has lived he would be reborn, with all the attributes of the various animals; such as the cunning of the Fox, the ferocity of the Tiger, etc., but that he would never re-appear again in a lower organism, for they thoroughly understood there is no retrogression in Nature and that all virbrates with progressive force and energy through myriads of successive births. We come, we go, each time ascending a step above the other, mounting the ladder of evolution, gaining experience on every rung and intertwined with the whole of organic and inorganic being, through which we have passed.

We climb the cycling path of evolution, from Infusoria to Protozoa, to Man. Step by step we advance through all the manifestations and differentiations in Nature's evolutionary processes, from primordial matter to humanity. Through ages innumerable we pass through variant forms in the varying kingdoms, and see our kith and kin on every hand. There is not only a relationship existing between the Macrocosm and the Microcosm, but a separate and intimate interrelation and interaction exists between their separate parts. Nature proclaims this grand and glorious Truth in our pre-natal experience, when the Microcosm of the individual demonstrates to us in miniature the Macrocosm of the Race.

During the gestative period, previous to birth, when first the protoplasm surrounds the germ and sets in vibration the life forces contained in its protoplasmic essence, causing our Proteus to vibrate through all the differentiations of Life, in his onward march through Nature's evolutionary processes, and clothes himself in all the various garments in nature's wardrobe in his long passage through the variant forms of life before he assumes the human embryo; he is continually changing in his progression to Man, passing through the various stages, from cell to infusora, worm, reptile, fish, including gills, quadruped, including tail; ever changing, until the mental development begins, then the caudal appendage commences to shorten and finally disappears and the embryo passes on to the human plane of development. During this period the embryo man demonstrates the evolution of the human race, through ages innumerable the human family came into the life of the world. From each germ-plasm of human being comes forth anew the life of the race; it goes through the same round as the species, and the life of the babe has repeated the evolutionary experience of mankind.

Mr. A. P. Sinnett, in "Transactions of the London Lodge of the Theosophical Society," No. 7, October, 1885, says: "That the human soul, once launched on the streams of evolution, as a human individuality, passes through alternate periods of physical, and relatively spiritual existence. It passes from the one plane, or stratum, or condition of nature to the other, under the guidance of its Karmic affinities; living in incarnations the life which its Karma has preordained; modifying its progress within the limitations of circumstances, and,—developing fresh Karma by its use or abuse of opportunities."

Now I firmly believe that the Ancient Egyptian Hierophants thoroughly understood this fact of the birth and immortality of the Soul as well as the re-incarnation of the Spirit and that once the Human Monad had demonstrated its individuality, by incarnating as a human individual, it could not pass back again, after the death of the human, by any see-saw process, into a lower animal organization, for there is no retrogression in Nature. There is a deal of difference between the *human* and the *brute*. In the former dwells the Manasaputras.

"*The Sons of Mind*" that have been through the long drifting ages, making a home for the reception of the Monad manifesting in the human kingdom and when once this "Mind-born Thinker" has manifested itself in man it could not under any circumstances go back and reincarnate in a lower animal, any more than it could return again in its molecular form, into the womb of its mother. The "Eternal Pilgrim" has, in its long journey through cycling ages, been waiting for the development of the perfect human body that was to become its home or dwelling-place, which, through myriads of years, had been developing for that especial purpose; but the animal as yet is not ready to receive this *Manasic entity*, it is not yet ready to become the habitation of the re-incarnating Ego, the Divine Thinker.

Evolution is a continual cycling progress, ever upward and onward, to higher planes of Spiritual unfoldment, but never backward; the animal is on a lower plane, and they are not ready to become the habitation of the "Sons of Mind," but are on the ascending cycle that will eventually bring them, through the law of evolution, to become the home of the Human Monad or "the Monad manifesting in the human kingdom," the dwelling place of the Divine Thinker.

In the Book of the Dead we find the soul of disembodied man announcing the victory of the soul over death, and that he lives in his spiritual body after dissolution. See 17: 22: "O ye who make the escort of the God, stretch out to me your arms, for I become one of you." Again, in 26: 5–6: "I open heaven; I do what was commanded in Memphis; I have knowledge of my heart; I am in possession of my heart; I am in possession of my arms; I am in possession of my legs, at the will of myself. My soul is not imprisoned in my body at the gates of Amenti," thus proving that, although the physical body had disintegrated, spiritual man continued to exist as a spiritual entity after death, because it is a part of the Divine Essence, the "Immutable and Unknowable to our physical senses, but manifest and clearly perceptible to our spiritual natures. Once imbued with that basic idea and the further conception that if it is Omnipresent, universal and eternal, like abstract Space itself, we must have emanated from it and must some day return to it."

Now if this abstruse Metaphysical, Theosophical and Psychological doctrine be true, then the thorough comprehension of the rest becomes very easy to understand, and we shall begin to know that "Life and Death, good and evil, past and future," are all empty words, or, at best, figures of speech. If the objective universe itself is but a passing illusion, on account of its beginning and finitude, then both Life and Death must also be aspects and illusions. They are changes of state, in fact, and no more. Real life is in the Spiritual consciousness of that life, *in a conscious existence in Spirit, not Matter;* and real Death is the limited perception of life, the impossibility of sensing consciousness, or even individual existence outside of form, or, at least, of some form of matter.

Those who sincerely reject the possibility of conscious life, divorced from matter and brain-substance, are *dead units.* The words of Paul, an Initiate, become comprehensible, " ye are dead and your life is hid with Christ in God," Col. 3 : 3, which is to say: Ye are personally dead matter, unconscious of its own spiritual essence, and your real life is hid with your divine Ego (Christos) in, or merged with, God (Atman); " now has it departed from you, ye soulless people." Speaking on esoteric lines, every irrevocably materialistic person is a DEAD MAN, a living automaton, in spite of his being endowed with great brain power. Listen to what Aryasanga says stating the same fact:

"That which is neither Spirit nor Matter, neither Light nor Darkness, but is verily the container and root of these, that thou art. The Root projects at every dawn its shadow on ITSELF, and that shadow thou callest Light and Life, O poor *dead* Form (this) Life Light streameth downward through the stairway of the seven worlds, the stairs, of which each step becomes denser and darker. It is of this seven-times-seven scale that thou art the faithful climber and mirror, O, little man ! Thou art this, but thou knowest it not.

"The higher triad Atma—Buddhi—Manas, may be recognized from the first lines of the quotation from the Egyptian papyrus. In the *Ritual,* now the *Book of the Dead,* the purified soul, the dual Manas, appears as ' the victim of the dark influence of the Dragon Apophis,' the physical personality of Kama-Rupic man, with his passions. If it has attained the final knowledge of the heavenly and infernal mysteries, the ' Gnosis '— the divine and the terrestrial mysteries of White and Black Magic—then the defunct personality will triumph over its enemy "—Death.

This alludes to the case of a complete reunion at the end of the earth life, of the lower Manas, full of the harvest of life with its Ego. But if Apophis conquers the soul then it cannot escape a *second* death. These few lines from a papyrus, many thousands of years old, contain a whole revelation, known in those days only to the Hierophants and the Initiates. The "harvest of life consists of the finest spiritual thoughts, of the noblest and most unselfish deeds of the personality, and the constant presence during its bliss after death, of all those it loved with divine spiritual devotion." *See Key to Theosophy, 147, et seq.*

Remember the teaching: The human Soul, Lower Manas, is the *only* and direct mediator between the personality and the divine Ego. That which goes to make up on this earth the *personality*, miscalled individuality by the majority, is the sum of all its mental, physical and spiritual characteristics, which, being impressed on the human soul, produce the *man.*

Now, of all these characteristics it is the purified thoughts alone which can be impressed on the higher, immortal Ego. This is done by the human soul merging again in its essence into its parent source, commingling with its divine Ego during life, and reuniting itself entirely with it after the death of the physical man. Therefore, unless Kama-Manas transmits to Buddhi-Manas such personal ideations and such consciousness of its *I* as can be assimilated by the divine Ego, nothing of that *I*, or personality, can survive in the Eternal.

Only that which is worthy of the immortal God within us, and identical in its nature with the divine quintessence, can survive; for in this case it is its own, the divine Ego's "shadow" or emanations which ascend to it and are indrawn by it into itself again, to become once more part of its own Essence. No noble thought, no grand aspiration, desire, or divine, immortal love, can come into the brain of the man of clay and settle there, except as a direct emanation from the highest to and through the lower Ego; all the rest, intellectual as it may seem, proceeds from the "shadow" the *lower mind*, in its association and co-mingling with Kama, and passes away and disappears forever. But the mental and spiritual ideation of the personal "I" return to it as part of the Ego's essence, and never fade out. Thus of the personality that was, only its spiritual experiences, the memory of all that is good and noble, with the consciousness of its " I " blended with that of all the other personal " I's " that preceded it, survive and become immortal.

There is no distinct or separate immortality for the men of earth outside the Ego which informed them. That Higher Ego is the sole bearer of all its *alter egos* on earth and their sole representative in the mental state called Devachan. As the last embodied personality, however, has a right to its own special state of bliss, unalloyed and free from the memories of all others, it is the *last life only which is fully and realistically vivid.*

Devachan is often compared to the happiest day in a series of many thousands of other " days " in the life of a person. The intensity of its happiness makes the man entirely forget all others, his past becoming obliterated. This is what we call the *Devachanic State* and the reward of the personality, and it is on this old idea that the hazy Christian notion of Paradise was built, borrowed with many other things from the Egyptian Mysteries, wherein the doctrine was enacted. And this is the meaning of the passage quoted in "Isis Unveiled" The Soul has triumphed over Apophis, the Dragon of Flesh. Henceforth, the individuality will live in eternity, in its highest and noblest elements, the memory of its past deeds, while the " characteristics " of the " Dragon " will be feeding out in Kama-Loca."

Sixteen Saviours—Lost Knowledge.

One evening Jesus lingered in the market place
Teaching the people of parables of truth and grace,
When in the square remote a crowd was seen to rise,
And stop with loathing gestures and abhorring cries.

The Master and His meek disciples went to see
What cause for this commotion and disgust could be,
And found a poor dead dog beside the gutter laid;
Revolting sight! at which each face its hate betrayed.

One held his nose, one shut his eyes, one turned away;
And all among themselves began aloud to say,—
"Detested creature! he pollutes the earth and air!"
"His eyes are blear!" "His ears are foul!" "His ribs are bare!"

"In his torn hide there's not a decent shoe-string left!"
"No doubt the execrable cur was hung for theft!"
Then Jesus spake, and dropped on him this saving wreath,—
"Even pearls are dark before the whiteness of his teeth!"

The pelting crowd grew silent and ashamed, like one
Rebuked by sight of wisdom higher than his own;
And one exclaimed, "No creature so accursed can be,
But some good thing in him a loving eye will see.
                                        —*From the Persian.*

CHAPTER XIV.

SIXTEEN SAVIOURS—LOST KNOWLEDGE.

THE profound philosophies taught in our beloved Ancient and Accepted Scottish Rite bodies of the Southern Jurisdiction were subjects for a discussion I held one day in San Francisco, California, with my friend and brother, the late C. M. Plummer, of the "Trestle Board." During our conversation we drifted to the teachings of Buddha, Zoroaster, Confucius, Pythagoras, Orpheus, Socrates and others. We soon found ourselves floundering in the depths of Christian Theology, Christ and Salvation, when Brother Plummer arose and walking to the shelves of his library, selected a copy of the "Trestle Board"—September, 1896. He turned to page 423, and handing it to me, said: "My dear Doctor, you and I think very much alike along these Theosophical, Philosophical and Metaphysical lines of thought, take this and read it and you will do me a personal favor by inserting it in your own work." I thanked him and read the article and give it to you verbatim; it is called "THE WORLD'S SAVIOURS."

"Many people have never heard of more than one Saviour and many more of no more than one crucifixion. Coming across an old book, recently, giving an account of no less than *sixteen* Saviours that have been crucified, we have compiled from it the following: They are named in the order of the prominence which they have attained by the number of their followers:

"1. CHRISHNA, OF INDIA, B. C. 1200. Among the sin-atoning gods who condescended, in ancient times, to forsake the throne of heaven and descend upon the plains of India, through human birth, to suffer and die for the sins and transgressions of the human race, the eighth Avatar or Saviour, may be considered the most important and the most exalted character, as he had the most conspicuous life, and commanded the most devout and the most universal homage. And while some of the other incarnate demigods were invested with only a limited measure of the infinite deity-ship, Chrishna, according to the teachings of their New Testament (the Ramazand), comprehended in himself 'a full measure of the Godhead bodily.' The evidence of his having been crucified is as conclusive as any other sacrificial or sin-atoning God whose name has been memorialized in history or embalmed as a sacred idol in the memories of his devoted worshippers.

"Mr. Moore, an English traveler and writer, in a large collection of drawings taken from the Hindoo sculptures and monuments, which he arranged together in a work entitled 'The Hindoo Pantheon,' has representing, suspended on the cross, the Hindoo crucified God and Son of God, 'our Lord and Saviour,' Chrishna, with holes pierced in his feet, evidently intended to represent the nail-holes made by the act of crucifixion. Mr. Higgins, who examined this work, which he found in the British Museum, makes report of a number of the transcript drawings, intended to represent the crucifixion of this oriental and mediatorial God, which we will here condense.

"In plate 98 this Saviour is represented with a hole in the top of one foot, just above the toes, where the nail was inserted in the act of crucifixion. In another drawing he is represented exactly in the form of a Romish Christian crucifix, but not fixed or fastened to a tree, though the legs and feet are arranged in the usual way, with nail holes in the latter. There is a halo of glory over it, emanating from the heavens above, just as we have seen Jesus Christ represented in a work by a Christian writer entitled 'Quarles Emblems,' also in other Christian books.

"In several of the *icons* (drawings) there are marks of holes in both feet, and in others in the hands only. In the first drawing which he consulted the marks are very faint, so as to be scarcely visible. In figures 4 and 5 of plate 11, the figures have nail-holes in both feet, while the hands are not represented. Figure 6 has on it the representation of a round hole in the side. To his collar or shirt hangs an emblem of a heart represented in the same manner as those attached to the imaginary likenesses of Jesus Christ, which may now be found in some Christian countries. Figure 91 has a hole in one foot, a nail through the other and a round nail or pin mark in one hand only, while the other is ornamented with a dove and a serpent, both emblems of the deity in the Christian Bible.

" The history of Christian Zeus (or Jeseus, as some writers spell it), is contained principally in the Baghavat-Gita, the episode portion of the Mahabarat Bible. The book is believed to be divinely inspired, like all other Bibles, and the Hindoos claim for it an antiquity of six thousand years. Like Christ, he was of humble origin, and like him had to encounter opposition and persecution. But he seems to have been more successful in the propagation of his doctrine, for it is declared he soon became surrounded by many earnest followers and the people in vast multitudes followed him, crying aloud, 'This indeed is the Redeemer promised to our fathers!'

" His pathway was thickly strewn with miracles, which consisted in healing the sick, curing lepers, restoring the dumb, deaf and the blind, raising the dead, aiding the weak, comforting the sorrow stricken, relieving the oppressed, casting out devils, etc. He came not ostensibly to destroy the previous religion, but to purify it of its impurities and preach a better doctrine. He came, as he declared, 'to reject evil and restore the reign of good, and redeem man from the consequences of the fall, and deliver the oppressed earth from its load of sin and suffering.' His disciples believed him to be God himself, and millions worshipped him as such in the time of Alexander the Great, B. C. 330.

" The hundreds of counterparts to the history of Christ, proving their histories to be almost identical, will be found enumerated in Chapter XXXII, such as : 1. His miraculous birth by a virgin ; 2. The mother and child being visited by shepherds, wise men and the angelic host, who joyously sang, 'In thy delivery, O favored among women, all nations shall have cause to exult;' 3. The edict of the tyrant ruler Cansa, ordering all the first born to be put to death ; 4. The miraculous escape of the mother and child from his bloody decree by the parting of the waves of the River Jumna to permit them to pass through on dry ground; 5. The early retirement of Chrishna to a desert; 6. His baptism or ablution in the River Ganges, corresponding to Christ's baptism in Jordan ; 7. His transfiguration at Madura, where he assured his disciples that present or absent I will always be with you ; 8. He had a favorite disciple (Arjoon), who was his bosom friend, as John was Christ's ; 9. He was anointed with oil by women, like Christ ; 10. A somewhat similar story is told of him—his disciples being enabled by him to catch large draughts of the finny prey in their nets. Like Christ he taught much by parables and precept.

"On one occasion, having returned from a ministerial journey, as he entered Madura, the people came out in crowds to meet him, strewing the ground with branches of cocoa-nut trees, and desiring to hear him. He addressed them in parables, the conclusion and moral of one of which, called the parable of the fishes, runs thus : 'And thus it is, O people of Madura, that you ought to protect the weak and each other, and not retaliate upon an enemy the wrong he may have done you.'

"Here we see the peace doctrine preached in all its purity. 'And thus it was,' says a writer, 'that Chrishna spread among the people the holy doctrines of purest morality, and initiated his hearers into the exalted principles of charity, of self-denial, and self-respect at a time when the desert countries of the west were inhabited only by savage tribes;' and we will add long before Christianity was thought of. Purity of life and spiritual insight, we are told, were distinguishing traits in the character of this oriental sin-atoning Saviour, and that 'he was often moved with compassion for the down trodden and the suffering.'

"Many of the precepts uttered by Chrishna display a profound wisdom and depth of thought equal to any of those attributed to Jesus Christ. In proof of the statement, we will recite a few of the examples out of the hundreds in our possession : 1. Those who do not control their passions cannot act properly towards others. 2. The evil we inflict upon others follow us as our shadows follow our bodies. 3. Only the humble are the beloved of God. 4. Virtue sustains the soul as the muscles sustain the body. 5. When the poor man knocks at your door, take him and administer to his wants, for the poor are the chosen of God (Christ said, 'God hath chosen the poor'). 6. Let your hand be always open to the unfortunate. 7. Look not upon a woman with unchaste desires. 8. Avoid envy, covetousness, falsehood, imposture and slander, and sexual desire. 9. Above all things, cultivate love for your neighbor. 10. When you die you leave your worldly wealth behind you ; but your virtue and vices follow after you. 11. Contemn riches and worldly honor. 12. Seek the company of the wicked in order to reform them. 13. Do good for its own sake, and expect not your reward for it on earth.

14. The soul is immortal, but must be pure and free from all sin and stain before it can return to Him who gave it. 15. The soul is inclined to good when it follows the onward light. 16. The soul is responsible to God for its actions, who has established rewards and punishments. 17. Cultivate that inward knowledge which teaches which is right and wrong. 18. Never take delight in another's misfortune. 19. It is better to forgive an injury than avenge it. 20. You can accomplish by kindness what you cannot by force. 21. A noble spirit finds a cure for injustice by forgetting. 22. Pardon the offense of others but not your own. 23. What you blame in others do not practice yourself. 24. By forgiving an enemy you make many friends. 25. Do right from hatred of evil, and not from fear of punishment. 26. A wise man corrects his own errors by observing those of others. 27. He who rules his temper conquers his greatest enemy. 28. The wise man governs his passions, but the fool obeys them. 29. Be at war with men's vices, but at peace with their persons. 30. There should be no disagreement between your lives and your doctrine. 31. Spend every minute as if it were the last. 32. Lead not one life in public and another in private. 33. Anger, in trying to torture others, punishes itself. 34. A disgraceful death is honorable when you die in a good cause. 35. By growing familiar with vices we learn to tolerate them easily. 36. We must master our evil propensities, or they will master us. 37. He who has conquered his propensities rules over a kingdom. 38. Protect, love and assist others, if you would serve God. 39. From thought springs the will, and from the will action, true or false, just or unjust. 40. As the sandal tree perfumes the axe which fells it, so the good man sheds fragrance on his enemies. 41. Spend a portion of each day in pious devotion. 42. To love the virtue of others is to brighten your own. 43. He who gives to the needy loses nothing himself. 44. A good, wise and benevolent man cannot be rich. 45. Much riches is a curse to the possessor. 46. The wounds of the soul are more important than those of the body. 47. The virtuous man is like the banyan tree, which shelters and protects all around it. 48. Money does not satisfy the love of gain, but only stimulates it. 49. Your greatest enemy is in your own bosom. 50. To flee when charged is to confess your own guilt. 51. The wound of conscience leaves a scar.

"We will cite a few examples relative to women: 1. He who is cursed by women is cursed by God. 2. God will punish him who laughs at woman's sufferings. 3. When woman is honored, God is honored. 4. The virtuous woman will have but one husband, and the right-minded man but one wife. 5. It is the highest crime to take advantage of the weakness of woman. 6. Woman should be loved, respected, and protected by husbands, fathers and brothers.

"II. Crucifixion of Hindoo Sakia, b. c. 600. How many gods who figured in Hindoo history suffered death upon the cross as atoning offerings for the sins of mankind is a point not clearly established by their sacred books. But the death of the God above named, known as Sakia, Buddha Sakia, or Muni is distinctly referred to by several writers, both Oriental and Christian, though there appears to be in Buddhist countries different accounts of the death of the famous and extensively worshipped sin-atoning Saviour.

"In some countries the story runs, a God was crucified by an arrow being driven through his body, which fastened him to a tree; the tree, with the arrow thus projecting at right angles, formed the cross, emblematical of the atoning sacrifice. Sakia, an account states was crucified by his enemies for the humble act of plucking a flower in a garden—doubtless seized on a mere pretext, rather than as being considered a crime.

"One of the accusations brought against Christ, it will be remembered, was that of plucking the ripened ears of corn on the Sabbath. And it is a remarkable circumstance, that in the pictures of Christian countries representing the Virgin Mary with the infant Jesus in her arms, either the child or the mother is frequently represented with a bunch of flowers in the hand. That his crucifixion was designed as a sin-atoning offering is evident from the following declaration found in his sacred biography, viz: 'He in mercy left Paradise, and came down to earth because he was filled with compassion for the sins and miseries of mankind. He sought to lead them into better paths, and took their suffering upon himself that he might expiate their crimes and mitigate the punishment they must otherwise inevitably undergo.'

"He believed, and taught his followers, that all sin is inevitably punished, either in this or the future life; and so great were his sympathy and tenderness, that he condescended to suffer that punishment himself by an ignominous death upon the cross, after which he descended in Hades (Hell) to suffer for a time (three days) for the inmates of that horrible prison, that he might show he sympathized with them. After his resurrection, and before his ascension to heaven, as well as during his earthly sojourn, he imparted to the world some beautiful, lofty and soul-elevating precepts. 'The object of his mission,' says a writer, 'was to instruct those who were straying from the right path, and expiate the sins of mortals by his own suffering and procure for them a happy entrance into Paradise by obedience to his precepts and prayers to his name.' 'His followers always speak of him as one with God from all eternity.' His most common title was 'the Saviour of the World.' He was also called 'the Benevolent One,' 'the Dispenser of Grace,' 'The Source of Life,' 'the Light of the World,' 'the True Light,' etc.

"His mother was a very pure, refined, pious and devout woman; never indulged in any impure thoughts, words or actions. She was so much esteemed for her virtues and for being the mother of a God, that an escort of ladies attended her wherever she went. The trees bowed before her as she passed through the forest, and flowers sprang up wherever her foot pressed the ground. She was saluted as 'the Holy Virgin, Queen of Heaven.' It is said that when her divine child was born, he stood upright and proclaimed, 'I will put an end to the sufferings and sorrows of the world.' And immediately a light shone round about the young Messiah.

"He spent much time in retirement and like Christ in another respect, was once tempted by a demon, who offered him all the honors and wealth of the world. But he rebuked the devil, saying, 'Begone; hinder me not.' He began, like Christ to preach his gospel and heal the sick when about twenty-eight years of age. And it is declared, 'The blind saw, the deaf heard, the dumb spoke, the lame danced, and the crooked became straight.' Hence the people declared, 'He is no mortal child but an incarnation of the Deity.' His religion was of a very superior character. He proclaimed, 'My law is a law of grace for all.' His religion knew no race, no sex, no caste, and no aristocratic priesthood.

"'It taught,' says Max Muller, 'the equality of all men, and the brotherhood of the human race.' 'All men, without regard to rank, birth or nation,' says Dunckar, 'form according to Buddha's view, one great suffering association in this earthly vale of tears; therefore the commandments of love, forbearance, patience, compassion, pity, brotherliness of all men.'

" Klaproth (a German professor of Oriental languages) says this religion is calculated to ennoble the human race. ' It is difficult to comprehend,' says a French writer (M. Laboulay) ' how men, not assisted by revelation, could have soared so high, and approached so near the truth.'

" Dunckar says this Oriental God 'taught self denial, chastity, temperance, the control of the passions, to bear injustice from others, to suffer death quietly, and without hate of your persecutor, to grieve not for one's own misfortune, but for those of others.' An investigation of their history will show that they lived up to these moral injunctions.

" Besides the five great commandments, says a Wesleyan missionary (Spense Hardy) in Dalimma Padam, ' every shade of vice, hypocrisy, anger, pride, suspicion, greediness, gossiping and cruelty to animals is guarded against by special precepts. Among the virtues recommended, we find not only reverence for parents, care of children, submission to authority, gratitude, moderation in all things, submission in time of trial, equanimity at all times, but virtues unknown in some systems of morality, such as the duty of forgiving injuries, and not rewarding evil for evil.' And we will add, both charity and love are specially recommended.

" We have it also upon the authority of Dunckar, that ' Buddha proclaimed that salvation and redemption have come for all, even the lowest and most abject classes.' For he broke down the iron castle of the Brahminical code which had so long ruled India, and aimed to place all mankind upon a level. His followers have been stigmatized by Christian professors as ' idolators ' but Sir John Bowring, in his ' Kingdom and People of Siam,' denies that they are idolators, ' because ' says he ' no Buddhist believes his image to be God, or anything more than an outward representation of Deity.' Their deific images are looked upon with the same views and feelings as a Christian venerates the photograph of his deceased friend. Hence if one is an idolator, the other is also.

" With respect to the charge of polytheism, missionary M. Huc says, ' that although their religion embraces many inferior deities who fill the same offices that angels do under the Christian. system;' yet, adds M. Huc, 'Monotheism is the real character of Buddhism,' and confirms the statement by the testimony of a Thibetan. It should be noted here, that although Buddhism succeeded in converting about three hundred million, or one-third of the inhabitants of the globe, it was never propagated by the sword, and never persecuted the disciples of other religions. Its conquests were made by a rational appeal to the human mind.

"Mr. Hodgson says, 'It recognizes the infinite capacity of the human intellect.' And St. Hilaire declares 'Love for all beings is its nucleus; and to love our enemies, and not persecute, are the virtues of this people.'

"Max Muller says, 'Its moral code, taken. by itself, is one of the most perfect the world has ever known.' Its five commandments are: 1. Thou shalt not kill. 2. Thou shalt not steal. 3. Thou shalt not commit adultery or any impurity. 4. Thou shalt not lie. 5. Thou shalt not intoxicate thyself. To establish the above cited doctrines and precepts, Buddha sent forth his disciples into the world to preach his gospel to every creature. And if any convert had committed a sin in word, thought, or deed, he was to confess and repent. One of the tracts which they distributed declares, 'There is undoubtedly a life after this in which the virtuous expect the rewards of their good deeds. . . . . . Judgment takes place immediately after death.

"Buddha and his followers set an example to the world of enduring opposition and persecution with great patience and non-resistance. And some of them suffered martyrdom rather than abandon their principles, and gloried in thus sealing their doctrines with their lives. A story is told of a rich merchant, by the name of Purna, forsaking all to follow his lord and Master; and also of his encountering and talking with a woman of low caste at a well, which reminds us of a similar incident in the history of Christ. But his enemies, becoming jealous and fearful of his growing power, finally crucified him near the foot of the Nepaul Mountains about B. C. 600. But after his death, burial and resurrection, we are told he ascended back to heaven, where millions of his followers believed he had existed with Brahma from all eternity.

"III. THAMMUZ OF SYRIA CRUCIFIED B. C. 1160. The fullest history extant of this God-Saviour is probably that of Ctesias (B. C. 400), author of 'Persika.' The poet has perpetuated his memory in rhyme:

> 'Trust, ye saints, your Lord restored ;
>   Trust ye in your risen Lord ;
> For the pains which Thammuz endured
>   Our salvation have procured.'

"Mr. Higgins informs us (Anac. Vol. I, page 246) that this God was crucified at the period above named, as a sin atoning offering. The stanza just quoted is predicated upon the following Greek text, translated by Godwin: 'Trust ye in God, for out of his loins salvation is come unto us.' Julius Firmicus speaks of this God 'rising from the dead for the salvation of the world.' The Christian writer Parkhurst alludes to this Saviour as preceding the advent of Christ, and as filling to some extent the same chapter in sacred history.

"IV. WITTOBA OF THE TELINGONESE CRUCIFIED B. C. 552. We have a very conclusive historical proof of the crucifixion of this heathen God. Mr. Higgins tells us: 'He is represented in his history with nail holes in his hands and the soles of his feet.' Nails, hammers and pinchers are constantly seen represented on his crucifixion, and are objects of adoration among his followers. The iron crown of Lombardy has within it a nail that is claimed as a true original, and is much admired and venerated on that account. The worship of this crucified God, according to our author prevails chiefly in the Travancore and other southern countries in the region of Madura.

"V. IAO OF NEPAUL CRUCIFIED B. C. 622. With respect to the crucifixion of this ancient Saviour we have this very definite and specific testimony, that ' he was crucified on a tree in Nepaul ' (see Gregorius, page 202). The name of this incarnate God and Oriental Saviour occurs frequently in the Holy Bibles and sacred books of other countries. Some suppose Iao (often spelt Jao) is the root of the name of the Jewish God Jehovah.

"VI. HESUS OF THE CELTIC DRUIDS CRUCIFIED B. C. 834. Mr. Higgins tell us that the Celtic Druids represent their God Hesus as having been crucified with a lamb one side and an elephant on the other, and that this occurred long before the Christian era. Also that a representation of it may now be seen upon the 'fire tower of Brechin.' In this symbolical representation of the crucifixion, the elephant being the largest animal known, was chosen to represent the sins of the world while the Lamb, from its proverbial innocent nature was chosen to represent the innocency of the victim (the God offered as a propitiatory sacrifice). And thus we have 'the Lamb of God taking away the sins of the world—symbolical language used with respect to the offering of Jesus Christ. And here is indicated very clearly the origin of the figure. It is evidently borrowed from the Druids. We have the statement of the above writer that the legend was found among the Canutes of Gaul long before Jesus Christ was known to history.

"VII. QUEXALCOTE OF MEXICO CRUCIFIED B. C. 587. Historic authority, relative to the crucifixion of this Mexican God, and to his execution upon the cross as a propitiatory sacrifice for the sins of mankind, is explicit, unequivocal and ineffaceable. The evidence is tangible, and indelibly engraved upon steel and metal plates. One of these plates represents him a's having been crucified on a mountain, another represents him as having been crucified in the heavens, as St. Justin tells us Christ was. According to another writer he is sometimes represented as having been nailed to a cross, and by other accounts as hanging with a cross in his hand.

"The 'Mexican Antiquities' (Vol. VI, page 166) says 'Quexalcote is represented in the Codex Borgianus as nailed to the cross' sometimes two thieves are represented as having been crucified with him. That the advent of the crucified Saviour and Mexican God was long anterior to the era of Christ is admitted by Christian writers. In the work above named (Codex Borgianus), may be found the account, not only of his crucifixion but his death and burial, descent into hell, and resurrection on the third day. And another work, entitled 'Codex Vaticanus' contains the story of his immaculate birth of a virgin mother by the name of Chimalman. Many other incidents are found related of him in his sacred biography, in which we found the most striking counterparts to the more modern gospel story of Jesus Christ, such as his forty days temptation and fasting, his' riding on an ass, his purification in the temple, his baptism and regeneration by water, forgiving of sins, being anointed with oil, etc. 'All these things, and many more, found related of this Mexican God in their sacred books' says Lord Kingsborough, a Christian writer, 'are curious and mysterious.'

"VIII QUIRINUS OF ROME CRUCIFIED B. C. 500.—The crucifixion of this Roman Saviour is briefly noticed by Mr. Higgins, and is remarkable for presenting, like other crucified Gods, several parallel features to that of the Judean Saviour, not only in the circumstances related as attending his crucifixion, but also in a considerable portion of his antecedent life. He is represented, like Christ; 1, as having been conceived and brought forth by a virgin; 2, his life was sought by the reigning king, Amulius; 3, he was of royal blood, his mother being of kingly descent; 4, he was 'put to death by wicked hands,' i. e. crucified; 5, at his mortal exit the whole earth is said to have been enveloped in darkness, as in the case of Christ, Chrishna and Prometheus. And finally, he is resurrected and ascends back to heaven.

"IX (ÆSCHYLUS) PROMETHEUS, B. C. 547.—In the account of the crucifixion of Prometheus of Caucasus, as furnished by Seneca, Hesiod and other writers, it is stated that he was nailed to an upright beam of timber, to which were affixed extended arms of wood, and that this cross was situated near the Caspian Straits. The modern story of this cruci- fied God, which represents him as having been bound to a rock for thirty years, while vultures preyed upon his vitals, Mr. Higgins pronounces an impious fraud. 'For,' says the learned historical writer, 'I have seen the account which declares he was nailed to a cross with hammer and nails.' Confirmatory of this statement is the declaration of Mr. Southwell, that 'he exposed himself to the wrath of God in his zeal to save mankind.' The poet, in portraying his propitiatory offering, says:

"'Lo streaming from the fatal tree,
His all-atoning blood,
Is this the Infinite?—yes, 'tis he—
Prometheus and a God.
Well might the sun in darkness hide,
And veil his glories in,
When God, the great Prometheus died,
For man, the creature's sin.'

" The 'New American Cyclopedia' (Vol. I, page 157), contains the following significant declaration relative to this sin-atoning Saviour: 'It is doubtful whether there is to be found in the whole range of Greek letters, deeper pathos than that of the divine woe of the beneficent demi-

ISLAND OF PHILÆ FROM THE ROCKS OF THE CATARACT.

god Prometheus, crucified on his Scythian crags for his love to mortals.' Here we have first-class authority for the truth of the crucifixion of this Oriental God.

"In 'Lempriere's Classical Dictionary,' ' Higgins' Anacalypsis,' and other works, may be found the following particulars relative to the final exit of the God above named, viz : 1. That the whole frame of nature became convulsed; 2, the earth shook, the rocks were rent, the graves were opened, and in a storm, which seemed to threaten the dissolution of the universe, the solemn scene forever closed, and 'Our Lord and Saviour' Prometheus, gave up the ghost. 'The cause for which he suffered,' says Mr. Southwell, ' was his love for the human race.' Mr. Taylor makes the statement in his Syntagma, that the whole story of Prometheus's crucifixion, burial and resurrection was acted in pantomime in Athens five hundred years before Christ, which proves its great antiquity. Minutius Felix, one of the most popular Christian writers of the second century (in his 'Octavius,' see 291), thus addresses the people of Rome: ' Your victorious trophies not only represent a simple cross, but a cross with man on it; ' and this *man* St. Jerome calls God. These coincidences furnish still further proof that the crucifixion of Gods has been very long prevalent among the heathen.

"X. CRUCIFIXION OF THULIS OF EGYPT, B. C. 1700.—Thulis of Egypt, whence comes ' Ultima Thule,' died the death of the cross about thirty-five hundred years ago. Ultima Thule was the island which marked the ultimate bounds of the extensive realms of the legitimate descendant of the Gods. This Egyptian Saviour appears also to have been known as Zulis, and with this name, Mr. Wilkinson tells us, ' his history is curiously illustrated in the sculptures made seventeen hundred years B. C. of a small retired chamber lying nearly over the western adytum of the temple.' We are told twenty-eight lotus plants near his grave indicate the number of years he lived on earth. After suffering a violent death, he was buried, but rose again, ascended into heaven, and there became ' the judge of the dead,' or souls in a future state. Wilkinson says he came down from heaven to benefit mankind, and that he was said to be ' full of grace and truth.'

"XI. CRUCIFIXION OF INDRA OF THIBET, B. C. 725.—The account of the God and Saviour Indra, may be found in Georgius, Thibetinum Alphabetum, page 230. In the work referred to may be found plates representing the Thibetan Saviour as having been nailed to the cross. There are five wounds, representing the five nail-holes, and the piercing of the side. The antiquity of the story is beyond dispute. Marvellous stories were told of the birth of the Divine Redeemer. The mother was a virgin of black complexion, and hence his complexion was of the ebony hue, as in the case of Christ and some other sin-atoning Saviours. He descended from heaven on a mission of benevolence, and ascended back to the heavenly mansion after his crucifixion. He led a life of strict celibacy, which he taught was essential to true holiness. He inculcated great tenderness toward all living beings. He could walk upon the waters or upon the air; could foretell future events with great accuracy. He practiced the most devout contemplation, severe discipline of the body and mind, and acquired the most complete subjection of his passions. He was worshipped as a God who had existed as a spirit from all eternity, and his followers were called 'Heavenly Teachers.'

"XII. ALCESTOS OF EURIPEDES, CRUCIFIED B. C. 600.—The 'English Classical Journal' (Vol. XXXVII) furnishes us with the story of another crucified God known as Alcestos—a female God or Goddess; and in this respect it is a novelty in sacred history, being the first, if not the only, example of a feminine God atoning for the sins of the world upon the cross. The doctrine of the trinity and atoning offering for sin was inculcated as a part of her religion.

"XIII. ATYS OF PHRYGIA, CRUCIFIED B. C. 1170.—Speaking of this crucified Messiah, the Anacalypsis informs us that several histories are given of him, but all concur in representing him as having been an atoning offering for sin. And the Latin phrase, '*suspensus lingo*," found in his history indicates the manner of his death. He was suspended on a tree, crucified, buried and rose again.

"XIV. CRITE OF CHALDEA, CRUCIFIED B. C. 1200.—The Chaldeans, as Mr. Higgins informs us, have noted in their sacred books the account of the crucifixion of a God with the above name. He was also known as 'the Redeemer,' and was styled 'the ever blessed son of God,' 'the Saviour of the Race,' 'the Atoning Offering for an angry God,' etc. And when he was offered up both heaven and earth were shaken to their foundation.

"XV. BALI OF ORISSA, CRUCIFIED B.C. 752.—We learn by the Oriental books that in the district of country known as Orissa, in Asia, they have a story of a crucified God, known by several names, including the above, all of which we are told signify 'Lord Second,' having reference to him as the second person or second member of the trinity, as most of the crucified Gods occupied that position in the triad of deities constituting the trinity, as indicated in the language 'Father, *Son* and Holy Ghost.' The son in all cases being the atoning offering, 'the Crucified Redeemer and the second person of the trinity.' This God Bali was also called Baliu, and sometimes Bel.

"The Anacalypsis informs us (Vol. I, 257) that monuments of this crucified Saviour, bearing great age, may be found amid the ruins of the magnificent city of Mahabalipore, partially buried amongst the figures in the temple.

"XVI. MITHRA OF PERSIA, CRUCIFIED B. C. 600.—This Persian God, according to Mr. Higgins, was 'slain upon the cross to make atonement for mankind and to take away the sins of the world.' He was reputedly born on the 25th day of December, and crucified on a tree. It is a remarkable circumstance that two Christian writers (Mr. Faber and Mr. Bryant) both speak of his 'being slain,' and yet both omit to speak of the manner in which he was put to death. And the same with respect to other crucified Gods of the Pagans. We might note other cases of crucifixion. DEVATAT OF SIAM, IXION OF ROME, APOLLONIUS OF TYANA IN CAPPADOCIA, are all reported in history as having 'died the death of the cross.'

"IXION, B. C. 400, according to NIMROD, was crucified on a wheel, the rim representing the world, and the spokes constituting the cross. It is declared 'He bore the burden of the world' (that is, 'the sins of the world') on his back while suspended on the cross. Hence he was sometimes called 'the crucified spirit of the world.' With respect to Appollonius, it is a remarkable, if not suspicious, circumstance which should not be passed unnoticed, that several writers, while they recount a long list of miracles and remarkable incidents in this Cappadocian Saviour, extending through his whole life, and forming a parallel to similar incidents of the Christian Saviour, say not a word regarding his crucifixion. And a similar course has been pursued with respect to Mithra and other sin-atoning Gods, including Chrishna and Prometheus, as before noticed."

By reference to Mackey's ' Lexicon of Freemasonry,' page 35, we learn that " Freemasons secretly taught the doctrine of the crucifixion, atonement and resurrection long anterior to the Christian era, and that similar doctrines were taught in ' all the ancient mysteries,' thus proving that the conception of these tenets of faith existed at a very early period of time." And it may be noted here that the doctrine of salvation by crucifixion had likewise, with most of the ancient forms of religious faith, an astronomical representation, *i. e.*, a representation on astronomical symbols. According to the emblematic figures comprised in their altar-worship, people were saved by the sun's crucifixion or crossification, realized by crossing over the equinoctial line into the season of spring, and thereby gave out a saving heat and light to the world, and stimulated the generative organs of animal and vegetable life. It was from this conception that the ancients were in the habit of carving or painting the organs of generation upon the walls of their holy temples. The blood of the grape, which was ripened by the heat of the sun, as he crossed over by resurrection into spring (*i. e.*, was crucified), was symbolically " the blood of the cross," or " the blood of the Lamb." That the world moves in cycles, and that history continually repeats itself, admits of no question, and so from the ruins of one Empire rises another, equally as grand, and the teachings of one age are as sure to come to the surface again as the motions of the earth upon its axis will apparently make the sun rise in the East and set in the West.

While it makes no difference from whom, whence, or where, originated the Truths of the so-called Christian teachings, one thing is certain in relation to the account of the " Sixteen Saviours," from Thulis down, and that is their teachings belong to the oldest metaphysical philosophies known to mankind and have been known to every epoch of the world's history. These Truths must have emanated from some reliable source, since they were embodied in all religious and metaphysical philosophies.

If we go back to the first days of Christianity we shall find the early fathers of the church turning the old pagan philosophies into new Christian teachings and that, too, in the very temples wherein had been practiced the ancient pagan rites. During the reign of Constantine these were readily transformed into sacred edifices for the growing sect of Christians. With slight alterations these temples were soon adapted to

Christian worship, while magnificent statues of Jupiter, with a few sweeping strokes of the chisel and a little plaster were transformed into God, the Son, or some Saint, and a priceless Venus into the Virgin Mary, the Mother of God. Where sounds of old pagan rites and Greek schools of Philosophy had vibrated for so many long centuries, were now to be heard the chanting of Psalms by monkish priests. The incense which had so long burned upon the altars, in honor of the pagan gods, may still be found swinging in the censers of the Romish Church of to-day.

Again Baptism does not belong exclusively to the Christian Church, nor did it originate with its teachings, for long ages before John the Baptist lived these rites were universally observed, being a mere relic of the early days of the world's history. Its use by the Christians is identical with that of the ancient Egyptian and Babylonian Mysteries, a symbol of regeneration and expiation of sin and a purification of the body. In nearly all the Mysteries baptism was considered to be indispensable. Purification of the body, by immersion in some of the sacred rivers, was an actual necessity before the candidate could be received and initiated into the sacred Mysteries of India. Christ himself was baptized by John the Baptist in the flowing waters of the river Jordan.

The Vedic Hymns praise the purifying powers of the sacred rivers of India and one of the most noted places is at the confluence of the three sacred rivers Jumna, Ganges and Sarasvati, at Allahabad. The natives claim three rivers to represent Matter, Spirit and Life. During my stay at this city I carefully examined the confluence of the two rivers, Jumna and Ganges, but could not find the third. I spoke to a Babu about it, when he took me down into an underground chamber of the old ruined palace of Akbar Khan and showed me a little water trickling down the wall and said, there is the evidence of the Sarasvati. The Zendavesta ascribe extraordinary virtues to the sacred waters of the holy river Ardvisura. The Hindu was purified by immersion in the sacred waters of the Ganges long centuries before Christ, and to-day the same ceremonies are performed by their descendants in nearly all of the rivers of India as well as the Ganges.

The Zarathustrians used pure filtered water for their purifications, in addition to prayers and certain other ceremonies which are preserved and practiced by the Parsees, after the same manner as by their great ancestors, long before Krishna descended upon the plains of India and gave to the people the sublime and beautiful teachings now as old as the world itself. This ceremony of immersion is still practiced as one of the most sacred and inexpressibly beautiful symbols of the purification of the heart by water as a pledge *of that* only which is Just, Right and True.

Christianity most assuredly extinguished the sacrificial fires of the pagans and she yet built far greater ones in endeavoring to bring the people into the fold of Holy Mother Church. I do not desire to speak against any religion or any philosophy. I only want to show that the teachings of Jesus and all those other Saviours had been taught long centuries before Abraham went down into the Land of Egypt and consequently they must have originated from some source. Therefore, if we search very carefully for the source, or fountain-head, of these pure Theosophical and Philosophical Truths we will find they originated in the " Land of the Vedas " and in the ancient Wisdom of India.

Many facts impress themselves upon our minds, in taking a survey of all the religions dominating the world in different ages. Their fundamental principles have been the same, though covered in many instances, with a mass of rubbish, while the eternal verities remain intact in each, only clothed in different vestments, making them difficult of recognition, excepting to the initiated. The very identity of these great and glorious Truths establishes the fact that each one of the sixteen Saviours must certainly have been Leaders and Martyrs of their race, who suffered and died for their love of humanity. That they were members of a Brotherhood of great spiritual Teachers, who endeavored to restore what a corrupt Priesthood had degraded, is to me a positive verity. These Teachers were most assuredly helped in their missions by the Adepts and members of the inferior degrees, who worked earnestly and faithfully to restore the Secret Doctrine of the Ancient Wisdom Religion. In like manner were the teachings of Christ, the Master, assisted by the Auditors, Catechumens and Faithful, during the struggles of the Christian Church against the old pagan philosophies, who was successful in restoring the glorious precepts of the Ancient Wisdom in Judea, Rome, Egypt and other places for a few centuries until it finally degenerated into Priestcraft and Sacerdotalism, when all those profound ethical teach-

SACRED LAKE OF THE MYSTERIES,

KARNAK.

ings of our Master were struck down and replaced by the "Holy Inquisition."

Masonry, a lineal descendant of the ancient Mysteries, conceals within her bosom symbols that will *reveal* to the student a profound knowledge of the ancient philosophies, older, by far, than the Vedas or the Zend-avesta. We have proof positive that these very symbols were designed by the Perfect Masters and Adepts, as a safe and sacred repository for the sublime teachings of the Secret Doctrine, as well as for the preservation of the Royal Secret, in order to convey to those generations yet unborn a knowledge of the Ancient Wisdom and the power of the "Lost Word." People may scoff and laugh at the claims of profound knowledge being contained in our symbols, though they cannot dispute their antiquity and dare not say they were fabricated by the builders of Rome, Greece or any other special nation, such as Egypt, Chaldea or Assyria. They are found in all of these countries, being inscribed upon the oldest monuments and statues known to exist in all parts of the world, and have come down to us through the drifting ages from the interior of India, possibly the plains of Gobi, where are to be found to-day records of a far higher civilization than is apparent in the dawn of this great twentieth century.

Go back to the distant ages of antiquity and search among the ruined empires of every nation throughout the earth ; study their mystic teachings and occult doctrines ; aye, each and every one of them, then study the sacred writings of these same people, examine carefully their Mystic Rites and ceremonies, and you will find proof positive of a "Secret Doctrine" running through them all, from the most remote ages to the present day. This Secret Doctrine is the container and contained of all Truths, carefully hidden from the profane; a great and sublime philosophy, the fountain of all Truth, the source of all Wisdom, the key to all the higher spiritual and intellectual qualifications.

The Wisdom itself, in fact, permeated all teachings, mystic rites and ceremonies everywhere, and in all its sublimity and grandeur it is to be found in the glorious symbols of our beloved Ancient and Accepted Scottish Rite. It will, however, require earnest and profound study before the student will be able to obtain the faintest glimmer of their meaning. He must concentrate his mind upon each and every one, and as I have hereinbefore stated, there is to be no jumping from one degree to another, skipping the symbology of those below. He must carefully study each and every symbol and allegory, until thoroughly understood, as presented to him, for the one below is the key to the one above. Like the sublime invocation of the Turanian Adept the meaning does not lie altogether in the symbol. The key must be found before we can thoroughly understand the ineffable Wisdom contained in the series that will transcend all we have ever known or dreamed of, and open to our view the great Truths taught by the Masters in every age.

During some of my lectures I have had many people come to me and say: " Well, Doctor, I enjoyed your ' talk ' very much, indeed, but when you spoke of lost Civilizations, Wisdom, Knowledge, etc., I can't believe it. Of course, I can very readily understand the Rise and Fall of empires, and that upon the ruins of one the foundations of another is laid; but you could never make me believe that the world was ever more civilized or enlightened than it is to-day, under the ' Light of the New Dispensation.' You may talk of the Lemurians and Atlanteans as much as you like, but I believe the world of to-day is just as full of knowledge and Wisdom as it ever was; and as to the sinking of those immense continents beneath the ocean, it is the height of absurdity."

Now, in answer to just such people, let me say this: During a visit to Southern California, to the city of San Jose, in the latter part of the year of 1899, I attended a Lecture illustrated by stereopticon views which showed the wondrous beauties of the Island of New Zealand, its magnificent rivers, streams, mountains and the gigantic tree ferns for which this country is noted; in fact, the Lecturer, a Maori, a native of the Island and a scholarly gentleman, a graduate of an English college, described to us not only the topographical features of the country, but its Flora and Fauna, as well as the manners and customs of the natives. After which he threw upon the screen a great number of Native Chiefs, their sons wives and daughters, calling our attention especially to the features of the young men and women, whose phrenological development would compare very favorably with our own Anglo-Saxon Race, both in beauty of expression and in evidences of a very high order of intellectual development.

He told us that he was on a Lecturing tour for the express purpose of making money to educate the native children of his country so as to preserve the last remnant of his Race. He said he knew that his people were doomed to pass away unless something were done for them. He also said it would be no use to try and raise the moral standard of the old people of his country. The young children, however, could be trained and educated so as to preserve their native characteristics, while living and growing up among the Anglo-Saxons who now dominated his country. He told us that in coming from his country, New Zealand, to the city of San Francisco he had visited quite a number of the islands in both the South and North Pacific Oceans, and on going ashore at the different islands "*en route*" he was very much surprised to note that the natives of the various places visited had the same peculiar characteristics as those of his own people. On arriving at the Sandwich Islands he went on shore at Honolulu, where he heard the natives in conversation, and was surprised to find that he could understand every word they said as they were speaking his own language, with very slight variations, which he described at the time, but I have since forgotten. He said it convinced him that the various Islands of Oceanica must at one time have formed a vast Continent, and he thoroughly believed the natives of these Islands to be lineal descendants of the Lost Continent of Lemuria.

After the lecture, on returning home, I thought considerably on what had been said by the lecturer, and after my meditation I began to realize that Knowledge could be lost, just as easily as a man could lose some trifling article out of his pocket; for instance: Would it not be possible for a tremendous seismic disturbance to occur, through some cause or another, and the poles of the earth be entirely changed from their present position, and America, with the whole of Europe, suddenly be forced beneath the ocean. Suppose all the civilized portions of the earth were wiped out of existence, submerged with all arts, sciences, philosophies, etc., a thousand fathoms below the surging ceaseless waves, with all history and record of civilization entirely lost, while from out the depths of the briny deep new continents should re-appear, to preserve the equilibrium of the earth's centre, giving to the islands of the Atlantic and Pacific Oceans their places once again as the sierrated peaks of magnificent mountain ranges, upon these various continents, while all that would remain of the lost ones would be the tops of the mountain ranges, forming islands which in many instances would be widely sepa-

22

rated one from the other, with possibly here and there a few hundred thousand people still in existence, who had been saved in some very extraordinary manner from this terrible cataclysm, this wrecking of a World.

The thought of intellectual development would stop right there, man would drop back into the Paleolithic age and self-preservation would be the dominant chord among them. .What a tremendous struggle would then take place for a mere existence, and it is self-evident that the civilization which had once been theirs would fall back into traditions and legends, to be handed down from one generation to another. It would grow more misty and hazy, more difficult of comprehension as the drifting centuries rolled along. Civilization would have to begin again with the life of a new race, as it were. After the obliteration of the older people, their children would not be able to understand anything, comparatively speaking, of the wondrous knowledge buried deep beneath the surging waves surrounding their island home. Knowledge would have to be obtained through long and bitter experience. No matter to what point their phrenological development had attained, they would again have to struggle along semi-barbarous paths before reaching any great intellectual development. It is therefore possible for knowledge to become entirely lost, though places may exist wherein may be stored and preserved the Knowledge and Wisdom pertaining to this lost civilization, as above stated, just as. in the plains of Gobi, or Thibet, for it is positively asserted that *there* in secret places are stored the remains of a far more ancient civilization than our own.

No doubt there are thousands of people, aye, millions, who would laugh to scorn this statement, but their laughing does not destroy or alter the fact of its existence. Let me repeat to you right here the apothegm of Narada, the ancient Hindu philosopher: *Never utter the words: I do not know this—therefore it is false.*

The Golden Fleece—Roman Eagle—Masonic Apron—What it Teaches.

The register! You're right;
There is my name in letters large and bold;
Thanks, Brother Tiler. Now will I unfold
　　My apron white.

Step this way to the light,
That all may see how clean it is and fair;
So, that is well. Now tie it on the square—
　　My apron white.

So let me ever wear—
finding my pleasure in a spotless name,
The honor of the Craft's unsullied fame—
　　My apron white.

—SYDNEY FREEMASON.

CHAPTER XV.

THE GOLDEN FLEECE—ROMAN EAGLE—MASONIC APRON— WHAT IT TEACHES.

IN this chapter, my dear Friends and Brothers, let me call your attention to the ceremony of the investiture of the Lamb-skin, or the white leather apron, the badge of a Mason. one of the most profound and deeply interesting symbols in Masonry, and one that is pregnant with occult meaning, one that demonstrates the ancient occult axiom of the Delphic Oracle—"Know thyself."

When first our Neophyte is invested with that most sublime emblem, the apron, he is told that it is more ancient than the "Golden Fleece" or "Roman Eagle," and that it is more honorable than the "Star and Garter," etc., etc. Now among all those who have been so told and so invested, how many are there who understand anything at all about the Golden Fleece and Roman Eagle, or the Honor pertaining to the Star and Garter? I will venture to say, that not one in a thousand knows anything at all about either one or the other, and still less of the profound symbology that is contained in the badge of a Mason—the white leather apron. Therefore, in order that you, my dear Brothers of all Rites, may be enabled to thoroughly understand something about these various subjects, I will write upon them for your especial edification.

In Grecian Mythology we find that Athămăs, the son of the King of Thessaly, married Nĕphĕlē (the cloud goddess), by whom she had a son Phrixus, and a daughter Helle. Some time afterward he fell in love with and married a mortal called Ino. This act of Athămăs in taking to wife a mortal aroused intense jealousy in the heart of Nĕphĕlē, and consequently she visited the earth with a drought, which Ino endeavored to avert by sacrificing her stepson, Phrixus, upon the Altar of Zeus Laphystius, through an oracle that she pretended to have received. But Nĕphĕlē, the mother of Phrixus, who was watching over him, sent him a ram, with a golden fleece, so that both himself and sister Helle

might be enabled to make their escape from their vindictive and treacherous stepmother, who sought to destroy them.

Phrixus and his sister now make their escape from Thessaly
upon the ram; but during their flight through the air Helle fell off
and was drowned in the waters below, and the place wherein she fell has
ever since borne the name "Hellespont." Phrixus arrived safely at the
city of Colchis, where he offered up the ram as a sacrifice to Zeus as the
"aider of flight" (Zeus Phyxius), and he made a present of its golden
fleece to King Acētēs, who hung it upon an oak in the sacred grove of
Ares (the son of Zeus by Hera, the Greek name for the God of War, and
which the Romans called Mars). Acētēs gave Phrixus his daughter
Chalciŏpē to wife, by whom he had two sons, whom he named Cytissōrus
and Argus, both of whom he eventually sent back to his home. Cytissōrus saved the life of his grandfather Athămăs from being sacrificed, and
Argus built the ship Argo which was named after him.

This vessel was the celebrated ship that carried the Argonauts in
their glorious expedition to recover the Golden Fleece, under the leader-
ship of Jason. They eventually accomplished their purpose by the help
of the king's daughter, Media, who was in love with Jason. The account
of this Argonautic expedition is well worth reading, as it will give you a
good account of the recovery of the wonderful Golden Fleece.

The Order of the Golden Fleece was founded by Phillip II, the Good,
Duke of Burgundy, on the 10th day of January, in the year 1429, on the
occasion of his marriage with the Infanta, Isabella of Portugal. This
Order was originally composed of thirty-one members, all of whom were
"*Gentilhommes de nom et d'armes, sans reproche.*" The office of Grand
Master passed to the house of Hapsburg in 1477, with the acquisition of
the dominions of Burgundy and the Netherlands.

In 1516 Pope Leo X consented to increase the number of the
Knights, including the Sovereign, to fifty-two, but at the present day the
statutes have been changed and the Sovereign is allowed to create just as
many Knights as he may deem wise, providing they be Catholics and are
of noble birth, but in the case of a nobleman of the Protestant belief a
papal sanction would have to be given before he could be legally installed
or created a Knight. After the accession of Charles V, in 1555, the
Spanish-Dutch line of the house of Austria remained in possession of the

Order, and in the year 1700 the Emperor Charles IV and also Phillip of
Spain both claimed the *sole* right to dominate the Order.   The Emperor
Charles IV carried away the archives of the Order to Vienna, where their
inauguration was solemnized in most magnificent splendor in the year
1713.   At the same time Phillip V of Spain claimed to be the legitimate
head of the Order, and as Grand Master he protested against the pretensions of the Emperor Charles IV.   They wrangled a long time between
themselves until the other powers interfered, when it was mutually or
tacitly agreed that both powers should have and hold their right to the
name, and that there should be two Orders of the Golden Fleece, known
as the Spanish and the Austrian.

The decoration of the Order is a golden ram pendent by a ring which
passes around its middle, and hangs from a jewel of very elaborate design,
with beautiful enamelling in different colors and the whole of which is
suspended from the collar of the Order.   Its motto is: "*Pretium non
vile*" (not to be condemned is the reward of labor), and the festal day is
St. Andrews.

I have not only given you an account of the Mythological idea of the
Golden Fleece, but also a description of the origin of an Order of Knight-
hood of the same name, which I hope will prove of interest to my very
dear Brothers and Friends.   I place a very high value on ancient Mythology, and I really believe that every intelligent man and Brother who
has not had the pleasure of reading Bacon's " Essays and Wisdom of the
Ancients," should most assuredly do so at their earliest convenience for
each and all will find a very great amount of wisdom contained in the
explanations of those so-called fables or mythological ideas of the Ancient
Greeks and Romans.

"MORE ANCIENT THAN THE ROMAN EAGLE."—Yes, the badge of a
Mason is far older than the so-called "Roman Eagle," because "The
Roman Eagle" came into existence just before the Cimbrian War and
previous to the commencement of the Christian Era.   We learn from
Xenophon and other ancient authorities, that the Eagle, with its wings
displayed, represented the standards of the Persians, long before the
"Roman Eagle" was even dreamed of, or Rhea Silvia fed the sacred
fire upon the altar of Alba-Longa, and there is no question in my mind
but that the Persians took this emblem from the ancient Assyrians, who

most assuredly carried it as their especial ensign, upon whose banners and staffs it appeared until Imperial Babylon, "Queen city of the World," with her conquering armies bowed their mighty heads beneath the yoke of Cyrus, from whom, no doubt, he borrowed this glorious emblem, the Golden Eagle with extended wings, and placed it upon his own standards as an emblem of Victory over his enemies.

An Eagle stripped of its feathers was carried upon the staffs and standards of the ancient Egyptians as their ensign, while the Lagides or Ptolemies carried as their ensign the head of a White Eagle, stripped; so you see that the Roman Eagle is of mere modern origin compared to its antiquity among those more ancient Empires of the world, for we find it in all ages, in every ancient nation as an emblem holding one of the most exalted places in their mythologies. In a great many nations this glorious bird was held sacred to the Sun, and we find a great many references made to it in the Bible. Like various other symbols it is lost in the hoary ages of antiquity, and like the Cross and Svastica, it belongs to no special age of the world's history; but the "Roman Eagle," that is very different, for the name itself shows from whence it originated.

In the year B. C. 155, Caius Marius, a farmer's son, was born at Arpinum (the birthplace of Cicero), and became, through his own individual exertions, one of the ablest generals of his day, and just before the Cimbrian War he consecrated the Eagle, with extended wings, to be the Roman standard, at the same time doing away with the Wolf, Horse, and the Boar, that had preceded it, and thus the "Roman Eagle" was carried at the head of every Legion of the Roman Empire throughout the world. From that time forward it was known through all the wars of that empire as the "Roman Eagle" or *Rome and her Eagles*, because before her mighty Legions and cohorts this king of birds was displayed and victory came to those sturdy warriors who fought under the outstretched pinions of their glorious "Roman Eagle."

The Eagle was adopted by our own country in the year 1793, and now bears upon her back the dominant coin of the world, the "Almighty Dollar," found in every country upon the face of the earth. The "Little Corporal" Napoleon I, adopted the Eagle in the year 1804. It was superseded by the Iris, or Fleur-de-lys in 1815, and it was again restored by Napoleon III in 1852.

The founding of secular chivalric orders originated during the time when Europe was in continued warfare among the different powers that dominated that continent, in imitation of the various ecclesiastic orders that preceded them. These orders were founded by the reigning sovereigns of the different countries for the express purpose of drawing into more friendly relations and union their prominent Knights and soldiers, so as to ally them, one with another, and at the same time for the purpose of rewarding those who had performed some special service to their King or their country, or to any one whom the Sovereign wished to especially honor, as a mark of esteem, with a special distinction. In this way he drew them nearer and closer to him as sworn friends and companions.

Standing at the head of all the great Orders of Knighthood which still maintain their pristine reputation is that of the Most Noble Order of the Garter that was founded by King Edward III, of England, about the middle of the fourteenth century. It is very difficult to state the exact date of the founding of this order for the simple reason that the original records were lost, and consequently the date is uncertain. The origin of this Order was, according to the legend pertaining to it, as follows:

King Edward III found a garter that had been dropped by the Countess of Salisbury at a ball. He stooped, picked it up and placed it around his leg, near the knee. His courtiers observing the act looked with questioning eyes at the King, when he responded to their looks by saying: "*Honi soit qui mal y pense*" (Evil be to him who evil thinks), or as some translate it: (shamed be he who thinks evil of it.) To this finding of a garter the foundation of this noble Order is ascribed and the distinguishing insignia, unlike other orders, is not the badge or collar, but the garter itself, consisting of a blue ribbon of velvet, edged with gold, having a golden buckle, worn upon the left leg of the gentlemen ; but when the sovereign is a woman it is always worn by her upon the left arm, and near the elbow.

The badge called the George, or Great George, is a representation of a figure of St. George in the act of killing the dragon, suspended from the collar of gold, composed of twenty-six coiled garters, connected together with links of a beautiful design. The lesser George is worn pendant from a blue ribbon over the left shoulder, which is an eight-pointed star (silver) having the cross of St. George in the middle, while around it is the garter itself, on which is inscribed the motto of the Order. In the year 1344, on the 19th day of January, it was placed under the protection of " God, the Virgin Mary, St. George of Cappadocia and St. Edward the Confessor."

The vesture of the order consists of a mantle of blue velvet, lined with white silk, with a hood and short tunic of crimson velvet ; a black velvet hat, surmounted with a plume of white ostrich feathers, in the center of which is a tuft of black heron feathers. Its members originally consisted of the Sovereign, the Prince of Wales and twenty-five Knight companions ; but it is now open to such other English princes and foreign Sovereigns as are entitled to the honor. The usual number of Knights were about fifty, all of whom were elected by the Knight companions themselves, but now they are appointed by the reigning Sovereign.

THE WHITE LEATHER APRON.—The most profound philosophical secrets of Masonry have been hidden in her symbols, wherein are to be found the deepest and most sublime Truths known to the ancient Mystic Philosophers of every age. No matter to what part of the world we force our investigation we shall find a series of symbols in each and every one of them as old as the world itself, symbols that contain the most sublime and profound Metaphysical and Theosophical Truths known to man. A knowledge of which will enable the student to come to an understanding of himself and his own potential forces latent within his heart, which will draw him closer to his God, purify his morals, elevate his soul and unfold to his view the sublime Truths contained in the Secret Doctrine. It will initiate him into the Wisdom of the ancient Mysteries and enable him to understand the teachings of Buddha, Zarathustra, Hermes, Confucius, Pythagoras, Orpheus, Socrates, Plato, in fact all the ancient philosophers of every age, who taught their pupils and followers a knowledge of God, Man and Nature, through a glorious symbology. These early philosophers threw aside all dogmas and creeds and awakened the dormant intellectual qualifications of their students by song, symbols and impressive exhibitions, which aroused their imagination and brought into use the latent faculties of thinking for themselves.

Now, my dear Brothers and Friends, I desire that each and every one of you shall have aroused within *yourselves* these latent faculties of understanding now dormant within *you ;* faculties that will enable each and every one of you to thoroughly comprehend those sublime and glorious symbols that permeate our beloved fraternity, so that you may live to learn and learn to know and meditate upon those profound Metaphysical, Philosophical and Theosophical emblems that we see in every degree of our beloved Scottish Rite.   It is a duty we owe to ourselves and our fellow man and Brother to earnestly study, until we thoroughly comprehend the profound philosophy which permeates our beloved fraternity.   In comprehending the full depth of its sublime teachings we shall realize that it is our *Duty* to enlighten and instruct our brother by the wayside, by showing him not only their Ineffable beauties, but to point out the path which will lead him on to a knowledge of himself and higher planes of spiritual unfoldment.

THE WHITE APRON.

I want no Fleece of Gold.
The symbol of fabled, fruitless quest,
To wear such now were but an idle jest,
    Worn out and old.

Give me no Eagle Roman,
Type of dominion, badge of servitude ;
No Emperor rules here ; however good,
    He is but human.

No Garter, and no Star—
Of old-world rank and wealth the symbols these,
A pompous show the multitude to please ;
    Leave such afar.

No Prince or Potentate
Shall ever place his Order on my breast ;
I would not choose to kneel at his behest
    Or on him to wait.

I serve no sceptered king,
I know not how to crouch at others' feet ;
It is not thus, I trow, that Masons meet—
    My apron bring !

This lambskin, soft and white,
Means brotherhood with neither guile nor strife ·
Means single-hearted purity of life—
Our actions right.

—*Sydney Free Mason.*

The Masonic Apron worn in the Blue Lodge should be made from a pure, unspotted white lamb skin, for *white* in every country and in every age has ever been an emblem of innocence and purity; in consequence of this fact Masonry has ever preserved this color and emblem from time immemorial. It has been used from the threshold to the summit of each and every degree of our most illustrious fraternity. . The symbol of a perfect square surmounted by a triangle is far older than the Babylonian or Egyptian Mysteries, and a knowledge of this most profound symbol will instruct and lead us on to the true meaning of the wise exhortation of the Delphic Oracle "*Know thyself.*"

The white leather Apron should be free from all garniture or device of any kind. It should never be substituted by silk, satin, fine linen or any other rich material, neither should it be decorated with rosettes or gold and silver trimmings, but just a simple, plain white lamb skin, with no distinctive decoration upon it. The only distinguishing feature about it should be the manner in which it is worn.

The Neophyte, on being invested with this sublime symbol, is taught to wear it with the bib or triangle fully displayed above the square, while in the second degree we find that the descent has been made and the apron, as now worn, represents a perfect square. In the next degree the ascent begins and we find the left hand corner of the apron changed, thus demonstrating to the Aspirant that the higher spiritual forces are beginning to dominate the lower animal propensities within, thus entirely changing the shape of the apron from the square to the triangle.

Now as the candidate advances into the higher degrees there are certain colors and decorations placed upon the apron, as distinguishing marks, and these various devices and decorations are always symbolical of the profound teachings that underlie the beautiful and profound ceremonies. Masonry is a "progressive science," and after the Neophyte has demonstrated that he has thoroughly learned the first lesson taught and

THE LITTLE TEMPLE OF MEDINET HABU

JACHIN AND BOAZ.

is keeping his promise, by endeavoring, with all his will and energy to subdue his passions and improve himself in Masonry, then and then only, is he permitted to place a distinguishing mark upon the spotless emblem by wearing it according to the ancient customs of the fraternity.

The Masonic apron is composed of a square and a triangle. The first represents the Lower Quaternary or animal man, while the Triangle with the point turned upwards, as in the Entered Apprentice degree, represents the Upper Triad, the imperishable part of man. Man is a sevenfold evolving human being, whose physical body is composed of a mass of living elemental units, that are vibrating within their cells, ever coming and going, continually changing, but ever preserving the body in the self-same mould, or form, that it received from the Hiranyagarbha and Tahbic Elementals.

The Seven Principles of Man are in their exoteric classification: 1st. THE PHYSICAL BODY. 2d. THE ASTRAL BODY. 3d. THE LIFE PRINCIPLE. 4th. KAMA. 5th. MANAS. 6th. BUDDHI. 7th. ATMA. (The order in which I have named the Principles is from Matter to Spirit.)

We will now consider these various principles and write upon them so that you, my dear friends and Brothers, may be enabled to understand the true meaning that underlies the profound symbology of the Masonic apron.

THE PHYSICAL BODY OF MAN, the *first* of the Seven Principles contains within itself all the various organs necessary for the development of the other principles and its own existence, and is built of the self-same material as all the other forms that are manifest to our physical senses, and is what the Hindu calls Prakriti or Matter. Now this Prakriti that goes to make up the physical body of Man is the very same kind of "*stuff*" that builds the waving corn, the rippling brook, the meadow and the mountain, the grasses of the field, or the dust and stones that we tramp beneath our feet. All are alike, and there is no difference between the material moleclues of the animal, or vegetable, mineral or man. They are all alike in essence and the only differentiation between them is their shape, for the molecules that go toward the upbuilding of one form are chemical compounds that are to be found in all others.

Both the Animal and the Vegetable kingdom are intimately related, one to the other, and whatever the plant has selected from the darkness of the earth or the surrounding atmosphere, is transferred and assimilated by Man, and the self-same atoms manifesting themselves in the molecular forms of the animals and vegetables of bygone ages, are the very same kind of cells vibrating in the organisms of our own bodies to-day.

"The molecule has in it the Seven Principles, in their Prakritic manifestations. As man, as a whole, contains every element that is found in the universe, and as there is nothing in the Macrocosm that is not in the Microcosm, so every molecule is, in its turn, the mirror of its universe, Man. It is this which renders man alone capable of conceiving the universe on this plane of existence; he has in him the Macrocosm and the Microcosm."

Man's Physical Body has its seven aspects, each aspect representing a Principle; then each of these has its own seven sub-divisions, each sub-division in its turn representing a Principle; and we have the "forty-nine fires" as seen in the Physical Body. It is because of this intricate correspondence, carried out in every detail, that men will ultimately be able to come into contact with every realm of being in the Universe.

Man may be studied from the various aspects above mentioned to a very great advantage by the student who is searching for more Light and a knowledge of himself, because each aspect represents a different principle, and, therefore, in his studying those different aspects or principles he will discover that his consciousness will function on these various aspects or planes of existence, states, or conditions of being. If he has aroused their latent forces and made them active and subservient to his WILL, then he can pass from one plane to another and function upon just as many as he has brought into activity. There are not many men who can function upon all planes, but the potentiality of being enabled to do so is latent within every man.

Annie Besant explains consciousness working on different planes very nicely in her "Seven Principles," pages 6 and 7, wherein she says: "A man may be conscious on the physical plane that is in his physical body, feeling hunger and thirst, the pain of a blow or a cut. But let the man be a soldier in the heat of battle and his consciousness will be centered in his passions, his emotions, and he may suffer a wound without knowing it, his consciousness being away from the physical plane, acting on the plane of passions and emotions; when the excitement is over, consciousness will pass back to the physical, and he will feel the pain of his wound. Let the man be a philosopher, and as he ponders over some knotty problem he will lose all consciousness of bodily wants, of emotions, of love and hatred; his consciousness will have passed to the plane of intellect, he will be "Abstracted," *i. e.*, drawn away from considerations pertaining to his bodily life and fixed on the plane of thought.

"Thus may a man live in these several conditions, one part or another of his nature being thrown into activity at any given time and an understanding of what man is, of his nature, of his powers, his possibilities, will be reached more easily and assimilated more usefully if he has studied along these clearly defined lines, than if he be left without analysis, a mere confused bundle of qualities and states."

According to the exoteric teachings of the ancient Egyptians Man was composed of Four Principles :—1st. The Physical Body. 2nd. The Ka or Astral Body. 3rd. The Bi or Ba, or the Soul. 4th. The Khoo or or Luminous Spark, the God in Man (see Chap. XIII of this work.)

Man, according to the Christian idea is composed of Body, Soul and Spirit, and yet, I am very sorry to say, that there are but very few who know the difference between the Soul and the Spirit, and in fact I believe this division into Body, Soul, and Spirit, has been kept separate from the general teachings of Christianity, because a careful.investigation of the three-fold division would simply prove that instead of three, there would be found seven.

The Astral Body or Linga Sharira is the *second* of the Seven Principles of Man. It is composed of a far more subtle matter than that of the Physical Body, and is not perceptible to our ordinary senses, as it is made up of Astral matter, a substance that is just beyond our physical senses, although Clairvoyants are enabled to see these bodies and describe them to us; but we ourselves are unable to do so, because the matter of which they are composed is in a finer state than we can see or feel.

The Linga Sharira is the exact duplicate of the Physical Body, like the Ka of the ancient Egyptians (described in Chap. XIII of this work.) It is often seen at spiritualistic meetings in so-called spirit manifestations, or materializations and in order that my readers may be enabled to understand the "Modus operandi" of the "spirit manifestations" I will say :

The Linga Sharira is the vehicle of the Life forces for the Physical Body and draws from the great ocean of Jiva the Prana to support the body. It gathers up the necessary properties from the surrounding kingdoms to give its counterpart, the Physical Body, the necessary life forces and energy for its continued existence. " Life " cannot pass immediately and directly from the subjective to the objective, for nature passes gradually from sphere to sphere, overleaping none.   The Linga Sharira serves as the intermediary between Prana and the Sthula Sharira (Physical Body), drawing Life from the ocean of Jiva and pumping it into the Physical Body as Prana.   For Life is in reality Divinity, Parabrahman, the Universal Deity.   But in order that it may manifest on the physical plane it must be assimilated to the matter of that plane ; this cannot be done directly, as the purely physical is too gross, and thus it needs a vehicle, the Linga Sharira.

If we should desire to investigate spirit manifestations we should go to some good spirit medium and watch very carefully the whole proceedings. The first thing we notice will be the medium going through a series of peculiar convulsive movements and twitchings of the various parts of the body, which very soon cease and the medium remains perfectly passive. Now, if we place our finger upon the medium's pulse we shall find it gradually dropping, and we will soon begin to realize that the life forces are leaving the physical in order to vitalize the Linga Sharira or Astral Body of the medium, which may now be seen oozing out from the left side of the body, in the shape of a greyish violet-colored vapor, that will gradually form itself into a duplicate of the medium's body, feature for feature, and if left undisturbed will stand beside the medium, attached to the body by a very slender thread.

If one goes to this meeting for the purpose of seeing some loved one who has passed away and if there should be no one present among the audience with a stronger *will* force than theirs, they will be enabled to mould the plastic Astral Body of the medium into any form they may desire and all those who are present will recognize the various forms as they are moulded by the will power alone. In proof of this fact let me quote you from Annie Besant's " Seven Principles," page 13.

" The Linga Sharira plays a great part in 'spiritualistic' phenomena. Here again the clairvoyant, seeing on the Astral plane, can help us. A clairvoyant can often see the Linga Sharira oozing out of the left side of the medium, and it is this ethereal double which often appears as the ' materialized spirit,' easily moulded into various shapes by the thought-currents of the sitters, and gaining strength and vitality as the medium sinks into a deep trance."

The Countess Wachtmeister, who is clairvoyant, says that she has seen the same " spirit" recognized as a near relative or friend by different sitters, each of whom saw it, according to his expectations, while to her own eyes it was the mere double of the medium. So again H. P. Blavatsky told me that when she was at the Eddy homestead, watching the remarkable series of phenomena there produced, she deliberately moulded the " spirit" which appeared into the likeness of persons known to herself and to no one else present, and the other sitters saw the types she produced by her own will-power, moulding the plastic astral matter of the Medium's Linga Sharira. And this Principle, in the form that we now find it as the duplicate of the medium's physical body and separated from it, is devoid of consciousness and perfectly senseless on the physical plane, although it contains the real organs of our senses.

I have spoken of this Principle as the centre of sensation Chapter X of this work. There is one thing I wish my readers to thoroughly understand and which is that the Ethereal double, and in fact Quaternary Man, is composed of molecules that are in-souled by Atoms; while the Upper Triad is atomic, containing all the potential forces of the lower Principles and at the same time all the higher spiritual forces that belong exclusively to *Atma, Buddhi, Manas*. I have already given you an account of the death of the physical body in Chapter X; but here let me give you an idea of what death means for this Ethereal Double, the *second* Principle of Man :

The physical and the Ethereal Body are both on the same plane, and are both molecular in their constitution. They are interdependent one to the other, therefore death to the physical body means the destruction of the other. Just before death occurs the Ethereal counterpart oozes forth from the left side of the physical body, in the manner described above; and when the last breath has been drawn and death claims

23

it, the thread that links the two together has broken, and those who are watching exclaim "he is dead." The Ethereal Double, now freed from its physical counterpart still remains with it, hovering around in its immediate neighborhood, just as the *Ka* of the ancient Egyptians (as already described), or as ghosts are often seen by people, either in the grave-yard or near the vault wherein the body has been deposited. It is very often seen revisiting the chamber where the death occurred and thus continues to act until the physical body disintegrates and becomes the "dust of the earth. Just as fast as the physical body decays and passes away the Ethereal double fades out with it until all that remains of either is faint glimmering violet-colored lights hovering over the graves of the dead, only seen by clairvoyants.

Before finishing on the Linga Sharira, I desire that you, my dear readers, should know that every Principle has its seven aspects, as I have hereinbefore stated; but, in addition to this every cell and organ in the body has its seven component parts, and the Principles are related in themselves to some special organ of the body. The *Spleen* belongs especially to this Second Principle, and like all the others, have their correspondences not only in every cell but in all the great organs of the body; for instance: The Brain is the centre of Intellectual Consciousness, having seven divisions, each one of which corresponds to one of the Seven Principles of the human body, and yet as a whole corresponds to Psycho-Intellectual Man. This assertion or statement is a positive fact and proves the great ' Truth" that every molecule is a mirror of the universe, and every microcosm the mirror of a macrocosm.

THE LIFE PRINCIPLE, "PRANA," is the *third* of the Seven Principles. Everything that exists in the Kosmos is bathed in an ocean of Jiva, or Life, and every form that we see around us, is permeated with its essence. The earth itself and all the stars glittering in the infinitude of space, are immersed in this great ocean. But that portion of Jiva that is in Man, and which permeates his whole being, is strictly speaking, Prana, or the "Breath of Life." It is what the Hebrew calls "*Nephesch*," and which at our birth is breathed into our nostrils with the *fourth* Principle and these two blended together, constitute the Vital Spark, giving *instinctual life* to both animal and Quaternary Man. Prana is an infinitesimal portion of the great ocean of Jiva, manifesting itself in molecular forms and the Linga Sharira is the *Upadhi* or Vehicle through which this Principle acts.

H. P. Blavatsky defines this vehicle as: "Upadhi means that through which a force acts. The word 'vehicle' is sometimes used to convey the same idea. If 'force' be regarded as acting, 'matter' is the Upadhi through which it acts. Thus the Lower Manas is the Upadhi through which the Higher can work; the Linga Sharira is the Upadhi through which Prana can work. The Sthula Sharira (physical body) is the Upadhi for all the Principles acting on the physical plane."

Nature is all one piece, and yet a unity, expressed in variety. All her changing differentiations and most extraordinary manifestations orginate from the same source. Rock. Plant, Animal, and Man have the same Life, differing only in degree; but the force is not so distinct in the lower as it is in the higher forms. A dog has the same life as the collar he wears upon his neck, or the house that shelters him from the sun or rain; for the simple reason that there is only ONE LIFE and everything is bathed in it; but in the dog it is manifested in a different manner from the collar, or the house, on account of their organic structure.

"All is life, and every atom of even mineral dust is a life, though beyond our comprehension and perception, because it is outside the range of the laws known to those who reject occultism." Nature streams in one continuous flow from the Absolute; every individual atom, even of her chaos, is peremeated by an adequate mind; every atom has its life and guiding directing force or energy.

Life is stratified, and but dimly sensed in the mineral and stone, and yet every particle of both mineral and stone are in a state of active vibration. It is filled with motion in the plant, and stands upon the boundary of *instinct;* while in the animal we find it filled with instinctual life and standing upon the very threshold of *reason;* but in Man we find the intellectual and truly spiritual dominating the animal propensities, which, with his reasoning faculties fully aroused, he can step across the threshold, lift the veil and stand within the presence of his God.

In him are the potential forces that will make him the highest being in Nature's evolutionary processes. He has climbed from out the dust of the earth upon every rung of the ladder of life. His body has been built from the bones and sinews of all below him; he has fed on all things, and existed in all forms from primordial matter to intellectual Man. The gases concentrate their forces in him, the very wind, rain, storm and sunshine hold him in solution. One of our most eminent scientists said: "He knows of Ox, Mastodon, Bird, and Plant, because he has just come out of them, and part of the egg-shell still adheres." The plowman, the plow, and the furrow, as well as the flowers and fruits of the field, the trees and the sunshine, which invigorates and stimulates growth, are all of the same "stuff." Prana or Life circulates throughout the physical body by way of the arteries and veins, impregnates every corpuscle with its life-giving forces, or energy, and reaches every part of the body in order to vivify and strengthen it, the heart being the medium through which it acts; compelled to action by the Linga Sharira, which is the vehicle of "these Pranic elements, the Devourers, which build up and destroy the human Body." It passes through the arterial system in all its wonderful ramifications, back through the veins into the heart and lungs again, and is continually forcing renewed Life and energy through all parts of the body.

KAMA, or THE DESIRE BODY is the *fourth* of the Seven Principles and completes our *Quaternary Man*, the emblem or symbol of which is the lower part of the badge of a Mason, a square. It (Kama) is often called the Animal Soul.

This Principle contains all our emotions and passions, such as love, anger, hate, jealousy, sexual desire, etc., all of which belong to the Kamic plane. This Principle is dual in its nature, for it has a desire for good and a desire for evil. It is continually lusting after things in order to gratify its animal passional nature and propensities.

What is known as desires of the Body have their origin in *Thought*, for thought occurs before the desire is formed. But this subject will be treated in the next Principle, "Manas." When evil tendencies and impulses have been thoroughly impressed on the physical nature, they cannot be at once reversed. The molecules of the body have been set in a Kamic direction and—though they have sufficient intelligence to discern between things on their own plane, *i. e.* to avoid things harmful to themselves—they cannot understand a change of direction, the impulse to which comes from a higher plane. If they are too suddenly and too violently forced into a reverse action, madness or death will result.

" The Kama during life does not form a Body which can be separated from the physical Body. It is intermolecular, answering molecule
for molecule to the physical Body and inseparable from it molecularly.
Thus it is a form, yet not a form ; a form within the physical Body, but
incapable of being projected outward as a form. This is the Inner, or
Astral Man, in whom are located the centres of sensation, the psychic
senses, and on whose intermolecular *rapport* with the physical Body all
sensation and purposive action depends. At death, every cell and molecule gives out this essence, and from it with the dregs of the Heranya-
garbha is formed, the separate Kama Rupa ; but this can never come
during life."

With Kama we have built up Quaternary Man, the animal pregnant
with instinct ; but *devoid of reason* it is simply a brute, as it were, that
dwells in the house that has been fitted up for the indwelling of the Mind.
It is now simply the personality, although a perfect entity, for it has a
body with its ethereal double, its life, animal soul, and all the passions
and desires of the lower animal, with just enough sense or instinct to eat
when it is hungry, seek shelter from the rain or storm, and yet, with all
its instinctual nature fully aroused, it is only an animal. It has no
intellectual reasoning faculties and can never develop above the animal,
until its Lord and Master, the Divine Thinker, enters fully into the
house that has been prepared for it, and by its presence makes it Man
and gives it both MIND and WILL.

MANAS, THE THINKER or MIND is the *fifth* of the Seven Principles.
In reaching the Upper Triad and Manas we come to one of the most
difficult and complicated of the Principles to understand, more especially
is this so of Lower Manas, which we will consider as a Principle in
order to study its workings in the Lower Quaternary.

One of the most important points about the Lower Manas is to comprehend the relationship existing between it and the Higher.

Manas is a Sanskrit word and comes from Man, the root of the Verb
to Think, and in this we will call Manas *The Thinker*, instead of *Mind*,
because this *fifth* Principle is the Re-incarnating Ego, the immortal, individual Man, that is described in the "Voice of the Silence" page 31, in the
exhortation addressed to the Neophyte for initiation : " Have perseverance
as one who doth for evermore endure. Thy shadows (personalities) live

and vanish ; that which is in thee shall live for ever, that which in thee *knows*, for it is knowledge, is not fleeting life ; it is the man that was, that is, and will be, for whom the hour shall never strike."

Madame H. P. Blavatsky gives a very clear description of this in the " Key to Theosophy," page 183-4 : " Try to imagine a ' Spirit,' a celestial Being, whether we call it by one name or another, divine in its essential nature, yet not pure enough to be *one with the* ALL, and having, in order to achieve this, to so purify its nature as to finally gain that goal. It can do so only by passing *individually* and *personally*, *i. e.*, spiritually and physically through every experience and feeling that exists in the manifold or differentiated Universe. It has, therefore, after having gained such experience in the lower kingdoms and having ascended higher and still higher with every rung on the ladder of being, to pass through every experience on the human planes. In its very essence it is THOUGHT, and is therefore called in its plurality *Manasa putra* ' the Sons of the (Universal) Mind.'

" *This individualized* ' Thought' is what we Theosophists call the *real* human EGO, the thinking entity imprisoned in a case of flesh and bones. This is surely a Spiritual Entity, not Matter, and such Entities are the incarnating EGOS that inform the bundle of animal matter called mankind and whose names are *Manasa* or ' Minds.' But once imprisoned, or incarnate, their essence becomes dual ; that is to say, the *rays* of the Eternal divine Mind, considered as individual entities, assume a two-fold attribute which is (*a*) their *essential* inherent characteristics, heaven-aspiring mind (*Higher Manas*), and (*b*) the human quality of thinking, or animal cogitation, rationalized, owing to the superiority of the human brain, the *Kama*-tending or Lower Manas. One gravitates toward Buddhi, the other tending downward, to the seat of passions and animal desires."

Now the house (Quaternary Man) that has been slowly built up for this " personal Ego," does not fully receive its glorious tenant at birth, like " the breath of Life," Kama-Prana, the " personality " is not individ-ualized until the child has reached the sixth or seventh year of its age ; but after that time our Thinker " dons his coat of Skin " and then he or she is held morally responsible for all their acts in *Thought or Deed*, and passes under the Law of Karma " before which period, even according to the canon of the Church and Law, no child is deemed responsible. In the Greek Eastern Church no child is allowed to go to confession before the age of seven, after which he is considered to have reached the age of reason."

Manas itself is a pure ray of Divine Light from the World Soul, in which there is no differentiation. It belongs to a higher plane than the gross molecular matter composing the form of Quaternary Man, and consequently cannot manifest in the physical Body. In order that it may be enabled to do so Manas becomes dual by evolving a Ray from its own Divine Light, clothing itself with Astral matter and entering into the human tabernacle, and thus becoming Lower Manas, whose vehicle is the Brain.

Its subdivisions correspond and are the organs of the subdivisions of the Thinker, and the convolutions of the cerebral hemisphere are shaped by the action of Thought which is being continually changed into far more complicated convolutions by the Thinker himself. It is Lower Manas that transforms animal man into the thinking, reasoning, human being.

Our Thinker has now reincarnated, clothing itself in a new personality, and in doing so has taken upon itself the sting of death, for this descent of spirit into matter is the Metaphysical, Theosophical and Philosophical conception of death. The very fact of it having passed into another personality brings with it a second death and that is the death in Kama Loka, or at least that particular portion of it which remains in the Kama Rupa, for just as soon as death takes possession of the physical body and this incarnation is finished Kama-Manas withdraws itself from the body and clothes itself with astral matter, that will have a conscious existence on this plane for a period of one hundred and fifty years. At the end of this period all of the unsullied portions of the Manasic Ray has disentangled itself from the Kama Rupa, taking with it all of the experiences gained during the earth life which are worthy of assimilation to the Higher Ego, and thus Manas again becomes One and the Kama Rupa eventually breaks up, leaving behind it a record of its misdeeds, the Tanhic Elementals.

It is during earth life, when the Divine Ray has descended into and incarnated in the flesh that it finds itself crucified between two thieves, for Kama tries to drag it down to its own animal, passional plane, or state, and at the same time its Father in Heaven is endeavoring to influence it to higher hopes and aspirations, to purer spiritual planes of Paradise.

This is where the battle rages between good and evil, or God and the Devil, and the battle-ground within man himself. Man receives immortality through the conquest of his own animal passional nature, therefore you must recognize the necessity for each and every human being to learn to subdue and purify Kama, so that its force and energy may be directed by its *Divine Master* Manas, for if this animal within us be so trained that the material instincts within us are killed, and it becomes subject to DIVINE WILL, then will we be assured that we shall be at one with our Father in Heaven, and like Christ, know that *He* and *I* are *One*.

Now do not think for one moment that by applying the forces of the subjugated Kama for the advancement of the intellectual qualifications latent within us that we kill out selfishness; we do not, for if you only pause to consider this fact, you will find that the more intellectual you desire to become, the less spiritual you will be, for intellect by itself is purely selfishness, for this reason intellectual development is a cold, heartless desire to gratify the personal *I*, and it is pure and unadulterated selfishness, with not a spark of Divine Love or Compassion.

" True knowledge is of Spirit, and in Spirit alone, and cannot be acquired in any other way, except through the region of the higher mind, the only plane from which we can penetrate the depths of the all-pervading Absoluteness. It is plainly to be seen that a man may be a morally good man and very intellectual, and at the same time not have the faintest glimmer of spirituality about him, in consequence of which, at death, he will be lost in the whirlpool of Kama Loka."

BUDDHI is the *sixth* of the Seven Principles of Man. It has no function on this physical plane, only when it is united to Manas, then it becomes Divine Consciousness. Buddhi is in itself so much higher than physical man that it cannot possibly enter into direct relationship with him, and only through and by its reflection can it manifest itself as Lower Manas. Buddhi is the *Upadhi* of the ONE ETERNAL ESSENCE; while Manas is the *Vahana* of Mahat the first principle of Universal Intelligence, Divine Ideation, and yet they are both of the same Eternal Essence of the ONE. As such they will be—ever exist, and neither can they ever be annihilated or destroyed, either in essence or consciousness, like the physical personality with its Linga Sharira and the animal soul with its Kamic elements and Kama Rupa, all of whom came from the realm of illusion (Maya), and they will most certainly return again to the realm from which they emanated, and vanish like snow in the hot rays of a summer's sun.

ATMA or ATMAN is the *seventh* Principle which completes the sublime and profound symbol of the badge of a Mason, or white leather apron. The last three Principles are symbolized by the triangle above the square.

H. P. Blavatsky states in the "Key to Theosophy:" "Atma is no individual property of any man, but is the Divine Essence which has no body, no form, which is imponderable, invisible and indivisible, that which does not *exist* and yet *is*, as the Buddhists say of Nirvana. It only overshadows the mortal; that which enters into him, and pervades the whole body, being only its Omnipresent rays, or light radiated through *Buddhi*, its vehicle and direct emanation."

Let me quote you from "Mystic Masonry," by Brother J. D. Buck, 32°: "Atma, Manas, Buddhi represents Father, Son and Holy Ghost. When Christ 'ascended to the Father' he raised his consciousness to the seventh or Atmic Plane, and became in fact (no longer in essence only) ONE WITH GOD." These three principles in man compose the Spiritual Soul; the Immortal part of man; while Atma-Buddhi constitute the Higher-Self, the latent or potential God in man. The lower quaternary Body, Life-Principle, Form-Body and Kama (or Desire) are symbolized by a square. To make it plain, let us say that the triangle incarnates in the square; that is, the Soul (spiritual) "descends into matter." The Body is the *vehicle* of Life; Life is the *vehicle* of the Astral Body; the Astral Body is the *vehicle* of Kama; Kama is the *vehicle* of Manas; Manas is the *vehicle* of Buddhi; and Buddhi is the *vehicle* of Atma. This is the orderly relation or sequence of the principles. But as already shown, man is not a mere aggregation of principles, any more than he is a conglomerate aggregation of atoms, molecules or cells. Just as atoms form molecules, molecules cells, cells tissues, tissues organs and organs the whole body; so the Principles, while preserving a similar orderly sequence in relation to each other, are at the same time *organized* in relation to the whole. That is, the Ego, the Thinker, unites with its vehicle, the Body."

Pyramids of Sakkarah—Lisht—Medum—The Fayum—Labyrinth.

There is a land where Time no count can keep,
  Where works of men imperishable seem;
  Where, through Death's barren solitude, doth gleam
Undying hope for them that sow and reap:
Yea, land of life, where death is but a deep
  Warm slumber, a communicable dream,
  Where, from the silent grave far voices stream
Of those who tell their secrets in their sleep.

—N. D. RAWNSLEY.

CHAPTER XVI.

PYRAMIDS OF SAKKARAH—LISHT—MEDUM—THE FAYUM—LABYRINTH.

THE Pyramids of Egypt, at Gizeh, situated in the most northern part of the site of ancient Memphis, received treatment in the eleventh Chapter of this work, while the reader will be taken in this Chapter to the extreme part of its southern line or boundary and visit the Pyramids of Sakkarah, Dashur, etc.

Having already described the Serapeum and the tomb of Tih, the necropolis of Sakkarah, which takes its name from the village located here, will constitute a continuation of my narrative. It is the oldest and at the same time the most modern of the cemeteries of ancient Memphis. It is four and one-half miles long, with an average breadth of three-fourths of a mile, and like the cemetery at Gizeh, properly speaking, belonged to the ancient capital of Lower Egypt (*Memphis*). The whole of this vast necropolis has been thoroughly searched by all kinds of people and exploring expeditions. Notwithstanding this fact the indefatigable efforts of Mariette Bay were rewarded by the discovery of the Serapeum as well as many other priceless relics of ancient Pharaonic History.

In our visit to the ruins of Memphis and to the Necropolis of Sakkarah we hired our donkeys at Bedrashen, a distance of about fifteen miles from Cairo, carrying our tents, provisions, etc., along with us, to enable us to camp just where we felt like, and remain as long as we desired, at any particular place, that we might explore the ruins of this ancient metropolis at our leisure.

After selecting our donkeys we started out across a dusty, sandy flat towards the little white-washed depot of Bedrashen. We rode across the track, and passed the squalid mud-hovels amid the date palms that composed the village, and rode on through a motley throng of villagers who had gathered in our path, shouting loudly for "baksheesh," while others were trying to dispose of their fruits and water, which they had for sale. We supplied ourselves abundantly with the fruit and continued on our way along the winding road leading to the celebrated necropolis of Sakkarah.

As we passed through the village of Bedrashen we noticed immense numbers of pigeons flying from their quarters on the walls of the square towers that were built expressly for their nesting places. As we rode along, shouting and laughing at the motley crowd, the dogs ran out and added their yelping chorus to swell the noise, for they ran beside us, barking loudly as we passed by. We soon left village and yelping curs behind and rode on through palm groves, fertile fields, and ponds of stagnant water, catching ever anon glimpses of the Pyramids of Gizeh, away off in the distance, and the mounds and groves of Mitraheny close at hand. We stopped to examine the statues of Rameses II., and continued our journey on towards Sakkarah. Leaving Mitraheny on our right we rode straight along until we turned sharp off to the right, skirting the village of Sakkarah, until we came to the regular camping ground, near the sycamore and well, a short distance north of the village, from which the Necropolis takes its name. Here we camped upon the site of one of the most ancient cities of the world's history.

We pitched our tents and fixed things up very comfortably, spending the night around our camp-fire, under one of the most magnificent moon and starlit nights I have ever seen in Egypt. As we sat there we chatted and talked of the grandeur of ancient Egypt, her lost arts and sciences, the decadence of her philosophies, and the wondrous knowledge possessed by the people by whom the Pyramids were built. These giant shapes were so clearly outlined in the silvery sheen of light softly falling around us, for the moon was at the full, the stars were as bright as electric lights, and as we stood looking around the voiceless city of the dead a picture of the scene was impressed upon my brain that will endure as long as life shall last. We awoke in the early morning and found the sun lighting up with rainbow tints the scenery around us, and the odor of the coffee and our morning meal came floating into the tent, giving us an appetite which was soon satisfied. After breakfast the shaggy little donkeys were brought around, and we were again soon riding off to the southwest, towards the southern group of

DISTANT VIEW OF THE PYRAMIDS OF GIZEH.

ruins at Sakkarah, among which are the *Mastaba Farun* and other tombs, as well as the ruined Pyramid of Pepi II.

In riding across this part of Memphis we find a vast difference in the debris under foot from that at Gizeh, for there it was of a very coarse, sandy, gravelly appearance, with very little else to be seen, but here in Sakkarah we can find all kinds of things, such as scraps of mummy cloths, bandages, fragments of mummy flesh, in fact the whole plateau is covered with relics of all kinds, from human bones to beads, scraps of pottery, broken funeral statuettes, etc.

It was a lovely morning as we started out on our way to visit the ruins of some of the most ancient monuments in the Necropolis of Memphis; stopping here and there before some point of interest, and seeing relics of a prehistoric civilization all around us, scattered about in utter confusion; we pass the ruins of an ancient Pyramid, close beside our path, and yet we did not stop to examine it because we wanted to look at and explore the ruined temples and tombs further on, which we deemed far worthier of our time and attention. There are quite a large number of tombs in this vicinity which have been opened up, carefully examined, and carefully covered again, for the purpose of preserving their interior decorations from the deteriorating effects of the air and the destructive hands of the vandal tourists that swarm through this ancient city of the dead, as well as through the whole of the Nile valley. We made our way directly towards the *Mastaba Farun*, which was originally opened and thoroughly explored by Mariette Bey, who believed it to be the resting place, or tomb, of King Unas, on account of some of the stones used in its construction having the name "Unas" inscribed upon them.

It is a kind of an oblong structure, built with splayed walls, the entrance to which is on the north side; but is now closed with barred gates and fastened, so that we were unable to gain admission to examine the interior. There are quite a number of ruined tombs and other structures in the immediate vicinity as well as numberless mummy pits. Close by is the Pyramid of Pepi II, in a very dilapidated condition, so much so that we gave up the idea of exploring it as the undertaking was considered too dangerous for us to make the attempt. We, therefore, mounted our donkeys and rode off in a northerly direction, that we might examine the Pyramid of Seker-em-sa-f, son of Pepi I, and elder brother of Pepi II, whose mummy was taken from this Pyramid in 1881, and considered the oldest known mummy of to-day. (For an account see Chapter XIII of this work.)

We visited all the Pyramids in the Pepi group and did not attempt to explore any of them excepting the one of Pepi I, into which we descended, and were well repaid for the labor, as the construction of the interior is widely different from those of Gizeh, or any other Pyramid we had heretofore examined. The hieroglyphic inscriptions here are of a pale bluish green color, as well as the interior decorations, and they are well worth seeing; but it was very dangerous to go prospecting around in the interior of this dilapidated monument, consequently we concluded to go over to some ruins which could be seen a short distance from us, off to the south-east, proving on close inspection to be the remains of a ruined Pyramid and the debris of numerous tombs, etc. Here we stopped awhile and hunted among the ruins to see if we could find some relics of these ancient people, in the shape of scarabs, or funeral statuettes, but after grubbing around for an hour or more I found a very small statuette some fragments of opalescent glass, a few beads, and a few pieces of very fine mummy cloth. Becoming satisfied with what we saw here we rode back to our camp, situated about three-quarters of an hour's ride to the north-east.

On returning to camp, weary and tired, we dismounted and soon refreshed ourselves with a good shower bath and found that our appetites had been very much sharpened by our fatiguing ride around this most remarkable plateau. Our welcome meal was soon served, to which we all did ample justice, when we lit our cigars and entered into a lengthy discussion on the religions and philosophies of the people whose remains were scattered around the length and breadth of this necropolis of Sakkarah, for from one end to the other may be seen the flesh and bones, as well as fragments of the cerement clothes that enwrapped them, evidencing rifled graves, and desecration of the dead.

The various tombs examined since we came into this country bear ample evidence that these ancient people were most assuredly filled with the idea of Death and a Future Life. It is very certain they were not Atheists, for they believed devoutly in God and a Life to come. This belief is in fact to be found in all religions throughout the world, but it was specially taught by the ancient Egyptians. The paintings upon the walls, in the interior, are evidences of their belief in a life to come; but we must remember that in the examination of the pictures upon the walls, we are not in the tomb proper, but only in the guest-chamber, far above the tomb itself. (See Chapter XIII of this work.)

The mummy was deposited in a pit below, while its double, the Ka, was supposed to take a great interest in all things earthly, and they thoroughly believed that it would be filled with joy in the success of their sons and daughters, after they themselves had gone to Amenti and they loved to come back and see the pictures of their families reaping rich harvests from the fields they had carefully tilled during their lives.

Just before sundown we saw and studied the very peculiar methods adopted by the sacred beetle of the ancient Egyptians *The Ateuchus Sacer*, the celebrated Scarabæus of the ancient people. They believed that there were no females among these sacred insects and that in order to propagate their species the Scarab would enclose a life germ within a ball of clay or the slime of the Nile mud, that this insect would mould or form itself into a little round ball, after which, it would push it backwards to the desired location and bury it in the sands of the desert and from this grave would arise another Beetle or Scarab that in due time would perform the self-same methods for the continuance of its species.

The Scarabæus was esteemed a very sacred insect among the ancient Egyptians, they considered it an emblem of Immortality and a symbol of the Sun, which demonstrated Life, Death and the Re-incarnation of the Spirit. It was emblematical of the Sun, because, just as the Scarabæus pushed the germ of a Future Life in a round ball of dirt, the Sun pushed the Earth from West to East, making the sun, from the earth, apparently rise or re-incarnate in the East once in every twenty-four hours, which is symbolical of the return of the Spirit to thread itself and its various personalities upon the sutratma of many lives. We retired early, as we anticipated a long day's work on the morrow, in visiting the Step-Pyramid, as well as other points of interest, in this most extraordinary necropolis of Sakkarah and vicinity.

In the morning we got up with the sun, took a slice of dry toast and a cup of coffee and went forth with our guns. Inside of an hour we

24

returned with between three and four dozen very fine quail and a nice lot of ducks, getting back in time for breakfast and an early start to the various places we had planned to visit. Mounting our little donkeys we went skurrying off to the North, riding over fragments of broken pottery, bricks, etc., with here and there large blocks of granite which once belonged to one of the most famous and populous cities of ancient Egypt. We rode up to the Pyramid of Unas which we found in a ruinous condition, and would not have been able to have seen the interior of this monument if it had not been for a party of Cook's tourists, who arrived there just about the same time we did and they having cards of admission and key to the iron gate, we were allowed to enter and examine the interior of this Pyramid with them.

The entrance to it was originally closed with immense blocks of sandstone, which obstructions must have required a vast amount of time and labor to remove, that admittance might be gained into the interior. To-day the entrance is provided with an iron gate, to prevent people going in without permission and destroying the interior decorations and chipping off pieces from the sarcophagus, etc. The entrance leads us into a chamber running off from which are two others, one on each side of this first or entrance chamber. The two larger ones contain quite a number of well-preserved funeral inscriptions and in the one to the right we saw a granite sarcophagus close to the alabaster walls, adorned with very nice paintings of plain simple patterns, whose colors are nearly as bright to-day as when first placed there by the artist B. C. 3,333. We saw here in these chambers the same class of hieroglyphic inscriptions of a bluish green color as those described in the Pyramid of Pepi I. but with this difference they are not in sunk relief, but just simply incised.

To the South and South-East of this Pyramid are the remains of the tombs of the various dynasties from the XVIII upward, to more modern times, but they have all been broken into and ransacked, for the purpose of gathering the priceless treasures and relics from their interiors, or to satisfy the curiosity of vandal explorers. To-day this plain is strewn with fragments of the dead, pieces of wood which formed the coffins, broken pottery, statuettes, mummy clothes, human bones, etc. Instead of rambling around trying to find a tomb that had not been examined before, we made our way to the largest and most celebrated monument of this group, the Step-Pyramid of Sakkarah, which is located about two hundred and fifty yards to the North-east of the Pyramid of Unas.

It is not built with a regular slope like any of the other pyramids from base to summit, neither is it a perfect square, nor does it face the cardinal points of the universe, being built in six stages that recedes one into the other and diminishes in height as well as in breadth. The lowest step being thirty-seven feet high and the upper one twenty-nine feet, and all being about six feet wide. The extreme height of the structure from the base to its summit is one hundred and sixty-seven feet. Much of this monument has been removed, possibly for building purposes in Cairo. The North and South sides measure three hundred and fifty-one feet two inches, and the East and West sides three hundred and ninety-three feet six inches, covering an area of a little over fifteen thousand square yards.

This Pyramid differs from others from the fact that it has four entrances, and the interior is a perfect maze of passages; but its chief peculiarity in the interior is the excavation seventy-seven feet deep by about twenty-four feet square, sunk immediately under the centre of this remarkable monument, the roof of this excavation being dome-shaped of rubble-work, originally supported by wooden rafters, which have long since decayed and fallen away, and the roof is held in place by the strength of the cement with which the rubble-work was made. The bottom of this shaft or excavation is paved with granite blocks, beneath which is a chamber ten feet long and five feet high, the entrance to which was covered up with an enormous block of granite weighing four tons. It is as difficult to describe the plan of the interior of this Pyramid as it is to find out what the monument was originally used for. Many of the chambers have been decorated with a series of bluish-green convex "tiles," on the backs of which are a number of hieroglyphics. General Minutoli entered this Pyramid in the year 1821 and discovered numerous very interesting relics in the various passages and chambers, among which was a gilded skull and two human feet that were ornamented in a most peculiar manner all of which were afterward lost at the mouth of the Elbe.

In many of the chambers and passages were found fragments of broken alabaster and marble vases, stars and broken ornaments that no doubt at one time formed the decorations of the different chambers in this most remarkable "Step Pyramid of Sakkarah." It is rather difficult to make the ascent of this monument alone; but with the help of the Arab guide I had no trouble, comparatively speaking, in reaching the top of the most extraordinary Pyramid. The view from the summit is not near so good as that from the larger one at Gizeh, not being near so high, consequently we could not expect so fine a view.

In rambling around among these Pyramids and tombs we met a party of travellers who were making arrangements for a trip to the Peninsula of Sinai; but had come out to this site of ancient Memphis for the express purpose of meeting some of my own party who had agreed to go with them, so instead of returning to Cairo they all rode over to our camp with us and we were very soon supplied with our evening meal, to which we all did ample justice. After the meal was over we lit our cigars and spent the evening in merriment and song, while the Arab servants and guides were making the necessary preparations for breaking camp. The next morning bright and early we packed our few personal traps, partook of a hasty meal, and rode off to Cairo, leaving the tents, baggage, etc., to be brought in by sumpter camels.

We arrived at Shepheard's dusty and tired, where we soon refreshed ourselves with a good bath and cooling drink from the fountain of Zem Zem, and that night we spent at the hotel with our departing friends. The next morning we wished them "bon voyage," as they started off on their long journey, to follow in the footsteps of the Israelites, to cross the Red Sea and explore the Sinaitic Peninsula. I did not remain in Cairo, as I was very anxious to get away and investigate the Tombs, Temples, Monuments, etc., of Upper Egypt; therefore the rest of us arranged for our boat to meet us at some point on the river to be decided on later, and in order to complete my investigations of the principal Pyramids of the Nile Valley I found that we would have to visit Rikka, to be able to examine the oldest monuments in the world, known as *The Pyramid and Mastabas of Medum.*

There are a great many authorities who believe the Step Pyramid of Sakkarah to be far older than any other fabric in the Nile Valley, basing their opinion or assertions upon the statement of Manetho, who attributes the Step Pyramid to Unenephus, who built the Pyramid at Cochome, as a

CORNER OF THE GREAT PYRAMID,

MAKING THE ASCENT.

monument to one of the Kings of the first Dynasty. Cochome was the Greek form of the hieroglyphic name Ka-kam " the Black Bull," which occurs on the " steles " and sarcophagi of the Apis tombs, as a place in the vicinity of the Necropolis. If this view be correct we have in the Step Pyramid the most ancient structure in the world. But there are numerous authorities who reject these statements, and assign its erection to one of the Kings of the fifth dynasty with very little evidence to prove their statements, consequently we are left to our own judgment in this matter. I shall describe the various monuments and leave it with you, my dear Brothers, as to which is the older.

Between three and four miles South of Sakkarah we find a group of Pyramids at Dashoor, they are four in number, two of stone and two of brick. The most Northern of the stone Pyramids is nearly as large as the Great Pyramid at Gizeh at the base, but is not nearly so high. It contains three chambers, lying one beyond the other, and they are constructed in a very peculiar manner, for the stones which form their sides overlap each other and draw in toward the roof, making it a pyramidical chamber, large at the bottom and very small at the top or ceiling. The other stone Pyramid is rather remarkable on account of the manner of its construction, it having been built at two different angles and is known as the " Blunted Pyramid." Its base is six hundred and nineteen feet long and its height three hundred and twenty-one feet. There was a very peculiar door used for closing the entrance to this Pyramid. It was hung on a horizontal stone hinge, and was discovered by W. Flinders Petrie during his researches among this group.

Mr. M. de Morgan made some very valuable discoveries in the years 1894-95 among the brick Pyramids of this group. He was very earnest and anxious in his explorations of these monuments, and gave the whole of his time and attention to the drifting into one of them, in order to find the regular passage or entrance into the interior. After he had drifted in to a considerable distance he discovered the real entrance, originally formed by the men who constructed the Pyramid itself, and as soon as he found this passage-way he began exploring the interior.

After traversing various passages, he had the good fortune to discover the burial place of two royal ladies belonging to the twelfth dynasty, whose tombs had not been disturbed since they were deposited there by tender hands, *thirty centuries before Christ*, and just as they had been laid to rest in those remote and by-gone days of prehistoric civilization, so were they found, with not a single article displaced or disturbed. The jewels and golden ornaments glistened as bright and beautiful upon them as when first placed there by their loving friends who laid them to rest, away back in the remote ages of the past. The whole of these jewels and ornaments, as well as many other interesting relics are to be seen to-day in room seven at the Gizeh Museum.

This same gentleman, in the year 1896, made some other very important discoveries. Not very far from the house in which he lived during his researches, and quite close to the barren plateau, are to be seen two low mounds formed from the remains of what was originally two brick Pyramids. He thought that possibly he might make new discoveries by investigating the ruins of these ancient monuments, and after considerable time and labor he was rewarded by finding the passage and chambers, which he thoroughly explored in search of relics. In the one farthest to the south he found two small black granite Pyramids about three feet high, and in one of the chambers discovered a very large sarcophagus of red granite with nothing inscribed on it. It is very difficult and dangerous to-day to search among the ruins of this Pyramid, as it is simply impossible to do so without the assistance of men and ropes to help you; and, in fact, will hardly repay one for the time and trouble expended in exploring its dark passages and chambers. The Northern mound contains a sarcophagus in one of the chambers, which can very readily be seen, but this is about all that would interest any one in this ancient ruin.

About nine miles south of this place are to be seen *The Pyramids of Lisht;* but they are in such a ruinous condition that it is not safe for any one to venture into them. Maspero attempted to thoroughly explore them, but he gave it up on account of finding so much water in them. About the same time that M. de Morgan was investigating the group at Dashoor in 1895, Mr. M. Guatier was exploring the ruins of these two Pyramids at Lisht, then considered unimportant, but after careful examination he found within them statues of Usertesen I, very fine specimens of ancient Egyptian sculpture, and later on discovered a very large altar that stood in a funerary chapel that had been built on the east side of the southernmost of the two Pyramids. It is exquisitely carved and is a very fine specimen of ancient Egyptian Art, being dedicated to Usertesen I. This place was, no doubt, the necropolis of one of the ancient cities of the Golden Age of Egypt, when Memphis was in the height of her glory, but to-day it is in utter ruin and naught remains to tell us of the vanished glory of this ancient city except the ruined monuments that I have just described and the few relics discovered within them.

It is fully twelve miles to the south of Lisht before we come to those ancient monuments of Egypt, *The Pyramids and Mastabas of Medum*, of which I have already spoken. Now, after carefully examining these wonderful fabrics, and devoting considerable study and much thought to the subject, I have come to the conclusion that they are the most ancient, in fact the oldest monuments in the world to-day, and for that reason, if no other, they are of especial interest to all men, and well deserving a visit from any one who goes to this most extraordinary part of the World, *The Valley of the Nile*.

One lovely morning we took passage on board a steamer that was going up the river, but stopped at Rikka for the accommodation of any one desiring to visit the celebrated monuments of a prehistoric age at Medum. It was a beautiful morning as our steamer pushed off from the bank, to ascend this glorious old river. There was a strong "etesian" wind blowing and the loud shouts of the sailors, as they hoisted their sails on some of the Dahabiyes, came floating to us over the bosom of the waters, reminding me of by-gone days, and the first time I visited Egypt and took passage on one of the Nile boats to examine the various points of interest that lay along its banks.

When I was a boy, it was the only way that one could travel on a trip to Upper Egypt. Ah! what enjoyable days they were to all of us; the boat was our home, our castle, for a few months at least, if no more. This floating home of ours had a peculiar charm and attraction that is difficult to explain. In our journeyings we could stop just when and where we wished. We could go off and hunt, or examine a tomb or temple at our leisure, and if the wind would not help us, we could always tie up to the bank and amuse ourselves in a dozen different ways. If I were going back to Egypt, to-day, to examine or explore the stupendous fabrics that adorn the banks of this grand old river Nile, I would take the Dahabiyeh in preference to any other mode of travel. Of course, one should not be pushed for time, but go with the understanding that you would have to depend principally upon the wind, with very little tow-path; and all those who travel on a Dahabiyeh will most assuredly enjoy it above all other modes of travel used in Egypt. If they should make the ascent of the first cataract in one of these Dahabiyehs, the memory of it would remain with them so long as life would last. The ride up the Nile on the steamer is very monotonous, between Gizeh and Rikka, for the banks of the river are quite low, and all the villages are very much alike, with but little to be seen, excepting the various groups of Pyramids which rise here and there into our view as we steam along, causing one to ponder upon the prehistoric people who built them and the knowledge to which they had attained, in quarrying and moving tremendous blocks of stone, in order to build those tremendous fabrics that have been the wonder and admiration of every age in the history of the world.

We landed at Rikka and secured donkeys to carry us out to this most remarkable Pyramid, standing seemingly upon a mound that was located fully an hour's ride from the river. It was a most delightful trip, and the great fabric that we are now approaching shines out resplendent in the glorious sunshine, in most exquisite coloring. We rode off down the track and turned into the square green fields of corn, beans, clover, etc., that ran up to the very foot of the necropolis of " Mi-Tum " Medum and the celebrated Pyramid itself, which is called by the fellaheen and Arabs " Harem-el-Kadab," or the False Pyramid. We now discovered that what we had taken to be a mound, upon which this famous Pyramid had been built, was simply the rubbish surrounding it at its base, formed no doubt from the outer casing which rose mound like all around the structure.

Mr. Flinders Petrie spent a great deal of time and patience in his explorations of the various points of interest among the tombs and temples of Medum, and has given to the world a vast amount of information in relation to these ancient buildings of the Third and Fourth dynasties. When first the stone composing this marvellous Pyramid was brought from the quarries it was most assuredly pure white limestone; but to-day it is of a beautiful orange hue, it having gradually changed, with the rolling centuries, from a pure white into a most magnificent yellow color, whose golden hues must be seen in order to be fully appreciated. This Pyramid rises in three stages above an apparent artificial mound, which is at least one hundred and twenty feet above the plain. The first stage above the mound is sixty-nine feet, the second twenty feet, and the third about twenty-three feet, the whole forming a square tower that rises in three stages, whose summit is fully two hundred and thirty feet above the level of the plain, having the appearance of some of the ancient mastabas of the old empire. The whole fabric seems to have lifted itself out of the brown mass of rubbish at its base into a most magnificent, glorious, shining golden tower that points upwards into the azure vault above. Once seen it will live in one's memory through all his life. The entrance to this Pyramid is situated on the north side, nearly fifty-four feet above the level of the desert sands, the passage descending at a certain angle for a distance of two hundred and thirty-four feet, where it falls upon a level passage-way of about forty feet in length, from the end of which a vertical shaft leads upwards into an empty chamber or tomb.

Maspero entered this Pyramid on the thirteenth day of December, 1882 ; when he found the passages and chambers he at once realized that it had been broken into and its sarcophagus and the contents taken therefrom. Mariette Bey states that the name of the king by whose order this Pyramid was erected for the repose of his own mummy is positively unknown, but there is every reason to believe that it was Sneferou, the predecessor of Cheops, for his tomb is unknown. This Pyramid is a most magnificent specimen of ancient Egyptian architecture, with its closely fitting joints and polished blocks of Mokattum limestone showing conclusively the rare excellence to which the ancient Egyptians had attained. Sneferou was, according to Bruysch Bey, the last king of the third dynasty B. C. 3766. Mariette Bey claims that the third dynasty commenced B. C. 4449, and that Sneferou was the first king of the fourth dynasty who reigned about B. C. 4235.

It was in the most northern mastaba of the necropolis of Medum that Mariette, in January, 1872, discovered two of the most marvellous portrait statues that has ever been found. They are almost life-size, and were carved out of limestone, being remarkable as the oldest known statues existing in the world to-day, and represent Ra-Hotep—son of Sneferou, "commander of the king's warriors, chief of the priests in the temple city of On, Heleopolis, the town of the Sun God Ra—and his princess wife, Nofrit, or Nefert, the beautiful—the king's granddaughter." Once seen these statues will never be forgotten, for the exquisite carvings are perfect and shows the wonderful skill and knowledge to which sculptors had attained in that early period, over six thousand years ago. The eyes of these wonderful statues once seen will so impress themselves upon you that you will always remember them, for they are perfectly life-like. The eyes are made of rock crystal, resting upon a back-ground of silver, which reflects the light in such a way that it appears as if they were eyes of a living human being.

In order that you may get the opinion of one of our greatest Egyptologists respecting these statues, I will quote you from Maspero's "Dawn of Civilization," page 363, wherein he states that these two statues were: "discovered in a tomb near Meydoum. According to the chronological table of Mariette, it is five thousand and eight hundred years old. Their rock crystal eyes are so bright that the Arabs employed in the excavation, fled in terror when they came upon the long-hidden chamber. They said that two afreets were sitting there ready to spring out and devour all intruders. These statues were discovered in a half ruined mastaba and have fortunately reached us without having suffered the least damage, almost without losing any of their original freshness. They are to be seen in the Gizeh Museum, just as they were when they were discovered by Mariette in the condition in which they left the hands of the workmen.

"Rahotpu (*Ra-Hotep*) was the son of a king possibly Snofrui (*Sneferou*); but despite his high origin I find something humble and retiring in his physiognomy. Nofrit (*Nefert*), on the contrary, has an imposing appearance, an indescribable air of resolution and command invests her whole person, and the sculptor has cleverly given an expression to it. She is represented with a robe with a pointed opening in the front; the shoulders, bosom, waist and hips are shown under the material of the dress with a purity and delicate grace which one does not always find in modern works of art. The wig secured on the forehead by a richly embroidered band, frames with its somewhat heavy masses the firm and rather plump face; the eyes are living, the nostrils breathe, the mouth smiles, and is about to speak. The Art of Egypt has at times been as fully inspired, it has never been more so than on the day in which it produced the statue Nofrit" (Nefert). Ra-Hotep sits with his right hand extended across his breast and his left upon his knee. He wears a simple jewel upon his neck and his body nude excepting for the waist-cloth that enwraps his loins. It is a most exquisite specimen of ancient Egyptian sculpture. There has never been a time in the history of Egypt when they could produce statuary more speaking and life-like than these two statues of Ra-Hotep and his charming wife, the Lady Nefert.

Medum has most assuredly furnished a great number of works of Art, which certainly goes to prove that sculpturing, frescoing, painting, etc., was most thoroughly comprehended by the artists who wrought them, when the Craftsman who worked in the Mokattum hills were quarrying the stones for the erection of the Pyramids in the extraordinary city of Memphis. The tomb in which Mr. Flinders Petrie made his headquarters during his explorations of this ancient necropolis, the tomb of Nefermaat, was a veritable treasure house of beautiful carvings, paintings, etc., illustrating the scenes of hawking, hunting, fishing and agricultural pursuits, very finely executed. It was in this tomb, or rather Lady Atot's chamber, that Mariette found the fresco of geese which now adorns the Gizeh Museum, and many other beautiful works of Art that were executed by these people long before the Sphinx looked to the East in the plains of Gizeh, across the desert sands of Arabia.

Students of hieroglyphics and ancient Art will find here in Medum a rich field to repay them for their time and trouble. The inscriptions found here upon these monuments present some of the oldest forms of writing, very clear, simple and beautiful in their grammatical construction as well as in clearly defined letters and carvings. Mariette Bey considered the tomb of Nefermaat to be the most carefully constructed and the best built tomb throughout the whole of the "Land of Egypt." The paintings are all well preserved, and many of them to-day are most exquisite specimens of Egyptian skill, although executed three thousand seven hundred and fifty years before Christ. The artists who executed the work show rare ability, as they painted and carved true to nature, for nothing is misrepresented, but each and all, in their proper colors and exact proportions. The Craftsmen who built the temple, or tomb, were thoroughly competent and well qualified to handle the enormous blocks of stone found here, and some of them *in the ceiling* measure twenty feet in length and fully three feet thick, weighing not less than forty tons each. This fact alone demonstrates to us, of the present day, the wondrous knowledge in Architecture possessed by the artisans who wrought long centuries before authenticated history. No one visiting the valley of the Nile should fail to see the celebrated tombs and temples of Medum and examine carefully the interior and exterior parts of these very remarkable relics of the " Golden Age of Egypt."

One of the most delightful places in which to spend a winter in Egypt is the Fayum. But few tourists go into this most interesting and fertile oasis that lies just one day's journey from the city of Cairo by rail or about three days on horseback; but all who take the time to go always come away charmed and delighted with their ramblings from one place to another, where the continual clamoring for " Baksheesh, O Hawadji " is seldom or never heard. For my part I much prefer the horseback ride to the cars, for the simple reason that one who goes on horseback will be enabled to take in the whole of the various groups of tombs, temples and Pyramids, from the plains of Gizeh to Medum, and either he or they will most assuredly enjoy the trip far better than they could in the hot dusty cars. If you ride on horseback you can rest when you wish, stop where you like, and examine the various points of interest at your leisure; while on the cars you would only be enabled to catch glimpses of tombs and temples that would well repay you to visit. Again, going on horseback you would be in a far better position to study the manners and customs of the fellaheen, who till the soil to-day in the same manner that their great ancestors did ere Joseph was sold into the " Land of bondage."

Beside all this you will be enabled to see the peculiar encampments of the Bedouin Arabs, who locate here in many of the fields rented from the fellaheen, and feed their camels and horses on the rich lucerne that grows here in such abundance. You will most certainly pass on your way a great many hunters who go out from Cairo to shoot over the cultivated fields that border the desert sands lying along your path, and considered to be the best place for quail shooting throughout the whole of Egypt.

But I do not wish to dwell too long upon the charms of horseback riding from the city of Cairo to the Fayum, for if I did this chapter would lengthen out to such an extent that I would be unable to describe this very interesting part of Egypt where Joseph lived and gave his name to one of the oldest canals in the " Land of Egypt."

The province or district in Egypt called the Fayum is a natural peculiar basin-shaped depression in the Libyan Desert, and is one of the most fertile provinces in the valley of the Nile. It is surrounded by desert sands, with the exception of the fringe of vegetation that adorns Bahr-Yusuf, which connects it with the river Nile and is about two hundred and seven miles in length. It flows into this fertile valley through a natural opening, caused by a peculiar trend of the Libyan chain of mountains, which a little north of Benisuef begin to circle off to the northwest, returning again toward the east and the river Nile. It has in its peculiar convolutions inclosed a very large tract of land, that was called by the ancient Egyptians *Arsinoe* and now known as the *Fayum*, coming from the Egyptian word " Phiom," signifying the sea, marsh or lake country, described in the hieroglyphic inscriptions of the fourth dynasty as " *Ta-she*," the land of the lake.

The opening of this valley is about four miles wide, through which the canal passes, and where it is divided into numerous branches that ramify from the main stem to the various parts of the valley, so as to irrigate and reclaim a vast amount of the desert sands (See Chapter VI of this work). The Fayum is noted for its fertility, as it produces an abundance from all seeds sown or planted in its remarkably rich soil. Here in this wonderful valley are to be seen large fields of corn, cotton, sugar cane, beans, clover, etc., besides all kinds of vegetables. It produces very fine grapes, from which they manufacture an excellent wine. This place is noted for its olives and it abounds in date palm groves, roses growing in rich profusion, while apricots, figs and other kinds of fruit are quite prolific. Considerable cattle is raised here, and since sugar-cane has been planted and found to do so well, a large number of sugar factories are to be found here.

This valley was the site of that ancient reservoir " Lake Moeris," the remains of which are to be plainly seen and traced to-day. It was originally used for the purpose of regulating the annual flow of the inundations of the river Nile, for irrigating the various parts of the " Land of Egypt." Strabo tells us that " Lake Moeris, owing to its size and depth, is capable of receiving the superabundance of water during the inundation, without overflowing the habitations and crops; but later, when the water subsides and after the lake has given up its excess through one of its two mouths, both it and the canal retain water enough for purposes of irrigation. This is accomplished by natural means; but at both ends of the canal there are also lock-gates, by means of which the engineer can regulate the influx and efflux of the water."

The cultivated part of this fertile valley is about twenty-five miles long by about thirty miles wide, and the district contains a population of two hundred thousand inhabitants, while the annual revenue is very nearly a million dollars. Its principal commerce is cotton, corn, cattle, mostly sheep, which are considered to be the best breed in the valley of the Nile. This province contains a large number of towns and villages, and is a perfect paradise for hunters, especially upon and around the borders of Berket el-Qurun (the lake of the Horn).

The water of this lake is very salty and brackish in midsummer, just before the annual inundations of the Nile. It lies considerably below the bed of the river, and is no doubt fed by the filtrations from the canals and the Nile. The view of the lake from the cultivated fields and uplands of the Fayum is just simply grand, as it lies nestling up against the fertile fields and vegetation that goes sloping down to the edge of the rippling waters, shining like a sea of burnished silver, glittering in the glorious sunlight from an unclouded sky, fairly dazzles one's vision. The various shades of green from the fertile fields, tamarisk bushes and dense palm groves lend a chàrm and fascination to the scene that is indescribably grand and beautiful. The lake is nearly thirty-five miles long and about seven miles wide, and its depth varies according to the season of the year. It lies at the foot of a richly cultivated upland on one side and bordered by the desert sands on the other, which stretches off into a series of rolling hills that connect with the rocky mountain chain which bounds our horizon in that direction. The lake abounds with fish, and *in the winter* there is not in the whole of Egypt a better place for hunting, for here are to be found quail in immense quantities and all kinds of aquatic birds fairly swarm from one end of the lake to the other, while among the tamarisk bushes and palm groves are to be found plenty of wolves and wild boar.

There are a few very interesting ruins at various points around this lake, and the principal ones are to be found about fifteen miles from the town of Nesla, and which is called *Quasr Qurun*, the remains of an ancient Egyptian temple, that is well worth visiting. It contains a great many chambers, stairways and passage-ways, giving unmistakable evidences of the good workmanship of the craftsmen who erected it. There are quite a number of ruins scattered around in this vicinity, and among them a number of arches of both stone and brick and partially demolished walls, around which can be found ancient copper coins, fragments of glass, etc., if you will take time to grub around in the sand among the ruins. On the borders of this lake, not far from Senhur, are to be found some old ruins called El-Hamman; in fact, we can find the remains of tombs, temples, reservoirs, etc., all around this lake, that will prove of deep interest to all those who visit them. Medinet el-Fayum, "The town of the Lake," is the capital of the Fayum, and has a population of about forty thousand inhabitants. It is a typical Egyptian town, with its long covered bazar and motley assemblage of people, who congregate there, and its baths, with Greek coffee houses, etc., etc., all going to make up a modern twentieth century town in the valley of the Nile. We notice that these people hold their regular markets on Sunday.

This town is located on one of the main branches of the Bahr Yusuf, where we could see the women continually going and coming at certain times to fill their heavy clay " goolahs " with water, to be used for their household; they carry these heavy " goolahs " upon their heads, with a peculiar grace that is truly remarkable. The canal runs through the town and is distributed to the various parts throughout this fertile valley by devices, such as water-wheels, flumes, etc. The canal in many places is more like a river, as it goes winding along by the houses and walls of the town, giving a charming effect to its surroundings, and reflecting the houses, trees and walls of the town in its flowing waters. There we can see the bearded wheat of ancient Egypt growing luxuriantly, very long in the ear, but short in the straw.

Every person who goes into the Fayum should not fail, upon any consideration, to get an introduction to the *Mudir* of the district, as it would be of very great assistance to either him or them in all their business transactions; but more especially if there is any trouble with the fellaheen, for horse, camel or donkey hire. There are no especial buildings in this modern town, that I cared for, and the only one of real interest that I noticed was the mosque of Quait Bey, which is in a very ruinous condition. It is a kind of a mosaic structure that contains various columns originally belonging to different buildings in the old city of Arsinoe, formerly Crocodopolis, the ancient Egyptian city of *Shat*, or *Pa-Sebek* ("the abode of Sebek"), who is represented with the head of a crocodile, and there in lake Moeris they used to keep this sacred animal, and worshipped it throughout the whole of the Arsinoite Nome in the ancient days of Egyptian history. In fact one of their triads that was worshipped here was Sebek, Hathor, and Horus.

Leo Africanus says, "The ancient city (*Pa-Sebek*) was built by one of the Pharaohs, on an elevated spot near a small canal from the Nile, at the time of the exodus of the Jews, after he had afflicted them with the drudgery of hauling stones and other laborious employments."

There are extensive ruins on the site of this ancient city, and many very important antiquities have been found here, also a large quantity of papyri, mostly Greek, and some of them written in hieroglyphics and hieratic characters dating back to the time of Rameses III.

It was here, within the Fayum, that the celebrated Labyrinth was built by Amen-em-hat III. It was a most extraordinary building and is said to contain three thousand chambers, half of which were subterranean and the other half lying above ground, and the whole of each series connected together by the most intricate passages and irregular corridors. It was considered very dangerous for any one to venture into the interior, without a guide, for fear of getting lost among the labyrinth of passages that ramified throughout the whole of this remarkable edifice.

Herodotus says that "the Temples of Ephesus and Samos may justly claim admiration and the Pyramids may be individually compared to many of the magnificent structures of Greece, but even these are inferior to the Labyrinth. It is composed of twelve courts all of which are covered, their entrances stand opposite to each other, six to the north and six to the south; one wall enclosing the whole. Of the apartments above the ground I can speak," continues Herodotus, "from my own personal knowledge and observation; of those below, from information I received. The Egyptians who had charge of the latter would not suffer me to see them; and their reason was, that in them were preserved the sacred crocodiles and the bodies of the Kings who constructed the Labyrinth. Of these, therefore, I do not presume to speak; but the upper apartments I myself visited, and I pronounce them amongst the grandest efforts of human industry and art. The almost infinite number of winding passages through the different courts excited my highest admiration; from spacious halls I passed through smaller chambers, and from them again to large and magnificent saloons, almost without end. The walls and ceiling are marble, the latter embellished with the most exquisite sculpture; around each court pillars of the richest and most polished marble are arranged, and at the termination of the Labyrinth stands a pyramid one hundred and sixty cubits high, approached by a subterranean passage, and with its exterior enriched by figures of animals."

The object of building this remarkable structure cannot be fully conjectured, nor will it ever be properly known. Neither should we have been enabled to have known anything, for certain about it, if Herodotus had not given us the above description and told of its exact location—at the entrance of the canal into Lake Moeris; and when Mr. Flinders Petrie, in 1887-8, started a systematic exploration at the supposed site of the Labyrinth and the Pyramid of Hawara he most assuredly settled many mooted questions. He not only found the site of the Labyrinth, but he found the remains of two statues whereon was inscribed the name of Amen-em-hat III, the creator of Lake Moeris and the Fayum, and also the pedestals upon which they stood, thus proving beyond the shadow of a doubt the assertions of Herodotus, who wrote of having seen two statues that stood upon the tops of two Pyramids that were erected in the middle of Lake Moeris. These two statues of Amen-em-hat III, were no doubt erected in commemoration of the work that he had done in reducing the size of the lake, deepening its waters, and in this way reclaiming a vast area of swampy marsh land that had long been submerged by the flooding waters of the river Nile.

Mr. Petrie, in the year 1889, opened the Pyramid of Hawara, wherein he expected to find at least the mummy of the original Pharaoh, who

25

founded the Labyrinth and made the Fayum a paradise; but he was very much disappointed upon entering the Pyramid and discovering the chamber, to find the sarcophagus of both Amen-em-hat and his daughter, Ptah-nef-eru, empty, with the lids of each lying askew on top of them.

One thing very remarkable about this chamber, was that it was carved from a single stone. The dimensions of this chamber are twenty-two feet, three and one-half inches long by seven feet ten inches wide, by six feet two inches high. The stone is of very hard quartzite sandstone, with walls very nearly three feet thick and weighing about one hundred and eighty tons.

Under the head of a mummy excavated at Hawara Mr. Petrie also found a large roll of papyrus, which contains almost the whole of the second book of "Homer's Iliad." This was not the property of some old, dried-up philologist, for it laid under the skull of a young lady, whose features are still attractive and very intellectual, finely chiselled and refined looking. Both the skull and the papyrus, together with the jet black tresses of this nameless Hypatia, are now in the Bodleian Library at Oxford. It is one of the three oldest manuscripts of "Homer's Iliad" known to exist. There are two others that also came from Egypt. They are all useful in correcting the received text. There is another Pyramid about five or six miles to the east of the Labyrinth which is called Illahun, or El-Lahun. Mr. Flinders Petrie penetrated this Pyramid and found many interesting things, but to-day it is hardly worth spending the time to visit it.

Sun Worship—Zodiac—Masonic Allegories.

By lustrous heralds led on high
The omniscient Sun ascends the sky,
His glory drawing every eye.
All-seeing Sun, the stars so bright
Which gleamed throughout the sombre night,
Now scared, like thieves, slink fast away,
Quenched by the splendor of thy ray.

Thy beams to men thy presence show;
Like blazing fires they seem to glow.
Conspicuous, rapid, source of light,
Thou makest all the welkin bright.
In sight of gods and mortal eyes,
In sight of heaven thou scal'st the skies.

Bright god, thou scann'st with searching ken
The doings all of busy men.
Thou stridest o'er the sky, thy rays
Create and measure out our days;
Thine eye all living things surveys.

Seven lucid mares thy chariot bear,
Self-yoked, athwart the fields of air,
Bright Surya, god with flaming hair,
That glow above the darkness, we
Beholding, upward soar to thee,
for there among the gods thy light
Supreme is seen, divinely bright.

—Translated from the Sanskrit by Dr. J. Muir.

CHAPTER XVII.

SUN WORSHIP—ZODIAC—MASONIC ALLEGORIES.

A CAREFUL examination of the religious beliefs of the people of the ancient world, and a study of their mode or manner of worship, will show that in a great many countries, and especially in the " Far East," God has been worshipped under the symbol of the Sun. For thousands of years men have worshipped this great luminary, the source of all light, whose very essence is Generation and Life; the container of both, for without the great and glorious Sun-God all the earth would be enwrapped in darkness and death. Its Light is emblematic of eternal verities and its heat of benevolence and love, thus constituting a fitting symbol of that great and incomprehensible Principle which holds the Kosmos in the hollow of His hand. They no doubt began to worship the Sun on account of observing the regularity of its motions, which knew no change

They observed that nations and cities would pass away and new ones arise upon the site of the old empires; that tombs, temples and enduring monuments would decay and crumble into dust, be scattered to the four cardinal points of the universe, and still the regularity of the Sun's motions underwent no change. He visited the old and new alike, and his light shone with unchanging rays upon all. To them his apparent journeyings around the earth was emblematic of Life, Death and the Re-incarnation of the Spirit or immortality of the Soul, and instilled into the very heart and mind of man, not only thoughts on the Immortality of the Soul, but of that Immutability symbolizing the Great Eternal Unknown God, to whom they offered up their most profound love and adoration.

Long centuries before the Delta of the Nile was formed or brought from the mountains of Abyssinia, within the throbbing bosom of old God Nilus it performed its diurnal motions with the same unchanging regularity and exactitude that it does to-day. It was that steadfast, immutable motion, whose course throughout the stellar world above, knowing no change, that caused men in every age and every epoch of the world's history to ascribe God-like attributes to this glorious Orb, which is the same to-day as when Abraham saw it glitter in the plains of Shinar, as it is now and ever will be, for ever and ever, the most splendid and magnificent object in all nature.

I do not wish to dwell upon the Sun-worshippers of the world; but will confine myself altogether to those of Egypt, and endeavor to show their proficiency in Astronomy and its relation to ancient Masonry. I have referred to the ancient legend of the slaying of *Osiris* by *Typhon*, in the third chapter of this work, which will no doubt prove interesting to you, my dear Brothers, for whom this book was written.

The worship of the Sun in Egypt was the same as in other countries, the basis of all religion. To them the forces emanating from this great and glorious luminary were as much a problem as they are to us, for Light, Heat and Electricity are as yet unsolved problems. We know that each one of them is manifested throughout the Kosmos; but those manifestations are as yet mysteries to us, and so far we do not nor cannot understand them, only in their effects.

The great god of the ancient Egyptians was Amun, represented by a man standing upright, wearing upon his head a flat cap, with two tall straight feathers, and holding in his left hand the sceptre, while in the right he holds the sign of Life. We sometimes find him seated as a mummy, with the same red cap and feathers, holding in his hands the sceptre, scourge and crook, in which position he is supposed to represent Amun-Osiris. He may be found identified with many other gods.

Herodotus tell us in Book II, 42, that "the Thebans and those who, like them, abstain from eating sheep, say they do it for this reason, that Jupiter (Amun) when Hercules desired to see him, at first refused, but on his persisting, cut off the head of a ram which he flayed and held it before him, clothing himself in the skin and showed himself to him in this form. And for this reason the Egyptians represent Jupiter with the head of a ram. And once a year, on the festival of Jupiter, they kill and flay a ram and clothe the statue of Jupiter in the manner described, and then bring near to it another statue of Hercules."

Jablonsky thought that Amun represented the Sun in Aries, and that the position of this Sun God *Ra*, at the four cardinal points of the universe at the four great seasons of the year, was the symbol of the Egyptian Gods Amun, Horus, Serapis and Harpocrates. Although there is no positive evidence of this being true, there being no actual confirmation of the above opinion, yet, the name *Ra*—Sun—is often found joined together as Amun Ra, which seems to indicate their relationship, or an original connection with the Solar god. We find upon many of the monuments throughout Egypt the name of *Amun Ra* that has been substituted for some other, and it has been so carefully and cleverly done that it is very difficult to ascertain what the original name could have been. According to Major Felix the obliterated characters " were a vulture flying, its body formed by an eye, holding in its claws a signet (Birch-Gallery of Antiq., page 2, note 12). The flying vulture was the emblem of the goddess of Elithyia, who corresponded with the Lucina of the Latins. Bunsen supposes that the ithypophallic Khem was the god for whom Amun was substituted." There are various authorities who believe that it was on account of some change in the religious system of these people.

According to ancient Egyptian history we find that Amen-hetep IV (who reigned B. C. 1400) apostatized from the faith of his Fathers, and there is certain evidence to prove that his mother was the cause of this backsliding, which occasioned him to change his faith and name. He induced a great many prominent men to follow his example, but could not influence the priests of Egypt, as they were bitterly opposed to his form of worship. He had to leave Thebes on account of opposition by the people, urged on no doubt by the priests, when they found that he had forsaken the True God for the heretical doctrines of his mother. Possibly it may have been the name of this king that was erased from the tombs and temples. Let me quote you from Murray, page 60, in relation to this matter. " The heretic King Amen-hetep IV, who, under the influence of his mother *Teie* endeavored to substitute a sort of Asiatic monotheism, under the form of the worship of the solar disk, for the official religion of Egypt.

" The cult and very name of Amen were proscribed, the name being erased from the monuments wherever it occurred, and the King changed his own name from Amen-hetep to Khu-n-Aten, ' the glory of the solar disk.' In the struggle which ensued between the Pharaoh and the powerful hierarchy of Thebes, Khu-n-Aten found himself obliged to leave the capital of his father and build a new one further north, called Khu-t-Aten, the site of which is now occupied by the village of Tel-el-Amarna and Haggi Qandil. Here he surrounded himself with the adherents of the new creed, most of whom seemed to have been Canaanites or other natives of Asia, and erected in it a temple to the solar disk, as well as a palace for himself, adorned with painting, sculpture, gold, bronze and inlaid work in precious stones. Along with the religious reforms had gone a reform in Art; the old hieratic canon of Egyptian art was abandoned and a striving for realism took its place. Adjoining the palace was ' the house of rolls' or record office, where the cuneiform tablets were discovered which have thrown so much light on the history of Egypt and Canaan in the century before the Exodus.

"The death of the King was followed by civil and religious war and the loss of the empire of Asia. The city of Khu-n-Aten was destroyed, not to be inhabited again, the Asiatic officials were driven from the country and the worship of Amen was restored." "The ancient Egyptians were the preservers if not the founders of Astronomy, and they claim to have been the teachers of the Chaldeans, whom they said were of their own stock and colony from Egypt " (see Herodotus, 2–82). The ancient Egyptians were most certainly very close observers of the aspects of the heavenly bodies and gave this science their most profound attention, for if we carefully examine the meaning of the different signs of the Zodiac, as well as the symbol, we shall find that the various constellations are all named after some event or occurrence which happened in the ancient days of Pharaonic history in the "Land of Egypt." Again, the very fact of the Pyramids, in the plains of Gizeh, standing geometrically correct in relation to their sides facing the four cardinal points of the universe, goes to prove their ability to establish an accurate meridian line.

There is no question but they divided the Solar year into twelve months and these into three hundred and sixty days which they afterwards added to the five intercalary days, thus making the year very nearly correct. But the name *Month* in their hieroglyphic inscriptions is represented by the crescent moon, consequently we judge from this that their months must originally have been Lunar, although they may have had both Lunar and Solar. Of this we are not positively certain and we do not know exactly when the Solar month was introduced. These months each had a name, which names have been preserved to us by many writers and they correspond to those of the "Julian Year" as follows: 1. Thoth —August; 2. Phaophi—September; 3. Athyr—October; 4. Choiak— November; 5. Tybi—December; 6. Mechir—January; 7. Phamenoth— February; 8. Pharmuthi—March; 9. Pacon—April; 10. Payni—May; 11. Epiphi—June; 12. Mesori—July.

Kenrick states in his " Ancient Egypt," Vol. I, page 277, that "When the Egyptians established the division of their years into twelve months of thirty days each, they may have reckoned the year at three hundred and sixty days; but at a very early period they had learned to intercalate five additional days. When this great correction of their calendar took place is uncertain. Syncellus, in the Laterculus, attributes it to Asseth, one of the Shepherd Kings; but Lepsius says that he has found traces of the five intercalary days, or *Epagomcnoc*, as the Greeks called them, in a grotto at Benihassan of the twelfth dynasty, that is before the invasion of the Shepherds. Their introduction into the year was expressed by an ingenious myth. Thoth (Hermes) the god of astronomy and calculation, played dice with the Moon and wins from her a seventieth (a round number for seventy-seconds) part of each of the three hundred and sixty days of which the year consisted, out of which fractional parts ($\frac{360}{72} = 5$) five entire days are composed. These days are consecrated to five gods whose worship thus seems to be indicated as of later origin; the first to Osiris, the second to Aureris, the third to Typhon, the fourth to Isis and the fifth to Nephthys. In the astronomical monument at the Rameseum, a vacant space is left between Mesori the last, and Thoth the first, of the Egyptian months, apparently to represent the intercalated days.

" But the intercalation of five days were not sufficient to bring the Egyptian calendar into harmony with the heavens. The true length of the Solar year exceeds three hundred and sixty-five days by nearly six hours. It is evident, therefore, that there would be an error in defect of a quarter of a day in every year, of a day in every four years, a month in every one hundred and twenty years, and a year of three hundred and sixty-five days, in fourteen hundred and sixty years. Without some further correction the Egyptian year would be an *annus vagus*; its true commencement and all the festivals, the time of which was reckoned from it, travelling in succession through all the days and months, just as our own were doing; but at a less rapid rate, and in a contrary direction, before the alteration of the Style. Herodotus appears not to have been aware that any correction had been applied to the calendar, or indeed required, since he praises the intercalation of five days, as bringing back the circle of the seasons to the same point. Diodorus, however, represents the priests of Thebes and Strabo, those of Heliopolis, as knowing the true length of the solar year and intercalating five days and a quarter. They furnish no evidence, however, of the antiquity of the practice, nor its adoption in civil life. Indeed Geminus of Rhodes who lived in the time of Sylla, expressly says that the priests did not intercalate the quarter day in order that the festivals might travel through the whole year, and 'the summer festival become a winter festival, and an autumn festival a spring festival.' Such a change implies that the original import of the festivals, some of which were closely connected with the season of the year, was no longer obvious. It is even said that the priests imposed on the sovereign at his inauguration an oath that he would keep up the old reckoning and not allow the quarter day to be intercalated. This again points to the time when the priests had become jealous of the civil power, and wished to perpetuate the confusion of the calendar, as the patricians did at Rome for their own purposes."

Now, I firmly believe that the ancient Egyptian Priesthood was thoroughly versed in all the Sciences; but more especially so in that of Astronomy, and carefully guarded the secrets of this Science from the people. By this means their despotic power was perpetuated and by keeping them in utter ignorance they could inspire a belief in their supernatural power and wisdom. Their predictions of eclipses of the sun and moon were watched by the masses with awe and superstitious dread, and each time the predictions were fulfilled these priests were credited with power to foretell other future events, such as years of famine or plenty, pestilence, earthquakes, inundations or changes in the various dynasties, along with other things of an astonishing nature. They were, in consequence, looked upon as prophets among the vulgar and lower classes, and we can readily see how carefully they would guard their secrets from the profane, that, by their superior knowledge, they might rule them with a rod of iron.

I previously stated that the ancient Egyptians worshipped the Sun, Moon, Stars and the river Nile, as gods, ascribing to them God-like attributes; being symbols to them of the Supreme Architect of the Universe, and to deny the divinity of either, or even permit any one else to do so, was considered the most horrible crime of which a man could be guilty. Thus through their superior knowledge and wisdom the rule of the Priesthood was supreme over those who had not seen the Light of Initiation and who could not understand the profound Truths veiled in Allegory and illustrated by symbols. For this reason an oath was imposed upon the King whereby he was not to divulge the secrets of the veiled Mysteries.

If we carefully examine the very name Freemason, the Dimensions of our Lodges, its coverings, its Lights, the positions of its Officers, etc., etc., we shall find that the astronomical allegories of the ancient Egyptians have been intimately blended with the Legend of Osiris and that these astronomical allegories and symbols, are the safe and sacred repositories of a profound Theosophical, Metaphysical and Philosophical Philosophy. An earnest search must be instituted that one may come to an understanding of the Sublimity and grandeur of the teachings of the Ancient Wisdom, embodied in the Secret Doctrine of the Princes and Adepts of our glorious Ancient and Accepted Scottish Rite. These have ever striven to make their fellow-man and Brother wiser and better than themselves, to assist him in following the dictates of his own conscience and the judgment of his *Higher self*, inciting him to be manly, true, self-reliant and independent. They have always been helpful in resisting spiritual Tyranny over their souls and consciences, by those striving to gain power by unworthy means, and have ever been faithful unto death to their Brother by the wayside. Let me quote you from that very valuable work "Stellar Theology and Masonic Astronomy," by Robert Hewitt Brown, 32°, page 35.

"The Sun rises in the *east* to open and govern the day, and sets in the west to close the labors of the same; while the Sun in the *south* admonishes the weary workman of his mid-day meal and calls him from labor to refreshment. Dr. Oliver informs us, in his dictionary, that the pedestal, with the volume of the sacred laws, is placed in the eastern part of the Lodge to signify that as the Sun rises in the east to open and enliven the day, so is the Worshipful Master placed in the east, to open the Lodge and instruct the brethren in Masonry."

Gadicke, another Masonic writer, says: "The Sun rises in the *east*, and the east is the place for the *Worshipful Master*, who is placed in the *east* to open the Lodge, and impart light, knowledge and instruction to all under his direction. When it arrives at its greatest altitude in the *south*, where its beams are most piercing and the cool shade most refreshing, it is then also well represented by the *Junior Warden*, who is placed in the *south* to observe its approach to meridian, and at the hour of noon to call the brethren from labor to refreshment. Still pursuing its course to the *west*, the Sun closes the day and lulls all nature to repose; it is then fitly represented by the *Senior Warden*, who is placed in the *west* to close the Lodge by the command of the Worshipful Master, after having rendered to every one the just reward of his labor." (I have quoted these authorities for the express purpose of showing that I do not stand alone in my assertions, see Chapter VIII, of this work.)

On page 34, "Stellar Theology," it is asked, "How ought every Lodge to be situated?" The answer is "Due east and west." Because, in the language of Dr. Hemming, a distinguished brother and Masonic writer, "the Sun, the glory of the Lord, rises in the east and sets in the west." It is again asked, "What are the dimensions and covering of a Lodge?" and answer is, "Its dimensions are without limit, and its covering no less than the clouded canopy or starry-decked heavens." Then the question is asked, "How many lights has a Lodge?" which is answered by Dr. Oliver, "a Lodge has three lights—one in the east, another in the west, and another in the south."

It is thus apparent that not only the position, form, dimensions, lights and furniture of the Lodge, but also its principal officers, their respective stations, and duties there, all have reference to the Sun.

It is my sincere conviction that all the incidents and allegories pertaining to Blue Masonry, or the Symbolic degrees, are true relics of Ancient Egyptian Astronomy, and are permeated with a far more profound meaning than is generally understood by a great majority of the craft to-day. Let me quote you once more from "Stellar Theology," page 109:

"If we view Masonry from a rational standpoint, and contemplate its mystic legends and allegories in their substance, without regard to the modern language, in which they are now clothed; if we investigate the meaning of its ceremonies, without regard to the specific words used in conducting them; if we study the signs, symbols and emblems, disregarding the erroneous modern applications given to many of them—the great antiquity of Masonry is apparent. It is now admitted on all sides that all the ancient Mysteries were identical and had a common origin from those of Egypt, a conclusion which has been reached by the same method of reasoning and comparison.

"The legend of Osiris is the parent stock from which all the others came, but in Greece and Asia Minor the name Osiris disappeared, and that of Dionysus and Bacchus were substituted, while in the Hebrew Tyrean temple legend, the name of Hiram is found. The claim, however, that the legend of Hiram is actual history, descriptive of events which really took place about the time of the building of King Solomon's temple, must be abandoned by the few who still blindly cling to it. Masonry can no longer hope to stand without criticism in this age of inquiry. There is a spirit abroad which does not hesitate to catch antiquity by its grey beard, stare into its wrinkled face, and demand upon what authority, of right reason, or authentic history it founds its pretensions.

"The Masonic traditions cannot hope to escape examination in its turn; and when it is examined, it will not stand the test, as claiming to be *historically* true. If, then, we have no explanation to offer, it must be discarded and take its place among many other exploded legends of the past. By showing, however, that it is not *intended* as an actual history, but is really a sublime allegory of great antiquity, teaching the profoundest truths of astronomy, and inculcating by an ancient system of types, symbols and emblems, an exalted code of morals, we at once reply to and disarm all that kind of criticism. The Masonic Fraternity is thus placed on a loftier plane and assumes a position which challenges the respect and admiration of both the learned and virtuous; the learned because they will thus be enabled to recognize it as the depository of an ancient system of scientific knowledge; the virtuous, because the Fraternity also stands revealed to them as having been in past ages the preserver of true worship and the teacher of morality and brotherly love.

"It has been the boast of Masonry that its ritual contained great scientific as well as moral truths. While this was plainly the fact as to the moral teachings of our Fraternity, to a large number of our most intelligent Brothers, the key which alone could unlock the Masonic treasury of *Scientific Truth* appeared to have been lost. We believe that key is at length restored; for, if the Masonic traditions and legends, with the ritual illustrating them, are regarded as *astronomical Allegories*, the light of scientific truth is at once seen to illuminate and permeate every part. If the explanations given in the foregoing pages are correct, any person who fully understands the meaning and intention of the legends and ceremonies, symbols and emblems of our Fraternity, is necessarily well informed as to the sciences of Astronomy and Geometry, which form the foundation of all the others.

"And why is not the explanation correct? Have you ever considered the 'caculus of probabilities,' as applied to a subject like this? That Masonry should contain a single allusion to the Sun, might *happen* and imply nothing. The same might be said if it contained but three or four; but when we find the name of the Fraternity, the form, dimensions, lights, ornaments and furniture of its Lodge, and all the emblems, symbols, ceremonies, words and signs, without exception, allude to the annual circuit of the sun—that astronomical ideas and solar symbols are interwoven into the very texture of the whole institution, and, what is still more significant, that there is such a *harmony of relation* existing between *all these astronomical allusions*, as to render the *whole ritual* capable of a perfect and natural interpretation as an astronomical allegory, *which is also one and complete*—is overwhelming, and amounts to a positive demonstration. There are millions of probabilities to one against the theory of the allegory being accidental, and not designed."

Now, if any earnest man or Mason will consider for a very short time upon the origin and antiquity of Ancient Masonry, he will realize at once that the guilds of practical operative Masons of Europe could never have designed or originated our glorious Fraternity of Masonry. The Builders of England, France, Germany and other European peoples,

were skilled mechanics and architects, no doubt, for the work of their
hands testify to the knowledge to which they had attained; but beyond
that they could not go, only in the case, possibly, of some of the more
prominent Architects, who were, most assuredly, not only skilful in the
Arts and Sciences, but intellectually informed upon the Religions and
Philosophies of the ancients, as well as those of their own age; while the
greater part of them were, no doubt, extremely ignorant, outside of their
professions, and nearly as well educated as the ordinary mechanic or
laborer of our own day, consequently it would have been simply impossible for them to have founded such an institution as our glorious Fraternity, if they had made the attempt.

Again, Freemasonry is, as I have previously stated, a peculiar
system of Morality, veiled in Allegory and illustrated by Symbols identical with those of the Ancient Mysteries, a fact which any thoughtful
student of Masonry will most assuredly recognize. If he will earnestly
study and carefully examine the ritualistic work of the Symbolic degrees,
compare them with what he can learn of the Ancient Mysteries, he will
certainly come to the conclusion that its antiquity rests upon an astronomical foundation, which can be traced back into remote ages of the
past, when all the grand truths embodied in those beautiful Allegories
were orally transmitted from generation to generation.

A thorough knowledge of the diurnal and annual motions of the
Sun-God *Ra*, will furnish a key to open up to his view a knowledge of
the sublime meaning which underlies the teachings, or ritualistic work,
of our Symbolic degrees, leading him on through the Lesser and into the
Greater Mysteries to the Ineffable degrees of the Ancient and Accepted
Scottish Rite of Masonry.

Christ himself taught by parables, not understood by many of his
own disciples, and so it is with the Allegories and Symbols of Masonry,
they are not understood or comprehended, I am sorry to say, by the great
majority of our Brethren. But they have the key to the solution of them
and if they would only give a little time and attention to the study of
those beautiful symbols permeating every one of our degrees, they would
soon begin to realize the sublime Theosophical and Philosophical Truths
embodied in the ritualistic work of our Glorious Fraternity. Brother
Buck says in his " Mystic Masonry:"

"The real secrets of Freemasonry lie in its Symbols, and the meaning of the Symbols reveals a profound philosophy and a universal science that has never been translated by man," and also states that " he desires to share the results of his personal observations with his Brothers, because it has revealed to him such priceless treasures, such precious jewels that will lead all who search to far greater discoveries. These jewels," he tells us, "have not been concealed by accident, but by design, in order that they might, in some future age, be restored. Even the *Stone* that was rejected and became lost in the rubbish, not only bears an emblem and contains a mark, but is itself, from first to last, with its surroundings, a method of restoration and final use, a symbol. It is the center of a five-pointed star, which is the Kabalistic sign of Man. In one direction, it symbolizes the five senses, lost in the rubbish of passion and self-gratification. When this rejected or lost stone is recovered and sent to the King of the Temple (Man's Higher Self), and is recognized and restored, the arch is complete, and the gate-way of the senses gives entrance to the ' Palace of the King.' The result is Light or Illumination. Such are the *Illuminati*."

The Zodiac is a broad belt in the heavens, 16° (*degrees*) wide. It is divided into twelve equal parts, called the Signs of the Zodiac. Each sign is 30° (*degrees*) long and divided in the centre by the Ecliptic, which cuts them into two equal parts, so that the Zodiac lies 8° (degrees) each side of the Ecliptic or apparent path of the Sun, around the Earth, a journey it accomplishes in about three hundred and sixty-five days, five hours.

When I was a boy at school we had an old rhyme by which we were taught to remember the various signs; it is as follows :

> The Ram, the Bull, the heavenly Twins
> Next the crab, the Lion shines,
> The Virgin, and the Scales,
> The Scorpion, Archer and the Goat
> The man that carries the Water-pot,
> The Fish with glittering tails.

The whole of the Stellar world was filled by the ancient Egyptian Astronomers with imaginary figures of men, animals, etc., plainly traced all over the Heavens. But to that great glittering belt, stretching its serpent-like coil around the starry vault above, which we call the Zodiac, they assigned the chief stars, because they laid along the path of their glorious Sun-God " Ra," who, in his journeyings through the twelve signs, enacts the part of Hercules, in performing the twelve labors ascribed to him.

According to the procession of the equinox, we find that the Sun does not reach the same point each year, and the one where he crosses at the opening of Spring, coming North, is called the *Vernal equinox*, while the one he crosses on his passage into the Southern hemisphere is called the *Autumnal equinox*. He reaches these two points the *Vernal* equinox, on or about the 21st day of March and the *Autumnal*, on or about the 21st day of September, at which time the days and nights are equal in both hemispheres. It reaches the solstitial point in the Northern hemisphere on or about the 21st day of June, when the days are longest and the nights the shortest in the North, and it attains the solstitial point in the Southern hemisphere on or about the 21st day of December when the days are longest and the nights are the shortest, South of the equator.

These two solstitial points, *Cancer and Capricorn*, were known to the ancients as the " Gates of Heaven," or the " Pillars of Hercules," beyond which the Sun never passed. These two columns are to be found in our Blue Lodges of to-day and they are represented in our rituals as a circle, with a point in the centre, between two parallel lines, demonstrating the sun between the tropic of Cancer and Capricorn, or the Pillars of Hercules.

Albert Pike says in " Morals and Dogmas," page 465 : " The image of the sign in which each of the four seasons commenced, became the form under which was figured the Sun of that particular season. The Lion's skin was worn by Hercules ; the horns of the Bull adorned the forehead of Bacchus and the autumnal serpent wound its long folds round the Statue of Serapis, 2,500 years before our era ; when those signs corresponded with the commencement of the seasons. When other constellations replaced them at those points, by means of the precession of the Equinoxes, those attributes were changed. Then the Ram furnished the horns for the head of the Sun, under the name of Jupiter Ammon. He was no longer born exposed to the waters of Aquarius, like Bacchus, nor

26

inclosed in an urn like the God Canopus; but in the Stables of Augeas or the Celestial Goat. He then completed his triumph, mounted on an Ass, in the constellation Cancer, which then occupied the Solstitial point of Summer.

"Other attributes the images of the Sun borrowed from the constellations which, by their rising and setting, fixed the points of the departure of the year, and the commencements of its four principal divisions.

"First the Bull and afterwards the Ram (called by the Persians the Lamb) was regarded as the regenerator of Nature, through his union with the Sun. Each, in his turn, was an emblem of the Sun overcoming the winter darkness, and repairing the disorders of Nature, which every year was regenerated under these Signs, after the Scorpion and Serpent of Autumn had brought upon it barrenness, disaster and darkness. Mithras was represented sitting on a Bull; and that animal was an image of Osiris; while the Greek Bacchus armed its front with its horns, and was pictured with its tail and feet.

. "The Constellations also became noteworthy to the husbandman, which .by their rising or setting, at morning or evening, indicated the coming of this period of renewed fruitfulness and new life. Capella, or the Kid Amalthea, whose horn is called that of abundance and whose place is over the equinoctional point, or Taurus; and the Pleiades that long indicated the Seasons, and gave rise to a multitude of poetic fables, were the most observed and celebrated in antiquity."

The ancient Egyptians named every star shining in the infinitude of space, and gave to the signs of the Zodiac the self-same names they bear to-day, from some event or occurrence which happened on or about the time of their rising in the east, in the early evening, or just after sunset, in the same manner that the appearance of Anubis upon the Eastern horizon indicated the approach of the annual inundations of the Nile, so the various constellations or signs of the Zodiac, appearing in the East about sunset, presages of some event of equal importance, or pointed out to them some duty that should not be neglected.

As an instance of this, Taurus signified when it was time to plow and till the soil, and to sow the seed for the reaping later on. When Virgo appeared, if old god Nilus had granted their request and overflowed the river banks at the proper time, and permitted the parched and thirsty soil to drink in sufficient to fructify the land and cause the seeds and plants to grow in abundance, then the Virgin harvest would soon be ready for the reaping. When Cancer appeared it informed them of the backward movement that is made by the Sun, apparently, in his descending course toward the Autumnal Equinox. The Lions, drinking from the river at certain times, indicate the approach of that constellation Leo, followed by the sign marking the Summer's Solstice, and the silver sickle of this constellation presaged the golden harvest of Virgo. This very welcome sign is represented as a beautiful Virgin, holding in her hand the ripened ear of wheat, indicating that the golden grain was now ready for the harvesting; then joy and gladness would fill the land, the people would rejoice and be happy throughout the Land of Egypt. Feasting, festivals and grand processions were always in order during years of abundance, but sorrow, woe and mourning when gaunt famine appeared. Libra, or the *balance*, told of equal days and nights in both hemispheres.

When the lurid Scorpio gazed across the sandy deserts of Arabia, it warned all those who travelled across the trackless waste of sands to be very careful, for on or about the time of its appearance the Simoon of the desert would begin to blow and produce terrific sand-storms, so dense and smothery that very often those who were caught in them would lose their lives, not being able to escape from them. At such times the wind would blow, fierce and strong, lifting stones, pieces of shells, etc., to dash them with dreadful force into the faces of unfortunate travelers, cutting the skin and flesh, drawing blood, and often causing intense pain, like the sting of a Scorpion, hence the name of this sign.

With Scorpio comes the most important signs of the Zodiac to the Masonic student, for now the Sun, having passed under the malign influence of the venomous Scorpio, becomes weak and weary when commencing the battle with the Archer, whose terrible darts wound him full sore, until finally overcome and slain by Sagittarius, and carried off by the terrible Capricornus into the depths of Winter Soistice where he remained for three days. Like the Goat which climbs the giddy heights of the mountain-side, where yawning chasms are tremendous, he re-incarnates once again and resurrected, comes forth from out the realms of darkness, sin and sorrow and suffering into grander heights of happiness and immortality.

Thus each and every sign of the Zodiac was fraught with a deep significance; but more especially to the initiated, because they, having the key to their esoteric meaning, saw in all the motions of the Sun along the Ecliptic a most profound, Sublime and Philosophical meaning which constituted the base of all religions and Philosophies. It is no wonder, therefore, that they viewed with awe and admiration the Birth, Life, Death and Re-incarnation of their glorious Sun-God Ra, for to them it demonstrated that there is no death, and proved the immortality of the soul.

The earnest Masonic student who is desirous of proving the antiquity of our glorious Fraternity, as well as to identify the teachings of our own beloved Scottish Rite with those of the ancient Mysteries, will have ample proof if he pursues his studies along these lines of Astronomical ideas and comes to an understanding of the true meaning underlying those sublime and beautiful symbols which have existed since time immemorial. On many of the coins and medals coined in different cities of the ancient world, are to be found carved or impressed the various signs of the Zodiac, Planets or Stars, showing the high estimation placed upon them by different people in different parts of the world.

In India the twelve signs of the Zodiac appeared complete on many coins, and on the medals struck to honor Antoninus are to be seen the greater portion of the magnificent signs which adorned the pathway of the Sun-God Ra, in his journey around the world.

Upon the medals of Antioch and the other Syrian cities appeared the RAM (*Aries*) and the crescent Moon. The Ram, singly, was the special Deity of Syria. The Egyptian Apis, or the sign TAURUS (*the Bull*), was engraved on the coins of many of the cities of Greece, Athens especially.

Many of the coins of Persia bore upon their face SAGITTARIUS, (*The Archer*). On the medals made in honor of the Kings of Comegena (a part of Syria above Cilicia), appeared SCORPIO (*The Scorpion*). On the seal of Locri (a town in Magna Gracia), was to be found HESPERUS, (*The Planet Venus*). And on the coins of Zeugma and other towns which adorned the banks of the Euphrates, in Mesopotamia, was carved the symbol so often and familiarly spoken of in connection with our beloved Fraternity—CARPRICORNUS, (THE GOAT).

"The Phœnicians and Egyptians," says Eusebius, "were the first who ascribed divinity to the sun, moon and stars, and regarded them as the sole causes of the production and destruction of all beings. From them went abroad, over all the world, all known opinions as to the generations and descent of the gods. Only the Hebrews looked beyond the visible world to an invisible Creator. All the rest of the world regarded as gods those luminous bodies which blaze in the firmament, offered them sacrifices, bowed down before them and raised neither their souls nor their worship above the visible heavens.

"The Chaldeans, Canaanites and Syrians, among whom Abraham lived, did the same. The Canaanites consecrated horses and chariots to the sun. The inhabitants of Emesa in Phœnicia adored him under the name of Elagabalus; and the sun as Hercules, was the great Deity of the Tyrians. The Syrians worshipped with fear and dread the stars of the constellation Pisces and consecrated images of them in their temples. The sun, as Adonis, was worshipped in Byblos and about Mount Lebanus. There was a magnificent temple of the sun at Palmyra, which was pillaged by the soldiers of Aurelian, who rebuilt it and dedicated it anew. The Pleiades, under the name of Succoth-Beneth, were worshipped by the Babylonian colonists who settled in the country of the Samaritans. Saturn, under the name Ramphan, was worshipped among the Copts. The planet Jupiter was worshipped as Bel or Baal; Mars as Malac, Melech or Moloch; Venus as Ashtaroth, or Astarte, and Mercury as Nebo, among the Syrians, Assyrians, Phœnicians and Canaanites. Sanchoniathon says that the earliest Phœnicians adored the Sun, whom they deemed sole Lord of the heavens, and honored him under the name BEEL-SAMIN, signifying *King of Heaven*. They raised columns to the elements, fire and air, or wind, and worshipped them, and Sabaeism, or the worship of the stars, flourished everywhere in Babylonia."

The Arabs, under a sky always clear and serene, adored the sun, moon and stars, as Abulfaragius informs us, and that each of the twelve Arab tribes invoked a particular star as its patron. The tribe *Hamyar* was consecrated to the sun, the tribe of *Cannah* to the moon, the tribe *Misa* was under the protection of the beautiful star in Tauras—Aldebaran; the tribe *Tai* under that of Canopus; the tribe *Kais*, of Sirius;

the tribes *Lackamus* and *Idamus* of Jupiter; the tribe *Asad* of Mercury; and so on.

The Saracens, in the time of Heraclius, worshipped Venus, whom they called CABAAR, or THE GREAT; and they swore by the sun, moon and stars. Shahaistan, an Arabic author, says that the Arabs and Indians before his time had temples dedicated to the Seven Planets. Albufaragius says that the Seven Great Primitive nations, from whom all the others descended, the Persians, Chaldeans, Greeks, Egyptians, Turks, Indians and Chinese, all originally were Sabeanists and worshipped the stars. They all, he says, like the Chaldeans, prayed, turning toward the North Pole, three times a day, at sunrise, noon and sunset, bowing themselves three times before the sun. They invoked the stars and intelligences which inhabited them, offered them sacrifices and called the fixed stars and planets gods.

Philo says that the Chaldeans regarded the stars as sovereign arbiters of the order of the world and did not look beyond the visible causes to any invisible or intellectual being. They regarded NATURE as the great divinity, which exercised its powers through the action of its parts, the sun, moon, planets and fixed stars, the successive revolutions of the seasons and the combined action of heaven and earth. The great feast of the Sabeans was when the sun reached the Vernal Equinox. They had five other feasts at the time when the five minor planets entered the signs in which they had their exaltation.

Diodorus Siculus informs us " that the Egyptians recognized two great Divinities, primary and eternal, the sun and moon, which they thought governed the world, and from which everything receives its nourishment and growth; that on them depended all the great work of generation and the perfection of all effects produced in nature. We know the two great Divinities of Egypt were Osiris and Isis, the greatest agents of nature; according to some, the sun and moon, and according to others, heaven and earth, or the active and passive principles of generation."

And we learn from Porphyry that Chaereman, a learned priest of Egypt, and many other learned men of that nation, said, that the Egyptians recognized as gods the stars comprising the Zodiac, and all those by their rising or setting marked its divisions; the subdivisions of the signs into decans, the horoscope, and the stars presiding therein, which are called Potent Chiefs of Heaven. Considering the Sun as the Great God, Architect, and Ruler of the World, they explained, not only the fable of Osiris and Isis, but generally all their sacred legends by the stars, by their appearance and disappearance, by their ascension, by the phases of the Moon, and the increase and diminution of her light; by the march of the Sun, the division of it and the heavens into two parts, one assigned to darkness and the other to light.

Diodorus also informs us "that the Egyptians acknowledged two great Gods, the Sun and Moon, or Osiris and Isis, who govern the world and regulate its administration by the dispensation of the seasons. . . . Such is the nature of these two great Divinities, that they impress an active and fecundating force, by which the generation is effected; the Sun, by heat and that spiritual principle which forms the breath of the winds; the Moon, by humidity and dryness; and both by the forces of the air which they share in common. By this beneficial influence everything is born, grows and vegetates. Wherefore this whole huge body in which nature resides, is maintained by the combined action of the Sun and Moon, and their five qualities—the principles, spiritual, fiery, dry, humid and airy."

Now we positively know that without these various principles nothing could grow, for every seed implanted within the bosom of "Mother Earth," requires Air to vitalize the Life essence, or Prana, within its quivering form, and moisture to swell the protoplasmic forces surrounding the germ. Under these conditions, therefore, the spirit lying dormant within the heart of the seed will at once manifest itself in growth and Life. These elements were recognized by the nations of antiquity, who looked upon the Sun, Moon and Stars as the embodiment and symbols of the Deity producing these elements, the real and essential cause of both Evolution and Involution, or of Generation and Destruction. According to Champollion:

"The tomb of Rameses V, at Thebes, contains tables of the constellations and of their influence for every hour, of every month of the year. Thus, in the latter half of the month of *Tobi*, Orion rules and influences, at the first hour, the *left arm;* Sirius at the second, influences *the heart;* the Twins, at the third, *the arms*, and so on." There is a papyrus in the

British Museum, of the age of Rameses III, which contains a division of the days of the year into lucky and unlucky ones. On the sarcophagus of Rameses IV, the twenty-four hours are represented, showing the antiquity of this division. Each has a star placed above it and a figure; twelve males, representing the day, have their faces turned toward the God Horus, the representative of the Sun; twelve females, towards a crocodile, the symbol of darkness.

In a great astronomical picture from the tombs at Beb-el-Melook, a variety of circumstances connected with the rising and setting of the stars are evidently indicated; but in the present state of our knowledge it is impossible to give the meaning of the Egyptian characters.

Donnelly, in his "Atlantis," page 454, says that: "There are actual astronomical calculations in existence, with calenders formed upon them, which eminent astronomers of England and France admit to be genuine, and true, and which carry back the antiquity of the science of astronomy, together with the constellations to within a few years of the Deluge, even on the longer chronology of the Septuagint (see "Miracles in Stone," page 142).

Josephus attributes the invention of the constellations to the family of the antediluvian Seth, the son of Adam, while Origen affirms that it was asserted in the Book of Enoch, that in the time of that patriarch the constellations were already divided and named. The Greeks associated the origin of Astronomy with Atlas and Hercules, Atlantean kings or heroes. The Egyptians regarded Taut (At?) or Thoth, or *At*-hotes, as the originator of both astronomy and the alphabet; doubtless he represented a civilized people by whom their country was originally colonized. Bailey and others assert that astronomy must have been established when the summer solstice was in the first degree of Virgo, and that the Solar and Lunar Zodiacs were of similar antiquity, which would be about four thousand years before the Christian Era.

"The signs of the Zodiac were certainly in use among the Egyptians one thousand seven hundred and twenty-two years before Christ. One of the learned men of our own day, who for fifty years labored to decipher the hieroglyphics of the ancients, found upon a mummy-case in the British Museum a delineation of the signs of the Zodiac, and the position of the planets; the date to which they pointed was the autumnal equinox of the year B. C. 1722.   Professor Mitchell, to whom the fact was communicated, employed his assistants to ascertain the exact position of the heavenly bodies belonging to our Solar system on the equinox of that year.   This was done and a diagram furnished by parties ignorant of his object, which showed that on the 7th of October, B. C. 1722, the moon and planets occupied the exact position in the heavens marked upon the coffin in the British Museum " (Goodrich's " Columbus," page 22).

And so it is with all astronomical statements, if we carefully examine them we shall find each and every one to be perfectly correct, and I consider this subject to be of the deepest interest, to not only the Masonic student, but to all men who are desirous of comprehending the profound depth of astronomical knowledge pertaining to the ancient people who lived in the Golden Age of Egypt.

A Voyage up the Nile—Description of Tombs and Temples—Pro Doric Columns.

"Smooth went our boat along the summer seas,

    Leaving—for so it seemed—a world behind,

    Its cares, its sounds, its shadows; we reclined

Upon the sunny deck, heard but the breeze

That whispered through the palms, or idly played

    With the lithe flag aloft—a forest scene

    On either side drew its slope line of green,

And hung the water's edge with shade.

Above thy woods, Memphis!—pyramids pale

    Peered as we passed; and Nile's soft azure hue,

    Gleaming 'mid the grey desert, met the view;

Where hung at intervals the scarce seen sail."

CHAPTER XVIII.

AFTER leaving the Fayum we made our way to Wasta, for the purpose of getting our mail, and went on up to Beni-Suef, by the cars,
as there was little to be seen that would interest any one on the
river between these two places. It becomes quite monotonous, simply
watching sandy banks, palm groves and the same peculiar features of the
villages we pass on our way into Upper Egypt. There is very little to
occasion amusement or to excite interest in the river scenery until you
begin to approach Beni-Suef.

This town has a population of about twelve thousand inhabitants, is
located twenty-two miles from Wasta and seventy-two from Cairo. It
contains both post and telegraph offices and a railway station, the steamers
stopping here, discharge their freight and passengers, and take on others
going to the South. It is very seldom though that passengers are left
here, excepting natives, or those Europeans and Americans who intend
going into the Fayum, by the road leading to the brick Pyramid of *El
Lahun.* They sometimes take on passengers who like ourselves have
"done" the Fayum. The wharfs and banks of the river are crowded
with quite a number of regular, dirty Nile boats, and there are a few buildings erected close to the river; but the town proper lies quite a way back
from the river front, the houses being built of sun-dried bricks of Nile
mud, present no new features to us. It has a bazar, fairly well supplied
with merchandise of the usual articles seen in such places; but there is
little of interest in this town, although it presents a very pretty view from
the river, for the island is well covered with vegetation of all kinds, and
the house of the Khedive looked quite charming peeping out from behind
its leafy screen. The chief industries of Beni-Suef are carpet and linen,
of a much inferior quality to what it was in the time of Leo Africanus,
when this town was noted for its manufacture of fine linen fabrics; in fact

it used to supply the whole of Egypt with flax, and exported large quantities to the various cities along the Mediterranean Sea.

From this place we start to do Upper Egypt in a Dahabiyeh, a mode of travel suiting myself and companions better than any other. It was, of course, more expensive than either cars or steamer; but we realized that wherever we should desire to stop, we would always have our home with us, on the river banks, with such comforts and accommodations as can only be truly appreciated and enjoyed. After long and weary tramping across the drifting desert sands, to examine some ruined tomb or temple, or some point of interest and come back to a refreshing bath, a good meal and the luxuries of a good, quiet resting place is an inexpressible convenience, I can assure you.

We had made all necessary arrangements for our boat, before leaving Cairo, to meet us at Beni-Suef. On our arrival at that place our Dragoman met us, and with the assistance of some of our sailors we were escorted, bag and baggage, to our clean and home-like quarters, where we found everything as nice and pleasant as could possibly be expected, under the circumstances, as we had arrived a day before our time. Under the superintendence of our *bijou* of a Dragoman we were, nevertheless, soon made as comfortable as could be desired, and that night, after dinner, we sat on the deck of our boat, under the glittering stars of an unclouded sky, smoking our cigars and chatting of the wonders of the Fayum, and on retiring were lulled to sleep by the rippling waters of the river Nile.

We were in no particular hurry to complete our journey, as my companions and I were going through this extraordinary country for the pleasure of seeing some of the stupendous fabrics belonging to the civilization of a prehistoric age. Accompanied by these genial associates I was going into the valley of the Nile with a determination to see all that was to be seen, and to study for myself the gigantic remains of the Tombs, Temples, Monuments and Mummies scattered promiscuously from one end of this interesting valley to the other, searching for evidences of our glorious fraternity amid the debris of departed ages. Realizing the immeasurable benefits conferred upon mankind by its teachings, descending from generation to generation, through all the vicissitudes and mutations of time, I was endeavoring, by these researches, to arrive at an

OUR FLOATING HOME—THE DAHABIYEH.

intelligent understanding of the Arts, Sciences and Philosophies belonging to the Ancient Egyptians long centuries before Homer sang of " Hundred gated Thebes."   My companions and I had travelled together through many parts of India, and had done considerable of Egypt in each other's company.   We thoroughly understood each other's peculiarities, and, consequently knew that no " Dahabiyeh Devil " could ever disturb the pleasure of our voyage.

Our berths had been selected before leaving Cairo, so that now everything had been nicely arranged for our comfort when we went on board our boat at this village of Beni Suef.   I had laid in an abundant supply of cigars, and a thousand and one other articles I would need during the voyage.   My companions had done the same; but before starting we strolled up to the bazar to make a few purchases and while we were looking at the various wares exposed for sale, my boy Salame, came rushing up to inform us that a fine fresh breeze was springing up from the North and that everything was in readiness for our departure, consequently we hurried off down to the wharf, stepped on board our dahabiyeh, the ropes were cast off, the sails hoisted and we went plowing along towards the steep and rocky cliffs which adorn the east bank of the Nile.

It reminded me of the happy days of long ago, to stand once more on board a dahabiyeh, to see the great big lateen sails swelling out before a good stiff north wind and hear the water rippling along under our quarter.   Our boat scudded along upon the bosom of this famous river and we watched the ever changing scenery of the fertile fields upon the banks, with occasionally here and there a village to attract our attention.   It was one continuous panorama of cotton, cane, clover, tasseled corn, sweet scented bean fields, purple lupins, and palm groves, with now and then the white-washed walls of a Sheik's tomb, or white minaret peeping out from amid the dense foliage surrounding them.   The tall black chimneys of some sugar plantation occasionally came into view, while pigeon towers, with clouds of fluttering birds around them, seemed ever to be coming and going.   We could hear at times the loud hoarse scream of a locomotive that was passing, the noise of which scared the white paddy birds and others from the banks of the river and the small islands dotting the stream on our way.

Every new village of mud-dried bricks was like the one just passed and the same river was rushing by, upon whose placid bosom drifted the magnificent barge of the renowned Cleopatra, now cut by the prow of our swiftly gliding boat. How dreamy the air and how beautiful the scenery! One must see for himself its wondrous charms, to be able fully to appreciate and enjoy the delightful pleasure of a voyage up the Nile in an Arab boat, manned by an Arab crew and under the supervision of a good Dragoman. It was one continuous round of ecstacy to be away from the cares of the world, with its pleasures and its pains, leaving civilization far behind as we sailed along upon the bosom of a mighty river.

Warburton says, in " Crescent and the Cross," page 180, " No words can convey an idea of the beauty and delightfulness of tropical weather, at least while any breeze from the north is blowing. There is a pleasure in the very act of breathing, a voluptuous consciousness that existence is a blessed thing; the pulse beats high, but calmly; the eye feels expanded, the chest heaves pleasurably as if air was a delicious draught to thirsty lungs, and the mind takes its coloring, and character from sensation. No thought of melancholy ever darkens over us; no painful sense of isolation or of loneliness, as day after day we pass on through silent deserts, upon the silent and solemn river. One seems, as it were removed into another state of existence; and all strifes and struggles of that from which we have emerged seem to fade, softened into indistinctness."

This mighty river has echoed to the demonstrated thoughts of a nation that had risen to wondrous heights of Science, Arts and Philosophies long centuries before the harps of Israel grew melodious with the songs of David; whose history can be deciphered, not only in the hieroglyphic inscriptions written with pens of steel and bronze and her mummied dead, but also in her works of Art which adorned the banks of this grand old river Nile before the dawn of history. These works demonstrate the extent of knowledge to which this ancient people had attained long centuries before Abraham came from Chaldea.

Who can tell when Egypt first began to develop, with gigantic strides, her onward march to civilization? How, when, or from whence she received her wondrous knowledge? We know not, and can only partially guess that she received it from the " Land of the Vedas." We can see the effect of the Wisdom that pertained to the people who built the stupendous Tombs, Temples and Monuments, whose ruins to-day lie scattered around, from one end of this remarkable valley to the other. Although a great majority of those extraordinary fabrics have crumbled into dust, becoming mixed with the drifting sands of the desert, and blown by the winds of heaven to the four cardinal points of the universe; yet, to-day, in this twentieth century, our most eminent men stand with bowed heads in admiration before the very vestiges of their departed glory. With silent but impressive tongues they impart to us the very thoughts of the people of ancient Egypt to whose knowledge and skill the world is indebted for these majestic tombs, temples and monolithic statues, whose very ruins command our most profound respect and admiration.

A sight in Upper Egypt never to be forgotten is the imposing effect of the setting sun upon the surrounding scenery. When the heat of the day has passed, the shadows of the palm trees lengthen out and go creeping across the Western bank, down into the flowing waters of the river. The deep recesses of the yellow cliffs of the mountains approach closer to the Nile, on the East, taking on a deep violet color, while their faces are lit up with a ruddy golden hue, changing again into a lovely roseate tinge, successively passing through all the colors of the rainbow. On the West bank the palms turn into a deeper bronze against the crimson and gold of the Western horizon, and as the glowing sun sank from our view, the mountains in the East changed to a very peculiar greenish grey color. The heavens above were illumined with an indescribable halo of glory, followed by a deep and beautiful blue, which gradually faded into a deeper and deeper tint, until finally the golden yellow, red and pink colors gradually dissolve and the blue became more clearly defined. One by one the stars began to appear in the azure vault above, a soft tremulous glow of twilight fell upon the scene, soon to fade away, and another day had passed and gone forever across the threshold of eternity. All that was left to remind us of its passing was the halo of light, the after-glow flashing up from the West-Gate in streams of light, lasting but for a short time, thus closing the day by the command of the Supreme Architect of the Universe, and darkness covered the face of the earth. From out the depths of the gloom came the lowing of cattle, the

27

voices of the fellaheen upon the banks of the river, as they return homeward from their labors of the day, and the swish of the waters of the river as our boat went sailing, with a light breeze, over the shimmering bosom of the glorious river Nile.

We passed islands thickly populated with paddy birds, rising in clouds at our approach and flying over to the western shore to disappear among the vegetation which lines its banks. We passed Bibba, with its peculiar looking Coptic convent, whose roof was covered with numerous little mud domes, and noticed quite a number of pelicans, herons, lapwings, purple Nile geese, and heard the shriek of the whistle of a locomotive as it went rushing by, with its motley crowd of passengers. As the sun went down in crimson and gold the wind died out and our captain sheered the boat into the bank of the river, the tall flapping sails were furled, and we tied up for the night under the glittering stars of an Egyptian sky.

Our sailors gathered around the fire for their evening meal and soon afterward the air resounded to their double pipe and drum. The guttural notes of an Arab love song rang out upon the stillness of the night, every verse of which was sung as a solo, but the last two lines were generally repeated by the whole crew, as a chorus, accompanied by clapping of hands, the beating of drum, and the shrill quick notes of the double pipe. They never seem to tire of singing, and every one of them seems to be fairly good performers on the pipe and drum. This latter instrument is simply an earthen vessel, with a skin stretched over the open end. (We afterwards procured two good tambourines for them.) They usually beat the drum as a tambourine with the open hand. Every night, whether sailing on the grand old river, or tied up to the bank, they gather in a circle and sing their songs and laugh and jest with each other like so many boys, until they tire, when they wrap themselves in their white capotes and seek the drowsy God. Some of these songs are quite humorous, others grave and sentimental. I shall quote you two songs that were translated especially for Eliot Warburton and his " Crescent and Cross : "

SERENADE.

" Come forth, bright girl, and midnight skies
    Will think that morning's gate uncloses ;
The dazzled dew will think thine eyes
    Are suns, and vanish from the roses.

Allah ! how my heart-strings stir !
Harp-like, touched by thought of her !
Holy prophet ! blessed be thou !
Fairest maiden, hear my vow !

" The rich red wine seems mantling high
Within thy cheeks so roseate glowing,
And beauty-drunkenness through mine eye
Is all my fevered heart o'erflowing.
Blessed Allah ! send thy grace !
Blessed Allah ! make my face
White, before thy presence dread
Wakes to life the slumbering dead.

The following is quite a favorite among the boatmen of the Nile :

THE MOTHER TO HER DAUGHTER.

MOTHER.

My daughter, 'tis time that thou wert wed,
Ten summers already have shone o'er thy head ;
I must find thee a husband, if, under the sun,
The conscript-catcher has left us one.

DAUGHTER.

Dear mother, one husband will never do
I have so much love, that I must have two ;
And I'll find for each, as you shall see,
More love than both can bring to me.

One husband shall carry a lance so bright ;
He shall roam the desert for spoil by night ;
And when morning lights up the dark palm-tree
He shall find sweet welcome home from me.

The other a sailor bold shall be ;
He shall fish all day in the deep blue sea ;
And when evening brings his hour of rest,
He shall find repose on this faithful breast.

MOTHER.

There's no chance, my child, of a double match
For men are scarce, and hard to catch ;
So I fear you *must* make one husband do,
And try to love him as well as two.

Our crew consisted of a Reis (Captain) a Pilot, twelve sailors, one good cook, a second cook, two good servants, a man to wash and iron and help in the cabin, one boy cook for the sailors and a dragoman who had charge of the whole outfit, subject of course to our special desire. These had been outlined in an agreement drawn up at our Consulate, duly signed and witnessed. I must certainly admit that the agreement was kept to the very letter, consequently the entire crew were liberally remembered when the question of bak-sheesh was considered at the expiration of our voyage.

Ah, what glorious nights were spent in our journey up that grand old river Nile. This night, especially, was enjoyable beyond expression, as each object around was enhanced and softened by the lovely moonlit rays. The very mountains stood out sharp and clearly defined under the silvery light of the brilliant moon; the radiant stars seemed to sparkle with indescribable splendor and beauty. Old god Nilus flowed quietly by, without a ripple upon its surface, and not a sound disturbed the silence of the night. The very air we breathed seemed full of quiet reverie, a dreamy indescribable feeling seemed to steal o'er us, and we were lost in our own thoughts. We were in the heart of the Land of the Pharaohs, upon the very river which bore upon its throbbing bosom the rush cradle wherein slept the infant Moses, and no doubt these very hills and banks have resounded to the laughter of Mark Antony and Cleopatra, with their attendants, as they floated o'er the flowing waters of the river in her gilded barge. Philosophers and learned men of every age have watched these self-same stars, under just as glorious a sky as shone down upon us that night. As we sat enwrapped in the majesty of its divine light memories of the grandeur of Egypt in her " Golden Age " came back to us and we saw, in fancy, the hundred gated Thebes, the glory of Memphian splendor, stately Heliopolis and the glorious cities of the dim and misty past, which, in imagination, we peopled again, as in the days of Ancient Egyptian splendor, when the Arts and Sciences were flourishing long before the Sphinx looked to the East. What an extraordinary panorama of events passed in review before us, comprising epochs of advanced knowledge, whose precepts and teachings were to be lost through successive ages; long processions of conquering armies and the domination of the imperial Cæsars, down to the Egypt of to-day.

Our reverie came abruptly to an end, and we retired to our cabin to dream in the arms of Morpheus, of white robed and leopard-clad priests, and vestal virgins performing their mystic rites and ceremonies, who crown us with laurel wreaths and lotus buds as they lead us up to their altar of Fire to receive the Light. As we prostrate ourselves before its radiance we awake with a start to find the Sun God Ra looking down upon us from his throne on high, and the jarring, jangling sound of a gong reverberating throughout the cabin, proclaiming the approach of our morning meal.

We took our regular morning plunge into the river, had our coffee presented to us by our dragoman, Hassan, who told us that we were close to the town of Feshn, and he pointed out to us the white-washed walls of the houses a short distance from the river,

This town is situated twenty-four miles from our starting-place, Beni Suef, and ninety-six miles from Cairo. It is surrounded with finely cultivated fields, gardens, palm groves, pomegranate trees, a variety of shrubs and all kinds of vegetables. We strolled out upon the bank of the river, gun in hand accompanied by Salame, and in a very short time we shot two or three brace of red-legged partridges, a couple of dozen quail and returned to the boat to enjoy our breakfast "*al fesco.*" As we sat under the awning, shaded from the glowing rays of the morning sun, our sailors harnessed themselves to the tow line and reis Abdallah sheered our boat off from the bank, and we went crawling along, accompanied by the sounding voices of the sailors upon the tow path. Soon a light air sprung up, our boat gathered head-way as the large sails swelled out, full and round before the freshening wind, when the men dropped the tow line, wrapped their scanty clothing around their heads, plunged into the river and came swimming alongside like so many tritons, with glistening skins and laughing faces, and as we sailed by the water front of Feshn, our sailors seemed to loose themselves in song and music. The sound of the drum, tambourines and pipes resounded over the river, the people gathered upon the banks and watched us as our boat went gliding by, like some gigantic bird o'er the sparkling waters.

A few miles above Feshn, upon the East bank of the river, we saw El-Kebi or Medinet el-Gahil, which marks the site of a very ancient Egyptian town. The site and fortifications can be plainly traced by the remains of the houses and ancient forts said to have been constructed by Men-Kheeper-Ra and Isis-em-Kheb against invasions from the North, on which side it is most strongly fortified. These fortifications run clear down to the river and out upon the rocks. We noticed that many of the bricks used in the building of this town and fortifications were marked with the names of both the High Priest of Thebes and his wife. There appears to have been a very fine stone quay or landing place, built quite close to the river and numerous tombs of all kinds just outside the town. The old city of *Hipponon* lies a couple of miles from these ruins, off to the South-east. In the ancient days of Pharaonic history it was the capital of the XVIIIth Nome of Upper Egypt. We passed *El-Fent,* located quite a distance back from the river, on the West bank amidst fertile fields, palm groves and gardens.

After rounding the bend of the river we saw *Malateya* and the site of some very ancient mounds, also, on the West bank, but close to the river, and for the first time in quite a distance, fields of waving grain again came into view upon the East bank, and just beyond this vegetation, under the shadow of the table mountain of *Gebel-Shekh Embarak,* we saw the site of an ancient city, which was in the height of its glory during the Roman domination. In this place we found the remains of an ancient flint manufactory, as the ground was literally strewn with flint implements of all kinds. The wind continued to blow softly in our favor, so we kept on our way southward, sailing by the rocky shores on the east and turning around the curving bank of the river, we sailed by a large island and discovered *Maghagha,* off to our right on the West bank surrounded by extensive sugar plantations.

There is a very large sugar factory here which is well worth seeing, besides a post-office and railway station. During the cane harvest it is a very busy place, but at other times is quite dull. The river here grew very wide, interspersed with several small islands, and a short distance above the town were numerous sand bars which seemed to be a favorite resort for all kinds of wild foul.

A little farther on we passed *Hagar-es-Salam,* the "Stone of Welfare," which is a large rock in the river, close to the shore. It had received its peculiar name from a superstition existing among the Nile boatmen. They believe a voyage down the river would not be prosperous until it is passed. We now noticed that the mountains bordering the river for quite a distance began to recede toward the East.

We passed Sharona on the East bank and Aba on the West, with ruins of ancient cities on both sides of the river. The wind freshened as we went careening along, by sand bars and small islands, inhabited by great flocks of birds who rose in clouds as we neared them.

We soon sighted *Abu Girga*, on the West bank, which boasts of a post-office besides a telegraph and railway station. It is a very fine looking place from the river, centered in a beautiful cultivated plain. The town is about half an hour's walk from the landing, surrounded with fine palm groves, flowering shrubs and some very extensive mounds. About eight miles to the West, on the *Bahr Yusuf*, and near the edge of the desert is located *Behnesa* (the ancient city of *Oxyrrhinkhos*), in the Nome of *Sep*, a point of departure for all desiring to visit the *Little Oasis* or *Woh el-Bahariya*, (*the Oasis Parva of the Romans*). It is about four days' journey from Behnesa and is reached, generally, by sumpter camels which travel about three to five miles per hour, on the average, although a great deal more can be got out of them if you push them hard.

There are a number of inhabited spots in this Oasis, but it is very unhealthy on account of the stagnant lakes or ponds of water which exhale a pernicious miasma, dangerous alike to natives and travellers, as it produces a very serious remittent fever, manifesting itself twice a year, in Summer and in Autumn. All those desirous of visiting this place should therefore do so either in the Winter or in the Spring, that they may escape the danger of this fever, which is very easily taken. Some fine gardens exist here, the best of which are to be found in the vicinity of El-Quasr. All kinds of fruit, such as pomegranates, bananas, oranges, apricots, figs, grapes, etc., grow in abundance. A number of hot springs also bubble up in this Oasis, the waters of which have a temperature of about 160° F. Very much finer dates are produced here than in any other part of the valley of the Nile. Their date palms yield in far greater abundance and the best are called *the Kaka*. It is from the date crop that they derive their principal revenue.

The city of *Oxyrrhynkhos* derives its name from a fish which the natives used to worship. The town, to-day, is of very little importance, the desert sands having drifted into large sand-dunes that extend all along the edge of the cultivated land, and on the southern part of the site of the old city, are mounds covered with sand, above which, have been erected several Sheik's tombs, while upon others we find large quantities of pottery, bricks, stones, columns, pieces of cornices and very peculiar looking altar-like stones, which go to prove the existence of a large city here at some time, whose size is demonstrated in the extent of the mounds.

There are some very interesting caverns to be seen a short distance to the northwest of the present town of Behnesa, one of which is decorated with a series of columns, but we are unable to explore and investigate them, as we would desire, on account of their being filled with water. The city of Oxyrrhynkhos was, during the fifth century, a stronghold of the Christians, and the town itself was noted for its churches, said to have been twelve in number. History informs us that the diocese contained ten thousand monks and twelve hundred nuns; its Egyptian name was *Pa-Maze*, and during the Arab domination it had quite a large population.

All around Abu Girga are to be found the ruined sites of ancient towns and cities, for instance, about three miles south of this place, and about a mile and a half from the river, we come to the town of El-Qes, the ancient site of *Kynopolis*—the "City of Dogs." It is here that Amubis was worshipped and all dogs held in great veneration by the ancient inhabitants, so much so that to kill one was considered the greatest crime which could be committed, and Plutarch tells how a quarrel once arose between these two Nomes of *Sep* and *Kynopolis*, requiring Roman intervention to settle. The citizens of each Nome, as it seems, had killed and eaten the sacred gods, or dog and fish, of the other, which act caused such bitter strife and ill-feeling that, as I have before stated, the Roman authority had to interfere. Some discussion has arisen as to the proof of the site of this city of *Kynopolis;* many historians place it upon the East bank, at Shekh Fadl, while according to Ptolemy it was situated upon an island of the Nile; but there is no evidence of such an island to-day, although Murray says:

"There is reason to believe that one branch of the Nile had been stopped in this spot, which once flowed to the west of El-Qes; and this would accord with the position of Kynopolis on an island, according to Ptolemy, and account for the statement of Mukkan that El-Qes was on the East bank." At Shekh Fadl there are to be found evidences of two small temples, the site of which is now occupied by a sugar factory, surrounded by very nice gardens, etc., in fact there are cultivated fields on the East bank the entire distance from Shekh Embarak, opposite Maghagah, to this place Shekh Fadl. Not far from here is where Father Sicard found quite a number of dog mummies, and in examining this subject we find the existence of more than one breed of dogs in Egypt in those days. There are in addition many other things which will possess great interest to the traveller or explorer in this vicinity.

In the morning we arose to find our boat under way, with just enough wind blowing to keep steerage way upon her; so we took our toast and coffee, lit a good cigar and went up under the awning to watch the surrounding scenery. As we watched the river bank receding we also noticed that the various sand spits were literally alive with all kinds of birds, such as the snow white pelican, flamingo, purple Nile geese, Ibis, Heron, plover, golden snipe, etc., etc., and saw away up in the azure sky an eagle watching its prey, far below him, while the pied kingfishers were plying their vocation. Flocks of sheep and many goats were browsing along the shore, while buffaloes and camels were to be seen under the care of some fellaheen, who was driving them along the path by the river, and all the time the songs of our sailors rang out upon the morning air in one continuous stream, like the flowing waters of the river itself, as they never seemed to tire of singing, and to tell the truth we had grown so accustomed to it we were beginning to like it, for it served to break the monotony of our voyage.

The gong rang out, and we went down the narrow steps to partake of an excellent meal, after which we came on deck again to see our sailors tracking along the tow-path, with their scanty costumes flapping as they went bobbing along, harnessed on to the tow-line, and the sound of their everlasting songs ringing out in unison to tramping footsteps. As we watched them the wind sprang up again, the ropes were dropped, they twisted their clothes around their heads, plunged into the river, clambered on board, loosed the great big sails, and once more we went careening along the sparkling waters up towards Kolosana, which is quite a large village on the west bank of the river, sixty-four miles from Beni Suef, and one hundred and thirty-six miles from Cairo.

It lies close to the river and presents quite a picturesque appearance from here, with its very fine-looking palm groves and fertile fields.

There is both post and telegraph offices here, as well as a railway station. The town is located on high mounds, and the bank of the river at this place is effected by the wash of its waters.

On the opposite side of the Nile, on its east bank, is the village of *Surariya*, and just beyond it are the ruins of some very ancient towns, as well as the remains of a very ancient temple in a rather out-of-the-way place among the rocks, which belonged to the nineteenth dynasty. The representations upon the walls show that the triad of Sebek, Hathor and Horus were worshipped here. Rameses III, Horus and the god Sebek, with the head of a crocodile, are plainly to be seen upon the walls. The hills recede close to this place, falling off to the southeast and forming the northern side of the Wady ed-Der. To the northwest of its mouth and about ten minutes' walk from the river are some very fine limestone quarries, wherein we found a painted grotto temple that had been dedicated to Hathor, and inscribed upon it were the names of Rameses II (Mer-en-Ptah), and Seti II.

Just beyond Kolosana we passed two large islands, and saw the cars go rushing by on their way south. The wind began to die out and our great sails began to flap idly in the calm of the evening, when our reis Abdallah again sheered the boat under the bank, and we tied up for the night a short distance north of the village of Samallut. It has a railway station with post and telegraph offices, and lies about half a mile from the river and about five miles south of Kolosana. This is quite a large town, conspicuous for a tall and graceful minaret rising from amidst a very fine grove of palm trees. The town is surrounded by fields of cane, clover, beans, etc., and there are some very good sugar factories located here. A little farther on, to the south, and on the east bank, are the lofty and precipitous cliffs of *Gebel et-Ter*, "Bird Mountain." Taking my gun and Salame along with me to carry the birds, we strolled down the river towards Kolosana, while Hassan took Musa along with him to make some purchases of butter, eggs, etc., at Samallut, to replenish our larder, while our sailors indulged themselves, by gathering in a circle in the usual way, to sing their customary songs. Salame and I soon had plenty of sport, for he enjoyed the retrieving process about as much I did knocking the birds over. In a very little while we found that we had bagged a lot of quail, over a dozen fine ducks, a few grouse and one very large snow-white pelican that I desired for a specimen. We then returned to the boat in time for my bath, and I dressed just as the gong rang out for dinner. After dinner we went on deck, threw ourselves into our nice cosy chairs under the awning, lit our cigars and watched the glorious sunset and the play of colors upon the high and lofty cliffs of Gebel et-Ter.

It would be simply impossible to express in words the gorgeous coloring, the play of lights and shades, the deep flush of crimson, pink, and gold, with the sweet, indescribable after-glow of a Nile sunset. I have watched the setting sun in many climes and countries, but never have I seen such glorious, inexpressible colorings of a sunset sky as I have witnessed in this wondrous valley of the Nile.

I conscientiously believe that to properly understand the history of this country one should begin in the Delta of the Nile and make a careful examination of the various ruins of tombs, temples, monuments, etc., as they go up the Nile, as by this means only will they be enabled to see some of the most ancient specimens of Egyptian architecture belonging to many cities which were in the height of their glory long centuries before Romulus and Remus laid the foundation of Rome. All who come into this valley to acquire a knowledge of Egyptian Architecture, etc., should. therefore, begin their study while coming up through Gizeh, Sakkarah, Medum, The Fayum, Beni Hassan, Tel el Amarna, Karnak and Luxor to the Island of Philæ. In this way each and all will be able to trace the peculiar style of architecture from the earliest Pharaonic age down to the decline of the Roman domination.

Again, before going into the "Land of Egypt," one should have *some* knowledge of the history of the country, its people, their manners and customs, by reason of which they would enjoy their journeyings more and would come back far better pleased and with a clearer understanding of what they had seen.

Under an awning, especially fitted up for our comfort and enjoyment, we passed many pleasant evenings. We had nice cosy, comfortable chairs, tables, rugs, cushions, etc., with a gun-rack quite convenient for our use, as we amused ourselves very often with our rifles and shot guns. We sat and talked on various subjects until we found ourselves yawning, when we retired to sleep. The loud *yallough* of Hassan to the crew awakened me and I found the sun flashing its light above the eastern mountains, and on reaching the deck found our boat was under way, with a light air astir, heading for the tall cliffs of Gebel et-Ter. It does not take long to reach the landing place on the north side of this mountain, upon whose flat top is located a Coptic convent. This place is also called *Der el-Adra,* and by many others *Der el-Bakara,* because in the days gone by travellers desiring to visit the convent were hoisted up by means of a pulley, but now they land to the north of the mountain and walk up steep rocky steps, which form a sort of path to the summit.

But very little is to be seen when the summit is reached, except the magnificent view of the surrounding country. The village is walled in and contains a number of squalid-looking houses, occupied by monks and laymen, with their wives and children. The monks claim to be shoemakers; but it seemed to me their principal occupation was that of begging, for no sooner does a boat appear in sight than they rush down to the river and swim off to it, actually fighting their way on board, and beg most lustily for alms, in many instances without a particle of clothing to hide their nakedness, and if the wind is scant they hang around and pester the life out of you. If they are driven off one side of the boat they will very soon appear on the other and in this way will cause you considerable annoyance, so the best thing to do is to give them baksheesh and let them go at their own "sweet will."

The convent, or church, is a very peculiar one, as it is partly underground, with the choir and sanctuary cut out of the solid rock. It is well worth a visit. There is a peculiar legend attached to this place. The Arabs believe that all kinds of birds flock to this mountain, once a year, in order to arrange the affairs of the whole feathered creation.

We came down to our boat and got rid of the jostling mendicant crowd, by going on board, after which our sailors punted her off into the stream, the sails were loosed and once more we were sailing along on our journey south. Our dragoman told us that he was glad we had passed this place in safety, for the last time he was sailing by this mountain a very sudden gust of wind turned the boat upon her beam-end. They were extremely fortunate, however, as not a life had been lost on account of the accident, they having righted her again and continued their voyage, minus some of their guns, etc., that were on the upper deck, and he said from that time he was always on the look-out for squalls while passing that mountain.

About five or six miles to the south of this convent are the site and ruins of Tehna, with its very large mounds, located about three-fourths of a mile from the river, under the rocky cliffs of the Eastern mountains, which have dwindled down into hills. A trip to this place will prove of more than passing interest to the traveller, because he will be enabled to see side by side, as it were, both the tombs of the earliest Pharaonic age and those that belonged to the very latest period of rock tombs of the Lagadie.

These tombs are built after the style of those at Memphis and consist of three distinct parts: 1st. The entrance chamber or chambers. 2nd. A very deep shaft. 3rd. The sepulchral vault, wherein is placed the sarcophagus for the mummy alone. The entrances to the different tombs vary in construction, as many of them are decorated with columns, while a great number are without them; but one thing they nearly all have in common, which is that the walls are all adorned with paintings taken from the daily life of the deceased and his family. It is just from such things as these that we have been enabled to study the manners and customs of these ancient people. The quarries are also very interesting places to visit, in fact there are many things in this vicinity which will repay one for the time and trouble expended in visiting them.

After returning from these jaunts we appreciated our comfortable quarters on board our floating home, as we were invariably tired and weary; but the comfort of a cooling bath and a good rest, after our long rambling tramp, added zest to our appetite for dinner, and fitted us to spend the evening on deck under the glittering stars, talking of these most extraordinary relics of ancient Egyptian splendor, constituting an ample recompense for the additional trifling expense. As there was no wind we tied up for the night, and long after the others had retired I sat up writing to friends at home and arranging my notes of the day for future use. I slept remarkably well and did not awake until Salame told me that the first gong had sounded for breakfast and was surprised on looking out my cabin window to see our boat crawling along, drawn by our sailors on the tow path, and to hear the same old inimitable refrain echoing o'er the waters, so, with rowing and punting we managed to reach Minia.

It is a very pretty and prosperous town one hundred and fifty-three miles from Cairo, very nicely located on the west bank of the river. It contains post and telegraph offices and a railway station. Minia is quite an important town, having a population of over sixteen thousand inhabitants, with two fairly good hotels and a number of stores, where one can purchase nearly all they may need, from different varieties of Manchester goods, to jams, jellies, patent medicines, etc., etc. A market was held here every Monday, and as we visited this place Saturday we agreed to remain over so that Hassan could buy the necessaries for our journey South. It was here in Minia that the first sugar factory was established in the "Land of Egypt," which is there to-day, not as it used to be, but very much enlarged and improved, with all the latest modern machinery. The inhabitants of this place are not very prepossessing in their appearance or their manners, and are generally very dirty, many of them swarming with vermin. Opthalmia and other diseases are quite prevalent among both sexes.

In many places throughout this country, one out of a score of people you meet, are either totally blind or partially so. I will venture to say that you may travel the wide world over and never in all your wanderings find so many one-eyed people as you will in the "Land of Egypt." The streets are extremely narrow, and very dusty, with no sidewalks, being usually filled with an ill-smelling lot of sullen, unfriendly, thieving people, both men and women.

We spent our Sunday on board the boat, arranging our notes, until the evening, when I went on shore and strolled off down the river, accompanied by Salame. On turning back toward our floating home we met a gentleman who was, like ourselves, out for an evening walk. I entered into conversation with him and found that he was returning to his home in England, after having spent a number of years in India. I invited him to dine with us, which invitation he most courteously accepted, and we spent the rest of the evening and far into the night talking of the "Land of the Vedas," Egypt and Ancient Masonry, of which I shall speak in the next chapter. The next morning we arose early and went on shore to visit the bazar and market-place. Hasson bought what he needed and I purchased a good supply of candles and magnesium wire to be used during our explorations among the tombs and temples farther South.

Everything in the nature of vegetables and fruits, as well as chickens, ducks, geese, turkeys, etc., were very cheap. Hassan bought a very fine sheep for our crew for $4.00, chickens sold for ten cents each, ducks the same, fine live geese from thirty-five cents to half a dollar, pigeons sold for twenty-five cents a dozen, while very large and excellent turkeys sold for seventy-five cents each. What a surging, dirty, clamoring crowd they were, yelling and shrieking at the top of their voices, bargaining one with the other for their ware. The burning sun during the time we were there was beating down upon us its fiery rays, and the dust, rising in smothering clouds, from the incessant tramping of feet made the air suffocating, and I was glad to get away from the place to enjoy myself with a good cigar on board the boat, watch the people walking on shore and the various boats and steamers upon the river.

Minia is a very busy place during the cane harvest, when the sugar factories are running. This is the proper time to visit them, to witness the process of extracting the juice, boiling, etc., which enters largely into the production of sugar. I sat here under the awning smoking and watching the people pass and repass, and the old fellow who keeps guard at the gate of the Khedive's summer palace, and the boats upon the river, until the gong rang for dinner. As there was no wind we concluded to remain at this place over night, on account of which the captain and crew had a grand fastasia, inviting a great many people from the other boats around us. As soon as our men began to beat their drums and tambourines the river bank became crowded with people, listening to both the vocal and instrumental music, not only of our own crew but that of their friends as well. They blew their pipes and beat their tambourines and drums, singing and dancing and performing various comic and grotesque antics, in fact, having one of the greatest times with this fantasia, burning fire works, etc., that we had ever witnessed. They kept it up for I do not know how long, as I went to bed and slept quietly all through the night.

Shortly after breakfast a light air sprang up that was favorable for us, so our sails were loosed, the boat punted off into the stream, when she soon began to gather headway, and off we go once more to the sounding songs of our sailors and the loud benedictions of the friends of our crew. We passed the thriving little town of Suadi, on the East bank, with its large sugar plantations; but we did not stop to examine either the mounds or the ruins of the town, said to be located there, but kept on, sailing by a rather large island, and as the wind began to freshen we soon came up to *Neslat ez-Zawiya*, a small village, around which there are many very interesting things to be seen. All the way from Suadi to Tel el-Amarna one can find ruins of tombs and temples, as well as very extensive quarries of the Roman period; but we did not stop to examine any, as we are very anxious to get to the tombs of Beni Hassan and explore them. About five miles from Minia we arrive at and pass *Zawiyet el-Mayyitin* at which place is located the modern cemetery of Minia.

In viewing their method of disposing of the dead to-day, and the ferrying of the bodies across the river, accompanied by the ululations of the women, will recall to the observer the same peculiar custom of the ancient Egyptians during the Golden Age of Egypt. Three times a year, in certain months, somewhere about the full of the moon, these people of Minia go over to their dead and make their offerings to them of dates, palm branches, etc. A short distance from here to the South, are the celebrated "Red mounds," a most interesting place to visit on account of the early tombs that were discovered here. It used to be in the days of the twelfth dynasty, possibly earlier, a manufactory of pottery and alabaster vases, and no doubt many beautiful specimens of the handiwork of these people, have been recovered from the tombs and temples in the different parts of Egypt, which are to be seen to-day, in the various museums throughout the world. A great number are still, doubtless, lying undiscovered beneath the shrouding sands of the desert. The ancient name of this place was *Hebu*, and it belonged to the Nome of *Mah*, in Upper Egypt.

Beni Hassan was at length reached, and we could see with our glasses the tombs and grottos that have been hollowed out in the side of the mountain. We had been warned by travellers and friends to be careful and have a good watch set both night and day, while stopping in this place, for it is noted as being one of the worst places for thieves to be found on the Nile. The villages have been the rendezvous for thieves for many long years; in fact, the old village was destroyed by order of Ibrahim Pasha, on account of the disreputable character of the inhabi-

ROCK TOMBS OF BENI HASSAN

tants; but they have returned again and rebuilt their hovels, and now the only thing to do is to keep a strict watch for them, both day and night. We gave our men extra baksheesh to be doubly careful during our stay. The tombs are located two miles from where we landed, so we hired donkeys, took candles and magnesium wire along, that we might examine their interior parts. We started upon our way, through palm groves and sand dunes, toward the mountains, our donkey boys making directly for one especial tomb, and that one is decorated with Doric columns. One of the first things we carefully examined was the columns at the entrance of this tomb, which most assuredly astonished us, as they were purely and simply Doric. After very careful examination, both of the outer and interior columns, we most certainly agreed with many other authorities that the Doric Order must have originated in Egypt, and that here in this very tomb were evidences of this fact. Champollin calls them *Proto Doric*, or *Pre Doric Columns*. And Lepsius bears out this assertion in his account of these remarkable columns.

The entrance to the first tombs is noted for its two beautiful octagonal columns, and in the inside chamber four sixteen-edged, fluted columns (referred to above) supporting three very fine painted arches. At the end of this chamber is a recess containing the dilapidated statues of the deceased and his two wives. He was named *Amenemha*, or *Ameni*, after a king of the eleventh dynasty. In the inscription which is upon both sides of the doorway, or entrance to the chamber, is an historical account of himself telling us that he was a General of infantry under Usertesen the First and Governor of the *Nome* of *Sah.* The paintings in this tomb are very interesting; but unfortunately they are not as bright and fresh as when I first saw them some years ago, but still they are well worthy a careful study. The next tomb that we visited was that of Khnem-Hetep, or Noum-Hotep, who was a priest of Horus and Anubis.

The pictures in this tomb, as I have said, are deserving of careful study, because, from such paintings only are we able to come to an understanding of the manners and customs of the people living in the Golden Age of Egyptian history; for here, like in the tomb of Tih, we may see carpenters, boatbuilders, weavers, potters, fullers, bakers, sculptors and others working at their trades, while other pictures represent

28

scenes of ploughing, sowing, reaping, harvesting, threshing and storing the grain, etc. Another represents a Nile boat taking the mummy of the deceased to Abydos (the grave of Osiris). There are fishing and hunting scenes, etc., etc., all of which are extremely instructive.

This tomb contains a very interesting painting upon the North wall, representing the immigration of some *Scmetic* tribe, for they all have very prominent aquiline noses and pointed black beards which plainly denotes their nationality. They are clothed differently from the Egyp-tians around them, and are evidently the advance guard of a new race into Egypt. It is the most ancient painting ever discovered, showing the immigration of an Asiatic race which afterward played such an important part in the government of this country.

We also visited *Spcos Artemidos*, a grotto, very much like those of Beni Hassan; it is called by the Arabs *Stable Antar*. This tomb was founded by Hatasu. or Thothmes III, of the eighteenth dynasty. We did not remain very long at this tomb, as it was getting on towards sun-down, and we were among a very hard class of people, so we mounted our little donkeys and rode back to our floating home; but before we reached the river I bought a few scarabs, a couple of mummied cats which bore their ear-marks in the smell, for although it must have been thirty cen-turies since they made night hideous with their yowlings, the odor of cat was plainly distinguished when handling them.

When we arrived at the river and our boat, the wind was blowing fair, so just as soon as we stepped on board the sails were loosed and off we went once again, still toward the South. We had time enough to take our bath and smoke a cigar when the gong rang out for dinner and our craft was bowling along before a good stiff breeze which would soon put us into Roda, nine miles from Beni Hassan. When we came on deck again the sun had set, the stars were out in all their resplendent glory, the wind was fair and our reis pointed out the lights of Roda, which we soon reached. The sails furled and our boat made fast to the bank of the river we again took seats under the awning, where, before we had finished our cigars, the crew had formed their circle and the pipe and drums rang out with the fluttering tambourines. I did not stop up to listen to their songs, but went down to sleep, as I was tired and weary from my ramb-lings amidst the tombs or grottos of Beni Hassan.

Ineffable Degrees—Thoughts on Ecclesiastes—I. N. R. I.

.

.

.

Remember now thy Creator in the days of thy youth, while the evil days come not, nor the years draw nigh, when thou shalt say, I have no pleasure in them.

—ECCLESIASTES 12 : 1.

CHAPTER XIX.

INEFFABLE DEGREES—THOUGHTS ON ECCLESIASTES—I. N. R. I.

THE Symbolic degrees are those conferred in the Blue Lodge and known as: 1st, The Entered Apprentice; 2nd, The Fellowcraft, and 3rd, The Master Mason. These degrees are recognized throughout the world universal as the most ancient. All those who have taken them have the pre-requisite of being elected to the higher degrees of the York Rite, or to be inducted into the sublime and Ineffable degrees conferred in our own beloved Ancient and Accepted Scottish Rite Bodies of both the Northern or Southern Jurisdictions. That is, providing the applicant is in good and regular standing, in some regularly constituted Lodge, working under a Charter or warrant from some Grand Lodge in the United States of America, or in good and regular standing in *any Foreign Lodge* that is recognized by the Grand Lodges of the United States of America. Then, if the applicant is found worthy and well qualified he will, most assuredly, be elected to receive those sublimely beautiful degrees from the 4th to the 14th inclusive, which are called Ineffable, in order to distinguish them from the Symbolic degrees of the Blue Lodge.

These degrees are known as 4° *Secret Master*, 5° *Perfect Master*, 6° *Intimate Secretary*, 7° *Provost and Judge*, 8° *Intendent of the Building*, 9° *Elu of the Nine*, 10° *Elu of the Fifteen*, 11° *Elu of the Twelve*, 12° *Master Architect*, 13° *Royal Arch of Solomon*, 14° *Grand Elect or Perfect Elu*. I have shown, in a previous chapter, that the first three degrees of Blue Masonry are based upon the ancient Astronomical Allegories of the Egyptians, whose Astronomical ideas and solar symbols are intimately woven into the very heart of our glorious Fraternity. The whole of which will be very readily understood and comprehended by the Masonic student who has risen to the Sublime heights of the Ineffable degrees of our own beloved Scottish Rite Masonry.

They are indescribably grand, sublimely beautiful and *truly Ineffable*. They can only be acquired, thoroughly appreciated and learned by all those who pass from the square to the compasses whose swinging leg circumscribes every moral virtue. They will then be enabled to thoroughly understand the true value of Secrecy, Obedience and Fidelity, and in passing from one to the other our Aspirant will soon realize that there is a vast difference between the York and Scottish Rite of Masonry.

He will realize that just as soon as he steps across the very threshold of Scottish Masonry, on his way to the higher degrees in our Lodge of Perfection, that he is entering upon a rich field of intellectual research so vast and so grand that our Neophyte will scarcely realize the sublimity and grandeur of its teachings. At first he will be so blinded, as it were, by the refulgent glory, that he will but dimly sense in darkness visible the sublime ceremonies, and from out their profound depths he will in Silence begin to realize that he carries the light of all Knowledge within his own heart; aye, within his own grasp, and will come to an understanding that, in order to acquire knowledge, we must look within for the Light of Truth and Wisdom.

Let me state right here, that I earnestly desire my readers to know that "The Key to each degree is the Aspirant himself," and we must ever remember that "it is not the fear of God which is the beginning of Wisdom, but the Knowledge of SELF which is WISDOM ITSELF."

We gain knowledge and information in reading the thoughts of others; but we only attain Wisdom or become Wise *when we read our own thoughts, or Think for ourselves.* By the LIGHT of TRUTH AND WISDOM we ponder upon Death, and realize *that there is no death*, and that there is no inorganic matter; that all molecular forms are pulsing with life, and so far as this physical body of man is concerned, the old *shard*, or *shell*, the Personality at death passes away never to appear again in that form. Every atom and molecule that went to build it, disintegrates and becomes the dust of the earth once again, while the Individuality lives, the immortal part of man never dies, but endures forever. This separation of the Personality and the Individuality is most beautifully described by Sir Edwin Arnold, as:

> "Faithful friends! It lies I know,
> Pale and white, and cold as snow;
> And ye say, 'Abdallah's dead!'
> Weeping at the feet and head.

> "I can see your falling tears,
> I can hear your sighs and prayers;
> Yet I smile and whisper this —
> I am not the thing you kiss;
> Cease your tears and let it lie.
> It was mine—it is not I.'
>
> "Sweet friends! What the women lave
> For its last bed in the grave,
> Is a hut which I am quitting,
> Is a garment no more fitting,
> Is a cage from which at last
> Like a hawk, my soul has passed.
>
> "What ye lift upon the bier
> Is not worth a wistful tear;
> 'Tis an empty seashell—one
> Out of which the pearl is gone;
> The shell is broken—it lies there
> The pearl. the all, the soul is here.
>
> "Now the long, long wonder ends;
> Yet ye weep, my erring friends,
> While the one whom ye call dead
> In unbroken bliss instead,
> Lives and loves you—lost, 'tis true,
> For the light as shines for you;
> But in the light ye can not see
> Of undisturbed felicity—
> Lives a life that never dies."

What we call Death comes to every one, it meets us everywhere; is ever by our side, and yet we should not fear it, for it is that which opens for us the portals to a Life Eternal. We must ever remember that it is our bounden duty to live so as to become Perfect Masters in very deed, and carefully follow the teachings that are embodied in our ineffable degrees by *doing unto others whatever you would justly wish that they should do unto you;* then will Wisdom, Power and Benevolence lead your footsteps on to higher planes where peace and concord reign supreme.

Be zealous in the Cause, Faithful to yourself and Brother, Benevolent and Charitable to the needy, ever striving to be the Peace-Maker, and you will be most assuredly recompensed in attaining a just reward—Perfection. Thus will you be qualified to do good and instruct your Brother in all of these truly ineffable degrees of our beloved Scottish Rite of Masonry.

Through all your life, in your dealings with your fellow-man, whenever placed in a position to do so, *always dispense impartial justice to all.* For it hath been written: " *With what judgment ye judge, ye shall be judged; and with what measure ye mete, it shall be measured to you again.*" Causes that are sown by every individual, each moment and every hour, produce their effects, and JUSTICE RULES THE WORLD.

The mighty wheel of Karmic Law brings to every man the Karmic effects of his every act; aye, his every thought! Our beloved Rite teaches us that we live in a world of our own making, or creating, and that all the thoughts generated in our brain go forth from it with a potency for good or evil. As they pass on in their mission, through the universe, they come in contact with others, for like attracts like, and they will receive from them some subtle essence, returning to the source from which they emanated far more heavily charged with powers for Good or Evil, and we shall reap the effects in bitterness of heart, or inexpressible joy and happiness, as the case may be.

We cannot, by any possible means, escape from ourselves, *for our own Thoughts are our own Judge,* that is Unerring, Precise and True. Eventually these very judgments will accumulate around us until we shall finally stand fully revealed before ourselves and our Brothers as we actually are—GOOD AND TRUE, or FALSE AND FORESWORN.

If we will only pause to consider, we shall realize how unqualified we are to judge of the actions of our fellow-men, and consequently should not, under any circumstances try to do so; as in the first place we have not the ability nor the necessary means to judge any one; and for the best of all reasons, we have not the *three great requisites* of a Judge, like the Supreme Architect of the Universe, OMNIPRESENCE, OMNIPOTENCE AND OMNISCIENCE. We should most assuredly thoroughly understand that each and every one of us is capable only of judging of but one person, *and that one is ourself*—and right there our judgment should cease.

We should also know that Judging and Discriminating are two different things and if we may not Judge we can discriminate. For instance, in recognizing a fault in our Brother we should not judge him for it; but rather sympathize with him in his inability to rise above it, therefore, it is our duty to give him generous sympathy, and not to be harsh with him, because he is entangled in the meshes of an irresistible force which compels him to act in the manner that he does. Each and every one of us possess those finer senses by which we are enabled to distinguish an hypocritical foe from a true friend, and by the development of which we can readily tell the true from the false, and develop a force that will give us help, in our every day life, among our Brothers by the wayside. There are a great many deeds performed by many men, deeds that we execrate; yet, if we ourselves were placed under the same conditions, and compelled by similar forces, we would doubtless act in the self-same way. *Therefore Judge not*, but if you are compelled or called upon to do so " decide justly and impartially, and do justice to all men."

Every Brother who has attained to the honor of " Intendent of the Building" should work most earnestly and faithfully for the benefit of our glorious Scottish Rite in particular, and Masonry in general, making Charity and Benevolence his watchwords, and practicing these virtues every hour and every day of his life. It will be his especial Duty to make himself thoroughly familiar with the esoteric teachings of Masonry and Masonic Jurisprudence, so that he will not be a mere drone among the zealous workers of this degree; but advance along the Masonic road which will ultimately lead him to those of Perfection, so that he may be enabled to explore the profound depths of Philosophy that lie beneath the surface of each and every one of our supremely beautiful *Ineffable Degrees*. In his endeavors to discover the true meaning of the Symbology, that permeates each and every one, he will most assuredly discover that they were intended to reveal far more than the symbol itself, for, as previously stated, Symbols were made to conceal, and not to reveal, in the generally accepted meaning of that word. It will only be, therefore, after long and earnest study, and profound meditation, that he will come to an understanding of their *true* significance. In the twinkling of an eye their meaning will finally flash across his brain and illuminate his mind, revealing to him the fact that Masonry is devoted to *all Truth*, not alone to Science and Philosophy, but more especially and particularly to Political and Religious Truths as well.

Many of our degrees were created in order to reward those Elus who had proved their worthiness to our glorious Fraternity by their Obedience, Fidelity and Devotion; not to the Fraternity only, but to the cause of suffering Humanity, the destruction of Ignorance, and the Liberty of the People. It is the *Duty* of every Brother to WORK, earnestly and untiringly, in the interest of his fellow man, his country, the destruction of Tyranny and Fanatacism and to champion the Rights of the People against Intolerance, Bigotry and Persecution. Masonry sits apart from all plots and conspiracies, and does not countenance either Licentiousness or Anarchy; but will always be a power for Liberty and Justice, believing that every man has the right to worship God according to the dictates of his own conscience; that no man or body of men, have a right to condemn another's faith or belief because it does not agree or conform to their own conception of Right or Wrong. All really good and true men, as well as Masons, are alike in their ideas respecting all forms of worship, as they tolerate all opinions, establishing a fellowship with all worthy men, without distinction to race, creed, cast, or color. True Masons are charitable to the faults of others, self-sacrificing to all men, speaking and acting well toward others, and if, by any means, they cannot speak a good word in praise of their fellowman and Brother, they prefer to remain silent, rather than say anything evil of any one.

Masonry is not a Religion, and he who would make it such falsifies its claims; as the Hindu, Bramin, Parsee, Jew or Christian can each, one and all, become members of our beloved Fraternity, provided they are found worthy and well qualified. Members of all denominations are to be found in all our Lodges, Chapters, Councils and Consistories throughout the world universal, and be he either Jew, Gentile, Hindu, Brahmin or Moslem, his belief will be respected by each member of our most glorious Fraternity.

Of course many pass through our portals, who are not worthy, and we are compelled to admit that there are *black sheep* within our fold, but by the Eternal God, Masonry never painted them black, for they were black at heart long before their petition was presented for admission into our beloved Fraternity.

In entering the fold of Masonry the first promise that is made by our aspirant is that "he will learn to subdue his passions and improve himself in Masonry," and this pledge must be given before our aspiring candidate can advance one step along the path which leads to LIGHT AND TRUTH.

As herein before stated, a man by simply joining a Masonic Lodge, does not at once become a good or better man. Its sublime teachings point out the path he should follow in order to perfect himself in Masonry, and it lies entirely with himself. whether or not, he will ever learn to subdue his passions.

In all our Institutions Black Sheep *crawl* in among us by some means or other; certain it is they get there, just as in our Churches of all denominations. We find some of the Clergy themselves, black-hearted, entirely unworthy the position they occupy. For my part I am truly sorry for this deplorable condition of things, and simply point out the fact of its being so. The only way that I can see to remedy this evil, is, for the examining committees to be more careful in searching for the True character of the applicants, and not depend upon their reputation, for it is not always safe to depend upon the reputation of any one, for this reason a man may have a good reputation and be apparently a grand good man, a jolly, jovial companion; but at heart he may be a most damnable, black-hearted scoundrel.

In conclusion let me say this: *Do not look at the financial condition of your treasury, but rather to the character of the Applicants themselves for the upbuilding of our beloved Fraternity.*

What right has any man, or body of men, to persecute and condemn another because he does not, and can not, believe as others command him to do? There are no two men constituted alike, neither are there two things exactly alike in the universe; consequently no man should be censured or praised because he believes that *Christ has come;* neither should we blame our fellow man because he believes that HE IS YET TO COME; or find fault with any man if he believes that *he never will come;* but, firmly believing that Christ, or the Christ principle, dwells in the heart of every man, and that every individual must be his own Saviour to work out his own redemption.

My dear Brothers and kind friends, if the so-called Light of the " New Dispensation " is not visible to either him or them, assuredly it is not your fault, nor their misfortune. *Truth* to one may not be *Truth* to another, and what may appear perfectly consistent to me, may seem to be the height of absurdity to you and others; but your thinking so does not make it so. Consequently we *must* certainly realize at some time, that it is one of the greatest of crimes for any man or body of men to condemn and punish others, simply because they do not believe as they do.

The Hindu, Brahmin, Jew or Moslem, has just as much right to condemn, persecute and punish us, as we have to revile and persecute them. There is no particular merit in a man being a Jew, Gentile, Mohammedan or Hindu.

No matter what his faith may be, it is dependent in a great measure, upon his birth-place, and to the Mother who bore him, for he drinks in with his Mother's milk the faith and belief which belongs to her. We shall find that these teachings are, in many instances, the most lasting, because he is so constituted as to need some system of worship, concrete and tangible, upon which to focus his hopes and aspirations, consequently he follows the form of worship, whose basic principles and rules, he learned at his Mother's knee.

It is self-evident that the country wherein we are born, and the religious belief of the Mother, are evidently mighty factors in the production of a belief in one thing and disbelief in another. All that Masonry demands of her applicants is a belief in the ONE GREAT GOD—*The Supreme Architect of the Universe,* who holds the Solar System within the hollow of his hand.

As Grand Master Architects, we are, or should be, thoroughly familiar with the various instruments belonging to this most beautiful degree, because it is actually necessary for the Aspirant to thoroughly understand everything pertaining to one degree, before entering upon another. Every sign and every symbol should be thoroughly comprehended by our aspiring Brothers, they should earnestly study and carefully examine each and every one, in order to comprehend their *true* meaning, for the most elementary symbol will make some demand upon their intelligence and attention, therefore a most profound study will be required before they will understand the beautful lessons which they teach. Then will they increase their knowledge, be in a far better condition to discharge the duties alloted to them, and better able to instruct other Brethren in need of more Light. It is far better to have Wisdom than riches, for the Wise are glad of heart always, while riches will take to itself wings and fly to the four corners of the earth. "Wisdom will remain with thee, and bring thee glory and honor when thou shalt, by earnest study and profound meditation, embrace her and hold her in thine arms; aye, within thine heart; then will she abide with thee and crown thee with glory that shall never die; for the words and deeds of the truly Wise will live for ever."

Life and Time are but a point within a circle, the centre of Eternity, and that point in the centre is a fitting emblem of the Deity, like the Pole star in the starry vault above:

> Self-centered in the boundless blue,
>   Calm dweller of the vast unknown;
> For ever tender, strong, and true,
>   Serenely from her distant throne,
> He gazes down the voiceless deep,
> While worlds are drifting at his feet,
> And mighty constellations sweep
> 'Round him like an endless fleet.
> The Northern Lights across him flame,
>   The glory of their dancing spheres;
> The morning star beneath him sing,
>   The chorus of creation's years.
> And while systems sink and rise,
>   And planets to each other nod,
> The light streams from his tranquil eye,
>   As steadfast as the Love of God.
>   —(REYNOLDS, of Lebanon Lodge, Tacoma, Washington.)

When the Sun has set in the golden West, and the evening star rises in the East, then will shine resplendent in the starry vault above the glorious Pole star which guides the Mason o'er the stormy seas of Time, and the Mariner o'er the trackless waste of waters, as true as the Word of God Himself.

The various degrees of Architecture are emblematical to us of the five different divisions of the Ancient and Accepted Scottish Rite of Masonry:

The Tuscan—of the three Blue Degrees or the Primitive Masonry.

The Doric—of the Ineffable Degrees, from the 4th to the 14th inclusive.

The Ionic—of the 15th and 16th, or the Council Degrees.

The Corinthian—of the 17th and 18th, or the Chapter Degrees.

The Composite—of the High Degrees from the 19th to the 32d inclusive.

We now pass from the working tools of the Architect and Geometrician. The trestle board, with all of its geometrical problems, we leave behind us and advance towards a profound Philosophy, and every degree we now receive is a step in that direction. Therefore, we now devote our time to researches among the ruins of ancient Temples, and to the history concerning them, wherein was discovered the Luminous Pedestal, Cubical stone, and the Ineffable long-lost Word, belonging to the Grand Elect and Perfect Mason.

The Luminous Pedestal, emblem of the physical body of man, is lighted up from within by the LIGHT OF REASON that permeates the heart of every man, and by which he turns the pages of the *Book of Nature*, and revels in the sublime and profound *Truths* revealed to him, through the Divine Light emanating from his own heart.

The physical body of each and every man is a *Great and Glorious Temple*, not made with hands. No sound of a gavel was heard at its construction. The winking of an eye-lid puts to shame all mechanism, and man's *Higher Self* is the Light within, a spark from the Divine Essence. I ask you, my dear reader and Brother, to turn up that Glorious Light of your Higher Self, so that it may illuminate your inner vision. Turn it up, good and strong, that you may be enabled to discover your *Higher Self*, and the potential forces latent within you; then will you realize that all things are within your own grasp.

The Cubical stone is a fit emblem of the Deity, because it contains, in miniature, all things in the Kosmos. The Master artist, given an Ashlar and proper tools, is capable of carving from it anything of which his mind may conceive, no matter what the thing may be; therefore, the Ashlar, or Cubical stone, typifies the Deity Himself, through whom are all things made manifest. He contains within himself all things, and He is, Himself, all manifest or unmanifested Nature.

TEMPLE OF RAMESES IV,

KARNAK.

The Lost Word we shall devote to another chapter, for now we gird upon our loins the sword of Knight-hood, and with golden spurs enter the Philosophical field of investigation, in search of "More Light."

Every Scottish Rite Mason; aye, every *true* Mason, is loyal to the cause of LIBERTY, EQUALITY AND UNIVERSAL BROTHERHOOD—because he knows full well that he himself is part of the *Divine Whole*, and that his fellow-man is another part, with equal rights to live, breathe and believe in a Deity according to his capabilities. Every True Mason will zealously assist his fellow-man in the upbuilding of the *Symbolic Temple*, the Holy House of the *Higher Self*, wherein he will find, not only the *Altar of Self-Sacrifice*, but the "*Antaskarana*," or the bridge that separates him from all for which his *soul* has yearned and longed, and he will realize that the letters L. D. P. mean something more than to simply pass over the three spans of *Ignorance, Bigotry and Intolerance*.

There was a time when our ancient Brethren were not allowed to think or act as their conscience dictated. Death was the penalty to all who belonged to our glorious and beloved Fraternity. It was proscribed; but still it was equally feared and dreaded. It was at this time that the meaning of the letters L. D. P. was veiled from the profane, and only understood by those who had assisted in the building of the *Temple*, with the trowel in one hand and the sword in the other. They recognized that the words of which the letters are simply the initials—signified *Liberte de Pensar;* that is—Liberty to Think, or Freedom of Thought and Conscience, with Political and Religious Liberty—a *cause* to which all Good and True Masons have ever devoted themselves.

The Bridge which spans the stream symbolizes the passage from Ignorance to Wisdom, from Slavery to Freedom, from Spiritual Bondage to Spiritual Freedom. In attaining to this glorious heritage of man we must distinctly understand that it is not gained in a day; but only after a long and continued struggle with our animal passional nature can we hope to accomplish the subjugation of our *Lower Self*, and in doing this we will have performed a deed greater than he who conquers a nation. We shall then be enabled to subdue Ignorance and Bigotry, trample beneath our feet Intolerance, Vice and Superstition, and pass across *Antaskarana* to Freedom, in the fullest sense of the word. It has been written that "The Initiates were many, but few wear the *Thyrsus*," and how few are there worthy? Every Brother should prove his Devotion and Fidelity to our beloved Fraternity and himself by deeds, not by words alone, then will not his merit go unrewarded.

Did you, my dear Brothers and readers, ever realize the profound depth of philosophical thought veiled in the twelfth chapter of Ecclesiastes? The beautiful and sublime significance is not very easily understood until we solve the meaning underlying the figurative language used therein. Therefore, for your special edification, we will endeavor to explain and interpret its true meaning, so that you may be enabled to realize its significance and beauty.

Verse 1, "Remember now thy Creator in the days of thy youth while the evil days come not, nor the years draw nigh, when thou shalt say, I have no pleasure in them.

2nd. "While the sun, or the light, or the moon, or the stars, be not darkened, nor the clouds return after the rain.

3rd. "In the days when the keepers of the house shall tremble, and the strong men shall bow themselves, and the grinders cease because they are few, and those that look out of the windows be darkened.

4th. "And the doors shall be shut in the street, when the sound of the grinding is low, and he shall rise up at the voice of the bird, and the daughters of music shall be brought low.

5th. "Also when they shall be afraid of that which is high, and fears shall be in the way, and the almond tree shall flourish, and the grasshopper shall be a burden, and desire shall fail, because man goeth to his long home, and the mourners go about the streets.

6th. "Or ever the silver cord be loosed, or the golden bowl be broken, or the pitcher be broken at the fountain, or the wheel broken at the cistern.

7th. "Then shall the dust return to the earth as it was: and the spirit shall return unto God who gave it."

You will notice, my dear Brothers and readers, that I especially call your attention to the first seven verses, and here is a synoptical interpretation:

1st. 'REMEMBER NOW THY CREATOR IN THE DAYS OF THY YOUTH, ETC."

This is the time that we should learn to control our animal passional nature, as well as the desires of the animal man within us, for if we let (KAMA) *our desires* master us in our youth, when temptation comes to us in Manhood, we are then, by force of habit, unable to control ourselves, and the "evil days" are nigh when we gratify our every wish. But the time will come to every man when he will say truthfully "I have no pleasure in them," The lust and frivolities of Life.

2nd. "WHILE THE SUN, OR THE LIGHT, ETC."

It is in the sunny days of our youth, or boyhood, and in the full radiance of Divine potential generative force, when the Moon, or female, tempts us before our eyes are darkened by age, that we should conquer self, then the dark clouds of evil deeds will never o'ershadow our declining years, for there will have been no rain, only joy and hope in a glorious future.

3rd. "IN THE DAY WHEN THE KEEPERS OF THE HOUSE, ETC."

The keepers of the house are man's lower animal nature, *Lower Manas* or the *Personality*, and his *Higher Ego or Higher Manas*, the Individuality. The Lower Manas includes the whole of the passional emotional desires and appetites, all its wants, such as sexual desire, hatred, love, pride, anger, etc., in fact, it is what goes to make our animal man, or as it is sometimes called, our *Animal Soul.* While the Higher Ego, or Manas, that dwells and acts in us, is the other keeper of the house. Now, between these two there is a continual battle being waged, for our Lower Manas, or Lower nature, animal like, is ever striving to gratify his evil desires, while our Higher Manas—a ray from the Divinity, is continually striving to curb the evil propensities of the animal Man. One is Good the other Evil, and thus the battle of Good and Evil, or God and the Devil, is continuously going on within us. And this is where we crucify Christ in our own heart, every day of our lives, if we permit our unbridled passions to dominate our *Higher Manas.* If we do so, *Lower Manas* drags down the Christ principle, to the level of its own *Animal Soul*, and thus Christ is crucified between two thieves—the *Human and Animal Souls.*

29

Now, my dear Brothers, I want you to thoroughly comprehend this very imporant assertion, or definition, and possibly you may be better enabled to understand me if I quote you from Brother J. D. Buck, 32° " Mystic Masonry," page 186:

" The Higher Self in man, called his ' God' or *Christos*, was formerly ' crucified between two thieves,' namely, the Higher and Lower Manas. Hence the saying, ' when I would do good, evil is present with me.' As the body is crucified (a symbol of death and suffering), the *Christos* says to one of the thieves: ' This day shalt thou be with me in paradise.' This refers to the Higher Manas, now freed from the lower nature. The other ' thief,' or the brain-mind, is left to perish with the physical body of Christos on the Cross of Time. It may thus be seen how the battle-ground of Man's lower nature, with the higher, is the Mind, and that self-conquest, and the higher evolution are synonymous."

"THE STRONG MEN,"

which is the dual nature of man, shall bow before the approach of Death.

"THE GRINDERS SHALL CEASE BECAUSE THEY ARE FEW."

Beautifully illustrates the approach of old age, for as it creeps upon us our teeth decay and grow less, and are few indeed, compared to those in the days of our youth.

"THOSE THAT LOOK OUT OF THE WINDOWS."

The Higher and Lower Manas, the *Human and Animal Souls*, no longer look forth from the windows (eyes) of the house, for the darkness of death o'er shadows it.

"THE DOORS SHALL BE SHUT IN THE STREETS."

Man grows deaf as old age comes upon him, and the *doors* (ears) *are shut in the street* on account of his sense of hearing failing him.

"THE SOUND OF THE GRINDING IS LOW."

Because now it is difficult for him to hear the most familiar sounds.

"RISE UP AT THE VOICE OF THE BIRD."

The soul was represented by the ancient Egyptians by a bird. It is the voice of his own spiritual Soul that tells him to awake and rise into *Life*, by passing through the portals of Death.

"THE DAUGHTERS OF MUSIC SHALL BE BROUGHT LOW."

The voice of Man, nearing old age and dissolution, fails him, and there is no music in him, for the organs that originally produced it have lost their vocal powers.

"WHEN THEY SHALL BE AFRAID OF THAT WHICH IS HIGH."

Higher and Lower Manas has, during earth-life, sown the seed of thoughts and acts, and now they are about to reap the harvest in the Karmic effects of what they had sown.

"THE ALMOND TREE SHALL FLOURISH."

In extreme old age man's hair shall grow as silvery white as the blossoms of the Almond tree. He now grows old and feeble and is unable to bear the slightest burden, the weight of a grasshopper would, comparatively speaking, be a burden unto him.

"AND DESIRE SHALL FAIL."

Desires naturally desert the aged. Life contains no pleasures for them— they wait.

"MAN GOETH TO HIS LONG HOME."

The long home signifies Death and the Future Life.

"AND THE MOURNERS GO ABOUT THE STREETS."

These are friends and relatives who mourn his death, for there is no man so bad but that there will be some one who will mourn for him.

"THE SILVER CORD BE LOOSED."

Is the thread of Life which binds the true man to the physical body. When it snaps in twain death ensues, the Spirit is freed, and the shard or shell is left behind, just in the same manner as in the hatching of a chicken; when the time comes, the chick pecks itself from out the old shard or shell, and goes forth into life and definition.

"THE GOLDEN BOWL BE BROKEN."

Is the head with its seven gateways to the senses, with its five attributes, container of the brain, that is looked upon as the organ of Consciousness and the seven Harmonies.

"OR THE PITCHER BE BROKEN AT THE FOUNTAIN, OR THE WHEEL BROKEN AT
THE CISTERN."

The "pitcher" is the left ventricle that empties into the *Aorta*. The "*Fountain*" is the heart itself. The "wheel" is the arterial and veinous system combined, through which the life-giving forces are continually circulating, and the "*Cistern*" is the right ventricle, into which the veinous blood is continually flowing. In order that you may better understand this let me explain to you the circulating system, which is two-fold.

There is the lesser and the greater circuit of circulation, as in all natural processes, there is no beginning, neither is there any end. But we will begin at (the Pitcher), the Left ventricle of the heart, from which the Arterial cherry red blood is "poured" into the Aorta, on its Life-giving mission throughout the whole of the body. At the extremities of the Arteries we have a system of capillaries, so very minute that the microscope is needed in order to detect them. These capillaries connect the Arterial with the Veinous system (forming the "wheel"), where marked chemical changes take place, converting the cherry red blood into the dark blue veinous. The veins bring back this used-up-blood to the heart again, emptying it into the right Auricle, from there it passes into the (cistern) Right ventricle, from which it is forcibly expelled by the contraction of the Heart ("Fountain"), into and through the pulmonary artery, which, by the way, carries veinous blood. In the Lungs it becomes electrified, oxygenized and vivified, when it is forced back to the heart again, entering at the Left Auricle, from whence it passes into the Left Ventricle and is started out once again on its life-giving journey throughout the whole of the Arterial ramifications.

The "Wheel" performs its revolution in this way and the whole of the body is built up from the circulating life-forces in the blood.

"THE DUST RETURN TO THE EARTH."

Which is plainly demonstrated by the disintegration of the physical body at Death.

"AND THE SPIRIT SHALL RETURN UNTO GOD WHO GAVE IT."

In reaching the first of the Philosophical degrees of our beloved Ancient and Accepted Scottish Rite, our worthy aspirant and Brother enters upon a glorious field, wherein he will find the True Light, which will lead him on to a knowledge of all that was lost, and the way to its *Recovery*. The ruins of empires will be at his feet, and their broken columns will be a verification to him of the wondrous knowledge that pertained to our Ancient Brethren. The understanding of which will give him courage to suffer and conquer in the Cause, and Strength to work for its final triumph. He will be devoted and consecrated to the service of *Truth, Justice and Virtue*, until, eventually, he will be found worthy to open the Great Book of the Law, by breaking the Seven Seals, and learn the True meaning of the great Truths contained within its sacred pages. Truths that have been gathered from the East and the West, and from out the heart of the sacred Books of all people.

The great banners of Masonry are FAITH, HOPE AND CHARITY, under which all men may gather from all nations and from every clime in the *One Great Cause*. Masonry is not a *Religion*, in the general accepted sense of that word, with Creeds and Dogmas compelling blind Faith in any part of it, and in the account of the suffering and Death of Christ, every Brother as I hereinbefore stated, may believe as he sees fit. Let me quote you once again from " Mystic Masonry," page 103 *et seq.*

" The candidate is taught not merely to tolerate another's religion, but to respect it as his own, though still adhering to that into which he was born. To make reasonable this obligation, he is shown through the Kabalah, or Secret Doctrine, that at the heart of every great religion lie the same eternal Truths. Forms and observances only differ. *The Ineffable Name* is spelled in many ways, yet the *Word* is one and eternal. Masonry is not a Universal Science, but a world-wide Religion owing allegiance to no one creed, and can adopt no sectarian dogma, as such, without thereby ceasing to be Masonic. Drawn from the Kabalah and taking the Jewish or Christian verbiage, or symbols, it but discerns in them universal truths, which it recognizes in all other religions. Many degrees have been Christianized, only to perish; as every degree eventually will, if circumscribed by narrow creeds, and dwarfed to the bigoted apprehension of a few sectarians, to exclude good men of any other communion. Is Jesus any the less *Christos* because Christna was called " The Good Shepherd?" or because the Mexican Christ was crucified between two thieves? or because Hiram was three days in a grave before he was resurrected? Are we not as selfish in our religion as in our other possessions? Then, why, is man, while cherishing as his most sacred possession the religion of his fathers, eternally seeking to degrade and destroy that of his Brother?

"The Great Republic, to which Brother Pike refers, is the Ideal of Masonry; the Genius that hovers, like a protecting angel, over the Lodge. Make it impossible for a Jew or Parsee, Buddhist or Brahmin, to enter any Lodge without witnessing the profanation of his sacred altars or contempt for his religion, and the angel hides her face and retreats from altars already profaned by unbrotherliness. Masonry is the Universal Religion only because, and only so long, as it embraces all religions. For this reason, and this alone, it is universal and eternal. Neither persecution nor misrepresentation can ever destroy it. It may find no place in a generation of bigots; it may retire for a century; but again comes a Master Builder with the key to the 'shut Palace of the King,' throws open the blinds, lets in the Light, kindles anew the fire on the sacred altar, clears away the rubbish, when behold! the tesselated pavement is as bright as when it first came from the quarries of Truth, the jewels are of pure gold and brighten at the touch, and the great Lights are undimmed and undecayed, 'When the candidate is ready the Master appears.' And men are yet so foolish and so vile as to imagine that they can destroy this heirloom of the ages: this heritage from the Immortals! No age is so dark as to quench entirely the Light of the Lodge; no persecution so bloody as to blot out its votaries; no anathemas of Popes so lasting as to count one second on its Dial of Time! These, one and all, serve only to keep the people in darkness, and retard the reign of Universal Brotherhood. Therefore, for humanity—the Great Orphan—the real Master laments. He smiles at the passions of Popes or Kings, and pities the folly of man. *He only waits*, indifferent as to results, knowing these to be under eternal Law; but ready and willing, whenever and wherever the instruction entering the listening ear may find lodgment in the faithful breast."

Masonry teaches toleration and the Union of all Religions and all philosophies. Within her temples the Jew, the Mohammedan, the Christian, the Buddhist, the Brahmin or Parsee, may stand beside a common altar, and be pledged upon the self-same emblems, and be devoted to the self-same cause that teaches to its members the duties they owe to their God, their fellow-man, and to themselves, and in this way we realize that it is our bounden duty to love our neighbor as ourself. Then will we discover the same truth that the rich man told unto Jesus that " there is no neighbor, and there is no self, all is in the Father, and of the Father, and in loving him I love all things."

We do not claim for any one creed more Truth than another, for in every religion there is a basis of Truth, as well as pure Morality. From the earliest ages men have believed in an unseen, governing and controlling and directing Power, and in every corner of the earth this Great Power has been located, by the various peoples of the earth, in Spatial depths around them.

Masonry does not teach the existence of an Anthropomorphic God, who is made in the image of man, with all the human attributes ; but, of course, if a brother desires to believe in such an one, it is his privilege so to do, and we should not, under any circumstances, revile him for his faith, or his God, be he Jew, Christian, Parsee or Hindu.

The so-called New Law, as taught by Jesus of Nazareth, is as old as the stars, and has been taught in every epoch of the world's history, and the sooner we understand this fact the better it will be for ourselves and our fellowman. We should never scoff at, or revile our Brother, because he believes God Loves him, when we believe God cannot Love any one, because God is Love and not Loving. Then if we believe that God is Love, let us follow the law of Love, by never permitting anything that a Brother may believe, say, or do, to offend us, so that the Law may be broken through our finite understanding of it. The Law of God passeth all understanding and we must learn, by experience, that it is better to love than to hate.

It is our bounden duty not to strive to be better than our Brother; but to be better than ourselves, by conquering self and subduing our passions. We should never forget that the more we have, the more we owe to our Brother, and that it is our duty to give abundantly of our store, to all those who are in need of our assistance. My dear Brothers, let me quote you from " Supernatural Religion," by an English clergyman, Vol. II, page 489:

" We gain infinitely more than we lose in abandoning belief in the Divine Revelation. Whilst we retain pure and unimpaired the treasure of Christian Morality, we relinquish nothing, but the debasing elements added to it by human superstition. We are no longer bound to believe a theology which outrages reason and moral sense. We are freed from base anthropomorphic views of God and His government of the universe; and from Jewish Mythology we rise to higher conceptions of an infinitely wise and beneficent Being, hidden from our finite minds, it is true, in the impenetrable glory of Divinity, but whose laws of wondrous comprehensiveness and perfection we can perceive in operation around us.

"We are no longer disturbed by visions of fitful interference with the order of Nature; but we recognize that the Being, who regulates the universe, is without variableness or shadow of turning. It is singular how little there is in the supposed Revelation of alleged information, however incredible, regarding that which is beyond the limits of human thought, but that little is of a character which reason declares to be the wildest delusion. Let no man, whose belief in the reality of a Divine Revelation may be destroyed by such an inquiry, complain that he has lost a precious possession, and that nothing is left but a blank. The Revelation not being a reality, that which he has lost was but an illusion, and that which is left is the Truth. If he be content with illusions, he will speedily be consoled; if he be a lover only of truth, instead of a blank he will recognize that the reality before him is full of great peace.

"If we know less than we supposed of man's destiny, we may at least rejoice that we are no longer compelled to believe that which is unworthy. The limits of thought once attained, we may well be unmoved in the assurance that all that we do know, of the regulation of the universe being so perfect and wise, all that we do not know must be equally so. Here enters the true and noble FAITH, which is the child of Reason. If we have believed a system, the details of which must at one time or another have shocked the mind of every intelligent man, and believed it simply because it was supposed to be revealed, we may equally believe in the wisdom and goodness of what is not revealed. The mere act of communication to us is nothing; FAITH in the perfect ordering of all things is independent of Revelation.

"The arguments so often employed by Theologians, that Divine Revelation is necessary for man, and that certain views contained in that Revelation are required by our moral consciousness, is purely imaginary, and derived from the Revelation which it seeks to maintain. The only thing absolutely necessary for man is TRUTH, and to that, and that alone, must our moral consciousness adapt itself."

It is asserted that when Christ was crucified upon the cross they placed above his head the Latin letters I. N. R. I., signifying, "Jesus Nazarenus, Rex Judæorum," (*Jesus of Nazareth, King of the Jews*). While others interpret the meaning of these initials quite differently, as: "IGNE *Natura* RENOVATUR *Integra*," Entire Nature is Renovated by Fire.

Dr. Wynn Westcott, *Fra Rosæ Crucis*, F. T. S., states in his "Hermetic Notes," in "Lucifer," Vol. VI, page 275, that "A very curious old Rosicrucian Manuscript passed through my hands a few years ago; it gave a new rendering to the initials I. N. R. I. The Christian meaning of which is known to all, and which has several Alchemic significations, such as *Igne Vitrum Roris Inventitur* ('by fire the Nitre of the dew is discovered'). Iammin Nour Ruach Iabesha, the Hebrew for ('Water, Fire, Air, Earth'). Igne Natura Regenerando Integrat ('Nature renews, in Regenerating by fire'). Igne Natura Renovatur Integra ('By fire Nature is renewed in its entirety').

"The rendering I now publish for the first time is *not* a simple use of initials, but the straining of the symbol shows the greater desire of denoting the doctrine: I. Ntra *vos* est Regum De I ('The kingdom of God is within you'). This seems to me a clear acknowledgment of the Higher Self within a man, which, if the Man rendered himself sufficiently pure and spiritual, can communicate with Powers above him and to him Divine.

"The same manuscript also gave this reading: 'In Nobis Regnum Intelligentia ('The Kingdom of the intelligence is in us'). From the same source comes also the following:

"Force arising in the *North* passes to the *South*. Intelligence arising in the South passes to the *North*. Initiation arising in the *East* passes to the *West*.

"But to crown the above let me state that the Jesuits, who have ever been the bitter, unscrupulous and uncompromising enemies of Masonry frame for it their own infamous phrase 'Justum Necare Regnas Impios:' 'It is Lawful to Slay Irreligious Kings.'" Yes, or any one else whom they considered Irreligious. From the above we find that there is quite a difference in the interpretations of the letters *claimed* to have been placed above the head of Christ upon the Cross, when crucified upon Calvary.

To-day there are millions. of people who never heard of him, and if they have, they do not believe in him, nor do they wish to do so; and yet, again, there are millions who do most earnestly and firmly believe that he was the Son of God, born of a Virgin, a Being of Divine Nature—in fact, that he was the Word made manifest in the flesh.

There are countless numbers who believe that he is yet to come, and they wait with patience the coming of the Redeemer. Again there are countless millions who believe that he was but a man, with all the attributes of man, and could not be God and Man at the same time. Others believe the whole life and acts of Christ to be but an Allegory. While there are a vast number of people, throughout the world universal, who believe most earnestly and sincerely that Christ, or Christos, dwells in the heart of every living, breathing Man to-day, and that he will never be more manifest in the world or our hearts than he is right now.

I claim that every man or Brother Mason has a perfect right to his own belief in this matter, and should be free from the sneers and scoffs of others, even though their views upon this subject do not coincide with his fellows. Masonry existed thousands of years before Christ was born, or dreamed of, and consequently it compels no man to believe either one way or the other. But before concluding this subject and chapter let me quote you from "Morals and Dogmas," page 524:

" We do not undervalue the importance of any Truth. We utter no word that can be deemed irreverent by any one, of any faith. We do not tell the Moslem that it is only important for him to believe that there is but one God, and wholly unessential whether Mahomet was his prophet. We do not tell the Hebrew that the Messiah whom he expects was born in Bethlehem nearly two thousand years ago; and that he is a heretic, because he will not so believe. And as little do we tell the sincere Christian that Jesus of Nazareth was but a man, like us, or his history but the unreal revival of an older legend. To do either is beyond our jurisdiction. Masonry, of no one age, belongs to all time; of no one religion it finds its great truths in all."

Every religion had a common origin, and underwent changes, from time to time, to suit the people of the various epochs in which they lived.

It was during the reign of Constantine, that the believers in the ancient teachings, were compelled to abandon their old faith and adopt the New, when all records of the Ancient Wisdom were sought for in order to destroy them.

The Secret Doctrine was the fountain and source of the Wisdom-Religion itself, whose doctrines were taught in the Ancient Mysteries, of which our own beloved Scottish Rite is a lineal descendant. All religions in existence to-day have descended from, and are related to, the Wisdom-Religion of India, which was the Primitive Wisdom Religion of the Ancient World. Masonry has preserved the sublimely beautiful teachings of this profound Wisdom in the various parts of her Ineffable and Philosophical Degrees, and evidences of the Truth of this statement are to be found in the Holy Doctrine and Royal Secret, and proves the antiquity of our most Illustrious Fraternity, and its relationship to the Indian, Mazdean and ancient Egyptian Mysteries.

We can trace the descent of the various Christian Sects, and prove they had a common origin, and that they all contain the same grand Truths, only clothed in different garments. Therefore, how foolish it is for men to quarrel over fictitious narratives, supposed to have happened in the early days of Christianity. They should be more charitable to the beliefs of others, more certain of their own, and should never, under any circumstances, dictate to any man what he should or should not believe. Masonry most assuredly does not claim any right to alter the belief of any Brother be he Jew, Gentile, Moslem or Hindu.

GRAND OFFICERS OF THE NORTHERN JURISDICTION.

Voyaging up the Nile—Examining Tombs and Temples—Paintings—Sculptures.

We have passed over cities in song renowned;
Silent they lie with the desert around;
We have passed o'er the river whose tide hath rolled,
All dark with the warrior-blood of old.

—F. HEMANS.

CHAPTER XX.

VOYAGING UP THE NILE—EXAMINING TOMBS AND TEMPLES—PAINTINGS—
SCULPTURES.

IT seems very difficult to add anything further to that which has already been told about Egypt and the ancient Egyptians, their tombs. temples, monuments and mummies, as well as to give additional information pertaining to their religion, arts, sciences and philosophies. I went into that country for the express purpose of examining for myself the most extraordinary ruins of those glorious temples which to-day lie scattered throughout the whole of Egypt, and to learn something pertaining to their ancient wisdom. In viewing these magnificent ruins, the work of the mighty Pharaohs of the "Golden Age" of Egypt, I was so filled with awe and admiration, with what I saw and learned, that I concluded to write an account of my researches in the land of "Old Khemi," the cradle of ancient Masonry. The land of the ancient Mysteries. The land that gave to Greece her culture and to Rome her civilization. The land that gave intellectual power to all who drank from that fountain from which Moses drew his wondrous knowledge and inspiration.

I shall therefore describe my journey up the river Nile, that I may give you a complete description of this most wonderful country, and that you may be enabled to trace from her tombs, temples, monuments and mummies the rise, progress, decline and fall of this most extraordinary Land of Egypt and her people.

This work is called "Egypt, The Cradle of Ancient Masonry," therefore I do not think that I should do you, or my subject justice, unless I gave you a thorough description of the valley of the Nile, her tombs, temples, monuments and mummies, while writing upon ancient Masonry and the profound philosophy that belongs to our most Illustrious Fraternity. I do most earnestly desire to impress upon your minds that Masonry originated in the "Land of the Vedas" and that it was cradled upon the banks of the Nile. I do not desire to give you a full account of what took place on our journey, but shall tell you of the various points of interest, giving descriptions of tombs, temples and monuments, interspersed with a few little incidents of our voyage, in order to vary the monotony of a trip of six hundred miles from Cairo to Philæ, in a Dahabiyeh, upon the bosom of one of the most interesting rivers in the world—the Nile.

We are now approaching the former home of the crocodile, but we shall find them very scarce on our journey. It is strange, but nevertheless true, that these saurians are never found below Minia, except on very rare occasions, although Herodotus speaks of them fighting with dolphins, at the mouth of the Nile; but, of course, this is a " fish story " of our learned and celebrated historian. The *hippopatamus* is never or seldom found below the *second cataract*, but occasionally there have been one or two found below it.

I arose early that morning at Roda. which is quite a large town, on the west bank of the Nile, containing post, telegraph offices and railway station, located close to the river. There is quite a large sugar factory here, and also several mosques and bazaars, and close to one of them Hassan purchased four hundred eggs for one dollar. Very nearly opposite this place, but a little to the northeast, on the east bank of the river, is the ruins of the celebrated city of Antinoe, which lies among the palm groves of *Shekh Abada.*

The city of Antinoe was built by order of the Emperor Hadrian, and the cause of its erection was as follows: Antinous, a young man of Bithynia, who dearly loved the Emperor, accompanied him on his journey into Egypt, where it appears that Hadrian was told by an oracle, that he could only secure happiness by sacrificing what he most dearly loved. The youth Antinous, hearing of this, cast himself into the bosom of old God Nilus, and was drowned. In commemoration of this event, Hadrian erected and dedicated this city, and instituted games and sacrifices to honor the young man who had died for love of him.

Shekh Abada is surrounded with a very fine palm grove, whose trees are noted for their size and beauty, among which lie a few pieces of stone and a corinthian capital scattered here and there, with some broken columns, etc. There are but very few ruins or relics to be found there to-day, belonging to the ancient city that originally stood here, for the reason that the Khedive burned all the stone that he could find for lime, to be used in the building of his sugar factory at Roda.

There are a great many Christian antiquities to be found in a little village called *Der Abu Honnes*, "The Convent of St. John." A short distance from here, there is a very ancient church located in a large quarry, in which many of the chambers were decorated with paintings that represent subjects taken from the New Testament. A little further on we reach the village of *Der en-Nakl*, "The convent of the Palms," near which is the tomb of Thoth-hetep, the son of Kai, wherein was found the celebrated picture of the transportation of a Colossus. It represents the method by which these people moved their immense stones, statues, monuments, etc., across the desert sands.

This figure shows a Colossus twenty feet in height upon a sled, fastened to it with ropes. There are little pads, or cushions, placed at different places around the statue, in order to prevent it from being chafed, or injured, in its removal or transportation. There are four very large ropes fastened to the sled, to each of which there are forty-three men stationed, making one hundred and seventy-two men in all, to pull the sled. Standing in the lap of the statue is the chanty man, clapping his hands and beating time, no doubt, to the song he sings, so that they may be enabled to pull in unison. There is a man pouring some kind of liquid upon the skids or planks so that it might slide along easier. It is a very instructive picture, and the only one that throws any light on the ancient methods of moving these immense monolithic stones, statues, etc., for the purpose of building and decorating their tombs and temples throughout the "Land of Egypt." There are many very interesting places to visit in this vicinity, on both sides of the river. We can find ruins of ancient cities with dilapidated tombs and temples in this Nome well worth seeing.

After leaving the tomb of Thoth-hetep we did not return to Shekh Abada, but kept right on to *Der el-Bersha*, because we had told Hassan to take the Dahabiyeh on to that place and await us there. Long before we got to our floating home we could hear the songs of our crew, echoing in the quiet evening air, as the lengthening shadows of the palms crept down toward the bosom of old God Nilus. We returned to our boat just

30

about sun down, and had time to refresh ourselves, with a bath, when dinner was served, to which we all did ample justice. If we ever appreciated a good comfortable home it was that night, for we had been riding, tramping and climbing around all day long, and were quite tired and weary. In fact so much so, that I sat down and arranged my notes, then went on deck, smoked a cigar, took a " brandy pawnee," and retired early, hoping that there would be a good favorable breeze in the morning, so that we might be enabled to reach *Haggi Quandil* the next day, as we were very desirous of visiting Tel el-Amarna.

I had a very refreshing night's rest and did not awake until the harsh and discordant notes of the gong rang out in the early morning. After toast and coffee, we went on deck and found a lovely morning, but not a breath of air astir. The mist was vanishing in the rays of the morning sun, and the river shone like burnished silver as our sailors went out upon the tow path and harnessed themselves to the towline, and our boat began to creep along at a snail's pace. Our men went jumping, singing, pulling and shouting like a lot of school boys, as if tracking in the hot sun was a pleasure and a pastime, instead of labor. I really believe that they liked to be out upon the tow path at times, and this appeared to be one of them, but, possibly, it was because we had told Hassan to tell our Reis Abdallah that we should give them a sheep, and what was needed for a grand fantasia, on our arrival at *Asyut,* where they were going to bake bread and have a day to themselves, to which we had agreed, and very likely this was the cause of their capers and jollity.

We went down to an enjoyable breakfast, and as we sat at the table chatting and talking of the paintings in the grottos of Beni Hassan, comparing them with those in the tomb of Tih, the air resounded with the word " Timseach " *crocodiles.* We hurried on deck, and on looking around we saw three large crocodiles basking in the rays of the morning sun. The boat was sheered into the bank, as Abdallah our captain knew that we were very anxious to get one if possible. They did not seem to be disturbed at the approach of our boat, so we took our rifles and clambered up the river bank, walking carefully and quietly along, until we came opposite the small island where we had seen them. Then creeping very cautiously up the bank toward the river, until we could see them lying in plain view, upon a sandy spit, not over two hundred and fifty yards distant, we agreed to shoot what appeared to be the largest one, and to the right of the "covey." We took steady aim, with a good rest for our rifles, pulled the triggers, and the one that we fired at gave one tremendous plunge and dragged himself to the river and disappeared from our sight, coloring the water red with its blood. The other waddled off down to the river, plunged in and disappeared.

We were very soon in our little boat, and arrived at the Island, when we found that one of the party had shot at one of the other crocodiles, the ball entering its mouth, severing the spinal cord. The ball was lying flattened among the broken bones just beneath the skin, and had actually not made a mark upon it. I inquired how such a shot had been made, and was informed that the crocodile was lying with its head and chest towards us, and that the shot had been aimed directly at its throat, but, just as the trigger was pulled, the crocodile lowered its head and the ball entered its mouth, broke and cut the spinal cord, and also the bones at the base of the brain, and laid him out quivering upon the sands.

It was quite a prize for us, and we were very glad to get it, and after taking it on board the dahabiyeh we measured it, and found that it was eight feet four inches from the end of its nose to the end of its tail. I have tried repeatedly to obtain another, but although I have shot a great many I was never able to capture a single one of them, for they all got away from me. On a previous trip I went far above the Khartum, when I secured over a dozen, besides some very fine Hippopotamus.

On arriving at the nearest point for us to visit the tombs of *Tel-el Amarna*, we saw a lot of donkeys, with Ali, one of our sailors, shouting to our captain to come in to the bank, for Hassan had sent him on from *Der-el-Barsha* to engage donkeys for us, and to have them in readiness for us by the time our boat would get there. The dahabiyeh was soon alongside the bank, when we scrambled ashore and mounted our little animals and were very soon scurrying off to the mountains with our guide in the lead. Our boat went on to *Haggi Quandil* to await our coming.

In the seventeenth chapter I referred to the King *Khu-n-Aten*, who left the city and home of his fathers on account of his very peculiar religious belief, and built for himself a New City and capital that was located here between *Tel-el-Amarna* and *Haggi Quandil*. Between these two places he built himself a most magnificent palace, a stupendous affair, whose interior apartments were decorated with gold and silver ornaments and inlaid with precious stones. He adorned it all with beautiful paintings, sculptures and magnificent specimens of ancient Egyptian works of art.

We were visiting the ruins of this palace and city for the purpose of examining for ourselves the site of the city and capital of *Khu-n-Aten.* The rock tombs of *Tel-el-Amarna* are quite a distance from the river, and were the repositories of the courtiers and various officials of the court of this once celebrated Pharaoh, who belonged to the eighteenth dynasty. These tombs form three different groups, and it is in the center one that we found the resting place of this great King and a few others that belonged to his dynasty and court. The great majority of these tombs, in the various groups, are entered through a fore-court, and upon the walls of nearly all the tombs that we visited were pictured incidents and scenes of royal life, etc. Lepsius and Mr. F. Petrie made some very valuable discoveries among these ruins. It was here that they found the celebrated clay tablets inscribed with the cuneiform characters of Babylon, and many with other peculiar characters written or inscribed upon them, representing the foreign correspondence between Khu-n-Aten and the Kings of Babylon, Assyria and other countries.

After viewing these interesting tombs, etc., we rode on to Haggi Quandil, where we soon found our boat and a couple of bottles of Bass' bitter beer which we took in order to get the fine sands out of our throats. There was a nice breeze blowing when we got on board, so the boat was punted off from the bank, the sails were loosed, and off we went again accompanied by the usual vocal music of our crew. After a bath and smoke the gong rang for dinner, and when we came on deck again we found our boat bowling along at a very rapid rate.

What a glorious night it was, the sky perfectly clear and cloudless, the stars shining down upon us with a sweet radiant light, the crescent moon setting in the west, the waters of the Nile shining with a soft shimmering glow, and there was nought to be heard but the water of the river rippling under our counter, and the low hum of the voices of our sailors, who sang their last song for the night, and were seeking the drowsy god. We retired to our cabin, put our notes in order and were soon off into the "Land of Nod," only to awaken in the early morning to find our boat tied up to the bank. Our sailors were getting their breakfast, and our own coffee and toast were handed to us, and as they were preparing for the tow-path we took our guns, intending to walk on ahead and shoot some quail, etc., but we had scarcely gone a hundred yards before a light air arose, when we turned back and got on board again. The boat was punted off into the stream, our sails loosed and we were off again with our big sails swelling out full and round, while our sailors squatted around and their songs rang out the same as usual.

The wind freshened and we went ploughing along through the water like a steamer, villages went drifting by and we saw the mountains and bluffs of Abu Feda away off to the south-east. We had been warned of the dangers of sudden squalls that apparently lurk in the cliffs of these mountains. Our captain, pilot, and in fact our whole crew, knew full well that this especial part of the river was very dangerous, and consequently every man was on the watch, but fortunately we had no trouble at all in passing these mountains, excepting a few sudden puffs from opposite quarters, and at one time we were caught flat aback, but just as suddenly our sails filled again and we continued on our journey before a good stiff breeze that sent us spinning along with terrific speed. The wind changed no more, and we very soon left the bluffs and mountains far behind us, and to tell the truth I was very glad of it. There are a great many strange stories told of accidents at that place, and it was not until we had left it far behind that our sailors seemed themselves again. We now saw *Manfalut*, with its towers and domes, which is quite a large town, situated about two miles from the river. It has post, telegraph offices and a railway station, with a population of about thirteen thousand inhabitants. It is a town of importance which we would liked to have seen, but as the wind was still blowing good and strong, we kept on our course towards Asyut.

After passing *Manfalut*, the valley widens out considerably, and we found both banks of the river extremely fertile and everything growing in luxuriant abundance; the air was pure and fresh, the sun was shining brilliantly from an unclouded sky, and the mountains in the distance had a soft glow of crimson light thrown around them, continually changing to deeper and softer tones; in fact, the whole scene was perfectly lovely. Every little turn in the river opened up a series of charming vistas that delighted the eye. As we went sailing along, the minarets and domes of Asyut were plainly visible, first on one side, and then on the other. We continued winding along with the sinuosities of the river, and it seemed as if we should never get there, for at one point it appeared as if we were leaving it behind us, but at length we turned the last bend, when our sailors started up their songs, laughed and danced in the greatest glee, and in a very little while we found our boat tied up at the port of Asyut " *El-Hamra* "—the town itself lying back in the plain and under the foot of a large mountain.

This place (*Asyut*) is the capital of middle Egypt. It has a number of hotels, post and telegraph offices located near the depot. There is one thing that we noticed in this place that is different from the rest of the towns between here and Cairo, and that is, there are quite a large number of houses here that are built in the European style. Asyut has a population of at least thirty-two thousand inhabitants, and there is a very fine college located here, for the accommodation of both boys and girls belonging to the American Mission. There are good baths and very fine bazaars to be found here ; also a cotton factory and several mosques, one of which is noted for its tall minaret. There is a market held here every Saturday, when the villagers come in from the surrounding country in order to dispose of their goods, and buy what they need for their own use. During this time the bazaars are filled to repletion, for here one can find all kinds of commodities that have been brought, not only from all parts of Egypt and Arabia, but also from Europe and America as well. We saw here in these bazaars very fine linen goods, embroidered leather goods of all kinds, and some very fine ostrich feathers, with numberless articles from the Soudan, and very conspicuously exposed were all varieties of the beautiful pottery they manufacture here. Any one who visited the World's Fair at Chicago, or the Mid-Winter Fair in San Francisco, must most certainly have noticed the beautiful bottles, pipe bowls, black tazzas, paper weights of both black and red pottery, and those exquisite coffee services, etc., all of which came from this place (*Asyut*).

This town rises out from amidst a very fine belt of palm trees, and a canal carries the water from the river to the town, whose banks are adorned with beautiful sycamore and fig trees. The canal reaches the Government Buildings and beyond it, and its banks form a very nice

VIEW OF THE CITY OF ASYUT.

promenade. We were very anxious to see about our letters, so we hurried off up town to the post office to enquire for our mail, and I was very glad indeed to receive two from home, three from friends in Cairo and Alexandria, and two from Lahore, India. Our sailors had this evening entirely to themselves, and as some of them belonged to this place, they asked for and received permission to go and visit some of their relations and friends. We spent the night ashore with some acquaintances whom we knew in Cairo, who were returning to the city, having been up as far as the second Cataract, and who were visiting the various points of interest on their way down the river. We arose early the next morning, having decided to visit some of the tombs, etc., that were located not far from here, and strolled down to the port of *El-Hamra* and to our Dahabiyeh.

We found that nearly the whole of our crew were off baking bread, so I sent Salame to pick out some good donkeys for us, while we supplied ourselves with candles, etc., for the trip. In a very short time Salame returned to tell us the donkeys were all ready, so we went on shore, mounted our little animals, and were soon speeding out along a very nice road that led up to the foot of the mountain, where we left our donkeys and clambered up to the tombs on foot.

The first one at which we stopped was called *Stabl Antar*, the entrance to which is fully thirty feet high and hewn out of the solid calcerous rock. We entered a vaulted corridor leading on to a great hall, with two side chambers, and a sanctuary, and found the ceilings of these tombs to be vaulted and ornamented with peculiar devices and designs which have been considered by a great many people who have visited these tombs to have originated from Greek patterns; but we know that could not be so, because these patterns and tombs were in existence long centuries before Greek Art was known. On some of the ceilings we could plainly trace the five pointed stars on a groundwork of yellow and blue, but it was very difficult to trace the designs, for they had been so blackened and discolored by smoke, disfigured and defaced by time, that it was very hard for one to trace the meaning of the devices, etc. Yet we could see upon some places, not completely disfigured and defaced, some very beautiful designs in light green, white and yellow, and on some of the walls we found traces of both male and female figures. On other parts of this tomb we found some of the walls covered with hieroglyphic inscriptions.

We visited another tomb called the "Soldiers' tomb," because of the rows of soldiers with immense shields, pictured upon the south wall, but the tomb is truly the resting place (or was) of *Tef-ab* the son of *Kheti;* and both Prof. Maspero and Mr. Griffith claimed that *Tef-ab* lived during the tenth dynasty, somewhere about B. C. 3000. *Where was Greek art then?*

The view from this mountain is magnificent. Lepsius claimed that it is the finest in Egypt. For my part I admit that it is a lovely view, but at the same time I think that there is equally as fine a one, if not superior, near Aswan, and also in the vicinity of Thebes there is some very beautiful scenery. We spent the greater portion of the day viewing these tombs among the calcerous rocks of this mountain, and in rambling around from one to the other we saw pieces of the mummied dead scattered in all directions, with shreds of mummy cloth, whitened bones, etc. We came down to where we had left our donkeys, mounted them, and inside of an hour we were on board our floating home, where we took our usual bath, smoked a cigar, and after dinner we strolled up town with our friends to see what we could of Asyut.

Returning along the embankment we passed a number of women slaves, perfectly nude, some washing, others filling their jars with water from the canal for household purposes. Some of these women were possessed of very fine figures, well developed, graceful in their carriage, and did not seem to notice our presence, but passed on their way with their jars posed upon their heads in a careless graceful manner. On our return to our boat we found our crew having a glorious time with their friends and relatives, whom they had invited to the "Fantasia." Their feast was o'er, their work was done, and now they were enjoying themselves to the fullest extent. We stood and watched them for quite awhile, then we all went into the cabin, and chatted with our friends. At last we parted from them, wishing them good night and "*bon voyage*" amidst a blaze of light, for our sailors were burning fireworks, etc.

After having parted from them we retired and slept soundly, and awoke the next morning to find Salame with our coffee and toast, of which we soon disposed. We sent for Hassan, in order to find out when he would be able to leave, he informed us that he desired to lay in a good stock of provisions, etc., at this place, which would be impossible to obtain farther south, and I noticed that he was not particularly anxious to leave for a couple of days, and as the rest were agreeable to remain I was satisfied. I sat down all the morning writing letters, while our sailors were all busy cutting up their bread (which they had baked) into very thin slices, which they lay in the hot rays of the sun, until it was as dry as a crisp, after which they stored it away in their lockers for future use. You would scarce credit the amount of bread those fellows had baked, for their use, between here and Aswan. I asked Hassan how much he thought it would weigh? He said that there was about two tons of it.

That night Hassan informed me that he had supplied himself with all that he would need for our trip to Aswan and asked me if he could have the next day to visit some friends. I told him certainly, so the next morning, he started off dressed up like some great Arabian potentate or plenipotentiary. I spent part of the day in writing, the other in sight seeing. At night Hassan returned and when he had arrayed himself in his every-day costume, he told me that everything was in readiness on board and that if the wind should spring up, at any time during the night, he would start again on our journey, but we did not care to travel by night if we could possibly avoid it, because we desired to see the country in the immediate vicinity, consequently we agreed to wait until the next morning before we started.

Ever since we came to this place there have been a persistent lot of fellows who were very desirous of selling us some of their pottery. Some of whom fairly took possession of our boat. They spread their wares all over the deck, as if it was their regular stall, or place for selling. We thought that if we bought a few things from them that they would pack up and leave; but it seemed to have a contrary effect for they stayed until quite late. At length our sailors commenced talking to them and in very pronounced language ordered them off and they went, but I firmly believe that if their wares were not so fragile that they would have remained with us over night.

After dinner we went for a stroll along the embankment and watched the people and talked of the decadence of Egyptian civilization, etc. We chatted and talked until after the sun had set and the stars shone forth from on high, in refulgent glory, as we retraced our steps to our floating home, and long before our arrival, we heard our sailors singing their everlasting songs. We retired and slept through it all, and awoke the next morning to find a dead calm, so we waited until after breakfast before sending our men to the tow-line. Just as we were discussing that subject, a light air sprang up, our sails were loosed and we began to gather a little headway and found *El-Hamra* dropping astern.

We now entered and passed through the most fertile part of the Nile Valley. The land lies low and the river banks are high, and are cut here and there by various canals for irrigation purposes, the waters of which flow out upon the land and cause all things to grow luxuriantly and in abundance. We now passed through fertile fields and meadows stored with sweet scented flowers, wherein were to be seen large flocks of sheep, and herds of buffaloes. Farther on we passed between gardens of cucumbers and various other vegetables and saw large fields of waving corn wherein could be hidden a squad of Lancers and their horses. We sailed by farms and villages and saw clover and lupins growing higher than a man's head, and immense fields of blossoming beans whose fragrant flowers filled the air with their delicious perfume. Again we passed through fields of waving corn, whose bright green color extended as far as the eye can reach, soon to be guarded by the slinger who will sit nodding at his post and *sometimes* use his sling to scare away the birds from the ripening ears. Continuing on we observed fields of cane and upon the banks of the river itself, we saw large quantities of pumpkin and squash shining like gold in the rays of the noon day sun.

This particular part of Egypt generally astonishes the tourist and traveller on account of the fertility of the soil and the wondrous growth of vegetation. Farms, towns, villages, Shadufs and Sakiyes, go drifting by and the changing scenery unfolds itself in one continuous panorama of charming vistas. The wind freshened and we went scudding along before a good stiff breeze and the scenery changed continuously. We passed high bluffs with here a farm and there a village, now a quarry, groves of palms, etc. *Abu Tig* fell astern, and was left behind as we went speeding along like a greyhound. Several Nile boats went lumbering along like an English collier heavily laden. *Mishta* was passed and now the Arabian hills began to draw closer to the river, and the strip of arable land upon the east bank grew narrower, and we saw the mounds of *Tahta* off the southwest. *Shekh Heridi* was soon observed on the east bank of the river and Tahta quite a distance inland on the west. With our glasses we could see very plainly the tombs that were cut into the face of the mountain of Shekh Heridi. Next we saw the square pigeon towers of *Passalon* where the arable land begins to widen out again upon the east bank, and we left *Maragah* behind us, passing quite a large cultivated island. Here we saw several hogs lying upon the bank of the river among a lot of sweet peas and vines loaded with squash, etc., but we soon stirred them up with a few fine bird shot just to see them run to cover. Unfortunately the wind that served us so well began to fail, and died out, so we tied up for the night in the bend of the river at a place called *Shendawwil* the ancient *Aphroditopolis.*

There is not much to be seen at this place, but after dinner we strolled up to the station and walked out along the track, and watched the glorious sunset and afterglow. How I wish, my dear brothers and readers, that you could have stood with me that evening and seen it as I did, for words cannot express the exquisite coloring of Nature's wardrobe, for she seemed to appear in her most charming hues in this wondrous valley of the Nile, the " Land of Egypt." As we sat under the awning that night, we noticed that the glorious stars seemed to have grown brighter. After a little while the golden moon came into view, and went sailing into grander heights from out the low refraction of the atmosphere, near the horizon, when it shone with a truer, purer and more brilliant light, looking like a burnished silver orb in the unclouded starry vault above, and lighting up the earth below with sweet, soft tones of wondrous light. As we sat and pondered upon the sublimity and grandeur of nature, the hum of voices from the distance, and the lowing of cattle came to us; the river was all aglow with a silver light, our sailors' songs were ended, and the wash of the river lingered with us, and as we retired it lulled us off to peaceful slumber.

Salame aroused us and presented our usual cup of coffee and toast, after which we went on deck to find a dead calm, owing to which we were compelled to tow and punt, for we were all anxious to reach " hundred-gated Thebes." Our sailors started out and harnessed themselves to the tow-line, and as they tugged upon the rope they sang their songs, chatted and laughed at each other, and although the sun was high in the heavens, and burning hot, they capered along and sang and danced as if towing was a most delightful pastime. We strolled on ahead and made some sketches, and when the boat came up we went on board for our luncheon.

The town of Suhag, situated about three hundred and ten miles from Cairo, was the next point of interest. It has a population of about nine thousand inhabitants, and is located close to the river. It has post, telegraph and railway offices, as well as Hotels, Bazaars, Mosques, etc. Here is where the irrigating canal begins, that carries the waters of the Nile to Asyut, irrigating that fertile plain and at the same time reclaiming as much of the Lybian desert as possible; it is called *Mohat Suhag*. A little over four miles inland from this place is located the celebrated "*White Monastery*" or convent of *Der-el-Abiad*, which is a very interesting place to visit; but the town of *Suhag* itself claims but very little of interest, consequently we pushed on to the steamboat and mail station *Ekhmin*. After turning the bend of the river, we found the merest strip of arable land on the east bank and the town of *Ekhmin*, which place we should never have been enabled to reach, if it had not been for a favorable wind that sprung up just before we reached Suhag, and pushed us on at a seven-mile gait, relieving our men from a very hard-day's work of towing and punting our boat. We dined as usual, and while we were enjoying our meal we were tied up to the bank of the river.

The town of *Ekhmin* is not far from the river, and it contains post and telegraph offices and a railway depot, etc. It is quite a town with a population of eighteen thousand inhabitants. It has a very fair bazaar and hotels, and a market-day is held here every Wednesday. At this place they manufacture those pretty check shawls that are worn so much by the "Sailors of the Nile." This town occupies the ancient site of *Khemmis* or *Panopolis*, and Strabo informs that this place was once famous for its linen manufactories and workers in stone. Herodotus says the inhabitants of this town (Panopolis) were the only Egyptians who favored Greek customs. The dealers in antiquities here will furnish you, or in fact any one, all kinds of relics from a mummy to a handful of scarabs, and if they should not have what you require they will manufacture it for you, while you wait.

HALL OF COLUMNS, TEMPLE OF DENDERAH.

The next day we arose with the sun and found a dead calm, so after our men had partaken of their morning meal, they went out on the tow-path and we were soon crawling along southward up the stream towards *Baliana*, but about ten o'clock the wind came up fresh and fair, when our sails were loosed and away we went ploughing along like a steamboat.

It was a delightful sensation to sit on deck under the awning, and watch the ever-changing scenery as we went scudding along the river, watching the towns and villages come and go. We found but a very scant strip of vegetation on the East bank, while on the West it stretches off for miles, with all kinds of vegetation growing abundantly. We now passed some islands that were cultivated, and arrived at, and left behind us the town of *Girga*. It is located close to the river, and is exposed to the wash of its waters. It was formerly the principal point of departure for Abydos, and the capital of Upper Egypt, but now it is simply the chief town of the province. Twenty-five years ago the town had not been touched by the river, but to-day it is being washed away by every passing steamer and the regular inundations of the river itself.

Passing more islands we very soon run up under the bank at *Baliana*, where we stopped in order to visit Abydos. Baliana has both post and telegraph offices and a railway station. At this place we hired donkeys for our trip to Abydos, which we had looked forward to with a great deal of pleasure. It is located about eight miles off to the South-west of Baliana, and it would take fully two hours to get there. Upon our arrival we sent Salame to engage donkeys for us as there was a "three-week" steamer due the following day, so we got our pick, and the next day arising, bright and early, we mounted our little animals and rode off to visit Abydos and vicinity. The road led out through fertile fields and palm groves until we at length arrived at Abydos, which Mariette called "The cradle of the Egyptian Monarch." We rode directly to the great temple of (Seti, the father of Rameses II.) of the XIX dynasty which is the Memnomium of Strabo.

The plan of this building is peculiar and many people are in doubt as to the meaning and object of its various parts. Like our Masonic temples and Scottish Rite Cathedrals, it is very difficult for the profane to determine the meaning and object of the various parts. To the initiate all is plain, and the meaning and object of everything is thoroughly understood, and the necessity of each part, in order to form the grand whole. We noticed on entering this temple that the pylon and walls, now in ruins, originally formed the *outer court*, which was to be plainly traced by the debris that clearly marked its outline.

The next *court* is in a far better condition for the simple reason that part of these walls have been preserved, and this *court* leads up to *the facade of the temple proper* and the *entrance* to the *first Hall*, which is decorated with a row of twelve columns. *The first Hall*, itself, has a double row of columns, twelve in each row ; the entrance is through two doors, one in the centre and the other on the extreme right, the middle one appears from its extreme width to have been the principal or main entrance, while the one on the right is quite narrow. The carvings on these columns are very peculiar, but more especially that portion which represents a kind of bat with human hands, in front of each there is a star with the hieroglyph *Neb* (Lord). This hall is long and narrow, but it must have been very imposing when magnificently draped, and the grand preliminary procession took place, preceding the regular initiatory services which were afterwards performed upon the aspiring Neophyte by the Master of the Holy House. To-day the roof has fallen down in many places, and it is only a question of time, when the lotus bud capitals will lie prone upon the earth, and be covered from sight by the dust of the dead past.

The second Hall is very much larger in height, length, and breadth, three rows of columns adorn this place, the first two have lotus bud capitals, but the third row starts from a raised platform just beyond the others. Behind these, and on the same level, there is a series of seven vaulted chambers, with passages leading into them. Between the opening of each are seven niches " for statuary " (?) but, may not these seven niches have been for the Hierophant and officers to have sat in during the initiatory services ? (I shall speak of this later on). Passing through the third chamber, from the north wall of the temple, we find ourselves in a small hall, whose roof is supported by ten columns, on the north of this hall and to the right of the entrance are two small chambers, and on the south end is a smaller hall, whose roof is supported by four columns, the entrance to which is through an opening in the centre. At the end of this smaller hall on the south there are two smaller chambers.

From the *second*, and largest hall, with the three rows of columns, there are two openings, the first one that is nearest to the vaulted chambers, is a very interesting hall or room, whose roof is supported by three columns, and on the west of this hall there are two oblong rooms whose vaulted ceilings are falling in to the room below. The other opening leads to a peristyle court that is adorned with six columns, and there are a great many other small halls and chambers off to the west of this court, but, it is here at the entrance to this hall, opposite the second and third row of the columns of the large hall, that is the most important part of the whole building because, on the right hand wall, on entering this ascending passage-way leading to the peristyle hall or court, was discovered the celebrated " Tablet of Abydos ".

Let me quote you from " Monuments of Upper Egypt " by Mariette Bey, page 147. " By way of information, we may add, that it was in the temple of Sethi, that we discovered a chronological table of kings, more complete and in a better state of preservation than that which has enriched the collection of the British Museum. Sethi as king and Rameses still as a prince, are there represented standing ; the one offering the sacrifice of fire, the other reciting the sacred hymn. Before them as a synoptical diagram, are the cartouches of seventy-six kings (Sethi has included himself among the number), to whom this homage is paid, and it is not without a certain emotion that one reads at the head of the proud list the name of Menes, the ancient and venerable founder of Egyptian monarchy ".

The discovery of this tablet has been of very great value to us, because it is an actual record of a list of Egypt's earliest kings, and recorded by one of Egypt's greatest rulers, who lived over thirty-four centuries ago. Of all the temples in Egypt, there is to-day no better specimens of Egyptian art and architecture, of the Middle Empire, than are to be found in the decorations of the temple itself of Seti at Abydos. There is no tomb or temple throughout the " Land of Egypt " that can show finer work than the exquisite carvings chiselled upon the walls in the celebrated temple of Seti at this place. The tombs of Tih and Phahhotep at Sakkarah do not show any more beautiful workmanship than is to be found here. I will not attempt to describe or explain the exquisite chisellings and decorations that have been inscribed upon the walls of the various halls, etc., of this most extraordinary temple of Seti, but, will refer my readers to Mariette, Rawlinson, Wilkinson and others for more information upon this famous *ruin*.

The temple of Rameses II is located a short distance to the north across a very high mound, and it, like that one of his father's, was dedicated to Osiris. It is somewhere about the same size of that of Seti's but it is in a much more dilapidated condition. Originally this temple was a most magnificent building, but to-day one can scarcely trace its outlines, for it has suffered far more from the ruthless hands of the destroyers, than it has from the all devastating hand of Time. From what information we can gain, and from our own personal observations, we find that there was a large open court surrounded by Osiride figures, which opened into the temple proper, the entrance to which was from the East through a gateway of sculptured red granite. We cannot gather very much information from these ruins to-day, but there is one thing that we are positive about, and that is, that the temple of Rameses was built of very much richer material than that which was used in the construction of his fathers; for we can plainly see in the temple of Rameses II, red and black granite and oriental alabaster lying all around among the debris. But in that one of Seti we find nothing excepting lime, and sandstone with which it was built.

We visited the Necropolis of Abydos and found it especially interesting as it contained graves from the sixth dynasty down. We spent quite a time in examining these ancient relics of ancient Egyptian history.

We retired early as we were all pretty well fagged out, and slept comfortably all through the night, and when Salame aroused me the next morning I felt refreshed from my long night's rest. After breakfast we went on shore with our guns and walked down the track with Salame following behind with a rifle. Our crew started out tracking, and by the time we arrived at the bend of the river we had bagged quite a lot of game. Here the river turns off sharp to the North of East, where we waited for the boat and got on board.

From *Bagura*, the Valley of the Nile and river runs nearly East and West as far as *Keneh*. We noticed now that the Dom-palm was more common and were to be seen in clusters, and were much finer looking than those farther north. At last we come to the island of *Denderah* which we passed and a landing was made on the West bank, just before reaching *Kench*, which is located on the East bank. We tied up here because we could very easily walk to the temple of *Denderah*, and not be bothered with donkeys or boys. About an hour after he had tied up to the bank, a glorious breeze sprung up and in our favor, after we had been tracking and punting, for three long days, trying to reach this place, where we were then moored. Such is luck. We retired early that night so as to get an early start the following morning to explore the temple of *Denderah* and its ruins.

In the morning, when Salame aroused us, the first rays of the sun had scattered the morning mist, and ushered in a glorious day and a pleasant breeze. We partook of our coffee and toast, and made preparations for an early start to the temple, so that after breakfast we were soon ready for our journey.

The foundation of this celebrated temple was laid by Ptolemy XI (*Auletes*) and it was not fully completed, so far as its decorations are concerned, until the time of Nero. It is a very fine specimen of Græco Egyptian Architecture, and shows upon its ovals the names of Augustus, Caligula, Tiberius, Domitian, Claudius, and Nero the very latest. This temple originally stood, like all other ancient Egyptian temples, in the centre of a vast enclosure generally made of rough bricks, whose walls were very high and extraordinary thick. These walls were pierced with regular openings, or entrance gates, into the inclosure and when they were closed, all that happened within the inclosure, or the interior of the temple, could neither be seen nor heard by the profane upon the outside. This temple of Denderah was dedicated to *Hathor*, the Egyptian Venus and it stands very nearly as perfect to-day as when it left the hands of the builders and decorators, excepting those carvings and paintings which have been so mutilated by the order of the early Christian fathers. These vandals destroyed and desecrated all the temples and sacred places of these ancient people by throwing down, and disfiguring their beautiful statues, robbing their sanctuaries and beating away the faces of every figure they could reach, both inside and outside, of not only this most magnificent structure, (with very few exceptions) but every other temple in the valley of the Nile.

31

Frank de Hess, D.D., in "Explorations in Bible Lands," says in relation to the preservation of the beautiful and elaborate scenes pictured upon the walls, etc., of many of the temples in Egypt, etc.: "Nothing could be more beautiful than some of the scenes here pictured, and the preservation of the coloring after so many centuries is truly wonderful. This is partly due to the following circumstances: When Theodosius, Bishop of Alexandria, in his pious but mistaken zeal issued his celebrated edict, A. D. 391, for the suppression of idolatry throughout Egypt, and ordered the temples to be divested of every vestige of idolatrous worship, when many works of Art were destroyed, and it is painful to see how with pick and chisel many of these beautiful temples have been defaced.

"Here, however (*Medinet Habu*), the bass-reliefs were so deeply cut in the hard granite, that instead of erasing the sculptures they merely plastered them over. This temple was afterwards converted into a Christian Church, as the frescoing clearly proves, and occasionally very ludicrous scenes are met with, where the stucco has partly fallen off. In one of the halls where the plastering has scaled off, may be seen a long procession of priests and princes, with Rameses III at their head, presenting their offerings and burning incense before Hathor, under the symbol of a cow, and just above, where the frescoing still adheres to the wall, may be seen St. Peter with the key and crosier, raising his hand, as if in the act of pronouncing a benediction on the pagan worshippers."

The entrance to the temple proper is from the east, and through a beautiful hypostyle hall fully fifty feet high, and one hundred and thirty-nine feet wide, adorned by twenty-four very fine columns, each of which has a capital of four Hathor heads, with cow's ears, surmounted by a house. The first or outer row of columns are connected by a series of balustrades, excepting between the two centre columns. Here was the gateway or entrance for the King and Hierophants who officiated in the ceremonies of initiation. While on each of the side walls there was a small door that was used no doubt by the priests and officials who assisted in the various ceremonies that took place within the *Sanctum Sanctorum*.

On entering into this beautiful temple, that is, coming in from out the bright sunlight outside, it will be some time before your eyes will become accustomed to the more subdued light of the interior, but by

ENTRANCE TO TEMPLE OF MEDINET HABU.

degrees you will be enabled to dimly see here and there the outlines of hieroglyphic inscriptions, royal ovals and fantastic forms of all kinds, such as scarabei, winged globes, hawk-headed, cow-headed and Ibis-headed figures all around you, and a feeling of awe will steal over you, as you stand in darkness visible, and recognize the symbolism of the hoary civilization of a prehistoric age.

All through this extraordinary temple are to be seen zodiacal emblems, figures seated on thrones, kings and divinities performing their mystic rites and ceremonies. In passing from one hall to another, and examining the various chambers, we get bewildered, as it were, in wandering around in the interior of this most extraordinary temple. Carvings of all kinds are to be seen all around us, the columns themselves are covered with divinities, in fact it would take me too long to describe them, consequently I will not attempt a description of these most extraordinary hieroglyphic carvings, paintings, etc., but rather refer you to Mariette, Lepsius, Maspero and others for their elucidation.

These sculptures are as perfect in detail and they look as beautiful to-day as when first the artist completed his work, and the designer saw his thoughts expressed in the decorations upon the walls, columns and ceilings of this magnificent temple. The hand of time has not injured them a particle, and what injury they have received has been from the early Christians, who, as I have herein above stated, beat and battered down all the statues, and disfigured the faces of all the carvings they could reach, otherwise this temple would have been as perfect to-day as when its halls resounded to the voices of the Hierophant and officers performing their mystic rites and ceremonies in the early days of the Christian era.

This is a most magnificent temple, its portico is majestic and impressive, with its massive columns, ponderous cornice and exquisitely carved frieze of kings, priests and warriors, in regular Egyptian Panathenaic procession, some of whom carry musical instruments and standards, and above all, as if o'ershadowing with its Divine essence, an enormous, winged egg, brooding as it were over the main entrance above the frieze. The decorations of the exterior and interior may seem very strange to many people who visit this temple, but each, and every one must admit that they are carved with masterly skill, and if you will examine the celebrated astronomical paintings upon the ceiling, the peculiar serpents in every variety of form, the massive columns or anything else, you will find them perfect specimens of what they were intended to represent. I especially desire to impress upon you this fact in relation to this temple. Although it is a most magnificent building, it does not represent the beauty of the early age of Ancient Egyptian Architectural design and beauty, and to the Art critics it only demonstrates the decadence of the Art under the Lagadi.

We came away charmed and delighted with our trip and walked back to our home the Dahabiyeh, and as they were taking her across to Keneh, we took our bath and refreshed ourselves with a good cigar, up under the awning. Soon after we moored the boat at Keneh we strolled up town, looked through the bazaars, came back again and found dinner awaiting us, after which we all went up town to see the *gawazi* (dancing girls). These dances were disgusting, but I do not need to describe them here, for since the " World's Fair " in Chicago these dances are well known.

The next morning we were fortunate enough to find a light air in our favor, so the sails were loosed, and we started off for Thebes, but only managed to get as far as *Neqada*, a small town on the West bank. The river scenery here was very fine, and the old town with its lofty pigeon towers, presented quite a quaint and picturesque appearance. Our whole talk was Thebes, and we talked of it until quite late.

The next morning our sailors were towing and punting, and after breakfast we went on deck and talked of the grandeur of Thebes, her ancient tombs, temples and monuments, that we soon were to explore, fully realizing the stupendous glory that belonged to Egypt in her Golden Age. As we turned the bend of the river, and saw *Qamula* a light breeze sprung up and we soon went spinning along over the waters. Very soon Hassan gave a shout and our whole crew burst forth in echoing yells Karnak! Luxor! etc. The pylons of Karnak came in sight and other points of interest. Our sailors struck up their songs, accompanied by drums, etc. The houses of the Consulates came in view with their flags fluttering in the breeze, the pigeon-towers of the village, Nile boats and Dahabiyehs dipping their flags, and firing their guns as we passed them. Our sails were furled and here we were at last, at the threshold of " Hundred-gated Thebes."

Masonic Teachings—Hindu Beggar—Roman Catholicism.

Slave to no sect, who takes no private road,
But looks through Nature up to Nature's God;
Pursues that chain which links th' immense design,
Joins heaven and earth, and mortal and divine.

—POPE.

CHAPTER XXI.

MASONIC TEACHINGS—HINDU BEGGAR—ROMAN CATHOLICISM.

EVERY man and brother who desires to thoroughly comprehend Masonry must be endowed with intellectual qualifications, in order to be enabled to understand and appreciate the grandeur and sublimity of its teachings. Therefore, if he is not intellectually inclined, he will never rise above the foundation of the Symbolic Degrees, but will become a mere drone in the busy hive of Masonry instead of an active worker. He will assuredly go through the various ceremonies of Initiation, Passing and Raising, receiving the degree of a Master Mason; but he will never become a Master, in very deed, until he has solved the various problems of its profound philosophies and understands the sublime teachings that permeate those ancient degrees—*then*, and *then only*, will he realize the true meaning of Brotherly Love, Relief and Truth. If he be true to his vows, he will be true to his fellow men, and will labor for the benefit and upbuilding of the human race by endeavoring to show them the Light of Truth, and help them on to a knowledge of the Law of Love and Righteousness.

It is the duty of every Mason to labor earnestly and incessantly for the advancement of his brother, both mentally and morally; teaching him that it is by the development of the intellectual qualifications that man begins to learn something about himself, and his own potential forces that are latent within. Because a man cannot read or write, that is no reason why he should not be enabled to learn to do so.

The acquisition of knowledge is a gift to some, but every living man, with a well balanced brain, has the potentiality of acquiring knowledge and becoming wise, by deep thought and earnest study. He must learn to think for himself; for, as a man thinks in the depth of his heart, so he becomes, and it will not be long before he will begin to realize that the key-note to WISDOM is MEDITATION. Then will he be enabled to trample beneath his feet the snarling serpent of IGNORANCE, FALSEHOOD and INTOLERANCE, and help humanity by showing them the Light of FREE THOUGHT, FREE SPEECH, *and a profound veneration for the Supreme Architect of the Universe.*

Masonry tolerates all religions, and emphatically asserts that *no man has the right to dictate to another what he shall or shall not believe,* and claims that *no one Religion possesses the whole of Truth,* and that every man has a perfect right to believe according to the dictates of his own conscience. Unless a man is allowed Freedom of Thought, he is not a Free man at all; for if Man is possessed of Free Will, and is not permitted to exercise it by following his own reasoning faculties, where is his freedom?

Every Religion, and the so-called Truths of "Inspired" writings, depend entirely upon the testimony of Man himself. The evidences brought forward by him are produced as proofs of the Truth of his assertions. Masonry claims that all men have the right to judge of the Truth of the claims put forward, and to examine the proofs of the various so-called "inspired" writings, and then to judge them, from a common sense reasoning standpoint. Then, if they stand the test of their investigations, it is Truth for them.

Man becomes what he WILLS himself to be, and he can never get outside of the world that he makes for himself. Death cannot destroy the seeds that he has sown, for they all in good time ripen, and he receives the fruition thereof. No confession, no repentance, no sacrifice, or imploring of God, can ever change the mighty Law of Cause and Effect (Karma). This Law is a law of perfect Justice, knowing neither Love nor Hate, but moves to perfect Righteousness. A man's Faith belongs to himself alone, as much as his reasoning faculties, and his freedom consists in being enabled to think and reason for himself, without let or hindrance, from any source at all whatever, exercising both to the uplifting of his *Lower Manas* (lower mind) to a higher plane of spiritual unfoldment, and thus dominating the *Kamic elements,* or animal propensities that are continually battling against his Higher Self. When he has accomplished this, subjugating the animal within, then he has conquered himself, and is worthy of more honor than he who has conquered kingdoms, for he has kept his " first vow," *and has learned to subdue his passions,* and in doing this he has improved himself in Masonry.

We find in " Morals and Dogmas," page 371 *et seq.*, that " Symbols were the almost universal language of ancient theology. They were the most obvious method of instruction; for, like nature herself, they addressed the understanding through the eye, and the most ancient expressions denoting communication of religious knowledge, signify ocular exhibition. The first teachers of mankind borrowed this method of instruction, and it comprised an endless store of pregnant hieroglyphics.

" The Ancient Sages, both barbarian and Greek, involved their meaning in similar indirections and enigmas; their lessons were conveyed either in visible symbols, or in those ' parables, and dark sayings of old' which the Israelites considered it a sacred duty to hand down unchanged to successive generations. The explanatory tokens employed by man, whether emblematical objects or actions, symbols or mystic ceremonies, were like the mystic signs and portents either in dreams or by the wayside, supposed to be significant of the intentions of the Gods; both required the aid of anxious thought and skilful interpretation. It was only by a correct appreciation of analogous problems of nature, that the will of Heaven could be understood by the Diviner, or the lessons of Wisdom become manifest to the Sage.

" The Mysteries were a series of symbols; and what was *spoken* there consisted wholly of accessory explanations of the act or image; sacred commentaries, explanatory of established symbols; with little of those independent traditions embodying physical or moral speculation, in which the elements or planets were the actors, and the creation and revolutions of the world were intermingled with recollectious of ancient events: and yet with so much of that also, that nature became her own expositor through the medium of an arbitrary symbolical instruction, and the ancient views of the relation between the human and divine received dramatic forms.

" There has ever been an intimate alliance between the two systems, the symbolic and the philosophical, in all the allegories of the monuments of all ages, in the symbolic writings of the priests of all nations, in the rituals of all secret and mysterious societies; there has been a constant series, an invariable uniformity of principles, which comes from an aggregate, vast, imposing and .true, composed of parts that fit harmoniously only there.

"Symbolical instruction is recommended by the constant and uniform usage of antiquity; and it has retained its influence throughout all ages, as a system of mysterious communication. The Deity, in his revelation to man, adopted the use of material images for the purpose of enforcing sublime truths, and Christ taught by symbols and parables.

"All the ideas of the Priests of Hindostan, Persia, Syria, Arabia, Chaldea and Phœnicia were known to the Egyptian Priests. The rational Indian Philosophy, after penetrating Persia and Chaldea, gave birth to the Egyptian Mysteries. We find that the use of Hieroglyphics was preceded in Egypt by that of the easily understood symbols and figures from the mineral, animal and vegetable kingdoms used by the Indians, Persians, and Chaldeans to express their thoughts; and in this primitive philosophy was the basis of the modern philosophy of Pythagoras and Plato.

"All the philosophers and legislators that made Antiquity illustrious were the pupils of the initiation; and all the beneficent modifications, in the religions of the different peoples instructed by them, were owing to their institution and extension of the Mysteries. In the chaos of popular superstitions those mysteries alone kept man from lapsing into absolute brutishness. Zoroaster and Confucius drew their doctrines from the mysteries that emanated from the Ancient Wisdom. Clemens, of Alexandria, speaking of the Great Mysteries, says: 'Here ends all instruction. Nature and all things are seen and known.' Had moral truths alone been taught the Initiate, the mysteries could never have deserved or received the magnificent eulogiums of the most enlightened men of Antiquity—of Pindar, Plutarch, Isocrates, Diodorus, Plato, Euripides, Socrates, Aristophanes, Cicero, Epictetus, Marcus Aurelius, and others;—philosophers hostile to the Sacerdotal Spirit, or historians devoted to the investigation of Truth. No: all the sciences were taught there; and those oral or written traditions briefly communicated, which reached back to the first age of the world."

Masonry, lineal descendent of those Ancient Mysteries, yields her glorious Truths to the earnest student who meditates upon the sublime and profound symbology of our most illustrious Fraternity, and to all those who diligently search, or seek, they will most assuredly find. But it must be thoroughly understood, that it will be very difficult to unveil

THE ARTIST'S CHOICE,

PHIL'A.

the secrets of her profound philosophies. They are only to be obtained by great mental exertion, but once they are unveiled, and comprehended, they will never be forgotten ; because what has been acquired through deep, earnest study, and a great mental exertion, is more easily remembered, and is generally more highly prized. Our own beloved Scottish Rite, like the Greater Mysteries, unfolds to her postulants, the true meaning of her profound symbology, so that they may be enabled to see the Light of Truth, in all its variant phases. Having acquired Knowledge and Wisdom, they should not be content with simply keeping it hid within their own heart, and be indifferent to the wants and needs of their fellow man and brother; but should ever strive to assist them along these lines of thought, so that they may be enabled to attain to the sublime Truths of the " *Holy Doctrine.* "

In order that we may be enabled to come to a thorough understanding of *Divine Wisdom*, we must light within our own heart the *Lamp of Reason*, and wander studiously among the rich field of Religion, Science and Philosophy, wherein will be found not only the " Holy Doctrine " but the Royal Secret. A knowledge of the one will unfold the other to all who earnestly desire the Truth in all its sublimity and grandeur. Reason and Meditation are *rays* of Divine Ideation which illuminates our mind and opens up to our consciousness Divine revelations.

In order that you, my dear readers and Brothers, may better understand my meaning let me say : When a man sits within the Light of Reason and Meditates upon the various problems of Religion, Science or Philosophy, no matter how difficult they may be to solve and understand, under the Light of Meditation, by concentrating his thoughts upon them he sets in vibration thought forces, that go out into the infinitude of space and into Divine Ideation, that return to him, bringing back with them a reflex action from the Divine Mind that illuminates his inner vision and the problem is solved. No matter what the subject or problem may be, or how difficult to understand, Concentration of the Mind will help us on to the solution of the greatest discoveries in all fields of investigation.

The law of vibration can be very easily proven to your entire satisfaction, and vibratory forces can be very clearly demonstrated, so that you may have ocular proof of the existence of them. Take a guitar, for instance, and tune it to a piano, and after they are in accord, set the guitar at the far end of a large room, or hall, then have some one strike the key note upon the piano, by which it was tuned, and we shall not only see the strings move, but hear them vibrate in harmony or unison, as the notes are struck upon the larger instrument. In the same manner in Concentration; the Mind of Man is a part of the Divine Mind and when, by profound Meditation and Concentration, we set up vibrations that pass out into the infinitude of space, they will come back to us illuminated by Divine Ideation, and thus we are enabled to discover the Truth for which we are searching, or solve the problem that we have been studying. Here we begin to see and understand that vibratory forces in *Thought or Act* are powerful factors for *Good or Evil.* We shall also realize that *Thoughts are Things*, that *Thoughts are Personal Entities*, and in knowing this to be a fact, we can better understand what is meant by the statement that " *Curses like chickens come home to roost.*"

> " You can never tell what your thoughts will do,
> In bringing you hate or love ;
> For thoughts are things, and their airy wings
> Are swifter than carrier doves.

> " They follow the law of the universe,
> Each thing must create its kind ;
> And they speed o'er the track, to bring you back
> Whatever went out from your mind."

The symbol of the Rose Croix is the pelican, tearing open its breast, in order to feed its young with its heart's blood, thus demonstrating to our Brothers of the Scottish Rite, Compassion and Love for our fellow Man, and teaches us that we should ever labor in the interest of humanity, by sacrificing ourselves, if need be, in a cause that all good, and true men should advocate : *Freedom of Thought, Freedom of Speech and Equal rights to Man throughout the world universal.* When Christ was asked by the lawyer, " Master, which is the great commandment in the law ? " Christ answered and said, " Love the Lord thy God with all thy heart. . . . This is the first and great commandment. . . . Thou shalt love thy neighbor as thyself." Matthew 22: 37–39.

How many are there who follow this advice ? The great majority of people simply live for themselves alone, believing that the gratification of the animal propensities is the height of human happiness. They are perfectly willing that their neighbor should sacrifice all his desires for either him or them, and consider it nothing but right and proper for him to do so, but they will never give anything in return for the sacrifice. Thus they demonstrate their selfishness. The love that the great majority of mankind has at heart, is the love of SELF. The fulfilment of the desires for their own good and selfish purposes, they consider to be true happiness. They will eventually find, however, that true happiness can never be attained by seeking it for ourselves alone, but only in sacrificing our own desires for the benefit of our fellow man, and in the practice of *selflessness*. It is far better to give than to receive. Therefore in seeking the happiness of others, doing good to all men, *because we know it to be our duty*, *asking nothing nor expecting anything in return*, is really and truly the *Law of Love;* which will lead us on to perfect bliss.

The man who has during the whole course of his life endeavored to accumulate vast wealth, and miser-like, hoards it away, gloating over untold sums of gold and precious gems, does not realize that not one pennyweight of it belongs to him in reality ; he has acquired it most certainly, but only as a loan, as it were, and just as he does with it, so will he reap reward or punishment. He cannot carry away with him beyond the grave one hair's weight of it, but the good that he has done with it, in deeds of charity and loving kindness, will be recorded and he will find, that that which he hath given away, that he will carry with him. The height of human happiness consists in man being enabled to truthfully say : I want nothing for myself alone in this world, and I live for the express purpose of helping my fellow man.

Masonry has ever labored to give humanity Freedom of Thought, Freedom of Speech, and a Free government, for the people and by the people, and all those who enter into the Holy House of the Temple should ever work to free their fellow man from the bonds of imposture and priestly arrogance. Man's birthright is freedom, but he has been enslaved by his fellow man.

Every Scottish Rite Mason who has the good of the fraternity at heart is a *Priest of Truth, of Toleration, of Philosophy*, and of *Rational Liberty*, and it is therefore his bounden DUTY, FIRST: to take *Tyranny*,

Injustice, and *Usurpation* by the throat, and by the assistance of his Brothers *Free the Human Race*, irrespective of *Creed, Caste* or *Color*, from all who would enslave it. SECOND: to *Free* his own country from *Despots* and *Despotism* and thus give to the people, both temporal and spiritual Freedom, which includes all the inalienable rights of Man.

To ever labor for the upbuilding of the human race is the DUTY of every true Man and Mason. They know full well that the greatest of all gifts to Man is *Manhood*. They also know that true Manhood can never be found in the mumbling chants and invocations of Romish Priests, or Sectarianism, and in religious Dogmas or Creeds. Our beloved Scottish Rite teaches us that our main object and *Duty* in life is for us to do *our* duty *to all men*, even to the neglect of our own personal comfort, ever and always striving to make others happy, because it is right for each and every man to do his Duty to all men, without hope of fee, or reward. Happiness will surely follow the man who performs his *duty*. At the same time we must ever remember that self-gratification should never be the incentive to do good, but to do it because it is right for us to do so. If Man would only practice Love and good fellowship to all men, and follow the teachings of our glorious Fraternity, Mankind would be far happier and this world would be a veritable paradise.

God commands us to do good, and Altruism has ever been taught by all the great Reformers, long centuries before our present Christian era. It is still taught and preached, but it is never or seldom ever practiced. This fact reminds me of an incident that happened to me in India, while travelling through that country a few years ago.

I was going from Dinapoor to Allahabad for the purpose of attending a celebrated *Mela*, that was to be held at the confluence of the Jumna with the Ganges, when I overtook a man who carried a beggar's bowl and staff. He seemed to be begging his way apparently from town to town. As I approached the man, I looked at him closely, and noticed that he was quite an athletic looking fellow, standing fully six feet two inches tall, with a very fine phrenological development, and from his expressive features I judged him to be a Frenchman, and said to him, in that language, *ete vous Francaise?* He replied to me in Italian, saying, "No, sir!" I answered him in that language, telling him that I could speak Italian, when he said to me in good plain English: " I am neither French nor Italian, sir; and why do you stop me upon the roadside and ask such questions ? Is there not room for you and me to pass, or is it customary in the country from which you come to accost the casual pedestrian and ask him all manner of questions ?"

To say the least, I was very much surprised, and said to him : " No, sir; it is certainly not customary to do so in any country I know, but being struck by your personal appearance, and seeing you in beggar's garb, I thought possibly that I could be of some assistance to you," at the same time, pulling out my purse in order to give him a few rupees, saying, " I have the greatest compassion for the poor in particular, and mankind in general. Seeing you begging your way along the road I wanted to help you." I then offered him some money, when he smiled upon me and said: " No, my dear sir, I have no need for money, these good people (pointing along the road) give me all that I need to eat and drink." I said : " That no doubt is quite true, your food is assured, but what about your sleeping at night, we all must rest." He answered me: " A neighboring tree furnishes me all the shelter that I need, and the glorious stellar vault above enwraps me in a Divine essence, and I sleep the refreshing sleep of childhood." I said to him : " Why do you not go to our Missionaries ? They would help you and give you more comfortable clothing than the yellow '*copra*' that you are wearing, besides you surely believe in the teachings of Christ, do you not ?"

He smiled upon me again and said, " Certainly, who is there that does not believe in those teachings of the Man of Nazareth ; but let me tell you, my dear sir, that there is not one word that the Lowly Nazarene preached, and practiced, that has not been taught and acted upon by all the Masters of every age, and each, and every one of those glorious Truths are embodied in all religions. They have been preached and practiced by all the Great Reformers long ages before *your* Christ was ever born or dreamed of, when He came down the winding way that led to Jerusalem, in order to take possession of His kingdom, riding bare-backed upon an Ass, with the glorious sunlight from heaven streaming down upon His bared head, light, that was free to all men. The people came flocking out from the City Gates, in order to welcome this so-called son of God, strewing palm leaves before Him, and shouting hosanna to the meek and lowly Nazarene, who in the humbleness of heart and humility of soul rode barefooted and bareheaded upon an Ass to preach *Love and Compassion to all men.* The people fell prone upon the earth in order to kiss the very hoof marks of the ass upon which He rode, because He taught Love in all its sublimity and grandeur, and He practiced what He preached, Compassion and Love to all Men.

"Now about the Missionaries that you ask me to go to. Do you think that they understand the practice of *selflessness* as the Master taught it?—I tell you No! they do not. The love that they have, is not so much for their fellow man, as you imagine, and the love that they have at heart, is the love of women, wine, fine clothes, fast horses, and above all, plenty of money, in order to gratify their animal passional nature. When they drive out in their carriages their runners who go before shout out in their language, 'Look out, the Great Man is coming!' These so-called teachers of the Lowly Nazarene would not walk ten rods barefooted to help any man unless they were well paid for doing so, or gained the credit of being an exception to the general rule."

Long after I had parted from him I thought that there was a great measure of Truth in what he had told me. I knew that the religious teaching of all the great Moral Reformers, long ages before the Christian Era, was Love and Compassion, and that they were not only preached but practiced.

The Religion of Buddha is full of the most beautiful and unselfish acts that have ever been taught in any age, for instance, "Be ye all of one mind, having compassion one of another; love as brethren; be pitiful; be courteous; not rendering evil for evil, or railing for railing; but contrawise, blessing." Again the teachings of Chrishna show a most profound depth of thought, that equals anything that is credited to Jesus Christ, for instance: "Above all things, cultivate love for your neighbor." "When you die you leave your worldly wealth behind you, but your virtue and vices follow after you." "Do good for its own sake, and expect not your reward for it on earth." *See Chapter XIV of this work.*

The Moral teachings of Christianity are sublimely grand, and beautiful, but they were preached and practiced centuries before the so-called, Light of the New Dispensation; and they are not new for they each and all originated in the Pagan philosophies of a prehistoric age. Our modern Ethics are most beautiful, and when we hear them read to us, they thrill us to the very centre of our being; but what are mere words without action.

H. P. Blavatsky says in the *Key to Theosophy*, page 238, "Self-sacrifice for practical good to save many or several people, Theosophy holds as far higher than self-abnegation for a sectarian idea, such as that of 'Saving the heathen from *damnation*,' for instance:—In our opinion, Father Damien, the young man of thirty who offered his whole life in sacrifice for the benefit and alleviation of the sufferings of the lepers of MOLOKAI, and who went to live for eighteen years alone with them, to finally catch the loathsome disease and die, *he has not died in vain.* He has given relief, and relative happiness to thousands of miserable wretches. He has brought to them consolation, mental and physical. He threw a streak of light into the black and dreary night of existence, the hopelessness of which is unparalleled in the records of human suffering. He was a *true Theosophist*, and his memory will live for ever in our annals. In our sight this poor Belgian priest stands immeasurably higher than—for instance—all those sincere but vainglorious fools, the Missionaries who have sacrified their lives in the South Sea Islands, or China. What good have they done? They went in one case to those who are not ripe for any truth; and in the other to a nation whose systems of religious philosophy are as grand as any, if only the men who have them would live up to the standard of Confucius, and their other sages. And they died victims of irresponsible cannibals and savages, and of popular fanaticism and hatred. Whereas, by going to the slums of Whitechapel, or some other such locality of those that stagnate right under the blazing sun of our civilization, full of Christian savages, and mental lepers, they might have done real good, and preserved their lives for a better and a worthier cause." *In all of which I do most heartily concur.*

We are certainly in great need of Missionaries in all our large cities, to work among many of the people, with whom we come in contact, every day of our lives. In every part of the civilized world, are to be found men and women, who are mere beasts of burden, who toil and live in squalor, misery, and ignorance. Women who are insensible to shame, and who revel in the luxuries that have been purchased by the loss of everything that women hold to be the brightest jewel in the crown of

32

true womanhood. Is there not a rich field for Missionary work at the very thresholds of our own homes? I have stated in a previous chapter of *this work*, that the world was never more full of open and unblushing vice than it is to-day. Our churches and ministers are unable to cope with it; they do not seem to understand the cause, and much less the remedy.

How often I have heard people laugh and scoff at the attempted harmony of the bands of the "Salvation Army." I tell you my dear Brothers, those people are doing a noble work. They may not furnish a grand rythmic harmony of sound, but they are most assuredly doing both grand and noble work in their efforts to raise the fallen and dissolute, to a higher plane of morality. In such work there is a wide, wide field for our Missionaries, and if they would only try to save our own heathen, who wander around the very thresholds of our own homes, they would be doing far more good than sacrificing their lives, and being barbecued upon a stack of their own tracts and bibles, and thus furnishing a rare feast to a lot of savages unable to understand either them or their teachings. They are being brutally murdered by the followers of Confucius, whose ethics are as beautiful and grand as our own code if properly understood.

To help our fellow man and to do the most good for the upbuilding of the human family, does not consist in losing our own lives, effecting no good results by the sacrifice; but to help our fellow man by sacrificing our own personal comfort and desires, to give to him from our own earnings and help him on to a higher plane of spiritual unfoldment, so that he may come to an understanding of himself is the *duty* that we owe to all men. We should ever remember, that wise aphorism of *Epictetus* "Be not diverted from your duty, *by any idle reflections the silly world may make upon you,* for their censures are not in your power, and consequently should not be any part of your concern."

Do good to all men, and try to recognize in the whole human race one great family of which you yourself are a part. Every true Knight Kadosh labors for the benefit of his fellow man and Brother in order to improve their condition both Mentally and Morally, teaching them never to submit to Oppression, Injustice and Usurpation; and whose watchwords are—Humility, Patience and Self-denial. They are always willing to hazard their lives for the welfare of their country, the interest of humanity, and to sacrifice their lives for their fellow man, if humanity may be benefited thereby.

The dogma of Masonry is that of Zarathustra and Hermes; its Law is progressive Initiation; its principles, Equality, regulated by Hierarchy and universal Fraternity. It is the continuation of the Greater Mysteries, and of the School of Alexandria, and it is the heir of all the ancient Initiations. It is the depository of the secrets of the Apocalypse and the Sohar. It is the conserver and preserver of the Wisdom pertaining to the Secret Doctrine. The object of its worship is TRUTH which is represented in our Lodges, Chapters, Councils and Consistories, by the LIGHT that it dispenses.

It antagonizes no creed, but tolerates all, and professes the teachings of the *Ancient Wisdom*, and claims that " THERE IS NO RELIGION HIGHER THAN TRUTH." It seeks TRUTH alone and strives to lead by *Degrees* all intellects to *Reason*, allowing every Brother to profess and practice any Religion or Philosophy that his conscience may dictate; or none if it be preferable to him, only asking that they believe in the Supreme Architect of the Universe. It is a Philanthropic and Scientific Fraternity that believes in and teaches the Fatherhood of God and the Brotherhood of Man, and that every man should have the right to *Freedom of Thought, Freedom of Speech* and *Freedom of Conscience.*

Through every age of the world's history, Masonry has ever been the Champion of the Rights of People, endeavoring to teach, practice, and disseminate a knowledge of Truth, among all men, throughout the world universal, ever striving to free them from their own animal passional nature and to free them from Ignorance, Bigotry, Intolerance, and Mental and Spiritual Slavery. It stands to-day at the head of human affairs, and will most assuredly guide and direct us safely on through the approaching Crisis to the inalienable *Rights of the People—Liberty of Thought, Freedom of Conscience and Free Government for the People and by the People.*

There has never been a time when our illustrious Fraternity conspired against the Government to which it owed due and lawful obedience, and it is always ready and willing to draw its sword in defence of the downtrodden and oppressed of every country. We have a bitter, vindictive, and relentless foe in Jesuitry, which would if it were possible, throw the world back again into the same conditions as when the fires flamed throughout the so-called civilized world in *Auto da fes* of the Romish Church, who have ever and always been the advocate, and upholder of the " *Nicolaitan* " theory—the rule of the priesthood over the People. Consequently she is the bitter foe of all that tends to enlighten and educate the masses, such as *Free Secular Schools*, a free press, freedom of thought and opinion, by which I mean—Religious Freedom, and as I have previously stated—*A Free Government for the People and by the People.*

It behooves every true Man and Mason to stand upon his guard against the interference of Jesuitry with our Secular Free Schools, conducted for the express purpose of instructing our children in pure secular learning. They may obtain herein a thorough and complete knowledge of reading, writing, and speaking the English language correctly, also arithmetic, with the higher branches of mathematics, as well as a thorough comprehension of History, Geography, etc. All of which is actually necessary not only for the future benefit of our American citizen, in particular, but for our beloved country in general, that her citizens should be men of education, intelligence and refinement. Men who are free from all bigotry, and intolerance of Creed and Dogmas such as pertain to the Romish Church, and her Jesuitical Bigots.

There has been much comment about " *Godless Schools* " promulgated most assuredly by our bitter foes the *Romish Church* and the *Jesuits ;* but my dear Friends and Brothers, it is the *Duty* of our Country to teach the KNOWN and not the *Unknown.* Every intellectual man will most assuredly come to an understanding of the Supreme Architect of the Universe, if he be permitted to light the lamp of his own reasoning faculties, and follow the dictates of his own conscience, by thinking for himself. He will never under any circumstance allow either Jesuit or Romish priests to attempt to compel him to believe, as he or they may desire. May the Good God preserve our Secular Schools and Free Institutions from the ruthless hands of what Pope Pius VII called his " *Sacred Militia* "—the Jesuists.

They are ever and always working and plotting to enter the thin end of the wedge into our Free Secular Schools, and destroy them. Our Laws and Constitution would be torn down and trampled beneath the feet of these bigoted and intolerant Jesuits, and a repetition of the horrors of the Inquisition would occur as it did during the "*Dark Ages*" and the Eve of Saint Bartholomew would be repeated, not only in our own country, but in every other that was not thoroughly under the dominion of the Romish Church.

There was quite a furore among the Jesuits and priests of the Romish Church, when the Prince of Wales succeeded his mother good Queen Victoria, and was crowned King of England, on account of the Oath that was taken by him at the time. In order that you may be enabled to thoroughly understand the nature of this Oath I will quote you from "Fifty Years of Masonry in California," Vol. II, page 537.

The following is the Coronation Oath, taken in Section VII of the Order of Coronation Ceremonies: "The sermon being ended, and his Majesty having in the presence of the two Houses of Parliament made and signed the Declaration, the Archbishop goeth to the King, and standing before him administers the Coronation Oath, first asking the King, 'Sir, is your Majesty willing to take the Oath?' And the King answering, 'I am willing.' The Archbishop ministereth these questions, and the King, having a copy of the printed Form and Order of the Coronation Services in his hands, answers each question severally as follows: '*Archbishop.*—Will you solemnly promise and swear to govern the people of the United Kingdom of Great Britain, and Ireland, and the dominions thereto belonging, according to the Statutes in Parliament agreed on, and the respective Laws and customs of the same? *King.*—I solemnly promise so to do. *Archbishop.*—Will you to the utmost of your power, maintain the laws of GOD, the true profession of the Gospel *and the Protestant Reformed Religion established by Law?* And will you maintain inviolably the Settlement of the United Church of England and Ireland, and the doctrine, worship, discipline, and government thereof, as by law established within England and Ireland, and the territories thereunto belonging? And will you preserve unto the bishops and clergy of England and Ireland, and to the churches there committed to their charge, all such rights and privileges as by law do or shall appertain to them or any of them? *King.*—All this I promise to do.

"Then the King arising out of his chair, supported as before, and assisted by the Lord Great Chamberlain, the Sword of State being carried

before him, shall go to the altar, and there, being uncovered, make his
solemn oath in the sight of all the people to observe the premises; laying his right hand upon the Holy Gospel in the Great Bible, which was
carried before him in the procession, and is now brought from the altar by
the Archbishop and tendered to him as he kneels upon the steps, saying
these words: King—'The things which I have here before promised I
will perform and keep. So help me, GOD.' Then the King kisseth the
book and signeth the Oath."

Now let us examine the form of oath taken by the Jesuits, and which
was published by "The Standard" of London, England, March 20th,
1901, and is as follows: "I, A. B., now in the presence of Almighty
God, the Blessed Virgin Mary, the Blessed Michael, the Blessed St. John
the Baptist, the Holy Apostles St. Peter and St. Paul, and all the Saints
and the Sacred Hosts of Heaven, and to you my Ghostly Father, do
declare from my heart, without mental reservation, that His Holiness
Pope Leo is Christ's Vicar General, and is the true and only Head of the
Catholic or Universal Church throughout the earth, and that, by the
virtue of the keys of binding and losing given to His Holiness by my
Saviour Jesus Christ, he hath power to depose heretical Kings, Princes,
States, Commonwealths and Governments, all being illegal without his
Sacred Confirmation, and that they may be safely destroyed. Therefore,
to the utmost of my power, I shall and will defend this doctrine, and
His Holiness' rights and customs against all usurpers, especially against
the new pretended authority, and the Church of England and all adherents in regard that they and she be usurpal and heretical, opposing the
Sacred Mother Church of Rome. I do renounce and disown any allegiance as due to any heretical King, Prince, or State named Protestant, or
obedience to any of their inferior Magistrates or officers.

"I do further declare the doctrine of the Church of England, of the
Calvinists, Huguenots, and of others of the name Protestant to be damnable, and they themselves are damned and to be damned that will not forsake the same. I do further declare that I will help, assist and advise all
or any of His Holiness' agents in any place in which I shall be, in
England, Scotland and Ireland, or in any other territory or Kingdom I
shall come to, and do my utmost to extirpate the heretical Protestant
doctrine, and to destroy all their pretended power, legal or otherwise.

" I do further promise and declare that notwithstanding I am dispensed to assume any religion heretical for propogating of the Mother Church's interest, to keep secret and private all her agents' counsels from time to time as they interest me, and not to divulge, directly or indirectly by word, writing, or circumstances whatsoever, but to execute all what shall be proposed, given in charge, or discovered unto me, by you my Ghostly Father.   All of which I, A. B., do swear by the Blessed Trinity and Blessed Sacrament, which I now am to receive, and on my part to keep inviolably, and do call the Heavenly and glorious Host of Heaven to witness these my real intentions, and to keep this, my Oath.   In testimony hereof I take this holy and blessed Sacrament of the Eucharist, and witness the same further with my hand and seal this —— day ——, Ann Dom., etc."

Now, if we compare the two Oaths, I am certain that you will agree with me that the English Protestants have far more complaint against the Romish Church and the black soldiers of Loyola (the Jesuits) than the Church of Rome and her "*Sacred Militia*" have against Protestants and the Oath of King Edward of England and her dependencies.

Papal Rome is the bitter foe of all English speaking people who are not under her control, and if she can by any means disrupt the Anglo-Saxon Race, her aim will be accomplished.   To-day her main object is to stir up strife and discord between England and America and thus destroy both if possible, then upon the ruins of two of the grandest nations of the earth, she would raise her standards and rule the world with a rod of iron. Her long war against humanity and human progress, Science and civilization, if successful, would be smothered in the smoke and flame of *Auto da Fes*, and Free Masonry would be stamped out of existence by those Ruthless and Intolerant Bigots, the Jesuits and Catholic priests.

I now quote you from General Albert Pike's answer to the letter of Pope Leo XIII, known as the letter, " Humanum Genus " :   " Thanks be unto the God of Hosts, from whom all glories are !   Free Masonry is mightier than the Church of Rome ; for it possesses the invincible might of the Spirit of the Age and of the convictions of Humanity ; and it will continue to grow in strength and greatness, while that Church, in love with and doting upon its old traditions, and incapable of learning anything, will continue to decay.   The palsied hand of the Papacy is too feeble to arrest the march of human progress. It cannot bring back the obsolete doctrine that Kings reign by divine right. In vain it will preach new Crusades against Free Masonry, or Heresy, or Republicanism. It will continue to sigh in vain for the return of the days of Phillip II and Mary of England, of Loyola, and Alva and Torquemada. If it succeeds in instigating the Kings of Spain and Portugal to engage in the work of extirpating Free Masonry, these will owe to it the speedy loss of their crowns. The world is no longer in a humor to be saddled and bitted like an ass, and ridden by Capuchins and Franciscans. Humanity has inhaled the fresh, keen winds of freedom, and escaped from companionship with the herds that chew the cud, and the inmates of stables and kennels, to the highlands of Liberty, Equality and Brotherhood.

" The world is not likely to forget the infallible Pope Urban VII. *Barberina* set his signature to the sentence which condemned to perpetual imprisonment, to abjuration, and to silence, Galileo Galilei, who, it is known, avoided being burned at the stake by denying on bended knees the deductions of positive science, which demonstrated the movement of the Earth, etc. . . . .

"Nor are Free Masons likely to forget that when the Bull of Clement XII, which Leo XIII now revives and re-enacts, was published; Cardinal Firrao explained the nature of the punishments which were requested to be inflicted on Masons, and what the kind of service was which the Pope demanded from ' the Secular Arm.'

" ' It is forbidden,' he said . . . . ' to affiliate one's self with the Societies of Masons . . . . UNDER PENALTY OF DEATH, AND OF CONFIS-CATION OF GOODS, AND TO DIE UNABSOLVED AND WITHOUT HOPE OF SALVATION.'

"Who will be audacious enough to censure us for replying defiantly to a decree which, by revivor of the Bull of Clement, condemns every Free Mason in the world to death, and confiscation, and damns him in advance to die without hope of salvation? The world has not forgotten that when Charles IX of France and the Duc de Guise at first disowned responsibility for the massacre of twenty thousand Protestants and others, on the eve, and after the Eve of St. Bartholomew, the Catholic Clergy assumed it. Heaven adopted it, they said: ' it was not the massacre of the king and the Duke: *it was the Justice of God.*' Then the slaughter re-commenced, of neighbor by neighbor, of women, of children, of children unborn, in order to extinguish families the wombs of the mothers were cut open, and the children torn from them for fear they might survive.

"Men remembered that at Saint Michael, the Jesuit Auger, sent thither from the college of Paris, announced to Bordeaux that the Archangel Michael had made the great massacre, and deplored the sluggishness of the Governor and Magistrates of Bordeaux. After the 24th of August there were feasts. The Catholic Clergy had theirs at Paris, on the 28th, and ordered a jubilee, to which the King and Court went, and returned thanks to God. And the King who proclaimed that he had caused Coligni to be killed, said that he would have poinarded him with his own hand, was flattered to intoxication by the praises and congratutions of Rome. Do men not remember that there were feasts and great gaities at Rome on account of the massacre? That the Pope chanted the *Te Deum Laudamus* and sent to 'his son,' Charles IX (to win for whom the whole credit of the massacre, the Cardinal of Lorraine moved Heaven and Earth) the Rose of Gold? was coined by Rome to commemorate it, and a painting of the bloody scene was made, and until lately hung in the Vatican?

"Free Masonry is strong enough, everywhere now, to defend itself, and does not dread even the Hierarchy of the Roman Church, with its great revenues, and its Cardinal Princes claiming to issue the decrees, and Bulletins of God, and to hold the keys with which it locks and unlocks, at pleasure, the Gates of Paradise. The Powers of Free Masonry, too, sending their words to one another over the four Continents and the great Islands of the Southern Seas, colonized by Englishmen, speak but with only the authority of reason, *Urbi et Orbi*, to men of free souls and high courage, and quick intelligence. 'It does not need that Free Masonry should take up arms of any sort against the Church of Rome. Science, the wider knowledge of what God is, learned from His works; the irresistible progress of Civilization, the Spirit of the Nineteenth Century; these are the sufficient avengers of the mutilations and murders of the long ages of a horrid Past. These have already avenged Humanity, and Free Masonry need not add another word, except these, that there are two questions to be asked and answered, thereunto demanded of all Roman Catholics in the United States, who are loyal to the Constitution of Government under which they live, patriotic citizens of the United States: *Does not your conscience tell you that what is now demanded of you by Pope Leo XIII, by the General of the Jesuits and the Chief Inquisitor is* TO ENGAGE ACTIVELY IN A CONSPIRACY AGAINST THAT CONSTITUTION OF GOVERNMENT, AND THE PRINCIPLES ON WHICH IT IS FOUNDED; AFTER THE DETHRONEMENT OF WHICH PRINCIPLES THAT CONSTITUTION OF GOVERNMENT COULD NOT LIVE AN HOUR?

"If you cannot see it in that light, *do not your conscience and common sense tell you that* TO APPROVE, AND FAVOR, AND GIVE AID AND ASSISTANCE TO AN OPEN CONSPIRACY AGAINST EVERY OTHER REPUBLIC, AND EVERY CONSTITUTIONAL MONARCHY IN THE WORLD, AND THE PRINCIPLES ON WHICH THEY ARE FOUNDED, IS TO PLAY A PART THAT IS INCONSISTENT WITH THE PRINCIPLES THAT YOU PROFESS TO BE GOVERNED BY HERE, IS IN OPPOSITION TO ALL THE SYMPATHIES OF THE COUNTRY IN WHICH YOU LIVE, AND IS HOSTILE TO THE INFLUENCES OF ITS EXAMPLE AMONG THE PEOPLE OF OTHER COUNTRIES, TREACHEROUS TO YOUR OWN COUNTRY, AND UNWORTHY OF AMERICAN CITIZENS. You will have to answer these questions; for they will not cease to be reiterated until you do; AND NOT BY FREE-MASONRY ALONE."

Let me quote you from an article by H. T. B., of Kansas City, Mo., published in the "Trestle Board" of June, 1896:—"The English-speaking race, rising from the sea of nations first lighted the fires of religious liberty in the British isles. The history of this race for eighteen hundred years has been a continuous struggle for religious and political freedom against the papal hierarchy, and nearly all its bloody and unceasing warfare has been in self-defence, or in defence of others of like faith, or for the purpose of extending the faith by enlargement of area.

"Excommunicated and opposed at times by nearly all the world at the instigation of Rome, it has disrupted its enemies and caused them to cripple each other, and has emerged stronger and wealthier than ever, until in our own day one-third of the world and its inhabitants is under its influence or direct rule, and the end is not yet. With all branches of this race united, no other power on earth can hold control, and Rome which aims at universal dominion is well aware of the fact. . . . "By flattery, and fanning the flames of jealousy, she strives to promote ill feeling between us and our natural allies, and would make us believe that the world is too small for both, and that their policy, no matter what it is, must be necessarily opposed to our interests.

"She urges that an alliance with the degraded and financially-impoverished South American despotisms (masquerading as republics), with their priest-ridden and rickety governments, with no trade, no enterprise and no love for us or our institutions, is preferable to the friendship of our own kith and kin, whose flag is the emblem of what we hold most dear, who offers free ports, free schools, free religious opinions, free press, free welcome and protection to all, who if she extends her territory makes no restrictions in favor of her own subjects, and under whose flag the missionary may proclaim his message assured of protection, who if she erred in the past has profited by experience, and now seeks to rule by wisdom and not by force, and has beyond contradiction improved the condition of all her colonies.

"What have we in common with any people on earth outside our own royal race? On what is the pretended friendship of Russia based but self-interest, and rivalry of England, and the desire to make a fool of us.

"Did France assist us through love, or because she hated Great Britain?

"What do the mongrel races of South America care for us except as a cats-paw to pull their chestnuts out of the fire, or as a defence behind which they can run riot and be impudent at will?

"If Rome loves our institutions as she professes to do, why does she not essay to introduce them where her will is sole authority? So far from this, here and in Canada, she would destroy our schools if she could; and, so far from upholding our institutions, with her followers in power, she has corrupted our nobly-conceived government until it has degenerated into a mixture of spasmodic anarchy, aggravated by a riot of trusts dominated by the wire-pulling of a short-sighted plutocracy.

"Luckily our people are awakening to the danger. The foreigner by sentiment, if not always by birth, is wresting the sceptre from our grasp, and we are in imminent danger of losing our birthright.

"Great Britain like ourselves, by reason of her views, has not a friend in the world, and undoubtedly her desire at the present time is to win our love and alliance, and to effect this is willing to sacrifice anything but honor and self-respect. There is room for both in the world. What she cannot control herself she would only be too glad to see controlled by a friendly, Protestant, English-speaking people like ourselves, and to save it from the clutches of her hereditary Foes."

Free Masonry neither fears, nor hates, any Sect or Society, but stands on guard to protect Humanity from the Intolerance of Jesuitry and the waning power of the Romish Church, and to give Man empire over himself, never permitting Tyranny, Fanaticism and Ignorant Brutality to dominate the world as they did in the days of old. "*Nekam Adonai.*"

Thebes—Colossi—Der-el-Bahari—Luxor—Karnak.

POEM FOUND INSCRIBED ON THE FRONT OF THE PEDESTAL
OF THE VOCAL MEMNON.

'Sea-born Thetis, learned Memnon suffered never pangs of dying.'

'Still, where Libyan mountains rise, sounds the voice of his loud
crying'—

'(Mountains which the Nile-stream, laving, parts from Thebes, the
hundred-gated)'—

'When he glows, through rays maternal with warm light illuminated.'

'But thy son who, never-sated, dreadful battle still was seeking,'

'Dumb in Troy and Thessaly, rests now, never speaking.'

—ASKLEPIODOTUS.

CHAPTER XXII.

THEBES—COLOSSI—DER-EL-BAHARI—LUXOR—KARNAK.

THE reader's attention was called in the closing part of Chapter XX to our arrival at the threshold of "Hundred-gated Thebes," conspicuously located on the banks of the river Nile, distant from Cairo about four hundred and fifty-four miles. Its origin is lost in the misty ages of the past, and according to the best authorities it is not so ancient as Memphis, the capital of Lower Egypt.

The next morning we arose bright and early, took our breakfast and with Hassan and Salame, preceded by our guide armed with a long spear, we rode out to visit the Colossi, distant about three miles. Our way led us along through cultivated fields, first winding one way then another, but all the time nearing our point of destination, the Colossi, for they are constantly in view.

These two statues sit looking out across the plains of Thebes, toward the ruined palaces of a vanished race; wearied, and worn, and crumbling into dust as the mighty ages roll along. They still preserve a sublime majesty even in their mutilated isolation. They are carved out of *breccia*, a kind of pebbly sandstone, and to this fact is due their preservation, for had they been composed of limestone they would have passed through the lime kiln and have been destroyed long ago. They both sit facing the Nile and looking to the East, and when it is high Nile they are surrounded with water that laps just above their feet.

Lepsius informs us that the Arabs called them *Sanamat*, or the idols. They are distant one from the other about twenty yards, and were originally monoliths, having been carved from a single block of breccia. Strabo informs us that they were thrown down by an earthquake somewhere about B.C. 27, and during the reign of Septimus Severus they were restored, but the work was very poorly executed. The most northern of the two is known as the *Vocal Statue of Memnon (Amenophis)* and called by the Arabs *Tama*, and the one to the south, *Shama*. This one is in a far better state of preservation than the other. The height of the statues themselves is very nearly fifty-two feet, and the height of the pedestal beneath them thirteen feet, which would make the entire height of the monument or statue close upon sixty-five feet. From the bottom of the feet to the top of the knees measures nineteen feet ten inches; the breadth across the shoulders nineteen feet and eight inches; the middle finger is four feet and six inches long; the foot of each figure is fully ten feet and six inches long, and the entire weight of the statue, throne and all, has been estimated at one thousand one hundred and seventy five tons. The northern pedestal, as well as from the feet to the knees, has been covered with beautiful Greek and Latin inscriptions, and quotations written by numerous people who no doubt came here to listen to the stony voice of Memnon. Some of these inscriptions bear the early date of the eleventh year of Nero.

To-day they are isolated and alone, but at one time they were surrounded with the magnificence of ancient Thebes, and formed the commencement of a most beautiful avenue that led up to the pylon of a temple. Judging from the size of the statues themselves, the temple must have been a most magnificent structure, but being composed of limestone it became food for the lime kiln, and passed through the voracious maw of that monster who destroyed thousands of priceless jewels belonging to Egypt in her Golden Age. The ruined site of the temple itself is covered with the shrouding desert sands, while these two ancient guardians of the temple sit majestically alone in silent solitude.

After leaving the Colossi we rode out toward *Medinet Habu*, situated at the foot of the Libyan range of mountains about a mile west from here. The road took us out along dikes, and cultivated fields, groups of dom palms, and beautiful gardens. There was not a breath of air stirring, and the sun shone down upon us with hot burning rays. We rode on our way until we found the rocks beginning to gather around us and eventually we found ourselves before the gates of Medinet Habu.

The ruins of this place consist of a small temple ·founded by *Queen Hatasu* daughter of Thothmes first of the XVIII dynasty, who erected it in honor of her father. A very much larger one was built by Rameses III, who was called *The Sesostris of Herodotus.*

THE COLOSSI,
THEBES.

This temple or palace is a noble specimen of ancient Egyptian Architecture. It is decorated with sculptures of all kinds, beautiful paintings, etc. It is one of the most magnificent temples to be found throughout the "Land of Egypt." Of course it does not begin to compare with the stupendous magnitude of Karnak, but its beautiful courts, superb columns, its most exquisite paintings and its peculiar style of walls, etc., lend a peculiar charm and fascination to it, making it a most attractive and interesting spot for the tourist and Masonic student to visit.

It is said to have been built by Rameses III as an offering to the " Gods of Egypt," in permitting him to gain a victory over his enemies. The paintings and sculptures within this temple demonstrate the complete triumph of an Egyptian Warrior King, not only triumphing over his enemies in battle, but in grand processional triumph, and sacred ceremonies after his conquest. There are many places where the pictures do not refer to war, captives, and slaves returning with spoils, but to hunting scenes, etc. In one of the upper apartments the King is surrounded by his *harem* in a variety of ways. He is also represented as playing a game of draughts with a lady, possibly some favorite of his harem. No matter what pictures we examine in this ancient temple, whether it is Rameses conquering a fleet of ships, or in his war chariot fighting and overcoming his enemies, or receiving the cut off hands of the conquered Libyans, or assisting in the mystic ceremonies within the temple, they are all of the deepest interest. If all those who go into this most extraordinary country for the purpose of carefully examining, not only the various tombs and temples, but those exquisite sculptures and paintings upon the walls, would only begin at the beginning of these decorations they would be enabled, in many instances, to trace the life and history of the whole reign of the King; his battles on sea, or on land, his spoils, his return, and welcome, the grand procession and glorious mystic ceremonies, and finally his interview with the Gods of Egypt *alone*. After which we find him enjoying the pleasure of the society of the ladies of his harem, in fact the whole series of pictures if properly linked together will give us a biographical sketch of his life and reign.

While we were examining the interior decorations of this charming temple, Hassan and Salame were preparing our luncheon, and before we

33

left we partook of refreshments in the hypostyle hall of this most extraordinary building, after which we mounted and rode off on our way to the Ramesseum which is located about a mile to the northeast.

This building is the mortuary temple of Rameses II, and the one that is described by Diodorus as the temple of Osymandyas, being *User-Maā-Ra*, otherwise Rameses II. The Ramesseum is a beautiful temple, and very much different from the great majority because it is not inclosed within walls, and shut out from the light of day. Here the free air circulates throughout the whole of the building, and we find no damp ill smelling odors within this temple, for the glorious rays of the sun god *Ra* illuminates its interior, and dispels the darkness and gloom that we find in nearly all others. Its architectural design and exquisite decorations will compare favorably with any other structure in the Valley of the Nile.

This temple was built by Rameses, and it was probably intended for the worship of the manes of this Great Warrior King, whose mummy was no doubt originally laid to rest within the sacred walls of this most magnificent fabric. To-day there is but very little of it remaining to guide either the traveller or student in his examination, yet they can still plainly trace the description of Diodorus amidst its ruins. We are perfectly assured, in our own mind, that it was originally the " Tomb of Osymandyas." Although it is in such a ruinous condition, we can still find evidences to prove Diodorus's description, from the first pylon to the largest statue in Egypt, which lies prone upon the ground. It still occupies the same place that it did when Cambyses hurled it from its original position in his mad rage. It lies there to-day disfigured and broken.

The battle scene with the lion, the fortress surrounded by water, and the golden stars on a blue ground, are still to be seen, in fact all the various things that were mentioned by Diodorus have been found in this temple. *Champollion* discovered here the figures of Thoth, the inventor of letters, and the goddess *Saf,* the " Lady of Letters," President of the Hall of Books, inscribed upon the jambs of a doorway which was no doubt the entrance to the Sacred Library that Diodorus describes—" The Dispensary of the Mind." Before leaving this very interesting ruin, I desire that you should know the dimensions of the colossal statue that was uninjured when Diodorus saw it in A. D. 60.

The leaders of the French expedition made some very careful measurements of this statue, which are as follows : Across the back from shoulder to shoulder, twenty-one feet six inches; across the chest from shoulder to shoulder, twenty-three feet four inches; across the face from ear to ear, six feet nine inches; length of the ear, three feet six inches; circumference of the arm close to the elbow, seventeen feet six inches; length of the forefinger, over three feet; length of the nail on the middle finger, seven and one-half inches, the breadth of the same nail being six inches; width of the foot across the toes, four feet six inches; and the height of this statue when in situ was fifty-seven feet six inches; the total weight of this most extraordinary statue being estimated by them at fully two million pounds.

About a half a mile to the north of the Ramesseum, and just beyond *Shekh 'Abd el-Qûrna*, and a short distance south of the ancient temple of *Der el-Bahari* is where Professor M. Maspero discovered the Royal mummies in the summer of 1881, and in relation to this find I will quote you from "Cleopatra's Needles" by the Rev. James King, M. A., an account of this wonderful discovery and their transportation to Gizeh, etc.

"Professor M. Maspero lately remarked that for years he had noticed with considerable astonishment, that many valuable Egyptian relics found their way in a mysterious manner to European Museums as well as to the private collections of European noblemen. He therefore suspected that the Arabs in the neighborhood of Thebes, in Upper Egypt, had discovered and were plundering some royal tomb. This suspicion was intensified by the fact that Mr. Colin Campbell, on returning to Cairo from a visit to Upper Egypt, showed to the Professor some pages of a royal ritual purchased from some Arabs at Thebes. M. Maspero accordingly made a journey to Thebes, and on arriving at the place conferred on the subject with Daoud Pasha, the governor of the district, and offered a handsome reward to any person who would give information of any recently discovered royal tombs. . . . Behind the *Ramesseum* is a terrace of rock-hewn tombs, occupied by the families of four brothers named *Abd-er-Rasoul*. The brothers professed to be guides and donkey masters, but in reality they made their livelihood by tomb breaking and mummy snatching. Suspicion at once fell upon them, and a mass of concurrent testimony pointed to the four brothers as the possessors of the secret.

"With the approval of the district governor, one of the brothers, *Ahmad-Abd-er-Rasoul*, was arrested and sent to prison at *Kench*, the chief town of the district. Here he remained in confinement for two months, and preserved an obstinate silence ; at length Mohammed, the eldest brother, fearing that Ahmad's constancy might give way, and fearing lest the family might lose the reward offered by Maspero, came to the governor and volunteered to divulge the secret. Having made his dispositions, the governor telegraphed to Cairo whither the Professor had returned.

"It was felt that no time should be lost. Accordingly M. Maspero empowered *Herr Emil Brugsch*, keeper of the Boolak Museum, and *Ahmed Effendi Kemal*, also of the Museum service, to proceed without delay to Upper Egypt. In a few hours from the arrival of the telegram the Boolak officials were on their way to Thebes. The distance of the journey is four hundred and fifty-four miles, and as a great part had to be undertaken by the Nile steamer, four days elapsed before they reached their destination, which they did on Wednesday, 6th of July, 1881.

"On the western side of the Theban plain rises a high mass of limestone rock enclosing two desolate valleys. One runs up behind the ridge into the very heart of the hills, and being entirely shut in by the limestone cliffs is a picture of wild desolation. The other valley runs up from the plain, and its mouth opens out towards the city of Thebes. 'The former is the Valley of the Tombs of the Kings—the Westminster Abbey of Thebes ; the latter the Tombs of the Priests and Princes—its Canterbury Cathedral.'

"High up among the limestone cliffs, and near the plateau overlooking the plain of Thebes, is the site of an old temple known as Der-el-Bahari. At this last named place, according to agreement, the Boolak officials met Mohammed-Abd-er-Rasoul, a spare, sullen fellow, who simply from the love of gold had agreed to divulge the grand secret. Pursuing his way among desolated tombs, and under the shadow of precipitous cliffs, he led his anxious followers to a spot described as 'unparalleled, even in the desert, for its gaunt solemnity.' Here, behind a huge fragment of fallen rock, perhaps dislodged for that purpose from the cliffs overhead, they were shown the entrance to a pit so ingeniously hidden that, to use their own words, 'one might have passed it twenty times without observing it.'

"The shaft of the pit proved to be six and a half feet square; and on being lowered by means of a rope, they touched the ground at a depth of about forty feet. Truth is sometimes stranger than fiction, and certainly nothing in romantic literature, can surpass in dramatic interest, the revelation which awaited the Boolak Officials in the subterranean sepulchral chambers of Der-el-Bahari. At the bottom of the shaft the explorers noticed a dark passage running westward; so, having lit their candles, they groped their way along the passage which ran in a straight line for twenty-three feet and then turned abruptly to the right, stretching away northward into the darkness.

"At the corner where the passage turned northward, they found a royal funeral canopy flung carelessly down in a tumbled heap. As they proceeded, they found the roof so low in some places that they were obliged to stoop, and in other parts the rocky floor was very uneven. At a distance of sixty feet from the corner, the explorers found themselves at the top of a flight of stairs roughly hewn out of the rock. Having descended these steps, each with his flickering candle in hand, they pursued their way along a passage slightly descending and penetrating deeper and farther into the heart of the mountain. As they proceeded the floor became more and more strewn with fragments of mummy cases and tattered pieces of mummy bandages. Presently they noticed boxes piled on the top of each other against the wall, and these boxes proved to be filled with statuettes, libation jars, and Canopic vases of precious alabaster. Then appeared several huge coffins of painted wood; and great was their joy when they gazed upon a crowd of mummy cases, some standing, some laid upon the ground, each fashioned in human form, with folded hands and solemn faces. On the breast of each was emblazoned the name and titles of the occupant. Words fail to describe the joyous excitement of the scholarly explorers, when among the group they read the names of Seti I, Thothmes II, Thothmes III, and Rameses II, surnamed The Great.

"The Boolak Officials had journeyed to *Thebes*, expecting at most to find a few mummies of petty princes, but on a sudden they were brought, as it were, face to face with the mightiest Kings of ancient Egypt, and confronted the remains of heroes whose exploits and fame filled the ancient world with awe more than three thousand years ago.

The explorers stood bewildered and could scarcely believe the testimony of their own eyes, and actually inquired of each other if they were not in a dream. At the end of a passage, one hundred and thirty feet from the bottom of the rock-cut passage, they stood at the entrance of a sepulchral chamber twenty-three feet long and thirteen feet wide literally piled to the roof with mummy cases of enormous size. The coffins were brilliant with color-gilding and varnish, and looked as fresh as if they had recently come out of the workshops of the *Memnonium.*

"Among the mummies of this Mortuary Chapel were found Kings, Queens, Princes and Princesses, besides royal and priestly personages of both sexes, all decendants of *Her Hor,* the founder of the line of priest kings known as the twenty-first dynasty. The chamber was manifestly the vault of the *Her Hor* family; while the mummies of their more illustrious predecessors of the eighteenth and nineteenth dynasties found in the approaches to the chamber, had evidently been brought there for the sake of safety. Each member of the family was buried with the usual mortuary outfit. One Queen, named *Isi-em-Keb* (Isis of Lower Egypt), was also furnished with a sumptous funeral repast, as well as a rich sepulchral toilet, consisting of ointment bottles, alabaster cups, goblets of exquisite variegated glass, and a large assortment of full-dress wigs curled and frizzed. As the funeral repast was designed for refreshment, so the sepulchral toilet was designed for the queen's use and adornment on the Resurrection morn, when the vivified dead, clothed, fed, anointed and perfumed, should leave the dark sepulchral chamber and go forth to the mansions of everlasting day.

"When the temporary excitement of the explorers had somewhat abated they felt no time was to be lost in securing their newly discovered treasures. Accordingly, three hundred Arabs were engaged from the neighboring villages; and working as they did with unabated vigor, without sleep, and without rest, they succeeded in cleaning out the sepulchral chamber, and the long passages of their valuable contents in the short space of forty-eight hours. All the mummies were then carefully packed in sail cloth, and matting, and carried across the plains of Thebes to the edge of the river. Thence they were rowed across the Nile to Luxor, there to lie in readiness for embarkation on the approach of the Nile Steamer.

"Some of the sarcophagi are of huge dimensions, the largest being that of *Nofretari* a queen of the eighteenth dynasty. The coffin is ten feet long, made of cartonnage, and style resembles one of the Osiride pillars of the temple of *Medinct Habu.* Its weight and size are so enormous that sixteen men were required to remove it. In spite of all difficulties, however, only five days elapsed from the time the Boolak Officials were lowered down the shaft until the precious relics lay ready for embarkment at Luxor.

"The Nile steamers did not arrive for three days, and during the time Messrs. Brugsch, and Kemal, and a few trustworthy Arabs kept constant guard over their treasure amid a fanatical people who regarded tomb breaking as the legitimate trade of the neighborhood. On the fourth morning the steamer arrived, and having received on board the royal mummies, steamed down the stream "*en route*" for the Boolak Museum. Meanwhile the news of the discovery had spread far and wide, and for fifty miles below Luxor, the villagers lined the banks of the river, not merely to catch a glimpse of the mummies on deck as the steamers passed by, but also to show respect for the mighty dead. Women with dishevelled hair ran along the banks shrieking the death wail; while men stood in solemn silence, and fired guns into the air to greet the mighty Pharaohs as they passed. Thus to the mummified bodies of Thothmes the Great, and Rameses the Great, and their illustrious compeers, the funeral honors paid to them three thousand years ago were in a measure, repeated as the mortal remains of the heroes sailed down the Nile on their way to Boolak.

"The principal personages found either as mummies, or represented by their mummy cases, include a King and Queen of the *seventeenth dynasty,* five Kings and four Queens of the *eighteenth dynasty,* and three successive Kings of the *nineteenth dynasty,* namely, *Rameses the Great, his Father and his Grandfather. The twentieth dynasty* strange to say is not represented; but belonging to *the twenty-first dynasty of royal priests* are four Queens, two Kings, a prince and a princess. These royal mummies belong to four dynasties, under which ancient Egypt reached the summit of her fame. Through the expulsion of the Hyksos invaders, and the extensive conquests of Thothmes III and Rameses the Great, the oppression of Israel in Egypt and the Exodus of the Hebrews, the colossal temples of Thebes, the royal sepulchres of the Valley of the Tombs of the Kings, the greater part of the Pharaonic obelisks, and the rock cut temples of the Nile Valley belong to this period.

"THOTHMES III.—Standing near the end of the long dark passage running Northward and not far from the threshold of the family vault of the priest kings, lay the sarcophagus of Thothmes III close to that of his brother Thothmes II. The mummy case was in a lamentable condition, and had evidently been broken into, and subjected to rough usage. On the lid, however, were recognized the well-known cartouches of this illustrious monarch. On opening the coffin the mummy itself was exposed to view, completely enshrouded with bandages; but a rent near the left breast shows that it had been exposed to the violence of tomb breakers. Placed inside the coffin and surrounding the body were found wreaths of flowers; larkspurs, acacias and lotuses. They looked as if but recently dried, and even their colors could be discerned. Long hieroglyphic texts found written on the bandages contained the seventeenth chapter of the 'Ritual of the Dead' and the 'Litanies of the Sun.' The body measured only five feet two inches; so that making due allowance for the shrinking and compression in the process of embalming, still it is manifest that Thothmes III was not a man of commanding stature; but in shortness of stature, as in brilliancy of conquest, finds his counterpart in Napoleon the Great.

"It was desirable in the interest of science to ascertain whether the mummy bearing the monogram of *Thothmes III*, was really the remains of that monarch. It was therefore unrolled. The inscription on the bandages established beyond all doubt, the fact that it was indeed the most distinguished of the kings of the brilliant XVIII dynasty, and once more, after an interval of *thirty-six centuries* humanity gazed on the features of the man who had conquered *Syria, Cyrus and Ethiopia*, and had raised Egypt to the highest pinnacle of her power; so that it was said in his reign 'she placed her frontiers where she pleased.' The spectacle was of brief duration; the remains proved to be in so fragile a state that there was only time to take a hasty photograph, and then the features crumbled to pieces and vanished like an apparition, and so passed from human view for ever. The director felt such remorse at the result that he refused to allow the unrolling of *Rameses the Great* for fear of a similar catastrophe. THOTHMES III was the man who overran *Palestine* with his armies *two hundred years before the birth of Moses*, and has left us a diary of his adventures; for, like *Cæser* he was an author as well as a soldier.

"It seemed so strange that though the body mouldered to dust, the flowers with which it had been wreathed were so wonderfully preserved. that even their color could be distinguished; yet a flower is the very type of ephemeral beauty, that passeth away and is gone almost as soon as born. A wasp which had been attracted by the floral treasures, and had entered the coffin at the moment of closing, was found dried up, but still perfect, having lasted better than the king whose emblem of sovereignty it had once been; now it was there to mock the embalmer's skill, and to add point to the sermon on the vanity of human pride, and power preached to us by the contents of that coffin. Inexorable is the decree, 'UNTO DUST THOU SHALT RETURN.'"

Following the same line of meditation, it is difficult to avoid a thought of the futility of human devices to achieve immortality. These Egyptian monarchs the veriest type of earthly grandeur and pride, whose rule was almost limitless, whose magnificent tombs seem built to outlast the hills, could find no better method of ensuring that their names should be held in remembrance, than the embalmment of their frail bodies. These remain, but in what a condition, and how degraded are the uses to which they are put. The spoil of an ignorant and thieving population, the pet curiosity of some wealthy tourist, who buys a royal mummy as he would buy the Sphinx if it were movable.

RAMESES II died about *thirteen centuries* before the Christian era. It is certain that this illustrious monarch was originally buried in the stately tomb of the magnificent subterranean sepulchre by royal order hewn out of the limestone cliffs in the VALLEY OF THE TOMBS OF THE KINGS. In the same valley his grandfather and father were laid to rest; so that these three mighty kings "all lay in glory, each in his own house." This burial place of the *Pharaohs* of the XVIII and XIX dynasties is in a deep gorge behind the Western hills of the *Theban* plain.

"The valley is the very ideal of desolation. Bare rocks without a particle of vegetation, overhanging and enclosing in a still narrower and narrower embrace, a valley as rocky, and bare as themselves—no human habitation visible—the stir of the city wholly excluded. Such is, such must always have been, the awful aspect of the resting-place of the THEBAN kings."

The sepulchres of this valley are of extraordinary grandeur. You enter a sculptured portal in the face of these wild cliffs, and find yourself in a long and lofty gallery, opening or narrowing as the case may be, into successive halls and chambers, all of which are covered with white stucco, brilliant with colors, fresh as they were thousands of years ago. The sepulchres are in fact magnificent palaces. Hewn out of the rock and painted with all the decorations of the tombs and temples. One of the most gorgeous of these sepulchral palaces, was that prepared in this valley by *Rameses II*, and after the burial of the king the portals were walled up, and the mummified body laid to rest in the vaulted hall till the morn of Resurrection. From a hieratic inscription found on the mummy case of *Rameses*, it appears that official *Inspectors of Tombs* visited this royal tomb in the sixth year of *Her-Hor*, the founder of the priestly line of kings; so that at least for two centuries the mummy of RAMESES THE GREAT lay undisturbed, in the original tomb prepared for its original reception.

From several papyri still extant, it appears that the neighborhood of Thebes at that period was like it is to-day, filled with robbers of the dead, or tomb breakers. Such being the dreadful state of insecurity during the latter period of the *twentieth dynasty* and throughout the whole of the *Her-Hor dynasty*, we are not surprised to find the mummy of *Rameses II*, and that of his grandfather *Rameses I*, removed for greater security from their own separate catacombs into the tomb of *his father Seti I*. In the sixteenth year of *Her-Hor*, that is ten years after the official inspection mentioned above, a commission of priests visited the three royal mummies in the tomb of *Seti*. On an entry found on the mummy case of *Seti and Rameses II*, the priests certify that the bodies are in an uninjured condition; but they deem it expedient, on grounds of safety, to transfer the three mummies to the tomb of *Ansera*, a queen of the seventeenth dynasty.

For ten years at least *Rameses'* body reposed in this abode; but in the year of *Pinotum* it was removed into "the eternal house" of *Amen-Hotep*. A fourth inscription on the breast bandage of *Rameses* relates how that, after resting for six years, the body was again carried back to the tomb of his father in "*the Valley of the Tombs of the Kings,*" a valley now called "*Bab el-Molook.*" How long the body remained in this resting place, and how many transfers it was subsequently subjected to, there exists no evidence to show; but after being exposed to many vicissitudes, the mummy of *Rameses II,* together with those of his royal relatives and many of his illustrious predecessors, was brought in as a refugee into the family vault of the *Her-Hor dynasty.* In this subterranean hiding place, buried deep in the heart of the *Theban Hills, Rameses the Great,* surrounded by a goodly company of thirty royal mummies, lay undisturbed and unseen by mortal eye *for three thousand years,* until a few years ago the lawless tomb breakers of Thebes burrowed into this sepulchral chamber.

The mummy-case containing *Rameses'* mummy is not the original one, for it belonged to the style of the *twenty-first dynasty,* and was probably made at the time of the official inspection of his tomb in the sixth year of *Her-Hor's* reign. It is made of unpainted sycamore wood, and the lid of the shape known as *Osirian,* that is, the deceased is represented in the well known attitude of *Osiris,* with arms across, and hands grasping a crook and flail. The eyes are inserted in enamel, while the eyebrows, eyelashes and beard are painted black. Upon the breast are the familiar cartouches of *Rameses II,* namely :—*Ra-user-Ma-sotep-en-Ra,* his prenomen ; and *Ra-me-su-Meri-Amen,* his nomen. The mummy itself is in good condition, and measures six feet; but as in the process of mummification, the larger bones were probably drawn closer together in their sockets. It seems self-evident that *Rameses* was a man of commanding appearance. It is thus satisfactory to know that the mighty *Sesostris* was a hero of great physical stature, that this conqueror of *Palestine* was in height equal to a grenadier. The outer shrouds of the body are made of rose colored linen and bound together by very strong bands. Within the outer shrouds, the mummy is swathed in original bandages ; and *Professor M. Maspero* has expressed his intention of removing these inner bandages, on some convenient opportunity, in the presence of scholars and medical witnesses.

It has been urged that since *Rameses XII, of the twentieth dynasty,* had a prenomen similar, though not identical, with the divine cartouche

of Rameses II, the mummy in question may be that of *Rameses XII.*
We have, however, shown that the mummies of *Rameses I, Seti I and
Rameses II* were exposed to the same vicissitudes, being buried, transferred and reburied again and again in the same vaults.   When therefore
we find in the sepulchre of *Der-el Bahari*, in juxta-position, the mummy
case of *Rameses I*, the mummy-case and acknowledged mummy of Seti I,
and on the mummy-case and shroud the well known cartouches of
Rameses II, the three standing in the relation of grandfather, father and
son, it seems that the evidence is overwhelming in favor of the mummy
in question being that of Rameses the Great.

The whole of these mummies were originally placed in the Boolak
Museum, but they are to be found to-day at the Gizeh Museum, which is
located a few miles from Cairo and close to the river.   This Museum is
open every day of the week to the general public, excepting Monday,
when a small admission fee is charged.   All these mummies have been
arranged, numbered and set up for general inspection, and what a
glorious company they are, for they represent the most mighty and
renowned Warrior Kings of ancient Egypt, and what an inexpressible
feeling comes over one in the presence of these illustrious mummied dead,
when we think that not one of them lived after B. C. 1000.

Before closing the account of these mummies I will quote you from
H. D. Rawnsley's " Notes for the Nile," page 84 *et seq.*, which will prove
that the mummy that was found with Rameses I, and Seti I, and known
as Rameses the Great was actually and truly the mummy of *Rameses II.*
" I had read in the Academy of July 3rd, 1886, the very startling and
accurate account of the unwrapping of the mummies of Rameses II and
Rameses III, which took place at the Bulak Museum June 1st, 1886.
There in the presence of His Highness Tewfik Pasha, Khedive of Egypt,
and their excellencies Mouctar Pasha Ghazi, High Commissioner of the
Sultan, Sir Drummond Wolf, Her Majesty's Consul, and other great
persons, M. Gastine Maspero, the director of the antiquities of Egypt, and
his subordinates, Messrs. Brugsch Bey and Bouriant, unrolled at nine
o'clock in the morning the royal mummies brought from *Der el Bahari*,
and marked in the catalogue Nos. 5229 and 5233.

" There was more of interest than at first sight attached to the
unwrapping of the royal mummy No. 5233, for though the coffin had

been found in close proximity to, and in company with, the coffins of Seti I and Rameses I, and though the coffin lid bore the nomen and pre-nomen of the illustrious Rameses II, it had been suggested by some Egyptologists that Rameses XII, of the XX dynasty, a man of no great noteworthiness, bore the similar divine name, or cartouche, as the Great Rameses the Second of the XIX dynasty. This coffin might contain the lesser notable's body, after all. The savants further pointed out the coffin-case was of the Osirian type of the XX or XXI dynasty; so that, as the royal assemblage gathered round coffin No. 5233, on the first of June, 1886, though Maspero was fully persuaded that the great Pharaoh's body lay before them, enveloped in its pink colored and yellow cerements, there was just enough element of doubt about it, to render his task intensely interesting as a work of identification, apart from the fact of the unveiling of a royal monarch.

"The *proces verbal* of the dates on the coffin lid pointed to the mummy being the mummy of the great king. It had been written in black ink on the sycamore coffin case, and gave the years six and six-teenth of the royal or high priest Her Hor Siamun, and the tenth year of the royal priest Pinotmou I, was traced on the first cerecloth or wrap-ping, just at the breast. The Khedive's attention was called to the inscription; he nodded assent, and the unwrapping went forward. Beneath the first envelope was discovered a band of cloth, wrapped round and round the body, then a second envelope or shroud, sewn and kept in its place by narrow bands from space to space; next came two layers of small bandages, and then a piece of fine linen, stretching from head to foot; on this was painted in red and black, a representation of the god-dess of creation out of nothing, *Nouit* or *Neith*, as prescribed by the ritual of the dead. The goddess in profile unmistakably resembled the delicate features of Seti I, the father of Rameses II, as made known by the bas-reliefs of Thebes and Abydos.

"This was proof, not positive, but looking very much as if the great son of Seti I lay therein. A band of brand-new material had been placed beneath this amulet of the goddess *Nouit;* then came a kind of quilt, of pieces of linen folded in squares, and stuck together by the bituminous preparation the embalmers had used. There was considerable excite-ment amongst the bystanders. This last covering was removed and lo,

" Among his perfumed wrappings Ram'ses lay,
   Son of the sun, and conqueror without peers ;
   The jewel-holes were in his rounded ears,
His thick lips closed above th' embalmer's clay ;
Unguent had turned his white locks amber-grey,
   But on his puissant chin fresh from the shears
   The thin hair gleamed which full three thousand years
Of careless sleep could never disarray.
Hands henna-stained across his ample breast
   Were laid in peace ; but through the narrow eyes
   Flamed fires no more beneath the forward brow,
His keen hawk nose such pride, such power expressed,
   Near Kadesh stream we heard the Hittite cries,
   And saw by Hebrews' toil San's temple cities grow.

" In less than a quarter of an hour from the commencement of the unwrapping, appeared from beneath its many cerements the great Sesostris himself, who had been embalmed with such care, and wrapped up so laboriously, over three thousand one hundred and eighty-six years ago."

I have devoted considerable space to the discovery of the royal mummies of Ancient Egypt, and to the unwrapping of Rameses the Great, because, after having visited Der el-Bahari and the place where they were found, I was very much interested in them, consequently I have written and quoted from the very best authorities, all that was to be gleaned in relation to these celebrated mummies so that you, my dear Brothers and readers, may thoroughly understand everything pertaining to them. I have been so intensely interested in taking notes, measuring and examining these most extraordinary tombs, temples and monolithic stones and statues, that the days have come and gone without note, and yet, we have not described half of what is to be seen on this western bank of the river Nile, but, as we were very anxious to see and examine Luxor and Karnak, we discharged our guide and hired another for our excursions upon the other side of the river, who was to direct our steps in search of " More Light " among those stupendous ruins of Luxor and Karnak. We spent that evening with some acquaintances we had made while examining the beautiful ruined temple of Medinet Habu.

The night was lovely, so after our dinner, we sat up under the awning, and talked until a late hour upon the various tombs and temples,

THE RAMESSEUM OR MEMNONIUM,

THEBES.

and the wondrous knowledge that pertained to those people who lived here in the "Golden Age" of Egypt. We drifted off into Scottish Masonry whose sublime philosophical and theosophical teachings emanated from the greater Mysteries of ancient Egypt, whose esoteric teachings were identical with the Indian and Mazdean of prehistoric ages.

Early the next morning we took our breakfast and started out on our way to examine the celebrated temples of Luxor and Karnak, so we landed upon the river bank and made our way direct to the temple of Luxor.

I first visited this temple many years ago with my father when I was a boy. I again visited it some years ago, on my return from India, at which time it was very difficult to move around in, for it was at that day literally filled with mud hovels of the Arabs, and it was nearly impossible to see anything at all whatever of the building proper, for it was a veritable village in itself containing a mosque. It was a very dirty village at that time, with very narrow filthy lanes or alleys through which to walk, amid stables, hen roosts, and pigeon houses that were plastered up against beautiful sculptured walls. There was so much confusion that I could not, under any circumstances, find out anything at all whatever in relation to the original plan of this especial part of the building, but to-day it is very much different, thanks to Professor Maspero, M. Grebaut and others, who have changed it most wonderfully, for they certainly had a very difficult task in clearing the temple of these Arab invaders.

They at first positively refused to sell their homes, or mud hovels in which they lived, and leave the temple. After long and tiresome negotiations were they induced to sell their mud houses and quit. There was one man Mustapha Aga, the British consul, who had built his consular residence between the columns of Horemeb, directly facing the river, and when he was approached in relation to buying him out, he asked them such an enormous price for his place, that it was simply impossible to do anything with him. He was a good kindly old fellow, and very hospitable, for his house was ever open to all travellers, but there was one thing that he was very peculiar about, and that was the selling of his home. It was not until this old fellow died that they were enabled to remove his residence from between the columns. Over forty other families had been bought out and got rid of, in one way or another, who rebuilt their homes upon the land that had been alloted to them.

The little native mosque gave them far more trouble than any other thing in the temple, but they continued in the good work until the year 1886, when they cleared the temple of the dirty accumulations of these people, whom they had bought out, until all that remained as evidences of their occupation was the little mud Mosque.

After the resignation of M. Maspero, M. Grabaut succeeded him, and followed up the work of the restoration of the temple. Any one who had visited it at the time I did, some years ago, would not to-day recognize it as the same building, for the dirty mud hovels, and accumulations of centuries have been removed from around the columns, clear down to the original pavement. During the performance of this work they discovered beneath "the rubbish of the temple," quite a number of magnificent colossal statues of Rameses II, in beautiful polished red granite.

The traveller who goes there to-day will see the ruins of a most magnificent temple of exquisite design and beauty, second only to that of the Grand temple of Karnak itself, of which this was originally the gateway, as it were, to the most stupendous building ever erected by the hand of man—The temple of Karnak.

One can very readily recognize the principal entrance, or pylon at Luxor, on account of the obelisk and colossi at the gateway. The companion stone to this remaining obelisk stands to-day in the famous *Place de la Concorde*. It was presented to the French government by Mohammed Ali and it cost them over a million francs to take from Luxor, and set it up in Paris, which was done in the year 1836. This stone is seventy-seven feet high, and about seven feet square at the base. The one still in situ measures about eighty-four feet in height, and seven feet six inches square at the base.

The pictures on the front of the towers represent battle scenes. The first hall that we enter is about one hundred and eight-six feet, by one hundred and sixty-eight feet. Upon the walls are historical representations of Egyptian victories, etc. A colonnade of about one hundred and seventy feet long, connects this hall with another one, that is not quite so large as the first one. As we continued our journey we at length found ourselves out of the temple at the west gate, standing facing the river, and the remains of a stone quay of the Roman age. We spent the day in this most extraordinary temple examining the various chambers, sanctuaries, columns, sculptures, etc., and were deeply interested in all we saw. It is so very difficult to describe the magnificence of these beautiful ruins, but you, I hope, will be enabled to get some idea of its beauty not only from my description, but from many of the illustrations of this temple of Luxor and Karnak.

We returned to our dahabiyeh tired and weary, and after dinner we smoked and chatted of what we had seen. Our sailors went ashore to visit the crew of another dahabiyeh, and assist them in a grand fantasia, and we could hear their voices and recognize their songs until we dropped off to sleep.

In the morning we landed at Luxor and hired donkeys, starting out along the avenue of sphinxes, that begins at the lone obelisk and extends for about two miles, from one temple to the other. We rode slowly down this avenue for more than a mile when the road turned slightly to the left. and we saw before us the pylon of Ptolemy III (*Eurgetus I*) through which we passed, and pushed on to the little temple of Rameses III. We did not stop here, only for a very short time, just peeped in, and turning sharp to the left we kept on, now toward the river, then to the right again until we arrived at another avenue of ram head sphinxes. At length we found ourselves before the main entrance of this wonderful temple of Karnak.

We now dismounted and stood before it in awe and admiration, for we were now at the threshold of this most stupendous and magnificent gateway of the grandest temple that was ever raised by the hands of man. One of the enormous towers is very nearly perfect, and its dimensions were three hundred and seventy feet broad, by one hundred and forty-two feet six inches high, with a depth of about fifty feet, so you can imagine what an enormous propylon it must be. One can readily make the ascent to the top from which they may obtain a beautiful view of the surrounding country, and all of these wonderful ruins.

What a sight the avenue of mutilated sphinxes must have been in the glorious days of ancient Egyptian splendor, before they were ravaged by the hand of time, or by those disreputable image breakers whose vandalism is visible throughout the whole of the Land of Egypt. No pen

34

can describe the magnificence, vastness and exquisite sculptures of this stupendous temple in its mutilated grandeur, as I saw it some few years ago. It must be seen to be fully appreciated and properly understood, for in no part of the world is there anything to compare with its magnitude and beauty, the splendor of which no man can describe.

We now passed through this enormous gateway and entered the outer court to the temple, it is two hundred and seventy-five feet deep by three hundred and thirty-eight feet wide, with a row of columns on each side, supporting a roof, which forms a regular corridor on both sides of the court, excepting where the temple of Rameses III projects into it through the south wall. At the end of this court we passed through another enormous gateway beautifully adorned with bas-reliefs and found ourselves in the celebrated hypostyle hall—the wonderful " Hall of Columns," the most beautiful and magnificent of its kind in the world to-day. It is one hundred and seventy feet long by three hundred and thirty-nine feet wide, whose roof is supported by one hundred and thirty-four most stupendous columns, twelve of which are twelve feet in diameter and sixty-two feet high, the other one hundred and twenty-two are nine feet in diameter and forty-two feet high, and all of them beautifully sculptured with kings, gods, etc., blazoned with royal names and emblems of all kinds. The immense stone beams that run from column to column are fully twenty-six feet long. I will not attempt to go into details in my description of this most magnificent temple, although as I stood among this forest of columns I seemed bewildered, and astonished, so much so that I could not find words wherein to express myself regarding this most marvellous building.

On my return from India I camped in this temple, and lived here within its sacred precincts for weeks, during which time I have carefully examined the various points of interest, in the vicinity, but more especially this temple itself. I have wandered from court to court, ever finding something new in every part of its pillared halls and corridors. I have at times stood, lost in admiration and wonder, beneath the shadows of its enormous columns and gazed up to their capitals whose summits rose nearly seventy feet above me. Six of our party, with outstretched arms, attempted to encircle some of these columns, but without success. This was my last visit to this celebrated temple and I still found many things

HYPOSTYLE HALL OF THE GREAT TEMPLE OF KARNAK.

that were new to me and which filled me with astonishment. For hours I rambled eagerly around among the ruins, lost in admiration of its magnitude and its mutilated grandeur. I realized that I stood within the walls of the grandest specimens of architectural design and beauty that have ever been executed by the hands of man, whose walls, columns, and pylons represent the torn, soiled, and ragged pages of the records of the most glorious dynasties of ancient Egyptian History.

Tired with our investigations we turned away very reluctantly, and remounting our donkeys rode back toward Luxor, deeply impressed by what we had seen, having spent the whole day in very carefully measuring and examining the various parts of this most extraordinary building. Luxor now has lost its charm for us and Karnak is the dominant chord, for we talked of it, we thought of it, aye, we dreamed of it, and even to-day in memory I can still see the depth of its shadows, and the dazzling light playing upon its pillared halls and glorious sculptures. From every point of view, or at any time, whether by the effulgent rays of a mid-day sun, at eventide, or even under the rays of the glorious moon, Karnak is at its best—Majestic, Silent and Impressive.

We at length arrived at the bank of the river, and were rowed to our dahabiyeh depositing our note books and traps in the cabin. We then strolled up to the postoffice and received two letters from home, and just as we returned the gong rang out the dinner hour. After which we informed Hassan, that we were ready to proceed on our journey, in the morning, if the wind should be in our favor. He told us that there was nothing that he needed, and that he had supplied himself abundantly for our journey southward. I spent the whole of the evening in writing letters and fixing up my notes, and retired early to sleep and rest, hoping for a favoring breeze in the morning.

Since I last visited this celebrated temple the French government has undertaken the restoration of this most stupendous building, and while they were endeavoring to execute the work in hand, M. Lazani found one of the ancient city gates, a very valuable discovery, and said to be the first of its kind ever found in this country. It has upon it the date of the eighteenth dynasty. There are quite a number of new discoveries now being brought to light that will be of great importance, not only to the Egyptologist, but to the Masonic student.

Ceremonies—Initiation—Blue Lodge—Transmigration—Mystery Language.

.

.

How poor, how rich, how abject, how august,
How complicate, how wonderful, is man!
How passing wonder he who made him such!
Who centred in our make such strange extremes.
from different natures marvellously mixed,
Connection exquisite of distant worlds!
Distinguished link in being's endless chain!
Midway from nothing to Deity!
A beam ethereal, sullied, and absorpt!
Though sullied and dishonored, still divine!
Dim miniature of greatness absolute!
An heir of glory! a frail child of dust!
Helpless immortal! insect infinite!
A worm! a God!—I tremble at myself,
And in myself am lost. At home, a stranger,
Thought wanders up and down, surprised, aghast,
And wondering at her own. How reason reels!
O, what a miracle to man is man!
Triumphantly distressed! What joy! what dread!
Alternately transported and alarmed!
What can preserve my life? or what destroy?
An angel's arm can't snatch me from the grave;
Legions of angels can't confine me there.

                                  —Dr. Edward Young.

CHAPTER XXIII.

CEREMONIES—INITIATION—BLUE LODGE—TRANSMIGRATION—MYSTERY
LANGUAGE.

FREE MASONRY has stepped across the threshold of another century, bringing with it those sublime and beautiful Truths that have ever been the admiration of the best men of every epoch of the world's history. Truths that were taught, practiced and thoroughly understood, long before the *Vedic hymns* were first chanted under the shadows of the Hindu Kush and Himalaya mountains, the home and birth-place of our great ancestors the *Aryan Race*. From which source it has found its way to every corner of the earth, and to-day the sun never sets upon our most Illustrious Fraternity. These great and glorious Truths which have been handed down to us were studied in the hoary ages of the past, under the dawning Light of a New Age and a New Race, by peoples whose visions were illuminated from the dying embers of the *Atlanteans and Lemurians*, races that have passed or are passing away, but who have left behind them the very essence and aroma of their ancient knowledge and civilization. The traditions connected with those older peoples have helped us on to the Light, Knowledge and Truth now taught behind the closed doors of our Lodges, Chapters Councils and Consistories of the Ancient and Accepted Scottish Rite.

Every intelligent Masonic student who is unprejudiced will realize the fact that Free Masonry has ramified from the GREAT LODGE OF THE PERFECT MASTERS AND ADEPTS OF INDIA. It has shaped the course of Empires, has controlled the destiny of all peoples upon the face of the earth, and is to-day a powerful factor used for the express purpose of helping humanity on to higher planes of intellectual development throughout the whole world, verifying the statements of our rituals in respect to its universality. Those sublime Truths and Ethics were in existence thousands of years before Egypt was populated by colonization from the "Land of the Vedas." Those colonists dominated the valley of the Nile by subjugating the primitive inhabitants, and decorating the banks of that mighty river Nile with most magnificent tombs, temples, splendid monuments and sculptures. Far back in the hoary ages of antiquity, in the dim dawn of approaching civilization, at which period fact and fiction were intimately blended to suit the capacity of the people, they strived to arouse the latent potential spiritual forces lying dormant like a precious jewel deep down in the heart of every living human being, helping them on to a knowledge of Light and Truth.

Many of those glorious Truths are to be found to-day pictured upon nearly all the tombs and temples of both India and Egypt. They are indelibly inscribed in hieroglyphic characters throughout the whole of the "Land of the Pharaohs," the land of mighty monuments and most stupendous specimens of cyclopean architecture. Many of these have been very difficult to understand, and for what purpose they were erected, and to-day upon their stony sides people look with bowed heads in awe and admiration. Their only history in many instances is carved upon those stony sides or the interior chambers. But in those stupendous pyramids that adorn the plains of Gizeh, and the Labyrinth at the Fayum, we can only dimly sense the intents and purposes for which they were erected. I do not dare to be more explicit regarding these most extraordinary monuments, but of one thing let me assure you, the great Pyramid was never intended for a "corn-bin," as some authorities have asserted. Both these most extraordinary monuments have stood for ages, silent and impressive, like the couchant Sphinx whose stony lips are sealed, and we are left in doubt as to the unsolved riddle. This monolithic monster represents a King and symbolizes the union of intellect and Power.

Murray informs us that "old Arab writers speak of it as a talisman to keep the sand away from the cultivated ground; and tradition at one time says that it was mutilated by a fanatical sheik in the fourteenth century, and that since then the sand had made great encroachments. Certainly in Abd el-Latif's time it appears not to have been disfigured as he speaks of the face as 'very beautiful,' and of the mouth as 'graceful and lovely, and as it were, smiling graciously,' and adds that the red color was quite bright and fresh. By the Arabs of the present day it is known as *Abu 'l-hol* (the Father of Terror)."

THE GREAT SPHINX.

It still lies nearly smothered beneath the drifting sands of the desert, looking to the East, watching the glorious constellations and signs of the Zodiac come and go, and the twinkling stars, whose radiant eyes peep out of the azure vault above from before the misty veil that guards the portals of eternal day. Yet still it lies crouching there, mute, dumb, but eloquent in its silent majesty, ever watching the endless centuries roll along the stream of time. It catches the dawning light of the glorious Sun-god *Ra*, and reflects it back in farewell benedictions to humanity, who stand watching and waiting from afar off the coming dawn of intellectual advancement, and true spiritual unfoldment, looking for the time when they will be enabled to lift their hands to its glorious light.

These stupendous tombs and temples of ancient Egypt, whose ruins are to be found throughout the length and breadth of this most wonderful valley of the river Nile, were most certainly never used for public worship, nor were the masses of the people ever admitted to observe the sacred rites and ceremonies that were performed by the King, or priests, during their initiative services. All that took place within the walls of these majestic temples was most assuredly well guarded from the prying eyes of the profane. It was only upon certain occasions, such as Initiation into the Greater Mysteries, or on certain days, that were set apart for the honoring of the local gods of the Nome or city, that they observed these local ceremonies. At such times the King clothed in most gorgeous vestments, followed by priests and officials of the temple carrying the divine images and flaunting banners, burning incense and chanting hymns. marched in a grand procession through the pillared halls and corridors. Very often they circled around the immense roof of the temple, and passed on through the sacred groves within the massive walls that inclosed them, then down to the sacred lake where certain ceremonies were performed, returning to the sanctuaries within the depths of the temple.

At such times, possibly from the distance, the populace might be enabled to catch a glimpse of the gorgeous pageantry, as the procession passed around the roof of the temple, but that was all. They never knew what took place within those walls; to them it was all a profound mystery. They were most certainly never allowed to participate in any of those most mysterious rites and ceremonies, in fact none were permitted to enter into the ranks of the procession, and assist in those sacred rites, but those of royal birth, priest, officials, and the Initiates of the Greater Mysteries. Here in these temples, upon the banks of the river Nile, were performed those profound, sublime, and awe-inspiring ceremonies, that have been spoken of and referred to, by the most eminent men of every age of the world's history.

These ancient Egyptian temples were used for the express purpose of preparation and initiation of candidates into the sublime and profound ceremonies of the Egyptian Mysteries. They were never used, as I have stated above, for public worship; of that we are positively certain. The interior of these most magnificent fabrics was fitted up with chambers, etc., wherein was stored the gorgeous robes, and paraphernalia used in the solemn initiatory services of those Rites for which Egypt was so noted. Some of these chambers were used for sacerdotal privacy, others for the preparation of the aspiring candidate into those most profound, supremely beautiful and awe-inspiring ceremonies.

There were a large number of other rooms and chambers used for different purposes, as well as large halls for processional services, and for actual initiation. Within these vast inclosures were sacred groves and lakes, that I have referred to above, each and every part of which were most assuredly used for some special purpose during the ceremonies of Initiation. When the Neophyte passed from the Lesser, into the Greater Mysteries, and received the Ineffable degrees, he began to realize that there was something more in it than a mere word, grip, token, and whispering meaningless phrases into a dead ear. In passing through the passages of the Pyramid we have to assume a crouching position and *stoop low, very low.* Many things are learned in examining these Pyramids and temples, not only of the Symbolic degrees, but of the Royal Arch as well. The things that are taught in the York Rites, we shall find, have a far deeper significance than is generally understood, by even those who perform and assist in the ceremonies of these degrees.

The true meaning of the various symbols are not fully explained to the candidate, and I am sorry to say that a great deal of the work that is done by those conferring the degrees, in our Symbolic Lodges, is seldom or ever properly understood. Even the principal officers who superintend the conferring of the degrees upon the aspiring candidate do not fully comprehend their import for the simple reason, they do not, as I have said thoroughly understand the true meaning themselves. They have the ritualistic work all right, and parrot-like, they are enabled to roll it off in eloquent phraseology, *but Ritualism is not Masonry.*

The deeper meaning, and profound knowledge that is contained in our most sublime, and glorious symbols, they do not, nor cannot understand, until, by deep earnest study, and profound meditation, they are enabled to comprehend them. They will most assuredly learn that the key note to the esoteric meaning of the Symbolic degrees is a thorough understanding of the first, or E. A.

Let me once again explain to you, my dear Brothers, that no man can ever acquire even a knowledge of mathematics without a thorough comprehension of Addition, Substraction, Multiplication, and Division, so it is with our glorious symbology of the first three degrees. Learn them, and understand them, and you will have the key that will lead you on to the discovery and solution of the most profound esoteric Truths that lie concealed in the glorious symbols of our Illustrous Fraternity. It will teach you the true meaning of " to travel in foreign countries and receive Master's wages," you will discover the " Lost word." It will reveal to you the true significance of the discovery of the stone that was rejected, and lost in the rubbish of the temple. It will explain to you the meaning of a square man, the temple of Solomon and the rebuilding of the temple. In fact all things will be made plain to you, and you will come to an understanding of your Higher Self, which knowledge will bring you in closer communion with your God, when you will positively understand and know that you and your Father are One.

The Secret Doctrine informs us that the King's Chamber in the Greater Pyramid, in the plains of Gizeh, was the Holy of Holies. " On the days of the mysteries of Initiation, the Candidate, representing the Solar God, had to descend into the Sarcophagus, and represent the energizing ray, entering into the fecund womb of nature. Emerging from it on the following morning, he typified the resurrection of Life after the change called Death. In the Great Mysteries his figurative " death " lasted two days, when with the Sun he arose on the third morning, after a last night of cruel trials. While the Postulant represented the Sun—the all-vivifying orb that 'resurrects' every morning but to impart life to all—

the Sarcophagus was symbolic of the female principle in Egypt. Its form and shape changed with every country, provided it remained a vessel, a symbolic 'nevis,' or boat-shaped vehicle, and a 'container' symbolically, of germs or the germ life. In India it is the 'Golden' Cow through which the Candidate for Brâhmanism has to pass if he desires to be a Brahman, and to become *Dvi-ja* born a *second* time."

It is positively asserted by certain writers that the various temples throughout the valley of the Nile were used for the express purpose of Initiation into the Ancient Egyptian Mysteries, and every thoughtful student will recognize this fact, if he will carefully examine them, as I have done.

Bædeker in his Upper Egypt, beginning at page 59, gives a very careful description of the temple of Seti I (*The Memnonium of Abydos*), which will be of great interest to the Masonic Student. He goes into details in reference to the Rites and Ceremonies that were performed therein, as well as in honor of the Divine Deceased (Osiris), whose name even the Great Herodotus shrank from breathing. The ancient Indian Mysteries, from which source all the others originated, were originally conferred upon the initiates in those cave temples for which that country is so celebrated, such as Elephanta, Ellora, Karli and many others which have been cut out of very hard porphyry rock, so far as the first three are concerned.

Let me quote you from "Morals and Dogmas," page 361: "The Indian Mysteries were celebrated in subterranean caverns and grottos hewn in the solid rock; and the Initiates adored the Deity, symbolized by the Solar Fire. The candidate, long wandering in darkness, truly wanted Light, and the worship taught him was the worship of God, the Source of Light. The vast Temple of Elephanta, perhaps the oldest in the world, hewn out of the solid rock, whose very large halls were used for Initiations; as were the still vaster caverns of Salsette with their three hundred apartments.

"The periods of initiation were regulated by the increase and decrease of the moon. The mysteries were divided into four steps or degrees. The Candidate might receive the first at eight years of age, when he was invested with the zennar (cable tow). Each degree dispensed something of perfection, 'Let the wretched man,' says the Hitopadesa, 'practice virtue, whenever he enjoys one of the three or four religious degrees; let him be even minded with all created things, and that disposition will be the source of virtue.'

"After various ceremonies, chiefly relating to the Unity, and Trinity of the Godhead, the Candidate was clothed in a linen garment without a seam, remained under the care of a Brahmin until he was twenty years of age, constantly studying and practicing the most rigid virtue. Then he underwent the severest probation for the second degree, in which he was sanctified by the sign of the cross, which, pointing to the four quarters of the compass, was honored as a striking symbol of the universe by many nations of antiquity, and was imitated by the Indians in the shape of their temples.

"Then he was admitted to the Holy Cavern, blazing with light, where in costly robes, sat, in the East, West and South, the three chief Hierophants, representing the Indian triune Deity. The ceremonies there commenced with an anthem to the Great God of Nature, and then followed this apostrophe: O mighty being greater than Brahma! we bow down before Thee as the primal Creator! Eternal God of Gods! The World's Mansion! Thou art the Incorruptible Being, distinct from all things transient! Thou art before all Gods, the Ancient Absolute Existence, and the Supreme Supporter of the Universe! Thou art the Supreme Mansion; and by Thee, O Infinite Form the Universe was spread abroad.

"The Candidate thus taught the first great primitive truth, was called upon to make a formal declaration, that he would be tractable and obedient to his superiors; that he would keep his body pure; govern his tongue, and observe a passive obedience in receiving the doctrines and traditions of the Fraternity; and the firmest secrecy in maintaining inviolable its hidden and abstruse mysteries. Then he was sprinkled with water (*whence our baptism*); certain words, now unknown were whispered in his ear; and he was divested of his shoes and made to go three times around the cavern. Hence our three circuits; hence we were neither barefoot nor shod: and the words were the Passwords of that Indian degree."

In these Ancient Mysteries of India the principal officers represented the *Tri-murti*—Brahma, Vishnu and Siva—the Hindu Trinity which furnished the Hebrew Triad of Sephira, Chockma and Binah. Brahma in the Indian mysteries represents the rising sun, the Creator and Container of the other two, rising into life and definition; Vishnu the Preserver and Conserver of all; and Siva the Destroyer and Transformer, thus forming a triangle of *Creation, Preservation* and *Transformation.* Brahma the *Master,* rising into Life, represents the Sun in the east; Vishnu in the south, the *Junior Warden,* the *Preserver* and *Giver;* Siva the *Senior Warden,* the Destroyer and Transformer; who transforms Light into Darkness, or day into night. During the ceremonies the candidate was baptized, and allegorically reborn, when he was taught to lead a true and purer life *not only in thought, but in act.*

The ceremonies of initiation were generally performed at midnight, in immense caverns amid darkness and gloom. Many of them were awful and appalling, for the candidate, in his journey through those terrible subterranean vaults and passages, was compelled to battle for his very life against the powers of Darkness, from which, if he succeeded, he came forth into *Light, Life* and *Joy,* when he was exalted and glorified. The Persians, like the Druids, built no temples, but worshipped in large circular enclosures the Sun God Mithras. The places wherein they adored the Sun were formed of immense blocks of unhewn stone, very much like those Druidical remains at Stonehenge, of Salisbury plains, England.

The Persians abominated images of any kind, and they considered that *Fire* was the only fit emblem of the Deity. From these people the Hebrews borrowed the idea and represented God as a flame of fire, which appeared to both Abraham and Moses, at Horeb and Mount Sinai. Both the Persian and Hebrew Lawgivers claim to have conversed with God, maintaining that the Deity instructed them in a system of pure worship, which was to be promulgated and taught to all those who were worthy to receive such exalted Truths, and who would devote themselves to the study of this higher and purer Philosophy. Zoroaster, or Zarathustra, soon became famous and his philosophical teachings brought to him, from all parts of the civilized world, the most eminent men who lived in that age, men who were anxious to improve themselves, by studying under a man whose name and fame had spread among the learned men throughout the four corners of the earth. I am referring to the ancient Persians, and to the time when first Zarathustra Spitama came forward as a reformer and leader of his people, long before the flight of the Israelites out of the " Land of Egypt." It is very difficult to find the exact date of his birth, or when he lived, but according to the best modern authorities we might place it anywhere between 2000 to 1000 B. C.

According to the most ancient *Gathas* (Psalms) Zarathustra pro-claimed himself " the reciter of the hymns, the messenger of Ahura-Mazda, the listener to the sacred words revealed by God." The name Zarathustra is a rather peculiar one, and in the language of those ancient people, it refers to some peculiar kind of a " camel," but of what species we are unable to determine. The Greeks transformed it into Zoroaster. William Jackson, Professor of Indo-Iranian Languages, Columbia University, places the date of his birth in the seventh century B. C., while Professor James T. Bixby, Ph. D., states that " the best modern authorities say from 2000 to 1200 B. C." But leaving the date of his birth out of the question, we know that he clothed himself in white priestly vestments, and assembled the people around the sacred Fire, and delivered an inaugural address, calling upon them to listen to the Words of *Ahura Mazda*, the ever living God, who speaks to them through him, by and with the holy flame of the sacred fire. In the early days of their history they worshipped and performed their initiatory ceremonies, into the Mazdean Mysteries, in immense caves fitted up expressly for that purpose. The grand final to these Mysteries was the triumph of Ormuzd, the Sun God, over the powers of Darkness.

I shall quote freely from our revered Brother Albert Pike throughout this chapter, because his ideas and mine are identical, in relation to the Ancient Mysteries. " Everywhere in the old Mysteries, and in all the symbolisms and ceremonial of the Hierophant was found the same mythical personages, who like Hermes, or Zoroaster, unites Human Attri-butes with divine, and is himself the God whose worship he introduced, teaching rude men the commencement of civilization, through the influ-ence of song, and connecting with the symbol of his death emblematic of that Nature, the most essential consolation of religion.

" The Mysteries embraced the three great doctrines of *Ancient Theosophy*. They treated of God, Man and Nature. Dionusos, whose Mysteries Orpheus is said to have founded, was the God of Nature, or of the moisture which is the life of Nature, who prepares in darkness the return of life and vegetation, or who is himself the Light and Change evolving their varieties. He was Theologically one with Hermes, Prometheus and Poseidon.

"In the Ægean Islands he is Butes, Dardanus, Himeros, or Imbros. In Crete he appears as Iesius or Zeus, whose worship remaining unveiled by the usual forms of mystery, betrayed to profane curiosity the symbols which, if irreverently contemplated, were sure to be misunderstood. In Asia he is the long-stoled Bassareus coalescing with the Sabazius of the Phrygian Corybantes: the same with the mystic Iacchus, nursling or son of Ceres, and with the dismembered Zagreus, son of Persephoné. In symbolical forms the mysteries exhibited the THE ONE, of which the MANIFOLD is an infinite illustration, containing a moral lesson calculated to guide the soul through life, and to cheer it in death.

"The story of Dionusos was profoundly significant. He was not only creator of the world, but guardian, liberator, and Saviour of the soul. God of the many-colored mantle, he was the resulting manifestation personified, the all in the many, the varied year life passing into innumerable forms.

"The spiritual regeneration of Man was typified in the Mysteries by the second birth of Dionusos as offspring of the highest; and the agents and symbols of that regeneration were the elements that effected Nature's periodical purification—the air, indicated by the mystic fan or winnow; the fire, signified by the torch; and the baptismal water, for water is not only cleanser of all things, but the genesis or source of all.

"Socrates says in the Phædo: 'It well appears that those who established the mysteries, or secret assemblies of the Initiated, were no contemptible personages, but men of great genius, who in the early ages strove to teach us, under enigmas. that he who shall go into the invisible regions without being purified, will be precipitated into the abyss; while he who arrives there, purged of the stains of this world, and accomplished in virtue, will be admitted to the dwelling place of the Deity.' Initiation was a school in which were taught the truths of primitive revelation, the existence and attributes of ONE God, the Immortality of the Soul, rewards and punishments not only in this but in a future life, the phenomena of Nature, the Arts, the Sciences, Morality, Legislature, Philosophy, Philanthropy, Psychology, Metaphysics, Animal Magnetism,

Telepathy and all Occult Sciences. Public odium was cast on those who were refused Initiation, and they were considered unworthy of public employment or private confidence, and were known as the profane, and were held in abhorrence and believed to be doomed to everlasting punishment. Bastards and slaves were excluded from initiation; and so were the Materialists or Epicurians, who denied the existence of the Supreme Architect of the Universe, and consequently the utility of Initiation.

"Eventually it came to be considered that the gates of Elysium would open only for the Initiates whose souls had been purified and regenerated in the sanctuaries or Holy of Holies. It was thoroughly understood that salvation or redemption was not to be obtained through Initiation alone, for Plato informs us that 'it was also necessary for the Soul to be purified from every sin; and the purification necessary was such as gave virtue, truth, wisdom, strength, justice and temperance.'

"The object of the ancient initiations being to ameliorate mankind and to perfect the intellectual part of man, the nature of the human soul, its origin, its destination, its relations to the body and to universal nature, all formed part of the mystic science; and to them in part the lessons given to the initiate were directed. For it was believed that initiation tended to his perfection, and to preventing the divine part within him, overloaded with matter gross and earthy, from being plunged into gloom, and impeded in its return to the Deity.

"The Soul with them was not a mere conception or abstraction; but a reality including in itself life and thought; or, rather, of whose essence it was to live and think. It was material; but not brute, inert, inactive, lifeless, motionless, formless, lightless matter. It was held to be active, reasoning, thinking, its natural home in the highest regions of the universe, whence it descended to illuminate, give form and movement to vivify, animate, and carry with itself the baser matter; and whither it unceasingly tends to reascend, when, and as soon as it can free itself from its connection with the matter. From that substance, divine, infinitely delicate and active, essentially luminous, the Souls of men were formed, and by it alone, uniting with and organizing their bodies, men *lived*."

This was the doctrine of Pythagoras, who learned it when he received the Egyptian Mysteries, and was the doctrine of all who by

35

means of the ceremonial of Initiation, thought to purify the soul. Virgil makes the spirit of Anchises teach it to Æneas: and all the expiations and lustrations used in the mysteries were but symbols of those intellectual ones by which the soul was to be purged of its vice-spots and stains, and freed of the incumbrance of its earthly prison, so that it might rise unimpeded to the source from whence it came. Hence sprang the doctrine of transmigration of souls; which Pythagoras taught as an allegory, and those who came after him received literally.

Plato, like him, drew his doctrines from the East and the mysteries, and undertook to translate the language of the symbols used there, into Philosophy; and to prove by argument and philosophical deduction what *felt* by the consciousness, the mysteries taught by symbols, as an indisputable fact—the Immortality of the Soul. Cicero did the same, and followed the mysteries in teaching that the Gods were but mortal men, who for their great virtues and signal services had deserved that their souls should, after death, be raised to that lofty rank. It being taught in the mysteries, by way of allegory, the meaning of which was not made known except to a select few, or, perhaps only at a later day, as an actual reality, that the souls of the vicious dead passed into the bodies of those animals to whose nature their vices had most affinity. It was also taught that the Soul could avoid these transmigrations, often successive and numerous, by the practice of virtue, which would acquit it of them, free it from the circle of successive generations and restore it at once to its source. Hence, nothing was so ardently prayed for by the initiator, says Proclus, as this happy fortune, which delivering them from the empire of evil, would restore them to their true life, and conduct them to the place of final rest.

This doctrine probably referred to those figures of animals and monsters which were exhibited to the Initiate, before allowing him to see the sacred light for which he sighed. I have already spoken upon this subject of Transmigration in the XIII Chapter of this work, and will only say—that once man has received the Divine light of Reason he could never retrograde, or go back into the lower animal kingdom. The Initiates into the Greater Mysteries were never taught any such idea; but they may have been told that if a man did not live a pure life on this earth, but pandered to his animal, passional nature, he would be reborn, with the attributes of the lower animals, such as the cunning of the fox, or the ferocity of the tiger, and this assertion is borne out by many of the Initiates themselves, for instance:

Hierocles, one of the most enthusiastic and celebrated followers of Pythagoras, emphatically asserts that " he who believes that the soul of man, after his death, will enter the body of a beast for his vices, or become a plant for his stupidity, is deceived; and is absolutely ignorant of the eternal form of the soul, which can never change; for, always remaining man, it is said to become God or beast, through virtue or vice; though it can become neither one nor the other by nature, but solely by resemblance of its inclinations to theirs."

Again Timœus of Locria, another of the Pythagorean school of Philosophy and an Initiate, tells us that " in order to alarm men, and prevent them from committing crimes, they menaced them with strong humiliations and punishments; even declaring that their souls would pass into new bodies—that of a coward into the body of a deer; that of a ravisher into the body of a wolf; that of a murderer into the body of some still more ferocious animal: and that of an impure sensualist into the body of a hog."

The more we force our investigations into the older forms of prehis-toric civilizations, and the religions and philosophies that pertained to them, the more beautiful, grand and sublime will those teachings that permeated them appear to us. We shall eventually discover that the great majority of those ancient peoples worshipped the ever living God under the symbol of the Sun, recognizing the fact, that they possessed a wonderful knowledge of Astronomy. The Arts and Sciences were thoroughly comprehended by them, and that there was a wonderful resemblance between the doctrines and worship of these ancient peoples. We are positively certain that the Mysteries of India, Chaldea, Assyria, Phœnicia and other countries were thoroughly known and comprehended by the Hierophants of Ancient Egypt, who instructed their initiates in all the profound Truths that pertained to the Greater Mysteries.

Each and every one who passed into the sanctuaries of these temples for initiation, were bound by the most terrible oaths, before they were even permitted to see, or know, anything at all whatever about the ceremonies they had to pass through. After they had seen the Light, they were then considered to be bound by a stronger tie, and were then permitted to perform their lustrations. They were then conducted into the regular initiatory ceremonials, where they underwent terrible ordeals and tremendous trials, both physically and mentally, before they were instructed in the sublime and glorious Truths and Wisdom which unfolded to them the proof of the Immortality of the Soul, the Reincarnation of the Spirit and the Doctrine of a Future Life, as well as the true meaning *of raising horizontals to perpendiculars upon the five points of fellowship.*

There are a great many Brothers, who firmly believe that the Blue Lodge, or Symbolic degrees, contain the whole of Masonry; but this assertion most assuredly proves that they have not delved very deep into the symbology of those first three degrees, or they would never make such an assertion. The first three rules of Arithmetic are the foundation of the science of numbers or Mathematics. But these first three rules do not demonstrate the higher branches of Mathematics, such as Proportion, Square root, Conic sections, Algebra. etc. Neither do these first three rules in themselves demonstrate the mutations and collocations that go to instruct us in those Higher branches of the "*Exact Sciences.*"

The seven notes of our scale in Music contain the whole of the demonstrated harmony of the Great Masters, but not until the combinations and collocations have been made do they produce the thoughts of the Masters in divine Harmony. In the same way the Blue or Symbolic degrees are only the foundation upon which have been erected the Higher Degrees of the York and our own beloved Scottish Rite.

It is stated in "Morals and Dogmas," page 819, "The symbols of the wise always become the idols of the ignorant multitude. The Blue Degrees are but the outer court or portico of the Temple. Part of the symbols are displayed there to the Initiate, but he is intentionally misled by false interpretations. It is not intended that he shall understand them; but it is intended that he shall imagine he understands them. Their true explication is reserved for the Adepts, the Princes of Masonry. The whole body of the Royal and Sacerdotal Art was hidden so carefully, centuries since, in the High Degrees as that it is even yet impossible to solve many of the enigmas which they contain. It is well enough for the mass of those called Masons to imagine that all is contained in the Blue

Degrees; and whoso attempts to undeceive them will labor in vain, and without any true reward violate his obligations as an Adept. Masonry is the veritable Sphinx, buried to the head in the sands heaped around it by the ages."

Our revered Brother Albert Pike has frequently written upon the first three degrees of Masonry, and his comparison of their being like the " broken columns of a roofless Druidic Temple in their rude and mutilated greatness " is perfectly correct, and every earnest student who will carefully examine the Symbolic degrees will most assuredly recognize their mutilated condition, and he will find that there is nothing complete or perfect in them. Even that which our candidate looks forward to has been lost, and he is given a substitute until future generations shall discover the lost one.

Yes, my dear Brothers, the first three degrees contain the whole of Masonry TO HIM WHO KNOWS. How I wish that I could talk to you and explain this seeming mystery, but as it is I can only hint at these things which I would like you to thoroughly understand. I have previously asserted, and I earnestly desire that you should comprehend that RITUALISM IS NOT MASONRY, for *that* may be changed at any time by the Grand Lecturers. But Masonry with its sublime and profound philosophies that have descended to us from the Wisdom Religion, through the Ancient Mysteries, is the same to-day and forever.

Her traditions carry us back to the most remote ages of antiquity, back beyond the dim dawn of prehistoric civilization, long before the hieratic inscriptions of Ancient Egypt were carved and painted within the tombs and temples throughout that wondrous Valley of the Nile. These to-day are, in many instances, undecipherable on account of the begrimed condition of the ceilings, walls, etc., and the vandal hands of the bigoted Christians, who mutilated so many of these temples, and to whom I have previously referred. Brother J. D. Buck, 32°, in "Mystic Masonry" (Introduction, VI *et seq.*) states that:

" Masonry deals largely with the Ethics and Symbolism of the Ancient Mysteries. The writer believes that through the well-timed efforts of Masons to-day, the grandest achievements in knowledge ever gained by man, which were originally concealed in the Greater Mysteries of Antiquity and in time became lost to the world, may be again recovered.

In the strictest sense, this knowledge has never really been lost, as there have always existed those who were possessed of the Great Secret. It was originally veiled in order to conceal it from the profane, and written in a universal language of Symbolism, that the wise among all nations and throughout all time might read it, as it were, in their own language. It was also written in parable and allegory so that the unlettered and common people might not be deprived of its wise precepts, and of its force in shaping character, dissipating ignorance, and inspiring hope. This Ancient Wisdom is the fountain from which Masonry takes its rise. The true Science of Symbolism in time became lost; the Temples of Initiation fell into decay, or were destroyed by priests, and potentates, jealous of their influence. For many weary centuries men have been trying to recover the lost key, and to restore the ancient wisdom from the parables and allegories in which it had been concealed. But progress in the inverse order is not only necessarily slow and uncertain, but all such attempts have, more or less, given rise to fantastic flights of the imagination, and resulted in confusion, rather than in enlightenment. The result has been to bring the whole subject under contempt, and to make the name "Mysticism" mean something vague and uncertain, if not altogether foolish to those ignorant of its true meaning."

The causes that have led up to the re-veiling of the Ancient Wisdom and Masonic Symbols have been many; some of which I have previously mentioned, such as Christian bigotry, ignorant fanaticism, misinterpretations and alterations, by those who desired to change the hieroglyphical inscriptions and symbols in order to suit their own ends and further their own designs. I have spoken about the destruction of the hieroglyphic inscriptions and sculptures in many of the temples throughout the "Land of Egypt."

"The Secret Doctrine" informs us in the Introduction to the "New Edition," page 24, Vol. I, as follows: "However superhuman the efforts of the early Christian Fathers to obliterate the Secret Doctrine from the very memory of man, they all failed. Truth can never be killed; hence the failure to sweep away entirely from the face of the earth every vestige of that ancient Wisdom, and to shackle and gag every witness who testified to it. Let one only think of the thousands, perhaps millions of MSS. burnt; of monuments with their too indiscreet inscriptions and

TEMPLE OF THE MYSTERIES,
THEBES.

pictorial symbols, pulverized to dust; of the bands of early hermits, and ascetics roaming about among the ruined cities of Upper and Lower Egypt, in desert and mountain, valley and highland, seeking for and eager to destroy every obelisk and pillar, scroll or parchment they could lay their hands on, if only it bore the symbols of the Tau, or any other sign borrowed and appropriated by the new faith—and he will then see plainly how it is that so little has remained of the records of the past. Verily, the fiendish spirit of fanatacism of early mediæval Christianity and of Islam, has loved from the first to dwell in darkness and ignorance *rather than Light and Truth.*"

I have repeatedly asserted, in this work, that I do most sincerely and firmly believe that the esoteric teachings of our glorious Fraternity originated in the " Land of the Vedas, and that every careful Masonic student will bear me out in this assertion, because they can by thorough investigation, trace all knowledge to this one source. I also firmly believe that the Wisdom Religion originated in the Great Lodge of Adepts and Perfect Masters who created it, and sent it echoing down the drifting centuries, where at times it has during the past, and even in our present Era, been hidden, in a measure, from our view, through like causes that I have already explained above. The very essence and aroma of the ancient teachings of the Indian, Mazdean, and Egyptian Religions emanated from this great primal fount: THE ANCIENT WISDOM RELIGION.

The real meaning of the great majority of our Masonic symbols, contains some of the most sublime Truths that were ever taught. To all those who were initiated and passed into the sanctuaries of the Temple these Truths will ever remain. Let me quote you once more the " Secret Doctrine " Introductory, Vol. I, page 27: " One more important point must be noticed, one that stands foremost in the series of proofs given of the existence of one primeval, universal Wisdom—at any rate for Christians, Kabalists and students. The teachings were, at least, partially known to several of the Fathers of the Church. It is maintained on purely historical grounds, that Origen, Synesius, and even Clemens Alexandrinus, had themselves been initiated into the mysteries before adding to the Neo-Platonism of the Alexandrian school, that of the Gnostics, under the Christian veil. More than this, some of the doctrines of the sacred schools, though by no means all, were preserved in the Vatican, and have since become part and parcel of the Mysteries, in the shape of disfigured additions made to the original Christian program by the Latin Church. Such is now the materialized dogma of the Immaculate Conception. This accounts for great persecutions set on foot by the Roman Catholic Church against Occultism, Masonry and heterodox Mysticism generally.

"The days of Constantine were the last turning point in history, the period of the supreme struggle, that ended in the Western world throttling the old religions in favor of the new one, built on their bodies. From thence the vista into the far distant past, beyond the Deluge and the Garden of Eden, began to be forcibly and relentlessly shut out by every fair and unfair means from the indiscreet gaze of posterity. Every issue was blocked up, every record upon which hands could be laid destroyed. Yet there remains enough, even among such mutilated records to warrant us in saying that there is in them every requisite evidence of a Parent Doctrine. Fragments have survived geological cataclysms, to tell the story ; and every survival shows evidences that the now secret Wisdom was once the fountain head, the ever-flowing perennial source, from which were fed all the streamlets—the later religions of all nations—from the first down to the last. This period, beginning with Buddha and Pythagoras at the one end and finishing with the Neo-Platonists, and Gnostics at the other, is the only focus left in History wherein converge for the last time the bright rays of light streaming from the Æons of times gone by, unobscured by the hand of bigotry and fanatacism."

What the world has lost through the bigotry, fanatacism and intolerance of the early Church Fathers will never be fully realized by the present generation, but there is one very great satisfaction to all, and that is the *Key* to the solution has never been lost and the LIGHT of the Ancient Wisdom will come forth once again, from the misty veil that enshrouds it, for the benefit of the human race. *Masonry, the lineal descendant of the Ancient Mysteries, contains that Key in her Symbology,* but in order that we may be thoroughly enabled to fully comprehend the sublimity and grandeur of these parables and allegories that are illustrated by symbols, we must work very carefully and zealously, and be guided by rules of analogy and correspondence. Then we shall find that our researches will lead us on to a knowledge of those sublime and glorious Truths that laid the foundation of the Indian, Mazdean and Egyptian Mysteries, afterwards ramified through the Chaldean and Babylonian Empires. It was from the Babylonian Magi that the ancient Hebrews drew their inspiration and Wisdom.

There is one thing I especially desire to call your attention to, and that is, DO NOT TAKE THE SYMBOL FOR THE THING SYMBOLIZED. *Masonry owes a great deal to the Hebrew people*, who have preserved to us a vast amount of priceless jewels they received from the Magi. These they have ever guarded from the profane and handed down to us in signs, symbols and records that will never be lost, but will live forever and be easily understood by each and every Neophyte who is *brought to Light* in our Lodges of the present day. If any of our most earnest students will only give their time and attention to the careful examination of the Kabala, and have their minds thoroughly illuminated by the Zohar, before they attempt to pass an opinion upon the "Mystery Language" of prehistoric ages, the language that is now called Symbolism, they will not only discover the *Truth* of the above assertions, but some of the Light, Knowledge, and Truth that illuminated the minds of the Hierophants of old, and also the great Pythagoras who taught in the sanctuaries over which they presided, the Wisdom that belonged to the *Great Lodge of Adepts of India.*

The Secret Doctrine informs us in Volume I, page 325 *et seq.*—"The proofs brought forward in corroboration of the old teachings are scattered widely throughout the old scriptures of ancient civilization. *The Puranas*, the *Zend Avesta*, and the old classics are full of such facts; but no one has ever taken the trouble of collecting and collating them together. The reason for this is that all such events were recorded symbolically; and the best scholars, the most acute minds, among our Aryanists and Egyptologists, have been too often darkened by one or anothers preconception, and still oftener, by one sided views of the secret meaning. Yet even a parable is a spoken symbol, a fiction or a fable, as some think; an allegorical representation, we say, of life realities, events and facts. And just as a moral was ever drawn from a parable, such moral being an actual truth, and fact in human life, so a historical, real event was deduced, by those versed in the hieratic sciences, from emblems and symbols recorded in the archives of the temple. The religious and esoteric history of every nation was imbedded in symbols· it was never expressed literally in so many words.

"All the thoughts and emotions, all the learning and knowledge, revealed, and acquired, of the early Races, found their pictorial expression in allegory and parable, Why? Because, *the spoken word has a potency not only unknown to, but even unsuspected, and naturally disbelieved in*, by the modern sages. Because sound and rythm are closely related to the four Elements of the Ancients; and because such or another vibration in the air is sure to awaken the corresponding Powers, union with which produces good or bad results, as the case may be. No student was ever allowed to recite historical, religious, or real events of any kind, in so many unmistakable words, lest the Powers connected with the event should be once more attracted. Such events were narrated only during Initiation, and every student had to record them in corresponding symbols, drawn out of his own mind and examined later by his Master, before they were finally accepted. Thus by degrees was the Chinese Alphabet created, as just before it the hieratic symbols were fixed upon in old Egypt. In the Chinese language, the characters of which may be read in any language, and which, as just said, is only a little less ancient than the Egyptian alphabet of Thoth, every word has its corresponding symbol in a pictorial form. This language possesses many thousands of such letters or logograms, each conveying the meaning of a whole word; for letters proper as we understand it, do not exist in the Chinese language, any more than they did in the Egyptian, till a far later period

" 'Thus a Japanese who does not understand one word of Chinese, meeting with a Chinaman who has never heard the language of the former, will communicate in writing with him, and they will understand each other perfectly—because their writing is symbolical.' . . . Recent discoveries made by great Mathematicians and Kabalists thus prove, beyond a shadow of doubt, that every theology, from the earliest down to the latest, has sprung, not only from a common source of abstract beliefs, but one universal Esoteric or Mystery Language. These scholars hold the key to the universal language of old, and have turned it successfully, though only *once*, in the hermetically closed door leading to the Hall of

Mysteries. The great archaic system known from prehistoric ages as the sacred Wisdom—Science, one that is contained and can be traced in every old as well as in every new religion, had, and still has, its universal language—suspected by the Mason Ragon—the language of the Hierophants, which has seven 'dialects,' so to speak, each referring and being specially appropriate, to one of the seven mysteries of Nature. Each had its own symbolism. Nature could thus be either read in its fulness, or viewed from one of its special aspects.

"The proof of this lies to this day, in the extreme difficulty which the Orientalist in general, and the Indianists, and Egyptologists in particular, experience in interpreting the Allegorical writings of the Aryans, and the hieratic records of old Egypt. This is because they will never remember that all the ancient records were written in a language which was universal, and known to all nations alike in days of old, but which is now intelligible only to the few. Like the Arabic figures which are understandable to men of every nation, or like the English word *and*, which becomes *et* for the Frenchman, *und* for the German, and so on, yet which may be expressed for all civilized nations in the simple sign &— so all the words of that Mystery Language signified the same thing to each man, of whatever nationality. There have been several men of note who have tried to re-establish such a universal and *philosophical* tongue. Delgarme, Wilkins, Leibnitz; but Demarmeux, in his *Pasigraphic*, is the only one who has proven its possibility. The scheme of Valentinius, called the 'Greek Kabalah,' based on the combinations of Greek letters, might serve as a model.

"The many sided facts of the Mystery Language have lent to the adoption of widely varied dogmas, and rites in the exotericism of the church rituals. It is these, again which are at the origin of most of the dogmas of the Christian Church; for instance, the Seven Sacraments, the Trinity, the Resurrection, the Seven Capital Sins, and the Seven Virtues. The Seven Keys to the Mystery Tongue, however, having always been in the keeping of the highest among the initiated Hierophants of antiquity; it is only the partial use of a few out of the seven, which passed, through the treason of some early Church Fathers—ex-Initiates of the Temples—into the hands of the new sect of the Nazarenes. Some of the early Popes were Initiates, but the last fragments of their knowledge have now fallen into the power of the Jesuits, who have turned them into a system of Sorcery.

"It is maintained that *India*—not confined to its present, but including its ancient boundaries—is the only country in the world which still has among her sons Adepts, who have the knowledge of all the seven sub-systems, and the key to the entire system. From the fall of Memphis, Egypt began to lose those keys one by one, and Chaldea had preserved only three in the days of Berosus. As for the Hebrews, in all their writings they show no more than a thorough knowledge of the astronomical, geometrical and numerical systems of symbolizing the human, and especially the physiological functions. They never had the higher Keys."

Now my dear Brothers and Friends, I do not wish you to think I am trying to introduce something into Masonry, which does not belong there, for every thing I have written, has been placed before you for your special investigation, so you may positively know that there is far more than Grips and Tokens in the beautiful symbols belonging to our most Illustrious Fraternity. It is in these glorious symbols that we shall find the Key by which we may be enabled to unlock the true meaning of those sublime philosophies which have commanded the most profound attention and admiration of the learned men of every epoch of the world's history, and *all* these profound Truths are open to *all* Masons who will diligently search and think for themselves.

The Gawazee—Exploring Temples and Tombs—Philæ and its Ruins—Nubia.

Loud is the sound of ballad-singers shouting,
While, with her wanton grace and paces pretty,
 Like some alluring, sly coquette,
 A dancer with her castagnettes
Displays herself in subtle pantomime
And singers chant an old Arabian ditty
 Of Saladin and of his time.

       —FREUDENBURG.

CHAPTER XXIV.

THE GAWAZEE—EXPLORING TEMPLES AND TOMBS—PHILÆ AND ITS RUINS—NUBIA.

THE Thebiad was one of the principal divisions of ancient Egypt, and was originally divided into ten nomes. There were ten halls in the Labyrinth that were specially allotted to the princes of Upper Egypt. It was divided by the river running through its entire length, and situated in a narrow valley that was, and is to-day, bounded by the Arabian hills on the west side, and the Libyan hills and desert on the other. It extended north as far as *Eshmunen* the Hermopolis Magna of the Greeks, and on the south as far as Asyut or Syene. We talked of the ancient glory of this wonderful city of Thebes and realized that it was the same old river that ran murmuring by, as when Seti and his son, the Great Rameses, beautified and adorned its banks with such wondrous works of art.

The sun shone bright and warm that day, and Memnon still sat looking to the east, but his voice was now hushed and his stony lips were as silent as the voices of the dead that surrounded him. The rising sun turned the Libyan hills into red and gold, and the marvellous play of colors were indescribable. The sky was just as blue, her fields were still marked with bright greens, yellow and brown, and the bean flower still shed its fragrance upon the morning air as in the days of old. The nights were supremely beautiful, the stars glittered in the azure vault above, and the splendid moon shone as beautiful and bright as when this majestic hundred-gated Thebes was in the height of her glory, and yet, nought but the ruins of this mighty city remain with us to tell of the wondrous knowledge that pertained to these warrior kings, and their vanished splendor.

We arose that morning and found a light air astir and Abdallah preparing to weigh the anchor, but it was not until nearly ten o'clock that the wind came out good and strong, our anchor was soon apeak, our big sails loosed and we bid adieu to Thebes. We passed swiftly by the grand pylon of Karnak and inside of an hour we drew up towards Erment, and very soon moored on the west bank, close to a sugar factory, four hundred and sixty-two miles from Cairo, and eight miles from Thebes. It was told us that there were some very interesting ruins at that place, but on our arrival we learned that they had been entirely destroyed for the purpose of building the sugar factory there, consequently as there was a light wind astir, we went on board again and started off for Eshne, but within about eight miles from that place the wind died out, the heat became intense and nearly unbearable, and hung like a heavy pall over all. Our great sails flapped idly to and fro with the motion of the boat as our sailors started out upon the tow path, and struck up their everlasting songs once more. We had dinner just as the sun went down, and we sat on deck until we saw the lights of Eshne, when we retired, and early the next morning we found that our boat was anchored off that place, which is located on the west bank of the Nile, four hundred and ninety miles from Cairo. This is the site of the old city of Latopolis, and derived its name from the Lato fish or Latus, that was worshipped here in the sanctuary of this temple. The people of this place claim that Moses was born here. It has a population of about ten thousand inhabitants and it is the headquarters of the Alme or Gawazee (dancing girls) of whom I have already spoken in a previous chapter.

Warburton, in "Crescent and the Cross," gives an account of the Alme, page 208, *et seq.*, which I believe will be of interest to you, my dear Brothers and readers, it is as follows: "The term Alme, or, in the plural *Awâlim*, means literally, a learned female. This epithet is only strictly applicable to singing women, whose music is sometimes of a very high order and their accomplishments in other respects so numerous, that they frequently obtain fifty guineas from a party for their exhibitions on one evening. The dancing girls belong to a very inferior order, and are termed *Gawazee* in the language of the country. These women used to have a settlement near Cairo, and attended all the marriages and other festivities of the beau monde there. The Moollahs, or Moslem divines, however, objected to them, not on account of their impropriety, but on the plea that the profane eyes of the '*Infidel*' ought not to gaze upon the women of the true faith. There was such an agitation raised

THE GAWAZEE, OR DANCING GIRLS.

on this subject, that the priests prevailed, and all the *Alme* were sent off to Eshne, five hundred miles up the river, by way of banishment, where they are allowed a small stipend, by the government, to keep them from starvation. The effects of this reformation produced frightful results, which I cannot allude to here, and Almeism still flourishes everywhere outside of the Cairene districts. . . . . . The dress of the Alme is very picturesque, and graceful, consisting of a short embroidered jacket fitting close, but open in the front, long loose trousers of almost transparent silk, a cashmere shawl wrapped round the loins, rather than the waist and light elegant turbans of muslin embroidered with gold. Their hair flows in dark curls down their shoulders, and glitters with small gold coins; their eyes are deeply but delicately painted with Kohl, which gives them a very languishing expression, and a profusion of showy ornaments glitters on their unveiled bosoms.

"When about to commence the Oriental ballet, the Alme exchanges this for a yet lighter dress, throws off her slippers and advances to the center of the room with a slow step and undulating form, that keep accurate time to the music of the reed-pipe and the castanets, on which she is accompanied by her attendants. She then, after a glance round upon her audience, throws herself at once and entirely into the part she intends to act; be it pensive, gay or tragic she seems to know no feeling, but that of the passion she represents. In some cases a whole romance is acted; an Arab girl, for instance, she listens at the door of her tent for the sound of her lover's horse, she chides his delay; he comes, she expresses her delight; he sinks to sleep, she watches over and dances around him; he departs, she is overwhelmed with grief. Generally the representation is more simple; the 'Wasp dance' is a favorite ballet of the latter class: the actress is standing musing in a pensive posture, when a wasp is supposed to fly into her bosom—her girdle—all about her; the music becomes rapid, she flies about in terror, darting her hand all over her person in pursuit of the insect, till she finds it was all a mistake; then smiling she expresses her pleasure and her relief in dance."

We started out to visit the temple of Eshne and found only a portico which was surrounded by houses, and the temple proper was covered with houses, it being very difficult to tell anything at all about it. The portico has been cleared of the rubbish and debris, and we recognized it as

36

belonging to the Roman period, for the cartouches belong to the various Roman Emperors. We did not care to stop at Eshne over night, but force of circumstances compelled us to remain. There was not a breath of wind astir, and Hassan had gone to visit a friend. so we spent that afternoon in rambling around the town visiting the bazaars, where we purchased a few articles, then went down to our dahabiyeh. After dinner we wrote a few letters, arranged our notes, and at night we went up to one of the principal coffee houses, and witnessed some of the dances of the Gawazee girls.

The very first dance was the "Wasp" dance that Warburton described, but like all the rest it soon began to express unbridled passion, when we turned away in disgust, throwing a few piasters as our offering. We strolled off down to our boat, smoked a cigar, and after a chat about what we had seen we retired for the night.

The next morning Salame aroused me from a sound slumber to hand me my morning coffee, and as I sat sipping it I looked out through the cabin window, and saw that we were under way, and would soon arrive at *El-Kab*, if the wind did not fail us; but by the time our breakfast was ready the wind had left us, and we had a lot of towing to do before reaching that place.

As we sat on deck that day we amused ourselves by shooting, and we bagged quite a lot of birds, some of which were beautiful specimens, and we preserved the skins for future use. We went crawling along slowly but surely with our big sails hanging from the yards, swaying backward and forward with every motion of the boat. We dropped off into a doze from which we were suddenly aroused by the shouts of our sailors, who came laughing and swimming on board, when the "*shogool*" was eased off our big sails swelled out full and round as the wind struck us on our port quarter, just before we got to El-Kab, the *Eilcithyes* of the ancients, or the "*City of Lucina.*" This was a very interesting place to visit, where there were some very fine rock tombs especially interesting. They would well repay any one for the time expended in examining them, but as I had visited these tombs and temples some years ago, and as the wind was blowing strongly in our favor and both Abdallah and Hassan urged us to go on, we took advantage of the wind and concluded to continue on to Edfu.

The decorations of the tombs and temples at El-Kab were in a very fair state of preservation when I saw them last. In the tomb of Paheri we were enabled to see farm scenes such as ploughing, sowing, reaping, in fact all kinds of field and farm work, river scenes, such as fishing, hunting, etc. There is one scene here that will be of great interest to the Masonic student, and that is the funeral procession and the *Judgment of the Dead.* One threshing scene in this tomb, where the oxen were treading out the golden grain, has the song of the driver inscribed above, which is translated as follows :

> Thresh for yourselves Oxen !
> Thresh for yourselves !
> Measure for yourselves !
> Measure for your Masters.

Mr. Gliddon renders it :

> Hie along oxen ! tread the corn faster ;
> The straw for yourselves,
> The corn for your master.

Some of the scenes here will be very interesting to the Scottish Rite Mason. We soon left this place (*El-Kab*) behind us with its yellow mountains, date palms, etc. As the wind was blowing fresh and strong we had earnestly desired to be enabled to anchor off Edfu.

After we passed El-Kab we ran by some very fertile islands, and noticed that the whole of the way from Eshne, the arable land upon the east bank of the river was very narrow, except in a very few places, but before we reached Edfu it began to widen out again. Our gong sounded the dinner hour and we went down to partake of it, and as we sat chatting over our nuts and wine the loud voices of our sailors rang out in song, we hurried up on deck and discovered the propylon of Edfu. We went gliding along, and as the shadows lengthened and twilight fell around us our sails were furled, and we were soon moored for the night under the glittering stars at Edfu, the *Appollinopolis Magna* of the Greeks.

Edfu has a post and telegraph office, and the steamers stop here every Tuesday and Friday for a couple of hours. We went on shore, and strolled up to the post office, and had quite a long chat with some gentlemen who were remaining over, so as to be enabled to visit the celebrated temple at that place ; so we made arrangements to visit it together the next morning. We went back to the dahabiyeh, and retired early, telling Hassan to have an early breakfast. The next morning Salame aroused me from a sound slumber, and finishing our morning meal, we started off with our new acquaintances to visit the celebrated temple, located about fifteen minutes ride from the river.

The temple lies directly West of the town, and it is entirely surrounded by the mud hovels of the natives; in fact, the whole of this most beautiful temple was covered, roof and all, with the mud dwellings of the people who lived here previous to 1864, when it was cleared of them by M. Mariette, who informs us as follows:

"The excavations of Edfu are the most extensive archæological work ever executed under the auspices of His Highness the Khedive (Ismail Pasha)." A few years ago the modern village had invaded the temple, its very terraces being covered over with dwellings, stables, storehouses of every kind. In the interior the chambers were filled with rubbish almost to the ceiling. The amount of time and trouble expended on the excavations will be realized on entering the temple, where every single line of inscription has now become perfectly accessible to the traveller, tourist and antiquarian.

There were sixty-four houses upon the roof of this temple that Mariette Bey removed, and with them the filth and vermin that went with these people; and to-day we are enabled to wander through all parts of this beautiful and perfect specimen of an ancient Egyptian Temple, with all its parts perfect, as in the early days of its completion. It resembles the temple of Dendcrah very closely in its general plan; in fact, they belong to the same period, and the inscriptions upon the walls of this temple refer continually to the same system of worship as was practiced in the temple of Denderah.

The inscriptions cover all parts of this temple, for every wall, column and ceiling is completely covered with hieroglyphic inscriptions that tell us of the use of the various halls, chambers, etc. Upon the walls of the Library is catalogued the books that were kept in it; in fact, every part of this beautiful temple tells its own story. It was one of the best preserved temples, in fact, one of the finest, that is to be found in this wondrous Valley of the Nile, because it is perfect in all its parts. The extreme length of this building, including the pylon and the circuit wall,

COLUMNS IN THE COURT OF THE TEMPLE OF EDFU.

is fully four hundred and fifty feet. The height of the pylon is very nearly one hundred and fifteen feet, and it has a frontage of one hundred and thirty-two feet; but if we include the pylon, its facade is two hundred and fifty feet.

On the front of this pylon are four cavities that were used for the purpose of securing the masts that decorated this most beautiful temple, into which they were no doubt fitted. There is an inscription here that tells us that they served for lightning conductors. Mariette believed that they must have been at least one hundred and fifty feet high.

Furlong informs us in his "Rivers of Life" that Solomon's temple was a very poor imitation of this temple at Edfu, and that it was upwards of fourteen times the size of the Hebrew Temple, and that one of the "halls" of the Edfu temple would swallow up the Jewish one entirely. We enjoyed ourselves very much, indeed, exploring the various halls and chambers of this very extraordinary temple, and after our careful examinations, we were soon on our way back to our very comfortable home the dahabiyeh, tired and weary, but extremely glad to know that we had been enabled to thoroughly examine and explore the most perfect temple in Egypt, that of Edfu.

The next morning bright and early found our crew towing and punting, trying to make *Gebel,* or *Hagar Silsilis* ("the mountain of the chain") as early as possible, located a distance of twenty-five miles from Edfu, and five hundred and forty-seven miles from Cairo; so that we might be able to visit the celebrated quarries, examine the monuments, and hurry on to Ombos. It was however not until late that night that we were able to moor close to the monuments, so Hassan informed us, for we had retired long before reaching there, and when Salame brought us our coffee in the morning we found ourselves moored near the West bank.

The river is very narrow here being not much over three hundred and fifty yards wide, with very lofty banks, abrupt and precipitous that come down to the river and inclose its very narrow quarters. We landed upon the east bank and visited the celebrated quarries from whence were taken those immense blocks of sandstone that have been used in the building of the great majority of temples throughout the whole of Upper Egypt.

There are quarries on both sides of the Nile, but we visited those on the east side first, on account of their extraordinary size. These quarries are open to the light of day, and demonstrate to the present generation, the wondrous knowledge of the craft in quarrying and handling the stupendous stones and carrying them to the river. It is remarkable to see the immense amount of work that has been done here, for the whole mountain has been cut into with the greatest of care, and proving to us of to-day, that they did not use explosives, of any kind whatever, in their methods of quarrying. The entrance to these quarries are through a long cutting clear through the solid rock, and upon all sides we found specimens of *graffti* (or scribblings), in both Greek and Demotic characters (writing used by the ancient Egyptian people not hieroglyphical). There were quite a number of things quarried here that have never been removed from this place, where they were originally carved or cut from the mountain side, such as Sphinxes, etc.

There were a great many things to be seen there that will prove of great interest to any one who will take the time and trouble to visit this place. The quarries on the West bank were not nearly so large as those on the other side of the river, for the stones had been quarried in a different manner entirely. These quarries are open to the sky and to the glorious light of day, but those on the East bank are quarried right into the cavernous depths of the mountain forming immense grottoes that were originally quarries; but which were afterwards used for tombs, temples, etc, while upon the walls of all are to be found hieroglyphic inscriptions. They have also been decorated with beautiful paintings and sculptures from the XVIII dynasty down to the Roman domination. Some of them are truly most magnificent specimens of ancient Egyptian Art. I specially refer to the bas-relief known as the "*Triumph of Horus.*"

We had a glorious time rambling around these quarries and grottoes, and examining the various points of interest on both banks of this wondrous old river Nile, at *Silsilis.* We retired rather early as we felt worn out with our investigations, and although our crew was having a grand old time, making the mountain ring and echo to their songs and laughter, we slept through it all, and awoke from our slumber the next morning refreshed. Salame brought us our toast and coffee, when we found by the motion of the boat, that we were under sail, and that we were scudding along through the waters before a good fresh breeze, running along toward Ombos, at the rate of about eight miles an hour, and while we were eating our breakfast we went careening along by *Fares.*

On coming on deck, after our morning meal, we sat under the awning and smoked cigars, noticing that there was but very little arable land upon either bank of the river. After awhile we saw a decided change, for fertile fields began to appear upon the east bank, and we very soon passed a small island that was well cultivated, and as our wind held good, we drew up to quite a large island called *Mansuriyeh,* which divides the river into two branches or channels. We entered the first or largest, when our course became nearly due east, and just as we reached the bend of the river, it turned due south again and we found ourselves at Ombos, five hundred and sixty-four miles from Cairo.

Kom Ombos is rapidly disappearing beneath the waters of the Nile, surely it is steadily falling into the river. This place, that was built to endure for ever, is rapidly being destroyed by the old God Nilus. Sebek, the deity that was worshipped here was also worshipped and adored at Silsilis, and the crocodile-headed god is found, not only upon the Stele in the quarries at Silsilis, but also in many parts of Ombos. As the wind continued to blow good and strong, we took advantage of it, and continued our journey southward toward Aswan. We spent a few hours at Ombos, but as there was not much to interest us there, we cast off our moorings, loosed our sails, and amid the sounding songs of our sailors, soon left it far behind us.

There was but very little to interest one as we sailed along the river, and there was a sameness about it that grew monotonous to all, so I sat on deck under the awning, and arranged my notes, while the others amused themselves with various problems in chess. Our boat went spinning along over the flowing waters of the river, until we began to notice a most decided change in the surrounding scenery, which now had a peculiar charm and beauty, that must be seen to be fully appreciated, for we now were approaching the scene of the Poet Juvenal's banishment, by Domitian, on account of offending Paris, the actor.

We were now enabled to see the mountains to the south, at whose feet nestles the beautiful island of Elephantine, which is about a mile in length and divides the river into two channels. It is a lovely island, with every foot of arable land thoroughly cultivated, with patches of cotton,

corn, beans, and castor-oil plants, etc. Thick palm groves gave a delightful charm and fascination to the scene, and from a distance, as the bright
sunlight fell streaming down upon it, the island was like a beautiful
jewel, for the play of colors upon its black syenite rocks, the golden
sand and the vivid greens combined to enhance the beauty of this place
beyond the power of words. It is a most interesting place to visit, and
will repay all those who may ramble around it. Although the ruins
were in a sadly dilapidated condition, we observed many things that
deeply interested us. We noticed that the symbols of the old pagan
philosophies were lying side by side with the cross that dethroned them,
and that both were superseded by Islamism.

The Church of Christ is extinct in Nubia, and it simply drags out
an existence in Upper Egypt in a very degraded form of worship, and all
that remains of Christianity on the borders of Nubia are a few crosses
indifferently cut upon the remains of some of the tombs and temples,
demonstrating that it did at one time reach to the first cataract and Philæ.
Those teachings have long since passed away. A few columns still
stand to mark the site of the temple of the ram-headed god *Khnum* or
Kneph, which was destroyed by direction of Mohammed Ali in the year
1822, for the purpose of erecting a palace for himself at Aswan. In order
to do this he destroyed a very beautiful temple erected by Amen-hotep of
the eighteenth dynasty. This king was a mighty warrior, and he was
exceedingly fond of building stupendous monuments and magnificent temples ; the celebrated Colossi " the Vocal Memnon " bears his name. He
was a wonderful king, who carried his conquering armies into the
Soudan, returning with spoils to adorn his country with splendid monuments, etc. The Nileometer is well worth a visit, for now it has been put
in proper working order, and to-day it is recording the rise and fall of the
river as it did in the early days of its completion.

There have been found upon this island of Elephantine a great
many things that have interested the scientific world, and among them
portions of a calendar of the time of Thothmes III, that records the rising
of *Anubis*, or the " dog star," nearly thirty-four centuries ago. There
are two villages on the island, the inhabitants of which seem to be
Nubians, and on the arrival of travellers upon this island they will crowd
around you, and offer all kinds of antiquities for sale, sometimes small

ROCK TOMBS AT GEBEL, OR HAGAR SILSILIS.

coins, and fragments of pottery, shells, etc. There is no doubt but that a great many of these so-called antiquities are manufactured like those at Thebes. At the southern end of the island one may frequently find fragments of inscribed terra-cotta vases, many of which are valuable. On the east bank, and opposite this island, is located the frontier town of Egypt *Aswan*, or as it is called by many writers "*Assouan*," or "*Syene*," distant five hundred and ninety miles from Cairo, in Latitude 24°, 5′, 23″ North, and 32°, 55′ East Longitude, which figures prove, that to-day, this town is not under the tropic of Cancer.

It was on account of a report spread throughout the "Land of Egypt" of a well in Aswan, wherein there was no shadow even at mid-day, which led the celebrated philosopher and mathematician Eratosthenes, who had charge of the Alexandrian Library, to measure the obliquity of the ecliptic, and also to measure a degree of the meridian. He discovered the exact circumference of the Earth, using the same methods in that day, that have been adopted by our own geometricians to-day. At the present time there is no well at Aswan in which the sun is reflected at noon, when it reaches its meridian height and glory, but, in the fourth century B. C. *Aswan was most certainly under the tropic of cancer*, and there is no doubt, but that there was a shadowless well at this place at that time.

We now found ourselves among a different class of people entirely, from those we had been accustomed to in our long journey up the Nile. The various articles they had for sale were also different. The town of Aswan is a very busy one, on account of its being the principal market town for the whole of the Soudan and Abyssinia. The streets of this place are very much like those of every other mud village throughout the whole of the "Land of Egypt," and the bazaars are just about the same, containing nearly all things usually found in the various towns in the valley of the Nile. A great deal more can be purchased here in Aswan, because a great many things are brought here, from the upper country, that are not always to be found in the bazaars of the towns below. There are quite a large number of cafes here, and each and every one have their regular dancing girls, who make night hideous with their mad revels.

It is extremely interesting to pass in among the tents of the merchants (who camp here) and to examine the various goods they have for sale. We were shown elephants tusks, henna leaves, lion, leopard, and in fact all kinds of skins; gum arabic, tamarinds and war implements of all kinds, etc. There is one thing most certain and that is you will find ostrich feathers much cheaper here than in any other place in Egypt. I paid fifty cents each for some beautiful black and grey ones, that you could not buy here in America for less than five or six dollars. The largest and most perfect white feathers can be bought for four or five dollars that would very much astonish some of your wives and daughters.

There are a great many things one ought to buy here besides ostrich feathers, well worth taking back with you, as "souvenirs." These comprise ivory rings, silver rings, armlets, beautiful basket work, and the aprons of leather fringe which form the costume of the Nubian women, and which are called "Madame Nubia." The people we met here were entirely different from those of Egypt. The turban was seldom seen excepting upon the heads of Egyptians or old men of Nubia. The great majority went around bare-headed and wore nothing to cover their heads, other than their thick matted hair, which was plentifully bedaubed with castor oil, as well as the whole of their bodies. The young men generally wore a small cloth around their loins of very scant dimensions, and the young women (*virgins*) simply wore "Madame Nubia." The older women wore a long blue robe, and the old men a long loose white one (?) and very often a turban. The women of Nubia do not cover their faces at all times with a veil, they seem to be more free to do as they please than the women of Egypt, and they are most assuredly far more virtuous. It was very peculiar to see both the young men and women shining like billiard balls, with their bodies glistening in the sun, smeared all over with castor oil, which was the prevailing fashion among the "elite" of Nubia.

There is just as much difference between Egypt and Nubia, as there is between the people of the two countries. The palm grows just as abundantly above Aswan as it does below, and the dates of Nubia are noted for their delicious flavor. In fact, they have been sought for, above all others, throughout all the eastern countries. The face of the whole country changed entirely beyond the island of Philæ, and the scenery became more wild and fantastic; the river was far narrower, and consequently more rapid. The arable land was much less, but the vegetation seemed to put on a brighter garb than that which we had been accustomed to in our long journey from Cairo to Philæ.

A great many men we met carried a spear and shield, the latter made from the tough hide of the hippopotamus. It has a large boss in the centre, with an iron bar across it, so that the hand can grasp it firmly when it is needed for defensive purposes. The language that we heard spoken was also very different from what we had been accustomed to, and is what the Egyptians call *Barabra*, and the people who speak it *Berberi*, which was no doubt the word or name from which we derive the word *Barbarian*. The ancient Egyptians considered all people who did not live in Egypt and speak their language to be *Barbarians.*

One of the most interesting places to visit in this vicinity is the celebrated granite quarries, located just beyond the Arab cemetery. Here we may see and examine the work of men who lived and wrought in these celebrated quarries long centuries before the foundation of Rome was laid. These specimens of their skill and workmanship are lying there to-day just as the workmen left them ages ago. It does not seem possible that those chips of granite which fell from the stroke of a gavel, were broken off long centuries before Rome was founded, or Romulus and Remus suckled. They look to-day as clean and bright as they did when they first fell before the hand of the craftsmen long centuries ago. As we stood looking down upon the handiwork of the men of the dim and misty past, we could hardly realize the bewildering stretch of time that had passed away since those ancient craftsmen laughed, chatted and worked in these quarries, and cut from the hard granite such tremendous blocks of stone apparently as easily as we of to-day would cut so much clay or chalk. This demonstrates to us of this present century, their thorough knowledge of quarrying immense blocks of stone without waste or injury to the quarry itself; and right here we have ocular demonstrations of their wondrous knowledge of mechanical arts, and their ability to transport such stupendous blocks of stone, to build or adorn their temples in the hoary ages of the past.

As I have previously stated, in Chapter III of this work, it is the height of absurdity to credit Archimedes with the invention of the lever or wedge, for here we see the practical application of the one, and the work in this place alone indicates the knowledge of the other. Here in these quarries we were enabled to see for ourselves, not only their methods of quarrying, but their manner of using the wedge for that purpose. The immense obelisk we saw here in the rough, which is nearly a hundred feet long, and fully eleven feet square at the larger end, testifies to this fact. We could see the holes that had been drilled along its entire length, for the express purpose of inserting wooden wedges, in order to detach it from the quarry.

There are many things to be found here that they have quarried, such as rough columns and various other peculiar shaped stones, intended, no doubt, for some especial purpose, that puzzled us immensely. No one who comes to this place should fail to visit these quarries, for they will most assuredly prove of great interest. I must certainly say that we enjoyed ourselves very much indeed, rambling around not only the quarries, but the town itself, watching the dahabiyehs making the ascent of the rapids, and purchasing the various articles to take back home to our friends as "souvenirs" from the borders of Nubia. As we did not take our dahabiyeh any farther than Aswan, we retained our Pilot, and as the crew remained with us, we made no change at all. If we had taken our boat up the cataract for a journey farther South, we should have been compelled to hire another Pilot, at least to direct our course, in the place of the one who had performed his duty so well in piloting our boat in safety from Cairo to the borders of Nubia, and the first cataract of the Nile.

The next morning we hired camels for the purpose of riding over to Mahatta, the first port in Nubia, after leaving Aswan. At this point goods or merchandise is unloaded for re-embarkation at Aswan, being destined for the different points below the cataract. Hassan had picked out all the camels necessary for our party, so bright and early we rode off with the worst lot of snarling, growling brutes that I had ever seen.

The great majority of my readers no doubt, understand how to mount a camel, but if they have never ridden one, it would be impossible for me to make them comprehend the sensation of the motion of one of these horrible brutes, the sumpter-camels. If the camel should walk with an even gait, you will be jostled backwards and forward, and you will wish that these animals had never existed, and will sigh for the donkey of Egypt. If he walks ahead briskly, with long swinging strides, you will be afraid that every joint in your body will be dislocated, if he does not stop. When he trots no words can express the horrible torture you are enduring, and if he should run,—well, only those who have trod the hot sands of the desert can fully explain the feeling of having "*to hold on.*"

When you are seated in the saddle, if you should happen to move, the miserable brute will try to bite your feet or legs, and should you try to compel him to go a different way from his own chosen route, he will turn his head and looking you snarlingly in the face swear at you in both Arabic and Berberi. If that does not compel you to leave him alone, why—he will lie right down and try to get you off.

A sumpter-camel is the most horrible thing in the world to try to ride. They are only fit for carrying heavy burdens across a trackless desert, under a burning tropical sun, and can be made to carry six or seven hundred pounds of pack goods all day long without stopping to drink. Mahatta is quite a small village that is used expressly for the purpose of shipping cargoes from the boats overland to Aswan, or receiving them for loading into the boats going into the Soudan or Abyssinia as the case may be, but since the British domination of this country the town of *Shellal* has taken its place. One can hire boats at either place for a voyage up to the second cataract and back, but they are very dirty with scarcely anything at all in the shape of furniture on board. They do not begin to compare with the clean, brightly painted, well fitted dahabiyehs of Egypt, but as we were not going up this time, we did not bother ourselves about transportation beyond the first cataract or Aswan.

We hired a Filucca to take us over to the " Holy Island " of Philæ, one of the most lovely spots in the whole of Egypt. There is no one who comes to this place who can help recognizing the grandeur and beauty of this most extraordinary Island and its picturesque surroundings, which are extremely grand, and which will charm and fascinate all who see it. On our trip from Mahatta to this lovely island, I was charmed and delighted in viewing this most exquisite piece of scenery. The tufted palms and pylons rise in their wondrous beauty seemingly from out the waters of the Nile, and the various columns and walls of the temple look as if they were new and in the height of their glory, just completed and ready for occupation. As we drew nearer to the Island everything looked beautiful, stately, magnificent, and as we gazed upon it from our boat upon the river, we saw that charming roofless temple called "Pharaoh's Bed." We were lost in thoughts of the glorious days of long ago, until the grating of the boat against the stones of an ancient landing place, aroused us from our reverie, when we sprang upon the gunwale of our boat, and climbed the steep bank, and stood enraptured before the glorious ruins of a magnificent temple, realizing that we were now viewing the crowning glory of our voyage.

The remains of the tombs and temples here are not vast, but they are extremely beautiful, and the impressions of the various ruins will forever remain with me so long as life shall last. Chief among these remains stands "Pharaoh's Bed," the beauties of which can never be fully described, any more than can the island itself. It has been sketched, painted and photographed from all points, but that alone cannot demonstrate its wondrous charm and beauty. What is a magnificent jewel without a setting? Of course we recognize its splendor, but the setting most assuredly enhances the beauty of the gem itself, and shows it off to the best advantage. In the same way, to get the full effect of this most lovely scene, we should approach the Island at certain times in a filucca upon the river, with the distant mountain as a back-ground, and the immense rocks framing it in, forming a most beautiful setting. It is under these conditions, with the mountain and rocks lit up with a play of colors indescribably grand, the tufted palms, glistening colonnades and pylons glowing in the changing light, like the scintillations of a most magnificent jewel, that we fail to find words wherein to express the beauty of the scene. You would fail, as I have to convey to you, my dear brothers and readers, the indescribable charm and beauty of the "Holy Island" of Philæ and its surroundings.

> " The footprints of an elder race are here,
>   And memories of an heroic time,
>   And shadows of the old mysterious faith ;
>   So that the isle seems haunted and strange sounds
>   Float on the wind through all its ruined depths.

> " ' By him who sleeps in Philæ '—such the oath
>   Which bound th' Egyptian's soul as with a chain
>   Imperishable, Ay, by Amun Ra,
>   The great Osiris—who lies slumbering here,
>   Lulled by the music of the flowing Nile.

KIOSQUE, OR PHARAOH'S BED,

PL. I.

> Ages have gone, and creeds, and dynasties,
> And a new order reigns o'er all the Earth ;
> Yet still the mighty Presence keeps the isle—
> Awful, serene, and grandly tranquil he,
> With Isis watching—restless in her love ! ''

This island was considered to be the most sacred spot in all the world to the ancient Egyptian. It is not very large, only about four hundred yards long, by about one hundred and fifty yards wide at its broadest part. To-day it is not inhabited, but there is a man who guards it, and who makes his home on an adjacent island. The most ancient building on this island of Philæ, was erected by Nectanebu II between the years B. C. 381 and 365, and all that remains of it to-day are a few columns, etc.

There are a great many things that will deeply interest the tourist on this lovely island, and all those who are desirous of examining the ruined temples of the various Ptolemies and Cæsars should camp upon it, and go over it very carefully so as to see all the varied beauties upon it, for it is " strewn with ruins." One of the most beautiful and pictur-esque of all of them is the *Kiosque*, commonly called " Pharaoh's Bed ;" which is located on the east side of the island, and is said to have been dedicated to Isis, or the Triad that was sacred to Philæ, which was— Osiris, Isis, and Horus. This temple is roofless, and was never com-pleted, but for all that it is a most charming spot and a most delightful place to enjoy an hour, and refresh yourself with luncheon, etc.

The cataract islands in the vicinity are well worth a visit, but more especially to the geologist and others who are desirous of seeing the many inscriptions, carved upon the rocks, many of which date back to the XI and XII dynasties. We had now completed a tour throughout the whole length and breadth of this most extraordinary country visiting and describing nearly all the ancient cities, and exploring the principal tombs and temples throughout both Upper and Lower Egypt, and we must cer-tainly say that we had derived an immense amount of pleasure in doing so.

After our trip to Philæ we return to Aswan, and to our dahabiyeh, tired and weary. During our absence our crew had baked their bread for the return voyage, and they now engaged in cleaning our boat from truck to kelson. We were going to remain here a few days as a caravan was expected to come in from the interior, and awaiting its arrival we remained within the roar of the foamy waters at Aswan.

The caravan arrived from the South with its strange looking Nubian attendants. It was a sight that will remain with us through all time, and whenever the name of Aswan or Camel is mentioned that strange, peculiar, barbaric procession comes back to me in all its peculiar features. There were somewhere about one hundred and twenty-five camels in line, and by the side of many of them walked barefooted a tall sturdy looking Nubian, whose shining bronze skin gave him the appearance of a living moving statue.

What strange looking bundles and packages the camels carry upon their backs, many of which are covered with raw hides containing elephants' tusks about ten or twelve feet long, some were carrying immense bundles of gum-arabic, wrapped up in skins and tied with long strips of hippopotamus hide. Others carried packages of the skins of all kinds of wild animals, and upon the backs of some of the camels were crates of wild beasts, one of which contained a litter of young lions that were quite playful. When the strange cortege halted to camp beside the river they formed quite a village of their own.

The leader of the caravan was a most magnificent specimen of a man, standing fully six feet and five inches tall; he was armed with regular old fashioned pistols and sword. We saw many who were armed with spear and shield, and occasionally they had an old fashioned brass mounted pistol stuck in their girdle, and many of them were armed with a club and sheath knife strapped around their arms. We mingled freely with the jostling crowd and found among them natives from nearly all parts of Africa and Abyssinia.

After they had camped and unloaded their camels, we went in among them and bought some beautiful leopard skins, ostrich feathers, spears, shields, ornaments and some very fine specimens of basket work, that had been manufactured by people who lived beyond Khartoum. These things Hassan and Salame took down to the dahabiyeh while we "dickered" for a lot of very fine curiosities from the Soudan.

The next morning we started on our return trip to Cairo, rowing through the day and drifting through the night. Sometimes we had a good breeze in our favor of which our captain and pilot took advantage, during such times our sailors would sing, dance and play their drums and pipes to their heart's content, for they were now " homeward bound."

Egypt is without doubt the most extraordinary, interesting and attractive country that the Masonic student should visit, in order to improve himself in the signs, symbols and allegories pertaining to Masonry. There he will have ocular demonstrations of the knowledge that was thoroughly comprehended by those ancient craftsmen, who lived upon the banks of the Nile, long centuries before the dawn of authenticated history. The ordinary traveler who desires to examine the ancient cities, tombs, temples, monuments and mummies of a pre-historic age, will find that there is no country on earth that will prove of greater interest to him than Egypt, and the Valley of the Nile.

Time has not robbed it of its peculiar charms and fascinations, but has rather given to it an atmosphere of mystery, that must be solved by actual searching among the ruins of this most wonderful country. If the student investigates and studies along the Valley of the Nile, he will discover many things that will prove the great antiquity of Egypt, and the wonderful knowledge that pertained to those people who built such stupendous fabrics in order to adorn and beautify the banks of this grand old river Nile. The Masonic student. if he be careful in his investigations, will have proof positive of the actual existence of the teachings of our own glorious Rite, in the fact that the people who migrated here laid the first stone of foundation, to establish themselves and their philosophies permanently upon the banks of one of the grandest, and most peculiar rivers in the world.

Greece and Rome were but the offshoots of this most wonderful civilization which originated in the Valley of Hindostan or the " Land of the Vedas," and which was Cradled on the banks of the Nile in the dim dawn of prehistoric ages. Egypt was a wonderful country with a knowledge of Social forms, Law and Order, long centuries before Abraham crossed the plains of Mamre in the company of angels, and the Hebrew people are modern when compared with the Ancient Egyptians. There is no question to the thinking man and Masonic student, but that Egypt, was not only the Cradle of Ancient Masonry, but the Cradle of the World's ancient civilization.

37

Cecrops carried with him to Greece, when he founded Cecropia, the wondrous knowledge that afterwards ramified through it, and which came down to the other peoples beautified, and enwrapped in the exquisite thought that gave to the world the Greek School of Philosophy and her marble miracles, and which also gave to Rome her boasted civilization. The effect of this has passed down through the drifting ages, throughout the whole of Europe, until we find it in this Twentieth Century dominating our own beloved America, with its wondrous teachings, proving the truth of the scriptures that " *There is no new thing under the sun,*" Eccl. 1-9. For instance.—

In our extradition treaties with other peoples we are now doing what was known and done in the " Golden Age of Egypt," for upon one of the walls, in the great temple of Karnak, we can find to-day written in hieroglyphic inscription an extradition treaty that was made between Rameses and Khetasira, Prince of Kheta (Hittites). This most valuable record can be seen upon a wall that juts out at right angles from the South wall of the temple, about sixty feet from the entrance to the temple, on that side of it. There is no doubt in my mind that this wall was built for the express purpose of recording this very valuable. record or treaty. It was placed under the especial protection of the gods that were worshipped by the peoples of both countries : " Sutekh of Kheta, Amen of Egypt and all the thousand gods, male and female ; the gods of the hills, of the rivers, of the great sea, of the winds and the clouds, of the Land of Kheta and of the Land of Egypt."

A great many people consider it to be a modern invention to hatch out chickens by the use of the incubator ; why, the ancient Egyptians hatched them out with natural heat, by simply burying the eggs in the sand and covering them up with manure. The modern Egyptians hatch them in ovens with a heat that is regulated for that purpose, and during the process of hatching they were carefully watched so as to keep the temperature even.

The modern nickle-in-the-slot machine is not new, for the ancient Egyptians used a simple machine for the purpose of supplying water for their lustrations, by baptism or washing, before entering their temples. The machine was worked by placing a small coin in a slit or slot, when it would drop down upon a perfectly balanced lever that would set in motion another sweep or lever, which would open a valve through which enough water would flow for their own especial use.

There is no question but that the knowledge that pertained to those ancient peoples was most profound and complete. All the scientific knowledge of the present day was thoroughly comprehended by the ancients, but there have been many things lost to the world, lost through fire, flood and the bigotry and fanatacism of many peoples, who destroyed what they could not, or would not, understand, and retarded the progress of the world in so doing.

Every religion that has ever been known is a fragment, *from the Ancient Wisdom Religion,* and like the most prominent to-day, they never can, nor never will, satisfy the demands of the devotees, because there is not one of them that is complete in itself, and consequently cannot, and does not, as a fragmentary portion, stand alone like the ANCIENT WISDOM RELIGION. This wondrous *Secret Doctrine,* this *Ancient Wisdom,* originally came from India and it followed in the footsteps of those peoples, who wandered from that country into Egypt and Chaldea, and was afterwards taught throughout Greece and Rome. It appears to-day, across the threshold of the twentieth century, as the one great force that will lead us on to LOVE AND RIGHTEOUSNESS.

Egypt is a wonderful country to-day; it has ever been a problem to the learned men of nearly every age, and we ourselves have stood with bowed head, in awe and admiration, before the stupendous ruins of these most extraordinary people. I have realized that those gigantic stones, quarried by the craftsmen of prehistoric ages, were like the great Sphinx—voiceless! but each and every one contains a history of its own, and represents a portion of the tattered pages of the historical records of this wonderful country and people.

There is a change coming over the various teachings of to-day, for the hand of inquiry and investigation is upon the throat of the various ISMS, and will not be downed, or satisfied with mysteries or parables, but will require the TRUTH—*the whole Truth,* for "THERE IS NO RELIGION HIGHER THAN TRUTH." The latter part of the nineteenth century witnessed a great revival of knowledge and scientific investigation that has excited widespread and profound attention, evidenced by the literature that has come to us across the threshold of the twentieth century,

Jewish Traditions and Customs—Cable Tow—Ceremonies of Ancient Initiation—Book of the Law.

Before thy mind thou to this study bend,
Invoke the gods to grant it a good end.
These if thy labor vanquish, thou shalt then
Know the connection both of gods and men;
How everything proceeds, or by what stayed;
And know (as far as fit to be surveyed)
Nature alike throughout; that thou mayest learn
Not to hope hopeless things, but all discern.

—PYTHAGORAS.

CHAPTER XXV.

JEWISH TRADITIONS AND CUSTOMS—CABLE TOW—CEREMONIES OF ANCIENT INITIATION—BOOK OF THE LAW.

REFERENCE was made to Traditions in a previous chapter of this work; but now I want you to thoroughly understand, that if it were not for traditions, we should not know the day of the week, the month, or the year that we are living in to-day. Therefore, in dealing with records that antedate authenticated history, as well as those symbols and allegories that belong to the Symbolic degrees of Free Masonry, we are compelled to depend upon Traditions for the elucidation and proper understanding of them.

TRADITION signifies the transmission of knowledge, opinions, manners, customs, etc., by oral communications from one generation to another. Now, in order that you may better understand me, let me inform you that amidst the writings of the ancient Hebrews we find that "the words of the Scribes are lovely, above the words of the Law; that the words of the Law are all weighty; that the words of the Elders are weightier than the words of the Prophets." By which is meant that the Traditions delivered to them by the Scribes and Elders in the Mishna and Talmud are to be considered of more value than the Holy Scriptures.

Without the aid of Traditions, said the Rabbins, our knowledge would be very limited. We glean from this same source that Hillel, a celebrated Jewish Rabbin; in fact, one of their greatest Sages, was tauntingly asked by a Cairoite: "Master, how can you prove that Tradition is true, and what evidence does it rest upon?" The Rabbin, pausing for a moment, crossing his arms over his breast and casting his eyes upwards in deep thought, then looking the man square in the face, said unto him: "Let me hear you repeat the first three letters of your alphabet." The man pronounced the letters "A B C," when the Sage said unto him: "How did you learn to pronounce those letters in that way, and no other?" The man replied: "I so learned them from my Father." "And in this way your son shall learn them from you," rejoined Hillel, "and this is Tradition."

And thus it was long ages before writing was known, the ancients handed down from Father to Son a knowledge of their manners, customs, Arts, Sciences and Philosophies, which have been the admiration of all men of every age of the world's history. The Wisdom that belonged to these ancient peoples, as well as their manners and customs, has stepped across the threshold of the twentieth century for our own especial edification. If we care to see *one* of the ancient customs of the Hebrew people, that has been handed down from generation to generation, let us go to one of their Abattoirs or slaughtering houses, where we may be enabled to see the Chocat kill a beef, in the same manner as it was done in the days of Abraham. They are just as particular now in performing the operation as they were then.

In order to kill a beef the Chocat uses a very long and sharp knife called a Chalef, of which he takes great care. It is honed or sharpened to a razor-like edge, and kept scrupulously clean; and when the Chocat desires to kill an animal for food, he cuts the throat with one continuous cut, being very careful not to touch the bone, for if he does, it is *Trifa*, or impure; but the veins and arteries must be severed by one continuous cut from ear to ear. After which, the heart and lungs are thoroughly examined, to see if the animal was healthy and fit for food. Then if any of the parts were found in an unhealthy condition, the body was marked *Trifa*, when it was divided in the centre and thrown away; but if everything was found to be healthy and pure, it was marked *Kosha*, or pure, and good and fit for food.

The Jewish people, at the time of their forced stay in Persia, were perfectly familiar with the doctrines of both Persia and India, and many of them held some of the highest offices under the Persian Empire. No matter where they lived, they soon attained to some of the most prominent positions in those various countries, such as governors, judges, etc. When Cyrus gave them their freedom, with permission to return to Jerusalem in order to rebuild their temple, all of them were not desirous of going, for there were a great number who were perfectly willing to remain in Persia, where their children had been born, who spoke the same language and, in fact, were like the people with whom they lived, having the same freedom. They may have been considered to be in bondage, but it is self-evident that they had equal rights among the Persians, with whom they lived, just as they are with us to-day.

Daniel was the Chief of the Babylonian College of Magi, and Minister and companion to the King. Mordecai became Prime Minister and Esther, his cousin, a Jewish damsel, became Queen, and helped her people. Look at Joseph, who was sold into bondage, and see to what prominence he attained! Disraeli, in our own time, became Prime Minister of England under Victoria. I tell you, my dear Brothers and Friends, that we owe a great deal to the Hebrew people. Moses gave to us the Decalogue, the very foundation of our Laws and civilization. The Word was made manifest in the body and blood of Christ, a Jew. In fact, we depend upon Jewish biographies for an account of his life and work.

Aristobulus and Philo Judæus were both Jews, and at the head of the Jewish Greek school of philosophy in Alexandria, where they labored earnestly and incessantly to prove that the Jewish Scriptures were simply allegories, that contained within themselves the most profound Truths and philosophies of every other country and peoples, and that Plato received some of his grandest thoughts from this source. Aristobulus himself positively asserted that the ethics of Aristotle demonstrated the esoteric teachings of the law of Moses, and Philo tried his utmost to reconcile the writings of Moses with the Pythagorean school of Philosophy. Josephus, the Jewish historian, has demonstrated in his works that the Essenes were identical with the Egyptian Theraputæ. Ammonius, a Christian philosopher, organized a Platonic school of Philosophy at Alexandria in A. D. 232. He strived in vain to reconcile the various religious sects, by having them give up their strife and bickerings, telling them that they were all possessed of the same glorious Truths, and that the first thing for them to believe in was, or should be, the Universal Brotherhood of Man, in fact he tried to verify the teachings of Aristobulus and Philo Judæus.

Albert Pike in "Morals and Dogmas," page 744, states that "All truly dogmatic religions have issued from the Kabalah and return to it; everything scientific and grand in the religious dreams of all the illuminati, Jacob Bœhme, Swendenborg, Saint Martin and others, is borrowed from the Kabalah; *all the Masonic associations owe to it their Secrets and their Symbols.* The Kabalah alone consecrates the alliance of the Universal Reason and the Divine Word; it establishes, by the counterpoises of two forces apparently opposite, the eternal balance of being; it alone reconciles Reason with Faith, Power with Liberty, Science with Mystery; it has the keys of the Present, the Past and the Future.

"The Bible with all the allegories it contains, expresses in an incomplete and veiled manner only, the religious science of the Hebrews. The doctrine of Moses and the Prophets, identical at bottom with that of the ancient Egyptians, also had its outward meaning and its veils. The Hebrew books were written only to recall to memory the traditions; and they were written in Symbols unintelligible to the Profane. The Pentateuch and the prophetic poems were merely elementary books of doctrines, morals or liturgy; and the true secret and traditional philosophy was only written afterward, under veils still less transparent. Thus was a second Bible born, unknown to, or rather uncomprehended by, the Christians; a collection, *they* say, of monstrous absurdities; a monument, the adept says, wherein is everything that the genius of philosophy and that of religion have ever formed or imagined of the sublime; a treasure surrounded by thorns; a diamond concealed in a rough dark stone.

"One is filled with admiration on penetrating into the Sanctuary of the Kabalah, at seeing a doctrine so logical, so simple, and at the same time so absolute. The necessary union of ideas and signs, the consecration of the most fundamental realities by the primitive characters; the Trinity of Words, Letters and Numbers; a philosophy simple as the alphabet, profound and Infinite as the Word; theorems more complete and luminous than those of Pythagoras; a theology summed up by counting on one's fingers; an Infinite which can be held in the hollow of an infant's hand; ten ciphers and twenty-two letters, a triangle, a square and a circle— these are all the elements of the Kabalah. These are the elementary principles of the written Word, reflection of that spoken Word that created the World."

From the preceding, my dear Brothers, you will see that the Hebrew peoples have been the medium through which we have received many very valuable Traditions, Symbols and Allegories, that are to be traced through the Symbolic into the Chapter and Council degrees of the York Rite. By careful examination we shall find that they are very much mixed up. But at the same time we shall find them all there, and the earnest student will find a rich field for investigation among the ruins of the Temple, where he will be enabled to discover valuable knowledge and information respecting the Symbology, Allegories and Traditions of the Fraternity. It will require a great deal of patience and perseverance before he will be enabled to unravel, not only the tangled skein of the symbolic degrees, but that of the Royal Arch and Council also.

One of the very first things he will discover will be that the secrets which lie concealed in our symbols and allegories are not taught openly in the Lodges, Chapters and Councils. They are known most certainly, but they are not given out promiscuously to every Brother. He is left to find the esoteric meaning of them, by and for himself alone. In his Entering, Passing and Raising in the Symbolic degrees he will realize that there are many things that will demand his time and most profound attention before he will find even a rudimentary explanation. But at length, when the first ray of "Light" permeates his mind, he will begin to realize that he is turning the tattered Archaic pages of a most profound and sublime philosophy. He will also discover that the key to the "Lost Word" is in his own hand. Again, when he and his companions wander among the fragmentary evidences of the Wisdom that belonged to the hoary civilization of a long, long past, he will not only see the "Light" but he will hear the faint echo of the "Lost Word" reverberating under the Living Arch. The "Light" will not illuminate his mind until he is ready to receive it, and the guttural vibrations of the Word itself will only be a paradox to him. When he passes into the higher degrees of our glorious Scottish Rite, thoroughly comprehending what he has already learned, through the Light he carries within his own heart, to illuminate his mind, every sound and word he has heard in the preceding degrees will be a priceless jewel to help him on to higher planes, and the unveiling of more profound and grander Truths that are embodied in our most Illustrious Fraternity, the Ancient and Accepted Scottish Rite.

A great many of the craft claim that the first three, or Blue Lodge degrees, contain the whole of Masonry. Well—so it does to him who knows.—But how many are there who do know? The whole of the sublime philosophical teachings of Masonry are latent in the Symbolic degrees, but it can never be thoroughly comprehended, until the Aspirant has taken the ineffable and profound philosophical degrees of our Scottish Rite.

Now my dear Brothers and friends, in order that you may fully understand me let me say, that the first three rules in arithmetic contain, in potentia, the whole of the science of numbers. We could not calculate anything without a knowledge of addition, subtraction and multiplication. Having just these three rules alone, what could we know of proportion, square root, mensuration, trigonometry, etc., until we thoroughly understood the combinations and collocations that elucidate the higher branches of mathematics? In the same manner, we may say that in music the octave contains, in potentia, all harmony; so it does, to those who know how to combine the various notes so as to produce the divine harmony of the masters, such as Mozart, Rossini, Meyerbeer, Mendelsshon and others.

I tell you, my dear friends, that the first three degrees of Masonry form the foundation upon which have been erected the " Higher degrees," these ineffable and sublimely beautiful philosophical degrees which have come down to us from the Indian, Mazdean and ancient Egyptian Mysteries.

Gil. W. Barnard says in the May number of " The Canadian Freemason," pages 336 *et seq.:* " Frequently we hear the remark that all of Freemasonry is contained in the first three degrees. . . . . . I cannot be justly charged with partiality when I claim that all that belongs to Freemasonry is not contained in the Lodge degrees. The Mark and Royal Arch degrees of the chapter, as well as those of Royal and Select Master, are not only essentially Masonic in character, but are as much needed for a proper understanding of our legends and mysteries as any part of the first three degrees. Some may say, (and truthfully) that the Masonic portions of the degrees mentioned were taken from the second and third degrees, but that only goes to prove my position. Another feature, and to me it is a much stronger argument for the usefulness of the so-called higher degrees, is that in the work of them we find an elaboration, and illustration in detail of the best and strongest points contained in the Lodge work. . . . . . Nothing is more Masonic than the teaching regarding the work and wages of the Mark Master, and equally so is the lesson contained in the Royal Arch, and the Grand Omnific Royal Arch Word. Holiness to the Lord is the essence of Freemasonry. . . . . . Brethren, it is true beyond a question in my experience that the lodge is strengthened, and made more useful through the lessons received by their members in chapter, council and commandery, and the beautiful, aye sublime teachings of the Ancient and Accepted Scottish Rite."

I have written upon this particular subject, my dear friends and Brothers, in order that you may thoroughly understand that IF the first three degrees do contain the whole of Masonry, the Master Mason will never be enabled to comprehend but the rudimentary parts of any of them. In fact he will never attain to a thorough knowledge of any one of them, until he has been initiated into the higher degrees of the Ancient and Accepted Scottish Rite, and then only, will he be enabled to thoroughly appreciate the beauty of the Symbolic degrees, and realize that although they do not include the whole of Masonry, they do most certainly contain the *key* to the sublime, profound Ineffable, Chivalric and Philosophical degrees of the Scottish Rite, which most assuredly contains the WHOLE OF MASONRY. Consequently every aspiring Brother who is desirous of fulfilling his first promise, to improve himself in Masonry, can never stop at the Third degree, because he has only been raised to *Light* and *Life*, so that he may be enabled to continue on to higher planes, and to a proper understanding of the profound Wisdom that pertains to the " Higher degrees " in Masonry. As he climbs, his view widens out, and his horizon expands. He will begin to realize not only the honor that has been conferred upon him, but also the duties and responsibilities that belong to all those who have been permitted to receive the glorious teachings that are embodied in the various Rites and Ceremonies of the "Higher Degrees." One of the first things impressed upon the candidate will be that—" Man should not live for himself alone."

I tell you my dear Brothers, that the " Cable Tow," binds us all in fraternal bonds of Love, uniting every Mason throughout the world universal, teaching them that by practicing the three principal tenets of the Fraternity—Brotherly Love, Virtue, and Truth we may demonstrate to the outer world that we not only teach, but practice morality, virtue, and are truthful in all our dealings with our fellow man. I assure you, my dear Brothers and Friends, that it is the *bounden Duty* of every Mason to be a good and unselfish man, to labor for the benefit of poor struggling humanity, the advancement of his fellow man; but above all to keep his *first vow* by *subduing his own animal passional nature*, and thus *improve himself in Masonry.*

Brother Albert Pike tells us in "Morals and Dogmas," page 112: "Be faithful to Masonry, which is to be faithful to the best interests of mankind. Labor, by precept and example, to elevate the standard of Masonic character, to enlarge its sphere of influence, to popularize its teachings, and to make all men know it for the Great Apostle of Peace, Harmony, and Good-will on earth among men; of Liberty, Equality, and Fraternity.

"Masonry is useful to all men: to the learned because it affords them the opportunity of exercising their talents upon subjects eminently worthy of their attention, to the illiterate, because it offers them important instruction; to the young, because it presents them with salutary precepts and good examples, and accustoms them to reflect on the proper mode of living; to the man of the world, whom it furnishes with noble and useful recreation; to the traveller, whom it enables to find friends and brothers in countries where else he would be isolated and solitary; to the worthy man in misfortune, to whom it gives assistance; to the afflicted, on whom it lavishes consolation; to the charitable man, whom it enables to do more good, by uniting with those who are charitable like himself; and to all who have souls capable of appreciating its importance, and of enjoying the charms of a friendship founded on the same principles of religion, morality and philanthrophy.

"A Freemason, therefore should be a man of honor and of conscience, preferring his duty to everything beside, even to his life; independent in his opinions, and of good morals; submissive to the laws, devoted to humanity, to his country, to his family; kind and indulgent to his brethren, friend of all virtuous men, and ready to assist his fellows by all means in his power."

I referred previously to the "cable tow," that binds us all in bonds of Love. This investiture comes down to us from ancient India. The god Siva of the Hindu Trinity is very often found represented in the character of a contemplative philosopher, with the Brahmanical thread around him. In which character he endeavors to teach men the necessity of subduing the animal passional nature within their own hearts. At the *Upanayana*, or Initiation, a boy was not considered worthy to receive the title *Dvi-ja* (twice born), until he had been invested with the sacred thread and spiritually regenerated by the act of investiture. In fact, no Brahman of the present day has any right to be called by any other name than *Vipra*, until he becomes initiated and invested with the yajnopvita or sacred thread, then he is known as Dvi-ja. This thread or cable tow (?) of the Hindu consists of three strands or threads, twisted into one thread, and three of these (three-fold strands) twisted together thus make a string or thread, of three times three, or nine strands in one.

Sir William Monier informs us in his " Brahmanism and Hinduism," page 378, that when a Brahman is " once invested with this hallowed symbol of second birth, the twice born man never parts with it. In this respect he has an advantage over his Christian brother. For the latter is admitted into the Church by a single ceremony performed in his infancy, and brought to his recollection by one other ceremony only; whereas the Indian twice-born man has a sacred symbol always in contact with his person, which must always be worn and its position changed during the performance of his daily religious services, constantly reminding him of his regenerate condition, and with its three white threads, united by a sacred knot (which they called *bramah granthi*) perpetually setting before him a typical representation of what may be called the triads of the Hindu religion. For example, it is probable that the triple form of the sacred thread symbolizes that the Supreme Being is Existence, Thought and Joy, that He has been manifested in three forms as Creator, Preserver, and Disintegrator of all material things; that He pervades the three worlds, Earth, Air and Heaven; that He has revealed His will in three principal books called the Rig, Yajur and Sāma Vedas, with other similar dogmas of the Hindu system in which the sacred number three constantly recurs."

When the Candidate was received into the Indian Mysteries, he was compelled to make the circuit of the cavern, being conducted through the ceremonies by an expert who held him by the " cable-tow " or sacred thread. Every time the Aspirant passed the meridian at the South, he would be taught to say that he followed the course of the sun god, from East to West, and West to East again. In fact, all through the Symbolic degrees he represented the sun, going to his death at the winter Solstice, being assaulted on his journey by the three wicked autumnal signs of Libra, Scorpio and Saggitarius, each one in turn attacking him on his downward path. Libra is the first to make the assault; then the deadly Scorpio inflicts a terrible stroke upon him; but it is Saggitarius who strikes the fatal blow with his quivering dart, which gives him his death and eventually lays the sun god low, for after being smitten with the fatal dart he staggers on until he falls dead at the winter Solstice.

"Morals and Dogmas," 361, tells us that: "The Initiate was invested with a cord of three threads, so twined as to make three times three, and called *Zennar*. Hence comes our cable-tow. It was an emblem of their triune Deity, the remembrance of whom we also preserve in the three chief officers of our Lodges, presiding in the three quarters of that Universe which our Lodges represent; in our three greater, and three lesser lights, our three movable and three immovable jewels, and the three pillars that support our Lodges.

"The Indian mysteries were celebrated in subterranean caverns and grottoes hewn in the solid rock; and the Initiates adored the Deity, symbolized by the solar fire. The candidate long wandering in darkness, truly wanted Light, and the worship taught him was the worship of God, the Source of Light."

Jos. E. Morcombe informs us in the "American Tyler," of September 15th, 1900: "That in the mysteries of India the aspirant was invested with a sacred cord or girdle, which he was commanded to wear next his skin, and by means of which his conductor might lead him through the caves of initiation. It consisted of a cord composed of three times three threads, and was said to possess the power of preserving its wearer from personal danger. Virgil says: 'I bind thee with three pieces of list, and I carry thee three times about the altar.' Pierson, without giving his authority, says that the word cable-tow is derived from the Hebrew words 'Kha-Ble Tu,' meaning 'the pledge.'

"The initiation into the ancient mysteries, occurring in temples or other places accounted holy, the aspirant was required to remove his

KOM-OMBUS — TEMPLE OF THE MYSTERIES.

shoes that the greater humility might be shown, and also that no pollution from the world without might be carried into the sacred precincts. When the Egyptians worshipped they removed their foot covering in token of reference. 'Worship the Gods with your feet uncovered,' is among the precepts of Pythagoras. In the Indian mysteries the aspirant was sprinkled with water in token of purification and then divested of his shoes. Ovid describes Madea as having arm, breast and knee made bare, and both feet made slip-shod. Dido according to Virgil, 'Now resolute on death, having one foot bare, ascend the altar.' . . . .

"Oliver quoting Tertullian says, 'the successful probationer for the Persian mysteries was brought into the cavern of initiation; where he was received upon the point of a sword pointed to his heart, by which he was slightly wounded.' The Greeks tested the fortitude of the neophyte upon his reception by the infliction of wounds with a heated iron or with the point of a sword, and this he must endure without shrinking. Entrance into the Mexican mysteries was gained after the candidate had been cut with knives or seared with heated stones or iron instruments."

The course of the candidate in the ancient initiations was from East to West by way of the South. He who was conducted through the caves of India was instructed to say: "I follow the course of the Sun in his benevolent path," at the same time making his movements and repeating the phrase each time upon reaching the South. On solemn occasions, the Druids passed three times in procession about their sacred enclosures, and thrice repeated their invocations. Nothing among the Ancient Britons was accounted sacred until it had been passed about in procession, according to the apparent path of the Sun. Going backward, or opposite to the Sun, was a Gothic method of invoking the infernal power.

The sun was worshipped by the Persians, who looked upon it as the source of all Light and Life. They saw in its diurnal and annual motions the immortality of the soul. In their Mithraic mysteries they practiced some of the most horrible cruelties upon all those who crossed through their portals for initiation. In fact, history informs us that they actually sacrificed some of the Aspirants who could not stand the terrible ordeals they had to pass through. These Mithraic mysteries were the principal of all others in Rome at the beginning of the Christian Era, or during the reign of Trojan. They grew into such terrible repute on account of the

38

horrible cruelties that were practiced during the initiatory services, that Adrianus prohibited the Mithraic rites and ceremonies in Rome during his reign. But, under that of Commodus (the cruel), they began to grow into surprising magnificence and splendor, when the horrible cruelties and tortures were renewed and continued. In fact the Emperor himself sacrificed a victim to Mithras. These Persian mysteries were generally practiced in caves amid the most gorgeous astronomical allegories, at which times the most cruel tests were required of all who were initiated.

In the Zoroastrian Caves of initiation, the magnificent stellary vault above or ceiling, was adorned with a central sun surrounded by the various planets, and the Zodiac was to be seen, starred in with gems and gold. Each star or planet represented the true place upon the roof or ceiling, in its relation to the central sun. The candidate in these mysteries was always received upon the point of a sharp sword that wounded his naked left breast, and caused the blood to flow freely from the wound. If he failed not, he would then be crowned with a circle of olive, and anointed with oil, his wound would be dressed, and afterwards he would be purified with Fire and Water, and permitted to pass through the seven stages of evolution, in order to reach perfection.

During these ceremonies he would undergo most trying ordeals and terrible trials, both mentally and physically, until he reached the topmost rung of the *ladder* of seven rounds. During his ascent, or initiatory path, he would pass through the valley of death where he would see the tortures of the damned in Hell. Eventually he would fall into the midst of the blessed, and be received with rejoicings by all the initiated and redeemed, who had gone before him, and who were especially assembled there to receive him on his arrival; he having passed through the valley of death to the representation of Life Eternal. Then the Archimagus, or Hierophant, clothed in most gorgeous vestments would receive him, and administer unto him the solemn obligation and vow that bound him to Secrecy and Obedience; after which all the various incidents of the initiatory services would be explained to him. He would be instructed in the true meaning of the legend of Ormuzd, and Ahriman, and intrusted with the meaning and nature of the One Absolute, known as ZERUANE AKHERENE.

The similarity of the various rites and ceremonies of the ancient mysteries most certainly demonstrates that they all had their origin in some ancient and primitive source, and from my own personal observations and researches, in the Eastern countries, I firmly believe that they have come down to us, as I have hereinbefore stated,—from India or the "Land of the Vedas." We also find that the three principal officers are always placed in the East, West and South, and in the Indian mysteries they represented the Indian Tri-une Deity,—Brahma, Vishnu, and Siva.

No matter where we force our investigations, either in India, Persia, Egypt or any of the other Eastern countries, we shall find that the very same events have been perpetuated by the use of the same rites, ceremonies, and symbols. This clearly demonstrates that although the people who practiced those peculiar ceremonies, and taught the same grand philosophy, and believed in the same grand Truths, were in many instances, widely separated one from the other; yet notwithstanding this fact, it must prove to the thinking Man and Mason, that it originated in some one source, and from some one people. Now I do most firmly believe that, *that* source was India, and that it ramified from there with those people who migrated from that country to Persia and the valley of the Nile. Thus from the very shadows of the Himalaya Mountains, the very cradle and birthplace of the Aryan Race, came the Indian, Mazdean and ancient Egyptian mysteries, of which our own beloved Scottish rite is a lineal descendant.

The removal of shoes from off one's feet is customary to-day in many countries, more especially is this so in Egypt, India, and other countries among the natives. This custom is as old as the Aryan Race itself. It is peculiar to see the large number of shoes lying around in the gateways or entrances to the Mosques of Egypt, Turkey and also the temples of India. At some of the Mosques I have visited during my travels in many of these Eastern countries, I was compelled to remove my shoes before they would permit me to enter within its sacred precincts, while at others they would furnish me covering to draw on over my own shoes, which in this case, seemed to answer the same purpose as removing my own. Many of these ancient customs of the East have been preserved and handed down from generation to generation, at the same time many others have become obsolete, and a great many entirely changed in order to suit another people's ideas.

The chequered pavement and tessellated border, with the star in the center, is very seldom seen upon the floor of our lodge rooms to-day, for it has been replaced by more gorgeous colorings, and the lessons which they taught are lost to our aspiring candidate of to-day, but future years will reproduce them.

The Ark of the Royal Arch has come down to us from the Ancient Egyptians, although we read that Moses was commanded to manufacture one (Exodus 25: 10), for the express purpose of holding the offerings of the people, who gave willingly to the Lord. It was considered so sacred that it is recorded that the Lord smote, or destroyed fifty thousand and three score people of Beth-Shemesh, because some of them simply looked into the Ark (see 1st Samuel 6: 19). The Jews certainly regarded it as the most sacred thing belonging to them and their religion, because, they declared, that it was a token of God's Covenant with His chosen people.

We find that in the ancient Egyptian mysteries, and also in those of Greece, they used similar boxes that were adorned very much like the Ark of the Covenant. This was long before they knew anything at all about the Hebrew people, or what took place in the Sanctum-Sanctorum of their temple in Jerusalem. In the early days of Egyptian history, the river Nile was the great highway for those people, and during their gorgeous ceremonial processions, when they exhibited many of their most sacred symbols, the chief among them was the image of their god or the image that represented him, placed in a *bari* or boat. It was sometimes exposed to the public gaze, at other times it was hidden from view by being placed inside a box or shrine and deposited in the middle of a boat or *bari*, wherein was laid the bodies of the embalmed dead, that were to be ferried across the river Nile for sepulture in the Libyan hills near Thebes.

These boats were represented, in the paintings of the ancient temples, artistically curved at both ends, in the center of which was placed the sacred shrine containing either the god himself or his creative organs, surrounded by the most sacred emblems of these ancient people. Now, it is on just such a model as this shrine, or chest, that the Ark of the Covenant, of the Jewish people, was constructed, and which is said to have contained " The tables of the Law, The Pot of Manna, and Aaron's budding rod." In the grand processions of these Ancient Egyptians, the ark or *bari* was richly decorated with most magnificent ornamentation of gold and precious gems, representing sacred emblems of the mysteries, and contained, as I have above stated, either the god himself or his *Lingham*, or the organs of generation of Osiris, which was emblematic of the sun god Ra.

This Egyptian Ark, or *bari*, was overshadowed by the wings of two kneeling figures of the goddess of Truth, both figures wearing the feather of Truth upon their heads. Now if we compare the Egyptian Ark with the Hebrew, we shall find a very close resemblance. I do not wish to make all these assertions, without proof from other writers, in relation to this subject, therefore I will quote you from Brother Hewitt Brown, 32°, " Stellar Theology," wherein he says, page 91–2 :

" The Ark was one of the principal features of the Egyptian Mysteries. Speaking of the religious ceremonies of the ancient Egyptians, Wilkinson says: 'One of the most important ceremonies was the ' procession of the shrines,' which is mentioned in the Rosetta Stone, and is frequently represented on the walls of the temples. The shrines were of two kinds, the one a sort of canopy, the other an ark, or sacred boat, which may be termed the great shrine. This was carried with great pomp by the priests, a certain number being selected for that duty, who supported it on their shoulders by means of long staves passing through metal rings at the side of the sledge on which it stood, who brought it into the temple, where it was placed on a stand or table, in order that the prescribed ceremonies might be performed before it. The same is said to have been the custom of the Jews in some of their religious processions, as in carrying the Ark 'to its place, in the oracle of the house, to the most holy place,' when the temple was built by Solomon,' (1 Kings 8). See *Ancient Egyptians*, Vol. I, page 267.

" ' Some of the sacred boats, or arks, contained the emblems of life and stability, which, when the veil was drawn aside, were partly seen, and others contained the figure of the divine spirit *Nef*, or *Nou*, and some presented the sacred beetle of the sun, overshadowed by the wings of the two figures of the goddess of *Themi* or Truth, which calls to mind the cherubim of the Jews, *Ancient Egyptians*, vol. I, page 270.' The principal difference between the Jewish and Egyptian Arks is that the Egyptian was more like a boat in shape, according to our ideas of a boat, while the Jewish ark is described as being of an oblong square form; this, however, it may be observed, was the exact form of Noah's 'ark,' as described by the Jewish historian in Gen. 6: 14–16. The idea of a boat is, therefore, characteristic of both of these ancient emblems, as, indeed, the very name 'ark' denotes. . . . .

"This mysterious ark or chest which figured in the Mysteries of Egypt much more nearly resembled the Jewish ark in form. After Typhon had slain Osiris he enclosed him in a *chest* and cast him into the sea (*river Nile*), thus plunging all heaven in grief and sadness. Isis, when she learned the melancholy news refused all consolation, despoiled herself of her ornaments, cut off her tresses, robed herself in the habiliments of mourning, and wandered forth through the world. Disconsolate and sorrowful, she traveled into all countries, seeking the mysterious chest which contained the body of the lost Osiris. In the meanwhile the chest was washed ashore at Byblos, and thrown into the centre of a *bush*, which having grown up into a beautiful tree, had entirely inclosed it. At length, however, the tree was cut down by a King of that country, and used by him in the construction of a new palace. But Isis finally learned the singular fate of the chest, and her persevering love was rewarded by the possession of it. The plant which thus indirectly led to the discovery of the mutilated body of Osiris was held sacred by the Egyptians.

"The whole story of the death of Osiris and the finding of his body is admitted to be an astronomical allegory of the death of the sun-god, slain by Typhon when the sun was in Scorpio, which was at that time on the autumnal equinox.

"Plutarch informs us that 'when the sun was in Scorpio, in the month of *Athyr*, the Egyptians inclosed the body of their god, Osiris, in an *ark* or *chest*, and during this ceremony a great annual festival was celebrated. Three days after the priests had inclosed Osiris in the ark, they pretended to have found him again. The death of Osiris was lamented by them when the sun, in Scorpio, descended to the lower hemisphere; and, when he arose at the vernal equinox, then Osiris was said to be born anew.'

"The use made of the ark, or sacred chest, in certain Masonic degrees, derives no one of its particulars from anything narrated in the Bible. On the contrary, it bears so striking an analogy to the ark of the Egyptian Mysteries as to at once disclose the original from which it was copied. The Masonic ark, like that of the Egyptian Mysteries, is lost or hidden, and after a difficult search it was at last found. The Masonic, it is true, does not, like the Egyptian one, contain the body of the slain sun-god, Osiris. It does, however, contain something symbolically representing the true God, and also certain matters which, it is claimed, lead to a superior knowledge of him. The analogy is, therefore, perfect, and the astronomical allegory is strictly preserved."

Albert Pike in "Morals and Dogmas," page 376, says: "When Isis first found the body, where it had floated ashore near Byblos, a shrub of *erica* or tamarisk near it had, by the virtue of the body, shot up into a tree around it, and protected it; and hence, our sprig of acacia. . . . .

"In the Mysteries, the nailing of the body of Osiris upon the chest or ark was termed *aphanism*, or disappearance (of the Sun at the Winter Solstice, below the Tropic of Capricorn), and the recovery of the different parts of his body by Isis, the *Euresis*, or finding. The Candidate went through a ceremony representing this, in all the Mysteries everywhere. The main facts in the fable were the same in all countries, and the prominent Deities were everywhere a male and a female.

"In Egypt they were Osiris and Isis; in India, Mahadeva and Bhavani; in Phœnicia, Thammuz (or Adonis) and Astarte; in Phrygia, Atys and Cybele; Persia, Mithras and Asis; in Samothrace and Greece, Dionusos, or Sabazeus and Rhea; in Britain, Hu and Ceridwen; and in Scandinavia, Woden and Frea; and in every instance these Divinities represented the Sun and Moon.

"The Mysteries of Osiris, Isis and Horus seem to have been the model of all the other ceremonies of initiation subsequently established among the different peoples of the old world. Those of Atys and Cybele, celebrated in Phrygia, those of Ceres and Proserpine, at Eleusis and many other places in Greece, were but copies of them. This we learn from Plutarch, Diodorus Siculus, Lactantius and other writers; and in the absence of direct testimony should necessarily infer it from the similarity of the adventures of these Deities, for the ancients held that Ceres of the

Greeks was the same as the Isis of the Egyptians, and Dionusos or Bacchus as Osiris."

My dear Brothers and Friends, you will see from the above that the
ark of the ancient Egyptians, and the ark of the Covenant of the Jewish
people was very much alike, and there is no question in my mind but
that the Hebrews copied their ark from that of the Egyptians, during the
time that they were held in captivity or bondage by those people, for
many of the pictures of the Osirian chest or ark that are to be seen upon
the walls of the various temples, in the valley of the Nile, will most certainly prove to be the pattern by which the Hebrew peoples made theirs.
I do not ask you, my dear Brothers, to go to Egypt in order to verify this
assertion, I simply ask you to look at some of the pictorial descriptions
of the interior decorations of the Egyptian tombs and temples, or to refer to
such a work as Kitto's Cyclopædia of Biblical Literature. Then compare
the ark of the Covenant with the ark of Osiris, and you will most assuredly agree with me upon this subject.

Now with respect to what is said to have been the contents of the
ark of the Covenant, let us consider this matter and carefully examine
what it is said to have contained. (*See* Hebrews 9 and 4.) Leaving
aside Aaron's budding rod (for account of which see Numbers 17th
chapter) and the Manna which the Lord rained down upon the children
of Israel when they sighed for the fleshpots of Egypt; (*see* Exodus 16th
chapter), we will confine ourselves to the "*Book* of the Law" and leave
the rod of Aaron and the pot of Manna out of our consideration.

In taking up the subject of the "Book of the Law" I feel that it will
interest every Masonic student, and will prove a most interesting subject
to all Royal Arch Masons. Their ancient traditions, which have been
preserved for so long a time within the Chapter, will now have to
undergo a test of investigation in order to prove the verity of the assertion, "Book of the Law." But no matter if we are able to prove that it
never existed, as is generally understood, the teachings that underlie the
sacred symbol, will ever remain one of the grandest features pertaining
to the rites and ceremonies of the Holy Royal Arch.

It is not with any irreverence toward the so-called "Book of the
Law" that I approach this subject, but it is with the most profound veneration for the writings contained in the Old Testament. I simply wish

to show you, my dear friends and companions, that it could not have been, what it is generally supposed to be, the canon of the Old Testament and the New combined; known as the " Holy Bible," which is generally used in the ceremonies of the Exaltation.

I have inquired in many countries by what authority it is used, but could get no definite information in relation to my question. Now this " Book of the Law " that is supposed to have been found and generally used in our Chapters of the Royal Arch is purely and simply the Holy Bible. I shall not enter into a long discussion upon the various translations of the Bible, or try to prove which one is the most correct, but will endeavor to find out something about the " Book that was Lost."

History informs us that after the captivity, when the Jews were rebuilding their temple under their leader Zerubbabel, and while this was going on, three very earnest sojourners applied for and received permission to assist in the good work, and that one of the very first things that resulted from their labors was the discovery of the " Book of the Law," which is said to have been lost since the time when Solomon lived and reigned. The " Book of the Law," long lost was now found, and they gave praise to the Lord, and from that time it has been preserved with other discoveries that were made at or about the same time.

Now, the only place in the Bible that refers to the discovery of the " Book of the Law " is in 2nd Kings, 22-8, where it tells us that Hilkiah, the High Priest, told Shapan, the Scribe, that he had discovered the " Book of the Law " in the house of the Lord, and possibly this discovery was the origin of the Book itself. There is one thing that is positively certain, and that is, the book that was found by our ancient companions did not include the New Testament with the account of the Life and Death of Christ, therefore we must omit that and confine ourselves strictly to the Old Testament, if we desire to find the " Book of the Law."

Now, if we are very careful in our investigations, we shall find that there is no certainty about the compilation of the various writings that compose the Old Testament, or by whom, or in what manner, or what time they were compiled. According to some of the Hebrew Rabbis, Ezra was the one who began the compilation of the many historical, poetical and prophetical writings that composed the Old Testament, but we do not consider this information as thoroughly reliable. There is one thing certain, however, and that is, the compilation was not made until after the exile. Ezra may possibly have commenced the compilation of this great work, which was, no doubt, continued by his successors, who eventually completed it, somewhere about the early part of the second century B. C.

In order to accomplish this great undertaking, it was necessary to write new works based upon the traditions of these people, until at last the work was finished. We now have the Old Testament, a very valuable and important collection of writings; but it is not the book for which we are looking. This compilation is not the " Book of the Law," although it may contain it. Therefore, in order to make our search complete, and our investigation thorough, we shall have to strike out those books that were composed after the reign of Solomon, and search for the book that had been lost for so many hundred years. Consequently we will begin our elimination with Ezra, Joel, Chronicles, Nehemiah, Ecclesiastes, Daniel, Malachi and Jonah, because these works were written after the Jews had been freed from their bondage in Persia, and, in fact, long after Ezra had died and their temple had been completed. We must also throw out those beautiful poetical works, the Psalms, Lamentations and the Song of Solomon, as well as the whole of those profound philosophical aphorisms that are contained in the Book of Proverbs.

We shall also have to eliminate Samuel, Ruth, Esther, Judges, Kings, Micah, Amos, Hosea, and, in fact, we are compelled to exclude the whole of the various works, or books, that go to make up the canon of the Old Testament, with the exception of the first five books, or the Pentateuch, which is composed of Genesis, Exodus, Leviticus, Numbers and Deuteronomy. Joshua may have been written at about the same time that the preceding works were composed; but we will leave Joshua aside, and continue our search in the Pentateuch for the long lost Book of the Law.

There is one thing that is positively certain, and that is, previous to the exile, there was no Old Testament such as we have to-day. There was, however, a great many writings no doubt held in great veneration by the Jewish people. The first form that all these promiscuous and scattered writings assumed was the Pentateuch, or the first five books compiled and bound together into one volume, which was really and truly a compendium of History and Law, beginning with the Creation of the Universe in Exodus, and ending with the death of Moses in Deuteronomy. These five books have been generally ascribed to Moses, but from the general concensus of opinions of various authorities, I find that no less than four different people were the authors of these books. In order to converge them, and make them appear the work of one hand, the redactor was compelled to put in additions of his own writings, so as to make them appear and read as one continuous history. But if you will go over these works carefully, you will easily discover where they have been pieced or connected together. After they were completed and formed into one volume it was called and known as "The law."

There are three distinct legal codes in the Pentateuch, and yet not one of them refers to either of the others, and in some cases they are contradictory. Now this fact alone would most assuredly prove that they were written by different authors. The *first* collection is said to have been given by God to Moses at Mount Sinai, and is known as the "*Book of the Covenant*," see Exodus, chapter 20. For an account of the *second*, see Leviticus, chapter 26. The *third* and last code, we find in Deuteronomy, was given to Moses on the East side of Jordan, Deuteronomy chapter 4, verse 44 to end of chapter, just before his death in the Land of Moab, in sight of the promised land, that the Lord showed unto Moses, but into which He would not permit him to enter, *see* Deut. 34.

I do not desire to enter into a discussion upon the statement that "*Moses was not the sole author of the Pentateuch*," but simply say that any companion who is in doubt upon this subject can easily verify the assertion by searching for the proof and judging for himself.

From the above we find that the Old Testament begins with the creation of the world and ends with the prophets, some time during the fourth century B. C. After the Babylonian captivity we also find that a compilation of these writings were collated, and thus formed the Canon of the Old Testament. In our search for the "Book of the Law" we have been compelled to cut out nearly all the books of that sacred volume in order to discover that which had been lost.

We now find ourselves with the Pentateuch, which contains three distinct Legal Codes, to which I have already referred. One of these must be the " Book of the Law," for they existed long before Solomon lived and reigned, and it was no doubt one of these that was deposited in the ark of the covenant with the Pot of Manna and the Budding Rod. I have not gone into this subject as deeply as I would wish, but I have given you a very cursory account of my search for the " Book of the Law," and thus I leave it in your hands for you to make your own deductions.

There is one thing, my dear friends and companions, that I am sure that we shall agree upon, and that is, the Canon of the Old Testament is not the " Book of the Law." In the closing words of this chapter I wish to call your attention to the fact that *Hilkiah the High Priest found and examined the " Book of the Law "* that was long lost, but now found, which *he handed to Shaphan the Scribe*, who also examined it and *passed it on to the King*, who exclaimed, " HOLINESS TO THE LORD."

Circumcision—Upon what the Ancient Craftsmen were Obligated—The Lost Word.

Hail, Ushas, daughter of the sky,
  Who, borne upon thy shining car
  By ruddy steeds from realms afar,
And ever lightening, drawing nigh:

Sweetly thou smilest, goddess fair,
  Disclosing all thy youthful grace,
  Thy bosom, thy radiant face,
And lustre of thy golden hair;

(So shines a fond and winning bride,
  Who robes her form in brilliant guise,
  And to her lord's admiring eyes
Displays her charms with conscious pride;

Or virgin by her mother decked,
  Who, glorying in her beauty, shows
  In every glance, her power she knows
All eyes to fix, all hearts subject;

Or actress, who, by skill in song
  And dance, and graceful gestures light
  And many-colored vestures bright,
Enchants the eager, gazing throng;

Or maid who, wont her limbs to lave
  In some cool stream among the woods,
  Where never vulgar eye intrudes,
Emerges fairer from the wave);

But closely by the amorous sun
  Pursued, and vanquished in the race,
  Thou soon art locked in his embrace,
And with him blendest into one.
          —*Paraphrased from the Rig Veda by Dr. Muir.*

CHAPTER XXVI.

CIRCUMCISION—UPON WHAT THE ANCIENT CRAFTSMEN WERE OBLIGATED—THE LOST WORD.

THE "Book of the Law" engaged our attention in the closing part of the preceding chapter, but I desire further to state that the Canon of the Old Testament was not and could not have been in existence during the reign of either David King of Israel, or his son Solomon, and that there were only a few scattered and promiscuous writings which were no doubt held as sacred by a great many people at that time. These writings composed a history and a variety of legal codes that were considered to have been written by Moses, and were known as the Pentateuch or the "Law of Moses," but which I have clearly proven were written by different people and at different times.

Now my dear Brothers and Friends, if there was no Bible in existence when David bought the land upon which to erect a temple to the most High God of Israel, or when our three Grand Masters laid its foundation, and only a few scattered and promiscuous writings were in existence, to which I have referred,—upon what were our ancient Brethren obligated at the building of the "House of the Lord?" Aye and long centuries before Moses received the "Decalogue" from God on Mount Sinai, or the Jews were a people!

This is a question that has often been asked me and one that I think will interest the "Royal Craft" wherever dispersed. Now my dear Fraters, we will endeavor to find the answer to that question. We know positively that those Craftsmen who wrought at the building of the Temple could not have been obligated upon the Bible, or the "Book of the Law," because they did not exist at that time. Therefore in order to find the answer to the question, we must look into the writings of those people which give us an account of the building of Solomon's Temple, its dimensions, etc. From the same source we will endeavor to find something pertaining to the Oaths and Obligations which were used at, or about the time this Temple was built on Mount Moriah. There is one thing certain and that is those people who lived at that time must have assumed obligations, and were sworn upon something which they considered to be the most sacred symbol known, upon which they took their solemn and binding obligations. In order to find what that symbol or emblem was, we will search the writings of the ancient Hebrews. One of the most sacred symbols or emblems that was known to the ancient Hebrew was the organs of generation or man's trinity. This fact is demonstrated through all the scriptures and ancient writings of the Jewish people.

We find that there is a great deal of importance placed by God upon the virile organs of man, so much so that we find in Genesis 17 : 2 that God informs Abraham that He would make a covenant with him and his chosen people, and the sign of the covenant was the circumcision of every male child among the Jewish people. Now God was very particular that this covenant should be kept by each and every one who belonged to the " chosen few," for we find in Exodus 4 : 24 that God would have slain the son of Moses, if his mother *Zipporah* had not mutilated her child with a sharp rock. Thus we find that God, himself, looked upon the virile organs, of every man among the Hebrews, to see that the covenant was kept to the very letter, thus compelling the " Children of Israel " to keep their covenant with him. But the case of Moses' son was not an isolated one, for when the Israelites fled from out the Land of Egypt and out of the House of Bondage, there were a great many who had been born in the wilderness, during their long wanderings, and who had not been subjected to the knife when they had reached the required eight days. The Lord knew it, and he commanded Joshua to " make sharp knives and circumcise again the children of Israel the second time," together with those who had never felt the knife. *See* Joshua, Chapter 5, Verses 2 to 5.

One of the strongest proofs to me of the sacredness of the generative organs of man, is in the beginning of the twenty-third chapter of Deuteronomy where we are told that he who is wounded in those parts, or by some unfortunate accident loses his organs of generation could not enter into the congregation of the Lord. In fact no one of the house of

Aaron was allowed to minister at the altar of the Lord if his generative organs were not perfect. *See* Leviticus 21 : 20.

From the above we find that the trinity of man (virile organs) was looked upon as something different from the other parts of the body, and hence was held as the most sacred symbol or emblem known to the ancient Hebrews. Such things being the case, we search and find that in the days of Abraham and Jacob, the people swore by, or upon, those organs of generation, or creative powers, for the simple reason that they considered the trinity of man to be emblematic of God the Creator. Through all the writings of these people we find this fact demonstrated, for instance, in Genesis, Chapter 24, Verse 2, we find the patriarch Abraham telling the chief of all his servants to "put I pray thee thy hand under my thigh," and swear by the Lord God of heaven to do his (Abraham's) bidding. Again we find in Genesis 47 : 29 that Jacob asks the same thing of Joseph, "put I pray thee thy hand under my thigh," when he made him swear to take him out of the " Land of Egypt " and bury him with his father, and Joseph obligated himself upon the generative organs of his father Jacob. Under the thigh, or loins signified upon the trinity of man, or the organs of generation.

Inman in his " Ancient Pagan and Modern Christian Symbolism," tells us that "' under my thigh,' is a euphemism for the words ' upon the symbol of the Creator.' I may point to two or three other passages in which the *thigh* (translated in the authorized version—loins) is used periphrastically : Genesis 46 : 26 and Exodus 1 : 5. See Ginsburg in Kitto's *Biblical Cyclopædia*, Vol. III, page 348, *s. v.* Oath.

" I have on two occasions read, although I failed to make a note of it, that an Arab during the Franco-Egyptian war, when accused by General Kleber of treachery, not only vehemently denied it, but when he saw himself still distrusted, he uncovered himself before the whole military staff, and swore upon his trinity that he was guiltless."

Throughout the whole of the Eastern countries, in the dim dawn of prehistoric ages, as well as at the present day, the virile organs of man, were and are held in the greatest of veneration by the different peoples of those countries. And I do most firmly believe that long before their sacred writings were in existence, the craftsmen of those ancient days were most assuredly obligated upon either his own trinity, or the phallus, or

39

linga stone, a symbol of the procreative forces of Nature. If the candidate was not sworn upon either of the above, he would most certainly have to be obligated upon their emblem, such as the—Sun, a flame, a burning torch, an erect serpent, or a tree, or stone that represented the phallus or creative powers of Man.

Throughout the whole of India the phallic worship is still practiced, as in the days of Guatama Buddha. This peculiar worship is still going on in nearly all the temples of India, and can be witnessed by any one in a great many of the temples, but not in all of them.

I remember sitting one day at the end of the temple of Elephanta in India, trying to decipher some ancient inscriptions, when a party of young women came into the sanctuary of the god Siva, who in this instance was represented under the symbol of the Linga stone, or the generative organ. They approached it and making their obeisance, scattered flowers before it, and pouring water (from out a chattie or small brass vessel that they carried with them) upon the stone one of them adjusted her dress, mounted the stone, muttered a few prayers or mantras and retired, when another took her place and repeated the performance. Before the last of them had finished her devotions I came out from the shadow and watched them. They did not seem to heed my presence at all, but kept on chatting with one another until all had paid their devotions to the God Siva.

But I do not wish to enter into a long discussion upon the phallic worship, but simply inform you of the great veneration that is given to the creative organs in India and all those eastern countries. They certainly believed it to be the most sacred emblem in existence and for that reason, as well as those above stated, I believe that the ancient craftsmen were obligated upon either their own trinity, or its symbol, long before and after their sacred writings were known.

No matter upon what the candidate was to be obligated the right hand should always be brought in contact with the sacred symbol of the Deity. In case that symbol was the sun, moon, star, or flowing river or something that could not be touched, the right hand would be held toward the object, with the palm forward and fingers unclosed. This mode of obligation refers to the most ancient days when the Vedas of India, the Zend-Avesta of the Parsees, and the Rituals of the Ancient

INTERIOR VIEW OF THE CAVE TEMPLE OF ELEPHANTA

BOMBAY, INDIA.

Egyptians were not known or written. But when the Vedas, Zend-Avesta, Rituals, Pentateuch, Koran, etc., were known and recognized as communications from the Deity, they eventually took the place of those more ancient methods, although they were often used conjointly.

Fort, in his " Early History and Antiquities of Freemasonry," tells us at page 193, *et seq*: " An oath of secrecy was administered to all initiates, and their secret conclaves were held at certain times and places. After the candidate had been properly instructed in the elements of the craft, the old manuscripts inform us, then one of the Seniors or Wardens held the book or holy-dome, and the initiate placing his hand upon it, took upon himself a solemn obligation to conceal all that he had previously been instructed in, and that he would endeavor to preserve the the charges of a Mason which were recited to him. . . . . Everything adopted for this purpose was presumed to be endowed with a high degree of holiness, and to such extreme was this conception carried, that a slave or bondman was debarred from the oath in its prescribed form.

" It was an almost invariable practice among the Norse nations to take the most sacred oaths with the face turned toward the rising Sun, and with the hand and fingers upraised. In the Seamund Edda, an oath was taken with the face to the southern sun. As previously stated, these obligations were assumed with the hand resting upon, or touching some material object. In nearly all cases this substance was adapted to the particular custom of a province, or was any animate or inanimate thing readily procured. Pagans swore with the hand grasping a blood smeared ring; Christians obligated themselves by the cross, relics of saints, by the book (missal) and bell; the latter was in consecrated use during ecclesiastic services. Ancient Scandinavians swore upon their swords, frequently by grass and trees, as appears from the following citation :

> ' Glasgerion swore a full grete othe,
> By oake; and ashe and thorne.'

" Oaths were also attested by water, fountains and streams, by rocks, cliffs and stones—the latter sometimes white, but the most sacred and binding obligation was made upon a blue stone altar. Ancient Northmen swore upon Thor's hammer. It was no unusual thing for persons solemnly to attest an oath by the beard, hair and eyes, or with the hand upon vestments. A judicial obligation was administered by touching the judge's staff of office. And for the same reason that warriors swore by the sword, also other people, in the less exciting spheres of domestic life, used house furniture. For example, travelers grasped the wagon-wheel, and horsemen their stirrups; sailors rested the hand upon the ship's railing. Operative masons or stonecutters, of the Middle Ages, perpetuated the Scandinavian custom of swearing upon common utensils, and used their tools in the solemn formality of an obligation—a usage still adhered to by the modern craft.

"The right hand was considered indispensable in mediæval oaths, to seize or touch the consecrated object. Frequently the hand was upraised in order to bring it in contact with the material object sworn by, and at the same time kneeling, divested of hat and weapon, was an essential element in the ceremony of assuming an oath. Ancient Jews called upon the holy name in attestation of the solemnity of their obligation, with the hand placed indifferently above or beneath the thigh. But the most impressive oath taken by the Israelites, was that in and by the sacred name of Jehova."

We also find on page 171, of this same work, that "The charges recited were binding upon each and every member of the Masonic fraternity, and were sworn to be observed to the utmost, under the sanction of God, the holy-dome, and upon the Book." In a note below we find a reference to the *holy-dome* which reads as follows: "Evidently derived from a very old form of administering an oath, upon the shrine in which the sacred relics of some martyred saint were enclosed. The chest or box in which these bones were contained was usually constructed in imitation of a small house. Hence *holy*, with direct reference to the sanctity of the relics, and *domus* (Latin for house) by gradual elision into holidomus, later holy-dome."

One of the most interesting subjects to me in Masonry has been the Tradition of the LOST WORD, which we are told was lost, and that a substitute word is given that is to be used until future generations shall recover the original. Now, I claim that the "Word" was never lost, and that this "Word" has always been in use, not only in the first three degrees, but in the Royal Arch as well, where we shall find it distinctly pronounced. Therefore, in order that you may be enabled to come to a thorough understanding of the "Lost Word," I will write upon this matter for your especial edification.

There is an ancient Masonic legend that informs us that "Enoch, under the inspirations of the Most High, built a secret temple underground, consisting of *nine* vaults or arches, situated perpendicularly under each other. A triangular plate of gold, each side of which was a cubit long, and enriched with precious stones, was fixed to a stone of *agate* of the same form. On this plate of gold was engraved the 'word' or true name of God; and this was placed on a cubical stone, and deposited in the *ninth*, or *lowest*, arch. In consequence of the deluge, all knowledge of this secret temple was lost, together with the sacred and ineffable or unutterable name, for ages. The long-lost word was subsequently found in this long-forgotten subterranean temple by David, when digging the foundation for the temple afterward built by Solomon his son." Tradition informs us that once a year the High Priest of the temple would perform the most solemn ceremonies and purify himself for the express purpose of pronouncing the True Name, the grand Omnific Word, by which the sins of the children of Israel would be atoned for.

This mysterious Word was always spoken amid the clashing of cymbals, or a great noise made by the people, in order to drown the intonations of the Grand Word, when uttered by the *one* man of the Jewish peoples who was allowed to do so, and this man was the Grand High-Priest himself. Long before the day of the Atonement approached the High-Priest would purify himself by fasting and other most solemn ceremonies that had to be performed in solitude and prayer. Everything depended upon him being pure himself, for upon this rested his power of performing the ceremonies and receiving the forgiveness of the sins of the children of Israel. If the prescribed rites and ceremonies were not conformed to, the result would bring upon the High-Priest instantaneous death, consequently he would be very particular, and when all things were ready and the time had arrived, he would pass into the temple, and in solemn silence proceed into the middle chamber, the Sanctum Sanctorum, or Holy of Holies, where he would retire behind the veil, and stand in the Divine Light, the resplendent presence of the Deity himself. Then and there, in and by the light of the Shekinah, he would pronounce the sacred name that had been placed there by Divine command (*see* 1st

Kings, 9 : 3), and by that name alone he would ask for the forgiveness of the sins of the children of Israel.

"The Jews consider the True Name of God to be irrecoverably lost by disuse, and regard its pronunciation as one of the mysteries that will be revealed at the coming of their Messiah. And they attribute its loss to the illegality of applying the Masoretic points to so sacred a name by which a knowledge of the proper vowels is forgotten."

In reading this account, one would imagine that the sacred word belonged solely and exclusively to the Hebrew peoples, but in our researches we find that it also belongs to the Indian, Mazdean and Ancient Egyptian Mysteries, and that it originated in the "Land of the Vedas."

The Word was also found in the Phœnician Creed, as in all those of Asia, a Word of God, written in starry characters, by the planetary Divinities and communicated by the Demi-Gods, as a profound mystery, to the higher classes of the human race, to be communicated by them to mankind and created the world. The faith of the Phœnicians was an emanation from that ancient worship of the Stars, which is the creed of Zoroaster alone, and is connected with a faith in one God. Light and Fire are the most important agents in the Phœnician faith. There is a race of children of the Light. They adored the Heaven with its Lights, deeming it the Supreme God.

The Mysteries among the Chinese and Japanese came from India, and were founded on the same principle, and with similar rites. The word given to the new Initiate was *O-mi-to Fo*, in which we recognize the A. U. M. of the ancient Hindu which represented their trinity of Brahma, Vishnu and Siva. The code of Manu, Book II, 265 — states that: "The Primitive Holy Syllable, composed of three letters, in which the Vedic Triad is comprised, is to be kept secret as another Triple Veda; HE who knows the mystic value of this Syllable, knows the Veda."

Albert Pike in "Morals and Dogmas," pp. 584, says that: "ATHOM or ATHOM-RE, was the Chief and Oldest Supreme God of Upper Egypt, worshipped at Thebes; the same as the O. M. or A. U. M. of the Hindū, whose name was unpronounceable, and who, like the *Brehm* of the latter people, was 'The Being that was, and is, and is to come; the Great God, the Great Omnipotent, Omniscient, and Omnipresent One, the Greatest in the Universe, the Lord;' whose emblem was a perfect sphere, showing

PYLON OF TEMPLE,

KARNAK.

that He was first, last, midst, and without end; superior to all Nature-Gods, and all personifications of Powers, Element, and Luminaries; symbolized by Light, the Principle of Life."

A. U. M. is the profound salutation of the Aryan Adept, son of the Fifth Race, who always begins and ends his devotional concentrations, or appeals to non-human Presences with this triliteral word which represents, the for ever concealed primeval triune differentiation, not *from*, but *in*, the ONE ABSOLUTE, and is therefore symbolized by the Tetractys (or the 4, thus: 1+2-3+4=10), which was the symbol of the Kosmos, as containing within itself, the point, the line, the superficies, the solid; in other words, the essentials of all forms. Its mystical representation is the point within the triangle. The Decad, or perfect number, is contained in the Four as above stated.

"OM-MANI" murmurs the Turanian Adept, the descendant of the Fourth Race, and after pausing he adds "PADME-HUM." This famous invocation is very erroneously translated, by the Orientalists, as meaning, "*O the Jewel in the Lotus*." For although literally, OM is a syllable sacred to the Deity, PADME means "in the Lotus," and "MANI" is any precious stone; still, neither the words themselves, nor their symbolical meaning are thus really correctly rendered.

In this, the most sacred of Eastern formulas, not only has every syllable a secret potency, producing a definite result, but the whole invocation has seven different meanings, and can produce seven distinct results, each of which may differ from the other. The seven meanings, and the seven results depend upon the intonation which is given to the whole formula, and to each of its syllables; and even the numerical value of the letters is added to or diminished, according as such or another rythm, is made use of. Let the student remember that number underlies form, and number guides sound and that Number lies at the root of the manifested Universe.

The mystic sentence, "*Om Mani Padme Hum*," when rightly understood, instead of being composed of the almost meaningless words, "O, the Jewel in the Lotus," contains a reference to the indissoluble union between Man and the Universe, rendered in seven different ways and having the capability of seven different applications, to as many planes of thought and action.

From whatever aspect we examine it, it means: "I am that I am;" "I am in thee, and thou art in me," or esoterically, "O, my God within me.". For there is, most certainly, a God in each human being, for man was and will re-become God. The sentence points to the indissoluble union between Man and the Universe. For the Lotus is the universal symbol of Kosmos as the absolute totality, and the Jewel is Spiritual Man or God. To the student who would delve into the *Vedas* and study the Esoteric Sciences with double object: (*a*) of proving Man to be identical in spiritual, and physical essence with both the Absolute Principle, and with God in Nature; and (*b*) of demonstrating the presence in him of the same potential powers as exist in the creative forces in Nature—to such an one a perfect knowledge of the correspondences between Colors, Sounds, and Numbers is the first requisite. As already said, the sacred formula of the Far East, "*Om Mani Padme Hum,*" is the one best calculated to make these correspondential qualities and functions clear to the learned.

The Veda seems nonsensical to us, only so far as we do not understand and read it aright. It is the oldest monument of human thought, the most venerable record in the world; and if it contains, as I think it does, those philosophical ideas that are reproduced and developed in our philosophy and religion, then it is the most interesting monument of human thought.

"We owe to *it* and the Zend-Avesta, and not to the Hebrew Books all our philosophical ideas about God, the immortality of the Soul, and the Trinity, and the doctrines taught by St. John and St. Paul." And Masonry owes to them her Symbols and the doctrines of which these are the symbols, as I have explained before. The Sacred Monosyllable is unquestionably concealed in certain symbolic Words in Free Masonry; and Aryan Migrations and Victories, no doubt, made it known to the sages all over the Orient.

It is for this reason that I have gone into the subject, so that you, my dear Brothers and Friends, may gain "More Light" on the so-called "Lost Word."

There is no question in my mind, but the real Word belonged to the Aryan race, long centuries before it was separated into the Iran, and Indu-Aryan branches, who originally formed the one great Aryan people and the Irano-Aryan branch carried away with them the esoteric knowledge that was common to both. Thus we find it in the *Agni, Ushas, Mithra* of the Fire worshippers, as their God and his manifestations of which we shall speak later on.

Brother J. D. Buck, 32°, states in his "Mystic Masonry," page 244, *et seq.:* "In the Tetragrammaton, or four lettered name of the Deity, the Greek followers of Pythagoras found a glyphic by which they both expressed and concealed their philosophy, and it is the Hebrew tetrad IHVH or—'Yod, hé, vau, hé,' that is introduced into Masonry with the Pythagorean art speech. The devout Hebrew, in reading the sacred Text, when he came to the sacred tetrad IHVH, substituted the word *Adonai* (Lord), and if the word was written with the points of Alhim, he called it *Elohom.* This custom is preserved in Masonry by giving the candidate a substitute for the Master's Word. The Hebrew tetrad 'Yod, hé, vau, hé,' is produced by repeating the 'hé.' The root word is a triad, and the quaternary is undoubtedly a blind. The Sacred Word is found in the mysteries as a binary, a trinary, and a quaternary; as with the Hindoos we have the OM and the *Aum,* indicating different methods of pronouncing the sacred name. The Pythagorean Tetraktys is represented by numbers, 1, 2, 3, 4 = 10, and by points or 'Yods' in the form of a triangle; this is called the 'lesser tetraktys' while a triangle composed of eight rows in the same form and containing thirty-six 'Yods,' or points, is called the 'greater Tetraktys.' This corresponds to the three lesser lights, and the three greater lights of the Blue Lodge, though the monitorial explanations in the lodge are, to say the least, incomplete. In the Pythagorean philosophy both the lesser and the greater tetraktys are represented by equilateral triangles, and the points, in either case, form the angles of a series of lesser triangles. In the lesser tetraktys these triangles are altogether nine, or three times three. In the greater they count forty-nine, or seven times seven; and in each case the series runs from the apex to the base, 1, 3, 5, for the lesser, and 1, 3, 5, 7, 9, 11, 13 for the greater tetraktys, or by a series of odd numbers: while the points before the triangles are formed, run consecutively, 1, 2, 3, 4, 5, 6, 7, 8. These symbols were thus used as 'odd' and 'even' to carry a philosophical meaning and to illustrate the doctrine of Emanation.

A great many Masons are under the impression that the sacred Tetragrammaton, the four lettered name of the Hebrew God, generally pronounced *Jehovah*, to be the true word, but in that they are greatly mistaken, for the Grand Omnific Word existed long before the Hebrews were a people.

Now if the long lost Word was really and truly a word, it could be just as well concealed in the name of the Hebrew Deity, as in any other. But the word we are searching for belongs to the ancient days, when the Aryan race separated into the Indo and Irano Aryans, and the *Word* belonged to both, and we find that it was carried away by the great ancestors of the Persian Magi. At the same time it was retained by the Ancient Brahmans in India, and although we may not know the true pronunciation of the Word, we do most certainly believe that its symbol is A. U. M.

Brother Buck says that, " the Hebrews seem to have derived their Tetraktys from the Chaldo-Egyptian Mysteries, and these may be traced to the Zoroastrian Fire Philosophy, till finally the Word is A∴ U∴ M∴ In both Persian or Zend and in Sanscrit, these three letters are found in many names that designate fire, flame, spirit, essence, etc. This again is glyphic form of expression. Every emanation is a trinity; and Fire, Flame, and Light are the most perfect synthesis of this tri-unity. Consider the expressions, 'The Lord is a consuming fire;' 'Since God is Light, and never but in unapproached Light dwelt from eternity,' etc.

" The symbol is found in all Scriptures, but only in the Mysteries was the meaning thus symbolized made known. Here, then, is the origin of all the *trinities* found in Masonry, the plainest of which are the *trinities* of Light, and the most superficial explanations are found connected with the three lesser Lights of the Lodge."

Brother Albert Pike, quoting from the sacred writings of the far East says : " He who knows the Mystic value of the Syllable knows the Names of which it is the sign and hieroglyph and the doctrine which these names express and teach, knows the Vedas. For they are the expression of those thoughts, and are comprised in the Trinity of which the Word is the sign and representation. The Word *is* the three Names. It, A. U. M., is the Trinity, as Ahura is the Deity. And this Trinity is the essence of the three Vedas, that which has expressed itself in them and whose out-flowings as thoughts they are. It was THE Vedas, before they were uttered, and when they existed in IT as thoughts unuttered. And that it is the essence of all Speech and Words, means that it is the divine Intellect, of which all human intellects are rays, and all Speech and Words the utterance of these intellects."

Triliteral words are supposed to have originated with the birth of the Aryan race, and to that end I have delved into the ancient writing of many peoples, in order to verify that statement. I soon began to realize that the word A. U. M. is the oldest and most sacred word known to man, and I firmly believe that it came down to us from a language that antedates all others known to us to-day. I further believe the source from which it emanated to have been the lost continent of Atlantis.

Donnelly tells us in his "Atlantis" that "Modern civilization is Atlantean. Without the thousands of years of development which were had in Atlantis, modern civilization could not have existed. The inventive faculty of the present age is taking up the great delegated work of creation where Atlantis left it thousands of years ago."

Our very learned Brother, Albert Pike, also states: " That the Word A. U. M. is the oldest Sacred and Ineffable Word, only to be lettered, of which we have any hint in history or etymology; that it belonged to a language older than any now known to us by any monumental records, and of which the Sanscrit, Zend, Persian, Arabic, Phœnician, Egyptian, Assyrian, and Hebrew were but dialects; that it was a Sacred Word in the Paropamisus [a ridge of mountains at the North of India, called the *Stony Girdle*, or Indian Caucasus—The Author], or Tartary beyond the Himalayas, before the emigrations into Southern Hindustan, Persia, Egypt or Chaldea, by which the Aryan Race flowed forth from their northern homes; and that, by these and other successive emigrations, it was conveyed everywhere with the mysteries.

" In the Punjab, the oldest Vedic Hymns were composed, and being compiled with some later ones, thousands of years afterwards, became the Rig-Veda, in ten Parts or Books called Mandalas. After most of these had been composed, the Indo-Aryans occupied the Ganges country, conquering the dark-skinned native tribes as they advanced, until they reached the Indian Ocean; and, in the meantime, the Brahmanic religion grew up among them, and the Veda, wholly misunderstood, became the source or cause of a thousand monstrously absurd legends and grave superstitions.

"Even now, the Brahmanic Commentators only for the most part mistranslate and misinterpret the Veda; and not one among them, nor a single European Commentator knows what many of the texts mean, nor what any of the Vedic Deities (except three or four unmistakable ones) really were. Hundreds of texts are a perfect enigma yet, to all of them. Hundreds more they all misunderstand.

"As to the word OM, there is not a Brahman in the world, nor a scholar or Commentator in Europe or America, that knows its real origin or what it meant and means."

The word A. U. M. is the original of _Amen._ Now amen is not a Hebrew term, but, like the word Hallelujah, was borrowed by the Jews, and Greeks from the Chaldeans. The latter word is often found repeated in certain magical inscriptions upon cups and urns among the Babylonian and Ninivean relics. Amen does not mean "_so be it_" or "_verily_," but signified in the hoary antiquity of prehistoric ages almost the same as A. U. M. The Jewish Tanaim (Initiate) used it for the same reason as the Aryan Adepts use A. U. M., and with a like success. The numerical value of A M e N in Hebrew letters being ninety-one, the same as the full value of Y H V H, twenty-six, and A D O N a Y, sixty-five, or taken together, ninety-one. Both words mean the affirmation of the being, or existence, of the sexless "Lord" within us. The Yod hé vau hé, Y H V H, or male-female on the terrestrial plane, as invented by the Jews, and now made out to mean _Jehovah,_ but which signifies in reality and literally "giving being" and "receiving life."

The "Secret Doctrine" tells us that "Esoteric Science teaches that every sound in the visible world awakens its corresponding sound in the invisible realms, and arouses to action some force or other on the occult side of nature. Moreover, every sound corresponds to a color, and a number (a potency spiritual, psychic or physical) and to a sensation on some plane. All these find an echo in every one of the so far developed elements, and even on the terrestrial plane, in the Lives that swarm in the terrene atmosphere, thus prompting them to action."

Brother Albert Pike informs us that "this mystic word was perpetuated among the Hebrews, for those who understood, by the word _Amn_ or *Amen*, for ages meaningless to all men, and all explanations of which hitherto have been absurdities, at first intentionally so; though it is identically the name of the Egyptian Mediator-God, the Lamb of God, or ram-headed Deity, AMun. In Buddha or Krishna the mysterious child, new Incarnation of the Divine Creative Wisdom, the First-begotten, the First Emanation, the Logos or Word, were the three persons of the Trimurti or Indian Deity, and each was the sacred mysterious never-to-be-spoken OM, symbolized by the *Palm-tree* and the Phœnix.

"The same word is also found in the Greek Ompha and Omphalos, and in the Hebrew word Omn-u-Al which we absurdly read Immanuel or Emanuel. Bacchus, too, was called Omadion. In the sign of the Planet Mercury, Representative of Hermes Trismegistos and of Khûmm, the Mediator of the Trinity of Schlomoth, or Wisdom. the Divine Intellect, Khûmm the Monarch, or the Divine Power, and himself, we find the three persons of the Oriental Trinity, in the Circle, the Crescent, and the Cross (☿ ', the Circle representing the Divine Generative Energy, the Crescent the Productive Capacity and the Cross the uttered Universe. A. U. M. or O. M. is emphatically called, by the Brahmins, the monosyllable ' I. A. M.' says Krishna, in the *Ghita*, ' of things transient, the Beginning, the Middle and the End; I. A. M. the monosyllable among words.' A Brahmin, says Manu, ' beginning and ending a lecture on the Veda, must always pronounce to himself the syllable O M.'

" This word was only permitted to be pronounced by the letters, for its pronunciation as one word was said to make earth tremble, and even the angels of Heaven to quake for fear. It was not the word that contained the secret meaning, but the separate letters of the word, as in the case with the Hebrew word A. G. L. A., which is the initials of four words that compose a phrase; and with אביע, composed of the initials of the names of the four ' Worlds,' Atsiluth, Briah, Yetsirah and Asiah."

The A and the O were the good and the evil Principle of the Median Magi of Zoroaster, and Manes, the Light, and the Shadow or Darkness. Also they represented the Male Energy and Female Productive Capacity; whence, in the Kabalah, the Sephira Benignity is represented as Male, and the Sephira Severity as Female. Hence, also, we find them, and the whole Sacred word, in the Latin verb AMO, *I love;*

as in the name of the Great Egyptian God Athom, and in the Median and Persian Ormuzd, Ahriman and Mithras.

Sir Monier Williams informs us in his "Brahmanism and Hinduism" that "this most sacred of all Hindu utterances, made up of the three letters A. U. M., and symbolical of the triple manifestation of the Supreme Being in the Tri-murti or Triad of gods, Brahma, Vishnu and Siva, is constantly repeated. It is as sacred as the name Jehovah with the Jews, but not too sacred for utterance.

"Manu describes it as a monosyllable, imperishable and eternal as the Supreme Being himself. After Om comes the utterance of the names of the three worlds, Earth (Bhūr), Atmosphere (Bhuvah), Heaven (Svar), to which are often added the four higher heavens, Mahah, Janah, Tapah and Satya. The utterances of these seven names—called the seven Vyāhritis—preceded in each case by the syllable Om, is an act of homage to all the beings inhabiting the seven worlds. It is supposed to induce purity of thought, and to prepare the worshipper for offering up his first prayer."

The Bactrian King Zarathustra (Golden Splendor) was called by the Greeks Zoroaster. He revived the ancient religion of Ahura Mazda and developed an extinct civilization that had existed thousands of years before Zarathustra was born. This hoary civilization existed on the Plateau of Iran, that extends from the valley of the Indus to the valley of the Euphrates on its western boundary and the whole surrounded by vast mountain ranges. It derived its name Iran from the original name of the Race "*Eron*," who first settled upon that high table land, that is located between the Hindoo Kush and river Oxus. This location may be said to be the cradle of the religion of both the Medes and Persians, and also the birth place of Zarathustra himself. The date of this extinct civilization is lost in the hoary ages of antiquity, and like the birth of this celebrated Adept, king and reformer, it is very difficult to find the exact date.

Our revered Brother, Albert Pike, in his FILIATION OF IDEAS, tells us that, "Aristoteles and Eudoxus, according to Plinius, place Zarathustra six thousand years before the death of Plato; Hermippus five thousand years before the Trojan War. Plato died 348 B. C., so that the two dates substantially agree, making the date of Zarathustra six thousand three hundred, or six thousand three hundred and fifty years before our era. Baron Bunsen, whose faith as a Christian is unimpeachable, assigns a date several thousand years earlier than that, to the first Aryan Emigration; while he assigns to the legendary Egyptian King Menes only the date of 3,645 B.C. It is certain that Zarathustra lived in Bactria, and that many ages passed before the Iranian race had so increased as to have emigrated to and conquered in succession Margiana, Parthia, Media and Persia, and to have become the great and wealthy and luxurious people over whom Kurush (Cyrus) and Darayvuch (Darius) reigned."

Ahura Mazda was, to Zarathustra, precisely what God is to us, a Spirit (in the vagueness of that word); a Power, Force and Person, yet not cognizable by the intellect, and of whom no definition could be attempted. He was THE FATHER, in the sense in which the equivalent of that word was then used. Fire being his "Son," He was Father of the Fire, *i. e.*, its Source and Producer; the SUBSTANCE from which it flowed forth, the Source of His Emanations. Aditi, Space, was Mother of the Planets, because in it their being began. Daksh, Strength, was Father of the Fire, because it caused the friction that produced the Fire from the wood; as Rudra, the potency of Fire which causes rarefaction, and ascension, and movements in the air, was "Father" of the Winds.

Zarathustra's Avesta ("the Law") or the Zend-Avesta ("Comment on the Law") embodies a great deal that had been written in the early language of the ancient Persians, consequently it is of the greatest importance to all those philologists who are desirous of comparing the various early Aryan tongues. The ethics and religious teachings of these ancient people are also of the greatest importance, especially to those who are interested in the religion of the oldest inhabitants of Iran or ancient Persia.

The language in which the Zend-Avesta was originally written, from all we can learn, was with the arrow head, or wedge shaped cuneiform letters like those that are still to be found carved upon the rocks in Persia, where they are to be seen to-day, perfectly legible, although they have been forgotten for more than two thousand years. They have remained there perfectly unintelligible, until our Scholars and Students have discovered their real meaning, consequently we are enabled to interpret and understand the dead language of these people, just as we are enabled to decipher and comprehend the meaning of the hieroglyphics that belonged to the ancient Egyptians. Thus we are enabled to compare Zarathustra's system of Theology.

Ahura-Mazda or Ormuzd was worshipped as the Wise and Good principle that dominated the Kosmos, and he is always represented by fire, light, or the sun, which was called by these ancient people the Son of Ahura-Mazda, who was himself the Supreme Diety of the followers of Zarathustra.

Albert Pike says that " Ahura-Mazda, the Light-Radiance, was the Supreme God, the God of Gods, Source, Origin, Creator, Father of All; the Light, his Manifestations, and Out-shining, the Celestial Luminaries His Creatures through and by which produced from Him, He revealed Himself, His Self as Light Essence.

"Cpenta Mainyu, was His Intellect-Self, God as Intelligence or Mind, the Divine Intellect, considered as a Person but imminent in the Deity. And Vohu-Manô Mind-being Intellect with outward being, the Divine Intellect, Cpenta Mainyu, revealed, and acting in the Universe was the Utterence, Effluence, Emanation, Out-flowing of the Divine Wisdom; the Logos or Word of Plato, St. John and the Gnostics.

" Vohu-Manô reveals Himself in every Aryan Intellect. All good Thought, all true Intelligence is Vohu-Manô inspiring Humanity and revealing Himself in it. The Mantras, or Prayers, Hymns and all good, and righteous Words, the Vedas, and Gathas, are His 'deeds,' his utterances, his Words and Speech."

Let me quote you a few lines from the Avesta so that you may better understand the teachings : " I celebrate the glorious Ormuzd, the greatest and best; all-perfect, all-powerful, all-wise, all-beautiful, all-pure, sole source of true knowledge, and real happiness ; him who hath created us, him who hath formed us, him who sustains us, the wisest of all intelligences.

" Zoroaster asked, what was the Word existing before the heaven, the water, the earth, before fire the Son of Ormuzd (the sun), before the whole existing world, before every good thing created by Ormuzd ? Then answered Ormuzd :—It was the All of the Word Creator, most holy Zoroaster, and he in the existing world who remembers the All of the Word

Creator, *or utters it when remembered, or chants it when uttered, or cele-brates it when chanted*, his soul will I thrice lead across the bridge to a better world, a better existence, better truth, better days."

Thus we find that a sacred trilateral Word or monosyllable existed among all the ancient people of the earth, and in the Indian, Mazdean, Egyptian, Hebrew and others we have most assuredly shown it to you. For in the Indian we find it hidden in the names of the triune Deity, Brahma, Vishnu and Siva. In the Mazdean we find the sacred Word concealed in AHURA-MAZDA, CPENTA-MAINYU, and VOHU MANO, and also in AGNI Fire, USHAS the Dawn, and MITRA, the Morning Star.

In the names of the ancient Egyptian Deities we find it hidden in Athom, Amon, or Khem-Amun. And in the Hebrew we are enabled to recognize it in Adom, Khurom, as well as in the Greek, Ompha, and Omphalos.

In the teachings of our Fraternity we find the sacred Word or mono-syllable hidden in the so-called Hebrew names of the three wicked ones Jubel*a*, Jubel*o*, Jubel*um*, but as these names were most assuredly not Hebrew they were invented for the express purpose of concealing the sacred Word, and what makes it doubly sure, is that it is also given in the sub-stitute Word itself, and as we climb the ascending ladder, we find it again, but this time vibrating under the living Arch.

Albert Pike informs us that,—The Mason, in his Lodge, surrounded by the Venerable Symbols of the Orient, sits, symbolically, in the centre of the Universe, and in the immediate presence of the Deity who made and rules it. He has been robbed, it is true, of that great Symbol, the Master—Mason's Word, while those whose predecessors took it, dispute among themselves what it is; and he has received in lieu of it only a Substite, which he may have been told means, " Marrow in the bones," or, " What is this the Builder?" and which having no symbolic meaning to him, and no sanctity, is valueless.

But the Great triads remain, and he may, with their aid, recover the lost Word. Each of these is a symbol of the Deity, and before each he should bow in silent adoration; for they have come to him from a Past that had ended before History began. The Master is Hermes, the Divine Word, Utterance, and Revelation of the Divine Wisdom; the Senior Warden represents the Divine Omnipotence; and the Junior

40

Warden the Harmony and Beauty that are the result of the equilibrium of Infinite Wisdom and Infinite Power.

I have often told you in the early pages of this work, in speaking of the esoteric teachings of Masonry, that every *word* and *symbol* contains a most profound meaning, and every Tradition and Allegory embodies far more than is dreamed of by those who have not seen the Light. Therefore, in order to thoroughly comprehend what the Words, Symbols, Traditions, etc. signify, we must give them our most profound attention, ever remembering that the Symbol must not be taken for the things symbolized.

We are told in the "Sohar" III, page 152 *et seq*, that: "We must believe that every word of the Doctrine contains in it a loftier sense, and a higher mystery. *The narratives of the Doctrine are its cloak.* Woe unto him who takes the covering for the Doctrine itself! *The simple look only at the garment,* that is, upon the legends of the Doctrine. They know no more. The Adepts, on the contrary, see not the cloak alone, *but that which the cloak covers.* . . . . Every Word *hides* in itself a profound meaning. *Every legend contains more than the event which it seems to recite.* This Holy and Profound Doctrine is the true Doctrine." And right here, my dear Brothers, let me tell you that: *He who thoroughly understands the Holy Doctrine,* KNOWS THE ROYAL SECRET.

Albert Pike, in his readings, tells us that "There are, perhaps, few *thinking* Masons to whom it has not seemed strange that the TRUE WORD, promised to every Master Mason, is not given to every one, but only a substitute that is not an approximation to the lost Word, but a mere trivial, ordinary Pass-Word not even alluding to the Deity. The Royal Arch American degree, is a modern invention, it perpetuates the Triangle, derived from the degree as known in England, and places on the sides of it the word, JAH, BEL, and ON, in some regions modified into or replaced by JEHABULUM, or JABULUM. The three words first mentioned are, in the Hebrew, יה, בעל, and אן or און; two of which only, at the most, are tri-literal; and the whole do not make three times three. I doubt if they are not a modern substitution by mere guess, for Jabulum or Jehabulum, a word said to be inscribed on one of the nine arches, and the name of an officer of the Lodge of Perfection.

" It is true, what is generally understood to be the Word of a Master-Mason, was at one time given in the Master's degree; but not as found amid or under the ruins, at the rebuilding of the Temple. Everything that relates to that rebuilding has a concealed reference to the destruction and hoped-for revival of the Order of the temple."

What is most worth knowing in Masonry is never very openly taught. The symbols are displayed; but they are mute. It is by hints only, and those the least noticeable and apparently insignificant, that the Initiate is put upon the track of the hidden secret. A word seemingly used at random, and as it were by chance, long escapes notice, and at last attracts the attention of some enquiring mind, and gives the clue that leads to new discoveries. " Many of these, by the manipulations of *improvers* of the work, and audacious mediocrity, like that of Preston and Webb, have disappeared forever and meaningless trivialities have taken their places. Some remain, proofs of the great antiquity of Masonry, much more convincing than all the babble of those whose business is to invent, and pervert, and not discover."

Masonry tortured out of shape by these interpreters, no longer Secret, and the Holy Doctrine is no longer the Sanctum Regnum or Holy Empire, and its ceremonies become trivial and puerile. No greater insults have ever been offered to the human understanding than most commentaries upon the Blue degrees. Every Brother will have to find the proper definition of the Master's Word for himself, just as he will have to discover the true meaning of Solomon's Temple, the Holy Doctrine, or the Royal Secret. All those who have passed through our portals and received the Light, will no doubt speculate upon the " Lost Word," but unless either he or they, are students of our symbology they will never believe that it lies concealed in the Third degree, consequently they will never recognize the key to it, or the tri-literal word that composes it. But if by deep thought and earnest study they discover this long lost Syllable, it will have no very great signification to them, in fact, they would hardly believe that it was the " Long Lost Word " of which they have the substitute. Yet if they examine *that,* very studiously, they will find that it has been carefully hidden in the substitute word itself. After either he or they have discovered the Word it will have no peculiar meaning to them, because they do not know that every letter in the alphabet, whether divided into three, four, or seven septuaries, or forty-nine letters, has its own color or shade of color. But let me assure you, that he who has learned the colors of the letters of the alphabet, and the corresponding numbers of the seven and the forty-nine colors and shades, on the scale of planes, and forces, and knows their respective order in the seven planes, will easily master the art of bringing them into affinity or interplay.

No matter where we search for the "Long lost Word" it takes us back to the language used by the great ancestors of our race the Indo-Aryan and although its true meaning has been lost to the Fraternity in general; yet I firmly believe that it is known and understood and that it is still pronounced by some of the descendants of the ancient Hindus and Brahmins whose lives, have, like their ancestors been devoted to the upbuilding of the human race. No matter where we force our investigations, we shall most assuredly go back to the A. U. M. of the "Land of the Vedas."

Brother Buck informs us in "Mystic Masonry": "The legend of the Lost Word and the Potency of the Ineffable Name are inseparable. They are the glyphics of Paradise Lost, and Paradise Regained; or of the Fall and the Redemption of man. So also is the legend of re-building the temple, a glyphic of Initiation, which is the same as Regeneration and Evolution.

"This ancient Wisdom belongs in a special sense to Masonry, for it has done most of any organization of modern times to preserve the ancient landmarks, and has honored and protected the sacred symbols. If Masonry has made only a superficial use of these hoary secrets, and their deeper meaning is still unknown to the craft, it is equally unknown to all others, except as the result of genuine initiation. One may know that a thing exists, where it is to be found, and that it is above all price, without knowing, to the last analysis, what it is. Such is the secret to the Lost Word, or the Ineffable Name. Its secret lies in exact vibrations under mathematical and synchronous relations; and its Law is Equilibrium, or Eternal Harmony.

Beginning with our Blue Lodge degrees we shall find this triliteral word, as I have before said, in the names of the three wicked ones Jubela, Jubelo and Jubelum, which forms the sacred monosyllable, and upon close investigation of these names we will most assuredly discover, that they are mere inventions, wherein to conceal the *Sacred Word* from all those who were not ready to receive it, and yet to preserve it for future ages, when it could be given back again to be used instead of its substitute, although (as I have previously stated) a careful search in that word itself will reveal to us its presence. In fact when a companion Mason is preparing for work, among the ancient symbols of the hoary ages of a prehistoric civilization, and amid the ruins of the temple, to search for the " Long lost Word," he will hear it as agreed, in unity, under the living arch, when if he be a student he will stand bewildered and perplexed, unable to hardly understand what he hears, and yet he will know that there is a far more sacred meaning to it than is generally understood by the great majority and he will intuitionally know that the *Long Lost* is not a WORD, but a SOUND

> Dear Brethren of the Mystic Tie,
>   The night is waning fast,
> Our work is done, our feast is o'er,
>   This song must be our last;
> Good night, good night, the farewell cry,
>   Repeat the parting strain,
> Happy to meet, Sorry to part,
>   Happy to meet again.
>   —*Final Toast.*

Printed in the United States
997900003B